NEW TESTAMENT CRITICISM & INTERPRETATION

NEW TESTAMENT CRITICISM & INTERPRETATION

EDITORS
DAVID ALAN BLACK & DAVID S. DOCKERY

ZondervanPublishingHouse
Academic and Professional Books
Grand Rapids, Michigan

A Division of HarperCollins*Publishers*

New Testament Criticism and Interpretation
Copyright © 1991 by David Alan Black and David S. Dockery

Requests for information should be addressed to:
Zondervan Publishing House
Academic and Professional Books
1415 Lake Drive S.E.
Grand Rapids, Michigan 49506

Library of Congress Cataloging-in-Publication Data

New Testament criticism and interpretation : essays on methods and issues /
David Alan Black and David S. Dockery.
    p.   cm.
    Includes bibliographical references and indexes.
    ISBN 0-310-51911-X (alk. paper)
    1. Bible. N.T.–Hermeneutics. 2. Bible. N.T.–Criticism, interpretation,
etc. I. Black, David Alan, 1952- . II. Dockery, David S.
    BS2331.N475 1991
    225.6–dc20   90-23879
                                                      CIP

Edited by Robert D. Wood
Cover Design by Vicki Heetderks

Printed in the United States of America

91 92 93 94 95 96 / AM / 10 9 8 7 6 5 4 3 2 1

To our New Testament students
past, present, and future

Contents

Part Three
SPECIAL ISSUES IN
NEW TESTAMENT INTERPRETATION

Acknowledgments

For the editors it has been a gratifying and stimulating task to work with the contributors to this volume. It is with grateful appreciation that we acknowledge their diligence, scholarship, and friendship. Special thanks are also due to the people at Zondervan Publishing House, who have superbly performed the tasks of receipting, processing, and readying the essays for publication. The contribution of Len Goss, Imprint Editor of Academie Books, was a major one, and we acknowledge it gladly. Finally, as with all our writings, this book is a small expression of esteem and love to our families for their constant support and encouragement of our work.

Editors' Preface

North American evangelicals have focused on the issues of biblical inspiration, authority, and interpretation for the past three decades. During this period several major conferences have been held, numerous issues have been debated, and many books have been written on these topics. One might reasonably ask, "Why another book on these subjects?" Certainly this is a legitimate question. Yet while much ink has been spilled over matters of inspiration and authority, works combining these concerns with issues of biblical criticism in general and New Testament studies in particular have been few.

For many years American evangelicals assumed that a high view of Scripture was incompatible with the employment of higher-critical methods. While Moses Stuart, the great nineteenth-century scholar, actually served as the pioneer introducing American Christianity to the field of biblical criticism, it was the work of Ned B. Stonehouse and George Eldon Ladd that paved the way for recent discussions among American evangelicals. Of course, neither Stonehouse nor Ladd provided a final answer to questions about the relationship of biblical inspiration and biblical criticism, and these issues will undoubtedly continue to be debated. One thing, however, is certain: If American evangelicals are to have an impact in the academy and in the church, they must enter into dialogue with contemporary scholarship. Mark Noll, in his penetrating analysis of evangelical scholarship entitled *Between Faith and Criticism*, has issued an invitation for American evangelicals to do just that. In one sense, the present book is a response to that invitation, though its primary audience is not the academy so much as it is the student who is being introduced to the world of New Testament studies.

The authors of this symposium, representing a wide

variety of denominational affiliations, share in common an affirmation of the Bible's divine inspiration and human authorship. The contributors unashamedly approach the New Testament as the written Word of God. Simultaneously they recognize that because the Bible is a divine-human book, it must be treated as both equal to and yet more than an ordinary book. To deny that the Bible should be studied through the use of literary and critical methodologies is to treat the Bible as less than human, less than historical, and less than literature. Bringing these presuppositions to their task, the authors have sought to articulate evangelical perspectives on current issues and methods in New Testament study.

It has not been the desire of the editors to select authors who would echo the editors' opinions on each and every matter. The contributors have been given freedom to explore and express their findings on these matters with the sole proviso that students be able to understand the methods, issues, and concerns involved. That the authors occasionally disagree among themselves only points to the rich variety of thought present in the growing evangelical movement. Each essay includes a list of works for additional study. These bibliographies are not intended to be complete nor to represent the most up-to-date works in the field. The books have been selected with students in mind to introduce them to the broad issues from a variety of perspectives.

A previous book by George Ladd entitled *The New Testament and Criticism* (1967), together with a symposium edited by I. Howard Marshall under the title *New Testament Interpretation* (1977), serve as forerunners to this volume. This work, however, is considerably broader in focus and brings these previous discussions up-to-date. In particular, we have written with college and seminary students in mind. Our aim is to help them grow in their love for the New Testament and to enable them to interpret God's Word with greater skill and understanding. It is our fervent hope that the church will be strengthened and our Lord will be glorified through these efforts.

Soli Deo Gloria

David Alan Black
David S. Dockery

PART ONE
INTRODUCTION

Chapter One

Authority, Hermeneutics, and Criticism

Peter H. Davids

Peter H. Davids

Peter H. Davids is Professor of Biblical Studies and New Testament at Canadian Theological Seminary in Regina, Saskatchewan. He is a graduate of Wheaton College (A.B.), Trinity Evangelical Divinity School (M.Div.), and the University of Manchester (Ph.D.). His articles have appeared in such journals as *New Testament Studies*, *Journal of the Evangelical Theological Society*, *Evangelical Quarterly*, *Themelios*, and *Sojourners*. He has also contributed to *Baker's Encyclopedia of the Bible*, *Oxford Companion to the Bible*, and *Dictionary of Evangelical Theology*. He is the author of *James* (Hendrickson), *The Epistle of James* (Eerdmans), and *The First Epistle of Peter* (Eerdmans).

Chapter One

Authority, Hermeneutics, and Criticism

I grew up in a church that stressed it was a "New Testament church" having no creed or procedural handbook other than the Bible. But then I went away to Wheaton College, and for the first time in my life had to live with good Christian fellows who went to different churches than I did and who were not persuaded by my arguments that our particular style of meeting was the one sanctioned by Scripture. This created a crisis in my life, for here were Christians reading the same Bible and claiming it as their authority and yet interpreting it differently. This was a crisis in hermeneutics, for we were differing in how we understood the text.

In the same college were many students who were critical of the church. Their argument was that the evangelical church talked a lot about biblical authority but did little actually to obey the commands of Scripture. It was, they argued, a faith of "cheap grace" without works. Other students had given up their faith entirely and did not see the relevance of Scripture to their lives. For them it was a historic book, the shaper of parts of their culture, but something to be left behind in their parental home. These groups of students, I noticed, were having a crisis in authority, the one group calling their elders to take the authority of Scripture more seriously, and the other group having lost any belief in the authority of Scripture.

Finally, when I left college and went on to seminary and then graduate school, I had to face the variety of critical methodologies discussed in this book. I personally found this challenging, for I believed I was learning to interpret Scripture more nearly accurately and therefore would be able to obey it more exactly. For me, criticism was an aid to biblical authority. But there were two other responses to this same challenge. Some of my friends felt that in giving up their old interpretations of Scripture they also had to give up the authority of Scripture. For them, biblical criticism relativized Scripture. Other friends argued that if these tools were needed to understand Scripture, then the layperson was in a hopeless state when it came to obeying Scripture. They felt hostile toward critical methodologies, for to them these tools were distancing Scripture from them and thus making them dependent upon scholars. They resented this removal of biblical authority out of their grasp. It is these issues we will address in this essay, setting the stage for much of the discussion in this book.

THE MEANING OF BIBLICAL AUTHORITY

First, what does it mean that Scripture has authority? Although we might describe authority in several ways, for our purposes there are two types of authority, intrinsic and extrinsic. Intrinsic authority is that which something or someone possesses due to what it or he or she is. People with guns have such authority, for they can enforce their demands. A law of nature has similar authority, in that life will operate according to it whether or not anyone knows about it or believes in it. Extrinsic authority, on the other hand, is the authority that someone or something possesses because people ascribe such authority to them. Presidents and prime ministers have this type of authority, for when the minute people refuse to grant them authority they are powerless. Likewise the laws of a government have only extrinsic authority, as when the speed limit is set at one speed, but the police will enforce only a higher limit because the people are all driving faster than the legal limit.

When we write about scriptural authority, we are not talking about its intrinsic authority. That topic would turn this into an essay on the doctrine of Scripture. Rather, we assume with 2 Timothy 3:16 that all Scripture is "God-breathed" and thus has intrinsic authority.[1] What Scripture says, God says. This truth stands whether or not anyone ever obeys Scripture, for it does not gain its intrinsic authority from the consensus of a religious community, but from the fact that God has put into the volume a description of reality (i.e., his will) as it is.

Given, then, that Scripture has God's authority, there is still the issue of extrinsic authority. That is, from the human point of view we must recognize that Scripture is authoritative and then understand and respond to it appropriately, i.e., with obedience. It is at this point that the issues of criticism and hermeneutics come into play. As readers we may or may not understand the message, which is where hermeneutics comes in, or critical studies may either obscure or clarify the reality of the authority. The real issue is whether the authority that God put into Scripture is received by human beings and is then translated into obedience. If there is no obedience, then all the discussions about authority are no more than abstractions. While we assume that Scripture will have the last say in the Day of Judgment, as far as today is concerned it is not functioning in an authoritative way unless we human beings respond to it.

AUTHORITY AND HERMENEUTICS

The first issue, then, is hermeneutics. God did not dictate the New Testament from heaven in some sort of divine language, just as Jesus did not appear in his full glory. Rather, God chose to preserve the letters of Paul as he struggled with correcting problems in the churches he founded (totally unconscious that people 2000 years later would be reading his letters); he inspired Luke (how he did we have no idea nor whether Luke was aware the impulse was divine) to write a two-volume history of the Christian movement; and he chose John on Patmos to receive an extraordinary vision and to communicate it to seven Asian churches.[2] This points out to us that God produced Scripture within the process of daily life. Just as no one noticed Jesus growing up or differentiated him from other young carpenters they knew, so also the scriptural revelation was "incarnate" within the process of human life. No one noticed that it was being produced. Even its authors for the most part were not aware that they were writing Scripture. At times they were aware of writing divine commands to this or that community, but that is a long way from having any idea that one is writing Scripture, the basic document of the church of God around the world. Only in 2 Peter 3:16 do we catch a glimmer that already, late in the New Testament period, some of Paul's writings were beginning to be considered as Scripture. We may object to this method of production, but we may as well object that the Gospel was announced to the world through human means, not through angelic voices from heaven. God being God chose to give revelation in his own way and did not consult human beings to discover whether we had better ideas.

While Scripture's form may at first appear problematic, it has profound implications for hermeneutics, the science of interpretation. The New Testament is human speech, human beings writing to others. Therefore, it needs to be understood as human speech. This is helpful to us, for we constantly interpret human speech; it would be problematic if we had to learn some divine language to understand God's communication. But at the same time there are problems involved in our interpretation. We human beings take our thoughts and encode them in a series of symbols (either oral sounds or written symbols for those sounds) that we share in common with others in our community. A different community will assign different meanings to the same symbols. For example, the English word "hell" means something quite different than the German *hell* (which means "light," as in *hell braun*, meaning "light brown"). What is more, the same symbol may have a different meaning depending on what other symbols it is combined with. For example, "green" means something different in "The house was green" than in "It was a greenhouse" or than in "He turned green as the ship pitched on the waves." Therefore, to understand Scripture we should know how the author and his community used their symbols.

It is at this point that hermeneutics begins, for, on the one hand, some people have tended to see the symbols of Scripture (i.e., the words of Greek or, in translation, English) as taking on a life of their own separate from the author's culture. It disturbs them when one suggests that as we come to understand the author's thought-world better we must change our understanding of what appears to be a word with a clear meaning. Thus if one argues that in 1 Timothy 2:9–15 the Greek term *gunē* meant within that cultural context "wife," not "woman,"[3] some folk will feel threatened because it has "always" been understood as "woman" (at least in English translations), while others will respond, "Let's see whether this is new and correct information that does in fact assist us in understanding and obeying the message of Scripture more accurately." In each case a different stance on hermeneutics has been taken. We have argued that the second position is more in keeping with the nature of language; it also allows one to accept new information and change interpretation without losing a sense of the authority of Scripture. But to the former group, those taking the second position may appear to be rejecting biblical authority, for that is what *they* would have to do to change their response to the text. The groundwork is thus laid for a discussion about interpretation to become (falsely) a discussion about authority, with charges and countercharges.

The issue of hermeneutics becomes more complicated when we move beyond the understanding of a single text, which itself is not always easy, to the understanding of Scripture as a whole. For example, since the Reformation the adherents of the Lutheran and Reformed traditions have tended to view the Pauline writings (particularly Galatians and Romans) as the center of the New Testament, with all other texts being interpreted in the light of these writings. This has also been true of Dispensationalist hermeneutics. But the Anabaptist tradition (and to a large degree the Roman Catholic tradition) has tended to put the Gospels in the center, with Paul being interpreted in that light. Furthermore, partly based on this difference, there has been an ongoing argument as to whether the Old Testament directions to Israel should be fulfilled in the secular state or instead obeyed in a spiritual form within the community of believers. These differences in hermeneutics came to a head in the Reformation period, with each group calling the other disobedient to Scripture and condemning the other to hell (and at times to prison, torture, and execution). Yet each was attempting to be obedient to Scripture; each side felt that Scripture was fully authoritative. Unfortunately, they did not discuss hermeneutics but theology, and because these underlying issues were not addressed, they ended up in a dialogue of the deaf. A similar impasse often occurs today when evangelicals discuss such issues as participation in war or the role of women in ministry.[4]

Finally, there is yet another set of hermeneutical problems when one attempts to translate obedience in the New Testament period into obedience in our culture. For example, in 1 Corinthians 11:2–16 Paul discusses what appears to be the wearing of veils by women when they prayed or prophesied in church.[5] For some Christians this means that Christian women should wear veils (usually reduced to hats) in church today, despite the fact that such items are now either archaic curiosities or elements of fashion rather than that they carry any of the possible meanings they had in Paul's day. Cultural differences in meaning are for these Christians irrelevant. Other Christians observe that the veil in Paul's day was probably a sign of marriage. In western culture the sign of marriage is a wedding ring. Thus a cultural translation might be made that Christian women should wear their wedding rings when ministering, or, by extension (since rings are less likely to be thrown aside than veils), they should not dishonor their marriage by the manner in which they minister. This is consistent with Paul's usual order of putting marriage and other forms of holiness before ministry. The first group sees itself as obeying Scripture and all others as disobedient to a clear command (although in many cases their women neither pray nor prophesy in church, which is presumed by Paul). The second group, however, also sees itself as obeying Scripture and might accuse the first group of failing to obey Paul's meaning in trying to obey the letter of the text. Again, there is no difference between the two groups about the authority of Scripture, but there is a lot of difference about hermeneutics and in particular about how one is to apply Scripture in a different culture. And while this particular issue may appear to be a trivial concern of a small section of the church, the same principles apply to a much wider spectrum of issues.

The upshot of this discussion is that differences in hermeneutics are not necessarily differences in ascribing authority to Scripture. If the mistake is made of confusing the two issues, then there will be no way of solving the problem. Rather, hermeneutical refinement is part of an ongoing process among many evangelicals to understand what John or Paul or Luke really meant (and therefore what God meant), and then to obey that message more carefully.

AUTHORITY AND CRITICISM

Turning to the issue of criticism, we face a more difficult situation. Some types of critical study will hardly disturb the one who is interested in the issue of authority. For example, the goal of textual criticism is to provide the text that is closest to what the original author actually wrote. Not only are the findings relatively inoffensive, but the goals are in line with the interests of those committed to biblical authority.[6] On the other hand, tradition criticism, a term that covers some aspects of both form and redaction criticism and that looks at the gospel tradition as something that changed considerably within the oral period (approximately A.D. 30–50) before the Gospels were written, can be threatening. Therefore, the real issue is how to respond. This essay is not the place to give a detailed critique of tradition criticism and related methodologies, for that is the job of other authors in this book, but we can discuss the appropriate attitude that enables one to come to terms with such areas of study.

First, it is necessary to separate the methodology from the skeptical presuppositions of some of its practitioners, including in many cases its originators. Luke claims that he used sources (Lk 1:1–4), so it is no surprise to discover that the other evangelists did also (source criticism). It is clear that a miracle story "looks" different than a proverb of Jesus, but a study of the forms in which such materials circulated does not have to imply that one is less genuine than the other (form criticism). The fact that Paul apparently quotes a hymn in Philippians 2:6–11 does not make him any less inspired (or the hymn any less a part of Scripture) than does his quotation of pagan poets in Acts 17:28. For some this may indicate the presence of "more primitive pre-Pauline" material, but in fact Paul presumably quotes what any author would quote, material he agrees with that says what he wants to say well (source and redaction criticism).

The truth is that many of these methodologies have been used by people who did have skeptical assumptions, for whom sayings of Jesus were creations of the later church unless proved to be genuine, or for whom material that was not actually created by Paul was in some way to be discounted. One does not have to hold such assumptions, however, to profit from the methodology. We can work from a basis of faith and piety as well as from a basis of skepticism and doubt. Indeed, the same tools that some have used to support their doubt will be used by other scholars to support their faith. And scholars on both sides can make good and poor use of their tools. Some are blinded by their personal beliefs and engage in circular reasoning and special pleading. Others can bracket their beliefs and come to conclusions that all applaud, whatever their position of belief or doubt. Those committed to the authority of Scripture need to be able to separate the facts that scholars observe from the faith-positions they may have mixed with them (and that may distort some of their data). This is what good scholarship is all about.

Second, we must again think about hermeneutics when we consider the issue of criticism. If the authority of Scripture rests in what the original author intended to communicate to his or her first readers, i.e., in the message in its original cultural context, then anything that clarifies the author's intentions is desirable. Let us take a series of examples.

Not one of the Gospels names its author (even the Fourth Gospel does not name its author, although in chapter 21 it does indicate—without naming him—the disciple who was either the author or the source of at least the second half of the Gospel). Thus there is no *biblical* authority at stake in arguing who wrote what, although there may be a lot of *traditional* authority at risk. On the other hand, in the epistles (except Hebrews and the Johannine epistles) the author is identified, so there is an issue of biblical authority at stake in the matter of authorship, unless one can show that in the ancient world pseudonymity was in fact accepted and thus that no deception was intended. In that (hypothetical) case we moderns would be wrongly assuming that the apparent claim of authorship was a true claim of authorship, but the ancient writer and reader would have read it as something like "in the spirit of _____." If that could be proved, then no biblical authority would rest in the claim of authorship (even though for centuries the church has read it as a true claim). On the other hand, if that cannot be proved, then biblical authority is truly at stake.

Moving one step beyond the authorship issue, we do know from the ancient world that authorship does not imply that the author himself actually wrote the document. Paul, for example, claims he followed normal practice and actually wrote only the last few lines of his letters (cf. 2Th 3:17; Gal 6:11). The rest was dictated. Did Paul give any freedom to his secretaries, who were often trusted co-workers? That should not bother us so long as the author "signed the letter."[7] Were some works, for example James, written after the death of the author from materials he had composed during his lifetime?[8] That would not be surprising in the ancient world, and James's sayings and sermons were *his* message, not that of whoever might have put them together.

Furthermore, we must read the documents in the context of the accepted canons of writing in the ancient world. Surely Peter did not deliver a five minute sermon on Pentecost (Ac 2). But every educated ancient reader (and most who could read were educated) knew that the standard practice of historians was to summarize what a speaker said. It was not expected that the author of Acts would have given a verbatim account. It was acceptable to put the speaker's thoughts into one's own words (much like the abstract of a book or article today). Indeed, it was even acceptable to make up a speech from the types of things the speaker was known to have said on other occasions. The author of Acts appears to have been a conservative historian within the context of his day.

Similar things can be said about the Gospels. In each, the words of Jesus at some point (whether by the evangelist or by someone who passed the tradition on to him) had to be translated from Aramaic into Greek. And at times they needed to be expanded to make sense in a different culture. For example, Mark 10:12 has the clause, "If [a wife] divorces her husband and marries another man, she commits adultery." This statement carried Jesus' thought into the Roman world, where Mark was written, but it was an impossible idea in a Palestinian context, where women could not divorce.[9] Thus Matthew omits it altogether, and Luke changes it to a passive ("The woman who has been divorced by her husband"). Did Mark accurately communicate Jesus' message of no divorce to the Roman world where women could and did divorce their husbands, expanding Jesus' saying to make it clear that it applied to women as well as men? Did Matthew and Luke shorten Mark to make it fit a Palestinian context, or did they know the original form of the saying? The point is that the ancient reader would never have raised such issues. So long as Mark communicated what Jesus meant, they were satisfied. From our modern point of view we might want more careful expansion. But the evangelists never went to our schools or wrote in our culture.[10] Their intentions need to be read within the context of their culture. Here critical study can be a help, for it shows what the evangelists (and others) actually did intend. And we can thereby get a clearer idea of what meaning is actually blessed with biblical authority (as differentiated from meanings we happen to read into the text).

Third, we have to remember that biblical authority rests in the canonical form of Scripture, not in real or hypothetical original forms. Certainly Scripture deserves the detailed study that it has been given. After all, if it is authoritative, and especially if God's authority rests in it, it is of supreme importance. In that case exploring the total way in which it was produced, its historical and cultural background and all that is involved with it, is worthwhile. But that does not mean that if we can discover the earlier forms of this or that work we have something more authoritative. For example, suppose that the "Q" source (the term used for the material that Matthew and Luke have in common but that is not in Mark; this material is mostly sayings of Jesus) turned out to be a written document and was discovered by an archaeologist. This would not be more authoritative than Matthew and Luke. It would not even be Scripture. How much more true is it that the hypothetical reconstructions of such sources or the original form of sayings (to the degree we are now capable of discovering them) or the Aramaic form of words of Jesus (created through a back translation of Gospel texts in an attempt to obtain what he actually said) are not Scripture. The same is true whether we are considering Gospels, Acts (e.g., if a transcript of Paul's trial in Caesarea were found), or epistles (e.g., Paul's lost letters or the letter of the church in Corinth to Paul). None of these are Scripture. We do not come to something more authoritative by delineating them.

What, then, is the use of such study? It reveals the method used by the scriptural author. The more we know about his or her sources, the better we can state what the authors of Scripture intended to communicate. And it is in that communication that biblical authority lies. There is an antiquarian interest in some phases of the study of development, but the goal of the biblical scholar is in the end to understand the meaning of the text better.

Something similar can be said about historical and sociological study. For example, Robert Banks wrote a book, *Going to Church in the First Century*,[11] an excellent example of taking what can be discovered about first-century house churches and turning it into an imaginative narrative. This illustrates two things. First, church in the first century was different from church today. Second, there is a lot of information about his social circumstances that Paul never intended to communicate but that can be teased out of what he does say by those who know about the social and historical context of the ancient world. We note, on the one hand, that this information is very useful. The more we know about the context of Paul (or any other New Testament author) and his readers, with whose lifestyle and social situation Paul was undoubtedly in touch, the better we are able to understand the communication between them. Knowing that the churches were house churches, for example, explains why the "elect lady" (KJV) of 2 John (probably a church) is not to receive false teachers "into [her] house" (v. 10). This is not referring to allowing false teachers to enter someone's home, but to receiving them into the gathering of the church where they could do damage. On the other hand, this sociological and cultural information is not Scripture. We have not added to biblical authority by discovering this information, but we may have clarified what it was that the author was trying to communicate (and what his first readers probably understood instantly) and therefore what message the authority of the Bible stands behind.

This distinction becomes important in that at times there is a tendency to try to imitate the social and cultural situation of the early church. That the early church met in houses is information that we now know. But because we know this does not mean that the Bible teaches that churches should meet in houses. That the early church celebrated the Lord's Supper as a full communal meal we also know (in fact, it was the mid-third century before the final shift to a symbolic meal was made), but because the Scripture makes no point of this means that there is no biblical command to return to this practice. Something similar might be said about baptismal practices. In other words, just because Scripture gives incidental evidence that the church did something in a certain way or that a person held a certain attitude does not mean that the author was making any attempt to communicate that information nor that we should imitate it. It would certainly be permissible to meet in houses and celebrate communion as a communal meal; it might even be advisable for any number of reasons; but the most we can claim biblical authority for is that the Scripture gives evidence that this or that was done in the early church, not that it teaches that this should be done.

Fourth, when doing scholarly research, it is necessary to maintain firmly in mind the categories of suspended judgment and paradox. God did choose to create Scripture through human processes, i.e., in an incarnational manner. Paul, as we noted, wrote his letters to answer problems in the churches he was addressing. The Gospels were likewise written to meet the needs of certain individuals or communities. The works themselves were written in locations stretching from at least Jerusalem to Rome and at times ranging from perhaps A.D. 50 to A.D. 96. This means first of all that there are many gaps in information we would like to fill in. We would love a detailed description of a single baptismal service, for example. We would like to know what Paul thought about abortion. We would also like him to explain how 1 Corinthians 15, which looks forward to transformation at the return of Christ, fits with 2 Corinthians 5, which appears to speak of transformation at death; or tell us exactly what he had explained to the Thessalonians (2Th 2:5). The fact is that we do not have this information. That does not injure biblical authority, for the authority is in what exists, not in what does not exist. But it does mean that we need to be careful that we do not fill in the gaps and claim biblical authority for the resulting teaching.

At the same time there are places in which teachings appear to clash. I cited above an example from Paul. Another would be the order of appearances of Jesus after his resurrection. One approach to such problems is to force a reconciliation, however improbable it may seem. To such people a forced harmony is at least better than ambiguity. Another approach would be to point quickly to as many of these situations as possible without attempting any reconciliation in order to relativize biblical authority.[12] Both of these approaches have their value. There are times when harmonizing accounts comes naturally and is appropriate. Yet when the harmonization is forced and seems a desperate resort, such an approach would appear to come more from an insecurity about biblical authority than a commitment to it. It is also important to be open to the possibility of tensions in Scripture, for it is a poor defense to biblical authority to take a stance that no data, however well established, could ever convince us to abandon our position. Yet a quick resort to contradiction appears to this writer to stem as much from prejudice or a fear of biblical authority as from dispassionate scholarly research.

Once we realize that our data are incomplete, however, we realize that we do not necessarily have to select either of the approaches mentioned. We can suspend judgment, realizing that we do not have complete data. This could be an approach to the resurrection appearances. The basic facts of the Resurrection are very clear in all accounts. Yet we may have to suspend judgment about who it was to whom the risen Jesus appeared first, second, etc. We cannot at this distance fill in the gaps and cross-examine the witnesses. But our experience with similar unique and shocking events in modern life (e.g., traffic accidents) should convince us that a variety of difficult-if-not-impossible-to-reconcile reports is precisely what we might expect to receive.

In the case of Paul we might resort to paradox. Is it possible that the transformation of human beings occurs at their death and at the second coming of Christ and yet there is only one transformation? Yes, it is possible. We might not be able to determine how to work it out, but they are not necessarily self-contradictory. They are, however, paradoxical. So are a number of teachings in Paul. No wonder Peter found Paul hard to understand (2Pe 3:16). We are in good company if we have the same problem.

The New Testament did not come to us as a code of Christian behavior (like a new Mosaic law) or a systematic theology. Nor is there an exhaustive history of either Jesus or the early church within the corpus. If we expect these we will be disappointed, and critical studies will likely shake us severely. But if we accept the Scripture as it was written, as occasional writings through which God wishes to communicate what we need to know, not necessarily what we would like to know, then we can hold to both biblical authority and critical methodology.

The sum of this discussion is that the critical study of Scripture can clarify the message that the authors were trying to communicate either by showing how the author came to produce his or her work (through examining sources) or by clarifying the context in which the message was communicated. But it cannot increase the authority of Scripture or find new material of the same level of authority. And while critical methodologies have undoubtedly led to a doubting of biblical authority by some, that is not their necessary conclusion, but one resulting from assumptions connected to them or perhaps even a misuse of the method.

AUTHORITY AND FUNCTIONAL CANON

Yet one more issue needs to be discussed. There is a tendency for each church community to respond selectively to Scripture. In critical scholarship this is referred to as the "canon within the canon," the part of Scripture that really functions as Scripture for a given scholar or group. The fact that German scholarship in particular has not been shaken by the criticism of the historicity of the Gospels or the authorship of most epistles other than Paul's main letters (his *Hauptbriefe*, Romans–2 Corinthians) is no surprise in that, as was mentioned above, the center of the Lutheran and Reformed canon has tended to be exactly these main letters of Paul (especially Romans and Galatians). The real center of authority has been preserved for such scholars even if little of the historical Jesus or the later letters of the New Testament are left.

We have rejected such an approach on two grounds. First, we do not believe that this is the necessary conclusion of the critical methodologies. Second, we do not believe that one has any real authority if he or she removes material from its context. To snatch a few paragraphs from this chapter and read them out of the context of the whole would be to distort their meaning. To look at Paul in isolation from the teaching of Jesus is to distort Paul's message and thus not to draw from biblical authority at all. But before we quickly condemn a particular school of thought, it is important to realize that for each community there is probably some such canon within a canon functioning. The difference is that some are conscious of it and others are not.

One example of this is found in ways a particular tradition uses biblical sections. For example, if a tradition's canon centered on Paul, one might find that Gospel texts were rarely preached on, and when they were used in sermons they functioned mainly as illustrations of an underlying Pauline text. That would mean that the teaching of the Gospels themselves would rarely if ever be heard in that community.[13] The church might assert that the Gospels were fully authoritative, but the Gospels would not function as authorities in its preaching.

Another example would be the use a church makes of

certain books or parts of books. The epistle of James is a case in point. Because it is difficult to reconcile it with Paul, it has tended to be sidelined and ignored in many churches. But within that book some passages are even more thoroughly ignored. For example, James 5:14–18 argues that if a person in a church is ill the elders should come and pray and that this prayer of faith will heal the sick individual. Furthermore, Christians are to confess their sins to each other and pray for one another that they may be healed. A year or so after I completed a doctoral thesis on James it occurred to me that I had never in over twenty years in the church heard of an instance in which James 5:14ff. had been followed, although there was no lack of sick people in the churches I had known. In other words, while the text in James was in the Bibles that the hundreds of Christians and dozens of elders I had known had in their homes (and as often as not in their hands every Sunday), it had apparently not functioned as an authoritative text for them. It was not that anyone had chosen to disobey the text. It was simply that it had been ignored in teaching and preaching. When the Scripture was read, it simply was not seen. For all practical purposes it was not in the canon.

While I have given a single example above, each tradition has its own groups of "texts to ignore." This is never stated explicitly, for if it were the texts would not be ignored. Rather, the focus of the community or the tradition is such that some texts are never read, or if they are read they appear irrelevant and are passed over quickly. The texts have their own intrinsic authority, but in that community they have no extrinsic authority.

This forms an argument, not for giving up traditions and church fellowships (for any other tradition or denomination or even a non-denominational fellowship would have the same problem in a different area), but for hermeneutical reflection and critical study. Hermeneutical discussion assists one in discovering how one is interpreting Scripture and thus what one might be filtering out of Scripture. Interaction with the full world of critical scholarship means that one is looking at Scripture from a variety of angles and traditions, many of which will be different from one's own. The result will be a tendency to see one's own blind spots and correct the shortcomings of one's theology. Even if one disagrees with a position, if the disagreement is expressed carefully and thoughtfully he or she has learned and exposed possible areas of ignorance. Yet one further aid to biblical authority is helpful, and that is working with Christians in a variety of churches and cultures. To return to the example above, it was while teaching in Germany that I learned African elders in Tanzania were teaching missionaries to pray for the sick in obedience to James 5. Those elders had come from a different culture without the same set of blinders (they surely had others), and when they came to that passage it seemed natural to them to see and obey it. They were in turn able to assist their German teachers to widen their sphere of practical biblical obedience. Our Two-Thirds World brothers and sisters have much to teach us, as we have much to teach them. Something similar happens, although to a lesser degree, when we work closely with Christians in traditions different from ours. We may never adopt their theology or practice as a whole, but such ongoing experiences will assist in revealing to us texts we have not been reading and give us new perspectives on texts we have been reading.

This topic, then brings our discussion full circle. The New Testament is authoritative. We have discussed ways we recognize this authority, i.e., extrinsic authority, and the contribution of hermeneutics and criticism to this process. While noting the dangers, we have tried to argue that both hermeneutical reflection and critical study can in fact assist us in more nearly accurately understanding the Scripture and thus set the stage for the recognition of its authority in obedience. But that is precisely the issue. No study of Scripture can of itself produce obedience. Unless Scripture is obeyed, it has in practice no present authority for those individuals or communities that are not obeying it. It is for a heart set to obey and for the carrying out of understanding in obedience that we have implicitly argued. Only when that happens will biblical authority be a truly meaningful category in our lives.

BIBLIOGRAPHY

Carson, D. A., and J. D. Woodbridge, eds. *Hermeneutics, Authority and Canon*. Grand Rapids: Zondervan, 1986.

_____. *Scripture and Truth*. Grand Rapids: Zondervan, 1983.

Conn, Harvey M. ed. *Inerrancy and Hermeneutic*. Grand Rapids: Baker, 1988.

Farrow, D. *The Word of Truth and Disputes about Words*. Winona Lake, Ind.: Carpenter Books, 1987.

Garrett, D. A., and R. R. Melick, eds. *Authority and Interpretation: A Baptist Perspective*. Grand Rapids: Baker, 1987.

Gnuse, R. *The Authority of the Bible*. New York: Paulist, 1985.

Marshall, I. H. *Biblical Inspiration*. Grand Rapids: Eerdmans, 1982.

McKim, Donald K. *What Christians Believe About the Bible*. Nashville: Nelson, 1985.

Morris, L. *I Believe in Revelation*. Grand Rapids: Eerdmans, 1976.

Nixon, R. "The Authority of the New Testament." In *New Testament Interpretation: Essays on Principles and Methods*, edited by I. H. Marshall, 334–51. Grand Rapids: Eerdmans, 1977. The rest of this symposium volume is also relevant.

Noll, Mark A. *Between Faith and Criticism*. San Francisco: Harper, 1986.

Pinnock, C. H. *The Scripture Principle*. San Francisco: Harper, 1984.

Radmacher, E. D., and R. D. Preus, eds. *Hermeneutics, Inerrancy, and the Bible*. Grand Rapids: Zondervan, 1984.

Ridderbos, Herman. *Studies in Scripture and Its Authority*. Grand Rapids: Eerdmans, 1978.

Rogers, Jack B. and Donald K. McKim. *The Authority and Interpretation of the Bible*. San Francisco: Harper, 1979.

Zehr, P. M. *Biblical Criticism in the Life of the Church*. Scottdale, Pa.: Herald Press, 1986.

NOTES

[1]For further information on the issue of the intrinsic authority of Scripture, see L. Morris, *I Believe in Revelation* (Grand Rapids: Eerdmans, 1976); C. H. Pinnock, "The Inspiration of Scripture and the Authority of Jesus Christ," in J. W. Montgomery, ed., *God's Inerrant Word* (Minneapolis: Bethany, 1974), 201-18; and C. H. Pinnock, *The Scripture Principle* (San Francisco: Harper, 1984), especially pp. 3–82.

[2]Numerous visions and related phenomena are repeated in the New Testament, but John's was extraordinary in (1) the command to send it to a group of churches, (2) its extent, and (3) its significance. It is more comparable to the experience Paul refers to in 2 Corinthians 12 than to the visions of Acts.

[3]As R. Remin recently did in "1 Timothy 2:12: Woman or Wife?," *His Dominion* 14:3 (1988): 2–14. E. Earle Ellis takes a similar position in *Pauline Theology: Ministry and Society* (Grand Rapids: Eerdmans, 1989).

In none of the examples in this essay does this writer intend to take sides, although the examples chosen are ones that have intrinsic attractiveness and should be taken seriously as a basis for further research.

[4]For a careful study of the hermeneutical differences involved in these arguments, see W. M. Swartley, *Slavery, Sabbath, War, and Women: Case Issues in Biblical Interpretation* (Scottdale, Pa.: Herald Press, 1983). See also R. K. Johnston, *Evangelicals at an Impasse: Biblical Authority in Practice* (Atlanta: John Knox, 1979), although this book goes beyond purely hermeneutical concerns.

[5]There are a number of interpretations of what Paul is talking about. Some argue that the Greek *katakaluptō* and its related terms referred to a veil, while others believe that it referred to a particular hair style, i.e., braided hair put up on the head. See J. B. Hurley, *Man and Woman in Biblical Perspective* (Grand Rapids: Zondervan, 1981), 168–71, for the evidence for this latter position. But for the purposes of this article the term "veil" is accurate enough to indicate a way of covering the head (whether with cloth or with hair) that signified a married woman.

[6]The major battles of textual criticism were fought over the issue of whether 1 John 5:7b, Mark 16:9–20, and John 7:53–8:11 were part of the original texts of their respective works. In each case textual scholars from a variety of perspectives have argued uniformly in the negative. No other large blocks of text are similarly in doubt. So for the most part textual criticism deals with the details of a word or a phrase, which rarely upsets people, although differing schools of textual criticism may argue heatedly. Naturally, the fact that a given passage did not occur in the autograph of a document does not mean that it is not canonical in that it may have been in that form of the document generally recognized as canon by the church. But that is an issue of canon, not of textual criticism.

[7]In the case of 1 Peter at least the totality of the Greek style of the letter must be attributed to a secretary if one is to argue that 2 Peter is also a product of Simon Peter. Cf. P. H. Davids, *The Epistle of 1 Peter* (NICNT; Grand Rapids: Eerdmans, 1990).

[8]Cf. P. H. Davids, *James* (The New International Biblical Commentary; Peabody, Mass.: Hendrickson, 1989) and *The Epistle of James* (NIGTC; Grand Rapids: Eerdmans, 1982).

[9]In Palestine, a wife could not divorce her husband, even in cases in which the wife needed to initiate a divorce, e.g., if the husband went to sea and did not return and it could be assumed that he had either abandoned his wife or died on the journey. She must in that case petition the court to divorce her in the name of her husband. Thus even if he were not present, he did the divorcing.

[10]For example, in John 3 the author never indicates where the words of Jesus leave off and his own begin. His culture did not use

quotation marks, just as James did not use them in James 5:12 where he quotes what we know from Matthew 5:33–37 to have been a saying of Jesus. The concern for exact quotation was not part of that culture. Of course, for the modern evangelical they are both equally inspired since we argue that God inspired the book, not necessarily the sources.

[11]R. Banks, *Going to Church in the First Century* (Chipping Norton, NSW, Australia: Hexagon, 1980). The church in question is Priscilla and Aquilla's house church in Rome because it was the easiest social context to describe.

[12]An example of this would be J. T. Sanders, *Ethics in the New Testament* (Philadelphia: Fortress, 1975), who, after arguing that the New Testament contains several contradictory ethical stances, chooses a humanistic ethic on the basis of James 2.

[13]This is a real example, but I avoid naming the interpretive tradition so as not to appear to be attacking a particular school of thought.

Chapter Two

New Testament Interpretation: A Historical Survey

David S. Dockery

David S. Dockery

David S. Dockery is Academic Editor for Broadman Press and Assistant Professor of New Testament at Southern Baptist Theological Seminary in Louisville, Kentucky. He holds degrees from the University of Alabama (B.S.), Grace Theological Seminary (M.Div.), Southwestern Baptist Seminary (M.Div.), Texas Christian University (M.A.), and the University of Texas (Ph.D.). A founding editor of the *Criswell Theological Review*, he has published articles in that journal as well as in numerous others, including *Grace Theological Journal*, *Wesleyan Theological Journal*, *Theological Educator*, *Review and Expositor*, and *Journal of the Evangelical Theological Society*. He has also coedited *Baptist Theologians* and *The People of God: Essays on the Believer's Church*, both for Broadman Press. He currently serves as the general editor of the *Holman Bible Handbook* (Holman) and *The New American Commentary* (Broadman), for which he is preparing the volume on 1–2 Peter and Jude. He is also completing *Biblical Interpretation Then and Now* for Baker Book House.

Chapter Two

New Testament Interpretation: A Historical Survey

New Testament interpretation has had as its goal the discovery of the meaning of the writings of the New Testament. Throughout the history of the church different people or schools have offered different ways to interpret the biblical texts and convey that interpretation to their contemporaries. Even for those in the early centuries of the church, and especially for twentieth-century interpreters, the New Testament has posed a considerable challenge because it was written in languages and cultures quite different from those of the respective generations. Too often these differences have been neglected and thus, at various times, interpreters have made the New Testament sound more like a medieval document or a contemporary political statement. Our purpose in this chapter is to reflect on these different interpretations in order to recognize that we stand on the shoulders of numerous others who have gone before us when we attempt to interpret the New Testament. There are many strengths and brilliant insights from which we can learn as well as weaknesses and pitfalls to be avoided from studying the history of interpretation. We shall begin with Scripture's own interpretation of itself, then move to examine the interpretations during successive periods of church history. While we will offer some analysis and evaluation along the way, our purposes are primarily descriptive.

THE BACKGROUND AND BEGINNINGS OF NEW TESTAMENT INTERPRETATION

Christian interpretation of Scripture has inherited, from its birth, the approaches to interpretation found in the writings of intertestamental Judaism as well as those of the contemporary Graeco-Roman world. From this dual heritage Christian interpretation has adopted characteristics of extreme literalism and extreme fancifulness. The first resulted from an unquestioning belief in the divine origin, nature, and authority of the Scripture, word by word. The latter developed from a desire to discover a deeper meaning hidden in the Bible or to sanction certain practices either not mentioned or even contradicted by the written word. Because of this heritage there was an observable continuity with the hermeneutical methods of the rabbis and Philo as well as the followers of Plato and Aristotle. Yet there was also a discontinuity as Christianity attempted to break with Judaism and surrounding Graeco-Roman religions to establish its uniqueness.

The New Testament's interpretation of the old was primarily typological and Christocentric. As F. F. Bruce has rightly noted, "The interpretation of the Old Testament in the New is a subject on which books are still being written and examination candidates still questioned."[1] There are few examples for our purposes regarding the way the latter parts of the New Testament interpreted the earlier sections.[2] Examples, however, include the way the church principles of 1 Corinthians were reset in Ephesians and reapplied in another way in the Pastoral Epistles. Second Peter mentions those who twisted the letters of Paul (3:16). An important passage in 2 Peter 1:20 (NASB) reads, "No prophecy of Scripture is a matter of one's own interpretation." This appears to recognize that an informal rule of faith served as the proper guide to interpret the Bible. Certainly in light of the following verse (v. 21), we learn the apostolic church recognized that the doctrine of inspiration did not guarantee that the Scriptures were easily or rightly understood.

INTERPRETATION IN THE POST-APOSTOLIC PERIOD

The Apostolic Fathers in the second century found the true understanding of the Bible in the teaching of the apostles. The rise of Gnosticism and other challenges to accepted orthodoxy caused a hermeneutical shift. The result was a contextual development that sought to wrestle with the hermeneutical confusion and ambiguity in the struggle for orthodoxy.[3] In order to demonstrate the unity of Scripture and its message, an authoritative framework was implemented by Irenaeus (ca. A.D. 130–200) and Tertullian (ca. A.D. 155–225) to handle such matters. Irenaeus has been described by R. M. Grant as "the father of authoritative exegesis in the church."[4] With Irenaeus we discover the first clear evidence of a Christian Bible and also a framework of interpretation in the church's rule of faith.[5] Continuing the Christological emphasis of the apostles, these early exegetes also emphasized that the rule of faith outlined the theological story that found its focus in the incarnate Lord.

Problematically, with his defensive posture Tertullian shifted the issue from a right understanding of Scripture to the more sharply stated issue of whether the heretics even had a right to read Holy Scripture.[6] Moreover, interpreting Scripture through this theological grid often forced the New Testament text into a preconceived set of theological convictions. The authoritative framework tended to divorce the text from its literary or historical context. Yet in light of the challenges faced by the second-century church, this hermeneutical approach was the only proper response. Included in this approach was a continuity with the typological-Christological method of the apostles and Justin Martyr (ca. A.D. 100–165?). The authoritative response resulted in a hermeneutical circle that safeguarded the church's message but reduced the possibility of creativity among individual interpreters.

THE SCHOOLS OF ALEXANDRIA AND ANTIOCH

With the rise of the Alexandrian school in the third century, an obvious innovational development arose in the church as scriptural exegesis reached new heights. The innovation of allegorical interpretation grew out of its own context. Adapting the allegorical interpretation of Philo and the philosophical framework of Platonism, biblical hermeneutics in Clement (ca. A.D. 150–215) and Origen (ca. A.D. 185–254) moved beyond the defensive posture of Irenaeus and Tertullian.[8] Clement's work initiated the allegorical method, but Origen was the premier exegete of the period. While several Christian writers of the second and third centuries engaged in biblical interpretation, Origen brought the touch of a master to what had been nothing much more than the exercise of amateurs.[9]

Origen created a three-fold hermeneutical methodology

that emphasized the spiritual sense.[10] He thought that Scripture had three different yet complementary meanings: 1) literal or physical sense, 2) a moral or psychical sense, and 3) an allegorical or intellectual sense. In his spiritualization of Scripture, he often "out Philo-ed Philo." The spiritual sense served an apologetic purpose against the Gnostic and other challenges, but primarily it served a pastoral purpose to mature the souls of the faithful.[11] While Origen rejected the authoritative framework of Irenaeus, he nevertheless sought to remain faithful to the church's rule of faith.[12] Origen's genius and allegorical hermeneutic occasionally led him down wrongheaded paths. Yet the allegorical method, at a critical moment in church history, made it possible to uphold the rationality of the Christian faith. Origen's total worldview brought the Alexandrian hermeneutic to new heights, not only in its methodology but in its spirit.[13] Alexandrian hermeneutics was primarily practical and its interpretation of Scripture cannot be understood until this is realized.

The successors of Origen were challenged by the school of Antioch and its emphasis on a literal and historical interpretation. The development that brought about the Antiochene school took place within the context of the maturing church's Christological debates.[14] The Antiochenes emphasized a theology and a hermeneutic that focused on the human and the historical, informed by an Aristotelian philosophy. In reaction to the Platonism and allegorical hermeneutics of the Alexandrians, the Antiochenes responded with a mature understanding of grammatical, historical, and contextual hermeneutics.[15] If hermeneutics is both an art and science, the Alexandrians emphasized the aspect of art while the Antiochenes raised interpretation to the level of a science. The mature interpretation of Theodore of Mopsuestia (ca. A.D. 350–428)[16] and John Chrysostom (ca. A.D. 354–407),[17] while literal, was not a crude or wooden literalism that failed to recognize figures of speech in the biblical text. Their emphasis on the human element of the text allowed for a critical reading that accounted for doctrinal development within the New Testament text, even within a single author.[18] The author-oriented perspective of the Antiochenes' objective hermeneutic represented a new advancement in patristic exegesis.

Both Alexandrians and Antiochenes recognized a plenary sense in Scripture.[19] The difference between their understanding of the fuller sense rested in their view of its scope and purpose. The Antiochenes limited the plenary sense to historical correspondences while the Alexandrians' limitations were generally their own creativity. The Alexandrian allegorical approach led the soul into a realm of true knowledge where the vision of truth could be discovered.[20] The Antiochene purpose led humans into a truly moral life developing in goodness and maturity that would continue into eternity.[21]

TOWARD A THEOLOGICAL HERMENEUTIC

As the church moved into the fifth century, there developed an eclectic and multifaceted hermeneutical practice that sometimes emphasized the literal and historical, and sometimes the allegorical, but always the canonical and theological. The consensus began to develop because of the dominating Christological controversies of the fifth century.[22] With Jerome (ca. A.D. 341–420) and Augustine (A.D. 354–430) in the West and Theodoret of Cyrrhus (ca. A.D. 393–466) in the East, a convergence emerged toward a textual, canonical, and theological interpretation of the Old and New Testaments. The contribution of this period was the emphasis on the biblical canon whereby a text was interpreted in its larger context, understood as the biblical canon.[23] The canon established parameters for validating spiritualized interpretations so that the historical meaning remained primary. Especially in the interpretive work of Augustine and Theodoret the rule of faith and Catholic tradition played a dominant role.[24] Neither the allegorical practices of Alexandria nor the historical emphases of Antioch dominated. A balanced hermeneutic emerged that impacted hermeneutical practices in the Middle Ages as well as in postreformation times. The eclectic fifth-century hermeneutic was shaped by 1) pastoral and theological concerns, 2) presuppositions that viewed the text from the standpoint of faith, and 3) interpretations that produced edification among the saints (Jerome),[25] love toward God and neighbor (Augustine),[26] and benefit and blessing for the church (Theodoret).[27]

THE MIDDLE AGES

From the time of Augustine, the church, following the lead of John Cassian (d. ca. 433), subscribed to a theory of the fourfold Scripture.[28] These four senses were 1) literal, 2) allegorical, 3) tropological or moral, and 4) anagogical.[29] The literal sense of Scripture could and usually did nurture the virtues of faith, hope, and love; but when it did not, the interpreter could appeal to three additional virtues, each sense corresponding to one of the virtues. The allegorical sense referred to the church and its faith, what it was to believe. The tropological sense referred to individuals and what they should do, corresponding to love. The anagogical sense pointed to the church's future expectation, corresponding to hope.

Bernard of Clairvaux (1090–1153) clearly explicated this fourfold approach. In the fourteenth century Nicholas of Lyra (1265–1349) summarized this medieval hermeneutical approach in a much quoted rhyme:

> Littera gesta doucet
> (The letter teaches facts)
> Quid credas allegoria
> (allegory what one should believe)
> Moralis quid agas
> (tropology what one should do)
> Quo tendas anagogia
> (anagogy where one should aspire).

For example, the city of Jerusalem, in all of its appearances in Scripture was understood literally as a Jewish city, allegorically as the church of Christ, tropologically as the souls of women and men, and anagogically as the heavenly city.[30]

Thomas Aquinas (1224–1274) wanted to establish the spiritual sense more securely in the literal sense than it had been grounded in earlier medieval thought. He returned to the distinction between things and signs as in Augustine, but because of his Aristotelianism he preferred "things" and "words."[31] In Scripture, the things designated by words can themselves have the character of a sign. He maintained that the literal sense of Scripture has to do with the sign-character of things. Thus, he was able to demonstrate that the spiritual sense of Scripture was always based on the literal sense and derived from it.[32] Also, he equated the literal sense as the meaning of the text intended by the author.[33] The medieval exegetes and theologians admitted that the words of Scripture contained a meaning in the historical situation in which they were first uttered, but overall they denied that the final and full meaning of those words was restricted to what the first audience thought or heard.

REFORMATION HERMENEUTICS

Martin Luther (1483–1546), the great Reformer, started his career as a biblical interpreter by employing the allegorical method but later abandoned it.[34] Yet it was Desiderius Erasmus (1466–1536) more so than Luther, who through the influence of John Colet (1466–1519) rediscovered the priority of the literal sense.[35] As the chief founder of modern biblical criticism and hermeneutics, he must always hold a cherished position among interpreters of the New Testament. Erasmus exemplified the finest in renaissance scholarship that emphasized the original sources. The ultimate source to which he returned was the Greek New Testament. Coupled with the return to the sources was a truly historical understanding of ancient texts, but he also desired that the texts bring edification to the readers through the spiritual sense as well.[36] His hermeneutical approach developed toward a more critical-historical and philological approach as his method matured, though he always, following his hero, Origen, emphasized the spiritual sense as well.

Erasmus recognized the need for a Greek Testament as early as 1507, and from 1511 onward he carefully studied and collated more Greek manuscripts of the New Testament than has been generally realized. He produced successive editions of the Greek New Testament in 1516, 1519, 1522, 1527, and 1535. In 1516 he published a revised Vulgate alongside his Greek text. His own fresh Latin translation appeared in 1519. From 1517 onward, he produced several editions of his own paraphrases of the New Testament Epistles and Gospels.[37]

As significant and innovative as Erasmus' works were, the pivotal figures in New Testament studies during the Reformation period were Martin Luther and John Calvin (1509–1564). Calvin was the greatest exegete of the Reformation. He developed the grammatical-historical exegetical method as revived by Erasmus, focusing the place of meaning in the historical interpretation and developing the spiritual message from the text.[38] In his commentary on Romans, he inscribed a dedication that read:

Since it is almost the interpreter's only task to unfold the mind of the writer whom he has undertaken to expound, he misses his mark, or at least strays outside his limits, by the extent to which he leads his readers away from the meaning of his author. . . . It is presumptuous and almost blasphemous to turn the meaning of scripture around without due care, as though it were some game that we were playing. And yet many scholars have done this at one time.[39]

While Erasmus and Luther broke tradition to establish a new Protestant hermeneutic, Calvin exemplified it with his touch of genius. Where Luther was bold, sweeping, and prophetic, Calvin was more scholarly and painstaking. Luther was a prophet, a preacher; Calvin a scholarly lecturer. Indeed in the eyes of some he is regarded as the greatest interpreter in the history of the Christian church.[40]

Luther wrote important commentaries on Romans and Galatians. He failed to find equal value in all the writings of the New Testament, judging those that most clearly conveyed the biblical gospel to be superior. He observed:

In short, St. John's Gospel and his first Epistle; St. Paul's Epistles, especially those to the Romans, Galatians and Ephesians; and St. Peter's first Epistle—these are the books which show you Christ and teach everything which is necessary and blessed for you to know, even if you never see or hear any other book or teaching. Therefore in comparison with them St. James's Epistle is a right strawy epistle, for it has no evangelical quality about it.[41]

Calvin wrote commentaries on every book in the New Testament except Revelation and 2 and 3 John. His works evidence an applied theological exegesis. Always insisting that Scripture interprets Scripture, Calvin rejected allegorical interpretation and emphasized the necessity of examining the historical and literary context while comparing Scriptures which treated common subjects.[42]

POST-REFORMATION INTERPRETATION: SCHOLASTICISM, PIETISM, AND RATIONALISM

It is commonly believed that the followers of the Reformers shrank from the exegetical creativity and freedom employed by Luther and Calvin. They instead produced their expositions along newly established theological boundaries, which resulted in a Protestant scholasticism. Yet as F. F. Bruce has noted, there were several independent thinkers during this period including Matthias Flacius Illyricus (1520–1575), Joachim Camerarius (1500–1574), Hugo Grotius (1583–1645), John Lightfoot (1602–1675), Christian Schöttgen (1687–1751), and Johann Jakob Wettstein (1693–1754).[43]

It is true, however, that the followers of Luther and Calvin tended to systematize their exegesis into an Aristotelian mold.[44] Primarily this approach was exemplified on the Lutheran side in Philip Melanchthon (1497–1560) and on the Calvinist side by Francis Turretin (1623–1687). This new form of scholasticism exercised an authoritative and dogmatic hermeneutic. The new scholasticism coupled with the rise of the Enlightenment, which rejected both authoritative and dogmatic approaches, issued in two reactions: 1) a new-found pietism in Philipp Jakob Spener (1635–1705) and August Herman Franke (1663–1727),[45] and 2) a historical-critical method that stressed the importance of the historical over against the theological interpretation of the New Testament pioneered by Johann Salamo Semler (1725–1791) and Johann David Michaelis (1717–1791).[46]

The most valuable contribution for New Testament studies from the Pietist tradition came from John Albert Bengel (1687–1752). He was the first scholar to classify the New Testament Greek manuscripts into families on the basis of various similarities. His commentary, the well-known *Gnomon of the New Testament* (1742), served as a model for its combination of historical roots, explanation of figures of speech, and suggestions for devotional applications.[47]

Philosophical and theological rationalism provided much of the foundation for the rise of historical-criticism. The rationalism of R. Descartes (1506–1650), T. Hobbes (1588–1679), B. Spinoza (1632–1677), and J. Locke (1632–1704) greatly influenced biblical and theological studies. H. S. Reimarus (1694–1768) and G. E. Lessing (1729–1781) subsumed biblical revelation under the role of reason. F. D. E. Schleiermacher (1768–1834) combined aspects of pietism (experience) with rationalism and developed new hermeneutical concerns. Schleiermacher granted that the historical-critical approach helped disclose the intention of the biblical writers in the context of their day, but he also raised the question of what their message might mean to readers and hearers in a different age and culture. In so doing, he became not only the "Father of Theological Liberalism," but also the "Father of Modern Hermeneutics."[48]

THE MODERN PERIOD

Historical-Criticism

A new approach to New Testament interpretation was introduced by J. Semler, who approached the New Testament text only on a historical basis. Unsatisfied with the pietist tradition, Semler made a distinction between the "word of God," which has abiding authority unto salvation, and the "scriptures," which contain information important only for the times in which they were written. Inspiration had given way to "objective" history.[49] A contemporary, Johann A. Ernesti, in his *Institutio Interpretis Novi Testamenti* (1761), applied to the New Testament the philological-historical method he had successfully used earlier in editing classical texts. Though F. Lau has considered Ernesti as "the father of the profane scientific interpretation of the Bible," Semler is better viewed as father of historical-critical study. Ernesti did not divorce historical study from biblical inspiration and continued to affirm the complete truthfulness of the Bible.[50] J. D. Michaelis introduced a new discipline, "Introduction to the New Testament," seeking to interpret the New Testament without dogmatic presuppositions.

In the seventeenth century B. Spinoza argued the importance of asking questions about the authorship, date, and purpose of the writings. Michaelis tackled these questions and determined that those New Testament books not actually written by apostles were neither inspired nor canonical. Semler and Michaelis approached the New Testament apart from confessional or theological concerns. Together they should be acknowledged as pioneers of historical-critical interpretation of the New Testament.[51] Historical criticism is used as a comprehensive term designating several techniques to discover the historical situation, the sources behind the writings, the literary style and relationships, the date, authorship, approach to composition, destination, and recipients. In contrast to textual criticism, which was known as "lower criticism," historical criticism was called "higher criticism," but this term is now virtually obsolete.

Gospel Studies

Johann Jakob Griesbach (1745–1812), the pupil of Semler, refused to harmonize the Synoptic Gospels and separated John's Gospel from the Synoptics, thus advancing beyond the historical issues of his mentors to a focus on literary relationships in the New Testament. Griesbach was not the first to raise these issues. Tatian (ca. A.D. 170) developed his *Diatessaron*, a harmony of all four gospels. The Reformers recognized the harmony of Matthew, Mark, and Luke. Griesbach, however, marked the transition in an obvious way from the Reformation approach to the modern period by his treatment of the Gospels. He proposed that Matthew was written first and Mark last, positing that it was a digest of the other Synoptics.[52] His work was published as *Synopsis Evangeliorum* (1776). G. E. Lessing proposed in *Neue Hypothese über die Evangelisten als bloss menschliche Geschichtsschreiber* (1778) that the Gospels were different translations or fragments of an older Aramaic *Gospel of the Nazarenes*. J. G. Eichhorn (1752–1827), a pupil of Michaelis, advanced Lessing's idea by proposing nine different gospels developed from the Aramaic *Gospel*. He suggested that the Synoptics were the final results of this complicated literary process.[53]

The Tübingen scholar G. C. Storr (1746–1804), a supernaturalist, convincingly explained the absence of large portions of material from Mark's gospel by suggesting that Mark was the initial Gospel penned. This Marcan priority hypothesis was advanced by K. Lachmann (1793–1851) and H. J. Holtzmann (1832–1910). Although it has been challenged in recent years by W. R. Farmer, J. B. Orchard, and several of their followers, the priority of Mark is the prominent position among most New Testament scholars today. These issues are clearly and carefully explained and evaluated by Scot McKnight in his chapter on source criticism later in this book.[55]

Unity and Diversity

During this period near the end of the eighteenth century, biblical theology, distinct from dogmatic theology, was introduced by J. P. Gabler (1753–1826). In his inaugural speech as professor of theology at the University of Altdorf in 1787, he outlined his understanding of biblical theology. He indicated that the New Testament authors must be interpreted in the light of their own historical contexts, and that in comparing these writings with each other, their differences must be acknowledged. Gabler, a rationalist, disavowed New Testament miracles. Similarly he failed to acknowledge a unity in diversity in the theology of the New Testament, instead focusing on irreconcilable differences. The result was a New Testament that included only kernels of confessional truth that were not limited by historical conditioning.[56]

This line of thought was developed significantly in the epoch-making work of Ferdinand Christian Baur (1792–1860). Baur was convinced that a deep gulf existed in early Christianity between the Jerusalem church and the Pauline mission. He and other members of the infamous Tübingen School reconstructed the history of the apostolic and sub-apostolic age by postulating a major antithesis between Peter and Paul. The solution for Baur came in his suggested synthesis that the New Testament writings were not first-century apostolic documents but second-century works that presented a developing catholicism. This "tendency criticism" came to dominate New Testament research and still strongly influences various schools of thought. Further research has shown that there is greater unity than allowed for by either Gabler or Baur.

The Tübingen school exaggerated the antithesis, failed to recognize Peter's role as a reconciler, and miscalculated the time involved in the advancement and development of early Christianity. The turning point in this research came from J. B. Lightfoot (1829–1889), who demonstrated the early date of the writings of the Apostolic Fathers.[57] Biblical theology has moved in different directions, reflecting various nuances, each wrestling with the theological contributions of the biblical writers, the unity, diversity and development in the New Testament.[58] Important works in this regard are W. Bauer's *Orthodoxy and Heresy in Earliest Christianity* (1934); H. Koester and J. Robinson, *Trajectories Through Earliest Christianity* (1971); and J. D. G. Dunn, *Unity and Diversity in the New Testament* (1977). Robert Sloan examines these themes in greater detail in his chapter in this volume.

Quest for the Historical Jesus

Simultaneous with Baur's work and building on the work of Gospel criticism, several scholars began a quest for the "historical Jesus." The purpose of the quest was to reconstruct the Gospels and the sources behind the Gospels to understand and interpret Jesus in purely historical and human categories. The phrase achieved widespread usage from the title of Albert Schweitzer's (1875–1965) volume, *The Quest for the Historical Jesus* (1906). Originally published as *From Reimarus to Wrede*, Schweitzer summarized over 250 authors who, from the end of the eighteenth century to the beginning of the twentieth, investigated the life of Jesus.[59]

The primary scholars examined were H. S. Reimarus (1694–1768), H. E. G. Paulus (1761–1851), F. D. E. Schleiermacher (1768–1834), D. F. Strauss (1801–1874), and W. Wrede (1859–1906). Reimarus separated the teachings of Jesus from what the apostles taught about him, suggesting that the apostles' teaching was a fabrication of their own theology. Paulus continued this line of thinking and rejected the miraculous events in the life of Jesus claiming that the observers of those events misunderstood natural events as "miracles." Paulus generally distrusted anything outside of rational thought.

Schleiermacher's *Leben Jesu* was published posthumously in 1864 based on lecture notes transcribed by a student. Schleiermacher differentiated between the Jesus of history in the Synoptics and the Christ of faith in the Fourth Gospel. Strauss, perhaps as radical as any "questor," rejected the idea that God could intervene in this world. He thus rejected the idea of incarnation and reconstructed the gospel story in mythological fashion. What was created by Schleiermacher and Strauss was an either/or choice: either Jesus was historical or supernatural; he was the Jesus of the Synoptic presentation or of the Johannine picture.

Wrede argued that the Gospels were not intended to be historical works, but were written as biased theology; thus the historical Jesus could not be discovered in the Gospels. Schweitzer reviewed all of these, and with J. Weiss (1863–1914) concluded that the kingdom proclamation of Jesus should be understood from a thoroughgoing eschatological perspective.[60] R. Bultmann (1884–1976) declared that the historical Jesus was inaccessible to the historian.[61] Most nineteenth- and early twentieth-century New Testament scholars felt the importance of interacting with this movement. T. W. Manson's infamous words point to this seeming necessity: "Indeed, it may be said of all theological schools of thought: By their lives of Jesus ye shall know them."[62] The problems were created by either/or choices when the Gospel picture is both/and. Jesus is historical (man) and supernatural (God), and the portraits in the Synoptics and John are complementary not contradictory. Jesus inaugurated the kingdom, but the kingdom yet awaits a consummation.

The psychological quest closed with Bultmann, but was reopened with Bultmann's students, J. Robinson and E. Käsemann. They began an existential quest that was little more profitable than the previous one. What was important about this new exploration was that Bultmann's disciples were rejecting the teaching of their mentor. Outside the Bultmannian circle, J. Jeremias, C. H. Dodd, T. W. Manson, and V. Taylor raised opposition to the old quest and the new one.[63] The relation of history to theology is further addressed by D. Hagner's chapter in this book.

American Reformed Exegesis

While these innovative questions were pursued, primarily in Europe, we must not neglect the able exegesis being carried out in North America during these centuries. America's greatest theologian, Jonathan Edwards (1703–1758), undertook two major exegetical projects seeking to advance a Reformed theological exegesis, though he was open to multiple levels of meaning in the biblical text. He was not bound to the literal sense but assumed that every passage held the possibility of multiple interpretations. In the same passage he often found a literal meaning, a statement about Christ, the church, and last things (heaven/hell). Edwards' spiritual approach has greatly influenced American pulpits for two centuries.[64]

A more consistent echo of the Calvinist tradition's grammatical-historical exegesis was advanced at Princeton Seminary in the nineteenth century. Charles Hodge (1797–1878) published masterful volumes on Romans, Ephesians, 1 and 2 Corinthians from 1835–1859. Other Princetonians, J. A. Alexander, A. A. Hodge, and B. B. Warfield, also contributed to the advancement of the theological exposition of the New Testament, which so influenced the work of J. G. Machen and N. B. Stonehouse.[65] This approach combined with the British evangelical tradition has greatly shaped the American evangelical understanding of New Testament interpretation.

Baptists in America have also made significant contributions to New Testament studies. Moses Stuart, the great Andover scholar, primarily concentrated his work in Old Testament, but also wrote important New Testament commentaries that interacted with critical European scholarship. His commentary on Romans served as a model for handling difficult textual and grammatical issues. A. T. Robertson, a prolific scholar, wrote commentaries, grammatical works, and textual studies. His *Word Pictures* remains a standard for pastors and teachers. His massive grammar continues to serve as a valuable resource for New Testament scholars, even though linguistic research has reversed some of his findings. Robertson's father-in-law, John A. Broadus, contributed significant studies in New Testament and preaching. Chief among these was his commentary on Matthew in the important *American Commentary* series edited by A. Hovey. George E. Ladd stands at the forefront of American Baptist and evangelical scholarship with his first-rate New Testament theology, his studies on the kingdom in the New Testament, and his pioneering efforts in New Testament criticism.

British Contributions

British scholarship at this time advanced a historical-critical interpretation of the New Testament, but generally the Cambridge trio of J. B. Lightfoot (1828–1889), B. F. Westcott (1825–1901), and J. A. Hort (1828–1892) reached different conclusions from their German counterparts. As previously noted Lightfoot refuted the Tübingen school's unwarranted conclusions regarding the supposed conflict between Pauline and Petrine movements in the apostolic church. He also wrote exemplary commentaries on several Pauline epistles including Galatians, Philippians, and Colossians.

Westcott and Hort are best known for their 1881 critical edition of the Greek New Testament. They also made other significant contributions including Hort's commentaries on 1 Peter, James, and Revelation. Westcott produced a major survey of the New Testament canon (1855) and outstanding commentaries on John's gospel, John's epistles, and Hebrews. These three masterful exegetes modeled an exacting scholarship that brilliantly influenced men like C. H. Dodd, T. W. Manson, and the New Testament evangelical giants of this generation, F. F. Bruce and I. Howard Marshall.

Form Criticism

All twentieth-century New Testament scholarship has had to reckon with the influential Marburg scholar Rudolf Bultmann. His form-critical approach advanced what had been proposed by source-critical and tradition-critical approaches via his existential hermeneutic. Tradition criticism moved the concerns of source criticism beyond the written sources, endeavoring to trace the course of the transmission of these oral or written traditions. Form criticism attempts to reconstruct the various New Testament "forms" of the preliminary tradition by classifying the principal forms such as legal, poetic, legends, parables, etc. The process includes examining these to discover the contents of the forms, how they were handed down, and what their successive life settings were until they assumed their present shape and position. Some scholars have undertaken to recover the exact words of Jesus by removing the so-called additions attached to the sayings in the course of transmission. The threefold interpretation task works back from 1) interpretation of the present gospels through 2) interpretation of the tradition lying behind them to 3) reconstruction of the proclamation of Jesus. This framework was applied to the Gospels almost independently by K. L. Schmidt in *The Framework of the Story of Jesus* (1919); M. Diebelius in *From Tradition to Gospel* (1919), and Bultmann in *History of the Synoptic Tradition* (1921). Further exposition and evaluation will be offered by D. Bock in the chapter on form criticism.

When this approach is applied to New Testament epistles, form criticism of another type seeks to recognize the form of a forensic argument or rhetorical situation, which also incorporates the concerns of rhetorical criticism. H. D. Betz has pioneered this approach by applying form criticism to Galatians.[66] Likewise, the work of George Kennedy in this field is worthy of special mention.

Redaction Criticism

Redaction criticism moved beyond the findings of form criticism as the limits of form criticism became apparent. Redaction criticism developed out of a concern to see the relationship of authors to written sources. This approach has four basic concerns: 1) the original situation of the Gospel event or saying, 2) the tradition and process of transmission, 3) the situation in the early church, and 4) the situation and purpose of the writer/editor. Basic to redaction criticism is the theological motivation of the author/redactor. Redaction criticism is concerned with the entire framework, not individual units of material. Pioneering studies using this method included H. Conzelmann's *The Theology of Luke* (1954); W. Marxen's *Mark the Evangelist* (1959); and G. Bornkamm, G. Barth, and H. J. Held's *Tradition and Interpretation in Matthew* (1960). Grant Osborne treats this subject in the present volume including a thorough analysis and evaluation.

Genre Criticism

Genre criticism seeks to identify the genre of the New Testament writing by the interrelation of the form, style, and content. Writings grouped together by content may belong to the same genre, but similarity of content alone is not a sufficient criterion. One of the chief criteria is how the writings function. Thus the classification of genres is really not so much to classify as to clarify. The four major genres of the New Testament, according to style, content, form, and function, are gospels, letters/epistles, Acts, and apocalyptic. These four overlap at times and all include numerous subcategories such as parable, hymn, poetry, rhetoric, diatribe, sermon, prophecy, liturgy, and other figures of speech and literary devices.[67] Craig Blomberg ably tackles these issues in the second section of this book.

CONTEMPORARY HERMENEUTICS

Foundational hermeneutical theories have grown up alongside the specific interests and methods outlined in the previous pages. These contemporary hermeneutical concerns have produced new approaches in recent years. In order to understand the background of these approaches we will outline the major hermeneutical discussions of the past two centuries. A. Thiselton has performed an invaluable service for New Testament studies with his monumental work on contemporary hermeneutics titled *Two Horizons* (1980).

The critical methods we have noted are generally built on an author-oriented hermeneutical perspective. Advocates of this position such as K. Stendahl and J. L. McKenzie writing in the *Journal of Biblical Literature* (1958) defined interpretation as determining the meaning intended by the human author and understood by the original readers.[68] This approach considered the meaning of texts to be stable and univocal, and its meaning in the original setting is where meaning is located. Such an understanding can be traced to J. A. Ernesti and Friedrich Schleiermacher.

Schleiermacher contended for a pre-understanding that must take place before interpretation can happen.[69] Understanding, for Schleiermacher, was related to the author's intention. The early Schleiermacher in his section on grammatical interpretation articulated some of the most incisive statements found in all hermeneutical literature on the principles for grasping what an author willed to communicate. The ultimate aim, however, was to get through to an author's unique individuality, a psychological interpretation. Interpretation required a knowledge of grammatical concerns, but also a divinatory intuition through empathy with and imagination of the author's experience. The interpreter attempts to divine the author so that one transforms oneself into another and seeks an immediate knowledge of the author's individuality.[70]

But this was not enough for Schleiermacher. He argued that the interpreter can potentially understand the author's work as well as or even better than the author.[71] W. Dilthey carried on this tradition by making the goal of interpretation that of inducing in oneself an imitation of life that is not native to him or her. He postulated the idea of a universal human nature that could make this possible, yet he conceded that an author's personality could not be fully grasped.[72] The most notable theorist of an author-oriented approach in the contemporary discussion is E. D. Hirsch.[73] He works in the Schleiermacher tradition, but has modified it by moving toward a more grammatical and, therefore, more objective direction. In many ways these insights reflect the best of the Antiochene school,

Erasmus, Calvin, the Princetonians, the Cambridge trio, and the historical-critical tradition.

Yet the author-oriented approach moved from an emphasis on epistemology in Schleiermacher to an existential emphasis with M. Heidegger (1889–1976) and Bultmann. With Heidegger came an increasing skepticism toward the possibility of achieving determinate meaning in textual interpretation. In his classic works, *Being and Time* (E.T. 1962) and *On the Way to Language* (E.T. 1971), Heidegger shifted the emphasis away from historical concerns of the text to a priori concerns of the interpreter.[74] Indeed, understanding was generated from the interpreter's existential awareness of human possibilities. From this level of awareness, understanding moved from cognition to expression in the use of language. He affirmed that what came to expression in discourse was the projection of an understanding of the possibility of human being.[75] The interpreter became the source of meaning as emphasis shifted from the author to the reader, and even to the core of the reader's being.

It is well known that Bultmann was primarily responsible for Heidegger's views entering the field of New Testament studies.[76] Bultmann's concern was not the objectifying language of the New Testament, but the existential possibilities of human being projected through it. One such possibility obviously rested in the New Testament concept of faith. He noted the New Testament was written from the vantage point of faith and called for a faith response from its readers.[77] Denying any coherent doctrinal norm in the New Testament, Bultmann claimed that by faith, New Testament doctrine, couched in the objectifying mode of language, which he called "myth," was to be interpreted in terms of the primordial possibilities of human being.[78] His program of demythologizing was not intended to remove myth from the New Testament but to existentialize it. Understanding occurs when the existential possibilities of the language of faith are appropriated by faith and result in a new self-understanding.

Bultmann thought biblical exegesis without prior understanding an impossibility.[79] By de-emphasizing the cognitive aspects of the biblical text and shifting the notion of interpretation to existential encounter, Bultmann redirected the focus of New Testament interpretation in the twentieth century.

The discussion has been refined and redirected by Hans-Georg Gadamer, a student of the Marburg scholars. His classic work, *Truth and Method* (E.T. 1975), stresses the distance that separates contemporary readers from ancient texts, like the New Testament, in terms of time, culture, and language. He also emphasized the prejudgments interpreters bring to the text as well as the way tradition impinges on how they read texts. The goal is not to understand the author's intention or the text's historical meaning, but to focus on what the text says to present readers. Interpretation is best pictured as a conversation in which two people try to come to a common understanding about some matter which is of interest to both.

Gadamer also contends that an ancient text is not a fixed depository of univocal language, but an exposition of something whose meaning exceeds the text.[80] Language, he maintains, is always polyvalent and analogical. The text contains a fullness of meaning by which its very nature can never be exhausted. Meaning, then, always exceeds the conscious intention of the author.[81]

Paul Ricoeur (1913–), in some ways, theoretically combines the concerns of author-oriented hermeneutics and reader-oriented hermeneutics.[82] While Ricoeur agrees that a text has intentionality, he stresses that when reading texts, the author generally is not present to be questioned about ambiguous meaning in the text. In contrast to Gadamer, Ricoeur posits that a text's meaning is intelligible across historical and cultural distance. Because of the nature of writing, the text opens up the text world to the interpreter. The interpreter may then enter that world and appropriate the possibilities that it offers. What is understood or appropriated, then, is not necessarily the author's intended meaning or the historical situation of the original author or readers but the text itself.[83] It is in this sense that Ricoeur can claim that Romans, Galatians, 1 Peter or John's Gospel can be addressed to contemporary readers as much as to original readers. Building on the shift in hermeneutics from finding meaning[84] in the author's intention or author's results to uncovering meaning in the text itself or the reader via existential encounter or shared conversation, current New Testament methods and approaches also have shifted the idea of interpretation away from the author. The final section of our survey will briefly note these recent developments.

RECENT DEVELOPMENTS

Though historical criticism continues to be immensely productive in some circles, there is a wide-ranging outlook suggesting that it has seen its best days.[85] Several chapters in this volume focus on these new ideas. One thing that has happened with these recent approaches is different questions have been asked and new insights have emerged.

Sociological criticism recognizes that conditioning factors helped to shape and focus the religious aspiration of the New Testament period.[86] The sociological approach is also interested in the New Testament's value for religious goals today. Several liberation[87] and feminist[88] models have come to the forefront asking how the New Testament was influenced by societal pressures and prejudices, and how, if at all, similar pressures and prejudices can be understood and addressed today.

Structuralism, based on the findings of C. Levi-Strauss, *Structural Anthropology* (1960), and F. de Saussure, *Course on General Linguistics* (1966), is concerned not with the formal structure of a unit of tradition, but with the deep structure of human self-expression. Daniel Patte, more than any other scholar, has advocated the possibilities of structuralism for New Testament studies.[89] One of the issues involved in this approach, as well as the other recent contributions, revolves around the value or lack of value of historical issues. There is even a strong contention by some for an antihistoricism, believing that historical criticism is illegitimate and without value.

Closely related, and at times indistinguishable, are new classifications of literary criticism called narrative criticism, compositional criticism, or rhetorical criticism. These models seek to understand not the history behind the text nor the historical situation of the original authors or readers nor even their understanding of themselves as human beings but the text itself. Two Johannine scholars have been prominent in the employment of this perspective: R. Alan Culpepper, *Anatomy of the Fourth Gospel* (Philadelphia: Fortress, 1983) and Paul Duke, *Irony in the Fourth Gospel* (Atlanta: John Knox, 1985). Their work follows in the path of Frank Kermode. Fresh ground is being plowed in many areas of the New Testament, particularly in the Gospels, such as Jack D. Kingsbury's works on Matthew and

Mark. The goal of such an approach is to discover the intertextual keys that allow the text to reveal itself.

A final observation about canonical criticism closes our survey. Originally voiced as a protest against preoccupation with the authenticity and forms of the Jesus tradition, canonical criticism has shifted the emphasis in interpretation back to the existing text in its canonical framework. Initially developed as an Old Testament discipline by J. A. Sanders, *Torah and Canon* (1972) and *Canon and Community* (1984), and B. S. Childs, *Introduction to the Old Testament as Scripture* (1979), the approach has expanded the concerns of redaction criticism to see how the canonical shape and the place of the book in the canon also impact interpretation. Childs' work has pioneered the entrance of this discipline into New Testament studies.[90]

Studies in canonical criticism have developed alongside parallel concerns in the area of New Testament canon. Questions addressed in these recent works include the traditional concerns of canon as well as the matters of authorship and inspiration, pseudonymity, and the place of tradition. Four works, among others, are worthy of special notice: D. G. Meade's *Pseudonymity and Canon*, Bruce Metzger's *The New Testament Canon*, Lee M. McDonald's *The Formation of the Christian Biblical Canon*, and F. F. Bruce's *The Canon of Scripture*. The answers to issues addressed above have received various responses in these volumes, indicating that much work still remains to be done in this area.

The space limitation of our chapter will not permit us to note interpretation issues in particular books. A fine survey of these matters can be found in *The New Testament and Its Modern Interpreters* (1988), edited by E. J. Epp and G. J. MacRae. Obviously the current state of New Testament studies is as diverse and varied as is its history. As someone has well said, "The field of New Testament studies is an inch wide and a mile deep." We have not come close to reaching these depths in this overview. I hope, however, that the survey introduces the reader to issues that will be addressed in the remainder of this volume. It is important to recognize that the articles are written by men and women who accept the New Testament as God's Word written by human authors.[91] Each recognizes the importance of the Holy Spirit's illuminating work in the process of interpretation. Our goal is to build on the initial chapters, which affirm the full inspiration and authority of the New

Testament and acknowledge the diversity of our past. We therefore approach our God-called task as interpreters and theologians with a simultaneous confidence in the Scripture illumined by the Spirit that points us to Christ and a sanctified tolerance and humility, recognizing that all interpretation is open to further correction and revision.

BIBLIOGRAPHY

Ackroyd, P. R., and C. F. Evans, eds. *Cambridge History of the Bible*. 3 vols. Cambridge: Cambridge University Press, 1970.

Bruce, F. F. "The History of New Testament Study." In *New Testament Interpretation: Essays on Principles and Methods*, edited by I. Howard Marshall. Grand Rapids: Eerdmans, 1977.

Dockery, David S. *Biblical Interpretation Then and Now*. Grand Rapids: Baker, 1991.

Grant, Robert M., and David Tracey. *A Short History of the Interpretation of the Bible*. Philadelphia: Fortress, 1984.

Kugel, James L., and Rowan A. Greer. *Early Biblical Interpretation*. Philadelphia: Westminster, 1986.

Kümmel, W. G. *The New Testament: The History of the Investigation of Its Problems*. Trans. S. M. Gilmour and H. C. Kee. Nashville: Abingdon, 1972.

Neill, Stephen and T. Wright. *The Interpretation of the New Testament 1861–1986*. 2d ed. New York: Oxford, 1988.

Rogerson, John, Christopher Rowland, and Barnabas Lindars SSF. *The Study and Use of the Bible*. Grand Rapids: Eerdmans, 1988.

Silva, Moíses. *Has the Church Misread the Bible?* Grand Rapids: Zondervan, 1987.

Thiselton, Anthony. *Two Horizons: New Testament Hermeneutics and Philosophical Description*. Grand Rapids: Eerdmans, 1980.

NOTES

[1]F. F. Bruce, "The History of New Testament Study," in *New Testament Interpretation: Essays on Principles and Methods*, ed. I. Howard Marshall (Grand Rapids: Eerdmans, 1977), 21; also see the chapter in this book by Klyne Snodgrass.

[2]The chapters on "Redaction Criticism" by Grant Osborne and "Canonical Criticism" by Mikeal Parsons will touch on these matters.

[3]Cf. Walter Bauer, *Orthodoxy and Heresy in Earliest Christianity*, ed. Robert Kraft and Gerhard Krodel (Philadelphia: Fortress, 1971), 61–194; Harold O. J. Brown, *Heresies* (Garden City, N.Y.: Doubleday, 1984), 38–94.

[4]Robert M. Grant with David Tracy, *A Short History of the Interpretation of the Bible*, rev. ed. (Philadelphia: Fortress, 1984), 55.

[5]Irenaeus, *Against Heresies* 1.10, 22; 2.25; 3.4; cf. Rowan A. Greer, "The Dog and the Mushrooms: Irenaeus' View of the Valentinians Assessed," in *The Rediscovery of Gnosticism*, vol. 1 of *The School of Valentine*, ed. Bentley Layton (Leiden: Brill, 1980), 146–75.

[6]Karlfried Froehlich, trans. and ed., *Biblical Interpretation in the Early Church* (Philadelphia: Fortress, 1984), 13–15.

[7]Cf. Oskar Skarsaune, *Proof from Prophecy: A Study in Justin Martyr's Proof-Text Tradition* (Leiden: Brill, 1987); also Willis A. Shotwell, *The Biblical Exegesis of Justin Martyr* (London: SPCK, 1965).

[8]Cf. James L. Kugel and Rowan A. Greer, *Early Biblical Interpretation* (Philadelphia: Westminster, 1986), 177–99.

[9]R. P. C. Hanson, *Allegory and Event: A Study of the Sources and Significance of Origen's Interpretation of Scripture* (London: SCM, 1959), 360.

[10]Origen, *De Principiis* 4.2.4–17; cf. J. N. D. Kelly, *Early Christian Doctrines* (New York: Harper, 1960), 70–75. Origen built his model on his translation of Proverbs 22:20, "Write them in a three-fold way."

[11]Cf. Karen J. Torjesen, "Hermeneutical Procedure and Theological Structure in Origen's Exegesis," (Ph.D. dissertation, Claremont Graduate School, 1982).

[12]See R. P. C. Hanson, *Origen's Doctrine of Tradition* (London: SPCK, 1954); also Albert C. Outler, "Origen and the Regulae Fidei," in *Church History* 8 (1939): 212–21.

[13]Joseph Wilson Tirgg, *Origen: The Bible and Philosophy in the Third-Century Church* (Atlanta: John Knox, 1983), 31–75; Dan G. McCartney, "Literal and Allegorical Interpretation in Origen's Contra Celsum," in *Westminster Theological Journal* 48 (1986): 281–301.

[14]Cf. F. A. Sullivan, *The Christology of Theodore of Mopsuestia* (Rome: Gregorian University Press, 1956); also R. A. Norris, *Manhood and Christ: A Study in the Christology of Theodore of Mopseustia* (Oxford: Clarendon, 1963).

[15]Jacques Guillet, "Les exegeses d'Alexandrie et d'Antioche: conflit ou Malentendu?" in *Recherches de science religieuse* 34 (1957): 275–302, is incorrect in concluding that the differences between the two schools were caused only by a fundamental misunderstanding of each other.

[16]Cf. Rowan A. Greer, *Theodore of Mopsuestia: Exegete and Theologian* (London: Faith, 1961).

[17]Cf. Donald Attwater, *St. John Chrysostom: Pastor and Preacher* (London: Harvill, 1959).

[18]See the discussion concerning the Antiochene treatment of the Apostle Paul in Maurice F. Wiles, *The Divine Apostle: The Interpretation of St. Paul's Epistles in the Early Church* (Cambridge: Cambridge University Press, 1967).

[19]Raymond E. Brown, *The Sensus Plenior of Holy Scripture* (Baltimore: St. Mary's University Press, 1955), 46.

[20]Cf. Origen, *Contra Celsum* 4.49. He contended that if the biblical text is divine, it must bear allegorical meaning. If a text cannot be interpreted allegorically, it must then be relegated to a state of unimportance.

[21]Cf. Chrysostom, *Expositions in the Psalms* 46.1.

[22]R. L. Wilken, "Tradition, Exegesis and the Christological Controversies," *Church History* 34 (1965): 123–45.

[23]See the discussion on Jerome and Augustine in H. F. D. Sparks, "Jerome as Biblical Scholar," and Gerald Bonner, "Augustine as Biblical Scholar" in *Cambridge History of the Bible*, eds. P. R. Ackroyd and C. F. Evans, 3 vols. (Cambridge: Cambridge University Press, 1970), 510–63.

[24]Augustine, *On Christian Doctrine* 3.2. In 3.5, he referred to the *praescriptio fidei*.

[25]See J. N. D. Kelly, *Jerome: His Life, Writings and Controversies* (London: Duckworth, 1975), 264–73.

[26]Augustine, *On Christian Doctrine* 3.15.

[27]Theodoret, *Letters* 16.

[28]Beryl Smalley, *The Study of the Bible in the Middle Ages* (2d ed., Oxford: Blackwell, 1952), 26–36; cf. Gillian R. Evans, *The Language and Logic of the Bible: The Earlier Middle Ages* (Cambridge: Cambridge University Press, 1984).

[29]Robert E. McNally, *The Bible in the Early Middle Ages* (Westminster, Md.: Newman, 1959), 50–54.

[30]See James Houston's introduction in Bernard of Clairvaux, *The Love of God and Spiritual Friendship*, ed. with an extended introduction by J. Houston (Portland: Multnomah, 1983), 32–33; Beryl Smalley, "The Bible in the Middle Ages," in *The Church's Use of the Bible Past and Present*, ed. D. E. Nineham (London: Macmillan, 1963), 60; John Rogerson, Christopher Rowland, Barnabas Lindars SSF, *The Study and Use of the Bible* (Grand Rapids: Eerdmans, 1988), 274–94.

[31]David C. Steinmetz, "The Superiority of Precritical Exegesis," *Theology Today* 27 (1980): 31–32; cf. F. Van Steenberghen, *Aristotle in the West: The Origins of Latin Aristotelianism*, trans. Leonard Johnston (Louvain: E. Nauwelaerts, 1955), 62–63.

[32]Cf. Thomas Aquinas, *On Interpretation*, trans. J. T. Oesterle (Milwaukee: Marquette University Press, 1962).

[33]Cf. B. Moeller, "Scripture, Tradition, and Sacrament in the Middle Ages and in Luther," in *Holy Book and Holy Tradition*, ed. F. F. Bruce and E. G. Rupp (Manchester: Manchester University Press, 1968), 120–22; also E. Gilson, *The Christian Philosophy of St. Thomas Aquinas*, trans. L. K. Shook (London: Victor Gollancz, 1957), 20–21.

[34]Cf. Raymond Barry Shelton, "Martin Luther's Concept of Biblical Interpretation in Historical Perspective," (Ph.D. dissertation, Fuller Theological Seminary, 1974); also Jaroslav Pelikan, *Luther the Expositor* (St. Louis: Concordia, 1959). Also see David S. Dockery, "The Christological Hermeneutics of Martin Luther," in *Grace Theological Journal* 4 (1983): 189–203.

[35]A. Rabil, *Erasmus and the New Testament: The Mind of a Christian Humanist* (San Antonio: Trinity University Press, 1972), 43–45; cf. J. H. Bentley, *Humanist and Holy Writ* (Princeton: Princeton University Press, 1983), 115–26.

[36]Cf. J. W. Aldridge, *The Hermeneutics of Erasmus* (Richmond: John Knox, 1966); also J. B. Payne, *Erasmus: His Theology of the Sacraments* (New York: Bratcher, 1970), 54–70.

[37]Traditionally negative evaluations have been given to Erasmus' work, e.g., A. T. Robertson, *An Introduction to the Textual Criticism of the New Testament* (New York: Doubleday, 1925), 19–20; Bruce M. Metzger, *The Text of the New Testament* (Oxford: Oxford University Press, 1968), 97–103. Recently more balanced and positive renderings have been offered by Bentley, *Humanist and Holy Writ*, 114ff.; and Henk Jan DeJonge, "The Character of Erasmus' Translation of the New Testament as Reflected in His Translation of Hebrews 9," in *The Journal of Medieval and Renaissance Studies* 14 (1984): 81–87; idem, "*Novum Testamentum A Nobis Versum*: The Essence of Erasmus' Edition of the New Testament," in *Journal of Theological Studies* 35 (1984): 394–413.

[38]Hans-Joachim Kraus, "Calvin's Exegetical Principles," in *Interpretation* 31 (1977): 8–18; cf. Timothy George, *Theology of the Reformers* (Nashville: Broadman, 1988).

[39]John Calvin, *The Epistles of Paul the Apostle to the Romans and to the Thessalonians*, ed. D. W. Torrance and T. F. Torrance (Grand Rapids: Eerdmans, 1961), 1.4.

[40]Even a rival like J. Arminius said Calvin's interpretation of Scripture was incomparable, saying, "He stands above others, above most, indeed, above all." Cited by C. Bangs, *Arminius: A Study in the Dutch Reformation* (Nashville: Abingdon, 1971), 287–88.

[41]Martin Luther, *Luther's Works*, ed. J. Pelikan (St. Louis: Concordia, 1955), 35:361–62.

[42]Cf. P. A. Verhoef, "Luther and Calvin's Exegetical Library," in *Calvin Theological Journal* 3 (1968): 5–20; also B. A. Gerrish, *The Old Protestantism and the New: Essays on the Reformation Heritage* (Chicago: University of Chicago, 1982), 51–68.

[43]Bruce, "History of New Testament Study," 34–37; also see W. G. Kümmel, *The New Testament: The History of the Investigation of Its Problems*, trans. S. M. Gilmour and H. C. Kee (Nashville: Abingdon, 1972), 27–28.

[44]Cf. J. P. Donnelly, "Calvinist Thomism," in *Victor* 7 (1976): 441–51; also J. K. S. Reid, *The Authority of Scripture: A Study of Reformation and Post-Reformation Understanding of the Bible* (London: Methuen, 1962).

[45]Spener, in *Pia Desideria* (1675) offered six proposals for reform that became a short summary of pietism. Chief among these proposals was the appeal for a more extensive use of the Word of God among us. The Bible must be the chief means for reform. See J. O. Duke, "Pietism versus Establishment: The Halle Phase," in *Classical Quarterly* 72 (1978): 3–16; K. J. Stein, "Philip Jacob Spener's Hope for Better Times: Contribution in Controversy," in *Classical Quarterly* 73 (1979): 3–20.

[46]Edgar Krentz, *The Historical-Critical Method* (Philadelphia: Fortress, 1975), 16–23.

[47]Johann Albert Bengel, *Gnomon of the New Testament*, ed. Andrew R. Fausset, 5 vols. (Edinburgh: T. & T. Clark, 1857–1858); cf. W. C. Kaiser, Jr., *Toward an Exegetical Theology* (Grand Rapids: Baker, 1981), 60–63.

[48]F. D. E. Schleiermacher, *Hermeneutics: The Handwritten Manuscripts*, ed. H. Kimmerle, trans. James Duke and H. J. Forstman (Missoula, Mont.: Scholar's, 1977).

[49]Kümmel, *The New Testament*, 19; Stephen Neill, *The Interpretation of the New Testament 1861–1961* (London: Oxford, 1966), 65.

[50]F. Lau, *Neue Deeustsche Biographie* (Berlin: Duncker & Humbolt, 1959), 4:605.

[51]Cf. Hans W. Frei, *The Eclipse of Biblical Narrative* (New Haven: Yale, 1974), 111–12; Craig Blomberg, *The Historical Reliability of the Gospels* (Downers Grove, Ill.: InterVarsity, 1987), 5–7.

[52]Cf. W. R. Farmer, *The Synoptic Problem* (New York: Macmillan, 1964); for a concise overview of the history of this issue, see D. Guthrie, *New Testament Introduction* (Downers Grove, Ill.: InterVarsity, 1970), 121–87.

[53]Kümmel, *The New Testament*, 77–79.

[54]Ibid., 75–77.

[55]See also Scot McKnight, *Interpreting the Synoptic Gospels* (Grand Rapids: Baker, 1989); cf. C. M. Tuckett, *The Revival of the Griesbach Hypothesis* (Cambridge: University Press, 1983).

[56]Kümmel, *The New Testament*, 98–104.

[57]Neill, *Interpretation of the New Testament*, 18–28, 33–57. Also see Carey C. Newman, "Images of the Church in Acts," *People of God*, ed. P. Basden and D. Dockery (Nashville: Broadman, 1991).

[58]Important theologians, among many, include J. von Hoffman (1810–1877); A. Schlatter (1852–1938); K. Barth (1886–1968); R. Bult-

mann (1884–1976); C. H. Dodd (1884–1973); J. Jeremias (1900-1979); O. Cullmann (1902–); G. E. Ladd (1911–1982); and D. Guthrie.

[59]See D. E. Nineham, "Schweitzer Revisited," in *Explorations in Theology* 1 (London: SCM, 1977), 112–33.

[60]D. Luhrmann, *An Itinerary for New Testament Study*, trans. J. Bowden (Philadelphia: Trinity, 1989), 67–69.

[61]R. Bultmann, *The History of the Synoptic Tradition* (New York: Harper, 1968).

[62]T. W. Manson, "The Failure of Liberalism to Interpret the Bible as the Word of God," in *The Interpretation of the Bible*, ed. C. W. Dugmore (London: SPCK, 1944), 92, though the Cambridge trio of Lightfoot, Hort, and Westcott neglected this area in their research.

[63]See I. H. Marshall, *I Believe in the Historical Jesus* (Grand Rapids: Eerdmans, 1977).

[64]Stephen J. Stein, "The Quest for the Spiritual Sense: The Biblical Hermeneutics of Jonathan Edwards," in *Harvard Theological Review* 70 (1977): 99–113.

[65]See M. Silva, "Old Princeton, Westminster, and Inerrancy," in *Inerrancy and Hermeneutic* (Grand Rapids: Baker, 1988), 67–80.

[66]H. D. Betz, *Galatians* (Philadelphia: Fortress, 1979).

[67]R. P. Martin, "Approaches to New Testament Exegesis," *New Testament Interpretation*, 229–47.

[68]K. Stendahl, "Implications of Form Criticism and Tradition Criticism for Biblical Interpretation," in *Journal of Biblical Literature* 77 (1958): 33–38; J. L. McKenzie, "Problems of Hermeneutics in Roman Catholic Exegesis," in *Journal of Biblical Literature* 77 (1958): 197–204.

[69]Schleiermacher, *Hermeneutics*, 141; cf. Hans-Georg Gadamer, "The Problem of Language in Schleiermacher's Hermeneutic," in *Journal for Theology and Church* 7 (1970): 70–76.

[70]Anthony Thiselton, *Two Horizons: New Testament Hermeneutics and Philosophical Description* (Grand Rapids: Eerdmans, 1980), 103–6.

[71]Cf. R. E. Palmer, *Hermeneutics* (Evanston: Northwestern University Press, 1969), 98–113.

[72]W. Dilthey, "Die Entstehung der Hermeneutik," *Gesammelte Schriften* (Stuttgart: Teubner, 1964), 5:324–30.

[73]Cf. E. D. Hirsch, *Validity in Interpretation* (New Haven: Yale, 1967); *idem, The Aims of Interpretation* (Chicago: University of Chicago, 1976).

[74]Cf. Thiselton, *Two Horizons*, 143–204.

[75]Cf. J. Vines and D. Allen, "Hermeneutics, Exegesis, and Proclamation," in *Criswell Theological Review* 1 (1987): 310–12.

[76]M. Silva, *Has the Church Misread the Bible?* (Grand Rapids: Zondervan, 1987), 115–17.

[77]R. Bultmann, *Theology of the New Testament*, trans. K. Grobel, 2 vols. (New York: Scribner's, 1955), 2: 130–35.

[78]R. Bultmann, *Kerygma and Myth*, ed. H. W. Bartsch (London: SCM, 1953); *idem*, *Jesus Christ and Mythology* (London: SCM, 1960).

[79]So he brilliantly articulated in his classic article, "Is Exegesis without Presuppositions Possible?" in *Existence and Faith*, ed. S. Ogden (London: Hodder and Stoughton, 1961), 289–96.

[80]Gadamer, "Problem of Language," 90–92; also cf. Thiselton, *Two Horizons*, 304–19.

[81]David S. Dockery, "Author? Reader? Text? Toward a Hermeneutical Synthesis," in *Theological Educator* (1988): 7–16.

[82]Cf. P. Ricoeur, *Interpretation Theory: Discourse and the Surplus of Meaning* (Fort Worth: Texas Christian University Press, 1976); *idem*, *Essays in Biblical Interpretation* (Philadelphia: Fortress, 1980).

[83]Cf. Peter Cotterell and Max Turner, *Linguistics and Biblical Interpretation* (Downers Grove, Ill.: InterVarsity, 1989); also R. E. Longacre, *The Grammar of Discourse* (New York: Plenum, 1983).

[84]G. B. Caird, *The Language and Imagery of the Bible* (Philadelphia: Westminster, 1980), 61, has discussed the difficulty of defining or identifying meaning. As carefully as anyone, Caird has detailed the concept of "meaning" and discovering "meaning" (see pp. 32–61). He distinguishes between meaning R (referent), meaning S (sense), meaning V (value), meaning E (entailment), and meaning I (intention).

[85]See Gerhard Maier, *The End of the Historical-Critical Method* (St. Louis: Concordia, 1977); Peter Stuhlmacher, *Historical Criticism and Theological Interpretation: Towards a Hermeneutics of Consent*, trans. R. A. Harrisville (Philadelphia: Fortress, 1977); and David C. Steinmetz, "The Superiority of Precritical Exegesis," 27–38.

[86]One of the finest examples of sociological interpretation can be found in W. A. Meeks, *The First Urban Christians: The Social Word of the Apostle Paul* (New Haven: Yale, 1983).

[87]E.g., J. M. Bonino, *Doing Theology in a Revolutionary Situation* (Philadelphia: Fortress, 1975).

[88]E.g., E. S. Fiorenza, *In Memory of Her: A Feminist Theological Reconstruction of Christian Origins* (New York: Crossroad, 1983).

[89]See D. M. Patte, *The Gospel According to Matthew: A Structural Commentary on Matthew's Faith* (Philadelphia: Fortress, 1987); and *idem*, *Structural Exegesis: From Theory to Practice* (Philadelphia: Fortress, 1978).

[90]B. S. Childs, *The New Testament as Canon: An Introduction* (Philadelphia: Westminster, 1984); also see the discussion in F. F. Bruce, "Canon, Criticism, and Interpretation," in *The Canon of Scripture* (Downers Grove, Ill.: InterVarsity, 1988), 284–97.

[91]See David S. Dockery, "The Divine-Human Authorship of Inspired Scripture," in *Authority and Interpretation*, ed. D. Garrett and R. Melick (Grand Rapids: Baker, 1987), 13–43.

Chapter Three

The New Testament, History, and the Historical-Critical Method

Donald A. Hagner

Donald A. Hagner

Donald A. Hagner is Professor of New Testament at Fuller
Theological Seminary in Pasadena, California. He is a graduate
of Northwestern University (B.A.), Fuller Theological Seminary
(B.D., Th.M.), and the University of Manchester (Ph.D.). He
also did post-graduate study at Cambridge, Lund, and
Tübingen universities. Before going to Fuller, he taught at
Wheaton College in Illinois. His publications include *The Use of
the Old and New Testaments in Clement of Rome* (Brill), *Hebrews*
(Hendrickson), *The Jewish Reclamation of Jesus* (Zondervan), and
Pauline Studies (coeditor, Eerdmans). He is currently completing
the volume on Matthew for *Word Biblical Commentary* (Word).

Chapter Three

The New Testament, History, and the Historical-Critical Method

It is revealing if also discouraging to hear the attempt of the average person on the street (and many in the churches too!) to define Christianity. Most of the time such definitions will refer to a way of life (a code of ethics) or a way of thinking (a philosophy). Even where a reference to faith is made, faith is thought of more in terms of the believing subject rather than what is believed, and if the latter does come into view, it is usually left abstract such as in the expressions "faith in God" or "faith in Jesus." Popular definitions of this kind, although of course they are often partially true, fail to grasp the very essence of Christianity, which according to the New Testament involved the activity of God in history, preeminently through and in his Son, Jesus Christ.

The present essay explores the importance of history to the New Testament, with the consequent indispensability of the historical-critical method, looks specifically at the issue of the historical Jesus, examines the historical-critical method, and concludes with some reflections on the use of the historical-critical method.

THE IMPORTANCE OF HISTORY

True Christianity, the Christianity of the New Testament documents, is absolutely dependent on history. At the heart of New Testament faith is the assertion that "God was in Christ reconciling the world to Himself" (2Co 5:19 NASB). The incarnation, death, and resurrection of Jesus Christ as real events in time and space, i.e., as historical realities, are the indispensable foundation of Christian faith. To my mind, then, Christianity is best defined as the recitation of, the celebration of, and the participation in God's acts in history, which as the New Testament writings emphasize have found their culmination in Jesus Christ. Referring to the gospel narratives, H. Zahrnt writes: "Here, then, we have not the eternal event of myth but unique, unrepeatable history; not an idea but a happening; not a cultic drama, but history in earnest."[1] Lesslie Newbigin puts it concisely when he describes Christianity as "primarily news and only secondarily views."[2]

It is this reality, that God has accomplished our salvation in the historical process, that constitutes the *glory* of our faith. God has acted not only among human beings in history, but now in the climax of his saving purposes he has acted in, through, and as a Man fully enmeshed in the life of this world. The Incarnation, along with its goal, the Cross, is thus the supreme paradigm of Christianity: "[Christ Jesus] emptied himself, taking the form of a servant, being born in the likeness of men. And being found in human form he humbled himself and became obedient unto death, even death on a cross" (Php 2:7f. RSV).

But if in this sense the historical character of the Christian faith is its glory, it is also unfortunately its *stumbling block* to many. Can the Christian faith depend so absolutely on whether or not certain things happened in history? If the answer must be, as I believe, an unqualified yes, then are we not dependent upon, not to say at the mercy of, the historian and the results of historical research? Here the answer must also be yes, but in this case a seriously qualified one. Without question the essence of our faith is by its very nature subject to historical investigation. But the historian, at least by the standards of the scientific historiography that began to emerge especially in the nineteenth century, is unable to say anything about God or indeed anything supernatural, i.e., outside the normal chain of cause and effect. This a priori limitation hardly puts the "scientific" historian in an advantageous position to study the Bible! And it is hardly appropriate for Christians to feel completely bound by such "historical" reasoning. Nevertheless, we cannot wash our hands of the necessity of historical evidence and historical research. We will be returning to this problem at the end of the essay, but for now we need only to note the problem, and to comment that a religion that has as its essence a code of ethics or a system of ideas does not face the difficulties in view here.

It is not, however, merely in the bare events of salvation history themselves that Christianity is so utterly dependent on history. In an equally important sense, Christianity is absolutely dependent upon the *interpretation* of God's acts in history and not least of the work of Christ. That interpretation, together with the record of the events, is itself fully a part of the historical process, i.e., it is given by specific individuals in specific places and at specific times. It is not merely in the deeds themselves that God reveals himself, but in the accompanying interpretation of those deeds in the Bible. Revelation thus takes place through a deed/word or event/interpretation complex.[3] The record of history is simultaneously an interpretation of history that is itself mediated through history; the documents themselves are a part of and a product of history. This is simply to say in another way what is central to the proper understanding of the Bible, something that cannot be overstressed: *the word of God comes to us through the words of human beings.*[4]

It follows from the preceding paragraphs that Christianity and the New Testament writings can be adequately understood only when they are understood historically. The New Testament is in one sense like the Incarnation: it is historically conditioned. The Bible is the word of God, but in it God has spoken in a lisping way.[5] Because revelation comes to us in and through history, historical criticism is not an option but a necessity. "Criticism" here means the making of informed judgments. In this sense no one who attempts to interpret or explain the Bible in any way can avoid the "critical" method.[6] The fact is that the truthfulness (at least at one level) and the meaning of the New Testament can be determined only through historical study. Critical study of the Bible of this kind was being done long before the invention of the so-called historical-critical method.

There is a sense, then, in which it is fair to say that God has entrusted his purposes for the world to the historical process. For whatever reason, God has chosen to accomplish redemption through the historical event of the life and death of his Son. This supreme redemptive act was itself preceded by a whole series of redemptive acts in history (e.g., in the lives of the patriarchs, in the Exodus, and in the history of Israel) that both anticipated it and prepared its way. As we have seen, furthermore, God has entrusted the recording of these events and their interpretation to human beings who were a part of the historical process. To be sure, these persons were inspired by God for their tasks, that is, they were led into the truth by the Spirit, but not in such a way as to obliterate or even bypass their historical identity and context. Even beyond this, God has entrusted his word to the historical process in the formation of the canon, which rests upon human decisions,[7] and in the transmission of the text of the New Testament, which was copied by hand for nearly fifteen centuries.[8]

The necessity of seeing New Testament theology as a decidedly historical discipline, rather than as a subspecies of dogmatics, goes back to as early as the 1787 essay of J. P. Gabler entitled "A discourse on the proper distinction between biblical and dogmatic theology and the correct delimitation of their boundaries."[9] In the nineteenth century this historical orientation to New Testament theology was continued by F. C. Baur and the so-called Tübingen school. Most influential, however, was the programmatic essay of W. Wrede published in 1897, entitled "Concerning the task and methods of the so-called New Testament theology."[10] Wrede, like Gabler, took exception to the "doctrinal approach," wherein New Testament theology was reduced essentially to prooftexting in order to support doctrines already held. He proposed instead that New Testament theology be conceived of as a history of early Christian thought, based on the description of the religious experience that underlay the documents.

It cannot be denied that for all the blind alleys we have been led down through the historical orientation to New Testament theology, we have at the same time reaped enormous benefits from it. We have become sensitive to the variety of theological perspectives represented in the NT. We have been made aware of the crucial importance of the specific and many-faceted historical realities that determined what the different New Testament writers wrote and how they wrote. We now realize something of the extent of development within the New Testament itself, of the tensions that existed already in the early church, of the impact of the surrounding milieu upon the thinking of the New Testament writers. We have become increasingly aware, in short, of the full humanity of these writers and of the full extent to which they were enmeshed in their various socio-cultural environments, and how in turn that affected what they wrote. The rich resources represented by the major exegetical commentary series that have become available in recent years owe very much to the historical orientation to the New Testament.

Not all of this has been without its problems for evangelicals, and evangelical scholarship is still in the process of coming to terms with much of it.[11] One problematic issue, that of the historical Jesus, illustrates some of the difficulties caused by the historical approach as it is commonly practiced.

THE HISTORICAL JESUS

For the evangelical, historical criticism is at its most destructive in its assessment of the historical Jesus.[12] If the statements concerning the importance of history to the Christian faith made at the beginning of this essay are true, it is obvious that the identity of Jesus, established to no small extent by his deeds and his words, his death and the reality of his resurrection, are all of inestimable importance. Yet it is precisely these things, except for the death of Jesus, that are frequently denied historical reality by scholars using the historical-critical method.

It had become fashionable in the nineteenth century to write lives of Jesus that attempted to make sense of him in terms of the humanistic values and the antisupernatural temperament of that era. Albert Schweitzer, who documented this stream of literature in his scintillating book *Quest of the Historical Jesus*, described the outcome in unforgettable language: "Those who are fond of talking about negative theology can find their account here. There is nothing more negative than the result of the critical study of the Life of Jesus." The Jesus arrived at was "a figure designed by rationalism, endowed with life by liberalism, and clothed by modern theology in an historical garb."[13] Reading the documents historically led Schweitzer to the conclusion that Jesus was an apocalyptic preacher with a message of imminent doom, not the gentlemanly nineteenth-century European humanitarian these books had portrayed.[14]

Although such scholars as Weiss, Schweitzer, and Wrede were correct in their dismantling of the Jesus reconstructed by nineteenth-century liberalism and in pointing to the central historical importance of apocalyptic eschatology to the understanding of Jesus, they shared the widespread a priori bias of the post-Enlightenment perspective against the supernatural. They thus rejected much of the gospel records as necessarily unhistorical and were thereby kept from arriving at a more adequate picture of Jesus. The historical Jesus as they understood him, in short, remained quite different from the Jesus confessed by the church.

Rudolf Bultmann, whose towering figure dominated New Testament scholarship for much of the twentieth century, came to the conclusion that the impact of the resurrection experience or faith (note, not event) so colored, not to say transformed, the gospel records of Jesus' ministry that it was nearly impossible to know anything of the historical Jesus: "I do indeed think that we can now know almost nothing concerning the life and personality of Jesus since the early Christian sources show no interest in either, are moreover fragmentary and often legendary; and other sources about Jesus do not exist."[16]

This stress on the impossibility of deriving accurate historical knowledge concerning Jesus from the Gospels has continued among more recent followers of Bultmann. Norman Perrin articulated this skepticism in an exaggeration even more astounding than Bultmann's: "So far as we can tell today, there is no single pericope anywhere in the Gospels, the present purpose of which is to preserve a historical reminiscence of the earthly Jesus."[16]

Bultmann's pervasive skepticism was challenged by his own students, led by Ernst Käsemann, the initiator of the so-called new quest for the historical Jesus.[17] The argument was that Bultmann's Jesus was so insubstantial that his view entailed a new Docetism.[18] It should be possible from the Gospels, even as we have them, to say much more about the human Jesus, these scholars maintained. While this development was certainly a step in the right direction, it should be noted that in no way was it a retreat from the antisupernatural attitude of Bultmann or his predecessors. What was looked for was knowledge of the uniqueness of Jesus as a teacher and healer—knowledge that indeed indicated God's special purpose for and through Jesus but that still left an enormous gap between the historical Jesus and the Christology of the post-Resurrection church. Thus, although the new quest allows more for the uniqueness of Jesus over against his contemporaries, like the old quest it too operates on the naturalistic assumptions of nineteenth-century scientific historiography.[19]

Recently in the United States attention has again been turned to the historical Jesus by means of the highly-publicized work of the "Jesus Seminar" organized by Robert W. Funk. When Funk was about to attempt a book on Jesus, he began to look for a collection of "reliable" historical data concerning Jesus with which he might begin. When he found that there was no such body of material agreed upon by scholars, he began a project to arrive at just such a consensus. He gathered a group of willing scholars who had been making their way through the Synoptic Gospels examining the words of Jesus (as eventually they will the deeds of Jesus) to determine whether Jesus said (and did) what is recorded there.[20] The results have been far more negative than positive. And what is to be noted is not so much simply the bulk of the material that is voted down but the nature of what is regarded as inauthentic.

What is immediately obvious is that the same or very similar presuppositions are at work here as were operative in the early part of this century, for example in the skepticism of a Bultmann. In particular, the widely used criteria for authenticity, especially that of "dissimilarity," which has at best only a very limited usefulness, seem to be applied with a heavy hand. It is often forgotten that these criteria are only effective in establishing the probability of a minimal core of material and are hardly suitable for anything more than a mere beginning in drawing up an estimate of the historical Jesus. Even a brief look at these criteria will make this clear.

Of the three main criteria,[21] the first, that of "dissimilarity," is at once the most determinative—that is, the one that exercises a controlling role over the others—and the most problematic. According to this criterion, only sayings of Jesus that are dissimilar both to Judaism and early Christianity can be safely attributed to the historical Jesus. Admittedly this can serve as a starting point of sorts, but it should also be immediately obvious that the resultant picture of Jesus will be both fragmentary and eccentric. As others have pointed out, what is arrived at through the use of this criterion will be what was distinctive to Jesus, but not necessarily what was truly characteristic of him.[22] It is on the one hand the height of absurdity to think that Jesus would have been uninfluenced by his Jewish background and environment. On the other hand, it is sheer prejudice and equally absurd to conclude that the teaching of Jesus must be wholly discontinuous with that of the early church.

This last point is so important that it deserves some further comment. The view that the post-Resurrection church held a view of Jesus that departed radically from the historical Jesus as he really was has dominated radical-critical scholarship from the time of Reimarus.[23] In this view it was the faith of the church that was responsible for the metamorphosis of an innocent charismatic teacher and healer into the Son of God, i.e., the unique manifestation of God in history. This view is no longer argued; it is assumed. It has indeed become the a priori starting point from which a whole host of inferences are quickly drawn. It is worth pointing out that an antisupernaturalism lies at the root of this viewpoint. That is, *ex hypothesi* the historical Jesus cannot have been the person the early church alleged him to be; he therefore cannot have said and done much that is reported of him in the Gospels.

It should be obvious that despite the dominant influence of this perspective in much past and current study of the Gospels, it rests almost exclusively on a questionable a priori assumption. To be sure, one must allow for the impact of the Resurrection on the transmission of the tradition concerning Jesus and its eventual appearance in the form of the Gospels. The stories are now repeated with the advantage of hindsight and with decidedly kerygmatic purposes. This influence should not be underestimated. But the fact that the faith of the church has influenced the Gospel narratives by no means need entail the transformation of Jesus into something he was not. Indeed, the latter conclusion raises a host of its own difficulties, including not least the moral integrity of the apostolic witness and the continuing availability of eyewitness control.[24] Was the church really capable of the kind and extent of creativity that this theory demands of it?

The point of the preceding paragraphs is merely to call attention to the unjustifiable assumptions that underlie the commonly used criterion of dissimilarity. The criterion guarantees the outcome: no material that is in agreement with the church's view of Jesus can be accepted as historical. But this is not only an implausible conclusion in itself (provided one has not ruled out the possibility of the supernatural in history), but it leaves the historian with the enormous difficulty of accounting for the rise of the faith of the church in opposition to what the historical Jesus was really about.

When one attempts to get some perspective on the issue, it is astonishing how this single criterion has dominated and continues to dominate in the search for the historical Jesus. That a perspective such as this, so clearly the result of a questionable a priori and so dubious methodologically, can gain such authority among biblical scholars readily explains the inadequacy of so much contemporary study of the historical Jesus.

Two other main criteria for establishing the authenticity of the sayings of Jesus that should be mentioned here also have limited usefulness. The criterion of multiple attestation may rightly enhance our confidence in certain material because it occurs in more than one strand of the Gospel tradition (e.g., Mark and Q, Mark and Matthew, Mark and Luke). Although this criterion was originally intended in this positive sense, it has frequently been used negatively to imply that material found in only one strand is regarded as automatically suspect. But given the fact that tradition shared by the three synoptic evangelists or by any two of them is extremely small and selective when compared with all that Jesus said and did, why should one resist the idea that individual synoptists may have picked up elements of the historical tradition that had not found their way into, say, Mark or Q? Can one safely dismiss from consideration as unhistorical material that is found in only one evangelist (e.g., M material, unique to Matthew, which suffers particularly)?

The third criterion, that of coherence, is again useful, but only to a degree. Everything here depends of course on the initial core of material that is accepted as historical. If, for example, one begins with a core determined solely by the principle of dissimilarity, obviously the resultant picture will be skewed accordingly. Generally the criterion of coherence also tends to underestimate the complexity that inheres in historical reality. That is, by its nature this criterion assumes reality to be far more monochromatic than it usually is. If the ministry of Jesus and the environment into which he came were anything like what the Gospels say they were, a monochromatic portrait of the historical Jesus can hardly be thought to suffice. An obvious related difficulty is the subjectivity involved in determining whether any particular item is to be understood as cohering with another.

These criteria, together with others that could be mentioned, will in fact take us only a short way toward the goal of arriving at an accurate representation of the historical Jesus. There will of course be some value in seeing what can be ascertained concerning Jesus using these authenticity criteria. Some of the resultant conclusions may be put together and shown to be consistent with and to some degree in continuity with the church's later estimate of Jesus. But if, as we have seen previously, research into the historical Jesus insists upon what amounts to an a priori conclusion that the historical Jesus cannot have been what the church came to believe concerning him and what they presented him as in the Gospels, then it is obvious that the results of its methodology, including the use of the criteria of authenticity, are predetermined.

To say under such circumstances that the burden of proof lies upon those who accept the authenticity of a saying of Jesus[25] is to make an impossible demand. No classical historian approaches the documents of antiquity with such a great degree of skepticism, since to do so would seriously undermine the very possibility of historical knowledge. On the other hand, it may be too easy simply to assert that the burden of proof lies only upon those who deny the authenticity of a saying.[26] The burden of proof—and really what is in view here is not proof but, as with all historical knowledge, the establishment of a reasonable degree of probability—cannot be altogether shunned by those who maintain the authenticity of a saying.[27] That is, while the post-Resurrection perspective of the church can hardly have created *ex nihilo* the view of Jesus contained in the Gospels, the possibility of some modification of the tradition is a reality that cannot be ignored. But for the historian who would do justice to the full range of materials being studied, the fairest approach would be to assume "that all material is potentially authentic."[28]

It is clear that especially where the study of the historical Jesus is concerned, scholars—far more than they are generally prone to admit—let their presuppositions largely govern the conclusions to which they come. We must now return to the question of the historical-critical method and examine the presuppositions commonly regarded as inherent in it. If the historical-critical method is indispensable for understanding the

New Testament, what are we to do with its apparent a priori bias against the possibility of God acting in history? Is there a way out of this impasse?

THE HISTORICAL-CRITICAL METHOD

As is well known, the historical-critical method has its origins in the epistemological revolution of the Enlightenment that gave birth to scientific study itself. The exhilarating freedom brought by the beginnings of the scientific method with its emphasis on hard data and reasoning meant an unrestrained questioning of authority and dogma. It seemed that the scientific method held the key to all knowledge. As it had removed the mystery from nature, and much of the consequent superstition, so too it would make possible a correct (non-ecclesiastical and undogmatic) understanding of the Bible. As V. P. Furnish puts it: "Now the Bible itself is on the way to being viewed as a datum of world history, as first of all an object, not to be believed, but to be observed, investigated and rationally understood."[29]

The trouble was that the scientific method had made its impressive advances precisely on the basis of its naturalism, its insistence on the absolute character of unbroken chains of cause and effect. The seemingly natural conclusion was that if historical criticism was also to be scientific, it too had to be conducted on a naturalistic basis. There was no room in the scientific worldview for the supernatural, and thus the Bible had to be understood differently.

Scientific historiography came to be a method "based on assumptions quite irreconcilable with traditional belief."[30] This became very obvious in the classical formulation of the "purely historical" method[31] outlined early in this century by the German philosopher Ernst Troeltsch, who stressed the following three principles.[32] The first is that of *criticism*, namely that all historical knowledge is a matter of probability and thus always open for revision. To this few would object.

The second and far more problematic principle is that of *analogy*. Here it is stipulated that only that which is analogous with what we have experienced can have a claim to being accepted as historical. Thus, for example, if we do not experience the raising of the dead in our day, no claim about the raising of the dead in the past can be accepted. Obviously this amounts to saying that nothing unique can happen in history. Like the criteria for authenticity already discussed, this may seem to be a "safe" way to proceed, but underlying this principle is the presupposition that our experience must be exactly like experience of the past and that the past must have been exactly like the present—an assumption that is obviously indefensible. Such a posited uniformity goes against the occasional occurrence of the surprising and the unpredictable in history. It presupposes a degree of knowledge that is simply unavailable to us. And of course it begs the question we are considering. This principle will not take us very far in reconstructing the past as it has been reported to us and as it may actually have been because it automatically excludes the testimony of ostensibly reliable witnesses. History, unlike science, has as its subject what is by nature unrepeatable. Its reality is available to us only indirectly through those who have left written records.

The third principle, that of *correlation*, maintains that all of reality is interconnected through an inviolable network of cause and effect. With this principle it is assumed that all of reality is like one large untorn tapestry, a self-contained complex reality that cannot be intruded upon from outside of itself. This a priori conviction, as we have already seen, obviously rules out the possibility of causation from outside the system. By definition, and again on the scientific model, the supernatural cannot occur, i.e., God cannot act in history.[33]

What we encounter here is a form of positivism, i.e., the insistence that knowledge be defined as only that which can be established by positive facts of the sort one arrives at through the scientific method. This historicism, as it is commonly called, is however no longer defensible because the scientific model upon which it is based has in the twentieth century been shaken to its foundations. The modern scientific revolutions initiated by Albert Einstein's reconceptualization of physical reality and by new fields of research such as quantum physics have necessitated a radical assessment of the Newtonian worldview. Recent philosophers of science such as Thomas Kuhn have called attention to the importance of these new developments.[34] To be sure, we still have to reckon with the reality of cause and effect in historical study. But the modern revolutions in science should teach us not only something of our own inescapable subjectivity as observers, but also that we cannot bank on a causation that is limited strictly to that which is immediately perceptible.[35]

More recent philosophers of history have begun to take these things into account.[36] Epistemologically, for example, they have had to admit that there is no such thing as bare fact without interpretation, that there is no interpreter who is a *tabula rasa*, that every interpretation is partial, necessarily assumes a specific perspective, and is value-laden. In philosophy itself, postmodern epistemology takes a holistic approach to the achievement of knowledge by insisting upon the validation of truth claims in terms of whole networks of theory rather than upon the attainment of separate, indubitable, and hence "foundational" facts. Postmodernism further points to the crucial role of the interpreter's community in determining the conventions of language as well as in arbitrating standards of truth.[37]

It is not surprising, given the current mood sketched in the preceding paragraphs, to find more and more biblical scholars—and by no means not only those of a conservative bent—turning away from the historical-critical method. We have already called attention to some of the weaknesses of a historical method that is modeled on the scientific method. When we add to these the recent trends in epistemology, the historical-critical method may seem doomed. There is in fact at the present among biblical scholars a rapidly growing retreat from the study of the Bible as history to what must be called the newer literary criticism.[38] The newest methods are decidedly ahistorical, focusing on the one hand upon the Bible as an object in itself, i.e., as pure literature to be understood in a nonreferential sense,[39] and on the other hand, and closely related, upon reader-oriented interpretation, i.e., where every reader constitutes his or her understanding of the text, each of which has equal validity.[40]

There is no need to deny the truth contained in these new trends. It is true that the Bible bears the characteristics of what may genuinely be called literature and that the study of these characteristics can be illuminating. It is also true that every reader unavoidably constitutes the meaning of the text. (It may be questioned, however, whether every reading of the text is therefore necessarily an adequate one, and whether this admission makes it futile to quest after the meaning of an author.) But it remains a fact that the biblical writings are largely concerned with recorded history and that therefore ahistorical approaches can be only partially satisfactory. If justice is to be done to the nature of these writings, there can be no escape from the necessity of responsible historical inquiry. All approaches that ignore or are oblivious to the historical claims in the Bible involve interpretive methodologies that can only be called docetic.[41]

It has become extremely important in our day to insist upon the indispensability of the historical-critical method. Early in this century it was reactionary fundamentalists who declared the historical-critical method invalid and illegitimate. In the middle of the century moderates pronounced biblical theology dead because of its inability to cope with the negative conclusions of historical-criticism. Now at the end of the century liberals are declaring the bankruptcy of the historical-critical method itself. This is hardly to be received by evangelicals as good news because with the abandonment of the method comes the abandonment of a historical understanding of the Bible and hence a biblical understanding of the Christian faith. In the current climate, it is the evangelicals—namely those who are committed to the truthfulness of the gospel in all its historical concreteness—above all who must not give up on the possibility of historical knowledge and hence of the vital importance of the historical-critical method.

The way out of the quandary is neither to continue to use the historical-critical method as classically conceived nor to abandon it outright because of its destructive past, but rather to modify it so as to make it more appropriate to the material being studied. But is this possible?

MODIFICATION OF THE
HISTORICAL-CRITICAL METHOD

We have seen that the older positivistic scientific method is simply unsuitable as a paradigm for the study of history. The newer understandings of scientific method seem far more promising. Nevertheless, because of their differences, it may be that science and history will require methods based on different models. This is not to say that history can afford to be any less rigorous in its own methodology than science is in its. Historical study, even of the Bible, cannot afford to be uncritical, i.e., naive and credulous. We must briefly discuss the key issue—the historian and the supernatural—before we conclude with some specific suggestions for the modification of the historical-critical method.

One of the main points I have argued is that an a priori exclusion of the possibility of the supernatural, God acting in history, is unjustifiable. There is no way that we can know that causation from outside the system we ordinarily experience cannot occur. Contrary to the fear of many historians, openness to the possibility of the supernatural does not entail the acceptance of every claim that a supernatural event has occurred. Every such claim must be evaluated case by case with attention to such things as the nature of the event[42] and especially the evidence backing up the claim. In the latter the extent and character of the witness to the event are especially important. Where, for example, we have eyewitness control of more than a few witnesses, e.g., as in the case of the resurrected Jesus (cf. 1Co 15:5ff.), the probability of the occurrence of an event escalates accordingly. Because one is open to the supernatural in history, one does not abandon critical judgment. Quite the contrary. In the face of reports of supernatural events, we must demand particularly convincing evidence, more than where ordinary events are in view. Apart from this special demand, historical judgment should be no different here than in the assessment of other historical narratives.

Another criterion that can be properly used in the evaluation of claims concerning supernatural reports involves what may be called, for lack of a better phrase, contextual appropriateness. Here there is an unavoidable subjective element. But an undeniable difference exists between most of the miracles recorded, for example, in the New Testament Apocrypha and those of the New Testament itself. The former are often bizarre (e.g., the boy Jesus lengthening a short beam in his father's carpenter shop; Peter's talking dog) and have a contrived, ad hoc character that detracts from their historical plausibility, even for one who may be open to the possibility of the supernatural itself. By contrast, most of the miracles in the New Testament reflect a restraint untypical of authors who have allowed their imaginations to run rampant in an ostensibly good cause. In the main they lack the ad hoc character that points to invention for convenience. Most important, almost without exception they fit well into the ministry and purpose of

Jesus, involving as they do both the manifestation and demonstration of the reality of the kingdom he announces.

There is an economy of the miraculous in the New Testament. This is not to deny that Jesus had an extensive healing ministry. As the healing summary passages show (e.g., Mt 4:23f.), the New Testament evangelists have been selective in what they have chosen to record, the Gospel of John being the most selective of all. The miracles of Jesus are part and parcel of his ministry, not deeds of magic performed to impress, to get him out of tight spots, or to make life easier for himself or his disciples.

The historian should be impressed by this economy. It suggests that the historian who is open to the possibility of the supernatural is functioning in an appropriate mode when he or she prefers explanations that depend on natural, ordinary causation wherever possible, and refuses to appeal to supernatural causation to get out of a tight spot, unless the evidence considered on its own terms is sufficiently compelling.

A historical-critical method open to the possibility of the supernatural must nevertheless retain its critical acumen. Although from the historian's perspective it is highly improbable that the faith of the post-Resurrection church can have been responsible for the wholesale creation of the Christology of the Gospels, that the faith and hindsight of the church has had a not inconsiderable impact on the transmission of the tradition can hardly be denied. Here again the judgments that are made concerning the extent of the modification of the tradition will be necessarily subjective, but the historian *qua* historian cannot avoid making them. Evangelical scholars in particular must be allowed the freedom to make such judgments.

The historical-critical method is indispensable to any adequate and accurate understanding of the Bible, but only where it is tempered by an openness to the possibility of supernatural causation in the historical process. Without this tempering of the method it is clearly inappropriate and ineffective, given the fact that the Bible is after all the story of God acting in history. In short, without this tempering the method can only be destructive. One of the great challenges currently facing evangelical biblical scholarship is precisely that of modifying the historical-critical method so that it becomes productive and constructive.[43] This challenge is demanding since it involves, as we have seen, such special fields as philosophy, epistemology, language, and logic. With an acknowledgment of the complexity and depth of these issues, I want in the concluding paragraphs of this essay merely to indicate in a summarizing way at least some of the elements that must be involved in the required modification of the historical-critical method.

1. *The historical-critical method must reject the limitations of the positivistic scientific model.* As we have seen, that model is itself based on the science of the eighteenth and nineteenth centuries and a worldview that has been seriously shaken by the science of our century. Apart from the additional query concerning the appropriateness of this model to the writing of history of any kind, the utter incompatibility of the assumptions of this model with the subject matter of the Bible should raise questions about its suitability. When what is being studied is essentially demolished in the process, it is worth asking whether the right tool has been used.

2. *The historical-critical method must be open to the transcendent, i.e., to the possibility of divine causation.* This is obviously the corollary of the preceding point, but it is so important that it needs separate emphasis. In view here is not the outright acceptance of the supernatural, but at least an openness to its possibility. What must be disallowed is the a priori rejection of every such claim in principle, without any attention to or regard for the strength and character of the witness by which the claim is made (see number 4 below). Openness to the possibility of the supernatural by no means leads to chaos in historical research. God's involvement in the historical process occurs most often in and through human agency and ordinary causation, working with these rather than against them. We are not in a situation where "anything goes," or where critical judgment no longer has a role to play. If the essence of Christianity can be summed up in the Incarnation, we can conclude that the transcendent enters fully and is fully taken up in the historical process.

3. *The historical-critical method must pursue without restriction the explanation that best explains the phenomena under investigation.* One might think that this is hardly a modification of the method in question. Has not the historical-critical method always favored the best explanation of what is under investigation? This has indeed been the case—but note carefully, at least

as the method has been practiced by some—only as long as the explanation was a naturalistic one. The result is that every evangelical biblical scholar who has attended professional meetings has had the experience of hearing the most ludicrous attempts to explain such things as the resurrection of Jesus, the conversion of Paul, or the birth of the church, with far-fetched and unconvincing arguments—all because the possibility of supernatural causation was ruled out from the start. The best, indeed the only convincing explanation of these things and others like them is in the acceptance of the work of God in history. If one insists on a purely naturalistic explanation one is thereby forced to choose an inferior explanation.

4. *The historical-critical method must test the reliability of historical witness using the same criteria and having the same resultant confidence whether what is in view involves the natural or the supernatural.* Perhaps more attention must be given to the quality, circumstances, character, etc., of the witnesses to a supernatural event than to an ordinary event. But it is frequently the case that the strength of the witness to the miraculous in the New Testament records stands up under the brightest light of scrutiny. Yet because of unfortunate and unjustified presuppositions, historical-critical scholars never bother to assess the strength of such testimony. Their bias rejects any such claim without any further discussion. And thus potentially historical evidence is unfairly dismissed.

5. *The historical-critical method must consider the role of the community in the transmission of the tradition not simply as potentially negative but as potentially positive.* Historical-critical scholars have focused so intensely on the extent to which the community may have transformed the tradition concerning Jesus that they have neglected the positive role of the community, and especially the apostolic circle, in the protection and preservation of the tradition.[44] It is admittedly not an either/or. The early Christian community both shapes the tradition in the light of its post-Resurrection knowledge *and* passes it on faithfully as authentic historical witness to the Jesus of history. But the tradition concerning Jesus in the Gospels, including the Gospel of John, is to be seen as a faithful (by which I mean trustworthy) interpretive account of the historical Jesus and thus deserves the respect of historical scholars.

Modifications such as these can make the historical-critical method the neutral and useful tool it should be in studying the

Bible. Unfortunately most of those who practice the historical-critical method today, encumbered by naturalistic assumptions as we have seen, in fact abuse that method. It is wrong to let them have their way in defining the historical-critical method as that which must exclude the supernatural from the start. It is hardly surprising that the method has become notorious among faithful Christians and is perceived as the enemy rather than the friend of the Bible. In the same way, it is wrong to imply that the historical-critical method was first practiced in the wake of the Enlightenment. Historical and critical study of the Bible was practiced long before the eighteenth century. What *was* new at that time was the fateful excluding of God from the historical process.

In reality most modern manifestations of the historical-critical method have been an abuse of the method. What is needed now in our increasingly secular world is a fresh, responsible, and constructive use of this method to study, explore, and understand aright the foundational documents of our faith. As Robert Morgan has noted, "The conflict is thus no longer between faith and reason but between a reasonable faith and a faithless reason."[45] If evangelical scholars—those open to the reality of God's saving activity in history—cannot be called upon and expected to do this with all honesty and integrity, then who can? Only the use of a historical-critical method not vitiated by an anti-supernatural bias can show that what we believe is worth believing and can thus bring an authority to the Gospel we proclaim.[46]

BIBLIOGRAPHY

Brown, C. *History and Faith*. Grand Rapids: Zondervan, 1987.

Hahn, F. *Historical Investigation and New Testament Faith*. Philadelphia: Fortress, 1983.

Harvey, V. A. *The Historian and the Believer*. Philadelphia: Westminster, 1966.

Keck, L. E., *A Future for the Historical Jesus*. Philadelphia: Fortress, 1981.

Krentz, E. *The Historical-Critical Method*. Philadelphia: Fortress, 1975.

Ladd, G. E. *The New Testament and Criticism*. Grand Rapids: Eerdmans, 1967.

Marshall, I. H. *I Believe in the Historical Jesus*. Grand Rapids: Eerdmans, 1977.

Mitton, C. L. *Jesus: The Fact Behind the Faith*. Grand Rapids: Eerdmans, 1974.

Nash, R. H.. *Christian Faith and Historical Understanding*. Grand Rapids: Zondervan, 1984.

Poythress, V. S.. *Science and Hermeneutics*. Grand Rapids: Zondervan, 1988.

Richardson, A.. *History Sacred and Profane*. London: SCM, 1964.

NOTES

[1]H. Zahrnt, *The Historical Jesus*, trans. by J. S. Bowden from the German original of 1960 (New York and Evanston: Harper, 1963), 65.

[2]L. Newbigin, *A Faith for This One World?* (New York: Harper, 1961), 45.

[3]Depending upon O. Cullmann, G. E. Ladd put great stress upon this dual nature of revelation. See *A Theology of the New Testament* (Grand Rapids: Eerdmans, 1974), 30ff.; "The Problem of History in Contemporary New Testament Interpretation," in *Studia Evangelica* V [= *TU* 103], 3d International Congress, Oxford, 1965, Part II, The New Testament Message (Berlin, 1968), 99f.

[4]G. E. Ladd made effective use of this formula in his *The New Testament and Criticism* (Grand Rapids: Eerdmans, 1967).

[5]"For who is so devoid of intellect as not to understand that God, in so speaking, lisps with us as nurses are wont to do with little children?" Calvin, *Institutes*, 1.13.1. See further the stimulating article of F. L. Battles, "God Was Accommodating Himself to Human Capacity," in *Interp* 31.1 (1977): 19–38.

[6]The strength of this statement needs to be appreciated. All interpretation involves making critical judgments, i.e., appraisals of one kind or another. If a person hoped somehow to avoid using his or her critical faculty by simply repeating the text of Scripture, critical judgment would nevertheless be involved in choosing a translation. Even reading the Greek text of the New Testament depends upon its critical reconstruction in the editions available. The only alternative to the use of critical judgment is absolute silence.

[7]Two recent, excellent studies of the emergence of the New Testament canon are: B. M. Metzger, *The Canon of the New Testament* (New York: Oxford University Press, 1987) and F. F. Bruce, *The Canon of Scripture* (Downers Grove, Ill.: InterVarsity, 1988).

[8]See B. M. Metzger, *The Text of the New Testament: Its Transmission, Corruption, and Restoration*, 2d ed. (New York: Oxford University Press, 1968) and K. & B. Aland, *The Text of the New Testament*, translated by E.

F. Rhodes from the German original of 1981 (Grand Rapids/Leiden: Eerdmans/Brill, 1987).

[9]Conveniently available in English translation in the article of J. Sandys-Wunsch and L. Eldredge, "J. P. Gabler and the Distinction Between Biblical and Dogmatic Theology: Translation, Commentary, and Discussion of his Originality," in *Scot Journ of Theol* 33 (1980): 133–58.

[10]Translated into English by Robert Morgan in *The Nature of New Testament Theology*, SBTh 2.25 (Naperville, Ill.: Allenson, 1973), 68–116.

[11]An interesting history of the maturing of evangelical scholarship together with description of some lingering tensions among evangelicals can be found in M. A. Noll, *Between Faith and Criticism* (San Francisco: Harper, 1986).

[12]Although I prefer to use the phrase "the Jesus of history" to refer to Jesus as he actually was, I use "the historical Jesus" here because it is commonly used in this way. Strictly speaking, however, the "historical Jesus" has come to refer to the artificial construct of the historian.

[13]A. Schweitzer, *Quest of the Historical Jesus*, trans. W. Montgomery from the German original of 1906 [*Von Reimarus zu Wrede*] (New York: Macmillan, 1961), 398.

[14]For a stimulating review of the late eighteenth- and nineteenth-century scholarship on Jesus, see C. Brown, *Jesus in European Protestant Thought 1778–1860* (Durham, N.C.: Labyrinth, 1985), available also from Baker Book House, Grand Rapids. For more attention to methodological problems, see H. Anderson, *Jesus and Christian Origins* (New York: Oxford University Press, 1964); and C. A. Evans, "The Historical Jesus and Christian Faith: A Critical Assessment of a Scholarly Problem," *Christian Scholar's Review* 18.1 (1988): 48–63.

[15]R. Bultmann, *Jesus and the Word*, trans. L. P. Smith and E. H. Lantero from the 1934 German original (New York: Scribner's, 1958), 8.

[16]N. Perrin, *Rediscovering the Teaching of Jesus* (London: SCM, 1967), 16.

[17]The new quest dates to Käsemann's 1953 essay "Das Problem des historischen Jesus," available in English translation by W. J. Montague, in Käsemann's *Essays on New Testament Themes* (Philadelphia: Fortress, 1982), 15–47. J. M. Robinson documented the new quest in his *A New Quest of the Historical Jesus*, SBTh 25 (London: SCM, 1959).

[18]Docetism was an ancient heresy wherein the humanity of Christ was only an appearance and not a fact. Bultmann's skepticism had all but eclipsed the human Jesus in favor of the Christ of the kerygma, and thus his perspective was in effect docetic.

[19]T. Wright has described what he calls the emergence of a "third quest," which makes constructive use of especially Jewish materials to arrive at a more adequate picture of Jesus. Although, to be sure, there

are some good signs, e.g., in the books of B. F. Meyer and A. Harvey in particular, Wright must admit a revealing point: neither Christology nor the Resurrection has been addressed in the third quest. But these are precisely the issues that will decide whether the newest generation of Jesus research can really go beyond the new quest. See S. Neill and T. Wright, *The Interpretation of the New Testament 1861–1986*, 2d ed. (New York: Oxford University Press, 1988), 379–403.

[20]The first major publication of the seminar is now available and contains the story of the beginning of the seminar (pp. ix–xv) as well as an account of its method (pp. 1–23), including its voting procedure using red, pink, gray, and black beads (from certain acceptance to certain refusal of the authenticity of an item). Those who read their newspapers—for the seminar is hungry for publicity—will not have to be told that "the trend of critical assessment is abundantly clear: only a very small portion of the words attributed to Jesus actually go back to him" (p. 14). *The Parables of Jesus. Red Letter Edition* (Sonoma, Calif.: Polebridge, 1988). The Jewish scholar Jacob Neusner describes the work of the seminar as representing "either the greatest scholarly hoax since the Piltdown Man or the utter bankruptcy of New Testament studies—I hope the former," *Understanding Seeking Faith: Essays on the Case of Judaism*, Brown Judaic Studies 116 (Atlanta: Scholars, 1986), 25. Personally I find most exasperating the repeated assertions that the seminar represents what critical scholarship concludes. At best, however, the seminar represents the views of some, but by no means all, critical scholars.

[21]The three main criteria are those set forth for example by N. Perrin, *Rediscovering the Teaching of Jesus*, 39–47. For helpful discussions of these and other criteria of authenticity, see R. H. Stein, "The 'Criteria' for Authenticity," in *Gospel Perspectives*, vol. 1, eds., R. T. France and D. Wenham (Sheffield: JSOT Press, 1980), 225–63 and C. A. Evans, "Authenticity Criteria in Life of Jesus Research," *Christian Scholars' Review* 19.1 (1989): 6–31, with helpful illustrations.

[22]See especially M. Hooker, "On Using the Wrong Tool," *Theology* 75 (1972): 570–81.

[23]The radical-critical study of Jesus began with G. E. Lessing's publication in 1778 of the work of H. S. Reimarus (who had died a decade earlier). Schweitzer thus begins his documentation of the quest with Reimarus. Reimarus' work is available in English translation: *Reimarus: Fragments*, trans. R. S. Fraser; ed., C. H. Talbert (Philadelphia: Fortress, 1970).

[24]It is worth quoting again the well-known, somewhat playful words of Vincent Taylor: "It is on this question of eyewitness that Form Criticism presents a very vulnerable front. If the Form Critics are right, the disciples must have been translated to heaven immediately after the Resurrection." *The Formation of the Gospel Tradition* (London: Macmillan, 1968), 41.

[25]Thus, e.g., N. Perrin, *What is Redaction Criticism?* (Philadelphia: Fortress, 1969), 70.

[26]J. Jeremias argues that it is the inauthenticity, not the authenticity, of material that must be demonstrated. *New Testament Theology. The Proclamation of Jesus,* trans. J. Bowden from the German original of the same year (London: SCM, 1971), 37. Stein's view should also be noted, where he calls attention to the importance of eyewitness testimony and suggests that in such circumstances, "The burden of proof should rest upon those who would deny the historicity of the events reported." "The 'Criteria' for Authenticity," 226.

[27]So, rightly, C. A. Evans, "Authenticity Criteria in Life of Jesus Research," 30.

[28]Evans, ibid., 31.

[29]V. P. Furnish, "Historical Criticism of the New Testament: A Survey of Origins," *BJRL* 56 (1974): 368.

[30]Van A. Harvey, *The Historian and the Believer* (Philadelphia: Westminster, 1966), 5.

[31]For L. Goppelt, it is this so-called purely historical approach and not the historical-critical method as such—which cannot be avoided—that has misled New Testament scholarship in the modern era. See his helpful review of the history of the discipline of New Testament theology in *Theology of the New Testament,* trans. J. E. Alsup from the German original of 1975, vol. 1 (Grand Rapids: Eerdmans, 1981), 251–81.

[32]Troeltsch's important article on method, "Ueber historische und dogmatische Methode in der Theologie," in *Gesammelte Schriften,* Zweiter Band, 2d ed., 1922 (Aalen: Scientia, 1962, in cooperation with J. C. B. Mohr), 729–53, will soon be available in an English translation to be published by Robert Morgan.

[33]See D. P. Fuller, "The Fundamental Presupposition of the Historical Method," *Theol Zeitschrift* 24 (1968): 93–101.

[34]See T. S. Kuhn, *The Structure of Scientific Revolutions* 2d ed. (Chicago: University of Chicago Press, 1970).

[35]See A. Richardson, *The Bible in the Age of Science* (London: SCM, 1961) and V. S. Poythress, *Science and Hermeneutics* (Grand Rapids: Zondervan, 1988).

[36]An account of these developments can be found in C. Brown, *History and Faith* (Grand Rapids: Zondervan, 1987) and R. N. Nash, *Christian Faith and Historical Understanding* (Grand Rapids: Zondervan, 1984).

[37]On postmodernism, see the especially helpful article by N. Murphy and J. Wm. McClendon, Jr., "Distinguishing Modern and Postmodern Theologies," *Modern Theology* 5.3 (1989): 191–214.

[38]This newer literary criticism is to be distinguished from the traditional literary criticism, i.e., the study of a variety of literary features of the biblical text, which scholars have applied to the Bible for

quite a long time. Now the Bible is being approached as a work of literature in its own right. For a useful introduction, see Tremper Longman III, *Literary Approaches to Biblical Interpretation* (Grand Rapids: Zondervan, 1987).

[39]That is, the Bible is self-contained and need not refer to anything outside itself for us to receive its truth. It is like a novel that can communicate various kinds of truth to a reader even though the story did not actually happen. The question of the historicity of events recorded in the Bible becomes a non-issue.

[40]See E. V. McKnight, *Post-Modern Use of the Bible. The Emergence of Reader-Oriented Criticism* (Nashville: Abingdon, 1988). The influence of the deconstruction is unmistakable here.

[41]That is, the historical existence, acts, and claims of persons in the Bible become irrelevant. The stories have only the appearance of actual historicity.

[42]By this I simply mean that some miracles by their nature are more reasonable and more easily defensible than others. This point is developed in the next paragraph.

[43]Martin Hengel has effectively addressed this problem in "Historische Methoden und theologische Auslegung des Neuen Testaments," *Kerygma und Dogma* 19 (1973): 85–90, available in English translation in his *Acts and the History of Earliest Christianity* (Philadelphia: Fortress, 1979), 129–36.

[44]One of the finest books available on this is B. Gerhardsson, *The Origins of the Gospel Traditions* (Philadelphia: Fortress, 1979). See too his *The Gospel Tradition* (Malmö: CWK Gleerup, 1986).

[45]R. Morgan, "The Historical Jesus and the Theology of the New Testament," in *The Glory of Christ in the New Testament*, Memorial volume for G. B. Caird; L. D. Hurst and N. T. Wright, eds. (Oxford: Clarendon, 1987), 199.

[46]I should like to acknowledge my indebtedness to Drs. Robert Guelich, Nancey Murphy, and Marianne Meye Thompson, my colleagues at Fuller Seminary, who kindly read this manuscript and offered helpful suggestions for its improvement.

PART TWO

BASIC METHODS IN NEW TESTAMENT CRITICISM

Chapter Four

Textual Criticism

Michael W. Holmes

Michael W. Holmes

Michael W. Holmes is Professor of Biblical Studies and Early Christianity at Bethel College in St. Paul, Minnesota. He holds degrees from the University of California at Santa Barbara (B.A.), Trinity Evangelical Divinity School (M.A.), and Princeton Theological Seminary (Ph.D.). He is the editor of *The Apostolic Fathers* (Baker) and the author of numerous articles appearing in such journals as *New Testament Studies*, *Journal of Biblical Literature*, *Themelios*, *Trinity Journal*, and *Journal of the Evangelical Theological Society*. He is a leading member of the Society of Biblical Literature's New Testament Textual Criticism section and is also active in the Institute for Biblical Research.

Chapter Four

Textual Criticism

In an age of mass-produced books and copy machines that enable us to obtain virtually on demand perfect copies of almost anything, it is difficult to imagine just how hard it was to obtain a reliable copy of a book before the invention of printing. All copying was done by hand (thus books produced in this way are called *manuscripts*), and this slow, laborious, and expensive[1] process was subject to all the vagaries and corrupting influences and effects of the human mind and body. Consequently no two copies of a book were identical, and neither perfectly represented the exemplar (model) from which they were copied.[2] This means, among other things, that all surviving manuscripts of the New Testament differ (sometimes widely) among themselves.

This would be, of course, of no great significance if the originals were available; one could then ignore the imperfect copies and simply consult the original to determine exactly what an author wrote. But this is not possible, since no autograph of any classical, biblical, or early patristic writer is extant today. This means that our only access to any of these writers is via the surviving imperfect copies. These two circumstances make *textual criticism*—the art and science of recovering the original text of a document—a necessary and foundational step in the study of any ancient author or book. It is, after all, somewhat difficult to study or interpret a document accurately unless one first knows exactly what that document says.

New Testament textual criticism involves three major tasks: (1) the gathering and organization of evidence, including especially the collation (comparison) of manuscripts (= MSS) with one another to ascertain where errors and alterations have produced variations in the text, and the study of how and why these variations happened; (2) the evaluation and assessment of the significance and implications of the evidence with a view to determining which of the variant readings most likely represents the original text; and (3) the reconstruction of the history of the transmission of the text, to the extent allowed by the available evidence.

This chapter will focus primarily on the first two areas, though there will be opportunity to say something about the third area as well. After discussing in greater detail the causes of variation in MSS and surveying the available resources for recovering the original text, we will consider the methodological approaches and practical guidelines textual critics utilize to reconstruct, with a high degree of confidence, the original text of the New Testament from the mass of variations and errors among the extant copies.

CAUSES OF ERROR

Both the format of books and the mechanics of the copying process facilitated the commission of errors when copying a book. Books were written in *scriptio continua* (i.e., without breaks between words) with minimal punctuation or other aids for the reader, generally in either one wide column or several narrow ones per page.[3] Thus it was not difficult to misread the text or lose one's place while copying. Scribes would often inadvertently skip between words or syllables with similar beginnings or endings,[4] the result being either the loss or duplication of material.[5] The steps involved in the copying process itself—reading the text, remembering it, and writing it down[6]—offered easy opportunity to misread the text, rearrange word order, or substitute a more familiar word or better remembered phrase for a less common or unusual one.[7] Fatigue,[8] poor eyesight or hearing, or simple stupidity could also contribute to errors in copying.

Not all alterations, however, were inadvertent. Harmonization, for example, could be deliberate as well as unintentional, and as Greek grammar, syntax, and style changed over the centuries scribes often "updated" the text to conform to current standards or substituted a more refined or literary term for a colloquial one.[9] Sometimes a scribe would venture to correct what appeared to him to be an error or difficulty in his exemplar; if done unskillfully, this not infrequently resulted in the replacement of one error by another or a compounding of the initial problem. Occasionally the text was altered for doctrinal reasons.[10] Orthodox and heretics alike leveled this charge against their opponents, though the surviving evidence suggests that the charge was more frequent than the reality.

These, then, are some of the reasons why there are variations in all extant copies of the New Testament, and thus why textual criticism is a necessary and foundational step in the interpretation of the New Testament. In a sense, textual criticism involves the *reversal* of the process of corruption described above. That is, the textual critic seeks to understand the transmission process and the causes and effects of corruption that produced imperfect copies from the originals, in order to reverse the process and thus work back from these surviving imperfect copies to reconstruct the lost originals.

SOURCES OF INFORMATION ABOUT THE TEXT

New Testament textual criticism enjoys an embarrassment of riches with regard to sources of information about the New Testament text. Unlike many classical texts, which have been preserved in only a few late copies or, in extreme cases, only a single, now-destroyed copy, there exist today thousands of copies of the New Testament in several ancient languages. In addition, almost all of the Greek New Testament can be reconstructed on the basis of quotations by ancient writers. For ease of reference scholars have grouped these sources under three headings: Greek manuscripts, ancient versions, and patristic citations.

Greek Manuscripts

The Greek manuscripts are categorized, somewhat arbitrarily, on the basis of either writing material, style, or format. First are the papyri, manuscripts of the Greek New Testament written on papyrus, an ancient paper-like writing material. These MSS, which include some of the oldest surviving copies,[11] are designated by a Gothic "p" followed by a superscript Arabic numeral (e.g., p^{46}). Today the remains of about ninety-six papyrus MSS are known, most of which are extremely fragmentary. Some of the better preserved and more important witnesses in this category include p[45] (third century; substantial parts of Gospels and Acts), p[46] (ca. 200; Pauline epistles), p[66] (ca. 200; large parts of John), p[72] (third/fourth centuries; parts of 1–2 Peter, Jude), and p[75] (early third century; over half of Luke and John).[12]

Continuous-text Greek MSS written on material other than papyrus (usually parchment, though after the twelfth century increasingly on paper) are subdivided on the basis of writing style. Uncial MSS (MSS written in a formal literary style of unconnected capital letters) initially were designated by letters of the alphabet; when these proved insufficient, the Greek and then Hebrew alphabets were used. Because of the confusion engendered, numbers prefixed with a zero (e.g., 01, 02) were eventually assigned to these MSS. Today only the most famous of the uncials continue to be known by their original letters; these include codices Sinaiticus (ℵ/01; mid-fourth century), Alexandrinus (A/02; early fifth century), Vaticanus (B/03; early fourth century), Bezae (D/05; fifth century), Washingtonianus (W/032; fourth/fifth centuries), and Koridethi (Θ/038; ninth century). Today about 263 uncial MSS are recognized.[13]

Minuscule MSS were written in a smaller cursive style that was developed in the eighth or ninth century. As this style was faster and more space-efficient than the uncial, it enabled books to be produced more cheaply. Minuscule MSS are identified by a simple Arabic numeral; the list now runs through at least 2812.[14] Some of the more significant minuscules include groups or "families" headed by 1 and 13 (symbols: f^1 and f^{13}), and 28, 33, 81, 323, 565, 614, 700, 892, 1241, 1424, 1739, and 2495.

Lectionaries are books containing selections from Scripture for use in worship and other services. These comprise the final category of Greek witnesses, and are identified by an Arabic number preceded by a script ell (e.g., ℓ32). Over twenty-two hundred lectionary MSS are known to exist today.

In all, something over five thousand witnesses to the Greek New Testament are extant today. Many (if not most) of these, it should be noted, are fragmentary or incomplete. Only three uncials (ℵ/01, A/02, and C/04) and fifty-six minuscules contain the entire New Testament; another two uncials and 147 minuscules lack only Revelation.[15] As for content, the Gospels are found in 2,328 MSS, the Acts and Catholic letters in 655, the Pauline letters in 779, and Revelation in 287. With regard to date, over sixty-five percent are from the eleventh through fourteenth centuries, while less than two and a half percent (125 total) are from the first five centuries.[16]

Ancient Versions

As Christianity spread into regions and social strata where Greek was not understood, there arose the need for translations of the New Testament. By about A.D. 180 the process of translating the New Testament into Latin, Syriac, and Coptic was underway. The Latin eventually developed into at least two major forms, the Old Latin or Itala and the Vulgate (of which over 8000 MSS are known), while the Syriac and Coptic exist in a number of versions and dialects. Later translations include Armenian, Georgian, Ethiopic, Gothic, and Old Church Slavonic; in several instances these translations were the first literary work in that particular language, and occasionally, as in the case of the Gothic, an alphabet first had to be created.[17]

Because the roots of some of these early versions antedate the vast majority of the Greek MSS, they are valuable historical witnesses to the transmission of the New Testament text, particularly regarding the form of the text in various regions or provinces. Limitations, however, in the ability of these languages to represent aspects of Greek grammar and syntax (e.g., Latin has no definite article) restrict their value at some points.[18]

Patristic Citations

Early Christian writers frequently quoted the New Testament in their writings and sermons, often at length, and many wrote commentaries on it. Together these constitute another important source of information about the New Testament text. "Indeed, so extensive are these citations that if all other sources for our knowledge of the text of the New Testament were destroyed, they would be sufficient alone for the reconstruction of practically the entire New Testament."[19] Their particular value lies in the help they provide in dating and localizing variant readings and text-types. Like the versions, however, their value is sometimes limited, in this case by a tendency to cite from memory or adapt a quotation to its context. Thus it can be difficult to determine whether a reading represents a genuine Greek variant or merely the author's adaptation of the text.[20] Nevertheless, these citations represent an important additional source of information.

The sheer volume of the information available to the New Testament textual critic makes it practically certain that the original text has been preserved somewhere among the surviving witnesses.[21] Thus only very rarely is it necessary to consider the possibility of textual emendation (the proposal of a reading not found in any extant witness). This is in sharp contrast to the textual criticism of the Old Testament, classical, and patristic texts where textual emendation is routinely necessary.

CLASSIFICATION AND GENEALOGICAL RELATIONSHIPS OF MSS

The volume of information also means that at times textual questions can become technical and difficult. To be sure, computer applications have eliminated some of the drudgery involved; even so, simply gathering all the evidence for a particular problem, not to mention analyzing and evaluating it, can be a formidable challenge.

The phenomenon of genealogical relationships and the classification of MSS into certain broad textual traditions (text-types) do, however, alleviate the problem significantly. In normal circumstances, MSS copied from a distinctive model will themselves exhibit those distinctive elements. Because they share these elements by virtue of a common parent, they may be said to be genetically related, or to have a genealogical relationship. Now in the case of the New Testament, as it was being copied throughout the Roman Empire, distinctive variations that arose in one region or area and which came to characterize MSS copied in that region would not, except by occasional sheer coincidence, occur in the same way or pattern in MSS copied elsewhere from different exemplars. On the basis of these particular patterns it is possible to group most MSS into one of three broad text-types, the Alexandrian, the Western, and the Byzantine.[22] Each of these text-types, identified on the basis of a high degree of agreement between certain MSS over both a set of readings peculiar to a text-type and the total area of variation, has a distinctive character and history.

The Alexandrian text-type, so named because most of the MSS belonging to it have come from Egypt, at one time was thought to be a carefully edited, late third-century recension (edition), a product of Alexandrian classical scholarship applied to the New Testament. But new discoveries, especially p[75] and p[46], have demonstrated that this text-type was already in existence well before the end of the second century. Thus it appears to represent the result of a carefully controlled and supervised process of copying and transmission. Primary representatives include p[46], p[66], p[75], ℵ, B, and Origen; secondary[23] witnesses include C L W 33 892 1739 and later Alexandrian fathers like Didymus.[24]

The Western[25] text-type, equally as old as the Alexandrian, is more widely attested geographically; major witnesses derive from North Africa, Italy, Gaul, Syria, and Egypt. But it lacks the homogeneity and consistency of relationships characteristic of the other two texts. It appears to represent a tradition of uncontrolled copying, editing, and translation; it is typified by harmonistic tendencies, paraphrasing and substitution of synonyms, additions (sometimes long[26]), and a small but theologically significant group of omissions. Major representatives include codex Bezae (D/05); p[45] ℵ W in the Gospels (all in part only), D/06 F G in the Pauline epistles, the Old Latin and Old Syriac versions, and Tatian, Irenaeus, Cyprian, and Tertullian among the fathers.

The Byzantine text-type, also known as the Koine, Syrian, or Majority text, comprises about eighty percent of all known MSS. While scattered individual Byzantine readings are known to be ancient, the Byzantine text-type as such—that is, as an identifiable pattern of distinctive variants and agreements— first appears only in the mid-fourth century among a group of fathers associated with Antioch. Thus it is the largest and latest of the three major text-types, and, in view of the obvious secondary character of many of its distinctive readings,[27] also the least valuable for recovering the original text.

The phenomenon of genealogical relationships is important not only for classifying MSS but for evaluating them as well. When evaluating witnesses and text-types, the genealogical principle means that *MSS must be weighed rather than counted*. The total number of MSS supporting a particular variant *in and of itself* is of little significance. Consider the following diagram, in which the first level (X) represents the now-lost original reading of a document and the second level represents copies of it (each letter stands for one copy):

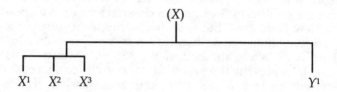

Of the four surviving copies in this hypothetical case, three read X and one reads Y. If one were to decide the original reading by simply counting MSS, one would conclude, in this case correctly, that the original read X.

But suppose that X^3 was destroyed in a persecution and that Y^1 was utilized by a scriptorium as an exemplar for several additional copies. The diagram would now look like this:

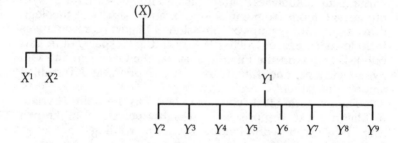

Here a count of the eleven surviving MSS would lead one to conclude, on the basis of the nine Y versus two X tally, that the original reading was Y. But in this case that conclusion would be wrong! Because Y^2 through Y^9 are all copies of Y^1, they add nothing to the weight or significance of Y^1.

In short, since even ten thousand copies of a mistake are still a mistake, the number of MSS in a given text-type or supporting a particular reading is of little intrinsic significance. Manuscript readings and text-types must be evaluated on the basis of their probable origin, character, and other consider- ations. This explains why the Byzantine text-type is of lesser importance than the other two, even though it comprises over eighty percent of all known MSS. Its distinctive readings consistently betray themselves, on the basis of historically verifiable criteria,[28] as secondary and derivitive, rather than original, despite their numerical preponderance.

THE RECOVERY OF THE TEXT
OF THE NEW TESTAMENT

Almost as soon as there were multiple copies of the books of the New Testament, people were aware that there were differences among the MSS.[29] But while early Christians (and some pagans as well) were aware of variations among the MSS, it was not until the late Renaissance that there were any systematic efforts to attempt to recover the original text of the New Testament.

Erasmus of Rotterdam, the man primarily responsible for the first published edition of the Greek New Testament,[30] reveals in his *Annotations* on the New Testament a well-developed critical sense of the causes of errors and variations in New Testament MSS and of criteria for discerning the original reading. He utilizes, at least in embryonic form, many of the analytic tools developed by later scholars.[31]

The text he edited was not, however, equal in quality to his methods, largely because of the severely limited manuscript resources with which he had to work.[32] Consequently his text ended up representing in printed form a late corrupt form of the Byzantine text-type. Because it was first on the market and because of its low price, Erasmus's Greek New Testament was widely influential and often reprinted without authorization. Even the later editions of such notable scholars as Robert Estienne (Stephanus) and Theodore Beza were essentially reprints of Erasmus. So dominant was this form of text that in 1633 a printer could boast that this was "the text which is now received by all" (*textum . . . nunc ab omnibus receptum*), from which arose the now common designation for this text, the "Textus Receptus," or TR. It was the basis of all the major European Protestant translations prior to 1881, including especially the King James of 1611, and unwarrantedly dominated the scholarly scene for over three hundred years.

Indeed, "so superstitious has been the reverence accorded the Textus Receptus that in some cases attempts to criticize or emend it have been regarded as akin to sacrilege";[33] those who dared to change the TR were vehemently attacked as heretics. As a result, scholars tended to relegate new manuscript discoveries or advances in methodology to the margins, the critical apparatus, or long appendices to their editions of the TR, and it is here that we must look for signs of progress beyond Erasmus.

Notable among those who advanced the discipline of textual criticism is J. A. Bengel (1687–1752). He recognized that many MSS could, on the basis of a shared pattern of variant readings, be classified into families or groups and that MSS must therefore be weighed rather than merely counted. He also expressed in classical form a still-fundamental principle for evaluating readings first utilized by Erasmus: the difficult reading is to be preferred to the easy one.[34] Other notable figures during this era include Richard Simon (1638–1712), John Mill (1645–1707), Richard Bentley (1662–1742), and J. J. Wettstein (1693–1754).[35]

The next fundamental advance was made by J. J. Griesbach (1745–1812), also known for his investigations of the Synoptic problem. Further developing Bengel's system of classifying MSS, he divided them into three major groups, which he termed Alexandrian, Western, and Byzantine. He also set out in substantial detail fifteen canons or criteria of textual criticism that continue, often in only slightly altered form, to be used today. Finally, he printed editions of the Greek New Testament in which he abandoned the text of the TR in many places and printed instead the form of text that his research had convinced him was closer to the original. His text, widely reprinted, was influential in England, Scotland, America, and on the Continent, and marks an important step away from the stultifying dominance of the TR. His influence upon the discipline, as Metzger notes, "can scarcely be overestimated."[36]

The first to make a clean break from the TR was Karl Lachmann (1793–1851), who in 1831 published an edition based solely upon the evidence of the earlier uncials, the Old Latin and Vulgate, and early patristic citations. In other words, rather than modifying the TR, as Bengel had done, Lachmann bypassed it entirely in favor of the oldest available evidence, and thus brought to fruition a proposal first set out by Bentley in 1716.

A weakness of Lachmann's edition was the still slender manuscript basis upon which it rested at points. That this is no longer the case for modern critics is due primarily to the tireless labors of Constantin Tischendorf (1815–1874). Best known for his dramatic discovery of codex Sinaiticus,[37] his enduring contribution was the discovery (he published twenty-two volumes of biblical texts) and assembling of textual evidence.[38] The critical apparatus of the eighth edition of his Greek New Testament, published in two large volumes,[39] remains an indispensable source of information even today.

The work of Lachmann, Tischendorf, and their predecessors set the stage for an epochal event in the history of New Testament textual criticism, the publication in 1881 of *The New Testament in the Original Greek*, by B. F. Westcott and F. J. A. Hort.[40] They contributed, in addition to a new edition of the Greek text, a fundamental statement of methodological principles upon which it was based and a reconstruction of the history of the text.[41] While new discoveries (especially the papyri) have led contemporary textual critics to lay aside Westcott and Hort's historical reconstruction, their methodology was so sound and insightful that these same discoveries have essentially confirmed their edition of the text.[42] So significant was their work that whereas it overshadows all previous efforts to recover the original text, almost all[43] fundamental progress since then has in some way been built upon or in relation to their foundation.[44]

Among the editions since Westcott and Hort, perhaps the most widely used for several decades was Eberhard Nestle's *Novum Testamentum Graece*, first published in 1898.[45] A handy pocket edition, the Nestle text was based upon the editions of Westcott and Hort, Tischendorf, and (after 1901) Bernhard Weiss; it thus represented the consensus of nineteenth-century scholarship. Under the successive editorship of Erwin Nestle, Kurt Aland, and now Barbara Aland, and with the assistance of the Institut für neutestamentliche Textforschung directed by the Alands, it has evolved into a critical text based no longer upon previous editions but solely upon manuscript evidence, which is presented along with numerous variant readings (over ten thousand) in a highly useful critical apparatus. Currently in its twenty-sixth edition,[46] "Nestle-Aland" (= NA[26]) is one of two forms of the standard critical text in use today.

The other is *The Greek New Testament* published by the United Bible Societies (= UBS[3]).[47] Intended for the use of translators, and edited by the same committee responsible for NA[26], it presents a much fuller apparatus for a smaller number of variants (ca. 1500). While differing with regard to punctuation, orthography, format, etc.,[48] the two editions present an identical text, and thus represent, in general if not in detail, the consensus of contemporary scholarship and research.[49]

CONTEMPORARY METHODOLOGICAL APPROACHES

The work of Lachmann and his predecessors marked a watershed in the application of a classical method of textual criticism, one that (for both the New Testament and the classics) relied heavily upon a stemmatic or genealogical approach. This approach sought to reconstruct a *stemma* or family tree of surviving MSS and then by working backward through the branches of the tradition to determine the most reliable or "best manuscript" upon which to base an edition.

But the work of Westcott and Hort and new discoveries and developments since their time have made it abundantly clear that this classical approach is unworkable in the case of the New Testament. Except in the case of certain small subgroups of MSS (e.g., "Family 1" [f^1] or "Family 13" [f^{13}]), it has not been possible to reconstruct a stemma for the textual tradition as a whole. This is because of (1) the relatively large number of MSS involved and (2) the widespread presence of mixture (or "cross-pollination") within the textual tradition.[50] That is, when copying, a scribe might utilize two exemplars, following now one and then the other, or he might correct his new copy against a different exemplar, which could be either older or more recent than the initial exemplar. Thus the lines of descent of a particular MS often may be said to be mixed or contaminated.

In practical terms this means that at any given point even the most reliable MS or group of MSS may be wrong and conversely (at least in theory) even a MS of very poor quality may occasionally preserve a true reading. Consequently there has emerged an approach that is best described as a *reasoned eclecticism*.[51] This approach seeks to apply to the New Testament all the tools and criteria developed by the classical method on a passage-by-passage basis. No one rule or principle can be applied nor any one MS (no matter how reliable) or group of MSS (no matter how large) followed in a mechanical or across-the-board fashion; each variation unit must be approached on its own merits and as possibly unique.

Differences in method today are largely a matter of

differing judgments as to the relative weight to be given to "external" evidence (i.e., the MSS themselves) over against "internal" evidence (i.e., considerations having to do with the habits, mistakes, and tendencies of scribes or the style and thought of an author).[52] There are, however, two notable exceptions. One is the so-called "rigorous eclecticism,"[53] which relies virtually exclusively on internal considerations and places little if any weight on external evidence; it treats the MSS as little more than a storehouse of readings to be evaluated on other grounds.[54] On the other extreme is the "Majority text method," embodied in *The Greek New Testament According to the Majority Text*.[55] This approach seeks to eliminate entirely any appeal to internal evidence, arguing instead that at any given point a variant that is supported by a majority of the MSS ought to be accepted as original.[56] But this essentially substitutes counting for reasoned criticism, and fails to realize that, as was pointed out above, MSS must be weighed, not simply counted, since ten thousand copies of a mistake do not make it any less a mistake.[57]

What the Majority text and the rigorous eclectic approaches have in common is a disregard for the history of the textual tradition. If, however, one takes the history of the text seriously, it becomes impossible to rely entirely upon either external or internal criteria alone. Instead, depending upon the facts in any given instance, a reasoned eclecticism applies a combination of internal and external considerations, evaluating the character of the variants in light of the manuscript evidence and vice versa in order to obtain a balanced view of the matter and as a check upon purely subjective tendencies.[58] This is the method and approach most widely practiced today and that lies behind, for example, recent translations such as the NRSV, REB, NASB, and NIV.

EVALUATING VARIANT READINGS: THE METHOD IN PRACTICE

A reasoned eclecticism seeks to follow one fundamental guideline that governs all other considerations: *the variant most likely to be original is the one that best accounts for the existence of the others.* That is, when confronted with two or more variant readings at some point in the text, it asks, "Which one best explains, in terms of both external and internal evidence, the origins of the others?" It is important to emphasize that "best accounts for" is here defined in terms of *both* external and internal considerations, because *prerequisite to reaching a judgment about a variant is the reconstruction of its history.* This is where both the Majority text and rigorous eclectic approaches fall short, in that they repeatedly contend for the originality of readings that cannot account for the historical (i.e., manuscript) evidence. Only the variant that can best account for *all* the evidence can seriously be considered as original.

Within the framework established by this fundamental guideline, several factors must be taken into consideration. Exactly which ones ought to be considered and how much weight is to be given to each depends upon the particular facts and circumstances in any given case. It may be helpful, therefore, to list the basic criteria for evaluating variant readings along with the various considerations that must be taken into account. We will then illustrate their application and use by means of some examples.

External Evidence

Four basic factors to consider when evaluating external evidence (i.e., the evidence provided by the MSS and other witnesses themselves) are: (1) the relative date of the witnesses (does the earlier[59] evidence support one variant more than the others? Are some variants without any early support? Or do all the readings have early support?); (2) the geographic distribution of the witnesses (generally, the broader the geographic distribution of the supporting witnesses the higher the probability that the variant may be original, assuming that remote witnesses are not otherwise related);[60] (3) the genealogical relationships among the MSS (one must determine whether the MSS supporting a variant represent a variety of text-types or are all from a single one, in which case it may be that a variant represents only a peculiarity of that text-type; also, once the reading of the text-type has been established, the addition of large numbers of additional witnesses of the same text-type does not appreciably affect matters); and (4) the relative quality of the witnesses.[61]

Internal Evidence

Internal evidence is of two kinds, *transcriptional* (having to do with the habits and practices of scribes) and *intrinsic* (having to do with the author's style and vocabulary). Each must be considered separately.

In evaluating transcriptional factors, it is a matter of asking whether any of the readings may be the result of slips, errors, or alterations in the copying process. In addition to the causes of error discussed above, one must take into account scribal tendencies to smooth over or resolve difficulties rather than create them, to harmonize passages, and to add rather than omit material.

As for intrinsic factors, the aim is to evaluate readings in light of what an author is most likely to have written. Factors to consider include the author's vocabulary and style, the flow of thought and logic of the immediate context (here exegesis may be decisive for the textual decision), congruence with the author's ideas or teachings, whether traditional material is being utilized, and, in the Gospels, the Aramaic background of Jesus' teachings.[62]

Not all these factors will apply in every case, of course, and it is not uncommon for two or more of them to conflict. This is why none of them can be applied or followed in a mechanical or thoughtless fashion and why the fundamental guideline must always be kept in mind: The variant most likely to be original is the one that best accounts for, in terms of both external and internal considerations, the origins of the others.

Summary

By now it should be clear that textual criticism is an art as well as a science. Like other historical disciplines it resists being reduced to a mechanical application of any one rule or set of rules. Each new variant confronts the critic with a potentially unique set of circumstances and data, and must be approached on that basis. Thus it is no surprise that two instances of variation may offer variants having identical external attestation and yet be evaluated quite differently on the basis of other considerations. As A. E. Housman so aptly and colorfully expressed it, textual criticism is not a branch of mathematics, nor indeed an exact science at all. It deals with . . . the frailties and aberrations of the human mind, and of its insubordinate servants, the human fingers. It therefore is not susceptible of hard-and-fast rules. It would be much easier if it were; and that is why people try to pretend that it is . . . Of course you can have hard-and-fast rules if you like, but then you will have false rules, and they will lead you wrong; because their simplicity will render them inapplicable to problems which are not simple, but complicated by the play of personality. . . . A textual critic engaged upon his business is not at all like Newton investigating the motions of the planets: he is much more like a dog hunting for fleas. If a dog hunted for fleas on mathematical principles, basing his researches on statistics of area and population, he would never catch a flea except by accident. They require to be treated as individuals; and every problem which presents itself to the textual critic must be regarded as possibly unique.[63]

Selected Examples

The following section attempts to illustrate by means of a discussion of selected variant readings some of the principles outlined above. Not every point touched on earlier can be mentioned here, of course, but the range and variety of the chosen examples should serve to give one a feel for how textual critics go about the business of applying these general considerations to specific problems.

It is customary to present the data of the Greek MSS, early versions, and early church fathers in the format of a *critical apparatus* (in Latin, *apparatus criticus*) to the passage under discussion. This offers a concise and precise way to present the mass of data available for most passages. Further to save space numerous abbreviations are used. To the uninitiated, a critical apparatus can appear intimidating. But with a little practice and some knowledge of the abbreviations used, it is possible to unpack the information presented in a critical apparatus without too much difficulty. Some common abbreviations and symbols used below include the following:

Byz	=	the reading of the majority of the Byzantine MSS
f^1, f^{13}	=	the "Family 1" or "Family 13" group of MSS

it	=	the Itala or Old Latin version (superscript letters indicate individual MSS)
vg	=	the Vulgate
sy^s	=	Sinaitic Syriac version
sy^c	=	Curetonian Syriac version
sy^p	=	Peshitta Syriac version
sy^h	=	Harclean Syriac version
sy^pal	=	Palestinian Syriac version
cop	=	Coptic version (the united witness of the dialects)
cop^sa	=	Coptic version, Sahidic dialect
cop^bo	=	Coptic version, Bohairic dialect
cop^pbo	=	Coptic version, Proto-Bohairic dialect
cop^ac2	=	Coptic version, Sub-Achmimic dialect
pc	=	a few (*pauci*)
pt	=	in part
marg	=	an alternate reading in the margin of a MS
*	=	reading of the original scribe of a MS (e.g., ℵ*)
c	=	reading of the corrector of a MS (e.g., ℵ^c)
2,3,4	=	readings of successive correctors of a MS

The first example will provide both a critical apparatus and a narrative listing of the evidence; successive examples will provide only a critical apparatus.

Luke 11:2, 4

What are the opening and closing words of the Lord's Prayer in the Gospel according to Luke?[64] The MSS offer the following possibilities:

11:2　　*Father* p^75 ℵ B f^1 700 pc vg sy^s Marcion Origen
　　　　Our Father L pc
　　　　Our Father in heaven A C D K P W X Δ Θ Π Ψ f^13
　　　　28 565 892 1010 1071 1241 Byz it sy^c,p,h cop

11:4　　*temptation* p^75 ℵ*,2 B L f^1 700 pc vg sy^s cop^sa,bo(pt)
　　　　Marcion Tertullian Origen
　　　　temptation but deliver us from the evil one ℵ^1 A C D K
　　　　W X Δ Θ Π Ψ f^13 28 33 565 892 1010 1071 1241
　　　　Byz it sy^c,p,h cop^bo(pt)

When we unpack this apparatus, we find out the following information: In Luke 11:2, the prayer opens with the single word "Father" in Greek manuscripts p^75, ℵ , B, Family 1 (f^1),

700, and a few others, in the Latin Vulgate and Sinaitic Syriac among the versions, and Marcion and Origen among the early church fathers. It opens with "Our Father" in Greek manuscript L and a few others, while the opening line is "Our Father in heaven" in manuscripts A, C, D, K, P, W, X, Delta (Δ), Theta (Θ), Pi (Π), Upsilon (Ψ), Family 13 (f^{13}), 28, 565, 892, 1010, 1071, 1241, and the rest of the Byzantine text-type, and in the old Latin, the Curetonian, Peshitta, and Harclean Syriac, and the Coptic versions.

In 11:4, the prayer ends with "lead us not into temptation" in p^{75}, both the original reading and the second corrector of codex Sinaiticus (ℵ*,2), B, L, Family 1, 700, and a few other Greek MSS, in the Vulgate, the Sinaitic Syriac, the Sahidic Coptic and part of the Bohairic Coptic among the versions, and Marcion, Tertullian, and Origen among the early fathers. It ends with "lead us not into temptation but deliver us from the evil one" according to the first corrector of Sinaiticus (ℵ1), A, C, D, K, W, X, Δ, Θ, Π, Ψ, Family 13, 28, 33, 565, 892, 1010, 1071, 1241, and the rest of the Byzantine text-type, and in the Old Latin, the Curetonian, Peshitta, and Harclean Syriac, and part of the Bohairic Coptic versions.

Now that we have unpacked the apparatus and found out what the external evidence (i.e., the actual readings of the Greek manuscripts, the versions, and the church fathers) is, we are now in a position to evaluate it. In this instance, the support for the two sets[65] of variants is so similar that they may be evaluated together.

The first thing to evaluate is external evidence: date, geographical distribution, genealogical relationships, and relative quality. In purely numerical terms the support for the longer reading is overwhelming. When the evidence is weighed, however, rather than counted, the situation is rather different. In view of the conjunction of Western (e.g., D it sy^c) and Byzantine support (A, most uncial and almost all minuscule MSS) the longer reading clearly is an early one,[66] but p^{75} (early third century) and the patristic citations, especially Marcion (*ca.* 140), show that the shorter reading is even earlier. The longer reading is broadly supported by representatives of the secondary Alexandrian (e.g., C 33 892 cop^{sa,bo}), Western (D it sy^c), and Byzantine (A K W Δ Π most uncials and minuscules) textual traditions, the shorter largely by primary Alexandrian witnesses (p^{75} ℵ B Origen) and, significantly, the Vulgate and

Sinaitic Syriac. The geographic distribution of the witnesses for each is roughly similar; the shorter reading, however, has the edge in terms of relative quality.[67] Overall, then, the external evidence favors the shorter reading.

Internal evidence, it will be recalled, is of two kinds, transcriptional (having to do with the habits and practices of scribes) and intrinsic (having to do with the author's style and vocabulary). Since both the longer and shorter forms of the prayer are consistent with the style and teaching of Jesus, the key considerations in this instance are transcriptional in nature. As is the case today, in the ancient church the Matthean version of the Lord's prayer (6:9–13) was best known, memorized, and used in worship. In light of this fact, the fundamental guideline given above (the variant most likely to be original is the one that bests accounts for the existence of the others) may be applied by asking this question: which of the readings best explains the rise of the others? Specifically, in this instance is a scribe more likely to have shortened the longer Lukan reading (thereby creating a discrepancy between Matthew and Luke) or added to the shorter Lukan form in order to harmonize it to the much more familiar Matthean version? The answer is clear: if the longer reading were original, it is virtually inconceivable that a scribe would cut out such well-known phrases, whereas if the shorter reading is original, it is easy to account for the rise of the longer reading as the result of inadvertent or deliberate assimilation to the better known Matthean form of the prayer. In short, the shorter reading can account for the rise of the longer, but not vice-versa.

Note how in this case both external and internal considerations favor the shorter reading. This convergence of evidence demonstrates conclusively that it represents the original text of the Lucan form of the Lord's Prayer.

John 6:69

The difference between the New King James and the New International versions of John 6:69—"You are the Christ, the Son of the living God" versus "You are the Holy One of God"—only hints at the extent of variation in this text. The textual evidence reads as follows:

(1) *the Christ the Son of the living God* K (Δ) Θᶜ Π Ψ 0250
    *f*¹³ 28 700 892 1071 1241 *Byz* itᵖᵗ syᵖ·ʰ copᵇᵒ⁽ᵖᵗ⁾
(2) *the Christ the Son of God* C³ Θ *f*¹ 33 565 *pc* itᵖᵗ syˢ
(3) *the Son of God* itᵇ syᶜ
(4) *the Christ* Tertullian
(5) *the Christ the Holy One of God* p⁶⁶ copˢᵃ⁽ᵖᵗ⁾, ᵃᶜ²,ᵇᵒ
(6) *the Holy One of God* p⁷⁵ ℵ B C* D L W copˢᵃ⁽¹ᵐˢ⁾, ᵖᵇᵒ

An initial assessment suggests (barring some consideration to
the contrary) that readings (2), (3), (4), and (5) should probably
be set aside on the basis of their slim external support. With
regard to internal considerations, these readings appear upon
further investigation to be the result of harmonization to or
conflation with parallel passages (John 11:27; 1:49; and Mark
8:29 respectively), an observation that clinches the case against
them. Readings (1), which has good Byzantine (K Δ Π 700 *Byz*)
and some versional (itᵖᵗ syᵖ·ʰ) and secondary Alexandrian (892
copᵇᵒ⁽ᵖᵗ⁾) support, and (6), which has support from Alexandrian
(p⁷⁵ B C L W) and Western (ℵ [in John 1:1–8:38] D) witnesses,
require further attention.

Both readings have parallels elsewhere in the Gospel
accounts: (1) parallels Matthew 16:16, the disciples' confession
at Caesarea Philippi (the Synoptic episode parallel to John 6:60–
71), while (6) parallels Mark 1:24/Luke 4:34, where an unclean
spirit about to be cast out acknowledges that Jesus is "the Holy
One of God." Conceivably either reading could be explained as
the result of assimilation to the parallel passage. It seems far
more likely, however, that scribes would harmonize (6) to
Matthew 16:16, and thereby remove a discrepancy between the
two parallel episodes, than that they would create a discrepancy by replacing (1) with words spoken elsewhere only by an
unclean spirit. Thus one may conclude that transcriptional
considerations clearly favor (6).

The same may be said for intrinsic considerations. In v. 69
Peter says "we have come to know," or "we have recognized
the truth" (*pepisteukamen*), implying a new depth of insight on
the part of the disciples. Yet the essence of the other variants
here—that Jesus is Messiah and Son of God—was already
confessed as early as 1:41 and 1:49. Variant (6), however—"the
Holy One [*hagios*] of God"—is appropriate as the disciples'
response to the events recorded in John 6. Furthermore, it also
sets up, in a typically Johannine way, 10:36 (the Father

sanctified [*hēgiasen*] and sent Jesus into the world) and 17:19 (Jesus sanctifies [*hagiazō*] himself for the disciples' sake). Of all the variants it best fits both the immediate context and the structural development of the book as a whole.

Thus all three lines of evidence—external, transcriptional, and intrinsic—come together in support of variant (6) as the reading that best meets our basic guideline. We may in this case be virtually certain that "the Holy One of God" represents the original text of John 6:69.

John 5:44

Though much less complex than the last example, this variant is of interest because of the similar alignment of the MSS evidence. Consideration of other factors, however, leads to a different conclusion. In the phrase "yet you do not seek the praise that comes from the only God" one finds these variants:

> *the only One [tou monou]* p[66] p[75] B W it[a,b] cop[sa,ac2] cop[pbo,bo(pt)]

> *the only God [tou monou theou]* ℵ A D K L Δ Θ Π Ψ 063 0210 *f*[1].[13] 28 33 565 700 892 1071 1241 *Byz* it vg sy[c.p.h.pal] cop[bo(pt)]

While the Alexandrian support (p[66] p[75] B W cop[sa,bo]) for the shorter reading is early and very impressive, internal considerations suggest that in this instance it is also wrong. First, *God* (*theou*) appears to be required by the context, a point confirmed by the observation that John nowhere else calls God "the only One." Second, the accidental omission of $\overline{\Theta Y}$ (*theta upsilon*, the customary Greek contraction of *theou* [God]) from the sequence TOYMONOY$\overline{\Theta Y}$OY (*TOUMONOU*$\overline{THU}$*OU*, remembering that the earliest manuscripts were written in continuous capitals) seems more likely than its insertion. Thus both intrinsic and transcriptional considerations favor the inclusion of *theou*, which in addition has substantial external support (secondary Alexandrian [L 33 892 cop[ho(pt)]], Western [ℵ D it sy[c]], and Byzantine [A K Δ Π *Byz*]). It seems relatively certain, therefore, that here the longer reading is original, rather than the shorter.

Matthew 22:13

Three forms of the king's instructions to his servants are found in the MSS at this point:

(1) *binding [deō] him hand and foot, toss [ekballō] him. . .* ℵ
    B L Θ 085 *f*¹ (*f*¹³) 700 892 *pc* (sy^p) cop
(2) *seize [airō] him hand and foot and throw [ballō] him. . .* D
    it (sy^s,c) Irenaeus Lucifer of Calaris
(3) *binding [deō] him hand and foot, seize [airō] him and toss
    [ekballō] him. . .* C (M) W (Φ) 0138 (565 1241 1424) *Byz*
    it^f (sy^h)

Variant (3), the Byzantine reading, is easily accounted for as a combination of (1) and (2), whereas it is not possible to derive both (1) and (2) from (3), as a little experimentation will demonstrate. Hence it may be set aside as a clever (but obviously secondary) conflation of the other two variants.

The differences between (1) and (2) are (a) *deō* ("bind") versus *airō* ("seize"); (b) *ekballō* ("toss") versus *ballō* ("throw"); and (c) subordination (participle + verb) versus parataxis (two verbs joined by "and"). In this instance transcriptional considerations are of little help in choosing between the two variants since the differences are obviously not accidental. It is just possible that *airō* has been deliberately substituted for *deō* because it was thought to be more suited to the setting (why bind someone just to toss him out of the banquet hall?), but this is too slim a point to carry much weight. Intrinsic factors are also indecisive. On the basis of usage all four verbs under evaluation may be said to be equally Matthean (*deō* occurs ten times, *airō* nineteen, *ballō* thirty-four, and *ekballō* twenty-eight times in Matthew), and while Matthew generally prefers subordination to parataxis (a point in favor of the first reading), this can be turned around to favor (2) as the more unusual construction (and thus more likely to be altered). In short, in this instance internal considerations either cancel each other out or are indecisive.

Hence it is necessary to make the decision solely on external grounds. Here Westcott and Hort's dictum—knowledge of documents should precede judgment upon readings[68]—comes into play. For the Western textual tradition, and particularly D, its leading witness, exhibits a decided tendency toward substitutions and revisions (of which the above variant is typical), which almost always prove to be secondary rather than original. The Alexandrian text-type, on the other hand, manifests a consistent freedom from these types of secondary alterations. In instances like this, therefore, when a decision must be made on purely external grounds, one is justified in preferring the Alexandrian reading and adopting (1) as the text of 22:13.

Summary

The preceding examples should serve to (1) illustrate the application of the primary guideline given above, (2) demonstrate that no one manuscript or textual tradition is always right, and (3) make clear that no one rule, consideration, group of MSS, etc., can be followed or applied to textual problems in a mechanical or thoughtless fashion. Every textual problem must be approached on its own terms; all the critic can learn about MSS, about scribes, about the author, must be brought to bear on it. Above all, the fundamental guideline must be kept in mind: Which variant best accounts for the origin of the others? The variant that, after thoughtful consideration of all the evidence, best satisfies this question will almost invariably best represent the original text.

THE SIGNIFICANCE OF
TEXTUAL CRITICISM FOR EXEGESIS

Before one can understand an author, one must know what the author wrote. Thus textual criticism is foundational to all study of the New Testament; one cannot hope to produce fruitful work without a reliable textual basis. Moreover, for many of the methods and approaches described elsewhere in this book, textual criticism is critically important. Source and redaction criticism, for example, involve the close study of sometimes small details and differences between the Gospels, details and differences that frequently involve textual variants. The textual choices one makes on this level often have a noticeable impact upon one's results.[69]

In practical terms, obtaining a reliable text means for most students utilizing one of the two excellent critical editions available today, either UBS[3] or NA[26]. But the availability of reliable critical editions produced by a committee of experts should not lull the student into thinking that textual criticism is an avoidable technicality, or that textual variants and their accompanying apparatus may be safely ignored. There are two reasons for this.

First, even so distinguished a group as the editorial committee responsible for the UBS[3] and NA[26] texts slips occasionally, and its work is sometimes capable of being improved. The student should always work through any variants in a passage being exegeted. In most cases she or he will find the committee's work convincing. At times, however, good reasons may be found for adopting another reading as more likely to be original,[70] and such decisions will of course affect one's exegesis.[71]

Second, the doing of textual criticism often leads to exegetical insights that might otherwise be missed. Textual decisions often require the closest attention to an author's style, thought, and argument, which are all in turn crucial to sound exegesis. The reverse also happens, as the exegesis of a passage may be decisive for the resolution of a textual difficulty within it.[72] Either way, attention to textual difficulties lays the basis for good exegesis. In a fundamental sense, therefore, textual criticism is not just preparatory to exegesis but part and parcel of it.

BIBLIOGRAPHY

Basic Works

Aland, Kurt and Barbara. *The Text of the New Testament: An Introduction to the Critical Editions and to the Theory and Practice of Modern Textual Criticism.* 2d ed., rev. and enlarged. Trans. by E. F. Rhodes. Leiden/Grand Rapids: Brill/Eerdmans, 1989.

Fee, Gordon D. "The Textual Criticism of the New Testament." In *The Expositor's Bible Commentary*, vol. 1. Ed. by F. E. Gaebelein. Grand Rapids: Zondervan, 1979, 419–33.

Finegan, Jack. *Encountering New Testament Manuscripts: A Working Introduction to Textual Criticism.* Grand Rapids: Eerdmans, 1974.

Metzger, Bruce M. *The Text of the New Testament: Its Transmission, Corruption, and Restoration.* 2d ed. New York/Oxford: Oxford University Press, 1968; 3d ed. forthcoming.

_____. *A Textual Commentary on the Greek New Testament: A Companion Volume to the United Bible Societies' Greek New Testament*. 3d ed. London/New York: United Bible Societies, 1971; rev. ed. 1975.

For Further Reading

Aland, Kurt. *Studien zur Überlieferung des Neuen Testaments und seines Textes*. Berlin: de Gruyter, 1967.

Birdsall, J. Neville. "The New Testament Text." In *The Cambridge History of the Bible*. Vol. 1: *From the Beginnings to Jerome*. Ed. by P. R. Ackroyd and C. F. Evans. Cambridge: University Press, 1979, 308–77.

Colwell, Ernest C. *Studies in Methodology in Textual Criticism of the New Testament*. Leiden: Brill, 1969.

Epp, Eldon J. "Textual Criticism." In *The New Testament and Its Modern Interpreters*. Ed. by E. J. Epp and George W. MacRae. Atlanta: Scholars Press, 1989, 75–126.

Fee, Gordon D. "P75, p66, and Origen: The Myth of Early Textual Recension in Alexandria." In *New Dimensions in New Testament Study*. Ed. by R. N. Longenecker and M. C. Tenney. Grand Rapids: Eerdmans, 1974, 19–45.

_____. "Rigorous or Reasoned Eclecticism—Which?" In *Studies in New Testament Language and Text: Essays in Honour of George D. Kilpatrick on the Occasion of His Sixty-fifth Birthday*. Ed. by J. K. Elliott. Leiden: Brill, 1976, 174–97.

Kenyon, F. G. *The Text of the Greek Bible*. 3d ed. revised and augmented by A. W. Adams. London: Duckworth, 1975.

Lagrange, M.-J. *Critique textuelle*. II. *La Critique rationnelle*. 2d ed. Paris: Gabalda, 1935.

Metzger, Bruce M. *The Early Versions of the New Testament: Their Origin, Transmission, and Limitations*. Oxford: Clarendon, 1977.

Reynolds, L. D., and Wilson, N. G. *Scribes and Scholars: A Guide to the Transmission of Greek and Latin Literature*. 2d ed. Oxford: Clarendon, 1974.

Westcott, B. F., and Hort, F. J. A. *The New Testament in the Original Greek*, [ii] *Introduction* [and] *Appendix*. Cambridge: Macmillan, 1881; 2d ed. 1896.

Zuntz, G. *The Text of the Epistles: A Disquisition Upon the Corpus Paulinum*. London: The British Academy, 1953.

NOTES

[1]Codex Sinaiticus, for example, a parchment manuscript that originally contained the entire Greek Bible, is estimated to have required the hides of approximately 360 sheep and goats.

[2]A professional scriptorium, or copy center, employed people to correct the work of the scribes, and was capable of turning out high quality work. But with regard to New Testament manuscripts, production under such careful control appears to have been the exception rather than the rule.

[3]In the second century Christians seem to have been among the first to abandon the scroll for the less expensive and more convenient codex or book format. Out of a group of 476 non-Christian second-century papyri from Egypt, over ninety-seven percent are scrolls, while all the Christian papyri from the same period and area are in codex form (J. Finegan, *Encountering New Testament Manuscripts* [Grand Rapids: Eerdmans, 1974], 29). See further the fundamental study by C. H. Roberts, *Manuscript, Society, and Belief in Early Christian Egypt* (London: Oxford University Press for The British Academy, 1979).

[4]This phenomenon is termed *homoioarcton, homoiomeson,* or *homoioteleuton,* depending on whether the beginning, middle, or end of a word is involved.

[5]In Matthew 5:19–20, e.g., the phrase "the kingdom of heaven" occurs at the end of verses 19a, 19b, and 20. A few scribes have skipped from the first occurrence to the second, thus eliminating 19b; one has skipped from the first to the third, thereby eliminating all of 19b and 20.

[6]The use of dictation, common in scriptoria, added another step and opportunity for error, particularly in the case of homonyms. The well-known variation in Romans 5:1 between "let us have peace" (*echōmen*) and "we have peace" (*echomen*; both words were pronounced alike) exemplifies this problem.

[7]The substitution of the frequently repeated Matthean form of the Lord's prayer for the less-familiar Lucan form in Luke 11 (see the first example below) is a good example of the latter phenomenon.

[8]A scribe's note in an Armenian MS (cited by B. M. Metzger, *The Text of the New Testament: Its Transmission, Corruption, and Restoration,* 2d ed. [New York and Oxford: Oxford University Press, 1968], 18) mentions that it is snowing heavily outside, the ink is frozen, and his hand is numb. Others complain of the physical discomfort involved in copying for six or more hours a day. Little wonder that copies were less than perfect!

[9]An ancient historian records an incident around A.D. 350 in which a man was publicly rebuked for substituting the Attic word *skimpous* for the colloquial Koine *krabbatos* ("pallet") in John 5:8 (cited by Metzger, *Text,* 196).

[10]As in Luke 3:22, where "You are my son; today I have begotten you" (as in NRSV[margin] and REB[margin]; cf. Ps 2:7) has been replaced by the less problematic "You are my beloved son; with you I am well pleased" (as in NRSV, NIV, NASB, REB; cf. Mk 1:11).

[11]P[52] (ca. 125, containing Jn 18:31–33, 37–38) is the earliest known MS of any part of the New Testament thus far identified. Claims that portions of Mark have been identified among the manuscript fragments of the Dead Sea Scrolls from Qumran are unconvincing (for bibliographic details of the discussion see B. M. Metzger, *Manuscripts of the Greek Bible* [New York and Oxford: Oxford University Press, 1981], 24 n41, 62 n1). The recent proposal by Y. K. Kim ("Palaeographical Dating of p[46] to the Later First Century," *Biblica* 69 [1988]: 248–57) that p[46] (widely dated to ca. 200) should be dated prior to the end of the first century has yet to be assessed.

[12]For a descriptive list of the papyri see K. and B. Aland, *The Text of the New Testament. An Introduction to the Critical Editions and to the Theory and Practice of Modern Textual Criticism*, 2d ed. rev. and enlarged (Grand Rapids: Eerdmans, 1989), 96–102 [through p[96]].

[13]Although the uncial numbers now run up to 0301, for a number of reasons only 263 different MSS are recognized; see Aland, *Text*, 106. For a descriptive list see Aland, *Text*, 107–28, and for greater detail on selected uncials see Metzger, *Text*, 42–61.

[14]For a descriptive list of selected minuscules see Aland, *Text*, 129–40, and Metzger, *Text*, 61–66.

[15]According to Aland, *Text*, 78. Strictly speaking, A and C are now incomplete, although they do contain at least part of every New Testament book.

[16]For these and other statistics see Aland, *Text*, 78–83.

[17]See B. M. Metzger, *The Early Versions of the New Testament: Their Origin, Transmission, and Limitations* (Oxford: Clarendon, 1977); for briefer treatments see Metzger, *Text*, 67–86, and Aland, *Text*, 185-214.

[18]See especially the sections on limitations in Metzger, *Early Versions*.

[19]Metzger, *Text*, 86.

[20]See Metzger, *Text*, 86–88. For a useful annotated list of early Church Fathers, see Aland, *Text*, 215–21.

[21]Indeed, in view of the attention that is rightly focused on the places where the evidence differs, it is worth noting just how much of the New Testament is well established. A survey by the Alands reveals that of the 7,947 verses in the Greek New Testament, seven major editions are in complete agreement regarding 4,999, or 62.9% (Aland, *Text*, 28–29). If one were to leave aside certain idiosyncracies and minor differences between these editions, it may be estimated that the number of verses about which there is substantial agreement approaches 90% of the total. To be sure, the remaining differences can be substantial and important, and fully merit the attention given to them

over the centuries by textual critics. One should not neglect, however, to keep them in perspective, especially as people unacquainted with textual matters are sometimes shocked to encounter statements to the effect that "there are over 30,000 errors in the New Testament." The intended implication is that the New Testament is unreliable. Such statements are uninformed and inaccurate. If one defines "error" broadly enough, to include, e.g., spelling mistakes or differences, then it is true that there are tens if not hundreds of thousands of "errors" among the 5000+ manuscripts of the New Testament. But this hardly affects the reliability of the New Testament itself, since wherever some MSS are in error, others have accurately preserved the original text.

[22]The so-called Caesarean text was for several decades thought to comprise a fourth text-type of the Gospels (the classic expression of this view is by B. H. Streeter, *The Four Gospels. A Study in Origins*. 5th impression [London: Macmillan, 1936]). This has recently been shown not to be the case. See B. M. Metzger, "The Caesarean Text of the Gospels," *Chapters in the History of New Testament Textual Criticism* (Leiden/Grand Rapids: Brill/Eerdmans, 1963), 42–72, and L. W. Hurtado, *Text-Critical Methodology and the Pre-Caesarean Text: Codex W in the Gospel of Mark* (Grand Rapids: Eerdmans, 1981).

[23]Labels used by other writers for the two subdivisions of this text-type ("primary" and "secondary") include "neutral" and "Alexandrian" (Westcott and Hort); "Proto-Alexandrian" and "Later Alexandrian" (B. M. Metzger, *A Textual Commentary on the Greek New Testament* [London and New York: United Bible Societies, 1971; corr. ed. 1975]); and "Alexandrian" and "Egyptian" (Aland, *Text*).

[24]For a more detailed listing of witnesses in all three text-types, as well as other important witnesses, categorized according to Gospels, Acts, Pauline Epistles, Catholic Epistles, and Revelation, see Tables 1–5 in M. W. Holmes, "New Testament Textual Criticism," in *Introducing New Testament Interpretation*, ed. by Scot McKnight (Grand Rapids: Baker, 1989), 53–74, or Metzger, *Textual Commentary*, xxviii–xxxi.

[25]The term "Western" is somewhat misleading. It was first applied to this particular textual tradition at a time when the only witnesses to it did have ties to the West, i.e., Rome, North Africa, and Gaul. Discoveries since then, however, have made it clear that this early textual tradition was widely disseminated throughout the Roman Empire and may have originated in the East, perhaps in Egypt. The continued use of the term today is largely a matter of custom and convenience.

[26]The Western text of Acts, for example, is over eight percent longer than the Alexandrian text of the same book.

[27]These betray decided tendencies toward smoothing out grammar, supplying assumed words or pronouns, harmonization, removal

of ambiguity, and conflation (combination) of readings found in the Alexandrian and Western text-types.

[28]For selected examples see G. D. Fee, "Modern Textual Criticism and the Revival of the *Textus Receptus*," *JETS* 21 (1978): 31–33.

[29]Already Irenaeus (ca. 175), for example, reports that while some copies read "616" at Revelation 13:18, "all good and ancient copies" read "666" (Irenaeus, *Against Heresies* 5.30.1). Scholars such as Origen (ca. 185–253) and Jerome (ca. 342–420) noted and discussed variances among MSS (see Bruce M. Metzger, "Explicit References in the Works of Origen to Variant Readings in New Testament Manuscripts," in *Biblical and Patristic Studies in Memory of Robert Pierce Casey*, ed. by J. N. Birdsall and R. W. Thomson [Freiburg: Herder, 1963], 78–95, repr. in Metzger, *Historical and Literary Studies* [Leiden/Grand Rapids: Brill/Eerdmans, 1968], 88–103; and "St. Jerome's Explicit References to Variant Readings in Manuscripts of the New Testament," in *Text and Interpretation. Studies in the New Testament presented to Matthew Black*, ed. by E. Best and R. McL. Wilson [Cambridge: Cambridge University Press, 1979], 179–90), and marginal and/or interlinear notes and comments remain as testimony to the occasional concern of now-anonymous editors to recover a "good and ancient" form of the text. Overall, however, there is little evidence of any sustained effort to choose between variant readings.

[30]The first *printed* edition of the Greek New Testament (part of a multilingual edition of the entire Bible known as the Complutensian Polyglot) was the product of a group of Spanish scholars at the University of Alcala (= Complutum in Latin), who finished their work in 1514. But it was not until 1520 that they were able to obtain permission to release it.

[31]See Jerry H. Bentley, *Humanists and Holy Writ: New Testament Scholarship in the Renaissance* (Princeton: Princeton University Press, 1983), 112–61.

[32]For the first edition he relied primarily upon MS 2 of the Gospels and MS 2 of the Acts and Catholic Epistles; his sources of corrections were MS 817 (Gospels) and MS 4 (Acts and Catholic Epistles). His main source for the Pauline Epistles was MS 7 (Bentley, *Humanists*, 127–29). His only source for Revelation, MS 1, was missing the last six verses. Erasmus filled in the gap by translating from the Vulgate back into Greek; his self-made text includes readings not found in any known Greek MS. He did make numerous corrections in later editions (including the definitive fourth) on the basis of later collations of a substantial number of MSS, but these were not enough to affect the basic character of his original edition.

[33]Metzger, *Text*, 106.

[34]This principle recognizes that a scribe is far more likely to make a difficult reading easier than he is to create a difficult or awkward reading out of one that presents no difficulty. Thus, e.g., in Mark 1:2

(which cites first Malachi 3:1 and then Isaiah 40:3) the original reading is certainly "in Isaiah the prophet" and not "in the prophets." The former is the "harder reading," in that it raises a question or difficulty for the reader while the latter does not.

[35]On Mill, Bentley, and Wettstein, see Metzger, *Text*, 107–15, and for the often-neglected Simon, L. D. Reynolds and N. G. Wilson, *Scribes and Scholars. A Guide to the Transmission of Greek and Latin Literature*, 2d ed. (Oxford: Clarendon, 1974), 169–70, 244.

[36]Metzger, *Text*, 121.

[37]For details of this fascinating story see Metzger, *Text*, 42–45, and for more recent developments J. H. Charlesworth, *The New Discoveries in St. Catherine's Monastery: A Preliminary Report on the Manuscripts* (American Schools of Oriental Research, 1981).

[38]Somewhat overshadowed by Tischendorf's fame is the work of his English colleague, S. P. Tregelles (1813–1875). A careful and systematic worker, his examination of nearly all the then-known uncials and most of the leading minuscules contributed greatly to an accurate knowledge of the evidence. Unlike Tischendorf, who rushed out a new edition almost every time he discovered a new manuscript, Tregelles focused his effort upon a single definitive edition, which, preceded by a statement of his own critical principles (*An Account of the Printed Text of the Greek New Testament. . .*[London, 1854]), appeared between 1857 and 1872. Cf. Metzger, *Text*, 127–28.

[39]Constantinus Tischendorf, *Novum Testamentum Graece. . .Editio octava critica maior*, 2 vols. (Leipzig, 1869–1872). A third volume of *Prolegomena* was edited by the American scholar C. R. Gregory (Leipzig, 1884, 1890, 1894); it later appeared in a German translation, with additions and corrections, under the title *Textkritik des Neuen Testamentes* (Leipzig, 1900–1909).

[40]B. F. Westcott and F. J. A. Hort, *The New Testament in the Original Greek*, 2 vols. (Cambridge, 1881–1882). Volume 1 contains the Greek text, while volume 2 contains an *Introduction* setting out their method and principles and an *Appendix* of notes on select readings.

[41]For a brief survey and assessment see Metzger, *Text*, 129–35.

[42]E.g., the text of the two most recent and widely-used editions, NA[26] and UBS[3], stands closer to the text of Westcott and Hort than it does to any other text published since Tischendorf.

[43]A notable exception is the industrious, idiosyncratic, and ultimately misdirected efforts of H. F. von Soden (*Die Schriften des Neuen Testaments in ihrer ältesten erreichbaren Textgestalt hergestellt auf Grund ihrer Textgeschichte*), which appeared in three large parts between 1902 and 1913. Cf. Metzger, *Text*, 139–43.

[44]Cf. on this point the important article by E. J. Epp, "Textual Criticism," in *The New Testament and Its Modern Interpreters*, ed. by E. J. Epp and G. W. MacRae (Atlanta: Scholars, 1989, 75–126), and his earlier articles to which he there refers. A different view is offered by

Kurt Aland, "The Twentieth-Century Interlude in New Testament Textual Criticism," in Best and Wilson, *Text and Interpretation*, 1–14.

[45]See Aland, *Text*, 19–22, or Metzger, *Text*, 144.

[46]Nestle-Aland, *Novum Testamentum Graece*, 26th ed. (Stuttgart: Deutsche Bibelstiftung, 1979).

[47]First edition, 1966; 3d edition (corrected), 1983.

[48]For a discussion of their distinctive features and aims, and an introduction to their use and textual symbols, see Aland, *Text*, 30–36, 43–47, 222–67.

[49]And, it may be added, the essential basis of nearly every recent major translation, including the NASB, TEV, NIV, NAB, and New Revised Standard Version (NRSV). In fact, the Westcott and Hort/Nestle-Aland/UBS textual tradition underlies virtually all major European and American Protestant translations of the last century, beginning with the Revised Version of 1881 (which utilized materials supplied by Westcott and Hort during the translation process). The sole significant exception among English translations is the NKJV, which continues to be based upon the Textus Receptus, which was essentially the textual basis of the KJV. But whereas in their day the KJV translators utilized the best—and only—text available to them, the NKJV follows what is now the worst text available. Even proponents of the Majority text recognize that the TR is a corrupt representative of the Majority text-type, differing from it in over 1800 instances. As a consequence of following the TR, the NKJV both includes words, phrases, and even sentences (cf. Acts 8:37) that never were part of the original text of Scripture and also omits parts that are original (cf. 1Jn 3:1).

[50]A related factor is the circumstance that almost all of the extant MSS are "orphans," without a parent, offspring, or siblings. Thus many of the genealogical links helpful in constructing a stemma are missing. As Metzger observes, "Instances of a known copy of another manuscript are exceedingly rare, which suggests that only a very small percentage of manuscripts have survived" (Metzger, *Manuscripts*, 54).

[51]Sometimes referred to as "rational criticism" (M.-J. Lagrange) or the "local-genealogical" method (Aland, *Text*, 34, 291).

[52]To give just two illustrations: the editors of the United Bible Societies' *The Greek New Testament* (UBS[3]) tend to follow, when all other criteria are equal, the reading of the Alexandrian witnesses; the editors of the NIV appear to have a tendency to prefer the reading that best harmonizes with other passages.

[53]Exemplified most notably by G. D. Kilpatrick and J. K. Elliott; see J. K. Elliott, "Keeping up with Recent Studies XV. New Testament Textual Criticism," *Expository Times* 99 (1987): 40-45, esp. 43–44.

[54]Cf. Elliott ("Keeping Up," 43): "I think it is perfectly feasible to try to reconstruct the original text by applying *only* internal criteria. . . . According to this method . . . the manuscripts are of

importance primarily as bearers of readings. . . . (The number or age of the manuscripts supporting the readings are of little significance)." For a detailed critique see G. D. Fee, "Rigorous or Reasoned Eclecticism—Which?," *Studies in New Testament Language and Text*, ed. by J. K. Elliott (Leiden: Brill, 1976), 174–97.

⁵⁵Zane C. Hodges and A. L. Farstad, eds., *The Greek New Testament According to the Majority Text* (Nashville, Camden, and New York: Nelson, 1982).

⁵⁶As Hodges puts it,

> Under normal circumstances the older a text is than its rivals, the greater are its chances to survive in a plurality or a majority of the texts extant at any subsequent period. But the *oldest* text of all is the autograph. Thus it ought to be taken for granted that, barring some radical dislocation in the history of transmission, a majority of texts will be far more likely to represent correctly the character of the original than a small minority of texts. This is especially true when the ratio is an overwhelming 8:2. Under any reasonably normal transmissional conditions, it would be for all practical purposes quite impossible for a later text-form to secure so one-sided a preponderance of extant witnesses. (Zane C. Hodges, "A Defense of the Majority Text," [printed syllabus notes, Dallas Theological Seminary, n.d.], 4).

In short, acceptance of modern critical texts "constitutes nothing less than a wholesale rejection of probabilities on a sweeping scale!" (Hodges, "Defense," 9). His entire case, however, rests upon a single assumption—that the transmission of the New Testament has occurred under "reasonably normal" conditions, that there has been no "radical dislocation in the history of transmission"—and that assumption is false. The history of transmission has been radically dislocated; examples include the destruction of MSS and entire libraries during times of persecution and the Muslim conquests. Thus readings once known to be in the minority are today dominant, and vice-versa; this fact alone rules out any attempt to do textual criticism by counting or statistical means. See further the critique and bibliography in M. W. Holmes, "The 'Majority text debate': new form of an old issue," *Themelios* 8 (1983): 13–19.

⁵⁷Moreover, in practice this "method" suffers from an internal contradiction. Hodges and Farstad place a great deal of importance upon the construction of a genealogical stemma of MSS, one result being a text that in numerous places is supported by only a *minority* of MSS. Cf. Daniel B. Wallace, "Some Second Thoughts on the Majority Text," *Bibliotheca Sacra* 146 (1989): 270–90, especially 279–85; and Holmes, "The 'Majority text debate'," 18.

[58]The best introductory (and now classic) treatment of this approach is still that of Metzger, *Text*, 207–46.

[59]It must be remembered, of course, that a late MS or witness may preserve a very early form of the text; e.g., MS 1739 (tenth century) preserves a text closely related to p[46] (ca. 200).

[60]It is also true, however, as in linguistics, that change often affects remote areas last, if at all; hence a true reading may be preserved in only a few witnesses from the fringes of the MSS tradition.

[61]This may well be the most difficult of the four external factors to ascertain, and perhaps the most subjective. But it is an observable fact that certain MSS display fewer readings that are obviously secondary (conflations, stylistic improvements, harmonizations, etc.) or scribal slips than do other MSS, which suggests that they are the product of a more controlled copying process, and therefore may be judged more likely to preserve an uncontaminated form of the text.

[62]Intrinsic considerations are often the most subjective kind of evidence the text critic must take into account, since at any particular point an author may have deviated from his usual style or lexical preference for the sake of variety, if nothing else. At times, however, it can be decisive in judging between readings and for this reason must never be neglected.

[63]A. E. Housman, "The Application of Thought to Textual Criticism," in *Selected Prose*, ed. by John Carter (Cambridge: Cambridge University Press, 1961), 132–33.

[64]There are also several other variations of a similar character within the prayer, but due to considerations of space and clarity we will focus only on these two places.

[65]Given that the third reading in 11:2 (*Our Father*) has very slim external attestation (L *pc*) and that the addition of "our" is almost certainly due to the influence of Matthew 6:9, it may be confidently set aside as a secondary or corrupt reading.

[66]Since these two textual traditions began to go their separate ways by the end of the second century, a reading broadly attested by both text-types likely antedates the split and hence must be reckoned as a very old reading.

[67]This is based upon the demonstrable fact that at those places where the original text is established beyond doubt, the Alexandrian text-type preserves the original reading far more frequently than do either of the other two text-types combined. But since at any particular point any of the text-types or MSS may be in error, this consideration of relative quality generally comes into play only in those cases where there are no other more weighty considerations upon which to base a decision, or when the other evidence is so evenly balanced that a decision is difficult. In these circumstances one will most likely pick the

original text if one picks the Alexandrian reading. Cf. the discussion of Matthew 22:13 below.

[68]Westcott and Hort, *Introduction*, 30.

[69]And, on occasion, vice versa: For some scholars, a particular view of the Synoptic problem has a decisive effect upon their textual decisions. Thus while textual decisions can affect one's view of the Synoptic problem, one's view of the Synoptic problem can affect one's textual choices. The danger of circular reasoning is apparent.

[70]Examples include Matthew 5:11 and 19:9, Mark 14:70, and 1 Corinthians 2:1. On Matthew 5:11 see M. W. Holmes, "The Text of Matthew 5:11," *NTS* 32 (1986): 283–86, and on 19:9 and Mark 14:70 see *idem*, "The Text of the Matthean Divorce Passages: A Comment on the Appeal to Harmonization in Textual Decisions," *JBL* 109 (1990): 651–64. On 1 Corinthians 2:1 see G. D. Fee, *The First Epistle to the Corinthians* (NICNT; Grand Rapids: Eerdmans, 1987), 88, 91.

[71]Compare, for example, the textual variants in Matthew 17:21 and Mark 9:29 (see the marginal notes in the RSV, NIV, NASB, or NKJV for details), which impact both one's interpretation and view of the Synoptic problem, or the variant in John 7:1: In place of "did not wish," some MSS read Jesus "did not have the authority" to go to Galilee. Clearly one's choice here is crucial to one's interpretation.

[72]See the discussion of John 6:69 above, for example, or the discussion of 1 Thessalonians 2:7 in either Metzger, *Text*, 230–33, or Holmes, "Textual Criticism," 69–70.

Chapter Five

Source Criticism

Scot McKnight

Scot McKnight

Scot McKnight is Assistant Professor of New Testament at Trinity Evangelical Divinity School in Deerfield, Illinois. He holds the B.A. from Grand Rapids Baptist College, the M.A.B.S. from Trinity Evangelical Divinity School, and the Ph.D. from the University of Nottingham. He is the author of *Interpreting the Synoptic Gospels* (Baker) and *A Light Among the Gentiles* (Fortress), and the editor of *Introducing New Testament Interpretation* (Baker). His articles have appeared in such journals as *Themelios*, *Trinity Journal*, and *Catalyst*. He is currently writing the volume on Matthew for the *New International Commentary on the New Testament* (Eerdmans) and the volume on James for the *Wycliffe Exegetical Commentary* (Moody). He also serves as coeditor of the two-volume *Dictionary of Jesus and the Gospels* (InterVarsity).

Chapter Five

Source Criticism

In the spring of my senior year in college I pulled a book from one of my shelves, and, knowing that the requirements for graduation were fulfilled and that I could now read simply for the pleasure of learning, I read the book from cover to cover. That book was R. P. Martin's *New Testament Foundations: A Guide for Christian Students. Vol. 1: The Four Gospels.*[1] The book raised what were, for me at least, some disturbing questions, and it answered these same questions in ways and with methods with which I was completely unfamiliar. The eleventh chapter, however, captivated me; that chapter covered the "The Synoptic Problem."[2] Here Martin assessed the literary relationship of the Synoptic Gospels and concluded that Mark, along with the hypothetical source Q, were the sources used by Matthew and Luke (along with other sources) when they composed their Gospels. I found this conclusion theoretically (at least) confirmed by Luke's statement of procedure (Lk 1:1–4) but also found myself dismayed, for I had never thought of the Evangelists proceeding in such a manner. Frankly I had a fuzzy dictation theory of inspiration and had never really entertained any "historical thinking" on the origin of the Synoptic Gospels.

Though at the time I could not foresee it, that book set the agenda for the interests in scholarship that remain with me to this day. I entered seminary with a host of questions about the Gospels, many of which were first raised by Martin, and I used that time to work through many fundamental issues about the Gospels—questions about historical reliability, about sources, and about the editorial activity of the Evangelists.

This chapter is concerned with one of those questions, namely, did the Evangelists of the Synoptic Gospels, under inspiration, use written sources when they wrote their Gospels? And, if so (and I believe they did), what is the relationship of the Synoptic Gospels to each other? For many these are disturbing questions. However, they must be asked and a reasonable answer ought to be given if we are to do our Gospel study with any sense of integrity.

THE PHENOMENA OF THE SYNOPTIC GOSPELS

I begin with observing that our Synoptic Gospels (Matthew, Mark, and Luke), when carefully compared in a synopsis,[3] show some remarkable signs of *similarity*. Thus, if one compares the *wording* of Matthew 3:7–10 and Luke 3:7–9 in parallel columns, one observes substantial similarity. (Similarity appears in regular type; dissimilarity in bold type.)

Matthew 3:7–10	Luke 3:7–9
But when he saw many of the Pharisees and Sadducees coming for baptism, he said to them, "You brood of vipers, who warned you to flee from the wrath to come? Therefore bring forth fruit in keeping with repentance; and do not **suppose that you can** say to yourselves, 'We have Abraham for our father'; for I say to you, that God is able from these stones to raise up children to Abraham. And the axe is already laid at the root of the trees; every tree therefore that does not bear good fruit is cut down and thrown into the fire."	**He therefore** *began* **saying to the multitudes who were going out to be baptized by him,** "You brood of vipers, who warned you to flee from the wrath to come? Therefore bring forth fruit_s in keeping with repentance, and do not **begin to** say to yourselves, 'We have Abraham for our father,' for I say to you that God is able from these stones to raise up children to Abraham. And **also** the axe is already laid at the root of the trees; every tree therefore that does not bear good fruit is cut down and thrown into the fire." (Translations from the NASB.)

Observe how the statement by John (Mt 3:7b–10; Lk 3:7b–9) is repeated by two authors in nearly identical language. The Greek text, apart from the introductory statements, shows only three variations, indicated by the underscore: (1) whereas Matthew has the singular "fruit" (3:8), Luke has "fruits" (3:8); (2) whereas Matthew has "do not suppose that you can" (3:9), Luke has "do not begin to" (3:8); (3) Luke has the added "also" at 3:9. Now, these differences do not count for much. Substantial similarities are evident, and it can be easily seen that one could be the source for the other or that each copied another source.

Yet we cannot stop here. The Gospels also demonstrate significant *dissimilarity* as can be seen in the introductory statements of each Evangelist. Apparently each Evangelist prepared his readers for the statements of John in a different way. Whereas Matthew has John addressing many of the Pharisees and Sadducees (3:7a), Luke records that John spoke to the crowds (3:7a).

What has been observed so far pertains to the *phenomenon of wording,* one of three phenomena (empirically observable facts) involved in the Synoptic Problem. The phenomenon of wording is recognized by anyone who reads the Synoptic Gospels and observes that different Evangelists record the same events often with the same words. A second is the *phenomenon of content,* namely that the Evangelists record similar events and sayings of Jesus. In fact, approximately ninety percent of Mark is found in Matthew and approximately fifty percent of Mark is found in Luke. Furthermore, approximately 235 verses, mostly sayings of Jesus, are common to Matthew and Luke but are not found in Mark.[4] Finally, the *phenomenon of order* describes the simple fact that at least two of the Evangelists agree almost all the time on the order of the events in the life of Jesus. This may be observed by anyone who will begin at Matthew 17:22–23; Mark 9:30–32; and Luke 9:43b–45. The next event is found only in Matthew (17:24–27). Then a common order is resumed: Matthew 18:1–5; Mark 9:33–37; Luke 9:46–48. Though Matthew does not record the next incident, both Mark and Luke do (cf. Mark 9:38–41; Luke 9:49–50). Again, two are united on the next event (Mt 18:6–9; Mk 9:42–50). The point is simple: two Evangelists almost always agree on the matter of order. These three phenomena (wording, content, and order) form the basis for the Synoptic Problem.

The study of these phenomena in the Synoptic Gospels is called *source criticism.* Source criticism "attempts to identify the written traditions behind the Gospels in order to determine the relationship of the Synoptics."[5] The precise relationship of the Synoptics to one another, a problem that naturally arises from the observations illustrated above, is called "the Synoptic Problem."[6]

THE IMPORTANCE OF SOURCE CRITICISM

It may be asked, "What significance does source criticism have for understanding the Gospels?" This is an important question, for if the discipline has no usefulness we may discard it as an interesting but irrelevant historical method. But the method is significant and is an assumption of most New Testament scholars today.

For instance, one of the standard editions of the Greek New Testament used by many students and scholars today is the United Bible Societies' text (UBS, 3d ed.). The editors of that text clearly state that they assume the Gospel writers were dependent on one another, and the editors utilize what I will describe below as the Oxford Hypothesis. The editor of a recent anthology of treatments on the Synoptic Problem has clearly expressed the crucial significance one's solution to the Synoptic Problem plays in New Testament studies:

> The synoptic problem lies at the heart of so many issues of New Testament scholarship that a change in our model of synoptic relationships affects meaningfully such other areas of New Testament research as form criticism, textual criticism, the quest of the historical Jesus, etc. The history of Christian theology, of early Christian sacraments, and of church institutions and government is affected significantly by our answer to the question of the order of composition of the synoptic gospels and the matter of their literary relationship. *Since Marcan priority is an assumption of so much of the research of the last century, many of the conclusions of that research would have to be redrawn and much of the literature rewritten if the consensus of scholarship were suddenly to shift.*[7]

In light of the significance of source criticism and the manifold implications it has for interpretation, it is not surprising that the particular conclusion one takes as to the precise relationship has generated great debate today. In fact, though the Oxford Hypothesis (see below) dominated Gospel scholarship for at least two generations, that theory has been under constant fire for nearly twenty-five years. There is today a revival of interest in this discussion. Consequently, the next section of this chapter will survey the history and development of source criticism and the Synoptic Problem.

THE HISTORY AND DEVELOPMENT
OF SOURCE CRITICISM

In the broadest of terms one can say that the story about source criticism has four chapters: (1) Earliest Christianity seems to have preferred the Augustinian Hypothesis, i.e., that Matthew was first, Mark second, and Luke third; (2) in the middle of the eighteenth century some scholars were moved by J. J. Griesbach to accept what we now call the Griesbach Hypothesis, i.e., that Matthew wrote first, that Luke used Matthew, and that Mark, conflating both Matthew and Luke into a briefer Gospel, wrote third; (3) at the end of the nineteenth century and in the first quarter of the twentieth, scholars converted *en masse* to the Oxford Hypothesis, a view that states that Mark and Q were used independently by both Matthew and Luke and that Matthew and Luke both had access to at least one other source or sources (called "M" and "L" respectively); and (4) since the middle of the twentieth century the discussion over the precise relationship of the Synoptic Gospels has been renewed with vigorous debate.

Augustinian Hypothesis[8]

The earliest comment in the earliest churches about the Gospels is from Papias, as found in Eusebius (*Church History* 3.39.15–16), and is worthy of repetition. According to Papias (ca. 60–138), Mark is an interpreter (or translator) of Peter, though Papias adds that Mark's design was not "in order" (*ou mentoi taxei*). Following his comments on Mark, Papias says that Matthew "composed the logia" (*ta logia synetaxato*) in a Hebraic style and that each person had to interpret (or translate) them as one was able.

Following Papias there is a widespread and fairly unanimous tradition regarding the origins and chronological order of the Synoptic Gospels.[9] The general consensus was that Matthew wrote his Gospel "among the Jews in their own tongue, when Peter and Paul were preaching the gospel at Rome and founding the Church."[10] After Matthew came Mark, the disciple and recorder of Peter. Then Luke, a follower of Paul, wrote his Gospel. Thus, the consensus of the early church seems to have been Matthew—Mark—Luke—i.e., the final canonical order is the chronological order. (However, these early traditions do not clearly speak of a literary relationship between Matthew, Mark, and Luke as if Luke used Mark and Matthew or as if Mark used Matthew. The interests of the early church were in the chronological order of the Gospels, their apostolic origin [or connection], and their historical reliability.)

This understanding received its definitive form in Augustine and, because of his stature, was bequeathed to the church as authoritative. Augustine's major statement follows: "Now, those four evangelists . . . are believed to have written in the order which follows: first Matthew, then Mark, thirdly, Luke, lastly John" (*Harmony* 1.2.3; cf. also 1.2.4; 4.10.11). This statement affirms what has been classically referred to as the *Augustinian Hypothesis*, namely, that the final canonical order is the chronological order.

This view of Augustine was the dominant view of the relationships of the Synoptics until J. J. Griesbach's formulation of a new theory. However, it needs to be said that Christian writers of this period (prior to Griesbach) were not seriously interested in the Synoptic Problem and simply repeated what tradition they had come to know. It must not be supposed that even Augustine was interested in this as a theoretical and historical problem; his concerns were with chronology, historical reliability, and theological presentation.[11]

Griesesbach Hypothesis: Two-Gospel Hypothesis

J. J. Griesbach (1745–1812) published two essays in Latin that both called into question the Augustinian Hypothesis as well as the then-developing view of Marcan priority and an Ur-Gospel theory.[12] He then formulated an entirely different theory as to how the Synoptic Gospels were related.[13] In brief, the Griesbach Hypothesis is that Matthew was written first; that Luke, using Matthew, was second; and that Mark, conflating both Matthew and Luke, was third.

At the time of Griesbach, few scholars accepted his theory.[14] However, in recent times, especially since the works of B. C. Butler and W. R. Farmer, the Griesbach Hypothesis has attracted a great deal of attention both to the problems in the Oxford Hypothesis and the plausibility of Griesbach's formulations.

Oxford Hypothesis: Two- or Four-Source Hypothesis

Contemporary with, though independent of, the Griesbach Hypothesis, the theory of Marcan priority developed in Europe until it was fully expounded at Oxford under the direction of W. Sanday, receiving its most complete exposition in the famous work of B. H. Streeter.[15]

When William Sanday organized his famous seminar on the Synoptic Problem in 1894, which convened three times per term until 1910, the dominant solution to the Synoptic Problem in England seems to have been the so-called "oral hypothesis."[16] For approximately fifteen years students and friends of Sanday gathered to go through a Synopsis paragraph-by-paragraph. The students surrounding Sanday included Sir J. C. Hawkins,[17] B. H. Streeter, and W. C. Allen.[18] The discussions were eventually brought to fruition in an influential volume entitled *Studies in the Synoptic Problem by Members of The University of Oxford*.[19] The value of this work today is largely historical, though it makes fascinating reading for anyone keenly interested in the decades that gave rise to the Oxford Hypothesis.

The singularly most influential source critic of Sanday's Oxford seminar was B. H. Streeter who, thirteen years after Sandays' *Studies* were published, completed the definitive work that expounded the Oxford Hypothesis.[20] Though scholars have criticized Streeter and modified his views here and there, it cannot be said that any one work on the Synoptic Problem has had more influence than his. In brief, Streeter contended that four sources were involved in the making of the Synoptic Gospels and, he maintained, both the dates and provenance of these sources can be discerned: (1) Q, containing those verses common to Matthew and Luke but not in Mark, was composed in Antioch in approximately 50 A.D.; (2) L, the original source for Luke's Gospel, was written in approximately 60 A.D. in Caesarea; (3) M, the source of the special material in Matthew, was written in Jerusalem in approximately 60 A.D.; (4) Mark was written in 66 A.D. in Rome; (5) the combination of Q and L was made by Luke, a companion of Paul, and the resultant document Streeter called "Proto-Luke"; (6) our canonical Luke is the result of conflating Proto-Luke with a special source for Luke 1–2 and the Gospel of Mark; this was accomplished in approximately 80 A.D., perhaps in Corinth; (7) Matthew wrote his Gospel in approximately 85 A.D. in Antioch and he did so by combining Mark, Q, M, and what Streeter called the "Antiochene Tradition." [21]

What has survived from this complex hypothesis, admittedly with many points that are easily challenged,[22] is what scholars now call the Two- or Four-Source Hypothesis. Thus, most adherents of the Oxford Hypothesis agree that there were at least two written sources: Q and Mark. Few today would contend that there was a written source M or L; fewer still adhere to the Proto-Luke hypothesis.[23] Nonetheless, in spite of its weaknesses, the essential theory of B. H. Streeter won the day and to this day is held by the majority of scholars

The Modern Debate

Of the more notable recent developments in the Synoptic Problem, three deserve mention. The first is a salty essay by A. M. Farrer that contests the necessity of Q. Instead, he maintains, it must be seriously queried whether or not it might be more useful (and accurate) to consider that Luke used Matthew, thus "dispensing with Q."[24]

A second development, surely the one most noteworthy, is the revival of the Griesbach Hypothesis, due largely to the pressing and persistent questions of W. R. Farmer. Because of the persuasive and administrative designs of Farmer (and other Griesbach proponents), five major international conferences have taken up the Synoptic Problem in a serious form.[25]

The revival of the Griesbach Hypothesis has not been unchallenged, however. In 1979 C. M. Tuckett successfully defended a Ph.D. dissertation on the Griesbach revival, and an abbreviated version of this dissertation followed (*The Revival of the Griesbach Hypothesis: An Analysis and Appraisal*).[26] Tuckett concludes that the Griesbach Hypothesis is not so satisfactory a solution to the Synoptic Problem as the Oxford Hypothesis.

A third area of great interest today is "Q research."[27] At the annual meetings of the Society of Biblical Literature major papers are read to discuss the original shape, order, and redactions of different Q texts. Alongside this official Seminar and the foundation for some of it has been the publication of two books that seek to provide a Q text in light of these modern discussions. These two texts have been composed by A. Polag[28] and J. S. Kloppenborg.[29] Even if some scholars doubt the existence of Q, vast amounts of research have gone into the Q question and it is far from abating.

EVALUATION OF SOURCE CRITICISM

Because so few scholars today adhere to the Augustinian Hypothesis, and because so much of contemporary discussions revolve around the Griesbach and Oxford Hypothesis, the Augustinian view will not be evaluated here. Instead, our focus is on the contemporary debate and, consequently, our discussion here becomes a little more technical and complicated. At many points it will be needful to have a Synopsis at hand.

AN EVALUATION OF THE GRIESBACH HYPOTHESIS

It is not possible to do justice to this position in such a short space. I will simply mention two strengths and a few weaknesses of the Griesbach Hypothesis.

Strengths of the Griesbach Hypothesis

Perhaps the greatest strength of the Griesbach proponents is their calling into question the sloppy logic of the Oxford Hypothesis, a position that had become by the middle of this century so dominant that almost any argument went unchallenged. In particular, B. H. Streeter in a classic statement has shown that the argument from order actually proves nothing: "The relative order of incidents and sections in Mark is in general supported by both Matthew and Luke; where either of them deserts Mark, the other is usually found supporting him."[30] Now this statement is patently circular, for it concludes (a little later) nothing more than it assumes: that Mark was used by Matthew and Luke.[31] Accordingly, a Griesbach proponent might describe the phenomenon of order like this: "Mark follows the order of Matthew and Luke, and whenever Matthew's or Luke's order diverge, Mark follows either one or the other."[32] This restates the phenomenon in a way that is just as unambiguous. A major contribution of modern Griesbach proponents is this: they have demonstrated that the phenomena of wording, contents, and order are nothing more than phenomena that are subject to several explanations.[33]

Another strength of this view is its careful attention to early

Christian statements. To my knowledge, no one in the history of the church has written so careful an analysis of early church testimony on the relationships of the Gospels as that by B. Orchard.[34] The Oxford proponents cannot simply dismiss early church traditions as wishful legends.[35]

Problems for the Griesbach Hypothesis

Though Griesbach proponents continually trumpet their successes (and there are some),[36] the majority of Gospel scholarship still holds tenaciously, though not now so naively, to the Oxford Hypothesis. Several arguments, therefore, have been lodged against the Griesbach Hypothesis.

First, far too frequently the Griesbach proponents do not seem to recognize the logical difference between an *explanation* and a *proof*. This is noticed most frequently when Griesbach proponents seek to show that the Griesbach Hypothesis makes most sense of the phenomenon of order simply because *its proponents can explain the order in light of their hypothesis*. I will illustrate this with only one example, but many others could be given.[37] I will pick on a statement of W. R. Farmer and show the inconclusive logic that is so typical of the Griesbach argumentation. In an article on how certain results of J. C. Hawkins and C. F. Burney would be more explicable on the basis of the Griesbach Hypothesis, Farmer makes this statement: "This [his careful explanation of how Luke used Matthew 24:1–17] is a perfectly comprehensible literary device, and *lends support to the hypothesis that Luke was using Matthew as his source.* . . ."[38] The first statement beginning with "This" is acceptable, for it is true that, *if Luke did use Matthew,* what he did to Matthew is a reasonable procedure. However, this does not lend "support to the hypothesis that Luke was using Matthew as his source" *because it assumes that Luke used Matthew.* In other words, Farmer (1) assumes that Luke used Matthew, (2) *explains* Luke's use of Matthew in light of his assumption, and then (3) concludes that this shows that Luke used Matthew.

The point I am making is simple but very important: an explanation is not necessarily a proof.[39] What is needed here is decisive evidence that Luke's use of Matthew is more credible than Matthew's use of Luke, or of Matthew's and Luke's independent use of a sayings source (Q), or of their mutual, but independent, use of Mark. This Farmer does not offer and so his explanation, though worthy as such, is not a proof. The Griesbach proponents too frequently resort to this procedure in their attempt to demonstrate their hypothesis, and it is nothing more than a circular argument.

Second, the assumed purpose of Mark in conflating Matthew and Luke goes contrary to clear evidence of what Mark did. It is laid down as an observable feature of Mark's redactional practice (assuming the Griesbach Hypothesis) that Mark recorded in his Gospel that "which deviated in no significant sense from the narrative to which the texts of Matthew and Luke bore concurrent testimony."[40] It is an easily demonstrable fact that this is *not* how Mark proceeded and, because this is not how Mark worked, a serious blow is dealt to the Griesbach Hypothesis. A careful analysis, for instance, of Matthew 13:31–32 and Luke 13:18–19 with Mark 4:30–32 yields just the opposite conclusion. C. M. Tuckett observed:

> For the overall picture, if Mark is using Matthew and Luke as his sources [at Mark 4:30–32], is that *Mark has carefully and systematically avoided everything that is common to Matthew and Luke: where they agree, Mark disagrees, and where Matthew disagrees with Luke, Mark follows Matthew closely.* Thus, Mark appears to have taken an intense dislike to Luke . . . and to have gone through Matthew's text, changing it where Matthew and Luke agree, but leaving it alone where they differ. Moreover, the result is, in places, grammatical chaos.[41]

If Mark avoids everything in common, then his procedure is not as Farmer says it is.[42]

Third, F. G. Downing has ably demonstrated that there are no contemporary parallels to the complicated kind of conflation assumed by Griesbach proponents to have been performed by Mark. The procedure for Mark, assuming the Griesbach Hypothesis, would have been a tedious and exacting process— sometimes lifting a word from Matthew, then one from Luke, and then a phrase from Matthew, then back to Luke, and so forth. In some recent work, Downing has shown that when we have clear instances of ancient historians using different sources covering the same material and who were compelled to conflate, the procedure was very simple. Instead of working through the different sources very carefully and adding one word from one source and another phrase from another source, producing a truly conflated text, the authors took one source as primary and then supplemented that source with larger conflated blocks. The Griesbach Hypothesis, he contends, goes contrary to everything we know about how historians thought of their procedure and how they actually practiced their historiography.[43] Downing's work deserves careful reading.

Fourth, so far as I can see, the Griesbach proponents have not dealt with the most decisive argument favoring the Oxford Hypothesis, namely, the argument from primitive language.[44] The most telling argument against the Griesbach Hypothesis is the accumulated answers to this question: which reading most likely gave rise to the other readings? Put differently, given Matthew's (or Luke's) rendering of a saying or event, is it likely that Mark is a later rendition of Matthew or Luke (or both), or is it more likely that Mark is the source for the others?[45] The answers so consistently move in the direction of Marcan priority that one is compelled either to adopt the Oxford Hypothesis or jettison text-critical procedures in use by all scholars today. I give but one example.

At Mark 7:31 Mark records what is, by all accounts, a trip of Jesus: "And again, Jesus left the regions of Tyre and went through Sidon to the Sea of Galilee through the middle of the regions of the Decapolis." On any reading of this text, Jesus has taken a strange route: a trip toward the southeast begins by going north, and one gets to this southeast destination, the Sea of Galilee, through a region of cities even further southeast than the Sea itself. What is noteworthy here is that Matthew's account of this trip is much easier to follow: "And departing from there [the regions of Tyre and Sidon], Jesus came to the Sea of Galilee" (15:29). For the purposes of the Synoptic Problem, we can ask a simple text-critical question: "Which reading most likely gave rise to the other?" And the answer, for all text-critics, would be that it is more likely that Mark gave rise to Matthew's clarification than for Mark to take this perfectly sensible statement of Matthew and make it obscure. What is at least more difficult to understand in Mark is easier to understand in Matthew. Mark is, therefore, more primitive and therefore probably prior to Matthew.

AN EVALUATION OF THE OXFORD HYPOTHESIS

In this section I want to explain the traditional arguments for the Oxford Hypothesis and then list a few of the problems I have pointed out regarding the adequacy of this solution. The Oxford Hypothesis, it will be remembered, argues that Matthew and Luke used the Gospel of Mark and the source Q, and that both Evangelists also had access to other material, conveniently dubbed "M" and "L."

Arguments in favor of this hypothesis fall naturally into two issues: the priority of Mark and the existence of Q. I begin with the arguments that favor Marcan priority.

Arguments for Marcan Priority

First, the Oxford Hypothesis is more probable because of the *linguistic phenomena*. Since I have mentioned this in the fourth criticism of the Griesbach Hypothesis, I will restate the argument and then give a couple of examples. Put simply, the linguistic phenomena of the Synoptic Gospels can be more easily explained if Mark is seen as prior to both Matthew and Luke than if Mark is seen as a later conflation of Luke and Matthew.[46]

At Mark 14:3 we find an unusual concurrence of two genitive absolutes in the same sentence; Matthew avoided this grammatical irregularity by rephrasing the first genitive absolute and turning the second into a finite verb (26:6). It is more likely that Matthew "corrected" Mark than that Mark took a perfectly normal expression and made it irregular.

A second example can be found at Mark 4:31 (parallels in Mt 13:31–32; Lk 13:19). Mark has a peculiar opening "as" clause that assumes some verb; this is followed by a masculine gender relative clause with a passive verb; and then Mark breaks all normal rules of grammar by turning the previous masculine relative pronoun into a neuter gender. My point is not that this is incompetent grammar; it is, however, peculiar. Matthew and Luke, on the other hand, have perfectly normal and simple grammatical constructions. It is much more likely that Matthew and Luke have "corrected" Mark than that Mark has taken normal constructions and created a gaffe. In the infamous words of B. H. Streeter in commenting on the cumulative effect of the linguistic phenomena when examining a synopsis, "How any one who has worked through those pages with a Synopsis of the Greek text can retain the slightest doubt of the original and primitive character of Mark I am unable to comprehend."[47]

Second, the Oxford Hypothesis is more probable because

of the *theological phenomena*.[48] One example will illustrate the point. At Mark 6:5–6 it is stated that Jesus was amazed at the unbelief of the Nazareth crowd and that he was *unable* to do any miracles there. Early Christians may very well have been bothered by this statement, since it could suggest the inability of Jesus, God incarnate, to do something. Such an impression, however, will not be given by Matthew. When he reports this narrative, in nearly identical terms, he states that Jesus "did not do many miracles there" (13:58). Now on the Griesbach Hypothesis one has to come up with an explanation why Mark would take a statement that in no way casts doubt on Jesus' ability (Mt 13:58) and created a theological problem, whereas the Oxford Hypothesis has a more probable account of the event. Matthew eliminated a theological difficulty. It is more probable that Matthew erased a theological problem than that Mark created one. This kind of observation, when comparing Matthew, Mark, and Luke, not only lends support to the Oxford Hypothesis, it makes it the most probable hypothesis.

Third, the Oxford Hypothesis is more probable because of the *redactional phenomena*. It is often argued that the consistency that has been found in either Matthew's or Luke's treatment of Mark is an argument in favor of Marcan priority. In other words, the coherency of the theory is an argument in its favor.[49] This is an important point, but the limitations of this argument need to be noted before an illustration is given. This argument is really nothing more than an explanation that makes good sense of the data; it is not, however, a decisive proof for Marcan priority. I quote from G. N. Stanton: "As far as Matthean scholarship is concerned, it has yet to be shown that any of the alternatives to the assumption that Matthew has used Mark and Q provides a more plausible and coherent account of Matthean redaction than the generally accepted view [Oxford Hypothesis]."[50]

One example of redactional activity from Matthew will illustrate the nature of this argument. No one who reads Matthew will fail to miss the importance he attaches to the term "righteousness." It is found seven times in Matthew (3:15; 5:6, 10, 20; 6:1, 33; 21:32). In addition, if one examines each of these in a synopsis, one observes that each is unparalleled. Thus, it appears that Matthew has consistently added the term to his sources because that term expresses what he wants to emphasize. One would have to ask, then, on the Griesbach or

Augustinian Hypothesis, why neither Luke nor Mark ever had any reason to use this term when using Matthew as a source. (It is simply not the case that Mark and Luke do not record traditions about doing God's will.) Further, one would have to provide reasons for Mark's or Luke's omission in each instance. These regular omissions of Matthew's particular emphases count heavily in favor of Matthew having added them. Furthermore, the notion of doing God's will (i.e., being righteous) is a dominant and consistent feature of Matthew's redactional presentation of discipleship.[51] In light of the absence of this Matthean theme in Mark and Luke and the pervasiveness of this theme in Matthew, it can be concluded that righteousness is a part of Matthew's redactional scheme. Accordingly, if one assumes Marcan priority (and the existence of Q) and then examines Matthew's emphasis on righteousness and doing God's will, one finds a consistent redactional tendency on the part of Matthew. This, it is argued, lends support to the Oxford Hypothesis; the hypothesis is coherent.

These three arguments demonstrate with a high degree of probability that Mark is prior to either Matthew or Luke. This is the first argument for the Oxford Hypothesis: Mark is prior to Matthew and Luke.

Arguments for the Existence of Q

The Oxford Hypothesis is more probable because *it is unlikely that Luke used Matthew; therefore, it is likely that they independently used another source (Q).* A fact to be noted here is that Matthew and Luke contain approximately 235 verses, mostly comprised of sayings of Jesus, that are not found in Mark. Most of these sayings are similar in wording—so much so that most would agree literary dependence is well-nigh certain. However, Matthew and Luke almost never record the same "Q" saying in the same location or order, though most scholars have concluded that Luke best preserved the original order of Q.[52] Thus, if one looks up Matthew 23:37–39 in a synopsis one finds a parallel at Luke 13:34–35. Two things can be observed for our purposes: (1) the saying of Jesus is recorded in almost identical Greek wording, and (2) each Evangelist records this saying in a different context. What I have been labeling "Q" in the present discussion is sometimes considered to be Luke's copying of Matthew. But there is sufficient evidence to suggest that Luke and Matthew are independent and that therefore a Q hypothesis is probable.[53] I turn now to these.

(1) When Matthew and Luke are recording the same event or saying that is also found in Mark, Luke never picks up the material that Matthew adds to Mark. Thus, it can be argued that Matthew and Luke are independent. For instance, both Matthew and Luke used Mark to record the baptism of Jesus (Mk 1:9–11; Mt 3:13–17; Lk 3:21–22). But none of the additions to Mark by Matthew (e.g., Mt 3:14–15) are added to Mark by Luke. If Luke is dependent on Matthew, then Luke made a conscious choice (almost) never to record Matthew's additions to Mark.

This observation can be extended: Luke also never included what we now call the "M" traditions, those incidents and sayings of Jesus found now only in Matthew. On first glance this could be taken as a logical error: Luke never records "M" traditions; "M" traditions are those traditions found only in Matthew; therefore, Luke by definition could not have included "M" traditions because then they would be classed as "Q" traditions. This is a fair observation. However, there is still an important observation here. Namely, Luke chose consistently not to include any narrative material added by Matthew to Mark (e.g., Mt 1:1–2:23; 27:62–66; 28:11–15) and seems regularly not to have included, for instance, parables not paralleled in Mark (e.g., Mt 13:24–30, 36–43, 44–46, 47–50, 51–52; 18:23–35; 20:1–16; 21:28–32), several of which are right to the heart of Luke's favorite themes: reversal of this world's values and the salvation of the unlikely. Even though this argument can easily turn into non-sensical circularity, it does have some value. Luke seems not to have known of these traditions and thus was independent of Matthew. This suggests the use of a common source (Q).

(2) After the temptation of Jesus, Luke and Matthew never place their common material in the same setting. The fact that this would almost certainly occur if Luke were using Matthew suggests that Matthew and Luke are independent and that they each used a common source (Q). The examples here could be easily multiplied. It is a known fact that Matthew has five discourses (5:1–7:29; 9:35–11:1; 13:1–52; 18:1–19:2; 23:1–26:2) and that the parallels to the sayings of Jesus found in Matthew's discourses are scattered throughout Luke (especially

in 6:20–8:3 and 9:51–18:14). That Luke did not place one of these sayings in the same setting that Matthew did suggests, if it does not prove, that Luke and Matthew are independent. Examples could be easily multiplied. The early observation of B. H. Streeter is worthy of repetition: "A theory which would make author capable of such a proceeding [Luke's treatment of Matthew's ordering of this non-Marcan material] would only be tenable if, on other grounds, we had reason to believe that he was a crank."[54]

(3) When Matthew and Luke contain material not found in Mark, sometimes it is Matthew and sometimes it is Luke that appears to be the more primitive. Again, this suggests that they are independent of each other and using a common source (Q). It must be frankly admitted that "more primitive" is a subjective factor. However, interpretation involves a certain measure of subjectivity and one ought not to discard this observation casually. Sometimes primitivity relates to theological understanding, but the standard observation has to do with which account of a saying of Jesus is more Semitic than the other. Assuming that Jesus spoke Aramaic, this criterion can be useful when used with caution. Two examples, one showing Matthew to be more primitive and the other Luke, will be given.

Matthew 7:9–11 records Jesus' statements on the goodness of God that can be trusted in prayer. The final statement is "how much more will your Father who is in the heavens give *good things* to those who ask him?" Luke, who also composed the Acts of the Apostles, which details the power of the Holy Spirit in the earliest churches, has a parallel to Matthew 7:9–11 that reads in this last line: "How much more will your Father who is from heaven give *the Holy Spirit* to those who ask him?" (Luke 11:13). By all accounts, Matthew's account is the more primitive (theologically speaking) than Luke's. Apparently, for Luke the "good things" of Matthew could be summarized (because they were focused) in the Holy Spirit—the essence of all good things.

On the other hand, Luke 14:26 seems to be more primitive than Matthew 10:37. Luke 14:26 reads, "If anyone comes to me and does not *hate* his father and mother and wife and children and brothers and sisters, and even his own soul, is not able to be my disciple." Matthew, on the other hand, showing a sensitivity to potential misunderstandings, edits out the Semitic idiom and writes, "The one who *loves* father or mother *more than* me is not worthy of me" (10:37). The more primitive Semitic idiom of Luke has been reexpressed by Matthew in both a historically reliable manner and in a way that cannot be misunderstood. This suggests that Luke's account is more primitive.

These two examples, one from Matthew and one from Luke, illustrate the argument being made for the independence of Matthew and Luke. If, say, Luke were dependent on Matthew, then one would expect that Matthew would be consistently more primitive, both in theology and language. In fact, neither Evangelist gets the consistent nod on primitivity, and the concluding inference is that this demonstrates that neither is more primitive because each Evangelist drew independently on a common source that was itself more primitive.

(4) It appears that at times Matthew and Luke record one saying of Jesus two different times in their Gospels. On these occasions, one time there is a parallel in Mark and the other time there is a parallel in Matthew or Luke. These sayings are called "doublets,"[55] and these doublets suggest that Matthew and Luke are independently drawing from two sources (Mark and Q). J. C. Hawkins listed twenty-two doublets in Matthew, one in Mark, and eleven in Luke.[56] Our concern is with those doublets in Matthew or Luke that have parallels in Mark and the other Gospel. A listing of these doublets follows:[57]

Marcan Tradition		"Q" Tradition
Mk 4:25	cf. Mt 13:12; Lk 8:18	Mt 25:29; Lk 19:26
Mk 8:34–35	cf. Mt 16:24–25; Lk 9:23–24	Mt 10:38–39; Lk 14:27; 17:33
Mk 8:38	cf. Mt 16:27; Lk 9:26	Mt 10:32–33; Lk 12:8–9
Mk 13:9, 13	cf. Mt 24:9, 13; Lk 21:12, 17, 19	Mt 10:19–20, 22; Lk 12:11–12

The presence of doublets suggests that Matthew and Luke both used Mark and another source from which they drew the second instance of the saying.[58]

(5) If Luke used Matthew it is almost impossible to propose a reasonable motive for what Luke would have had to do to Matthew. Thus, on the grounds of coherency, a Q hypothesis is more coherent than a Griesbach theory. This argument is subject to the same, if not even more, weaknesses that we encountered in the argument from order in the Griesbach Hypothesis. It is a fact that one could find, I

suppose, sufficient motives for anything Luke would have done to Matthew. Granted the explanatory nature of this argument, we still need to recognize the problems that must be dealt with by anyone who denies the independence of Matthew and Luke. If Luke is dependent on Matthew, then it is difficult for us to understand why he took beautiful structures, structures that have appealed to Christians since the beginning of the church (like the birth narratives of Matthew and the Sermon on the Mount), and broke them into separate pieces and then placed the pieces in much less pleasing places.[59] This argument, though not a proof, tends to favor the independence of Matthew and Luke and the existence of Q, and so deserves mention.

For these five reasons, it is improbable that Luke and Matthew are interdependent and it is probable that Matthew and Luke independently used a source of the sayings of Jesus that is now called "Q." The Oxford Hypothesis, arguing that Matthew and Luke both drew independently upon Mark and another source (Q), is the most probable theory of Gospel origins.

Problems for the Oxford Hypothesis

It must not be thought, however, that the Oxford Hypothesis is without its problems. Certainly it is the foremost theory for explaining the origins and the relationship of the Synoptic Gospels, but the critique of the Oxford Hypothesis in the last generation by Griesbach proponents has caused some important revisions, many of which are reflected in our previous discussion. What are the weaknesses of the Oxford Hypothesis? Three major problems must be mentioned.

First, the Oxford Hypothesis has not sufficiently struggled with the early Christian evidence on the origins of the Gospels. It is a noticeable feature that W. Sanday's Seminar, so far as I know, did not deal with the patristic evidence with sufficient rigor. It will just not do for Oxford proponents to dismiss patristic evidence as tendentious or, worse yet, precritical and naive. Examination of this evidence may lead to the conclusions that the patristic evidence is mistaken, but such a conclusion ought not to be drawn unless careful attention is given to the matter.

The major criticism of the Oxford Hypothesis has been the

observation of so-called "minor agreements" of Matthew and Luke against Mark. What are these? An agreement of Matthew and Luke against Mark is a term, expression, or entire incident in the life of Jesus that is related one way by Mark and in a different but identical way by both Matthew and Luke—and, assuming the Oxford Hypothesis, when Matthew and Luke are supposed to be unaware of each other's work. Thus, these are coincidental, independent, but identical alterations to Mark.

For example, I include a synopsis of Mark 1:41–43; Matthew 8:3; and Luke 5:13. Mark is in the middle to make the problem more visible.

Matthew 8:3	Mark 1:41–3	Luke 5:13
And _____	And *displaying compassion*	And _____
he stretched out *the* hand	he stretched out *his* hand	he stretched out *the* hand
and touched him, *saying*	and touched him *and said* to him	he touched him, *saying*
_____		_____
I will, be cleansed	I will, be cleansed	I will, be cleansed
And *immediately* his leprosy	And *immediately* his leprosy departed from him	And *immediately* his leprosy departed from him.
_____		
was cleansed.	and he was cleansed.	
_____	And warning him sternly,	_____
_____	immediately he sent him	_____
_____	away.	_____

From this synopsis several "minor agreements" can be observed. (1) Matthew and Luke agree against Mark in omitting "displaying compassion." (2) They both omit "his" from "his hand"; (3) They both alter "and said" to "saying." (4) Though not seen in English, when Mark records "immediately," both Matthew and Luke have another form of the word "immediately": Mark has *euthus* and Matthew and Luke have *eutheōs*. (5) Both Matthew and Luke omit the emotional charge of Jesus. Seen individually, one would not take notice of such "minor" changes, for changing Mark's typical "and said" to "saying" is typical both for Matthew and Luke (assuming the Oxford Hypothesis). But the significance of such a minor change becomes altogether more important when it is observed that within the space of three verses of Mark five "independent but identical" changes occur. This is more than a "minor agreement." And it must be admitted that these minor agreements work against the Oxford Hypothesis because they suggest a literary relationship between Matthew and Luke. Griesbach proponents explain these as Marcan alterations of Matthew and Luke where Luke has followed Matthew identically.

Thus, the minor agreements are not minor and deserve careful attention by Oxford proponents. One recent study by an Oxford proponent, C. M. Tuckett, has tackled the issue of the minor agreements, and his work is worthy of careful attention.[60] Tuckett contends that the minor agreements are not more easily explained by the Griesbach Hypothesis than by the Oxford Hypothesis. One of his examples will suffice. Matthew 21:23 and Luke 20:1 both describe Jesus as "teaching"; Mark 11:27, the parallel, and according to the Griesbach Hypothesis the conflation of the two, does not have "teaching." Griesbach proponents point to the "agreement" between Matthew and Luke against Mark and imply that the Oxford Hypothesis cannot make sense of this phenomenon. Tuckett, however, shows that Mark's plan—according to Griesbach—is to use the concurrent testimony (in this case, Matthew and Luke agreeing that Jesus was teaching) and does not do so. Further, since Mark often stresses the fact that Jesus was "teaching," its absence is even less explicable. After presenting a coherent explanation in light of the Oxford Hypothesis, Tuckett concludes: "On the theory of Marcan priority this agreement can be explained as due to independent editing, whilst on the GH [Griesbach Hypothesis], the text is very difficult to explain."[61] After examining a sufficient number of these minor agreements, Tuckett concludes his chapter with the following statement: "Whilst the minor agreements all present some difficulties for the 2DH [Two Document Hypothesis = Oxford Hypothesis], and whilst some of Streeter's own arguments were suspect (e.g. his stress on textual corruption), overall, the 2DH can often give a more coherent explanation of these arguments than can the GH."[62] If this is just a beginning for the Oxford Hypothesis on the road to serious working on the minor agreements, that future is bright because Tuckett has offered a serious challenge and a reasonable explanation for a great number of the minor agreements.

A final problem for the Oxford Hypothesis revolves around the difficulties encountered in Q studies. In particular, three problems stand out: (1) problems with the original wording,

(2) problems with the original contents, and (3) problems with speculative theories. I begin with the last. It goes without saying that some of the most fertile and imaginative theories of Synoptic studies have been raised by Q scholars. Scholars have inferred a Q tradition to a Q document, from a Q document to a Q author and his community, from a Q author and his community to redactional and theological ideas of the Q author and his community, even to the point that some scholars have convinced themselves that the Q community moved several times. The problem is with probability—and the multiplication of theories on the basis of a document that is already hypothetical does not increase one's chances of being accurate. The opposite is the case! In fact, I suspect that many Gospel students are put off by the speculative nature of Q scholarship.[63] I, for one, am convinced that there was at least a Q tradition that can be reasonably separated from our present Synoptic Gospels, but I am greatly suspicious of any theories that go much beyond the level of identifying the general contents and wording of such a tradition. To speak, then, of a Q redactor or a Q community strikes me as too speculative to be of use. Granted, these things are not impossibilities but they are so highly speculative that we are best left with suggestions.

Further problems arise when we try to determine the original wording of Q—did Q have "finger" or "Spirit" of God (cf. Mt 12:28; Lk 11:20)? Not only is wording a problem. Will it ever be possible for modern scholars to approach probability on the original contents and even order of this hypothetical document? For many scholars, discussion of the order of Q is so hypothetical to be well-nigh a waste of time.

For these reasons it is impossible to determine with rigor the original contents and wording, let alone order,[64] of Q. If we do not know even the complete shape of the "document," it is indeed hazardous to make speculative judgments about its author and his redactional activity, not to mention the community in which the author supposedly lived.

In spite of these problems, scholars of the Oxford Hypothesis have come to a fairly unanimous conclusion regarding the basic shape and contents of Q. It must not be supposed that it is all up for grabs. Rather, though the general contents are fairly agreed upon, it is when we need precision that we must admit that we do not have certain results.

These are three problems that the Oxford Hypothesis is

currently addressing. Though these problems have undoubt-edly taken some wind from the sails of the Oxford Hypothesis, it does not appear that the theory has been shaken to the point of surrender. The theory is simply being refined so that it fits more of the evidence.

It is not possible to evaluate carefully the other theories that were mentioned above. Virtually all scholars today fit either into the Griesbach or Oxford Hypothesis. Arguments for either of these are arguments contrary to the other theories. It remains for us now to apply one theory, the Oxford Hypothesis, to a New Testament passage. Our goal here is simply to show how an Oxford proponent would examine this text source-critically.[65] And our procedure will be to show how an Oxford proponent would explain what Luke has done to Mark.

EXEMPLAR: PETER'S CONFESSION AND THE MESSIAH'S RESPONSE

An introductory comment is necessary at this point. A source critic's work is a preliminary matter. A source critic is looking at the Synoptic passages in order to determine the sources of the Evangelist and, through that determination, to discern what is traditional and what is redactional. The historian will utilize the source critic's conclusions to write a "history of the tradition" of that event or saying; the redaction critic will use that information to examine why the Evangelist did what he did to his sources in order to explain that Evangelist's theology and church setting. Accordingly, the task below is preliminary. I will look at this one passage in light of the Oxford Hypothesis to show the source pattern. Chapter 7 on Redaction Criticism by G. R. Osborne will expound the significance of these findings for exegesis.

The passage to be examined is Peter's confession and the Messiah's response to Peter. The passage, in general, contains these elements, with the Lukan references: (1) The Situation and Question (9:18); (2) The General Responses (9:19); (3) Peter's Response (9:20); (4) Jesus' Response to Peter (9:21); (5) The Implications of the Confession (9:22–27): (5:1) For Jesus (9:22) and (5:2) For the Disciples (9:23–27). These five elements will provide the structure for our source-critical observations.

A source-critic looks at a given passage and, through tedious examination, asks, "Where did the Evangelist get this word or idea?" His or her work is careful and minute. Sometimes the source-critic discovers an amazing pattern of alteration; more frequently this is not the case. In the following source-critical observations I will at times point out a pattern of alteration. Most of our observations are little more than comparative remarks.

We have discussed above the phenomenon of order and it needs to be illustrated here. Whereas Mark's order and Matthew's order are virtually identical (from Mk 6:14–8:21; cf. Mt 14:1–16:12) with only one omission (Mk 8:14–21), Luke's order diverges markedly at this point. Luke joins the confession of Peter and the response of the Messiah to Peter to the feeding of 5000 (9:10–17 and 9:18–27). In effect, Luke "omits" Mark 6:45–8:26.[66] Thus, though the Evangelists do join the responses of Jesus to Peter's confession in identical fashion, the exact placement of the unit differs. According to the Griesbach Hypothesis, Mark has preferred Matthew here; according to the Oxford Hypothesis, Matthew witnesses to Mark's order when Luke does not. Both can explain the phenomena; neither proves the solution.

LUKE'S REDACTION OF MARK

The Situation and Question (Mk 8:27; Lk 9:18). Because Luke has placed this pericope in a different location, he provides some "glue" to put his sections together. Taking Mark's "and," Luke composes a transition that emphasizes Jesus' prayer life.[67] This is a fact not known in Mark and has evidently been discovered by Luke. Luke takes over Mark's verb, agreeing with Mark when Matthew does not and, though Matthew agrees with Mark on "men," Luke alters this to "the crowds."

The General Responses (Mk 8:19; Lk 9:19). Luke changes Mark's "said, saying" (*eipan, legontes*) to "said, saying" (*apokrithentes, eipan*). Though Luke alone follows Mark in two words in this sentence ("others," "that"), Matthew and Luke both dropped "and" and changed it to "but." Mark's phrase "one of the prophets" is altered by Luke to "a certain prophet of old has arisen."[68]

Peter's Response (Mk 8:29; Lk 9:20). Though Luke has taken Mark as his source here, Luke (1) adds "but he said"[69]; (2) puts the confession in the accusative case—a grammatical nicety since technically "the Messiah of God" is the predicate of "I" and "I" is in the accusative case; and (3) adds "of God" to "the Messiah." Furthermore, there are four "minor agreements" here: both Matthew and Luke (1) alter the accusative "them " to the dative "them";[70] (2) begin the response of Peter with a similarly added "but";[71] (3) change Mark's historical present ("he says") to an aorist indicative ("he said"); and (4) add "of God" to the Messiah, though Matthew's is part of a larger addition.

Jesus' Response to Peter (Mk 8:30; Lk 9:21). Luke betrays no awareness of Matthew's insertion of the revelation to Peter and thus moves directly to Jesus' demand not to make him known. And here we see the phenomenon of alternating agreement again: though Matthew diverges substantially in wording, Luke does not diverge so widely. In common, Luke follows Mark in (1) the verb used,[72] (2) the object, (3) the negative, and (4) the verb "say." However, Luke reshapes the saying by altering "and" to "but," by adding the verb "ordered" (cf. 5:14; 8:29, 56), and by using "this " for Mark's "concerning him." Here Mark is Luke's source, but Luke prefers his own diction.

The Implications of the Confession (Mk 8:31–9:1; Lk 9:22-27). This section has every appearance of being dependent on Mark. Here we have some evidence of Luke following Mark when Matthew diverges (cf. Lk 9:22, 26, 27). Overall, Luke's presentation is tidier and neater than Mark's.[73]

For Jesus (Mk 8:31–33; Lk 9:22). Luke chooses to make this verse subordinate to the previous command of silence, bringing the passion prediction into the very heart of the messianic secret; he does this by using "saying" as the introductory word to the prediction of the passion. This is a substitute for Mark's "and he began to teach them." Then Luke follows Mark for ten consecutive words,[74] and apart from some "minor agreements" follows Mark for the next twelve words.

At this point Mark continues with Peter's rebuke and Jesus' counter-rebuke: Luke drops this material altogether. Notice, however, that Matthew continues with this material, evincing proof for Mark as the "middle factor." A plausible motive for Luke's omission is his desire to avoid the unflattering aspects of Peter.

For the Disciples (Mk 8:34–9:1; Lk 9:23–27). Luke, having omitted the firm interchange between Jesus and Peter, joins the passion prediction to the prediction of discipleship passion by adding "but he was saying to all" (9:23).[75] Luke betrays an awareness of Mark's larger audience and makes this explicit with "to all." In the rest of Luke 9:23 and all of 9:24 we find only the following changes to Mark: (1) Luke uses the present tense of "come" (*erchesthai*) for Mark's "follow"; (2) he drops Mark's intensifying preposition (Mark: *aparnēsasthō*; Luke: *arnēsasthō*), (3) adds "daily" (cf. 11:3; 16:19; 19:47; 22:53) to Mark's "let him take up the cross";[76] (4) alters, along with Matthew, Mark's incorrect future to a subjunctive; (5) drops, along with Matthew, Mark's "and the Gospel"; and (6) adds "this" before the verb "will save."[77]

Luke changes Marks' grammar at Luke 9:25 by (1) putting Mark's object as the subject and turning the verb into a present middle-passive, (2) turning Mark's infinitives into participles, and (3) clarifying Mark's "forfeit his soul" with "destroying or forfeiting himself." Luke then drops Mark 8:37, apparently because of its redundancy. But it ought to be noticed that Matthew retained this element (16:26b)—Mark is shown again to be the middle factor.

Luke 9:26 is based on Mark 8:38. Apart from Luke's "correction" of Mark's conditional particle (*ean*), changing it to an indefinite (*an*), the first third of Luke 9:26 is identical to its Marcan parallel. Improving Mark's grammar, Luke drops Mark's "in this adulterous and sinful generation" and Mark's unnecessary "and."[78] Luke's alteration of Mark 8:38b is peculiar: he follows Mark for the first five words and then changes Mark's "glory of his father with his holy angels" to "his glory, and the Father's glory, and the glory of the holy angels."[79]

Luke again improves the grammar of Mark 9:1 (Lk 9:27) by omitting "and he was saying to them" and adding "but." Luke's use of "truly" (*alethōs*) is a Grecized form of the Hebrew "truly" (*amen*) (cf. 12:44; 21:3), evincing a later development than Mark's form. Luke's use of "here" (*autou*) is a legitimate (cf. Ac 18:19; 21:4), though unpredictable, substitute for Mark's "here" (*hōde*), and his substitute of the simpler relative "who" (*hoi*) is a slight refinement of Mark's indefinite "whoever" (*hoitines*). Luke then follows Mark until Luke drops Mark's final "having come in power."

In summary, the Oxford Hypothesis has much to commend it. The changes made by Matthew and Luke to Mark are typical and generally characteristic of their editorial procedures elsewhere. Secondly, their changes frequently improve Mark's grammar and diction. This counts heavily in favor of the Oxford Hypothesis. Thirdly, many of the changes are attributable to observable theological tendencies for these authors, as seen, for instance, in Luke's emphasis on prayer (9:18).

CONCLUSION

Source criticism involves the tedious procedure of going through the Gospels word-by-word looking for potential clues for priority and sources. The conclusions to such quests are merely historical. It remains for the redaction critic and interpreter to pick up these conclusions and explore them for their significance and motivation. Some of these have been suggested throughout this paper; an exposition of these awaits chapter 7.

BIBLIOGRAPHY

Farmer, W. R. *The Synoptic Problem*. London: Collier-Macmillan, 1964.

Guthrie, Donald. *New Testament Introduction*. Downers Grove, Ill.: InterVarsity, rev. 1989.

Küemmel, W. G. *New Testament Introduction*. Nashville, Abingdon, 1975.

Longstaff, Thomas R. W. and Page A. Thomas, eds. *The Synoptic Problem: A Bibliography 1716–1988*. Macon, Ga.: Mercer, 1988.

McKnight, Scot. *Interpreting the Synoptic Gospels*. Grand Rapids: Baker, 1988.

Stein, Robert H. *The Synoptic Problem: An Introduction*. Grand Rapids: Baker, 1987.

Stonehouse, Ned B. *Origins of the Synoptic Gospels*. Grand Rapids: Eerdmans, 1963.

Streeter, B. H. *The Four Gospels: A Study of Origins*. London: Macmillan, 1924.

Tuckett, C. M. *The Revival of the Griesbach Hypothesis*. Philadelphia: Fortress, 1983.

NOTES

[1]Grand Rapids: Eerdmans, 1975.

[2]Martin, *New Testament Foundations* 1.139–60.

[3]Several good synopses are available. The standard critical synopsis of the Gospels is K. Aland, *Synopsis Quattuor Evangeliorum* 13th ed. (Stuttgart: Deutsche Bibelgesellschaft, 1985). Because this synopsis contains no English translation, many students prefer K. Aland, *Synopsis of the Four Gospels* (7th ed.; New York: United Bible Societies, 1984). Other good synopses include A. Huck, H. Greeven, *Synopsis of the First Three Gospels* (Tübingen: J. C. B. Mohr, 1981; available from Eerdmans); B. Orchard, *A Synopsis of the Four Gospels in Greek: Arranged According to the Two-Gospel Hypothesis* (Macon, Ga.: Mercer University Press, 1983).

English synopses include K. Aland, *Synopsis of the Four Gospels* (7th ed.; New York: United Bible Societies, 1984); B. Orchard, *A Synopsis of the Four Gospels in Greek: Arranged According to the Two-Gospel Hypothesis* (Macon, Ga.: Mercer University Press, 1983); R. W. Funk, *New Gospel Parallels*. 2 vols. (Philadelphia: Fortress, 1985).

For a survey of the history of making synopses, cf. R. H. Stein, *The Synoptic Problem: An Introduction* (Grand Rapids: Baker, 1987), 16–25.

[4]This is commonly referred to as "Q," the first letter of the German word *Quelle*, meaning "source."

[5]S. McKnight, *Interpreting the Synoptic Gospels* (Grand Rapids: Baker, 1988), 34.

[6]The finest book available today on the Synoptic Problem and on issues pertaining to critical issues in the Synoptic Gospels is Stein, *Synoptic Problem*.

[7]A. J. Bellinzoni, Jr., *The Two-Source Hypothesis: A Critical Appraisal* (Macon, Ga.: Mercer University Press, 1985), 9. (Emphasis added.)

[8]A convenient collection of the early Christian comments (in their original language) on the origins of the Gospels is found in Aland, *Synopsis Quattuor*, 531-48. For discussion, cf. esp. B. Orchard, H. Riley, *The Order of the Synoptics: Why Three Synoptic Gospels?* (Macon, Ga.: Mercer University Press, 1987), 111–226.

[9]It must not be thought, however, that the early Christians were oblivious to chronological and historical problems. Tertullian, for instance, states: "It matters not that the arrangement of their narratives varies, so long as there is agreement on the essentials of the Faith" (*Against Marcion* 4.2.2; trans. Orchard, *Order*, 134). See also especially Augustine, *Harmony*.

[10]The wording is that of Irenaeus (*Against Heresies* 3.1.1; trans. Orchard, *Order*, 128). It is a known fact that Peter and Paul did not "found" the church at Rome, though this statement could be taken to mean "establishing through teaching subsequent to its genesis as a

church." Clement of Alexandria argues that Mark was written while Peter was alive (cf. his *Adumbrationes in epistolas canonicas*; text and trans. in Orchard, *Order*, 131; see also Eusebius, *Church History* 2.15). Irenaeus most likely suggests that Mark was not written until after the death of Peter and Paul (*Against Heresies* 3.1.1; trans. Orchard, *Order*, 128 and note "b." on p. 129).

[11]A recent defense of the Augustinian Hypothesis may be seen in B. C. Butler, *The Originality of St. Matthew: A Critique of the Two-Document Hypothesis* (Cambridge: Cambridge University Press, 1951).

[12]"Ur" means "original" in German. This "Ur-Gospel," it was argued, is not extant.

[13]The first essay, published in Jena in 1783, was *Inquiritur in fontes, unde Evangelistae suas de resurrectione Domini narrationes hauserint* Jena, 1783 [An Inquiry into the Sources from which the Evangelists drew their Narratives of the Resurrection of the Lord]; the second, more substantial essay, published also in Jena in 1789 and enlarged in 1794 was *Commentatio, qua Marci Evangelium totum e Matthaei et Lucae commentariis decerptum esse monstratur*, Jena, 1789, 1794 [The Theory in which it is proved that the whole of Mark's Gospel is derived from the works of Matthew and Luke]. The Latin text and translation of the second work can be found in B. Reicke and B. Orchard, "Commentatio" and "Demonstration," *J. J. Griesbach: Synoptic and Text-critical Studies 1776-1976* (SNTSMS 34; ed. B. Orchard, T. R. W. Longstaff; Cambridge: Cambridge University Press, 1978), 68-102, 103-35.

[14]A few useful studies about the history of the Griesbach hypothesis are G. Delling, "Johann Jakob Griesbach: His Life, Word and Times," and B. Reicke, "Griesbach's Answer to the Synoptic Question," both in *J. J. Griesbach: Synoptic and Text-Critical Studies 1776-1976* (SNTSMS 34; ed. B. Orchard, T. R. W. Longstaff; Cambridge: Cambridge University Press, 1978), 5-21 and 50-67; C. M. Tuckett, "The Griesbach Hypothesis in the 19th Century," *JSNT* 3 (1979): 29-60; Farmer, *Synoptic Problem*, 1-198; H. H. Stoldt, *History and Criticism of the Marcan Hypothesis* (Macon, Ga.: Mercer University Press, 1980); C. M. Tuckett, *The Revival of the Griesbach Hypothesis: An Analysis and Appraisal* (SNTSMS 44; Cambridge: Cambridge University Press, 1983).

[15]It is for this reason that I choose to call this theory the "Oxford Hypothesis." All historians recognize that the roots of the movement are in Germany and not England; however, no one will contest the fact that the view that became dominant was most clearly articulated by B. H. Streeter.

[16]For example, one can consult the standard work of B. F. Westcott, *An Introduction to the Study of the Gospels* (8th ed.; London: Macmillan 1895), 165-212, esp. 192-212, where Westcott puts each current theory to the test. It is clear that Sanday himself was dependent on the German scholar H. J. Holtzmann; cf., e.g., Farmer, *Synoptic Problem*, 51-63. (I must add that Farmer is unduly hard on

Sanday and explores too many unknowable psychological motivations on Sanday's part—motivations that are all but impossible for historians to discern.)

[17]See especially his *Horae Synopticae: Contributions to the Study of the Synoptic Problem* (2d ed.; reprinted; Grand Rapids: Baker, 1968 [=1909]). On Hawkins, see the statements of Neill, *Interpretation*, 126–27.

[18]Famous for his ICC volume on Matthew, a commentary singularly concerned with source-critical matters; cf. *A Critical and Exegetical Commentary on the Gospel According to S. Matthew* (3d ed.; Edinburgh: T & T Clark, 1912).

[19]Edited by W. Sanday (Oxford: Clarendon, 1911).

[20]Streeter, *Four Gospels*. For further details about Streeter, cf. Neill, *Interpretation*, 131–36.

[21]Streeter's famous chart can be found on p. 150 of *Four Gospels*.

[22]Streeter was hit hardest for suggesting order and date for these hypothetical sources. In short, he "knew too much" because he inferred more than the evidence allowed.

[23]See Martin, *NT Foundations* 1:152–6, for a sympathetic discussion.

[24]A. M. Farrer, "On Dispensing with Q," *Studies in the Gospels: Essays in Memory of R. H. Lightfoot* (ed. D.E. Nineham; Oxford: Basil Blackwell, 1955), 55–88.

[25]A survey of these conferences, with listings of major papers and participants, can be found in W. R. Farmer, ed., *New Synoptic Studies: The Cambridge Conference and Beyond* (Macon, Ga.: Mercer University Press, 1983), vii–xxiii.

[26]SNTSMS 44 (Cambridge: Cambridge University Press, 1983).

[27]A massive bibliographical undertaking has begun under the able direction of the bibliophile, D. M. Scholer. See his latest "Q Bibliography: 1981–1988," *Society of Biblical Literature Seminar Papers* (ed. D. J. Lull; Atlanta, Ga.: Scholars, 1988), 483–95. A more popular survey can be seen in H. Biggs, "The Q Debate since 1955," *Themelios* 6 (1981): 18–28.

[28]A. Polag, *Fragmenta Q. Textheft zur Logienquelle* (2d ed.; Neukirchen-Vluyn: Neukirchener Verlag, 1982). In spite of the German title, this book can be used easily by those who cannot read German but who can read Greek. There is an English introduction and key.

[29]J. S. Kloppenborg, *Q Parallels: Synopsis, Critical Notes, & Concordance* (Foundations & Facets, Reference Series; Sonoma, Calif.: Polebridge, 1988). This is the most complete Q text available and has a number of useful features: (1) the Greek and English texts for the parallels in question are given with the Greek words in common in boldface; (2) other parallels are provided with English translations; (3) a brief discussion of modern scholarship on the Q text is given;

(4) a Greek concordance is found; and (5) a useful bibliography is added.

[30]*Four Gospels*, 151 (cf. 161–62). The quotation is from Streeter's introductory précis; pp. 161–62 further expound this point and they do not show any sign of being aware of the circular nature of his argument.

[31]This is usually referred to as the Lachmann fallacy. A good critique of the Lachmann fallacy was made originally by Butler, *Originality*, 62–71.

[32]It is probably impossible to state the phenomenon of order in a way that is completely neutral. The most neutral statement I have seen is offered by Tuckett: "Whenever Matthew's order and Mark's order differ, Mark's order and Luke's order agree; and whenever Luke's order and Mark's order differ, Matthew's order and Mark's order agree." See "Arguments from Order," 198.

[33]The odd thing about the Griesbach proponents is that they, too, have committed a kind of Lachmann fallacy. Frequently, too frequently in fact, Griesbach theorists have concluded that the Griesbach Hypothesis is the only credible explanation of the phenomenon of order. But this is no more the case for the Griesbach Hypothesis than for the Oxford Hypothesis since *either hypothesis can readily explain the phenomenon of order.* See e.g., W. R. Farmer, "Modern Developments of Griesbach's Hypothesis," *NTS* 23 (1977): 275–95, esp. 293–95. "Farmer's fallacy" has been ably exposed by Tuckett, "Arguments from Order," 205–6. The same critique can be applied to H. Riley, *Order*, 3–18. The fallacy, simply stated, is to argue that a given hypothesis is the *only* hypothesis that can explain the phenomenon of order.

However, it needs to be observed that the phenomenon of order may have as its best explanation the Griesbach point of view. It is a notable feature that, as they put it, Mark "zigzags" in that he moves back and forth from Matthew to Luke, never retracing his steps. And, as Riley has stated of the Oxford Hypothesis, "At every point where Matthew ceases to follow Mark's order, whether for a short or longer period, Luke continues it; and wherever Luke ceases to follow Mark's order, Matthew in his turn continues it. There is surely an inescapable conclusion to be drawn from this. *If Matthew and Luke were dependent on Mark for the order of events, they must have agreed together that they would do this.* Without constant collaboration, the result would be quite impossible." From H. Riley, B. Orchard, *Order*, 7 (italics added). What Riley states is important and, I think, probably favors the Griesbach Hypothesis. However, as Tuckett has pointed out, the frequency of this phenomenon is "statistically insignificant" and ought not to be given the importance that it is by Griesbach proponents; cf. Tuckett, "Arguments from Order," 202–5.

[34]B. Orchard, *Order*, 111–221.

[35]See this kind of procedure in W. G. Kümmel, *Introduction to the New Testament* (rev. ed.; Nashville: Abingdon, 1975), 53–55.

[36]In a recent survey of the literature in preparation for this essay, I was amazed at the frequency of this self-congratulation. I will restrict the notations to four: W. R. Farmer, "Introduction," *New Synoptic Studies: The Cambridge Conference and Beyond* (ed. W. R. Farmer; Macon, Ga.: Mercer University Press, 1983), xx. (Here he cites statistics of those invited but one might ask, "Was it a fair sampling?"), xxi. ("The old consensus about Marcan Priority has gone. We can now recognize that we have entered a new era in Synoptic studies. . ."), xxviii. (Here he seems to assume that active writing on the Synoptic Problem is somehow a measure of statistics.) In the same volume, the essay by O. L. Cope is entitled "The Argument Revolves: The Pivotal Evidence for Marcan Priority Is Reversing Itself," 143–59; Dungan, "Abridgement," 87 (speaks of the "death-knell").

The most grievous statement of this sort is by Farmer, "Certain Results," 79–80, who states, "I take the situation to be this. Since Austin Farrer wrote 'On Dispensing with Q,' those who have followed his counsel to read Luke through carefully, to test whether there was any need to appeal to 'Q,' have uniformly, so far as I know, come to the same conclusion: there is no need for 'Q.' " Now this statement is inaccurate and a tendentious statement of the worst kind. Scholer, "Q Bibliography: 1981–1988," lists some 240 items, and the earlier bibliography of F. Neirynck was twenty-five pages long. Number counting probably favors belief in Q by a landslide, but this is not the issue. Farmer's statement is one that is woefully unfair and inaccurate.

The problem with this kind of argument is that it is exactly what Farmer criticized the Oxford Hypothesis for—majority opinion wins! What counts is evidence and logic, not the number of scholars one can find on one's side. And, to continue with this logic, I can think of only one major commentary published in the last twenty-five years that has argued for (or assumed) the Griesbach Hypothesis—C. S. Mann's robust *Mark: A New Translation with Introduction and Commentary* (AB 27; Garden City: Doubleday, 1987). This commentary, however, seems to be receiving more criticism than acceptance.

[37]For example, observe the explanatory nature of the proof given, or a simple assumption, and then the conclusion in favor of the Griesbach Hypothesis in the following sampling: it begins with J. J. Griesbach, "Demonstration," 108–13, 123–33 (observe, however, his apparent awareness of this kind of an assumption as a problem on p. 120) (trans. Orchard, "Demonstration"); H. Riley, B. Orchard, *Order*, 3–99, 229–74.

[38]"Certain Results," 91. Italics added.

[39]I do not wish to deny the importance of overall coherence for any theory being proposed. What I do want to point out is that explanations are not necessarily proofs. A similar, but consciously

aware, procedure is found in Tuckett, "Arguments from Order," 206–13; outlined originally in *idem, Revival,* 9–15, and used throughout his book.

[40]Farmer, *Synoptic Problem,* 79; cf. also 83, 217, 264.

[41]Tuckett, *Revival,* 80; italics added; see pp. 78–85 for the complete discussion.

[42]Another careful demonstration of the same kind of phenomenon can be found in F. G. Downing, "Towards the Rehabilitation of Q," *NTS* 11 (1964-65): 169–81; reprinted in Bellinzoni, *Two-Source Hypothesis,* 269–85.

[43]F. G. Downing, "Compositional Conventions and the Synoptic Problem," *JBL* 107 (1988): 69–85; "Redaction Criticism: Josephus' Antiquities and the Synoptic Problem, I, II," *JSNT* 8 (1980): 46–65; 9 (1980): 29–48.

[44]The most careful linguistic work to date from a Griesbach Hypothesis viewpoint is that of Farmer's student, D. Peabody, *Mark as Composer* (NGS 1; Macon, Ga.: Mercer University Press, 1988). But Peabody's work is surprisingly disappointing in conclusions regarding the Synoptic Problem. I know of no thorough response to the kind of linguistic phenomena pointed out by Hawkins, *Horae Synopticae,* 114–53. Consequently, the language factor remains the Achilles heel for the Griesbach Hypothesis.

[45]This is the classical argument put forward in convincing fashion by J. Fitzmyer. Cf. his "The Priority of Mark and the 'Q' Source in Luke," *Jesus and Man's Hope* (Pittsburgh: Pittsburgh Theological Seminary, 1970), 1.131–70, esp. 134–47.

[46]The best listing of these linguistic phenomena can be found in Hawkins, *Horae Synopticae,* 131–38, which deals with odd Marcan elements that are not found in the parallels in Matthew and Luke; these include unusual words and constructions (thirty-three examples), incomplete sentences (thirteen examples), and omission of conjunctions (twenty-one examples).

[47]Streeter, *Four Gospels,* 164. The next sentence, from the same page, is perhaps more frequently quoted: "But since there are, from time to time, ingenious persons who rush into print with theories to the contrary, I can only suppose, either that they have not been at pains to do this, or else that—like some of the highly cultivated people who think Bacon wrote Shakespeare, or that the British are the Lost Ten Tribes—they have eccentric views of what constitutes evidence." In spite of the rhetoric one hears here, it cannot be denied that the grammatical argument is the most important argument for the Oxford Hypothesis. And it remains a fact that the Griesbach proponents simply have not dealt with the phenomenon squarely.

[48]A good listing can be found in Hawkins, *Horae Synopticae ,* 117–25.

[49]This has been a major criterion for a solution to the Synoptic Problem for C. M. Tuckett; cf. his *Revival*, 9–15; "Arguments from Order," 205–13. See also J. M. Robinson, "On the *Gattung* of Mark (and John)," *Jesus and Man's Hope* (Pittsburgh: Pittsburgh Theological Seminary, 1970), 99–129, esp. 101–2: "In a generation in which the Synoptic problem has been largely dominant, the success of *Redaktionsgeschichte* [redaction criticism] in clarifying the theologies of Matthew and Luke on the assumption of dependence on Mark *is perhaps the most important new argument for Marcan priority*, just as perhaps the main ingredient lacking in William R. Farmer's argument for Marcan dependence on the other written Gospels is a convincing *Redaktionsgeschichte* of Mark based on that assumption." The same point is made by G. N. Stanton in his masterful survey of Matthean research; cf. "The Origin and Purpose of Matthew's Gospel: Matthean Scholarship from 1945 to 1980," *Aufstieg und Niedergang der Römischen Welt* (2.25.3; ed. H. Temporini, W. Haase; Berlin: de Gruyter, 1984), 1899–1903.

[50]G. N. Stanton, "Origin," 1902.

[51]Cf., e.g., B. Przybylski, *Righteousness in Matthew and His World of Thought* (SNTSMS 41; Cambridge: Cambridge University Press, 1980); R. Mohrland, *Matthew and Paul: A Comparison of Ethical Perspectives* (SNTSMS 48; Cambridge: Cambridge University Press, 1984), 7–26.

[52]A useful survey may be found in J. S. Kloppenborg, *The Formation of Q: Trajectories in Ancient Wisdom Collections* (SA&C; Philadelphia: Fortress, 1987), 64–80.

[53]A lucid defense of the Q hypothesis by an evangelical scholar can be seen in Stein, *Synoptic Problem*, 89–112. The classic defenses can be found in J. C. Hawkins, "Probabilities as to the So-called Double Tradition of St. Matthew and St. Luke," *Studies in the Synoptic Problem by Members of the University of Oxford* (ed. W. Sanday; Oxford: Clarendon, 1911), 95–138; Streeter, *Four Gospels*, 182–86. A useful commentary on Q is T. W. Manson, *The Sayings of Jesus* (London: SCM, 1949[–1937]).

[54]B. H. Streeter, *Four Gospels*, 183.

[55]A doublet by definition is a single saying of Jesus that was then reported by Mark and found its way into the "Q material." The Evangelists Matthew and Luke then picked the saying both from Mark and Q. Calling something a doublet does not necessarily mean that Jesus did not repeat the saying more than once. Calling something a doublet, however, speaks of the Evangelists drawing the same saying of Jesus from two different sources.

[56]Hawkins, *Horae Synopticae*, 80–107.

[57]From Martin, *New Testament Foundations* 1.145.

[58]Evangelists often appeal here to Jesus' repeating his own sayings. This is an altogether natural response and too often neglected by critical scholars. However, a fundamental question here is not, "Did Jesus repeat himself?" for the answer is, "Of course he did." Rather,

the question here is "Are the Evangelists obtaining their information from Mark or Q?" In other words, Jesus may have repeated himself, but the saying remains a doublet because Matthew or Luke have taken a saying from Mark and Q, and therefore that one-time saying has appeared twice.

[59]Critics of the Griesbach and Augustinian hypotheses continue to ask this question. Cf., e.g., Fitzmyer, "Priority," 149.

[60]*Revival*, 61–75. Streeter's solution to these was "to divide and conquer." What Streeter did was isolate the various kinds of minor agreements and examine them separately. By doing this he avoided the serious accumulation of agreements in a single location. Cf. Streeter, *Four Gospels*, 293–331, and the telling criticisms of Farmer, *Synoptic Problem*, 118–52 (though Farmer's tone is not productive).

[61]*Revival*, 67.

[62]*Revival*, 75.

[63]A brief survey of Q studies can be found in Kloppenborg, *Formation of Q*, 8–40. What will strike most readers is that some of the studies on Q are solid pieces whereas others are too speculative to be probable.

[64]Since Streeter there have been several major treatments of the original order of Q. These have been surveyed by Kloppenborg, *Formation of Q*, 64–80.

[65]Students will need to have a synopsis to follow the next section.

[66]This omission was discussed intensively in the early Oxford school. Cf. esp. J. C. Hawkins, "Three Limitations to St. Luke's Use of St. Mark's Gospel," *Studies in the Synoptic Problem by Members of the University of Oxford* (ed. W. Sanday; Oxford: Clarendon, 1911), 27–94, who argued that Luke intentionally omitted this section. On the other hand, Streeter, *Four Gospels*, 172–79, tentatively suggested that Luke's copy of Mark was mutilated at this point. Others have suggested an Ur-Gospel theory. Most Oxford proponents today seem to favor deliberate omission; cf., e.g., Fitzmyer, *Luke* 1.770–71.

[67]The style of the verse is Lukan. Cf. I. H. Marshall, *The Gospel of Luke: A Commentary on the Greek Text* (NIGTC; Grand Rapids: Eerdmans, 1978), 366; J. A. Fitzmyer, *The Gospel according to Luke* (2 vols.; AB 28, 28A; Garden City, N.Y.: Doubleday, 1981, 1985), 1.773–74.

[68]The language here is reminiscent of Luke 9:7–8 and shows Lukan style.

[69]This is a substitute for Mark's wordy "and he was asking them." The change of verbs may be to avoid repetition (cf. Mk 8:27 with Lk 9:18).

[70]The case, of course, is dictated by the verb used. Both have used "say," though Matthew uses the historical present and Luke the aorist indicative.

[71]Mark's answer is asyndeton; this may give sufficient reason for both Matthew and Luke to insert a conjunction.

[72]However, Luke uses a participle; Mark uses a finite verb.

[73]So Fitzmyer, *Luke* 1.783–84.

[74]Six of these words are singular agreements between Mark and Luke and are not the words of Matthew.

[75]Though Luke alters Mark's aorist to an imperfect, Matthew has the aorist, confirming again Mark's middle status.

[76]That Luke is concerned with a daily denial is also seen in the present tense "to come" at the beginning of 9:23.

[77]Such a word is not strictly necessary since it creates a "suspended subject clause," but such a grammatical feature is common to New Testament writers.

[78]Mark has "For whoever is ashamed of me. . ." and then has "and the Son of Man will be ashamed of him," leaving the first clause grammatically incomplete. Luke improves this by placing "this person" at the head of the second clause, even though Luke here leaves a typical suspended subject clause. Luke's grammar, though not stylistically pure, is better than Mark's, suggesting that Mark is prior. Furthermore, this is the second case of a doublet in this section; cf. Mark 8:38 and Luke 9:26 with Matthew 10:33 and Luke 12:9. Cf. above at Matthew's use of Mark 8:35.

[79]On the Oxford Hypothesis, this is difficult to explain since Luke, in effect, tones down the Christology of Mark 8:38 by giving the angels a glory separate from the Son of Man's. On the other hand, only in Luke does the Son of Man have a separate glory. Further, the Griesbach Hypothesis has just as much trouble with Luke's redaction since he has performed a similar operation on Matthew's saying—a saying that is similar to Mark's in the wording that concerns us here.

Chapter Six

Form Criticism

Darrell L. Bock

Darrell L. Bock

Darrell L. Bock is Associate Professor of New Testament Studies at Dallas Theological Seminary in Dallas, Texas. He is a graduate of the University of Texas (B.A.), Dallas Theological Seminary (Th.M.), and the University of Aberdeen (Ph.D.). His publications include *Proclamation From Prophecy and Pattern* (Sheffield), and essays in *Bibliotheca Sacra* and *Introducing New Testament Interpretation* (Baker). He recently completed a year of post-doctoral study at the University of Tübingen. He is currently writing the commentary on Luke for the *Wycliffe Exegetical Commentary* (Moody) and editing (with Craig Blaising) *Israel and the Church: Essays in Contemporary Dispensationalism* (Zondervan). He is also the New Testament editor of *A Biblical Theology of the Bible* for Moody Press.

Chapter Six

Form Criticism

When I was a child, there was a special moment when the teacher said, "Once upon a time." I knew it was time to hear a fairy tale. I also could count on the last words bringing joy and being something like, "And they lived happily ever after." Such is the nature of form. In a set format stories or events are told in certain ways, with certain stylistic or programmatic indicators that let the reader know the type of account that is present.

The five-minute newscast seeks a succinct presentation of the news, while a news commentary expresses opinion more overtly than a news report does. Both forms do have perspective (which is why news can be a subtle form of commentary!), but when commentary is explicitly present, one automatically knows the author is speaking his or her mind. News presentations will take on a certain form in order to get in as many details in as short a space as possible. Commentary tends to focus more on cause, effect, and significance. Such differences are differences of form and can help orient the audience to the content of what is presented.

In New Testament studies, especially in the Gospels, one often hears about issues of form. Pericopes appear with certain titles like "pronouncement story," "miracle story," "saying," "tale," "legend," "parable," "proverb," or "controversy account." The different titles indicate different concerns in the account. These are designed to be descriptive titles that help the interpreter understand the account, its structure, and its emphasis. But beyond description, Form Criticism has often moved into determining the historicity of an account by an appeal to "form" and *Sitz im Leben* (setting in life). What guides such analyses? Can one get from form to setting? Is Form Criticism helpful to New Testament study? What presuppositions produced it and are they valid? These are some of the questions this essay seeks to probe.

We shall pursue our topic in several parts. First, I will define the task of Form Criticism and briefly overview its axioms and history, including major categories Form Criticism has developed. Then I will evaluate these categories. Within this section evaluation will be made of the various groupings. Finally, I will summarize the benefits and limitations of the discipline with an illustration.

DEFINITION, AXIOMS, AND HISTORY OF FORM CRITICISM

Definition

Seventy years ago Form Criticism burst on the New Testament scene as the rising star of New Testament analysis.[1] It offered hope that this method would aid the interpreter to get at the thrust of what a passage's message was, especially since Source Criticism had, in the judgment of most, established the order and nature of written sources.[2] Form Criticism sought to get behind the written sources by studying the form of the individual units of the Gospels. It is both descriptive and historical. It seeks to describe the characteristics of existing forms in the New Testament and then attempts to investigate how those forms emerged in the history of the oral transmission of the church. The fundamental presupposition of the discipline is that stories about Jesus circulated in individual oral units before being fixed in written form. They were passed on as "popular" literature. The Gospel writers served more as "collectors," to use Dibelius' metaphor, than as "authors." Certain motives caused the accounts to be fixed in form, and those motives rested primarily in the edification and instruction of the early church community, who gave the stories their final shaping before they were fixed in the Gospels. In fact, when one thinks of the tradition, one should not think of the activity of an individual mind but of the activity of a community as the tradition is passed along. The individual accounts in the Gospels are but the last step in this developing tradition. Yet one can understand both the text and the history of the tradition better by analyzing what is present in the text.[3]

How then does one define Form Criticism? Bultmann, in analyzing his own work and that of Dibelius, explains it this way:

> I am entirely in agreement with M. Dibelius when he maintains that form-criticism is not simply an exercise in aesthetics nor yet simply a process of description and classification; that is to say, it does not consist of identifying the individual units of the tradition according to their aesthetic or other characteristics and placing them in their various categories. It is much rather "to discover the origin and the history of the particular units and thereby to throw some light on the history of the tradition before it took literary form." The proper understanding of form-criticism rests upon the judgment that the literature in which the life of a given community, even the primitive Christian community, has taken shape, springs out of the quite definite conditions and wants of life from which grows up a quite definite style and quite specific forms and categories. Thus every literary category has its "life situation" (*Sitz im Leben* Gunkel), whether it be worship in its different forms, or work, or hunting, or war. The *Sitz im Leben* is not, however, an individual historical event, but a typical situation or occupation in the life of a community.[4]

The citation shows clearly that Bultmann is not interested merely in descriptive classification. Rather, he wishes to use this classification of form as a means to determine what general social setting in the church allowed for the preservation and perpetuation of a given account. In short, Form Criticism is both descriptive and historical in its concerns. Form deals with description, and *Sitz im Leben* deals with history. In addition, the tracing of the form's history is really an aspect of Tradition Criticism. So in its comprehensive sense Form Criticism deals with literary questions (the forms), historical questions (the community setting), and theological development questions (the tradition history of the form's development).

A simple definition comes from F. F. Bruce: "Form criticism (Ger. *Formgeschichte*, 'form history') represents an endeavor to determine the oral prehistory of written documents or sources, and to classify the material according to the various 'forms' or categories or narrative, discourse, and so forth."[5] Now when practitioners speak of the setting in the church, they usually are thinking of forms that are used in preaching or that have settings in the liturgy, instruction, or ordinances of the church. Often a form is said to have value because it contributed to exhortation to the body, to the defense of the gospel, to instruction for baptism, or other such corporate concerns. Early Form Criticism tended to deny that the individual units were preserved simply because people were interested in knowing about the historical Jesus.

Axioms

The basic axioms of Form Criticism can be briefly stated, since the definitions have already raised many of the basic points.[6]

(1) The Gospels are "popular" or "folk" literature. They are not primarily the work of one person or one mind. They belong to the community. The stories passed through the communities where their shape was determined by the shared needs of the group.

(2) The material circulated for at least twenty years in oral form and in individual units. The only exception to this rule was the Passion material, which became a large unit fairly quickly because of apologetic needs. Often a citation like that of Papias, as recorded in Eusebius's *Ecclesiastical History* 3.39.4, is noted to show the ancient's love of the oral word. Papias said, "I supposed that things out of books did not profit me so much as the utterances of a voice which lives and abides."

(3) Units were used as the occasion required, and it was their usefulness that caused them to be retained. Occasionally stories were grouped together because they shared the same form or terms, but these instances were few.

(4) As the materials were used in the same types of settings they took on a particular form according to the function they had in the community, which is why the form can help surface the account's concern and thus be useful for analysis. Here is where *Sitz im Leben* enters the discussion. One could even speak of various settings such as the *Sitz im Leben Jesu* (a setting in Jesus' life) or the *Sitz im Leben Kirche* (a setting in the church). Early Form Criticism tended to look first for the setting in the church, as the various axioms concerns show. The tradition is the servant of the church's needs.

(5) One can assume that the Gospels, as we now have them, had the following sources: Mark, Q, special Matthean material (M), and special Lukan material (L). In other words, the results of Source Criticism in terms of Marcan priority are a given.

(6) Alongside Form Criticism came criteria by which to look for secondary elements. These criteria of authenticity are really a part of tradition historical analysis, but they indicate how far-reaching the task of Form Criticism was.[7] Three criteria were key: a) The *criterion of dissimilarity* argues that a saying was authentic when it could not emerge either from Judaism or from the early church. Skeptics of this criterion said that this gave us only the distinctive or minimalist Jesus. It also was a "guilty until innocent" approach. b) The *criterion of multiple attestation* said that those sayings that appear in variety of distinct sources are more likely to be authentic. The argument here is that such distribution is evidence of an early and widespread tradition. This category can be helpful, though it tends to suggest that an individual witness is not enough. c) The *criterion of coherence* is the most subjective category. It argues that the other sayings that fit together or cohere with already demonstrated authentic sayings are most likely to be authentic as well.

In addition, form critics tended to assume that accounts expanded as they got older. Dibelius's treatment of the forms tended to suggest that forms became more complicated. So additions in the parallels were looked on with skepticism. It is precisely this type of particular stylistic criterion that Sanders examined and found wanting.[8]

History

The foundations behind Form Criticism lie in biblical studies as it emerged in the eighteenth and nineteenth centuries. Johann Gottfried Herder (1796) studied folk poetry and applied what he learned about such popular literature to biblical studies. His work allowed the development of viewing the texts as popularly developed literature that passed through a community.[9] Franz Overbeck (1899) distinguished biblical literature from patristic texts and raised the issue of forms, while Hermann Jordan (1911) attempted to come up with a list of the various forms within the history of the canonical and post-canonical ancient church.[10] Jordan's list included narratives and historical books such as the Gospels and Acts, letters, apocalypses, speeches and sermons, apologies, dialogues, controversy writings, tracts, church ordinances, rules of faith, hermeneutical literature such as commentaries, and translations.[11] Finally Hermann Gunkel, especially influenced by Herder, applied his work to the investigation of the Old Testament, especially Genesis and the Psalms, and also emphasized the *Sitz im Leben*.[12]

Clearly by the time Diebelius and Schmidt wrote, the study of form was on the rise. The men responsible for developing Form Criticism simply applied the ongoing discussion to their disciplines. The attention Form Criticism received was partially because the originators were so thorough in terms of treating all the text. For example, Bultmann's study attempted to classify and discuss every Synoptic Gospel text. The new tool created great interest.

Eventually the high interest waned. There were two reasons. First, the work of Bultmann was so thorough and implied that little else needed to be done. On the other hand, some frustration set in with going behind the text, and some questions were raised about the fundamental suppositions of the method. Vincent Taylor expressed some reservations about the historical results of Form Criticism, while analyzing its presuppositions.[13] He particularly criticized Form Criticism's ignoring of the role of eyewitnesses and the refusal to see some basic structure in the various units of the tradition. Speaking of Form Criticism and eyewitnesses, he says, "It is on the question of eyewitnesses that form criticism presents a very vulnerable front. If the Form-Critics are right, the disciples must have been translated to heaven immediately after the Resurrection. As Bultmann sees it, the primitive community exists *in vacuo*, cut off from its founders by the walls of inexplicable ignorance. Like Robinson Crusoe it must do the best it can."[14] Later he says, "All this is absurd." Taylor represented a more conservative approach to Form Criticism. He did not doubt the existence of oral tradition or the influence of the community on the tradition. He simply did not see the tradition as floating out at sea without any anchor in the original setting.

The rise of Redaction Criticism in the 1950s brought the Gospel writers again to the fore as theologians and editors who helped shape and present Gospel material.[15] The image of the evangelists as collectors was forever lost as examination of the text revealed the synoptic writers had presented their material with their own emphases about Jesus. One can think here of the different order in the Temptation accounts, which shows either Matthew or Luke has presented the material in a distinct order to make a point (Mt 4:1–11—kingdom temptation last; Lk 4:1–13—temple temptation last.)

In addition, the rules of oral tradition were evaluated and found wanting, while the Jewish parallels for handling oral tradition showed that tradition could be passed on and remain relatively fixed.[16] So serious is the damage that some today regard as questionable many of the essential elements of the historical quest of the old Form Criticism.[17]

But efforts to focus on the more literary aspects of the discipline have not died. Klaus Berger has tried to classify most of the New Testament through comparison with other ancient writings and has been the most prolific writer in attempting to speak of the "new" Form Criticism[18] So the fate of Form Criticism is still to be decided, though aspects of the old Form Criticism are probably a relic of the past.[19]

THE BASIC FORMS DESCRIBED

We begin with the five basic categories that originally emerged from the discipline. Then we will briefly consider the new Form Criticism and its approach to classification.

Paradigms / Apophthegms / Pronouncement Stories

These accounts have five characteristics according to Dibelius.[20] First, they are stories that are rounded off. By this Dibelius means that the high point comes toward the end, either through a word or deed of Jesus. This is the reason Taylor preferred the name "pronouncement story," which certainly is a better title.[21] Bultmann had a different name for these accounts and divided them into "controversy" dialogues when opponents were present, "scholastic dialogues" when disciples were present, and biographical apophthegms where there is much more narrative detail present and where there is simply an event in which Jesus participates.[22] It should be noted that Bultmann regarded the controversy and scholastic texts as similar.

The second characteristic is that the narrative is brief and simple. There is little extra detail. Third, there is religious coloring in the account. This means that expressions describing actions have a religious tone to them, like "he preached to them" (Mk 2:2) or "he was grieved at their hardness of heart" (Mk 3:5). Fourth, the goal of the narrative is the didactic point that concludes or summarizes the account. It is the word from Jesus that counts. In short, it is a story with a punch line. Fifth, the account is useful for preaching purposes. Here one crosses from descriptive into historical categories. This is why the accounts are preserved. For Bultmann, the origin of these accounts is in the polemic atmosphere of the church (controversy dialogues) or in the desire simply to teach (scholastic dialogues) or for preaching (biographical apophthegms).

Some illustrations of such accounts are Controversy dialogue: Mark 2:23–28 (*Plucking Corn on the Sabbath*); Scholastic Dialogue: Mark 10:17–31 (*The Rich Young Man*); and Biographical Apophthegm: Luke 10:38–42 (*Mary and Martha*). Each account ends with a punch line and drives toward it. In the controversy, there is inherent conflict that is resolved in Jesus' remark. The tension in the scholastic dialogue is more a probe into what is so or how one should view something. The biographical account simply tells something that happened to Jesus that elicited a key saying. It is easy to see how the category, though broad, is a helpful description of the kind of account and its emphasis.

Tales / Novellen / Miracle Stories

These accounts are slightly more complex. The accounts are complete units in themselves and also have clear characteristics.[23] Bultmann again has subgroupings like Exorcisms, Healings, Raisings from the Dead, and Nature Miracles. The basis of the names are not really the form but the nature of the miracle. A more recent attempt at such analysis is that of Gerd Theissen.[24] Theissen speaks of Exorcisms, Healings, Epiphanies (Appearances), Rescue Miracles, Gift Miracles, and Rule Miracles. Again, the nature of the miracle dictates the title and is helpful in focusing on the thrust of the passage.

The characteristics are that the accounts are self contained, that they are descriptive, that details of the story are told with pleasure, that the malady is specified, and that there is a note of the healing's success. There is a lack of devotion in the account in that religious language is lacking and often there is an absence of teaching by Jesus, which makes this category distinct from the previous category of paradigm. Part of the pleasure in the account is the detail given to the nature of the malady, the means of healing, and the public reaction to the miracle.

Numerous examples exist: *The Leper* of Mark 1:40–45 (Healing); *The Stilling of the Storm* in Mark 4:35–41 (Nature Miracle); *The Healing of Jairus' Daughter and the Stilling of the Flow of Blood* in Mark 5:21–43 (Healing and Raising from the Dead); and *The Demons and the Swine* in Mark 5:1–20 (Exorcism). One can look at any of these accounts and trace the sequence of the traits.

Sayings / Parenesis or Exhortations / Parables

Here is the most varied category. This group of accounts deals with the individual teachings of Jesus that are not tied to a controversy or a simple event. In other words, they describe his discourse.[25] Again, there are subgroupings. Dibelius had maxims (Mt 12:34b: *Out of the Abundance of the Heart*; also called proverb or gnome); metaphor (Mk 4:21: *Is a Lamp Put under a Bushel?*); parable (Lk 15:1–7: *Lost Sheep*); prophetic call (Mt 5:3–12: *Beatitudes*); short command (Mt 18:10: *Do Not Despise Little Ones*); and extended command (Lk 6:27–49: *Sermon on the Plain*).[26] Most of these names are straightforward. The most difficult is the prophetic call, which is really a word of blessing or warning that comes from God through a prophet about what God will do or what will happen.

Bultmann's names differ but represent similar categories. First, he has Logia (or Wisdom), which equals Dibelius's maxims (Mk 3:24–26: *A Kingdom Divided Against Itself*). Second, he speaks of Prophetic or Apocalyptic Sayings, which equal the prophetic call as well as include parable and metaphor. This category is further subdivided into preaching of salvation (Lk 7:22–23: *The Blind See, etc.*); minatory sayings, which are threats of judgment or woe (Lk 6:24–26: *Woes to the Rich*); admonitions, which are warnings and include many parables (Lk 12:42–46: *Parable of the Stewards*); and, last of all, apocalyptic predictions (Mk 13:5–27: *Olivet Discourse*).

Third, Bultmann speaks of Legal Sayings and Church Rules. Some of these are metaphors or prophetic sayings as well. These are sayings that set down limits on life or that indicate where authority lies. Here he includes *The Sin Against the Spirit* in Luke 12:10; the *Instruction on Reconciliation* in Matthew 6:14–15; and the *Divorce Pericope* of Matthew 5:31–32.

Fourth, he speaks of "I sayings." These are mission statements about why Jesus has come or has been sent or how he acts. They usually start with "I have come" (Mk 2:17: *Not to Call the Righteous but Sinners*); or "I am sent" (Lk 4:43: *To Preach the Kingdom*); or "I have given/made" (Mk 1:17: *You Fishers of Men*). Any saying where Jesus speaks of his activity belongs here. Again, the separation of sayings into such groupings is helpful.

The fifth and final subunit under sayings are the similitudes. Here appear hyperbole (Mt 5:29–30: *Plucking out the Eye*); paradox (Mk 10:39: *The One who Seeks His Life Will Lose It*); metaphor (Mt 7:13–14: *The Narrow Gate*); and similitudes proper, which are the extended metaphors that also are known as parables (Lk 18:1–8: *The Nagging Widow*). Such parables can be short (Mt 13:33: *The Leaven*) or long (Lk 15:11–32: *The Prodigal Son*). Through such descriptive and distinguishing categories Form Criticism shows its strength and its value for study. The categories are an analytical and descriptive aid to the interpreter.[27]

Legends / Stories about Jesus

In this category, the story is told to exalt a saint or great figure.[28] It will be distinguished from the next category, myth, in that the figure's greatness in a legend does not include divine qualities. Bultmann used the title "Historical Stories and legends." The name "legend" is unfortunate because in English it suggests that the accounts are false. To comment on historicity is not the intent of the title, though it is true that for many form critics most of the accounts in this category are embellished beyond the historical realities. Bultmann's alternate name, "Historical Stories," is also a problem since he does not mean to suggest by that title that the stories are true historically. Either title is simply intended to describe an account that is interested in the life and adventures of Jesus for its own sake, without being concerned to recount his sayings or other such things. The problem of title caused Taylor to prefer the simple "Stories of Jesus." It is the best title for the category.

These accounts are interested in revealing the person of
Jesus or those around him. They underline how God has
marked the life of these individuals. The story of *Jesus as a
Twelve Year Old* in Luke 2:41–52 is an example of such an
account, though here the saying of Luke 2:49 also has an
important role to play.[29] Bultmann lacks Dibelius's category of
myth so his section includes what Dibelius called legend and
also what Dibelius called myth. Thus, *The Voice at the Baptism*
(Mk 1:9–11 and parallels), *The Triumphal Entry* (Mk 11:1–10 and
parallels), *Peter's Confession* (Mk 8:27–30 and parallels), and *The
Transfiguration* (Mk 9:2–8 and parallels) are among the accounts
that fall into this category for Bultmann. Apparently, Bultmann
found it difficult to sort out when "supernatural elements"
were or were not present or else he decided a distinction in
these two categories was not possible because so many of the
accounts had supernatural touches.

In fact, this category is the most elusive of all because in
many cases the text could be put elsewhere as well. Dibelius
puts *The Synagogue Speech* of Luke 4:16–21 here, but is this not a
prophetic call and a mission account? One senses that accounts
end up in this category because they are too supernaturally
charged. Even so, the category, rightly understood, is helpful
in pointing out that the person of Jesus is the issue in these
accounts. Usually something about his person, something
marvelous, is revealed in these accounts and is the point of the
unit.

The problem with this classification points to a warning
about form that needs attention. Sometimes there is the
complaint that one should not classify texts by content.[30] The
value of the complaint depends on what is meant by "content."
Guthrie is disturbed that some classifications look at the
supernatural content in the account and call the result legend or
myth as a result, when in fact the account differs little
otherwise from a pronouncement story, a miracle story, or a
saying. The validity of the complaint at this level is certainly
correct. Form cannot be used to determine historicity unless a
clear set of formal characteristics are present and clearly
established as part of the form, such as in the case of a parable.
Only then can a form be marked off as non-historical. In fact,
the claim was that legend and myth theoretically could contain
historical material, but often that was not in reality the case.
Thus the warning is a real one. The terms "legend" and

"myth" cannot be used to indicate historicity. If that is what they intend to communicate, then other terms might be better and clearer, such as "embellished accounts." This is why Taylor's "Stories about Jesus" is the best title for this category. All titles should be clear and used as intended, as descriptive categories of literary emphasis and focus. Issues of historicity have to be tackled at other levels by other approaches. Here is a case where Form Criticism can attempt to do too much with too little.

On the other hand, the classification of form by content can be helpful in determining subcategories within a larger category and can be helpful in describing the point of focus in an account. So the subclassifications of miracle stories and parables are helped when this procedure is applied. As always, defining terms and procedures carefully is the key, and generalizations should be examined carefully to see whether they have been established, rather than asserted.

Myths

The last category is Dibelius's alone.[31] These accounts deal with the "many sided doings of the gods." Here we move from Jesus the teacher to Jesus the divine figure. Again, the intent of the title is not necessarily to make a historical judgment, but the name is unfortunate in that it suggests the account is false when normal English usage is applied to the meaning of the term. In fact, many form critics do believe these accounts are embellishments about Jesus, but that was not the intent of the title. It is really a way of saying that God or Satan deals directly with Jesus in these accounts and that these encounters, in turn, point to the mystery of his person. So Dibelius has only a few events here. For him *the Baptism, the Temptation,* and *the Transfiguration* belong here. Once again, if the category name were not a problem, the description would prove helpful. Perhaps the name "Direct Supernatural Encounter Stories" would be a more neutral name to offer.

The New Form Criticism
Forms and Multiple Subforms

When one turns to the treatment of Berger, many of the old categories are gone, though they really have received new names.[32] In addition, Berger covers the passages of the entire New Testament. He does not limit himself to the Synoptic Gospels. He also is clear that his version of the discipline is distinct from tradition history. This separation is positive, though it means that the concerns of the "new" Form Criticism represent the emasculation of much of what was Form Criticism for Dibelius and Bultmann. This is something Berger is aware of and welcomes.[33] In short, the literary features of Form Criticism remain, but the issues of history and tradition are largely removed. This surgery on Form Criticism probably strikes some as no longer being Form Criticism, but what it represents is a slimmed down version that allows the tool to do what it does best, which is to describe.

Berger has four basic categories. The first is *Sammelgattungen* ("Collected Forms").[34] This is largely discourse material. Here he has pictorial texts, which include metaphors and parables, sentences, speeches, apophthegm, and argumentation, which are the controversy texts, whether apologetic, instructive, or diatribe. Second comes the *Symbuleutische Gattungen* ("Behavior Forms").[35] Here are found, among many others, parenesis, warnings, house rules, martyr warnings, blessings, woes, and community rules. Third come the (*Epideiktische Gattungen* ("Demonstration Texts").[36] These are texts about things, persons, or events that are to lead the reader to admiration or repulsion. Here we find acclamations ("you are worthy," "this one is"), hymns, doxologies, prayers, proclamation, judgments, "I sayings," visions, apocalyptic genres, miracle accounts, travel accounts, martyr accounts, conflict accounts, example accounts from the disciples, and summaries. We move into events or their significance in these accounts. Finally are the *Dikanische Gattungen* ("Decision Texts").[37] These are apologetic texts in one way or another that explain why something is done or how one should look at a matter. It should be noted that individual texts for Berger can fall into many categories at the same time, a departure from the older version of Form Criticism, which tended to hunt for the "pure" form and regarded most mixed forms as evidence of a position later in the given tradition's historical development.

What Berger gave up in leaving history behind he added by introducing numerous new categories on the literary side. Such detailed and thorough analysis is to be appreciated, but one wonders whether the simplicity of the old classifications has been lost in the plethora of options now provided and in the multiplied categories within which a text can function. Nonetheless, here is Form Criticism at its descriptive level carried out to its logical and detailed end. Only time will tell whether the pursuit of this degree of detail is helpful or whether a retreat to more general categories is advisable.

AN EXAMPLE: LUKE 5:1–11

Such a vast discipline with its many subcategories makes the choice of an example that is representative difficult. Luke 5:1-11 has the advantage of a rich history of discussion about its form that reveals both the strengths and weaknesses of the discipline. In examining this passage, we shall note the history of this discussion and show how the discipline wrestles with itself to understand a given text. We will do this by tracing the position of a variety of interpreters about the form of this passage, and note the strengths and weaknesses of their approach.

Dibelius called the account a "legend."[38] The major reason for the choice appears to be the miraculous catch, along with the detail about Peter's view of himself. Now Source Criticism had suggested that John 21:1–14 and Luke 5:1–11 were related to one another. Dibelius picks up on this and argues that John 21 is the later account, since Peter in Luke 5:8 does not confess his specific sin (and thus would be alluding to his denials); rather, he speaks of sin in general terms. He notes the passage is really a call-word and that it might in reality have been tied to a real catch of fish.

Dibelius's denial that Luke 5 comes from John 21 is a good example of careful observation that is frequent in Form Criticism. However, the tendency simply to assume the results of Source Criticism is not always good. Another assumption crippling the analysis is that similar events mean originally unified traditions. The possibility that Luke 5 and John 21 were distinct is not raised despite numerous differences in the events. Differences such as timing, the setting of the fishing, the role of the participants, and the contents of what Jesus says do not count sufficiently to overcome the belief that similarity is really identity. His treatment also tends to assume that accounts move from simple to more complex forms, since he seems to suggest a basic call and event was expanded into a more miraculous form.

Bultmann discussed the account as a nature miracle, though he argued that it really is a legend.[39] The reason for this distinction is not made clear. It evidences how difficult it is to keep categories distinct if supernatural contents create a shift in category. He argues that the original tradition was the saying of Luke 5:10, which has been expanded into its "symbolic actualization," that is, the miracle of Luke 5:4–8. He sees John 21 as the earlier account, though why this is so is not made clear. Perhaps the confession and Christology are considered to be more appropriate in the post-resurrection setting.

The category of nature miracle is an appropriate description of what Jesus does here. But again, old assumptions crowd in. The movement from simple to complex accounts fuels the suggestion that originally the simplest form of the tradition had only a saying. In addition, like the previous effort, there is no attempt to deal with the possibility that Luke 5 is distinct from John 21. Despite any superficial similarities, differences are treated as the work of the evangelists, rather than reckoning with the possibility that they are older or even signs of distinct traditions. Others have criticized the choice of "legend" for the account, noting that Peter's person and piety are not the focus of the account.[40]

Theissen called the account a "gift miracle."[41] This is another way to refer in more detail to a nature miracle. The gift miracle has three basic characteristics. 1) The miracle is spontaneous and surprising. This means the miracle worker initiates the miracle. There is no request for it. 2) The miracle is unobtrusive, which means the "how" of the miracle or the actions associated with it are absent. 3) The final demonstration of the miracle is stressed. This means that the consequences are detailed. All of these observations are true of Luke 5:1–11. Jesus does the miracle without lifting a finger. He simply says go out and toss the nets. The fishermen are left to deal with the (too great!) consequences in order to avoid the tragedy of sinking under the weight of the catch. The point of the miracle is that a situation of want is overcome. Theissen makes no mention of John 21 in his treatment. His handling of the text is reflective of more recent Form Criticism. His descriptive approach is helpful.

Fitzmyer calls the account a pronouncement story (Luke

5:10b) plus a miracle story.[42] The miracle serves the saying, which is why the emphasis is on the pronouncement part of the account. The combination was Luke's doing. Again strengths and weaknesses exist. The assumption that there is no such thing as a mixed form appears to force the conclusion that Luke has taken Mark 4:16–20 and joined it to another tradition to form this unit. This is not helpful. However, of more value is the observation, which certainly is correct that the key to the account is the saying, which in turn is set up by the miracle. In other words, Fitzmyer's double classification and description nicely prioritizes the elements within the story and notes that the punch line of Luke 5:10 is pivotal.

Talbert discusses the form of this text in great detail.[43] He argues that the text is a commission account, not a call. A commission account has an introduction (Luke 5:2), a confrontation (5:3), a commission (5:4), a protest (5:5), a reaction (5:8–9) and a reassurance (5:10), and a response (5:11). This is in contrast to the call that has Jesus coming, seeing, calling, and then the person(s) leaving and following.

This classification looks good on the surface, but it seems to suffer from overanalysis and shows that any classification should be examined carefully. For example, to call Luke 5:5 a protest is to undermine the very point of the verse. The verse really concerns Peter's faith, which despite appearances leads him *to obey* Jesus. Peter's remark is not a protest, but the expression of great faith. In addition, Luke 5:3 is hardly a confrontation. Finally, to distinguish between a call and a commission seems artificial.

Tiede briefly handles the passage with some sharp observations.[44] He speaks of an "epiphany-call," by which he means that the passage evidences a divine presence and makes a call to the fisherman to be a disciple. He compares the account in form to Exodus 3, Judges 6, and Isaiah 6. The center of the passage is Peter's faith, which leads to the manifestation of divine presence, which in turn is the basis of a call. The miracle is less crucial except to set up the call, since the miracle's material success is totally ignored, when the men leave behind their nets and vocation for a new call. The action of the account reinforces the point of the story and the priorities in it.

Here is helpful form critical work. The form is defined and the parts are placed in order of priority. In addition, parallels are noted that show other examples of the form.

Finally we look at Berger's handling of the text.[45] He complains that the title "miracle story" is a modern category and that often miracles can be placed in other categories more easily. Again, such a complaint depends on what one wishes to do with the account once it is placed in the category. If "miracle story" is a way to deny historicity, then his complaint has merit. It also is true that miracle accounts can often fit elsewhere. However, it also is the case that the category miracle stories and their subclassifications can be descriptively helpful, as Theissen's work shows.

Berger argues that the issue of an account like Luke 5 is Jesus' spiritual power and evinces the fellowship that he had with the disciples and shows the prominence of Peter. He speaks of a "mandatio," or mandate account, and also speaks of a "call history." Berger, unlike his predecessors, will use several categories at once. The mandate is an account in which there is an order by a superior to an inferior that is to be obeyed. Here is the call to cast the nets and the call to commission. The call history has precedent in 1 Kings 19:19–20 and is like Mark 1:19. Again, parallels are noted. He argues that the miracle is less important than the call and also speaks of subforms within the account, such as dialogue and "religious self witness," the latter describing Peter's exclamation that he is a sinner (Lk 5:8).

Many strengths are seen here. There is an absence of traditional historical speculation. The account is related in terms of form to other similar texts. There is a willingness to recognize mixed types. He prioritizes the parts to each other. He recognized the problem with the title "miracle story," though there may be an overreaction here. There is much here to work with in terms of exegesis.

One sees in the example a certain flexibility of category and a playing around with category titles. This is inevitable in a descriptive process where one is searching to be more precise. Now what could be the *Sitz im Leben* of such an account? How would it function in the church? Two motives seem clear. First, the account would explain the roots of the early disciples involvement in the church. How did they come to be called? What did they see in Jesus? The account shows the knowledge and authority of the one whom the church confesses as Savior. Second, the account articulates the mission of the church. The disciples are to be "fishers of men." They are to cast nets into the world and seek to rescue people from death. In this perspective, Peter is not just the first disciple, he is the exemplary disciple. All disciples share his call and can identify with his mission. The account seems to suggest these two emphases. As long as one does not deny that the origins of the tradition go back to the participants, this search for the *Sitz im Leben* in the church need not be a problem and in fact can help show the way to methods one might use to teach the account today.

SUMMARY

Form Criticism is not the center of New Testament exegesis. It is but one humble tool among many. It has the potential to be a blunt instrument that is not helpful in the exegetical task when it is used for things for which it was not designed. On the other hand, the descriptive features of the discipline and the hunting for parallels can be helpful in describing the focus, elements, and structure of a text's argument. In the hands of a skilled exegete who uses the tools of interpretation in a way that fits what they are capable of, Form Criticism can be a fruitful aid to understanding and to exposition.

BIBLIOGRAPHY

Beasley-Murray, George R. *Preaching the Gospel From the Gospels*. London: Lutterworth, 1965.

Bultmann, Rudolf. *The History of the Synoptic Tradition*. Oxford: Blackwell, 1968.

Doty, W. G. "The Discipline and Literature of New Testament Form Criticism." *Anglican Theological Review* 51 (1969): 257–321.

Ellis, E. E. "New Directions in Form Criticism." *Jesus Christus in Historie und Theologie*. Ed. G. Strecker. Tübingen: Mohr, 1975, 299–315.

France, R. T. "The Authenticity of the Sayings of Jesus." *History, Criticism, and Faith*. Ed. Colin Brown. Downers Grove, Ill.: InterVarsity, 1977.

Gerhardsson, Birger. *Memory and Manuscript: Oral Tradition and Written Transmission in Rabbinic Judaism and Early Christianity*. Trans. E. J. Sharpe. Lund: Gleerup, 1961.

McKnight, E. V. *What is Form Criticism?* Philadelphia: Fortress, 1969.

Manson, T. W. *The Teachings of Jesus: Studies of Its Form and Content.* Cambridge: Cambridge University Press, 1931.

NOTES

[1]The major ground breaking studies appeared in 1919. Though we will refer to updated, translated editions, the key studies were in German. Martin Dibelius, *Die Formgeschichte des Evangeliums*, and K. L. Schmidt, *Der Rahmen der Geschichte Jesu*, were both released in 1919. Two years later came the comprehensive and influential study by Bultmann, *Die Geschichte der synoptischen Tradition*.

[2]The history and nature of Source Criticism is the topic of the previous essay.

[3]Early in this study, Dibelius described his aim this way: "The right to read the Gospels from the standpoint of their form is the objective of the present volume." Later he says, "Further, the categories allow us to draw a conclusion as to what is called the *Sitz im Leben*, i.e., the historical and social stratum in which precisely these literary forms were developed." Finally, Dibelius again states, "The ultimate origin of the Form is the primitive Christian life itself." The English title of Dibelius's work, *From Tradition to Gospel*, summarizes the discipline's concern nicely. The quotations are from pp. 6, 7, and 8 of Dibelius, *From Tradition to Gospel*, 2d ed., trans. B. L. Woolf, (London: James Clarke & Co., 1971 trans. of 1933 ed.). The Dibelius metaphor of the evangelists as "collectors" can be found on pp. 3 and 59. The emphasis on gospel pericopes as "sociological" products, not as individual creations, can be found on p. 7.

[4]Bultmann, *The History of the Synoptic Tradition*, 3d ed., trans. J. Marsh (New York: Harper, 1963 trans. of 1958 ed.), 3–4.

[5]Bruce, "Criticism," *ISBE* 1:822.

[6]Such axioms are rarely listed in the early works. Rather, they are introduced in the opening remarks. So Dibelius, *From Tradition to Gospel*, 1–36, where he stresses the role of preaching as a major formative factor. Cf. Bultmann, *History of the Synoptic Tradition*, 1–7. Bultmann has one sentence on p. 3 that summarizes the approach: "The following investigation therefore sets out to give an account of the history of the *individual units of the tradition*, and how the tradition passed from a fluid state to the fixed form in which it meets us in the Synoptics and in some instances even outside of them."

[7]For this list, see David Catchpole, "Tradition History," in *New Testament Interpretation*, ed. by I. H. Marshall (Grand Rapids: Eerdmans, 1977), 174–77. A detailed article noting some eleven criteria is Robert Stein, "Criteria for Authenticity," in *Gospel Perspectives I*, ed. by

R. T. France and David Wenham (Sheffield: *JSOT*, 1980). The article is excellent for its scope, though it fails to distinguish when a criterion authenticates the exact wording of a saying versus only the conceptual thrust of the saying.

[8]E. P. Sanders, *The Tendencies of the Synoptic Tradition*, SNTSMS 9 (Cambridge: Cambridge University Press, 1969).

[9]K. Berger, *Einführung in die Formgeschichte*, UTB 144 (Tübingen: Franke, 1987), 63–67, traces Herder's influence.

[10]Ibid., 33–34, 56.

[11]Jordan, *Geschichte der altchristlichen Literatur* (Leipzig, 1911).

[12]E. Güttgemanns, *Candid Questions Concerning Gospel Form Criticism*, trans. by W. Doty (Pittsburgh: Pickwick, 1979 trans. of 1971 ed. with author's additions in 1978), 235–48, evaluates Gunkel's role. His prolific work was 1901–1932. Gunkel's work on Genesis was published in 1901.

[13]V. Taylor, *The Formation of the Gospel Tradition* (London: Macmillan, 1949 reprint of 1935 ed). The original volume was published in 1933 and came from lectures given in 1932.

[14]Ibid., 41. On the other hand, he says on p. 20, "I have no doubt that the value of form criticism is considerable." He speaks of a "tool with limited powers" here. If one may play with this picture a bit, one thinks of a standard screw driver that has been made into a Phillips screw driver and is no longer able to work with normal screws as a result. In this sense, the critics have argued that Form Criticism overstepped what the texts were capable of yielding.

[15]See the essay on Redaction Criticism that follows in this volume.

[16]Here one can mention the study of E. Güttgemanns and E. P. Sanders, *The Tendencies of the Synoptic Tradition*, SNTSMS 9 (Cambridge: Cambridge University Press, 1969) for the issue of the rules of transmission. Sanders especially showed that accounts both get simpler and more complex with time. There is no "rule" that applies. In addition, the examination of oral tradition in Judaism revealed the potential for very stable tradition; so H. Reisenfeld, *The Gospel Tradition and Its Beginnings: A Study in the Limits of Form Criticism* (London: Mowbray, 1957) and B. Gerhardsson, *Memory and Manuscript: Oral and Written Transmission in Rabbinic Judaism and Early Christianity* (Lund: Gleerup, 1961).

[17]K. Müller, "Neutestamentlicher Literaturüberlick (1)," *Pastoral-Theologie*, 78 (1989): 278. This article is an overview by a German New Testament scholar reviewing developments in New Testament study for pastors. He speaks of the Form Criticism of Bultmann and Diebelius as past, at least in terms of reconstructing the oral tradition; the assumption about the makeup of the Christian community; and the pursuit of *Sitz im Leben*. He notes that Form Criticism today is more interested in rhetorical issues and synchronic comparison than with diachronic study, by which he means they engage in contemporary

comparison with other New Testament works and outside sources, rather than reaching back through the tradition history. In other words, Form Criticism is moving in a descriptive, literary direction.

[18]K. Berger, *Formgeschichte des Neuen Testaments* (Heidelberg: Quelle & Meyer, 1984).

[19]Many treatments of Form Criticism in discussing the history of the movement also launch into a discussion of the New Quest for the historical Jesus, a movement started in Germany by Bultmann's students, who thought he was too negative on issues of historicity. This movement evidences the frustration with Form Criticism, but technically it is not part of the discipline itself and thus is not discussed here. Its presence is only to be noted.

[20]Dibelius, *From Tradition to Gospel*, 37–58.

[21]Taylor, *The Formation of the Gospel Tradition*, 30.

[22]Bultmann, *The History of the Synoptic Tradition*, 11–69.

[23]Dibelius, *From Tradition to Gospel*, 70–103; Bultmann, *The History of the Synoptic Tradition*, 209–44. Bultmann preferred the name "miracle story," as did Taylor, *The Formation of the Gospel Tradition*, 119–41.

[24]Gerd Theissen, *The Miracle Stories of the Early Christian Tradition*, trans. by Francis McDonaugh, ed. by John Riches (Philadelphia: Fortress, 1983 ed. of 1974 German ed.).

[25]Dibelius, *From Tradition to Gospel*, 233–65. He called them "Exhortation" or "Parenesis." Bultmann, *The History of the Synoptic Tradition*, 69–205. He spoke of "Dominical Sayings." Often the material in this category was also described as present in the source Q.

[26]The list of example passages here is mostly ours, since Dibelius does not supply a clear list for each category.

[27]Many have also attempted to subject the parables to a more comprehensive examination of form. By far the most famous attempts are: C. H. Dodd, *The Parables of the Kingdom*, rev. ed. (New York: Scribner's, 1961 ed. of original ed. in 1935) and J. Jeremias, *The Parables of Jesus*, 2d rev. ed., trans. by S. H. Hooke (New York: Scribner's, 1972 ed. of 1954 original). Here one can speak of kingdom parables, parables of the return, parables of discipleship, parables of mission, or parables about God. Again, the subcategories are determined by the topic at hand within the parable.

[28]Dibelius, *From Tradition to Gospel*, 104–32. Bultmann, *The History of the Synoptic Tradition*, 244–317.

[29]This raises the problem of "mixed forms," which will be addressed in our example below.

[30]So D. Guthrie, *New Testament Introduction* (Downers Grove, Ill.: InterVarsity, 1970 ed.), 211, point 1.

[31]Dibelius, *From Tradition to Gospel*, 266–86.

[32]Berger, *Formgeschichte des Neuen Testaments*.

[33]Ibid., 11–13.

[34]This category as well as the subsequent ones come from Berger, *Formgeschichte des Neuen Testaments*. The subgenres of this category are described on pp. 25–116. The translation of his titles are my own, since his work is currently available only in German.

[35]This is a rough translation of what is a difficult German term. Berger is clear on p. 18 of his work that behavior, injunction, or advice is the issue here. The subgenres are discussed on pp. 117–220.

[36]Another difficult term is present. The name comes from the Greek *epideiknymi*, which means "to point out something to someone" or "to show, demonstrate." Berger's description is on p. 18. The subgenres are on pp. 221–359.

[37]Again, Berger's choice of terms makes translation difficult. The burden of these texts is to lead the reader to a decision about a disputed matter. See pp. 18–19. In fact, Berger spends little time here, pp. 360–65.

[38]Dibelius, *From Tradition to Gospel*, 113.

[39]Bultmann, *The History of the Synoptic Tradition*, pp. 217–18 and 230.

[40]Schürmann, *Das Lukasevangelium*, Erster Teil, Herder's Theologischer Kommentar zum Neuen Testament, Band III (Freiburg: Herder, 1984 printing of 1968 ed.), 273, n. 79.

[41]Theissen, *The Miracle Stories of the Early Christian Tradition*, 104, 161–62, and esp. 321.

[42]J. Fitzmyer, *The Gospel according to Luke I-LX*, Anchor Bible 28 (Garden City, N.Y.: Doubleday, 1981), 562.

[43]C, Talbert, *Reading Luke* (New York: Crossroad, 1984), 60–61. His work is built on that of Hubbard, "Commissioning Stories in Luke–Acts: Their Antecedents, Form and Content," *Semeia* 8 (1977), 103–26.

[44]D. Tiede, *Luke*, Augsburg Commentary on the New Testament (Minneapolis: Augsburg, 1988), 115.

[45]Berger, *Formgeschichte des Neuen Testaments*, 305–6, 309–10, 316, 255 and 278.

Chapter Seven

Redaction Criticism

Grant R. Osborne

Grant R. Osborne

Grant R. Osborne is Professor of New Testament at Trinity Evangelical Divinity School in Deerfield, Illinois. He holds the B.A. from Fort Wayne Bible College, the M.A. from Trinity Evangelical Divinity School, and the Ph.D. from the University of Aberdeen. He also did post-doctoral studies at Cambridge and Marburg universities. His articles have appeared in such journals as *Evangelical Quarterly, Semeia, Trinity Journal,* and *Westminster Theological Journal.* He has also published *The Resurrection Narratives: A Redactional Study* (Baker), *Meaning and Significance: The Hermeneutical Spiral Between Text and Context* (IVP), *Handbook for Bible Study* (co-author; Baker), *The Bible in the Churches* (co-author; Paulist), and *Annotated Bibliography on the Bible and the Church* (Trinity). He currently serves as the editor for the forthcoming commentary series on the New Testament by InterVarsity Press.

Chapter Seven

Redaction Criticism

Four disciplines have been developed in this century that have special relevance for Gospel studies—Form Criticism, Tradition Criticism (usually considered not so much a "school" as a "method" used by Form and Redaction Criticism), Redaction Criticism, and Narrative or Literary Criticism. Each discipline presupposes the validity of and builds upon its predecessor, yet each also has originated partly because of inherent weaknesses in the preceding approaches. Form Criticism assumes that the gospel authors were mere "scissors-and-paste" editors who artificially strung together the traditions of Jesus, while Tradition Criticism concludes that since the traditions themselves were the product of a long period of oral development and often had little connection with the historical Jesus, the scholar has to remove those later additions to get at the "true" meaning of the stories. Both disciplines ignore the author (or "redactor"), considering that author of little value for the task of interpreting the Gospels. Redaction Criticism arose in the 1950s to correct this erroneous omission.

Redaction Criticism may be defined as a historical discipline that seeks to uncover the theology and setting of a writing by studying the ways the redactor or editor changed the traditions he inherited and the seams or transitions that the redactor utilized to link those traditions together. The creative force shifts from Jesus (the traditional view) and the early church (Form Criticism) to the author (Redaction Criticism).[1] There are two foci for the discipline: (1) the editorial alterations of the traditions (this is the primary concern of earlier redaction critics) and (2) the process by which the authors combined the traditions into a holistic work (this is called Composition

Criticism and is the goal of later redaction critics). Critics today use the two approaches together.

There are several elements in the process of redactional inquiry. First, Redaction Criticism builds upon the results of Source Criticism, which assumes that written or oral sources lay behind the Gospels, and studies the interdependence between those sources.[2] The general consensus[3] (called the two- or four-document hypothesis) is that there were two primary sources, Mark and Q (either a written or oral source containing sayings of Jesus and accounting for 235 verses common to Matthew and Luke but missing from Mark). In addition, both Matthew and Luke utilized their own sources (M and L) in constructing their Gospels. Redaction critics take this data and study the editorial alterations made to their sources by the individual evangelists. For instance, they will ask why Luke has added three sayings of Jesus in his crucifixion scene—"Father, forgive these people, for they don't know what they are doing" (23:34); "Today you will be with me in paradise" (23:43); and "Father, I commit my spirit to you" (23:46)—while omitting Mark's and Matthew's, "My God, my God, why have you forsaken me" (Mk 15:34; Mt 27:46).

Second, Redaction Criticism works with the results of Form and Tradition Criticism. Form critics seek the original or authentic tradition behind the final gospel form, while tradition critics try to discover the history or development of that tradition from the earliest to the final form in the Gospels. Redaction critics center upon the final stage of the editorial process, the evangelist's changes, believing that these are the clue to the intentions of the author and the situation of his community.[4] For instance, they would inquire about which of the sayings may have been added earlier in the tradition-history of the crucifixion narratives and which might be Luke's own contributions. The latter would provide the data for determining Luke's distinctive emphases.

Third, the primary goal of Redaction Criticism is to discern the theological message of each evangelist. This is accomplished both by asking *why* the changes were introduced into the final form of the traditions and by looking for consistent patterns in the ongoing composition of that Gospel. The alterations introduced in a Gospel begin to fall into certain categories or patterns, and these patterns denote redactional interests or theological tendencies that characterize that Gospel.[5] In Luke's crucifixion narrative, two such theological tendencies have emerged: (1) Jesus is portrayed as the quintessential innocent righteous martyr (seen in Luke's version of the centurion's cry, "Surely, this man is innocent," and in the Christological focus of the entire account); and (2) Luke's version is altered into an awesome scene of worship (two of the last sayings in Luke are prayers, and the negative elements of Mark and Matthew have been omitted). Furthermore, both of these emphases are part of larger patterns in Luke's Gospel.

Fourth, the setting or situation of the Lukan church is often surmised on the basis of these redactional tendencies. This is a highly controversial aspect of Redaction Criticism because of its speculative nature, but the majority of scholars continue to seek such conclusions in their studies. They believe that the changes were introduced by particular problems in the church behind each Gospel, and that by looking at the sociological factors hinted at in the text one can surmise the pastoral concerns that led to the final form. Thus the redaction critic elucidates not only the theological interests but also the ecclesiastical situation behind the editorial alterations. The portrayal of Jesus as the righteous martyr is said to be addressed to a church undergoing persecution, and the emphasis on worship presupposes a liturgical setting.

THE ORIGINS OF REDACTION CRITICISM

There were several precursors to Redaction Criticism, including Wilhelm Wrede's "messianic secret," Ned Stonehouse's study of the Christological emphases of the Synoptic Gospels, and R. H. Lightfoot's Bampton Lectures of 1934, which traced theological nuances in Mark's treatment of his sources.[6] In ways remarkably similar to the founding of Form Criticism in post-World War I Germany (via three scholars working independently—K. L. Schmidt, Martin Dibelius, and Rudolf Bultmann), Redaction Criticism began in post-World War II Germany with three scholars working independently— Gunther Bornkamm, Willi Marxsen, and Hans Conzelmann.

Bornkamm launched the movement with his 1948 article on "The Stilling of the Storm in Matthew," which was later combined with similar essays by two of his students in *Tradition and Interpretation in Matthew*.[7] By comparing Matthew 8:23–27 with Mark 4:35–41, Bornkamm argued that Matthew not only altered but reinterpreted the stilling of the storm scene in the direction of discipleship. While in Mark the miracle is predominant, for Bornkamm the central element in Matthew is the "little faith" of the disciples, which designates the difficult journey of the "little ship of the church." Thus Bornkamm concludes, "Matthew is not only a hander-on of the narrative, but also its oldest exegete."[8] In a 1954 article entitled "End-Expectation and Church in Matthew,"[9] Bornkamm expands his horizons to consider Matthew's Gospel as a whole, stating that for Matthew ecclesiology must be understood via eschatology; the church defines itself and its mission on the basis of the coming judgment that applies to believers as well as unbelievers. For instance, John the Baptist, with his message "Repent for the kingdom of heaven is at hand" (3:2, 4:17), becomes a proclaimer of the Christian gospel by anticipating Jesus' denunciation of false teachers in 3:2 and 7:15–23 (both messages for Matthew address the church in the "end times"). This article even more than the earlier one led to a flood of redaction-critical studies of Matthew, for it demonstrated the contribution that such an approach could make to an understanding of the theology of the first Gospel as a whole.

Hans Conzelmann first published his study of Luke in a 1952 article, "Zur Lukasanalyse,"[10] and later expanded it in 1954 into a monograph with the English title, *The Theology of St. Luke*.[11] Perrin writes, "If Gunther Bornkamm is the first of the true redaction critics, Hans Conzelmann is certainly the most important."[12] Conzelmann challenges the prevalent approach to Luke by arguing that he is self-consciously a theologian rather than a historian. Accepting the priority of Mark and studying Luke's editorial alterations of his Marcan source,[13] Conzelmann traces Luke's theological interests in a series of areas, beginning with geography and eschatology. The basic thesis is that the delay of the Parousia led Luke to replace the imminent eschatology of his predecessors with a salvation-historical framework centered upon a three-stage view of history: the time of Israel, which moved from the law and the prophets to John the Baptist; the time of Jesus, in which Satan is silent (4:13; 22:3) and salvation is present in "the center of time" (the original title of the book); and the time of the church, from the exaltation of Jesus to his return, characterized by persecution and temptation and overcome by the church as the messenger of salvation.

According to Conzelmann the central stage predominates, and in it eschatology reinterpreted as salvation history has caused Luke to redefine the ministry of Jesus. The kingdom has become a timeless entity, and the Parousia is no longer the focus. The brief interim of Mark has become an indefinite period, and the church is prepared by Jesus for a prolonged conflict in the world. Luke does this by positing three periods in Jesus' life and ministry: the ministry in Galilee (3:21–9:50), centering upon the gathering of the disciples; the travel narrative (9:51–19:27), in which the disciples are prepared for suffering; and the final events (19:28–23:49), in which suffering is actualized. In each section Jesus is seen as preparing the church to be the true Israel in the lengthy period before the final judgment.

Willi Marxsen in 1956 was the first to use the term *Redaktionsgeschichte* to describe the new movement, and the first and most influential portion of his *Mark the Evangelist*[14] is devoted to describing the differences between Form and Redaction Criticism. He argues that Form Criticism has missed a third *Sitz im Leben* behind the Gospels (in addition to the situation of Jesus and of the early church), namely that of the evangelist. In this way the Gospels are commentaries written backward in that they interpret the life of Jesus from the perspective of the evangelist and read each pericope or story from the standpoint of those episodes preceding it. Marxsen then applies this methodology to a study of Mark's Gospel, concluding that Mark emphasizes Galilee over Jerusalem due to the desperate situation of his community during the Jewish War of 66 A.D. Four separate but connected studies make up this second half of the book: John the Baptist, geography, the concept of "gospel," and Mark 13. His thesis is that, unlike Luke, Mark believed in an imminent Parousia, and his Gospel is a call to the church to flee the serious persecution and go to Galilee where the Parousia would occur. Details like the Baptist tradition or geographical references do not have independent historical value but function rather as theological pointers to Jesus and this message. Marxsen's thesis has been the least accepted of the three pioneers, but he was the first to develop a redaction critical methodology; and his introduction of the third *Sitz im Leben* has made a lasting contribution to the discipline.[15]

THE METHODOLOGY OF REDACTION CRITICISM

The challenge of Redaction Criticism is ascertaining with a fair degree of probability that one has discovered a redactional nuance. The discipline is prone to highly speculative theories because the conclusions depend entirely upon how one chooses and organizes the data. If the search is not complete and if the changes are not studied carefully, virtually opposite theories can be promulgated. For instance, Marxsen has argued that Mark was written to call Jewish Christians to the Parousia in Galilee, while Theodore Weeden has theorized that Mark wrote to confront a Hellenistic "divine-man" heresy by casting himself and his opponents in the form of a dramatic conflict between Jesus and his disciples. When Jesus is portrayed as castigating the disciples so thoroughly in Mark's Gospel, it is actually Mark castigating his opponents.[16] In both cases the evidence was not examined thoroughly, and few interpreters have followed either theory. Yet this sample demonstrates the necessity of a developed methodology to protect against such excesses.

The key to gospel research is a good Greek synopsis (Kurt Aland's *Synopsis* is the best). One begins by underlining the pericopes and noting which elements are found in one (Mark, M, or L source), two (Q, Mark and M against L, or Mark and L against M), three (the synoptics), or all four Gospels. When this step is completed the interpreter evaluates the data by utilizing tradition-critical, form-critical, and redaction-critical techniques.

TRADITION-CRITICAL ANALYSIS

The historical aspect is evaluated by applying the "criteria for authenticity" in order to determine the development of the tradition from Jesus through the early church to the evangelist. These criteria originated within Form Criticism but are universally accepted by redaction critics. For the most part they have been controlled by a "hermeneutics of suspicion" that places the burden of proof upon those who affirm the historicity of the pericope. Perrin says, "The burden of proof must lay on the claim to authenticity, and the difficulties of establishing that claim become very great—very great indeed but not impossible."[17] On the other hand, there has been a strong reaction to such implications, with many arguing that the text should be presumed innocent until proved guilty and that the burden should be upon the skeptic[18], while others assert that the scholar should at least be neutral and let the evidence decide.[19] I will organize the criteria somewhat historically, beginning with the "big three" mentioned in Perrin and Fuller and then proceeding loosely to others utilized by the critics.

Criterion of Dissimilarity. This is the most negative criterion. It assumes that whenever a saying can be paralleled in either Judaism or the early church it cannot be affirmed as authentic because it could have been derived from Jewish teaching or read back onto Jesus' lips by the early church. As such this criterion has come under severe criticism for its overly skeptical nature since it assumes that the historical Jesus had no ties with Judaism and no influence upon the church. But the kerygma hardly arose in a vacuum, and it is erroneous to shift the creative genius behind the Christian movement from Jesus to the early church. The resultant "critically assured minimum" ignores large amounts of authentic material.[20] Yet at the same time this criterion, when used positively (i.e., to authenticate rather than to disprove a pericope), does have value, for those passages that do meet the criterion are certainly trustworthy.[21]

Criterion of Multiple Attestation. Called the "cross-section method" by Fuller,[22] this criterion states that a saying (or pericope) is authentic if it is repeated in several or all of the primary sources behind the Gospels. For instance, if a saying is found in Mark, Q, M, L, and John it is considered a reliable tradition. Perrin uses this criterion to authenticate Jesus' concern for "tax collectors and sinners" (found in several of the sources), and Stein uses it to support the view that Jesus said that the kingdom of God was realized in his own person (Mk 2:21–22; Q = Lk 11:20; M = Mt 5:17; L = Lk 17:20–21; Jn 12:31).[23] Another version of this criterion asserts that if a saying appears in more than one form (e.g., parable, aphorism, or pronouncement story) it is verified.[24]

Criterion of Coherence. In actuality this criterion should be last, for it logically assumes that any pericope that is consistent or coheres with a passage already authenticated on the basis of the other criteria is itself acceptable. This means that such investigations do not have to be repeated whenever a saying or story is part of a larger pattern of sayings that have already been judged reliable. Of course, it is a secondary proof, for the passage depends for its validity upon the quality of argumentation used for the primary passage. Nevertheless, this criterion is widely accepted by scholars.

Criterion of Divergent Patterns. C. F. D. Moule has said, "It would appear that there are certain features in the story of Jesus, the retention of which can scarcely be explained except by their genuineness and durable quality, since everything else was hostile to their survival."[25] The well-known "pillar" sayings are an example, e.g., Mark 3:21 (Jesus' relatives think him insane), 10:18 ("Why do you call me good?"), or 13:32 (Jesus' ignorance regarding the coming of the end of the ages). Since these sayings are contrary to emphases of the early church, they at least were so firmly embedded in the tradition that the evangelist decided to include them.

Criterion of "Unintentional" Signs of History. When a story contains details that would suggest an eyewitness account and that demonstrate accurate knowledge of the environment surrounding the original event, it is more likely to be reliable. Mark and John have such details, and scholars have argued viably for their basic historicity. Of course, such could be simply the product of a good storyteller adding details to heighten the realism,[26] but when such Palestinian features and customs betray a real knowledge of the original scene, the details are less likely to be fictional additions and more likely to be authentic.

Criterion of Aramaic Linguistic Features. Joachim Jeremias and Matthew Black have especially stressed the presence of Aramaisms (since Jesus undoubtedly spoke Aramaic) as proof of authenticity. Jeremias for instance attempts to uncover an Aramaic original behind the Lord's Prayer as well as Aramaisms that prove the validity of Mark's account of the Lord's Supper.[27] Two basic criticisms have been leveled against this view: (1) Aramaic features could be the product of septuagintal influence, and (2) the presence of Semitic features demonstrates only that the saying stems from the Aramaic church—i.e., it does not prove that the saying comes from Jesus himself. Hence, while such criteria cannot "prove" that a saying or story is authentic, they do give it greater reliability and point to the probability of a valid tradition.

Criterion of Contradiction. Calvert and Stein[28] discuss the possibility that any saying or story that could not have occurred in the life of Jesus or that contradicts an existing authentic saying is invalid. The difficulty, of course, is in the application of this criterion. For instance, Matthew 22:7 (since the destruction and burning of the offending city could reflect a post-70 A.D. Gentile setting) and Mark 10:12 (since Jewish women could not divorce their husbands) are denied on these grounds. Yet the Matthew saying fits Old Testament and Near Eastern practices, and the Marcan divorce logion could actually stem from Herodias's divorce of her husband. Moreover, contradictions (e.g., Lk 14:26 on "hating" one's family vs. Lk 6:27 on honoring parents) are often such in appearance only. In short, this criterion could be valid only if such contradictions could be proved; however, the scholar must move with extreme caution lest such a "contradiction" exist more in the modern mind than in the ancient setting.

Tradition-critical analysis has more benefits than just anchoring stories in history. It also enables the scholar to detect how the traditions have been handled by the evangelists, and it provides the data for the form-critical and redaction-critical stages to follow. Nevertheless, demonstrating the reliability of the material is an important step in itself, for it anchors interpreters in history and helps them to realize they are not simply studying the ideas of Mark or Matthew (one danger of a redaction-critical approach) but the teachings of Jesus himself.

FORM-CRITICAL ANALYSIS

Before one can begin a detailed study of a pericope it is important to decide what form the story takes, e.g., pronouncement story (in which the details prepare for the climactic saying of Jesus); controversy narrative (similar to the pronouncement story but centering upon Jesus' conflict with the Jewish authorities); miracle story (of which there are several types, some centering upon discipleship, others upon Christology, still others upon cosmic conflict or the presence of the kingdom); dominical saying (short maxims, often without specific context; Bultmann further classifies these into wisdom logia, prophetic or apocalyptic sayings, legal sayings or church rules, "I" sayings, and similitudes); parable (often classified into similitudes or brief comparisons, example stories centering upon moral paradigms to be imitated, and one-, two-, or three-point parables depending upon the number of characters involved[29]); event or historical story (episodes in Jesus' life like the Baptism or Transfiguration—called "legends" by many form critics because of the predominance of the supernatural); and passion stories (considered a separate set of traditions though containing a variety of actual "forms").[30]

Identifying the form is important because each subgenre has its own set of hermeneutical principles to guide the interpreter.[31] For the scholar there are technical works on each of these formal types like pronouncement stories, miracles, or parables. In the final analysis the formal features help more in Composition Criticism than in Redaction Criticism, but these are two aspects of a larger whole, and therefore formal analysis is critical for a redactional understanding of the pericope.

REDACTION-CRITICAL ANALYSIS

This is the most detailed aspect and the one in which the Greek synopsis is the most critical. Each alteration of the source should be examined to see whether it is a redactional or stylistic change, i.e., whether the alteration has a theological purpose or is merely cosmetic, part of the evangelist's normal style. One complication is that Redaction Criticism is more easily done in Matthew and Luke (if one accepts Marcan priority) since identification of sources in Mark is highly speculative and since the Gospel of John is so independent of the Synoptics. Yet it is not impossible to analyze Mark and John in this way (though obviously the source-critical techniques do not readily apply). The following principles are intended to guide the student through the process as it applies to all four Gospels. There are two stages to the redaction-critical process: (1) the individual analysis of a single pericope, and (2) the holistic analysis of the entire Gospel. These are interdependent steps, for the material from the pericopes form the building blocks for the study of the whole, and the repetition of themes throughout the book is a critical control against an overzealous attempt to see every change as theologically motivated.

Individual Analysis. McKnight provides an excellent approach for underlining a pericope in the synopsis in order to delineate the particular emphases of each Gospel. There are six steps[32]: 1) Determine whether a true parallel exists; whether the accounts are independent (e.g., Mt 22:1–14 and Lk 14:16–24, which have few words in common and occur in separate places in the narrative); do not underline. 2) If the accounts are parallel, note those words that are not paralleled in the others (i.e., that are peculiar to that Gospel), and either do not underline them or underline them in brown. 3) Underline terms or phrases that are common to all three Synoptic Gospels in blue. 4) Where Mark and Matthew agree against Luke, underline in yellow or black. 5) Where Mark and Luke agree against Matthew, underline in green. 6) Material found in Matthew and Luke but not Mark (mostly Q sayings) should be underlined in red.[33] This procedure provides the raw data for the following analysis.

Noting the various relationships within the pericope on the basis of the underlining, the student evaluates the account from the standpoint of the evangelist and his sources. For Matthew and Luke steps two and six will tell the interpreter how each altered Mark or Q. By grouping the changes one can begin to see a pattern emerging and can detect certain theological nuances developing within the larger matrix of the story as a whole. For instance, Luke's version of the centurion's cry (23:47) says, "Surely, this man was innocent (*dikaios*)," while both Matthew and Mark have "Surely this was the Son of God." The alteration in Luke is in keeping with his stress throughout his passion narrative upon Jesus as the righteous martyr and is undoubtedly a redactional emphasis.[34]

Holistic Analysis. The preceding step is primarily utilized for Matthean and Lukan studies (for those who accept Marcan priority). The present step can be used in analyzing any of the four Gospels since it is not dependent upon a source-critical theory.[35] Here we would note again that the analysis of the individual pericopes become the building blocks for the larger study of the Gospel as a whole. Edgar McKnight calls this "the principle of comprehensiveness," quoting Schreiber: "All verses of Mark that are to be ascribed to the redaction of Mark with the help of the methods of analytical research provide the point of departure for establishing his theology, to the extent that in these verses scattered over the whole gospel a unified theological conception becomes visible."[36]

1) Study the Seams. The "seams" in a Gospel are the transitions (introductions and conclusions) that link episodes together and provide the setting and often the theological emphases for the passage. Since K. L. Schmidt's influential form-critical study of the Marcan seams[37], scholars have realized the importance of these units for critical research. One might note the synagogue ministry of Jesus in Mark 1:21 and

3:1, in which Jesus confronts the Jews via his authority in word and deed. Marcan Christology becomes apparent in the two seams by providing the setting for Jesus' ministry of confrontation.

2) Note the Summaries. Where an evangelist has summarized material, redactional emphases are particularly apparent. The recurrent themes of these passages provide clues to major theological overtones in the Gospel. One example might be Matthew 4:23 and 9:35, which are virtually identical in wording, which summarize Jesus' itinerant missionary activity, and which lead into the Sermon on the Mount and the Missionary Discourse respectively. The combination of teaching, preaching, and healing is a major theological emphasis of Matthew.[38"]

3) Note Editorial Asides and Insertions. Comments that are peculiar to a particular evangelist become invaluable guides to the direction the stories are taking. Mark often introduces such comments with *gar* ("for"), as in 1:16 ("for he was teaching them as one with authority, not like the scribes") or 2:15 ("for there were many like this [tax-collectors and sinners] who followed him"). In both instances the editorial aside points to the major emphasis of the passage. One of the better known examples is the series of editorial comments by John, as in 3:16–21, which is most likely the evangelist's commentary on the soteriological significance of the Nicodemus dialogue (3:1–15).[39]

4) Note Repeated or Favorite Words/Phrases. The repetition of a word or phrase is indicative of emphasis and functions at both the micro- (individual pericope) and macro- (whole Gospel) levels. For instance, in the healing of the demon-possessed child in Mark 9:14–29 the attempt of the demon to destroy the child is repeated four times (vv. 18, 20, 22, 26, none of which are found in the Matthean parallel [17:14–21]). Obviously Mark wants the reader to note the cosmic conflict taking place (a major Marcan theme). John, of course, is the master of this technique. Every term he favors is found nearly as often in his Gospel as in the rest of the New Testament together: *pisteuein* (ninety-eight times in John versus thirty-four total in the other Gospels); *zōē* (sixty-six of the 135 New Testament uses); *kosmos* (105 of the 185 New Testament uses); *alētheia* (eighty-five of the 163 New Testament uses). Each term is also a primary source of Johannine theology.

COMPOSITION-CRITICAL ANALYSIS

The task of delineating the theology of the evangelist is incomplete if one considers only the redactional changes, for the evangelist obviously intended that the tradition he decided to include be part of his theological message as well. This step reverses the tradition-critical approach above; instead of removing the tradition in order to identify the redactional changes, we now study the tradition as well as redaction to see how the whole fits together to produce the theological message. Here Redaction Criticism shades over into Literary or Narrative Criticism, for the interpreter now looks at the whole product as the source of theological emphases.[40]

Note the Structure. Rearrangement of the inherited tradition usually points to theological emphases. For instance, in the temptation narrative, Matthew (4:5–10) and Luke (4:5–12) reverse the order of the last two temptations, Matthew ending with the mountaintop temptation and Luke with the temple temptation. Most believe that Matthew has preserved the original order and that Luke places the temple scene last in order to conclude with Jesus at the temple in Jerusalem (a major thrust in Luke-Acts), although it could also be true that Matthew decided to conclude with a mountain scene (cf. Mt 5:1; 8:1; 14:23; 15:29; 17:1). Rearrangement may also occur at the macro-level. Mark and Luke do different things with Jesus' early Capernaum-based ministry. Mark places the call of the disciples at the beginning (1:16–20) in order to focus at the start on the issue of discipleship and only then goes into the Capernaum ministry, reserving the rejection at Nazareth for 6:1–6. Luke, however, starts with Jesus' inaugural address and rejection at Nazareth (4:16–30), reserving the call of the disciples for 5:1–11. Thus Luke begins with Christology rather than discipleship.

Study Intertextual Development. As the gospel narrative unfolds, the evangelist arranges his stories so that they interact with one another to produce the intended message. A primary maxim of Narrative Criticism is that this intertextual arrangement is not haphazard. In fact, intertextuality at the macro-level is the literary counterpart of Redaction Criticism at the macro-level, for the writer uses the same principles of selection, omission, and expansion to develop the narrative as a whole. This can be seen, for instance, in the strategic placement of the pericope of the healing of the blind man in Mark 8:22–26 (found only in Mark). At one level the pericope forms an inclusion with the healing of the deaf man in 7:31–37, thus framing the feeding of the four thousand and discipleship failure scenes (8:1–21) and stressing the need for spiritual healing on the part of the disciples. On a second level, as a two-stage miracle it leads into the two-stage healing of the disciples' misunderstanding via Peter's confession at Caesarea Philippi (8:27–33, in which Peter metaphorically sees Jesus' messianic status in "blurred" fashion) and the transfiguration (9:1–10, in which the disciples glimpse the true nature of Jesus). In this sense the miracle of 8:22–26 links together the discipleship emphases of Mark's middle section.

Study the Plot. This also is done at both the micro- and macro-levels. Plot refers to an interconnected sequence of events that centers on conflict and follows a cause-effect order. In studying plot we note the lines of causality, that is, how the characters interact and how the interplay of opposing forces builds to a climax. To discover this we chart the actantial units (the individual events and actions) and study the ebb and flow of the story line. Within Redaction Criticism the key is to compare the differing plots of the evangelists in order to determine their distinctive approaches and theological purposes in writing. The differences are often striking. Consider the resurrection narratives as an example. Mark has a linear flow centering upon discipleship failure and concluding with the women's failure to witness in 16:8; this is countered by Jesus' enigmatic promise to meet them in Galilee (14:28; 16:7), where they apparently will be reinstated (14:28 following v. 27). Matthew, on the other hand, centers upon the power of God overcoming the double attempt by the priests to thwart his ordained purpose (27:62–66; 27:11–15) via supernatural intervention (28:2–4) and by the universal authority of the Son passed on to the church in mission (28:18–20).[41]

Note the Setting and Style. These are also redactional peculiarities that enable the scholar to detect the theological message of the evangelist. The setting is the textual context within which the action occurs. As Rhoads and Michie state, this setting can have several functions: "generating atmosphere, determining conflict, revealing traits in the characters who must deal with problems or threats caused by the settings, offering commentary (sometimes ironic) on the action, and evoking associations and nuances of meaning present in the culture of the readers."[42] The evangelists, by giving the same or similar episode a different setting, can evoke various nuances of meaning. For instance, the parable of the lost sheep in Matthew is delivered to the disciples and church (18:12–14) and apparently refers to "straying" members, while in Luke 15:3–7 it is addressed to the Pharisees and scribes and refers to those outside the kingdom.[43] Style refers to the way the material has been arranged in the individual Gospels. There can be inclusio or chiasm, repetition, gaps, or omissions that draw the reader into the story in order to complete its meaning, antitheses, irony, or poetic parallelism. All these stylistic devices are utilized by the authors and should be carefully scrutinized by the reader as important clues to the theological message.

DANGERS OF REDACTION CRITICISM

Redaction Criticism has found a firm place in the list of hermeneutical tools, but by no means has it won universal acceptance. Evangelical and non-evangelical scholars alike have criticized its excesses, and some have argued that it should be discarded as an unworkable tool. The major problems must be considered carefully before we can evaluate its usefulness.

Dependence on the Four-Document Hypothesis. This is primarily a problem for those who doubt the Streeter solution accepted above. It is true that the issue of sources will never be settled with certainty, but it is also a fact that anyone studying the Gospels seriously must adopt some theory regarding the relationship between these Gospels, and the four-document hypothesis is clearly the best of the alternatives (see McKnight's article in this volume). Therefore we can proceed with confidence that Marcan priority is basically correct.

Historical Skepticism. Many critics proceed with the assumption that every redactional change is by definition a creation and thus cannot be historical. Yet this is a presupposition and by no means carries the day. Addition and omission are not criteria for historicity, but for style, selection, and emphasis. As Caird says, "Redaction criticism treat[s] the evangelists as interpreters, but all too often with the tacit assumption that to interpret is to misinterpret. Considering that they are themselves professional interpreters, it might seem wiser to allow for the possibility that an interpreter should occasionally be right."[44] Some evangelists have argued that this skepticism is inherent in the tool itself and that Redaction Criticism should therefore be discarded[45] This pessimism is as unwarranted as is the historical skepticism above. Anti-historical tendencies are not inherent in redaction critical methodology, and many studies have proceeded with a positive outlook toward the historicity of the pericopes.[46]

Rejection of Harmonization. Due to the excesses of some who answer all historical discrepancies by shallow harmonization, modern critics have too often refused any attempt to harmonize accounts. At the same time these scholars assume that any sayings, parables, or stories that are somewhat similar are variations of the same account, and their so-called "contradictions" are often just as shallow as the aforementioned harmonizations. Jesus was certainly an itinerant preacher/teacher who used variations of the same story or saying on more than one occasion, and it is often erroneous to assume that one is "more authentic" than the other.[47]

Tendency toward Fragmentation. Form criticism with its assumption that each pericope was an independent unit was certainly more guilty of fragmenting rather than unifying the Gospels, but Redaction Criticism has a similar problem when it studies only the additions to the tradition. Many have called this the "disintegration" process, and McKnight labels it the "problem of interpretative priority"[48] since the critic seeks meaning in the redaction rather than the tradition. The movement toward Composition Criticism has provided a good solution from within this school. Scholars now realize that theology comes from the pericope as a whole and not just from the alterations.

Overstatement. Many proponents of Redaction Criticism assume that every jot and tittle of the author's changes carries theological weight. They seem to forget that many changes are stylistic rather than theological and that the evangelists were often paraphrasing rather than quoting their sources verbatim. Again, Composition Criticism provides a corrective, for it demands that theological emphases be part of a larger pattern rather than be read into every individual change.

Subjectivism. The bewildering multiplicity of theories coming from redactional studies belies any pretence that the method leads to assured results. Carson goes so far as to claim that "the tools are incapable of providing an entirely neutral and agreed judgment as to what is authentic."[49] There is a great deal of truth to this charge, for each scholar seems to produce different results from the same data, results that suspiciously resemble the thesis with which the scholar began! This tendency is counteracted only by a judicious use of *all* the hermeneutical tools mentioned above in such a way that they challenge and correct excesses.

The Speculative Nature of "Sitz im Leben" Determinations. The preoccupation of many with the situation behind the evangelist's redactional changes provides probably the best evidence for the subjective nature of the whole enterprise. Attempts to describe the church behind Matthew's Gospel as Gentile or upper middle class or Jewish have established little except the academic morass behind such attempts. In fact, there is an implicit negativism within such an enterprise, for it assumes that redactional emphases are always due to problems in the evangelist's church and ignores the fact that many of the changes are the result of Christological or worship or historical interests. The solution is to recognize that the true place of a life-situation approach lies not in the speculative reconstruction of the church behind a Gospel but in the delineation of the evangelist's message to that church.

THE VALUE AND PLACE OF REDACTION CRITICISM

One could assume from these difficulties that Redaction Criticism is more trouble than it is worth. Such would be an unfortunate mistake. A careful methodology can remove or control most of these potential problems, and the values far outweigh the dangers. In fact, I would go so far as to say that any responsible study of the Gospels must proceed from a redaction- (and literary-) critical perspective. It can be claimed with virtual certainty that the Gospel writers were led by God to utilize sources in the production of their Gospels. Moreover, these sources (most likely Mark and Q behind Matthew and Luke as well as the special sources M and L) can be detected and should be utilized in any attempt to understand the Gospels more deeply. At the same time, the message is found in the pericope as a whole and not just in the redactional changes so the next step is to trace the message through a combination of tradition and redaction in the unified story and finally through the Gospel as a whole.

The values of such an approach are obvious. Redaction Criticism enables us to understand as never before how the process of inspiration took place in the production of the Gospels. Heretofore the authors of every book of the Bible were regarded as inspired, but the authors of the Gospels were ignored because these books contained the stories of Jesus. Now we can see how God inspired the evangelists to select, highlight, and emphasize certain aspects of the life of Jesus in order to speak to their readers. For the first time these writings have actually become "gospels," not just biographical accounts but "history with a message." These inspired authors did not just chronicle historical events but produced historical sermons, as God inspired the evangelists to take virtually the same set of stories and weave out of them individual tapestries of theological truth.

Until this school developed, most of us turned to the Epistles for theology because they were the didactic tools of the early church. Redactional studies have demonstrated that the Gospels are also theological; and in many ways this theology is even more exciting than that stemming from the Epistles, for it is presented through living relationships and enacted in dynamic events, thus producing a sort of case study workbook for theological understanding. In other words, the Gospels are not just theology taught but theology lived. As a result we have an exciting "new" source for the relevant presentation of God's truths.

Redaction Criticism enables the modern interpreter to reconstruct the theology of each evangelist by detecting how he used his sources to produce that intended message. While the theology comes out of the unified (tradition and redaction) product, redactional analysis provides a control that leads to greater precision and less subjectivism in uncovering the intended message. By itself, of course, a new subjectivism could arise, exemplified in those early studies (e.g., Conzelmann or Marxsen) that drew erroneous conclusions by studying only part of the evidence. However, composition analysis interacts with Redaction Criticism in such a way that the whole and the parts correct one another, with the redactional study providing the data and the compositional study analyzing it all together before making final conclusions.

Furthermore, the reader can appreciate the two-fold thrust of the Gospels better: they present the events and sayings of the historical Jesus (the historical component) in such a way that the stories speak to the church (the kerygmatic component). We dare not forget that the life and teachings of the historical Jesus are also an assured result of the study of the Gospels. We cannot trace with certainty the "footsteps of Jesus," since no Gospel gives a chronological (i.e., day by day or even month by month) account of Jesus' ministry; and we can seldom detect the *ipsissima verba* (exact words) of Jesus. But we can know the broad contours of his life and certainly the *ipsissima vox* (exact understanding) of his teaching.[50] In short, the Gospels are historical records that tell us about Jesus and about his life and teachings. While Redaction Criticism as a discipline centers upon the theological aspect, it does not neglect the historical factor. By its very nature it studies only the diverse theologies of the four evangelists, and in fact this diversity is what God inspired. However, it is valid and in some ways obligatory for us to put these diverse accounts together to produce a unified account of the life and teachings of Jesus,[51] so long as we recognize that we cannot do so with precision. For instance, we cannot harmonize the chronologies of John and the Synoptics in such a way as to know the precise order of events in Jesus' life, but we can know the broad contours, and that is sufficient. The way we must do this is not to ignore the results of Redaction Criticism but to work with them by harmonizing the diverse accounts and theologies of the separate Gospels into a unified record of Jesus' life and teaching.

Finally, Redaction Criticism is a preaching and not just an academic tool. When we contextualize the Gospels for our contemporary audiences, we must realize that the evangelists have already done so; they contextualized the life of Jesus for their own churches and thus provided a model to guide our own homiletical process. The Gospels have been shown to be inspired sermons ("gospel" means "a good news sermon") using the person and impact of Jesus upon three groups (the disciples, the crowds, and the Jewish leaders) to speak to their own contemporary world (evangelism) and church (exhortation). Therefore it is in keeping with the very nature of the Gospels to use them as a source for preaching. It is here that the true value of the *Sitz im Leben* (life-situation) approach to the Gospels can be found, not in determining the exact nature of the church behind, say, Matthew's Gospel, but in discovering Matthew's message to that church. As Stein says, "If one attributes divine authority to the Evangelists, we often possess not only a divine word from Jesus himself, but an authoritative interpretation of that word. We are doubly enriched in such instances."[52] In fact, one could argue that the true intention of the Gospels is incomplete until they are indeed preached. The true goal of hermeneutics is not so much the learned monograph as it is the sermon. The gospel (and Gospels) is not just the good news probed but the good news proclaimed.

Redaction Criticism is not an end in itself. It must be utilized along with other hermeneutical tools if it is to be effective. For instance, it should not be done without the historical-grammatical exegesis of the text itself, for exegesis will yield that detailed understanding of the pericope that Redaction Criticism by itself can never provide. On the other hand, redactional study will deepen one's knowledge regarding the evangelists' emphases. In other words, the two work together in the study of biblical narrative. Background study is another essential, for this draws the interpreter back into the historical dimensions of the text and protects the scholar from reading the story with a twentieth-century literary bias. When Redaction Criticism is placed within this larger hermeneutical paradigm, it is not only a valuable but an essential tool for understanding the God-inspired meaning that each evangelist gave to the story of Jesus the Christ in his Gospel.

BIBLIOGRAPHY

Bornkamm, G., G. Barth and H. J. Held. *Tradition and Interpretation in Matthew*. Philadelphia: Westminster, 1963.

Conzelmann, Hans. *The Theology of St. Luke*. New York: Harper, 1961.

Marshall, I. Howard. *Luke: Historian and Theologian*. Grand Rapids: Zondervan, 1971.

Marxsen, W. *Mark the Evangelist: Studies on the Redaction History of the Gospel*. Nashville: Abingdon, 1969.

Osborne, Grant. *The Resurrection Narratives: A Redaction Study*. Grand Rapids: Baker, 1984.

Perrin, Norman. *What Is Redaction Criticism?* Philadelphia: Fortress, 1970.

Stein R. H. "What Is Redaktionsgeschichte?" *Journal of Biblical Literature* 88 (1969): 45–56.

NOTES

[1]One should note here that in neither Form nor Redaction Criticism is Jesus the creative force. Both assume the negative results of Tradition Criticism, which concludes that the historical Jesus is an elusive presence in the Gospels.

[2]See the chapter "Source Criticism" in this volume. Robert H. Stein, *The Synoptic Problem: An Introduction* (Grand Rapids: Baker, 1987), 143, calls Source Criticism "the single most important tool of the redaction critic" because the changes that the evangelists chose to introduce into their sources guide the interpreter to their theological interests (see pp. 143–51).

[3]This has been challenged in recent years by the Griesbach Hypothesis, rejuvenated recently by Farmer and Orchard and arguing for Matthean priority. As McKnight shows above in his article on source criticism, however, this has far more problems than does the four-document hypothesis presented here.

[4]See the fine discussion of this in E. P. Sanders and Margaret Davies, *Studying the Synoptic Gospels* (Philadelphia: Trinity Press International, 1989), 201–02. They state that Redaction Criticism began when Bultmann's disciples reworked the final section of his *History of the Synoptic Tradition*, entitled "The Editing (*Redaktion*) of the Traditional Material."

[5]Scot McKnight, *Interpreting the Synoptic Gospels* (Grand Rapids: Baker, 1988), 85, notes the developing interest of the critics as they move "from minute alterations unique to an evangelist as compared with his inherited traditions to larger patterns (including literary strategies)." There are three successive stages: the process moves from (1) the detection of individual changes to (2) the discovery of patterns that indicate theological interest and finally to (3) noting the overall literary strategy of the author that led to those alterations. These three levels are obviously interdependent.

[6]Wilhelm Wrede, *The Messianic Secret*, trans. J. C. G. Greig (Cambridge: James Clarke, 1971, originally 1901); Ned B. Stonehouse, *The Witness of the Synoptic Gospels to Christ* (Grand Rapids: Baker, 1979, originally 1951); and R. H. Lightfoot, *History and Interpretation in the Gospels* (New York: Harper, n.d.). On the history of Redaction Criticism see also Norman Perrin, *What Is Redaction Criticism?* (Philadelphia: Fortress, 1969), 7–13, 21–24; McKnight, *Interpreting*, 87; and Moisés Silva, "Ned B. Stonehouse and Redaction Criticism, Part 1: The Witness of the Synoptic Evangelists to Christ," *Westminster Theological Journal* 40 (1977): 77–88.

[7]Gunther Bornkamm, Gerhard Barth, and H. J. Held, *Tradition and Interpretation in Matthew*, trans. P. Scott (Philadelphia: Westminster, 1963).

[8]Bornkamm, *Tradition*, 55. Joachim Rohde, *Rediscovering the Teaching of the Evangelists*, trans. D. M. Barton (Philadelphia: Westminster, 1968), 13, summarizes Bornkamm's conclusions: "By its connection with the sayings about discipleship, the stilling of the storm has become *kerygma* and a paradigm of the danger and glory of discipleship."

[9]Originally presented at a conference in 1954 under the title, "Matthew as Interpreter of the Words of the Lord" but expanded into the form found in *Tradition and Interpretation*, 15–51. There are four parts to the article dealing with eschatology, the law, Christology, and ecclesiology.

[10]Hans Conzelmann, "Zur Lukasanalyse," *Zeitschrift für Theologie und Kirche* 49 (1952): 16–33.

[11]Hans Conzelmann, *The Theology of St. Luke*, trans. G. Buswell (New York: Harper, 1960, German 1954).

[12]Perrin, *Redaction Criticism*, 28. Perrin believes that Conzelmann's work ranks with Bultmann's *History of the Synoptic Tradition* and Jeremias' *The Parables of Jesus* as one of the most important New Testament studies of our time.

[13]Conzelmann speaks of Luke's "critical attitude to tradition" as seen in his "positive formation of a new picture of history out of those already current, like stones used as parts of a new mosaic" (*Theology*, 12).

[14]Willi Marxsen, *Mark the Evangelist: Studies on the Redaction History of the Gospel*, trans. J. Boyce, D. Juel, W. Poehlmann, and R. A. Harrisville (New York: Abingdon, 1969, German 1956).

[15]For others who have utilized Redaction Criticism see Rohde, *Rediscovering, passim*; and for an updated discussion see Edgar V. McKnight, "Form and Redaction Criticism," in *The New Testament and Its Modern Interpreters*, ed. Eldon J. Epp and George W. McRae (Philadelphia: Fortress, 1989), 157–63.

[16]Theodore J. Weeden, *Mark—Traditions in Conflict* (Philadelphia: Fortress, 1971).

[17]Perrin, *Redaction Criticism*, 79.

[18]See Stewart C. Goetz and Craig L. Blomberg, "The Burden of Proof," *Journal for the Study of the New Testament* 11 (1981): 39–63; Grant R. Osborne, *The Resurrection Narratives: A Redactional Study* (Grand Rapids: Baker, 1984), 195–96.

[19]See Morna Hooker, "Christology and Methodology," *New Testament Studies* 17 (1970–71): 485. While accepting the reliability of the tradition, R. T. France, "The Authenticity of the Sayings of Jesus," *History, Criticism, and Faith*, ed. Colin Brown (Downers Grove, Ill.: InterVarsity, 1977), 117, says of the negative and positive burdens of proof that "both views are assumptions" and that "what we must both do is to examine our assumptions in the light of the available evidence." On the other hand, scholars on both sides are skeptical of

the viability of any such "neutral" position. See from the skeptical side E. P. Sanders, *Jesus and Judaism* (Philadelphia: Fortress, 1985), 13–14; from the positive side see Craig L. Blomberg, *The Historical Reliability of the Gospels* (Downers Grove, Ill.: InterVarsity, 1987), 241–42. Both believe that it is necessary to take a studied position while remaining open to the evidence.

[20]See Morna Hooker, "On Using the Wrong Tool," *Theology* 75 (1972): 570–81; and her "Christology," 481-85; cf. R. S. Barbour, *Traditio-Historical Criticism of the Gospels* (London: SPCK, 1972), 19–22.

[21]See Grant R. Osborne, "The Evangelical and Traditionsgeschichte," *Journal of the Evangelical Theological Society* 21/2 (1978): 122–23; and Robert H. Stein, "The 'Criteria' for Authenticity," *Gospel Perspectives*, vol. 1, ed. R. T. France and David Wenham (Sheffield: JSOT, 1980), 244–45.

[22]Reginald H. Fuller, *The Foundations of New Testament Christology* (New York: Scribner's, 1965), 96–97.

[23]Perrin, *Redaction Criticism*, 71; Stein, "Authenticity," 230.

[24]See Stein, "Authenticity," 232–33, who considers this a separate criterion ("of multiple forms"). However, it is so closely connected with the source-critical form that the two become one. Moreover, in most instances the two blend into a single criterion, as in the realized kingdom passages above that take the form of aphorisms or sayings (Mt 5:17; Jn 12:31), pronouncement stories (Mk 2:18–22; Lk 11:14–22), and parables (Mt 25).

[25]C. F. D. Moule, *The Phenomenon of the New Testament* (London: SCM, 1967), 62–63. See also Richard N. Longenecker, "Literary Criteria in the Life of Jesus Research," *Current Issues in Biblical and Patristic Interpretation*, ed. G. F. Hawthorne (Grand Rapids: Eerdmans, 1975), 227–28. R. S. A. Calvert, "An Examination of the Criteria for Distinguishing the Authentic Words of Jesus," *New Testament Studies* 18 (1972): 215; and Stein, "Authenticity," 247, extend this to material that does not fit the evangelist's purposes—for instance, positive statements about the disciples in Mark (contrary to Mark's stress on discipleship failure) or Matthew 11:13, "the prophets and the law prophesied until John" (contrary to Matthew's emphasis on the permanence of the law).

[26]So Hugh Anderson, *The Gospel of Mark* (London: Oliphants, 1976), 22.

[27]Joachim Jeremias, *New Testament Theology*, trans. J. Bowden (New York: Scribner's, 1971), 193-96, 288–92.

[28]Calvert, "Criteria," 212-13; Stein, "Authenticity," 248–50.

[29]See the excellent discussion in Craig L. Blomberg, *Interpreting the Parables* (Downers Grove, Ill.: InterVarsity, 1990).

[30]See the chapter on Form Criticism in this volume and the summary in McKnight, *Synoptic*, 74–76.

[31]For the best work on genre analysis from a practical perspective, see Gordon D. Fee and Douglas Stuart, *How to Read the Bible for All It's Worth* (Grand Rapids: Zondervan, 1981), especially chapters 7–8 on gospel and parable.

[32]McKnight, *Synoptic*, 41–44. He builds upon similar suggestions in Farmer (*Synopticon*) and Stein (*Synoptic Problem*). The colors mentioned are suggested by all three authors.

[33]These steps are directed only to the Synoptics and take no account of John. McKnight suggests highlighting agreements with John in yellow (if black is used for step four). While this does not indicate which Gospel John agrees with, a simple look across the synopsis will quickly provide that information.

[34]Luke also adds that the centurion was "stricken with awe before God," which adds an atmosphere of worship to the scene (the other Lukan emphasis in his crucifixion narrative).

[35]The following material is dependent largely upon Grant R. Osborne, "The Evangelical and Redaction Criticism: Critique and Methodology," *Journal of the Evangelical Theological Society* 22/4 (1979): 316–18; and Stein, *Synoptic Problem*, 251–58.

[36]McKnight, "Form and Redaction," 163, quoting Johannes Schreiber, "Die Christologie des Markusevangeliums: Beobachtungen zur Theologie und Komposition des zweiten Evangeliums," *Zeitschrift für Theologie und Kirche* 58 (1961), 154.

[37]Karl Ludwig Schmidt, *Der Rahmen der Geschichte Jesu: Literarkritische Untersuchungen zur ältesten Jesusüberlieferung* (Berlin: Trowitzsch und Sohn, 1919). Schmidt was another precursor of Redaction Criticism. He presupposed that the seams were non-historical and purely theological. Recently, however, studies in Audience Criticism among other disciplines have shown that the seams blend tradition and redaction.

[38]For a more detailed discussion of Matthean theological emphases, see D. A. Carson, "Matthew," *The Expositor's Bible Commentary, vol. 8*, ed. Frank E. Gaebelein (Grand Rapids: Zondervan, 1984), 120–21. For other Matthean summaries, see 7:28–29; 11:1; 15:30–31; for Marcan summaries, see 1:14–15, 28, 39; 2:13; 3:7–12; 6:53–56; 9:30–32; 10:32–34.

[39]See Merrill F. Tenney, "The Footnotes of John's Gospel," *Bibliothecra Sacra* 117 (1960): 350–64.

[40]McKnight, *Synoptic*, 135, goes so far as to say that "much of the good in literary criticism has already been exposed through redaction criticism in its 'composition criticism' emphases." While this is overstated, there is some truth in it, for composition criticism utilizes many of the tools (though not such perspectives as plot, characterization, or intended author). For an introduction to literary criticism, see R. A. Culpepper, *Anatomy of the Fourth Gospel* (Philadelphia: Fortress, 1983); and Rhoads and Michie (note 42). For an evangelical response,

see Tremper Longman III, *Literary Approaches to Biblical Interpretation* (Zondervan, 1987).

[41]For details on these and the other resurrection narratives, see my *Resurrection Narratives, passim.*

[42]David Rhoads and Donald Michie, *Mark as Story: An Introduction to the Narrative of a Gospel* (Philadelphia: Fortress, 1982), 63.

[43]See the excellent discussion in Stein, *Synoptic Problem*, 247-51, who argues strongly for the parable's historical veracity whether it was spoken on one occasion by Jesus or two. Stein and Blomberg, *Parables*, 83, prefer to see it as more likely a single parable placed in different settings "due to the amount of verbal and conceptual parallelism" (Blomberg), while Carson, "Matthew," 400, argues that it was a similar parable delivered by Jesus on two occasions because the parallels "are well within the bounds of repetition expected in an itinerant ministry." Either way, biblical authority is upheld.

[44]George B. Caird, "Study of the Gospels. III. Redaction Criticism," *Expository Times* 87 (1976): 172.

[45]See John Warwick Montgomery, "Why Has God Incarnate Suddenly Become Mythical?" in *Perspectives on Evangelical Theology*, ed. K. Kantzer and S. N. Gundry (Grand Rapids: Baker, 1979), 57–65; and Robert L. Thomas, "The Hermeneutics of Evangelical Redaction Criticism," *Journal of the Evangelical Theological Society* 29/4 (1986): 447–59.

[46]For articles chronicling this debate but with a more positive assessment of the discipline, see David L. Turner, "Evangelicals, Redaction Criticism, and the Current Inerrancy Crisis," *Grace Theological Journal* 4 (1983): 263–88; *idem*, "Evangelicals, Redaction Criticism and Inerrancy: The Debate Continues," *Grace Theological Journal* 5 (1984): 37–45; and Grant R. Osborne, "Round Four: The Redaction Debate Continues," *Journal of the Evangelical Theological Society* 28/4 (1985): 399–410.

[47]An excellent and balanced introduction to harmonization can be found in Craig L. Blomberg, "The Legitimacy and Limits of Harmonization," in *Hermeneutics, Authority, and Canon*, ed. D. A. Carson and John D. Woodbridge (Grand Rapids: Zondervan, 1986), 139–74.

[48]McKnight, *Synoptic*, 90.

[49]D. A. Carson, "Redaction Criticism: On the Legitimacy and Illegitimacy of a Literary Tool," in *Scripture and Truth*, ed. D. A. Carson and John D. Woodbridge (Grand Rapids: Zondervan, 1983), 126. He quotes Hooker, "Wrong Tool," 577: "Of course, NT scholars recognize the inadequacy of their tools; when different people look at the same passage, and all get different answers, the inadequacy is obvious, even to NT scholars! But they do not draw the logical deduction from this fact."

[50]Paul Feinberg, "The Meaning of Inerrancy," in *Inerrancy*, ed. Norman L. Geisler (Grand Rapids: Zondervan, 1979), 301, says,

"Inerrancy does not demand that the logia Jesu (the sayings of Jesus) contain the ipsissima verba (the exact words) of Jesus, only the ipsissima vox (the exact voice). . . .When a New Testament writer cites the sayings of Jesus, it need not be the case that Jesus said those exact words. Undoubtedly, the exact words of Jesus are to be found in the New Testament, but they need not be so in every instance. . . . With regard to the sayings of Jesus, what would count against inerrancy? The words in the sense of *ipsissima vox* were not uttered by Jesus, or the *ipsissima verba* were spoken by our Lord but so used by the writer that the meaning given by the writer is inconsistent with the intended meaning of Jesus" (italics his).

[51]A good book in this respect is Robert H. Stein, *The Method and Message of Jesus' Teachings* (Philadelphia: Westminster, 1978).

[52]Stein, *Synoptic Problem*, 270. See also Grant R. Osborne, "Preaching the Gospels: Methodology and Contextualization," *Journal of the Evangelical Theological Society* 27/1 (1984): 27–42.

Chapter Eight

Literary Criticism

Aída Besançon Spencer

Aída Besançon Spencer

Aída Besançon Spencer is Associate Professor of New Testament at Gordon-Conwell Theological Seminary in South Hamilton, Massachusetts. She earned the B.A. from Douglass College, the M.Div. and Th.M. from Princeton Theological Seminary, and the Ph.D. from Southern Baptist Theological Seminary. In 1989 she served as Visiting Scholar at Harvard Divinity School. Her articles have appeared in such journals as *Novum Testamentum, Journal of the Evangelical Theological Society, Daughters of Sarah*, and *Journal of Biblical Literature*. She has also written *Paul's Literary Style* (Eisenbrauns), *Beyond the Curse: Women Called to Ministry* (Nelson), and *2 Corinthians* (Zondervan).

Chapter Eight

Literary Criticism

The apostle Paul summarizes his letter to the Philippians with the well-quoted sentence:

> Finally, brothers, everything that is true, everything honorable, everything just, everything pure, everything pleasing, everything auspicious, if anything virtuous and if anything praiseworthy, these things consider; whatever also you learned and received and heard and saw in me, these things do; and the God of peace will be with you (4:8–9).

Dwelling on and doing these things will help the Philippians stand firm in the gospel in one spirit. Paul could have greatly decreased his word count and economized on his papyri by shortening this lengthy sentence (forty-six Greek words) to be briefer and more to the point: "If you think about moral matters and imitate me, God will be present among you and make you tranquil" (nineteen English words rather than the fifty words in the above translation; fifty-seven words NIV; fifty-eight words RSV; sixty-eight words KJV). Or, "Think about good things, imitate me, and God will be with you" (a snappy twelve words!).

Many Bible-as-Literature students have noticed and appreciated that the Bible writers have not simply stated commands without any concern for style or the manner of communication.[1] Because of his concern for style, Paul's words are much more powerful than any of these shortened sentences. Even if we as readers do not have any conscious awareness of style, we can still feel its effect. In this one brief sentence, part of a longer letter, Paul uses several figures of speech: anaphora (the repetition of the word "everything" at the beginning of four clauses), ellipsis (the omission of the verb "is" seven times), polysyndeton (the repetition of "and" three times), and periodic sentences (holding the main verbs "consider" and "do" to the end of their clauses).

What literary techniques does Paul use? And what effect do they have? These are the questions of literary criticism, which analyzes the style of something written. It is concerned with the aesthetic effects of language. Style concerns the choices (conscious or subconscious) an author makes among linguistic possibilities (not necessarily grammatical possibilities). Why should students of the Bible study the style of communication? How has style been studied? What is literary criticism? Finally, what are some contemporary examples of literary studies done in the New Testament? These four questions will be explored in this chapter.

WHY STUDY STYLE?

Analyzing Style Can Help the Reader Understand the Message Being Communicated

If someone were to tell us to think about moral and beautiful matters, we might agree: "Yes, that is a good idea." However, if that person were to tell us in a way that itself was moral and beautiful, then the very *means* of communication would reinforce the message being communicated. Whether the style mirrors the content or even clashes with the content adds to the total communication. Attention to style helps the reader understand more accurately and more precisely what the writer wants the reader to know. In Philippians 4:8–9, Paul reinforces his command to dwell on beautiful things by stating it in a beautiful way. Paul reinforces his message by having us dwell on the qualities themselves even before we know what we are supposed to do. By omitting the verb "to be" in the first clause he is then able to repeat seven moral and beautiful qualities: true, honorable, just, pure, pleasing, auspicious, virtuous, praiseworthy. The reader does not get bogged down in "is"s, but is enabled to focus on the qualities themselves. On the other hand, by repeating "everything" at the beginning of each subordinate clause, Paul creates a marked rhythm building up to his main clause: "these things—consider."

If we were to visualize these figures of speech, the first part of Paul's sentence might look like this:

Finally
    brothers [and sisters]

everything	that is	true,
everything		honorable,
everything		just,
everything		pure,
everything		pleasing,
everything		auspicious,
if anything		virtuous,
and if anything		praiseworthy,
		these things
		CONSIDER!

As Paul writes and as we read, we begin doing what he is going to command: we *consider* truth, honor, justice, purity, pleasure, auspiciousness, virtue, praiseworthiness. Paul's very manner of communication forces us to do what he wants us to do: dwell mentally on the good. And as we are peacefully dwelling on all that is true and honorable and just and pure (our emotions included with our thoughts), Paul surprises us with his command: "these things consider!"

Paul slows the rhythm in the second half of his sentence by placing "and" between each verb:

Whatever also
    you learned and received and heard and saw in me,
        these things DO—

Neither learning nor receiving nor hearing nor seeing is more important. Paul gives a sense of an extensive summary by repeating "and." With his words, Paul has painted a picture so that the Philippians could be reminded of what they saw when Paul was active among them. They were learning, receiving wisdom, hearing words, and seeing Paul act. Again, Paul surprises their recollections by breaking into this mental picture with the action they are to take: "these things DO!" Paul has balanced doing or action with considering or thinking. "These things consider" and "these things do" are parallel main clauses. Therefore, we understand that neither the mental thought nor the action (in this passage) is more important than the other. Both are essential. And then Paul tells us the result. Only after considering these things and doing these things will the God of peace be with the Philippians.

The more attention we as readers give to style, the more we will learn about the message. When the style clashes with the content, the style again adds to the total message. Oral communication communicates such divergence by tone: "I do not want an A in this course!" said with a pout might really be communicating "I would love to get an A but I think it is absolutely impossible; therefore, I am going to pretend I do not want one." Who could ever be so honest? Irony is a written way to express tone. In verbal irony the writer intends a word(s) to express a meaning directly opposite the literal meaning. When Paul tells the Corinthians, "Forgive me this injustice" (2Co 12:13), he neither wants forgiveness nor does he see his action as unjust. Not to allow the Corinthians to donate to his labors is not injustice. Rather, the point of his letter to them is to explain how his actions are loving. By taking Paul literally, a reader could totally misunderstand the intent of his words.

Analyzing the literary style of a passage helps the reader understand the cognitive message. The words expressed need to be compared to the stylistic features so that a total package is presented.

Analyzing Style Can Help the Reader Understand How to Communicate to Others

The grammarian A. T. Robertson writes:

> There was never a more nimble mind than that of Paul, and he knew how to adapt himself to every mood of his readers or hearers without any sacrifice of principle. It was no declaimer's tricks, but love for the souls of men that made him become all things to all men (1 Cor. 9:22). He could change his tone because he loved the Galatians even when they had been led astray (Gal. 4:20).[2]

Because Paul wants to present others mature in Christ, he is conscious of his style of writing. Similarly, we as readers can begin to understand better and to appreciate more how the manner of communication (style) can affect others for good. In Socrates' dialogue with Phaedrus he explains the importance of communication:

> Socrates: The method of the art of healing is much the same as that of rhetoric.

Phaedrus: How so?

Socrates: In both cases you must analyze a nature, in one that of the body and in the other that of the soul, if you are to proceed in a scientific manner, not merely by practice and routine, to impart health and strength to the body by prescribing medicine and diet, or by proper discourses and training to give to the soul the desired belief and virtue (Plato, *Phaedrus* 54).

When the lawyer wants to justify himself by asking, "And who is my neighbor?", Jesus replies with a story (Lk 10:29–37) because sometimes fiction can convict in a way non-fiction cannot. After comparing the style of 2 Corinthians 11:16–12:13, Romans 8:9–39, and Philippians 3:2–4:13, I discovered that Paul varies the manner in which he communicates in order to reach different goals with his audience and to appeal differently to different groups. The Corinthians are at war with Paul, so Paul becomes a Warrior. The Roman churches are unknown personally to Paul, so Paul becomes a Diplomat. The Philippians love and respect Paul, so Paul remains their Father.[3] If Paul (not to mention Jesus) placed such importance on the manner of communication, should not we, as disciples, do likewise?

Analyzing Style Can Help the Reader Appreciate God

Some people are hesitant to analyze style because then they expect to lose the magic of a passage or a presentation. However, if looking at style is enjoyable, we can in turn appreciate the New Testament writers and ultimately the God who inspires them. God who is Beauty employs beauty.[4] Seeing how the details of the Bible add meaning should make us more appreciative of the God who loves us enough to add those details. I enjoy looking at style because it hearkens back to a God who is concerned with beauty, detail, the means of communication. We humans are a symbolizing species because we are made in the image of a symbolizing God.[5] The theologian Augustine expresses it well: "The more these things seem to be obscured by figurative language, the sweeter they become when they are explained" (*On Christian Doctrine* 4.8.15). Giving attention to style can lead us to appreciate the New Testament, and ultimately God, more.

Analyzing Style Can Help the Reader Guard Against the Misuse of Style

No one is more susceptible to the misuse of style, which is to deceive, than the person who declares that style does not exist or should not exist or that style is not worth analyzing. We humans are not first and foremost abstract reasoning beings. We were created by God with a will. If we will the good, our reasoning can flow from that goodness. If we will the bad, our abstract reasoning can disguise that evil. Our emotions are a thermometer to our will. But emotions can be ignored if we will the good. Therefore, the person who is insensitive to style may find that other people might reach beyond their conscious awareness to their emotions and lead them to think or do what they might not otherwise think or do. I think the "superapostles" (2Co 11:5) were rhetorically impressive in their time. But the superapostles led the Corinthians to disregard and to despise their spiritual parent, Paul. Paul instead was not "a trained speaker" (2Co 11:6). The first-century A.D. writer Longinus says in a positive way about persuasive writers what could be used for negative goals:

> The effect of genius is not to persuade the audience but rather to transport them out of themselves. Invariably what inspires wonder casts a spell upon us and is always superior to what is merely convincing and pleasing. For our convictions are usually under our own control, while such passages exercise an irresistible power of mastery and get the upper hand with every member of the audience (*On the Sublime* 1).

If as listeners or readers we have become aware of style, we can observe manner of communication and decide consciously if the goal to which we are being led is a good one.

HOW HAS STYLE BEEN STUDIED?

If indeed looking at the style of the New Testament writers is important because the style can help the reader understand the message, communicate to others, appreciate God, and guard against the misuse of style, how have students of the Bible gone about their literary quests? William A. Beardslee suggests that literary criticism has had two main lines of tradition, both originating with Aristotle. In Aristotle's *Rhetoric*, content or the cognitive message "can stand on its own right, apart from the form." In Aristotle's *Poetics*, literary form is an essential part of the work.[6] In contrast, Seymour Chatman, citing E. A. Tenney (*Dictionary of World Literature*) finds the two main lines of tradition coming separately from Aristotle and Plato.[7] For Aristotle style is subordinate to truth. It is adornment, a technique that can be acquired. Style is the "dress of thoughts." Therefore, the details are important. For Plato style is an inevitable product of content. Plato would not dwell on techniques since the essence of style cannot be taught. Style is the "incarnation of thoughts."

Aristotle's two books deal with two different topics. *The Art of Rhetoric* primarily has to do with public speaking, but Aristotle broadens "rhetoric" to "the faculty of discovering the possible means of persuasion in reference to any subject whatever" (*Rhetoric* 1.2). Therefore, he discusses oral and written composition. Rhetoric mainly concerns prose or nonfiction (*Rhetoric* III.3,12). *The Poetics*, in contrast, has to do with creative or imaginative works, what is "not true" (*Poetics* 15). *Poiētikos* in Greek is "capable of making, creative, productive" as opposed to *praktikos*, which means "fit for or concerned with action, practical, representative of action."[8] The root of *poiētikos* is *poieō*, to do or make. In other words, in *The Poetics* Aristotle writes about fictional literature, the tragedy, comedy, and epic. In both works, but especially in *The Poetics*, Aristotle defines the function and construction of each genre.[9] But even in *The Art of Rhetoric* Aristotle writes about the suitable style for a written or an oral work.

In *The Poetics*, Aristotle does not so much claim that form is an essential part of a work as he defines what he thinks are the essential characteristics of each form. Aristotle in both works wants to teach the reader how to compose the best fictional or persuasive piece. Nevertheless, Beardslee has captured two different approaches to literature. The cognitive content has a life of its own that is studied from the particular (inward) out, and a life of its own that affects the content of anything within. In other words, in the first line of tradition (or perceptive mode), a reader could summarize the content or message of a work in new words. In the second line of tradition (or perceptive mode), a reader could never express the content in any form other than the original one because then the message would no longer be the same. As Marshall McLuhan said, "The Medium is the Message."[10]

In addition, in the first tradition, more attention is paid to an in-depth reading or close examination of the text. In order to understand the message, the work is looked at in detail to observe what is unique and particular. James Muilenburg, who is often cited as an exemplary in-depth literary Old Testament critic and who popularized the term "rhetorical criticism" in biblical studies, even went so far as to say that exclusive attention to the literary form "may actually obscure the thought and intention of the writer or speaker."[11] Stylistics, an interdisciplinary study using linguistics as a tool of literary criticism, would fit in this line of tradition. In the second tradition, genre becomes most important. The form must be classified with its family of forms, resulting in observation of what is common to all. In the first line of tradition, in the microcosm is the macrocosm. Leo Spitzer, a literary historian, wrote, "Any one outward feature [of a text] when sufficiently followed up to the center, must yield us insight into the artistic whole, whose unity will thus have been respected."[12] Or, "If we think of this globe as a sun-ball, and of the particular points as sunbeams, we may be sure that, just as from any particular sunbeam we may infer the live force which sends forth all the sunbeams, so we will be able to penetrate from any peripheral point of the work of art to its core."[13]

In the second line of tradition, in the macrocosm is the microcosm. For example, Amos Wilder writes, "The work of the author, finally, is determined by the genre he adopts. This is not a question of aesthetic form but of fundamental hermeneutic communication. In this sense the genre or medium of the work is of primordial importance and its meaning subtends all other aspects of meaning in the writing in question."[14]

In the *structuralist* movement, literary genres have "a semantic power in themselves."[15] This emphasis on form or genre would appeal to form critics, who envision the New Testament, especially the Gospels, as originally derived from separate oral literary forms with independent historical contexts. Amos N. Wilder is an example of a literary scholar who wedded literary criticism to form criticism by highlighting forms and genres, the larger aspects of style.[16] His impact on New Testament studies is decisive since literary studies tend to be done more on genre than on figures of speech.

The two archetypal approaches to literary analysis can be summarized on this chart:

First Line of Tradition	Second Line of Tradition
first perceptive mode	second perceptive mode
Aristotle's *Rhetoric*?	Aristotle's *Poetics*?
Aristotle (style is adornment)?	Plato (style is content)?
content can be separated from form	form essential to content
in-depth reading	study of genre or form
unique and particular	common and general
in microcosm is macrocosm	in macrocosm is microcosm
smaller aspects of style	larger aspects of style

People who claim allegiance to either line of tradition appear to be spinning off in opposite directions. Nevertheless, the unifying base for both emphases is a conviction that genuine literary criticism is concerned with the literary piece itself.[17] The work of art, the genre, the story, the passage, the phrase becomes the end in itself. To understand or to look at the text for its own sake is literary criticism.

WHAT IS LITERARY CRITICISM?

If we were to read several works on literary criticism, we would be assaulted with several contrasting definitions. Literary criticism could be:

1. Criticism done by specialists in literature;[18]
2. Criticism that deals with fiction or imaginative literature;[19]
3. "Judging books";[20]
4. The study of "the act of literary communication" where a literary text is a message "addressed by an author to a reader";
5. The interpretation of "the meaning of a piece of literature" by concentrating on the author, the text, the universe imitated in the work, and/or the reader;
6. "Traditional literary theory" is "a synchronic approach" that concentrates (usually) on the final form of the text, regardless of its prehistory;
7. "Study of style, *how* something is communicated by author(s) to reader(s)";[21]
8. "Study of beauty" or aesthetics and "people's response to it";

9. "Study of style, artistic means (in a text) for achieving effects upon the reader or audience";[22]
10. "Criticism of, having the nature of, or dealing with literature";[23]
11. "Higher criticism or the study of such questions as the authorship, date, place of writing, recipients, style, sources, integrity, and purpose of any piece of literature";[24]
12. Source criticism or investigation of "the sources and literary links of the New Testament writings";[25]
13. Literary-historical or form criticism, "the objective concern was not with the literary achievement of the individual writers but with the prehistory of the form of the material as they received it, with the preliterary growth of the primitive Christian tradition on the analogy of the development of folk tradition in general";
14. Redaction criticism, or the study of how the evangelists compiled their oral sources to express their own theology or the theologies of their communities;[26]
15. "The interpretation and evaluation of a literary work through the careful examination and analysis of the work itself on the basis of both internal factors (e.g., genre, structure, content, style, sources) and external factors (e.g., historical setting, social setting, biographical data, psychological information)."[27]

DEFINITIONS #1–3

The problem that Bible students must confront is that often we have imitated movements in literary studies without assessing the significance for the study of the Bible. Often literary criticism indeed is whatever is being done by specialists in fictional literature. But are critics of fictional literature necessarily doing something helpful? Moreover, although the Bible clearly contains fiction (parables, for example), if literary criticism deals with fiction, literary critics of the Bible will be encouraged to fictionalize what is historical. Is a Gospel really like the plot of a story? Can a Gospel be called a genre if it is unique? Are the early chapters of Genesis really a drama? Is poetry necessarily fiction? Moreover, should Bible interpreters evaluate or judge the aesthetic success of God's Word? The

methods employed in imaginative literature are not completely
appropriate for biblical studies if you believe, as I do, that the
Bible claims to be a historical revelation from God directly or
with God's perspective. If the Bible is historical, then literary
studies may deny its referential function.[28] In practice, the Bible
must be studied with methods from various disciplines. The
Bible is an historical document with literary features and claims
to be authoritative in a unique sense.

DEFINITIONS #10–15

Most New Testament handbooks, especially in years past,
have broadly defined literary criticism. The New Testament is
literature, and therefore any study of literature is literary.
Literary criticism includes historical questions such as authorship, date, place of writing, and recipients. The scope of
"literary" changes depending on the critic's hypotheses. If the
critic thinks the author may have used written sources, these
sources are searched out. If the critic thinks the author may
have collected oral tales, these tales and their sources are
searched out. If the critic think the author placed the oral tales
in some sort of sequence, then the author's purposes are
ascertained.

However, these criticisms are not "literary" criticism in that
their main goal is historical. Looking at the literary unit is a
means to an end: to understand the historical process. What
sources did this writer use? Which sayings were repeated in
what places and by whom? How did the writer combine
different forms? How can style of writing prove or disprove
who was the author? As Tremper Longman expresses well, in
source, form, and redaction criticism "the interpretive key is
thought to lie outside of the text itself in its origin or
background."[29] In genuine *literary* criticism, the critic is concerned with the literary text for its own sake. The literary unit is
the end, *not* the means to something else.

DEFINITIONS #4–9

Some aspects of traditional biblical "literary" or "higher"
criticism did include genuine literary criticism, as for example
determining the purpose of a specific piece of literature.
Nevertheless, literary criticism can be defined broadly as the

study of the meaning of a piece of literature, or more narrowly as the study of style, how something is communicated by author to reader. The author and the reader would have importance only in so far as they help the critic understand the meaning of the text itself. If literary criticism is simply interpreting the meaning of a piece of literature, almost every reader of the Bible would be a literary critic. What is John's main purpose in writing his Gospel? What do the speeches of Jesus mean? Why did Jesus use parables and proverbs? These are all questions that concern the final form of a literary piece.

My own inclination is to separate questions of what is said from how something is said. Only when people analyze the "how" and its impact on the "what" are they doing literary studies. R. S. Crane similarly writes that the essential thing for a literary critic is to understand "literary works in their character as works of art." To understand the meaning of a work is to know not *why* but *what* an author "is saying and his reasons for saying it (in the sense of its artistic rationale)."[30] Aristotle wrote, "It is not sufficient to know what one ought to say, but one must also know how to say it" (*Rhetoric* 3.1). Style includes not only the smaller aspects of word order, figurative or literal language, and other choices among linguistic possibilities, but also the larger aspects of choice of genre or form.[31] The author also has the option whether to stay within or without the bounds of a form. I think if the Bible student believes the Bible is God's revelation through time, then analysis of style should be descriptive or appreciative rather than derogatory.[32]

Thus my own definition of literary criticism is the study of the meaning of a text by means of the study of style, and how that meaning is communicated by author(s) to reader(s). Nevertheless, Longman's definition is one that will include many literary developments ("the interpretation of the meaning of a piece of literature by concentration on the author, the text, and/or the reader").[33] His definition includes the necessary historical work that needs to be done on the New Testament writings in order to understand them. My definition makes literary studies one aspect of comprehending a text. The historical context of author, reader, date, place of writing, and main purpose must be studied as well.

If redaction, form, and source criticism do not fit under Longman's definition of "literary" criticism, neither does structuralism nor deconstruction fit, although they are practices in some literary circles. Structuralism, which examines the deep structure of a text, studies the text only in order to understand the larger recurring human myths. Daniel Patte explains that the structural exegete attempts to uncover "the linguistic, narrative, or mythical structures of the text under consideration. Whether or not these structures were intended by the author is not a relevant question. . . . The structural analyst studies this language without concern for what the author meant (the traditionally understood semantic dimension of the text)."[34] The structuralist, in effect, studies language as a system of signs.

Deconstruction, founded on Nietzsche's philosophical view that life inherently has no meaning, does not even attempt to interpret the meaning of literary works. Deconstruction gives the reader a strategy of reading that attempts, according to Patricia A. Ward, "to undermine the primacy of rational discourse in the western metaphysical tradition. . . . Reading is a skillful military manoeuver which breaches the defenses (the line of reasoning) of a particular text, working from within the text itself."[35] In Jacques Derrida's essay, "Living On: Border Lines," he plays with words in a stream of consciousness, making word associations and setting two texts parallel with each other. He concludes, "How will they translate that? Of course, I have not kept my promise. This telegraphic band produces an untranslatable supplement, whether I wish it or not. . . . To speak of writing, of triumph, as *living on*, is to enunciate or denounce the manic fantasy."[36] In other words, texts cannot be interpreted because life itself has no meaning. It is a universe without God, the source of meaning.

Examining a text from a certain political perspective may or may not be literary in the sense of focusing on the text itself. For example, Joyce Quiring Erickson explains that "the task of feminist criticism is not only to highlight women's consciousness and experience but also to uncover ways in which that experience has been misunderstood or denigrated in the writings of men or masked and trivialized in the writings of women."[37]

Feminist critics can accentuate the feminist as reader, a way to interpret the text, or the feminist as author, the study of women as writers. Erickson argues that in addition feminist criticism is similar to Christian criticism in that "feminist critics have alerted us to the human tendency to make *others* of those who are different, especially of those who have less access to power than we."[38] The only danger here is going beyond the bounds of Christianity where ultimately some people are unacceptable to God. People should not be objects or "others" because they are different or less powerful. However, some people do make themselves "others" to the degree that they reject God's good for them.[39] A feminist reading can bring out perspectives that are in a work of art, but the reader has to beware of distorting a text as well.

A psychological criticism has a similar danger. If the text does not lend itself to a particular psychological interpretation, the perspective will not add meaning to the work itself. However, some works clearly are written along psychological lines. To ignore this psychological perspective is to miss some of the meaning of the work. For example, the popular Rambo movie "First Blood I" uses Freudian psychology to develop its message, because the unresolved psychological tensions of the Vietnam veterans are like the unresolved psychological stages of youth. The unresolved psychological stages of youth have to reassert themselves in the adult. When the veteran Rambo comes back from Vietnam to the United States and is mistreated, the United States becomes Vietnam. The woods begin to take on the sounds and vegetation of the jungle. American society has become a jungle. The psychological changes in Rambo then become symbolized by his long and tortuous progression through an underground passage under the "mine" (mind!). When he comes out, he erupts into psychotic violence.

Christians, too, bring a perspective to their reading. If they indeed are identifying with the ultimate Author of the New Testament writings, they should be able to understand them better. If they are experiencing what is described, they can identify the meaning more readily. But again, they must avoid the danger of reading into a text something that might be true but not necessarily present in a particular passage.

SOME CONTEMPORARY EXAMPLES OF LITERARY STUDIES ON THE NEW TESTAMENT

In summary, I am limiting my discussion of "literary studies" to those studies that look at the meaning of a New Testament book or passage by means of the study of style, and how that meaning is communicated by author(s) to reader(s). To understand the text for its own sake is the goal of the reader. Although the critic may concentrate on author, reader, or the universe imitated in the work, the interpretation of the text itself must be the main goal for the criticism to be "literary" rather than, for example, historical, political, or psychological. Literary studies in the New Testament can be classified on a continuum of those that accentuate the larger or smaller aspects of style.

Larger Aspects of Style

The largest aspect of style is to look at the genre of the entire "book," where genre is "a group of texts that bear one or more traits in common with each other."[40] David E. Aune in *The New Testament in Its Literary Environment* deals with the question of genre from a historical perspective and attempts to classify the Gospels and the Letters in their respective genres. The second level of style is the arrangement of parts, the narrative, the succession of events, the plot, and the purpose analyzed into an outline. Many New Testament literary studies have been done at these levels. For example, Hans Dieter Betz sees Galatians as an example of an apologetic letter genre, 2 Corinthians 8 as an administrative letter, and 2 Corinthians 9 as an advisory letter.[41] Many scholars have pointed out that Romans 16:1–2 is or has affinities to ancient letters of recommendation.[42] Charles H. Talbert in *Reading Luke: A Literary and Theological Commentary on the Third Gospel* studies the narrative construction of Luke, looking at the larger thought units and their relation to Lukan thought as a whole.[43] For example, he analyzes the three parables in Luke 15:1–32 together rather than looking at them independently.

R. Alan Culpepper takes some of Aristotle's categories (plot, character, diction, thought, spectacle, and song) and uses them to analyze the *Anatomy of the Fourth Gospel: A Study in Literary Design*. He looks at narrator, narrative time, plot, character, implicit commentary, and implied reader. For example, Culpepper writes that the prologue in John "establishes the antithetical norms which will be in conflict throughout the narrative: light and darkness, belief and unbelief, grace and truth and the law."[44] James L. Blevins takes seriously the apocalyptic genre of Revelation in his commentary. He suggests that worship services use some elements from drama in order to communicate the dramatic quality of Revelation: "This dramatic element stems from the fact that Revelation is dealing with visionary experiences. John saw the visions; he heard the beautiful music recorded in the book; he felt the force and power of the presence of God. John could not write down a visionary experience in prose, for he needed a dramatic medium to capture his experiences."[45]

Mary Ann Tolbert uses both semiotics and rhetorical criticism to give *Perspectives on the Parables*. However, her final example has two psychological readings of Luke 15:11–32. She sees the parable of the prodigal son as an "example of the parallel plot type" that "tends to encourage a comparison of the two [plots] with each other."[46] In that sense the parable is like a dream. The parable may also be seen as two sides of ambivalence. Both the father and the elder son speak to every individual's painful awareness of "his or her own emotional ambivalence towards those with whom attachment is most intimate and important."[47]

George A. Kennedy looks at the New Testament through the perspective of classical oratory or rhetoric. For example, he analyzes 2 Corinthians as judicial rhetoric because Paul is seeking to persuade the audience, the Corinthians, to make a judgment about events occurring in the past. In 2:14–17 Paul states his proposition: "(A) as men of sincerity, (B) as commissioned by God, (C) in the sight of God we speak in Christ."[48] Paul's "character witnesses" are the Corinthians themselves. Throughout Paul's proof he builds on the three topics in 2:17: "God's mercy, his own afflictions, and his desire to share God's comfort with the Corinthians."[49]

Without a doubt the New Testament has at least three genres: letter, narrative (Gospel, Acts), and apocalypse (Revelation).[50] The New Testament contains parable and possibly poetry. I personally think that genre critics can tend to force New Testament writings into forms that do not completely fit. Part of the danger of looking at form is to accentuate the common rather than the unique. The ancient Hebrews, for example, did not differentiate between parable, allegory, and saying as we do. The Hebrew word *mashal* refers to sayings (Dt 28:37), proverbs (1Sa 10:12), *and* allegories (Eze 17:1–24). Therefore, although the classification of genre should be welcomed, the application of such classification should be done carefully with attentiveness to the individual New Testament book. However, studying a book in light of its overall purpose is essential as a basis for all further study of any part or passage.

Smaller Aspects of Style

In the smaller aspects of style, the critic studies the use of language in a work. For this type of study, knowledge of New Testament Greek is essential. At a minimum, the use of a Greek-English New Testament interlinear is necessary. Every sentence has four basic possible types of sentence changes: addition, omission, substitution, and transposition. For example, when words like "and" are repeated (polysyndeton), that would be an addition change. If no conjunctions connect words (asyndeton), an omission is occurring. Substitution changes include figures of speech, such as metaphor; syntactical changes, such as an active or passive verb; and lexical changes, such as a popular or learned word. Changing the usual word order, which Greek allows, is an example of a transpositional change.

The analysis of Philippians 4:8–9 at the introduction of this chapter exemplifies one close examination of a passage.[51] In the Old Testament, James Muilenburg and Phyllis Trible have pursued the study of the smaller aspects of style. G. B. Caird highlighted metaphor in the Bible in *The Language and Imagery of the Bible*. He writes, for example, that metaphors can have varying degrees of correspondence between vehicle and tenor and varying degrees of development.[52] The correspondence between the judge and God in the parable in Luke 18:1–8 is limited to the aspect that both can determine verdicts. Many readers have misrepresented this parable by extending the degree of correspondence, concluding that Christians need to "keep coming" to God in prayer or "wear God out" or "storm the gates of heaven" in order to get a positive reply. However, the point of the parable is the contrast between God's righteousness and the judge's unrighteousness. Understanding the richness of many New Testament passages can be increased by analyzing to what degree a metaphor is developed.[53]

Michael R. Cosby has published a fine close reading of Hebrews 11. Cosby claims that the writer uses language forcefully and artistically to undergird and strengthen the claim that "those who please God are the ones who ignore earthly blessing and live their lives in the glorious hope of the promised heavenly rest."[54] For example, the writer of Hebrews uses anaphora, repeating the first word of a clause:

> Over and over "By faith. . . . By faith. . . . By faith. . ." impacts the listeners' ears, and the rhythm generated by this expression creates the impression that the speaker could go on giving examples *ad infinitum.* . . . The rhetorical effect is to make this definition seem to represent a statement of timeless truth for which examples can be marshalled from the beginning of human history to the present time.[55]

The contrast between the two methods of analyzing style is caught in the approach of each. Should the critic have a deductive approach, analyzing the goal and elements of a genre or form and then applying these common characteristics to a specific book or passage? Or should the critic have an inductive approach, reading and rereading a book or passage until an intuitive hypothesis is formed about the significance of how a particular stylistic feature relates to the whole? Both approaches have integrity and value. Probably some people tend to accentuate the general and common, and others the unique and particular. But the two approaches need to inform one another graciously.

SUMMARY

The first-century rhetorician Longinus believed that "a great style is the natural outcome of weighty thoughts, and sublime sayings naturally fall to people of spirit." In contrast, "those whose thoughts and habits all their lives long are petty and servile" cannot "flash out anything wonderful, worthy of immortal life" (*On the Sublime* 10). Since the New Testament was written by people with "weighty thoughts," inspired by the immortal God, is it any wonder that New Testament writers have written their narratives and letters with attention to style? What may appear to be superfluous may in fact be a key to the interpretation of a text and a key to communicating to others, appreciating God, and guarding against the misuse of style. Literary studies can be an opportunity, as Leo Spitzer says, "to retrace the beauty of God in this world."[56] He continues, "There are hidden beauties which do not reveal themselves at the first exploratory attempts (as the apologetic theologians know); in fact, all beauty has some mysterious quality which does not appear at first glance."[57] He adds, "Love, whether it be love for God, love for one's fellow men, or the love of art, can only gain by the effort of the human intellect to search for the reasons of its most sublime emotions, and to formulate them. It is only a frivolous love that cannot survive intellectual definition; great love prospers with understanding."[58] Attention to ways a writer communicates will not only add to understanding of a message but it can also serve as a means to worship God. Then indeed we "apologetic theologians" will know about God's hidden beauties.

I have defined literary criticism as the analysis of the meaning of a written text by means of the study of the style, and how that meaning is communicated by an author(s) to a reader(s). It includes the analysis of how form is related to meaning, and the aesthetic effects of language. The goal of literary study is not historical (the common purpose of "literary studies" in biblical criticism), but the study of the form, narrative, or sentence for its own sake. Since the New Testament claims to be historical (the word "which we have heard, which we have seen with our eyes, which we have looked upon and touched with our hands," 1Jn 1:1), the New Testament writings should not be treated identically in the way fiction is treated. Nevertheless, as literary communication, the New Testament does lend itself to many techniques of literary analysis.

We have looked at many examples of literary analysis in the New Testament, seeing how they can highlight the larger or smaller aspects of style. If wisdom calls people to seek her diligently because her "fruit is better than gold, even fine gold, and her yield than choice silver" (Pr 8:19), searching out the meaning of a text is one way to begin that search. What does wisdom say? How does wisdom say it? And then, how shall I obey her commands?

BIBLIOGRAPHY

Alter, Robert. *The Art of Biblical Narrative*. New York: Basic, 1981.

Aristotle. *The "Art" of Rhetoric.* Trans. John Henry Freese, The Loeb Classical Library. Cambridge, Mass.: Harvard University Press, 1926.

————. *The Poetics.* Trans. W. Hamilton Fyfe, The Loeb Classical Library. Cambridge, Mass.: Harvard University Press, 1927.

Beardslee, W. A. *Literary Criticism of the New Testament.* Philadelphia: Fortress, 1970.

Frye, N. *The Great Code: The Bible and Literature.* New York: Harcourt, 1982.

Kennedy, G. A. *New Testament Interpretation Through Rhetorical Criticism.* Chapel Hill, N. C.: University of North Carolina Press, 1984.

Longman III, Tremper. *Literary Approaches to Biblical Interpretation,* Foundations of Contemporary Interpretation, Vol. 3. Grand Rapids: Zondervan, 1987.

Lanham, Richard A. *A Handlist of Rhetorical Terms: A Guide for Students of English Literature.* Berkeley: University of California, 1968.

————. *Style: An Anti-Textbook.* New Haven: Yale University Press, 1974.

McKnight, Edgar V. *The Bible and the Reader: An Introduction to Literary Criticism.* Philadelphia: Fortress, 1985.

Ricoeur, Paul. *Essays on Biblical Interpretation.* Philadelphia: Fortress, 1980.

Ryken, Leland. *Words of Life: A Literary Introduction to the New Testament.* Grand Rapids: Baker, 1987.

————. "Literary Criticism of the Bible: Some Fallacies." *Literary Interpretations of Biblical Narratives,* eds. Kenneth R. R. Gros Louis, James S. Ackerman, and Thayer S. Warshaw. Nashville: Abingdon, 1974.

Spencer, Aída Besançon. *Paul's Literary Style: A Stylistic and Historical Comparison of II Corinthians 11:16–12:13, Romans 8:9–39, and Philippians 3:2–4:13,* An Evangelical Theological Society Monograph. Winona Lake: Eisenbrauns, 1984.

————. "God as a Symbolizing God: A Symbolic Hermeneutic." *Journal of the Evangelical Theological Society,* 24 (December 1981): 323–32.

Wellek, René. "Criticism, Literary." *Dictionary of the History of Ideas.* New York, Scribner, 1973, I:596–607.

NOTES

[1]For example, Leland Ryken writes, "Biblical literature constitutes a literary achievement of unavoidable importance and indisputable value." See his "Literary Criticism of the Bible: Some Fallacies," *Literary Interpretations of Biblical Narratives,* eds. Kenneth R. R. Gros Louis, James S. Ackerman, and Thayer S. Warshaw (Nashville: Abingdon, 1974), 40.

[2]A. T. Robertson, *A Grammar of the Greek New Testament in the Light of Historical Research* (Nashville: Broadman, 1934), 1199.

[3]Aída Besançon Spencer, *Paul's Literary Style: A Stylistic and Historical Comparison of II Corinthians 11:16–12:13, Romans 8:9–39, and Philippians 3:2–4:13,* An Evangelical Theological Society Monograph (Winona Lake: Eisenbrauns, 1984). For further defense of the importance of style read Richard A. Lanham, *Style: An Anti-Textbook* (New Haven: Yale University Press, 1974). Umberto Eco shows what great attention to style he placed in the writing of his best-selling novel in *Postscript to the Name of the Rose,* trans. W. Weaver (New York: Harcourt, 1984).

[4]Leland Ryken argues about literature in general: "In a Christian framework all truth is God's truth and all beauty God's beauty. Any discovery about the truth or beauty of literature is therefore a contribution toward the cultural mandate of subduing God's world for his glory." *Triumphs of the Imagination: Literature in Christian Perspective* (Downers Grove, Ill.: InterVarsity, 1979), 127.

[5]Aída Besançon Spencer, "God as a Symbolizing God: A Symbolic Hermeneutic," *Journal of the Evangelical Theological Society* 24 (1981): 323–32.

[6]William A. Beardslee, *Literary Criticism of the New Testament* (Philadelphia: Fortress, 1970), 3–4.

[7]*The Semantics of Style: Introduction to Structuralism,* ed. Michael Lane (New York: Basic Books, 1970), 124–25. See also R. A. Sayce, "Style in Literature," *Dictionary of the History of Ideas* (1973), IV, 330–33.

[8]Henry George Liddell and Robert Scott, *A Greek-English Lexicon* (9th ed.; Oxford: Clarendon Press, 1940), 1429, 1458.

[9]"Let us here deal with Poetry, its essence and its several species, with the characteristic function of each species and the way in which plots must be constructed if the poem is to be a success." *Poetics,* 1.

[10]Chapter 1, *Understanding Media: The Extensions of Man* (2d ed.; New York: New American Library, 1964).

[11]James Muilenburg, "Form Criticism and Beyond," *Journal of Biblical Literature* 88 (March 1969).

[12]Leo Spitzer, *Linguistics and Literary History: Essays in Stylistics* (Princeton: Princeton University Press, 1948), 42, 198.

[13]Ibid., 198.

[14]Amos Wilder, "Norman Perrin, *What is Redaction Criticism?*", *Christology and Modern Pilgrimage: A Discussion With Norman Perrin*, ed. Hans Dieter Betz (Claremont: New Testament Colloquium, 1971), 146.

[15]Daniel Patte, *What is Structural Exegesis?* (Philadelphia: Fortress, 1976), 18.

[16]For example, see his *Early Christian Rhetoric: The Language of the Gospel* (London: SCM, 1964).

[17]E.g., Leland Ryken writes, "One of the most serious fallacies in the study of biblical literature is the view that literary criticism of the Bible should be preoccupied with the process that produced the Bible as we know it. . . ."

"The conclusion is obvious: literary critics are opposed to a critical methodology that devotes its major attention to the process of composition instead of the text itself." *Literary Interpretations of Biblical Narratives*, 36–37.

Phyllis Trible in her introduction to literary criticism states that, according to rhetorical criticism, "the major clue to interpretation is the text itself." She agrees with her former professor James Muilenburg that rhetorical criticism is attention to the text itself, its own integrity, its dramatic structure, and its stylistic features. See her *God and the Rhetoric of Sexuality* (Philadelphia: Fortress, 1978), 8.

[18]Definitions 1, 2, 4, 5, 6 come from Tremper Longman III, *Literary Approaches to Biblical Interpretation* (Foundations of Contemporary Interpretation 3; Grand Rapids: Zondervan, 1987), 2–3, 9, 18, 22. However, I have added "universe imitated in the work" to definition five in accordance with M. H. Abrams, *The Mirror and the Lamp: Romantic Theory and the Critical Tradition* (New York: Oxford University Press, 1953), 6.

[19]In agreement with definition two, R. S. Crane defines literary criticism as "any reasoned discourse concerning works of imaginative literature the statements in which are primarily statements about the works themselves and appropriate to their character as productions of art." *The Idea of the Humanities and Other Essays: Critical and Historical*, II (Chicago: University of Chicago Press, 1967), 11, 16.

[20]C. S. Lewis, *An Experiment in Criticism* (Cambridge: Cambridge University Press, 1961), 1. The emphasis here is on the word "criticism," which comes from the Greek *kritikos*, "judge of literature." See René Welleck, "Criticism, Literary," *Dictionary of the History of Ideas* (1973):I:596. The word "style" itself can include this prescriptive, as opposed to a simply descriptive, aspect. See *Paul's Literary Style*, 25–26.

[21]E.g., Amos N. Wilder introduces his "literary approach" as a concern first of all "not so much with what the early Christians said as how they said it." *Early Christian Rhetoric*, 10.

[22]Definitions eight and nine are rejected by Longman as too narrow (*Literary Approaches*, 7–8). Definition eight is quoted from M.

H. Abrams' *A Glossary of Literary Terms*, 160. Often style is defined as the smaller aspects of style; however, style is a much broader term.

[23]*Webster's New Twentieth Century Dictionary* (ed. Jean L. McKechnie; 2d ed.; New York: Publishers Guild, 1962), 1055. René Welleck's definition of literary criticism is most similar to Webster's: "discourse about literature" or "the study of literature" including description, analysis, interpretation, and evaluation.

[24]George Eldon Ladd, *The New Testament and Criticism* (Grand Rapids: Eerdmans, 1967), 112.

[25]Definitions twelve and thirteen are from Werner Georg Kümmel, *Introduction to the New Testament*, trans. Howard Clark Kee (17th ed.; Nashville: Abingdon, 1975), 33. Rudolf Bultmann has a readable introduction in *Form Criticism: Two Essays on New Testament Research*, trans. F. C. Grant (New York: Harper, 1962).

[26]Donald Guthrie, for example, under the heading of "Literary Criticism," includes source, form, and redaction criticism. R. K. Harrison, B. K. Waltke, D. Guthrie, and G. D. Fee, *Biblical Criticism: Historical, Literary and Textual* (Grand Rapids: Zondervan, 1978), 98–110.

[27]David E. Aune, *The New Testament in Its Literary Environment* (Philadelphia: Westminster, 1987), 19.

[28]See Longman, *Literary Approaches*, 54–58. Edgar V. McKnight cites as his rationale for literary studies his inability to reconcile the historical Gospel accounts. He then highlights a reader-oriented study of literature that creates meaning in the reader's interpretation more than in the text itself: "Literature is what we read as literature." *The Bible and the Reader: An Introduction to Literary Criticism* (Philadelphia: Fortress, 1985), xvii, 9–10.

[29]Longman, *Literary Approaches*, 24.

[30]Crane, *Idea of the Humanities*, II, 12, 16. Phyllis Trible similarly writes: "Proper analysis of form yields proper articulation of meaning" (*God and the Rhetoric*, 8).

[31]R. A. Sayce defines style in both its smaller and larger aspects: use of language in a work of literature and the summary of formal characteristics common to a period, school, or genre, *Dictionary of the History of Ideas*, 330.

[32]Linguistics also studies style in a descriptive rather than a prescriptive manner. John Lyons, *Introduction to Theoretical Linguistics* (Cambridge: Cambridge University Press, 1968), 42–44.

[33]Longman, *Literary Approaches*, 63–68.

[34]Daniel Patte, *What is Structural Exegesis?*, 14–15. See also Daniel Patte, ed., *Semiology and Parables: An Exploration of the Possibilities Offered by Structuralism for Exegesis*, Pittsburgh Theological Monograph Series (Pittsburgh: Pickwick, 1976) and Robert Detweiler, *Story, Sign, and Self: Phenomenology and Structuralism as Literary Critical Methods* (Philadelphia: Fortress, 1978).

[35]Patricia A. Ward, "Revolutionary Strategies of Reading: A Review Article," *Christianity and Literature*, 33 (1983): 11.

[36]Harold Bloom, Paul DeMan, Jacques Derrida, Geoffrey H. Hartman, and J. Hillis Miller, *Deconstruction and Criticism* (New York: Seabury, 1979), 175–76.

[37]Joyce Quiring Erickson, "What Difference? The Theory and Practice of Feminist Criticism," *Christianity and Literature*, 33 (1983): 69. See also *Daughters of Sarah*, 15 (July/August 1989), which is an issue on "Women's Art: Creating and Transforming."

[38]Erickson, "What Difference?", 72.

[39]E.g., Rosemary Radford Ruether explains that "Feminist theology should not fall back on biblical exclusivism over against 'paganism.' It should not call for biblical religion as the 'true' foundation of feminism over against non-Christian traditions." "Feminist Theology and Spirituality," *Christian Feminism: Vision of a New Humanity*, ed. Judith L. Weidman (San Francisco: Harper, 1984), 15. Probably the desire to reject any lines between Christian vs. non-Christian foundationally goes back to a view of the Bible rather than to feminism per se. A biblical feminist would draw lines according to the Bible's guidelines.

[40]Longman, *Literary Approaches*, 76.

[41]Hans Dieter Betz, *Galatians* (Philadelphia: Fortress, 1979); *2 Corinthians 8 and 9: A Commentary on Two Administrative Letters of the Apostle Paul* (Philadelphia: Fortress, 1985).

[42]Spencer, *Paul's Literary Style*, 94.

[43]Charles H. Talbert, *Reading Luke: A Literary and Theological Commentary on the Third Gospel* (New York: Crossword, 1982).

[44]R. Alan Culpepper, *Anatomy of the Fourth Gospel: A Study in Literary Design* (Philadelphia: Fortress, 1983).

[45]James L. Blevins, *Revelation* (Atlanta: John Knox, 1984), 7.

[46]Mary Ann Tolbert, *Perspectives on the Parables: An Approach to Multiple Interpretations* (Philadelphia: Fortress, 1979), 34–50, 98–99.

[47]Tolbert, *Perspectives*, 109.

[48]George A. Kennedy, *New Testament Interpretation Through Rhetorical Criticism*, Studies in Religion (Chapel Hill: University of North Carolina Press, 1984), 87–88.

[49]Ibid., 89.

[50]Leland Ryken also writes that the New Testament has three main genres: narrative or story, letter or epistle, and vision or apocalypse. *Words of Life: A Literary Introduction to the New Testament* (Grand Rapids: Baker, 1987), 18.

[51]See Spencer, *Paul's Literary Style*, for additional examples. Appendix II defines commonly used New Testament rhetorical terms. See also Richard A. Lanham, *A Handlist of Rhetorical Terms: A Guide for Students of English Literature* (Berkeley: University of California Press, 1968). A study of the manner in which the extended metaphors

develop a consistent message in James may be found in "The Function of the Miserific and Beatific Images in the Letter of James," *Evangelical Journal*, 7 (1989): 3–14. The author's (with William D. Spencer) study of 2 *Corinthians*, Bible Study Commentary (Grand Rapids: Zondervan, 1989) also includes many literary observations such as of Paul's lists of sufferings in 2 Corinthians 4, 6, 11.

[52]G. B. Caird, *The Language and Imagery of the Bible* (Philadelphia: Westminster, 1980), 153–55.

[53]E.g., Jean-François Collange thinks that the metaphor of the footrace extends to Philippians 3:14, the "call." *L'Epitre de Saint Paul aux Philippiens.*, Commentaire du Nouveau Testament 10a (Neuchâtel: Delachaux and Niestlé, 1973), p. 118. Cf. Spencer, *Paul's Literary Style*, 201.

[54]Michael R. Cosby, "The Rhetorical Composition of Hebrews 11," *Journal of Biblical Literature*, 107 (June 1988): 258, 261, 273.

[55]Ibid., 261.

[56]Leo Spitzer, *Linguistics and Literary History*, 24, 30 n.l.

[57]Ibid., 30 n.l.

[58]Ibid.

Chapter Nine

Canonical Criticism

Mikeal C. Parsons

Mikeal C. Parsons

Mikeal C. Parsons is Assistant Professor of Religion at Baylor University in Waco, Texas. He holds degrees from the University of Wales (B.D.), Campbell University (B.A.), and Southern Baptist Theological Seminary (M.Div., Ph.D.). He is the author of *The Departure of Jesus in Luke-Acts (JSOT)* and of articles appearing in such journals as *New Testament Studies, Catholic Biblical Quarterly, Journal of Biblical Literature, Review and Expositor,* and *Perspectives in Religious Studies.* He is currently writing a narrative commentary on Acts, and is coediting (with R. I. Pervo) *Rethinking the Unity of "Luke-Acts"* for Fortress-Augsburg.

Chapter Nine

Canonical Criticism

INTRODUCTION

Along with sociological analysis and the newer literary criticism, canonical criticism is a fairly recent development in biblical studies compared to most of the other methods of interpretation considered in this volume. And since most of the "early" dialogue regarding canonical criticism has taken place among Old Testament scholars, the interest of New Testament scholars in this canonical approach is even more recent. In fact, the only introduction to the New Testament written from a perspective entirely committed to a canonical approach is that by the Old Testament scholar, Brevard Childs.

Canonical criticism emerged, in part, in response to a growing sense of the inadequacy of the historical-critical method in dealing with the message of the biblical texts. This dissatisfaction has ranged from those who wish to abandon the historical-critical method altogether to those who wish to subordinate historical criticism to some other interpretive matrix (such as the canon). Even among canon critics there is no consensus about the role historical criticism should play in their endeavors. Still, over the past decade, the canon has taken on new significance for many biblical scholars who are committed to taking the canon seriously, and a number of studies have attended to the historical and theological problems associated with the critical study of the canon.

Part of the problem in writing about canonical criticism is a lack of agreement about what canonical criticism is or what it ought to be. In fact, the phrase "canonical criticism" itself prejudices the argument in some minds, and terms like "canon criticism" or "canonical approach" or "canonical process approach" have been suggested as alternatives. Still, for reasons to be explained later, I will adopt the phrase "canonical criticism" as an appropriate label for a method of study that has as its primary focus the interpretation of the New Testament within its canonical context.

HISTORY OF CANONICAL CRITICISM

Despite the impact canonical criticism has made in biblical studies in recent years, summaries of this approach to the Bible are not readily accessible to the beginning student. Little substantive attention has been given to this subject in standard introductions to the Bible, especially the New Testament. This is true, in part, because canonical criticism is such a recent development and because so many of the standard introductions were written before this approach emerged on the scene. The dearth of treatments of canonical criticism in New Testament handbooks may be due also to the fact that the leading advocates of this approach are Old Testament scholars or experts in intertestamental literature. Often when canonical criticism has been treated in the introductions, it has received negative evaluation because the writer was either not sympathetic to or did not fully understand the approach.[1] Part of the problem also lies in the fact that there is no consensus among biblical scholars as to how canonical criticism ought to be done or, for that matter, whether or not the approach is even worth pursuing.

In this essay, I will attempt to help remedy this situation by providing a sympathetic yet critical look at the history, principles, and application of canonical criticism aimed at the beginning student. We will begin with a survey of the work of the two men who have most influenced the discussion of canonical criticism, Brevard Childs and James Sanders.

The Canonical Approach of Brevard Childs

Brevard Childs is Professor of Old Testament at Yale Divinity School. He received his theological training at Princeton Theological Seminary and the University of Heidelberg, and his Doctor of Theology degree from the University of Basel. He studied with some of the best known Old Testament scholars of the German tradition, including Walter Eichrodt, Gerhardt von

Rad, and Walter Zimmerli. Childs is recognized as one of the most skilled practitioners of the historical-critical method with which, as we shall see, he has become dissatisfied.[2]

A New Kind of Old Testament Criticism: "Interpretation in Faith." In 1964, Childs published a programmatic essay entitled, "Interpretation in Faith," in which he laid the foundation for his subsequent work.[3] Childs lamented the then widely accepted distinction made by Krister Stendahl between the task of biblical theology and that of systematic or dogmatic theology.[4] The task of biblical theology, according to Stendahl, is purely historical and descriptive: what did the text mean in its historical setting? The task of the systematic theologian, on the other hand, is constructive in providing a normative reading of the text: what does the text mean for the contemporary community of faith? Childs eschewed this bifurcation between what it meant/what it means and argued that the theological exegesis that one might reasonably expect to find in an Old Testament commentary must include both the descriptive and normative tasks.

Though at this point Childs does not use the phrase "canonical criticism" or "canonical approach," he does outline what such theological exegesis would entail. He proposes that theological exegesis must be developed within the "hermeneutical circle" by way of three dialectical relationships: 1) the single text is read in light of the whole Old Testament witness; 2) the Old Testament is read in light of the New Testament, and vice versa; and 3) the Old Testament is read in light of the theological reality itself and vice versa, that is, the interpreter seeks to hear *God's* Word in the text, not the words of Moses or John; their witness is a vehicle for the Word of God. Childs would later abandon this dialectical framing of the problem, but what is important in this article is the first indications of his frustrations with "the limitations of this exclusively historical method."[5]

A New Kind of Biblical Theology: Taking the Canon Seriously.[6] Childs' dissatisfaction with the accepted way of doing biblical theology emerged with full force with the publication of *Biblical Theology in Crisis* in 1970.[7] In this book, Childs traces the development of the Biblical Theology Movement in America from its origins in the early post-World War II years to its alleged demise in the 1960s.[8] Most of the book is devoted to a description of the essential features of the movement, its unresolved problems, and reasons for its failure.

For Childs, the principle reason for the movement's failure was that it did not take the canonical context seriously enough. At the conclusion of this book, Childs offers a brief but provocative proposal for a new way of doing Biblical theology within a canonical context. This canonical context involves taking the Old and New Testament together as constitutive of sacred Scripture.

Drawing upon the so-called "pre-critical" exegesis of the Reformers, especially Calvin, Childs argues that the "literal sense" of Scripture was its "plain sense . . . when interpreted within the canonical context of the church."[9] This view, according to Childs, is preferred to the eighteenth-century identification of the "literal sense" with the "historical sense." Thus, the canonical context, rather than the historical one, is the context that Childs argues must finally be granted the status of the privileged context for theological reflection. The original, historical context of a text is not to be ignored nor are the tools needed for such historical investigation; but for Childs, such historical reconstruction is subordinated to a new biblical theology that "takes as its primary task the disciplined theological reflection of the Bible in the context of the canon."[10]

A New Kind of Commentary: Understanding "The Scripture of the Church." Childs moved from theory to practice with the publication in 1974 of a commentary on Exodus in the Old Testament Library series.[11] He begins this much-heralded commentary with the following words: "The purpose of this commentary is unabashedly theological. Its concern is to understand Exodus as Scripture of the church. The exegesis arises as a theological discipline within the context of the canon and is directed toward the community of faith which lives by its confession of Jesus Christ."[12]

The concern to understand the text as the "scripture of the church" may be seen as clearly in the format of the commentary as in the exegesis of individual passages. Each section of the text follows the same structure. Following a fresh translation of the Hebrew in which he notes textual problems and unusual syntactical constructions, Childs examines the text with the typical historical tools of form criticism and tradition history. This section, in smaller type, is clearly subordinated to the next one dealing with the final form of the text that church and synagogue have accepted as the authoritative Word of God. Next, the Exodus passage is illumined by the (usually Christological) context of the New Testament. A section on the history of interpretation indicates how the passage has been understood across the generations of believing communities. Each section ends with theological reflections in which Childs attempts to construct a theology from his findings of the Old and New Testament contexts and the history of exegesis that can inform and enrich the contemporary community of faith.

With his Exodus commentary, Childs finally answers his own call to take the canon seriously. His theoretical foundations for this canonical approach, however, are still being formulated. It is not until the publication of his *Introduction to the Old Testament as Scripture* that Childs' reflections on the canonical context are fully articulated.

A New Kind of Introduction: The Old Testament as Scripture and the New Testament as Canon. Rarely has a book received such intensely varied responses as Childs' *Introduction to the Old Testament as Scripture.*[13] One scholar praised the work in glowing terms: "Childs' Introduction stands as a monumental contribution to Old Testament scholarship. It will be, appropriately, a significant factor in biblical studies for at least the balance of this century."[14] But another dismissed the work as "a new kind of obscurantism, one which while accepting the logic and many of the conclusions of past and present biblical criticism, yet dismisses it as relevant, barren and even harmful."[15] Such reactions are typical of the divisive reception this book has engendered.

One of the reasons for the negative reaction on the part of some is the decisive step Childs takes in this book to displace the historical-critical method and its concern for the original meaning of the text with his canonical approach and its concern for the canonical meaning of the text. Childs asks, "Is it possible to understand the Old Testament as canonical Scripture and yet to make full and consistent use of the critical tools?"[16] While Childs' answer is yes, he has so modified the purposes of the historical-critical method that many of his critics think he has in fact abandoned the historical-critical method altogether.

Perhaps the most important contribution Childs has made in this book to the development of a method of canonical exegesis is the introduction for the first time of the term "canonical shaping." Canonical shaping refers to the selection, collection, and ordering of the Old Testament materials. Though the identity of the canonical editors has been obscured by the editors themselves, at least one concern of theirs is preserved, namely "that a tradition from the past be transmitted in such a way that its authoritative claims be laid upon all successive generations of Israel."[17] For each individual book of the Old Testament, Childs discusses its canonical shape, that is the literary clues left by the editors to insure that the work would have enduring significance for subsequent generations of believers.

With the publication in 1984 of *The New Testament as Canon*, Childs for the first time turns his full attention to the implications of his canonical approach for New Testament interpretation. Responding to critics' charges that any serious canonical exegesis must incorporate the entire Christian canon into its findings, Childs attempts what few biblical scholars would dare do in an age of increasing specialization; he traverses the iron curtain that has separated the two Testaments in critical biblical scholarship. Childs reveals something of the cost when he acknowledges that he spent five years working early mornings and late nights on this research project in New Testament studies while simultaneously carrying a full teaching load in Old Testament studies at Yale Divinity School. The results are impressive.

In this Introduction, we have the most articulate statement to date of Childs' agenda. As in the counterpart introduction to the Old Testament, Childs engages historical-critical study of the New Testament over the past one hundred years. The breadth and depth of his knowledge of the history of interpretation of the New Testament is admirable. But such knowledge is generally used to demonstrate the inadequacy of historical criticism in dealing with the final form of the New Testament as the church received it. Perhaps the most helpful contribution of this volume for our purposes is the list of principles that Childs gives for canonical exegesis. We will deal with those tenets later in this essay.

Childs' Approach in Context. Any discussion of canonical criticism must take into account Childs' substantive contribution. Before turning to the work of James Sanders and an evaluation of the work done in canonical criticism to date, it might be helpful to set Childs' work in perspective by locating it within several relevant contexts.

In the Context of Old Testament Theology. Childs declared that the Biblical Theology Movement with its emphasis on a "canon within the canon" (G. E. Wright) was inadequate for theological exegesis of the Old Testament. Likewise, Childs charged that the attempts of older Old Testament theologies either to systematize Old Testament theology (Eichrodt) or to locate the center of Old Testament theology as "salvation history" via tradition history (von Rad) also failed. It is in the midst of these failures to come to terms with the theology of the Old Testament in the context of the Christian canon that Childs forged his unique approach. Childs' efforts are self-consciously theological, and it would be a mistake to label his efforts as anything else.

In the Context of "New Criticism." Despite the self-consciously theological nature of Childs' agenda, John Barton has made the interesting observation that much of Childs' proposal resembles the so-called "New Criticism," popular among American literary critics in the 1940s and 1950s. Childs himself recognizes common concerns between his canonical approach and modern literary theory, but he denies any non-theological origins for his agenda:

> The canonical study of the Old Testament shares an interest in common with several of the newer literary critical methods in its concern to do justice to the integrity of the text itself apart from diachronistic reconstruction. One thinks of the so-called "newer criticism" of English studies, of various forms of structural analysis, and of rhetorical criticism. Yet the canonical approach differs from a strictly literary approach by interpreting the biblical text in relation to a community of faith and practice for whom it serves a particular theological role as possessing divine authority. . . . The canonical approach is concerned to understand the nature of the theological shape of the text rather than to recover an original literary or aesthetic unity.[18]

Barton, while respecting Childs' own account of the route he took to canonical criticism, presses the connection between the literary interests of New Criticism and Childs. He argues:

> Whether or not he has been influenced by the New Criticism, it is hard to believe that his proposals would have taken just

this form, if the New Criticism had never existed. On all three counts—"emphasis on the text itself" as a finished product rather than as a vehicle for expressing an author's ideas; indifference to authorial intention; and concern for the integration of individual texts into a literary canon, which contributes to their meaning—Childs stands very close to the New Critics.[19]

Such links do not have to be intentional to be useful in placing Childs in a larger context of those biblical scholars whose own dissatisfaction with current historical criticism led to their self-conscious identification with the basic tenets of New Criticism.

In the Context of Yale Theology. As members of an intimate scholarly community, usually in the context of a university, divinity school or seminary, scholars tend to influence each others' thinking, often to the degree that schools of thought cluster around great intellectual centers. Childs himself has acknowledged the existence of a "New Yale Theology," an emerging consensus among the theology faculty at the university and the divinity school.[20] Mark Wallace has identified these theologians as Hans Frei, Paul Holmer, George Lindbeck, and David Kelsey and suggests: "The Yale theologians exhibit a cooperative attempt to forge a biblical alternative to mainstream theological liberalism that eschews both confessionalism and fundamentalism."[21]

Sharp differences among the Yale theologians preclude identifying these efforts as constitutive of a homogeneous movement or school. Nevertheless, Childs does recognize "a distinct family resemblance among several recent theological proposals stemming from Yale,"[22] and seems willing to identify himself with this "postliberal alternative" that seeks to redirect the Christian community's vision back to its scriptural sources and to the Bible's distinctive, even unique, vision of reality."[23]

Conclusion. "No man is an island entire of himself." This statement is certainly true of almost all biblical scholars and is certainly true of Brevard Childs. The preceding paragraphs have attempted to locate Childs within various theological, literary, and intellectual/social contexts. Such contextualization is not intended to diminish the unique contributions of Childs to biblical study, but to help the student understand the intricate social web in which all intellectual thought is inevitably embodied.

Childs is a leading figure in the study of the Bible in a

canonical context. To be sure, he represents only one approach to the canon, but his approach is widely known if not widely accepted. His emphasis on the final form of the canonical text as theologically normative is one to which we must return shortly.

James Sanders and the Canonical Process

James Sanders is the other figure closely associated with canonical criticism. In fact, it is Sanders who finally settled on the phrase "canonical criticism" as an apt description of the approach he takes. Since 1977, Sanders has served as Elizabeth Hay Bechtel Professor of Intertestamental and Biblical Studies at the School of Theology at Claremont and Professor of Religion at Claremont Graduate School. He formerly taught at Colgate Rochester Divinity School (1954–1966) and Union Theological Seminary in New York (1966–1977).

By his own admission, Sanders' academic pilgrimage has been unusual.[24] As a divinity student at Vanderbilt, Sanders planned to do doctoral studies in New Testament at Yale. After a year of study in Paris, he attended Hebrew Union College in Cincinnati to improve his knowledge of Jewish backgrounds to the New Testament before entering Yale. He stayed three years, earning his Ph.D. in Hebrew Bible and early Judaism under the supervision of Samuel Sandmel, a well-known Jewish biblical scholar. Upon completing his degree, Sanders took for eleven years a "temporary" position in Old Testament at Colgate Rochester Divinity School, never completing his plans to pursue graduate work in New Testament. He laments the division in the academic guild between Old and New Testament studies and in fact has maintained interest in both testaments. Though a Presbyterian by denominational affiliation, Sanders maintains, "Since my formation is largely French and Jewish I approach the New Testament first and foremost as but a part of Christian Scripture."[25] In addition to his work in canonical criticism, Sanders has worked extensively with the Qumran scrolls and their impact on New Testament studies. Below I will discuss Sanders' major contributions to the formation of canonical criticism.

Torah and Canon. In 1972, Sanders published *Torah and Canon.*[26] Though Sanders had explored the issue of canon in previous articles, this work was his first sustained effort to engage in reflection on the historical and theological problems associated with canon.[27] For Sanders, canonical criticism is a subdiscipline of exegesis that picks up the results of historical criticism (source, form, redaction) and seeks to determine the function of the ancient tradition in its historical context. Sanders is vitally interested in the historical processes that gave the canon its final shape.

In *Torah and Canon*, he first focuses on the canonical shape of the Torah and the historical processes that gave rise to it. He argues that the Torah story that begins with creation and continues with the promises made to Abraham of land and nationhood properly ends either in the fulfillment of the promises to Abraham of a land (Joshua) or of nationhood (Samuel-Kings). On the basis of the recitals or credos of faith found throughout the Torah, Sanders argues that in fact in preexilic Israel the Torah story did come in two versions: 1) Abraham to the Conquest; 2) Abraham to the Monarchy. How then, Sanders asks, does one explain the canonical shape of the Torah that ends in Deuteronomy with neither promise fulfilled?

His answer to this question is, in the words of Brevard Childs, "the most original part of the book."[28] Sanders turns to the historical context to explain the canonical shape of the Torah. His explanation is that the canonical redactors in reaction to the shock of the destruction of Jerusalem, the demise of the Davidic monarchy, and exile from their promised land relocated Jerusalem's true identity in the Mosaic torah. Thus, the final editors of the canon enabled Israel to survive even as the state and cult crumbled around them. In the rest of the book, Sanders shows how the Prophets and Writings understood the Torah story and made use of it in their new situations. Sanders sees in the process whereby the believing community adapted its sacred traditions to meet new situations the key for modern communities to transform our traditions in light of changing situations.

Canon and Community. Sanders' next book, *Canon and Community*, explores canonical criticism around two foci: canonical process and canonical hermeneutics.[29] The first, canonical process, is the extension of his argument in *Torah and Canon* that one must search for the historical traces of the ways the believing community of Israel repeated and modified its sacred traditions. According to Sanders, there were two periods of "intense canonical process": the exile in the sixth century, B.C.

and the destruction of the temple in the first century, A.D. Though during these periods the authoritative traditions were moving toward fixed stability (a five-book Torah was the product of the Exile; a fixed collection of writings the result of the destruction of the Herodian temple), the canonical process, according to Sanders continues into the modern period as Jewish and Christian communities receive and adapt their sacred Scriptures for new situations.

This emphasis on both the stability and adaptability of Scripture leads Sanders to discuss what he calls canonical hermeneutics. What modern communities need to do, Sanders argues, is to study the pattern of interpretation that the ancient communities used in adapting their Scriptures for us. Sanders had already developed this canonical hermeneutic in an earlier essay. The diagram reproduced below is accompanied by his explanation:

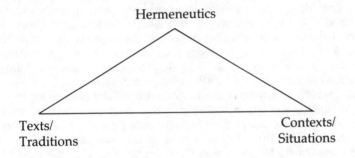

By texts is meant the common authoritative traditions employed and brought forward (re-resented) by the prophet to bear upon the situation to which he or she spoke in antiquity. Such traditions included both the authoritative forms of speech expected of prophets and the authoritative epic-historic traditions to which they appealed to legitimate their messages.

By contexts is meant the historical, cultural, social, political, economic, national, and international situations to which prophets applied the "texts." Context here, then, is not solely or even principally a literary reference (though often the literary context is determinative for meaning) but refers primarily to the full, three-dimensional situation in antiquity necessary to understand the significance of the literary record or unit under study.

By hermeneutics is meant the ancient theological mode, as well as literary technique, by which that application was made by the prophet, true or false—that is, how he or she read the "texts" and "contexts" *and* how he or she related them.[30]

Sanders proposes this triad of text, context, and hermeneutics as an interpretive paradigm for modern believing communities. We will evaluate this approach a little later in the essay.

From Sacred Story to Sacred Text. Sanders' most recent book, *From Sacred Story to Sacred Text* (1987), is a collection of nine essays previously published between 1975–1980 and one article that appears here for the first time. But this book is far more than simply a collection of diverse writings. It is what Sanders calls "a sort of pilgrimage into canonical criticism."[31] Sanders allows the interested reader to follow that pilgrimage by providing a clearly articulated prologue and epilogue, a brief introduction that sets these chronologically arranged essays in context, and a concluding essay (that shares its title with the book) that serves, so he suggests, "as an epitome, for the time being, to the pilgrimage."[32] In this last essay, Sanders defines canonical criticism as "a theocentric monotheizing hermeneutic," which he claims is the hermeneutic of the biblical writers.[33] It is this theocentric monotheizing that allows modern believing communities to adapt their Scriptures to new situations in ways analogous to the biblical world. And monotheizing in the modern world is "to pursue the oneness of God or the Integrity of Reality" that is perhaps the greatest challenge the human mind and spirit have ever encountered."[34] Thus like Childs, Sanders is able to overcome the distance between descriptive and constructive theology (what it means/what it meant) that traditional historical-critical methods had created (or at least acknowledged).

Sanders' Approach in Context. Like Childs, James Sanders owes much to his academic (students and colleagues) and ecclesial (pastors and lay persons) contexts. Sanders' own academic background prepared him well for his subsequent theological interests. As he himself notes, "What I learned in doing the dissertation has been extended in various ways but principally into research on canonical hermeneutics, those unrecorded hermeneutics that lie between all the lines of

Scripture where any authoritative community tradition, or international wisdom accepted as authoritative, is cited or alluded to and re-presented."[35]

Another interesting note to make here is that Sanders' emphasis on the canonical *process* meshes well with the interests of some of his colleagues at Claremont in process theology (e.g., John Cobb). While Sanders had already developed this interest before going to Claremont, it has surely been reinforced by the intellectual context there.[36]

Conclusion. Like Brevard Childs, James Sanders has devoted the better part of the last two decades in working out his own agenda for canonical criticism. For Sanders, canonical criticism involves sensitivity to the canonical processes whereby a sacred tradition was adapted to a new situation, thus bearing witness to Scripture's stability and adaptability. Further, canonical criticism involves developing a canonical hermeneutic that takes into account the triad of text, context, and hermeneutic. The last legacy that the biblical tradition has left to the modern communities of faith, according to Sanders, is a pattern of how to interpret ancient traditions in new situations.

EVALUATION OF CANONICAL CRITICISM

Though others have made contributions to the development of a canonical approach to the New Testament, Childs and Sanders stand head and shoulders above the others in terms of their influence in the dialogue. And though they share certain common interests and commitments, their approaches to the issue of canon are, at times, radically different. I will proceed, then, by comparing their work, noting the strengths and weaknesses of each approach. I will then enumerate the principles that seem most useful in the construction of an interpretive method that seeks to take the canon seriously. We will label that method "canonical criticism."

Agreements Between Childs and Sanders

Childs and Sanders share a number of common concerns in their attempts to take the canon seriously. First, both of them recognize the need to move the Christian canon to the center of hermeneutical discussions of how to interpret the Bible. Second, both of them also have sensed the inadequacy of the historical-critical method, though Childs is far more critical than Sanders. And third, both of them wish to see the Bible returned to its proper place in the believing community.

Disagreements Between Childs and Sanders

Despite these agreements, the differences between these two approaches are sharp. A commonly noted distinction is between Childs' emphasis on the canonical *product* and Sanders' emphasis on the canonical *process*. For Childs, the canonical product is the literature of the community in its final canonical form. It is the canonical text that is the reliable vehicle of the Word of God. For Sanders, on the other hand, the canonical process refers to use the community has made of its literature, adapting ancient traditions for new situations. While Sanders rightly points out that this distinction between canonical product and process is a simplification of the differences between himself and Childs, the nuance is helpful nonetheless.[37]

Another distinction between Sanders and Childs is in their regard for the usefulness of the historical-critical method. While it is true that both see the methods of form, source, and redaction criticism as generally practiced are open to serious challenge, Sanders is far more sympathetic to the use of such methods in reconstructing the canonical process described above. Childs, on the other hand, while often accepting the judgments of even the most radical historical-critical probes, dismisses the historical-critical method as irrelevant to the church and incompetent to deal with the theological character of Scripture. The difference between the two on this score may be illustrated by the fact that Childs disdains using the term "canonical criticism." He notes:

> I am unhappy with this term because it implies that the canonical approach is considered another historical critical technique which can take its place alongside of source criticism, form criticism, rhetorical criticism, and similar methods. I do not envision the approach to canon in this light. Rather, the issue at stake in relation to the canon turns on establishing a stance from which the Bible can be read as Scripture.[38]

Sanders, on the other hand, openly embraces the term canonical criticism as indicative of the way he wishes his approach to be complementary to historical criticism. In fact, Sanders is fond of saying that historical criticism is "a gift of God in due season."[39]

The extent of the canon is another point of contention. Childs repeatedly argues that the canonical approach must take into account the "full canonical context." Sanders, while sympathetic to Childs' position, also sees the positive contributions of the notion of a "canon within the canon," that is, the portion of Scripture that holds a more elevated, authoritative status than other parts. For Sanders, this canon within the canon is the Torah-Gospel to which other parts of the canon respond.

Strengths and Weaknesses

What are we to make of these differences, and how do we evaluate the approaches of Childs and Sanders in a way that allows us to forge a canonical criticism that is a useful method of interpretation? Much about the work of Childs and Sanders commends itself. Where they agree that the Christian canon has been largely neglected in contemporary hermeneutics, that the historical-critical method poses questions it has difficulty answering, and that the Bible properly deserves a central place in contemporary worshiping communities, I stand in agreement.

Where we must make progress—if we are to formulate a method of interpretation that takes the canon seriously—is in adjudicating those places of critical disagreement between Childs and Sanders. This may entail, at times, rejecting both proposals for yet a third.

The canonical product and the canonical process are both helpful ways of thinking, but both notions stand in need of modification. First, let us take up Childs' emphasis on the canonical product or final form of the text. For Childs, the canonical context is the only context for proper theological exegesis. For this reason, Childs rejects the reconstructed historical context of a text and, so it seems, the historical-critical methods of reconstruction along with it.[40] I would like to argue that the canonical meaning of a text is significant and often to be preferred over the historical meaning, i.e., the meaning derived from the historical-critical method. But it is not the *only* proper context for interpretation.

The difference here, as I see it, lies in our theoretical understanding of meaning. In a stimulating article, "The Sensus Literalis of Scripture: An Ancient and Modern Problem," Childs argues that, in the history of exegesis, the literal sense of Scripture has generally meant the "plain sense" of Scripture; and until the Enlightenment, the plain sense of Scripture was the canonical meaning.[41] The literal or plain sense of Scripture was used by the Reformers to control the wild allegorizations of the medieval church. After the Enlightenment and the genesis of historical criticism, the plain meaning of Scripture was equivalent to the original meaning of the text in its historical context as reconstructed by historical criticism. Childs' plea at the end of this article is that the notion of the plain sense (understood as the canonical sense) is a way out of the cul-de-sac into which historical criticism has led us. What is clear throughout this essay is Childs' theoretical assumption that a text has a single meaning. He simply wishes to shift the locus of that meaning from a historical to a canonical context.

Much more helpful to me has been the article by Reformation specialist David Steinmetz entitled, "The Superiority of Pre-critical Exegesis."[42] In this article, Steinmetz argues that rather than denouncing the fourfold exegesis of the medieval church, we should look to it as a way of escaping the reductionistic approaches of historical criticism. To be sure, Steinmetz is not suggesting that we return to the allegorical method per se, but that with the medieval exegetes (and he argues with some of the Reformers as well) we recognize the multivalency of the scriptural text. This is not to say that every text has a limitless number of interpretations or that we have no way of judging among interpretations. No, the text in its historical and canonical contexts constrains the number of interpretations available and provides textual clues for adjudicating among those interpretations to prevent an anarchy of readings. But still, as Steinmetz notes, the notion that every text has only one, single meaning (whether it is the historical or canonical) is a hermeneutically impoverished theory. He concludes, "The medieval theory of levels of meaning in the biblical text, with all its undoubted defects, flourished because it is true, while the modern theory of a single meaning, with all its demonstrable virtue, is false."[43]

The parables of Jesus are a good illustration of this point. It is unlikely that when Jesus originally told the parable of the good Samaritan it produced one interpretation among the hearers or that Jesus intended it to do so. Parables often have a redemptive ambiguity that allows for multiple interpretations. The interpretation of this parable in its original setting in part depended on the social location of the hearers: Were they priests, Levites, Samaritans, Jews? Males or females? And even today the parable can have a different meaning if we identify, for example, with the man in the ditch rather than with the Samaritan. Likewise the parable of the unjust judge in Luke has no less than four interpretations attached to it, all of them laying claim to be legitimate interpretations. F. F. Bruce has also recognized that "the establishment of the primary sense of a passage of scripture is not always such a straightforward matter as is commonly supposed."[44]

My point is that even in its original setting it is not always clear that a text (or saying or oral tradition) had a singular meaning, and to assume so may do violence to the text. As Steinmetz observed, "Until the historical-critical method becomes critical of its own theoretical foundations and develops a hermeneutical theory adequate to the nature of the text which it is interpreting, it will remain restricted—as it deserves to be— to the guild and the academy, where the question of truth can endlessly be deferred."[45] And Steinmetz's critique of historical criticism may aptly be applied to canonical approaches if they are theoretically underpinned by the notion that every text has only a single meaning, even if it is the *canonical* meaning.

It is at this point that I want to introduce a concept that is still much discussed in scholarly circles, namely the *sensus plenior* or "full sense" of Scripture. Though some prominent evangelicals, like Walter Kaiser, have rejected the concept of the *sensus plenior*, other confessional scholars have sensed the possibility of interpreting the *sensus plenior* in a canonical context.[46]

Douglas Oss has recently offered a penetrating analysis of the function of the *sensus plenior* in the context of the canon for evangelical hermeneutics.[47] Oss argues, "*sensus plenior*, here defined, refers to the recognition of the canon of Scripture as a single and unified literary work. Because it is one book, no part of the book can be properly understood apart from the whole."[48] He further elaborates:

Thus a biblically based *sensus plenior* considers a given text in the light of the fulness of revelation. Any deeper meaning for a text comes only from other biblical texts. Using this definition one cannot be accused of looking to a source outside the canon for the meaning of texts, nor of reading into a text something that is not there. The meaning is there by virtue of the organic relationship of the parts of Scripture to the whole of Scripture.[49]

Oss still is reluctant to give up the discussion of the single meaning of a text, particularly if the notion of multiple meanings postulates unrelated meanings emanating from the same text. But for Oss, the " 'single meaning' in a text refers to its unity of meaning. . . . Where a deeper meaning emerges as the result of reflection on either the relationships of a text to other texts or on the integration of texts into the canonical structure, it is the multi-dimensional nature of meaning that is coming to the fore."[50] While I see no reason to preserve the notion of a single meaning of Scripture, particularly in light of Oss's contention that reflection on the canon of Scripture may reveal the "multi-dimensional nature of meaning," I do concur with his contention that the canonical meaning(s) of a text—the *sensus plenior*, if you will—is integrally related to the historical meaning(s) of the text. The *sensus plenior* in this canonical context, then, will not tolerate unbridled allegorization. Rather, the full meaning(s) of the text, i.e., its canonical meaning(s) must be understood as intimately related to the historical sense of Scripture and vice versa. F. F. Bruce notes that "the plenary sense, to be valid, must be the plenary sense of the *biblical text*: it will remain that if its relationship and consistency with the primary sense be maintained."[51]

At times, that intimate relationship entails a fuller or deeper elaboration of the historical meaning(s); at times, it means that the historical sense is reshaped by the text's placement within the canon. But in either case, to argue a priori that the historical meaning of Scripture must always take precedence (as historical critics argue) or to argue a priori that the canonical meaning of Scripture must always be the privileged reading (as Childs and other canon critics maintain) is to diminish both the notion of meaning and the hermeneutical enterprise. To limit the exegete to the historical or canonical meaning of the text, particularly the exegete who sees himself

or herself as a theologian of the church, is needlessly reductionistic.[52] Bruce has commented wisely on this matter:

> . . .Professor Childs' "canonical" exegesis might point a way
> forward. But if it does, the way forward will be in essence the
> way of plenary interpretation—that is to say, a way which
> does not break loose from the primary sense, but expounds
> the text so as to reveal its relevance to human life today, just
> as the successive generations intervening between the origi-
> nal readers and ourselves have heard it speak to their
> varying conditions.[53]

By thus modifying Childs' emphasis on the canonical
meaning as the singular meaning, we are also able to address
another problem with Childs' approach. Childs pays little
attention to the issue of genre in dismissing the historical
approach. Certain New Testament genres, the epistle for
example, are much more open to historical investigation and
reconstruction than, say, narratives. Partly for this reason, we
know more about the historical situations of the recipients of
Paul's letters than we do the Gospels. We know more about the
social history of the Corinthian congregation than we do the
Lukan community. And such historical information is invaluable in interpreting Paul's Corinthian correspondence, while
historical reconstruction may serve only to confuse the interpretation of the third Gospel. To be sure, it is also helpful to
interpret 1 Corinthians in the context of the Pauline corpus or
the corpus in the context of the rest of the New Testament. But
why should we choose?

The Old Testament lacks such an immediate genre as the
epistle, and this fact might help explain some of the problems
in transition when we move to apply Childs' program, forged
as it is primarily on the Old Testament text, to the New
Testament. It also explains in part why Childs' approach is
often less convincing in his New Testament Introduction than
in his Old Testament Introduction. At any rate, while I shall
keep the emphasis on the canonical product in my version of
canonical criticism, I will not preclude the importance of the
historical context of either the composition or canonization of
the New Testament materials.

James Sanders' emphasis on the canonical process is, of
course, a helpful corrective here. Sanders attempts to take
seriously the historical factors that produced the final form of

the text (and precanonical forms as well). It is just such an emphasis that I will include in my version of canonical criticism. Where I disagree with Sanders is in the significance he attaches to this canonical process. If Childs is too reductionistic in his approach to the canon, Sanders may be too open. If Childs argues for the unity of the canonical witness, Sanders celebrates its plurality. For Sanders it is not biblical traditions that are authoritative, but the hermeneutical patterns or paradigms of the biblical writers who adapted these traditions to their situations that are hermeneutically determinative. While I agree that the hermeneutical patterns of the biblical communities have much to contribute to contemporary hermeneutics, I am not satisfied with the idea of replacing the religious authority of the canonical texts with the canonical hermeneutics of the writers. Most persons who hold a high view of Scripture will probably be troubled by this proposal since it confers authority, not on the text of Scripture, but on hermeneutical patterns that Sanders admits are often found only between the lines of the text.

The combination of the canonical product with the canonical process, however incompatible those two emphases may at first appear to be, will serve as the foundation of my version of canonical criticism developed below.

TENETS OF CANONICAL CRITICISM

Below are the tenets of canonical criticism that I propose to employ in this essay. In part, these principles draw upon the work of Childs and Sanders and attempt to synthesize aspects of their work. Like Childs, I propose to take seriously the canonical product of the New Testament writings, though I am unwilling in every case to absolutize the canonical meaning as the singular meaning. Like Sanders, I am interested in reconstructing the canonical process where it is possible to detect the traces of those historical factors, but I am unwilling to canonize the hermeneutical patterns discovered there to the denigration of the text itself. The particular shape of these principles, then, is a constructive effort on my part, and I have no illusions that either Childs or Sanders would be fully satisfied with this construal. I hope to articulate these tenets and my justification for them, however, in such a way that it may be useful to other scholars and students. Of course, one runs the risks of having the proposal viewed as idiosyncratic and therefore relegated to some marginalized position in the field.[54] Still, given the ferment now current in discussions of canonical criticism, if my proposal contributes to that debate in both academic and ecclesial circles, I will view it as a risk worth taking.

The Canonical Product: The Final Form of the Text

In dealing with the final form of the canonical text, canonical criticism is interested in both the canonical *shaping* of the text as well as the canonical *position* of the text. Below I will attempt to develop both of these lines of thinking.

Canonical Shaping. In *The New Testament as Canon*, Childs has a helpful list of guiding principles in a section entitled "Methodology of Canonical Exegesis." These principles might be described as typical of what Donn Morgan has called "micro-canonical analysis," which "studies a book or perhaps an even smaller unit."[55] Below are listed some of those principles, along with some examples from the New Testament. This list is to be taken as exemplary, not exhaustive. I have not included all of the items in Childs' list of principles; in some cases, I have slightly modified those I did choose. Certainly I have not exhausted all of the possible illustrations of these principles of canonical criticism.

The Overall Structure of the Book. Childs suggests that "one of the first places to look for indications of canonical shaping lies in the structure of the book."[56] He further argues that a "construal of the structure which in fact eliminates portions of the book should be viewed with suspicion."[57] This canonical perspective would affect our understanding, for example, of composite letters in the New Testament, i.e., letters composed of the fragments of two or more letters.

If there are any composite letters in the New Testament, then we have a case of the canonical structure of the book being different from the structure in its original composition. Perhaps the best candidate for such a phenomenon is 2 Corinthians. While the arguments of older scholarship for the presence of fragments from as many as five letters in 2 Corinthians have been seriously challenged, there seems to be an emerging consensus, even among conservative scholars, that 2 Corinthians is comprised of two letters, which are found in 1–9 and 10–13.[58] These two letters were probably brought together by the editor(s) responsible for the Pauline corpus. Canonical criticism would attempt to interpret the entirety of 2 Corinthians in its canonical context.[59]

Prescripts, Conclusions, and Superscriptions. According to Childs, "The purpose of the author is often most clearly stated in the prescript or in the conclusion."[60] These beginnings and endings often "were added during the final stages of canonization, but frequently give a valuable clue to how the church first heard the message."[61] In the prescript or salutation of Paul's letter to the Ephesians, some manuscripts read, "To the saints who are also faithful in Christ Jesus," omitting the words "in Ephesus" (see 1:1). The external evidence of the manuscript witnesses is divided, and it is difficult to know what the text read originally. Some scholars have assumed that Ephesians was written by the anonymous editor who was responsible for collecting Paul's letters into a corpus. On the other hand, others argue that the reference to Ephesians has been omitted to make the Epistle more readily acceptable as a universal or catholic letter. At any rate, the canonical shape of the Letter includes the reference, and—text-critical arguments aside—canonical criticism will attempt to make sense of this address in the context of the larger Pauline corpus.

The longer ending of Mark (16:9–20) shows all the marks of being the product of redactional activity with a canonical consciousness. Two facts support this assertion. First, whether Mark actually ended at 16:8 or whether the original ending was lost, the impetus to provide a proper conclusion to the Gospel no doubt was provided by the fourfold collection of the Gospels. Hence, from the perspective of the church, the "inadequacy" of Mark's conclusion stood in bold contrast with the other three Gospels, all of which brought their stories to an "appropriate" denouement with their accounts of the post-resurrection appearances of Jesus. Second, the contents of the longer ending of Mark reveal a clear dependence on the other canonical Gospels, even if there are some traditions that are independent of the canonical Gospels. Rather than dismissing the longer ending as useless and irrelevant, as historical criticism has largely chosen to do, the canonical critic would be most interested in the function of this ending in its canonical context and would attempt to make sense of Mark as it stands in its final form.

The canonical editors were most likely responsible for most

of the titles, or superscriptions, to the majority of the New Testament writings. While these titles for the most part reflect the ancient and honored traditions of the church and thus hold a certain authority, they were, in all likelihood, not part of the original composition. Rather, in some cases, the inclusion of the title may have coincided with the struggle for canonization. This is almost certainly true of the full title of Hebrews: "The Epistle of Paul the Apostle to the Hebrews." As Reginald Fuller has noted (tongue-in-cheek), the only problem with this superscription is that Hebrews is not an epistle in genre, it was not written by Paul the apostle, and it was not addressed to Hebrews (non-Christian Jews).[62] Still, a canonical critic would be interested in that title because it says something (along with the actual placement of Hebrews) about the role Hebrews played as a canonical coordinate between the Pauline Corpus and the collection of writings known as the General Epistles.

The Function of the Addressee. "A frequent indication of how the New Testament seeks to transcend its original historical context," Childs insists, "lies in carefully observing the function of the addressee of a composition."[63] Often the subsequent readers of Scripture are addressed only by "subtle analogies" though "at other times the disciples became an obvious transparency for the one obedient response of the church. . . ."[64] Both the Gospel of John (20:31) and the Gospel of Mark (13:14), from the perspective of canonical criticism, seek to encompass the larger Christian church by virtue of their use of direct address.[65]

Canonical Position. Another aspect of the canonical product or final form of the text has to do with the canonical position or placement of the document. "Macro-canonical analysis," as it has been labeled by Donn Morgan, focuses on an entire document or collection of writings such as the Torah or Prophets in the Old Testament or the Fourfold Gospel or Pauline Collection in the New.[66] Macro-canonical analysis might include "consideration of the sequences of books and their variations within particular canonical collections."[67] Such analyses in Old Testament studies often reflect on the various functions of a book whose order is different in the sequence of the Hebrew Bible and the Septuagint. In New Testament studies such examination might include the shift in the canonical function of a book whose order in some of the ancient manuscripts differs from that of the typical order we now know.

Long ago, E. J. Goodspeed observed that the New Testament is a "collection of collections."[68] Macro-canonical analysis takes that observation to heart. Several attempts have already been made at dealing with the collections of writings in the New Testament, including the Fourfold Gospel and the Pauline Collection. In addition, the place of Hebrews as the canonical coordinate between the Pauline Corpus and the General Epistles, Acts as a canonical bridge between the Gospels and Epistles, and Matthew as the canonical beginning of the New Testament have also been explored. The point is to take seriously the position of the New Testament writing as part of the canonical product and indicative of its canonical function.

Conclusion. Treating the New Testament as a canonical product entails close attention to the canonical shape of the writing for clues to the way the original text has been modified as it passed through the prism of canonization. From such clues we may glean insight into the meaning that the canonical editors attached to the writing. Additional clues for the function of a document or collection of documents within the canonical context may be derived from the placement of that writing within a smaller collection (Gospels or Epistles) or the collection within the larger canon. By identifying the marks of the canonical product, we may begin to understand the factors involved in the canonical process.

The Canonical Process:
Historical Factors in Canonization

To take seriously the canonical process that produced the canonical product described above requires that the student have some awareness of the historical factors involved in the canonization of the New Testament writings. In addition to the older studies of canon by Goodspeed, Knox, von Harnack, and van Campenhausen, a new wave of interest on the history of the canon has appeared recently in the works of Harry Gamble, F. F. Bruce, and Lee MacDonald.

Awareness of the theological and historical problems of the canon must include the origins and growth as well as the closure of the canon. Until we articulate a thoroughgoing historical reconstruction as to the factors involved in inclusion and exclusion of certain early Christian writings, we will continue to view the canonical process as an "accidental precipitate."[69] The unfortunate result is that we are forced either to accept the canon as a theological a priori with no historical explanation for reasons why these writings and not others or to reject the canon as irrelevant for historical and theological investigations. The history of the New Testament, while complicated, is perhaps less difficult to deal with historically and theologically than the Old Testament, and some progress is being made toward articulating a theory of canon that respects both its historical and theological dimensions.[70] I hope that such canonical critical endeavors might also contribute to our understanding of the composition, collection, and canonization of the New Testament writings.

APPLICATION OF CANONICAL CRITICISM: THE BOOK OF ACTS IN CANONICAL CONTEXT

As an exercise in canonical criticism, I will deal with the Acts of the Apostles in its canonical context. This is not exhaustive treatment of the issue, but serves rather as illustrative of the insights that canonical criticism may bring to bear on a particular problem in New Testament studies. We must begin by recognizing that the unity of Luke and Acts is axiomatic in current New Testament scholarship. W. Ward Gasque, for example, at the end of his exhaustive survey of Acts scholarship, concluded, "The primary gain of the recent criticism of Luke-Acts has been the recognition that the Gospel according to Luke and the Book of Acts are really two volumes of one work which must be considered together. Questions concerning purpose, theology, speeches, and historical value cannot be answered apart from a study of both volumes of Luke's two-volumed work."[71]

Henry J. Cadbury was the person most responsible for this *opinio communis*. In the preface to the 1958 edition of *The Making of Luke-Acts*, he writes, "It may help the reader place this 1927 publication in past history to remind us how many other books in English since then have employed the convenient hyphenated expression 'Luke-Acts.' "[72] It is remarkable that in a twenty-year period of New Testament research, which has witnessed a frontal assault on the entire historical-critical enterprise from the priority of Mark to the dominance of redaction criticism as *the* interpretive method in gospel studies, the notion of the unity of Luke-Acts has remained unscathed. What happens, though, when we attempt to take seriously the canonical context of the Acts of the Apostles?

Acts as a Canonical Product:
The Final Form of the Acts of the Apostles

The unity of the Lukan writings, as we have seen, is a construct of critical scholarship.[73] That John stands between canonical Luke and Acts, however, presents something of a problem for the notion that these two works form a single, continuous work. The fact that the two writings are not united in their canonical form is evidence that the first readers read them separately, and either actively and intentionally split a one-volume work into two to create these two works or passively introduced the individual scrolls at different points in the canonical order. While critical historical scholarship has insisted that Luke and Acts must be taken together against their canonical shape, it also insists that the Pauline letters must be taken individually against their canonical shape. From the perspective of canonical criticism, what, then, can we make of Acts as a canonical product as it stands in its final form in the Christian canon?

The Canonical Shape of Acts. Returning to our list of principles for canonical exegesis, there are a number of micro-canonical observations to be made about Acts.

Overall Structure of the Book. The overall structure of Acts moves from the story of the apostles after Jesus' ascension to the story of the travels of Paul and his companions. This structure contributes to its canonical position and is significant for its canonical function—assertions that will be demonstrated later in the section on the canonical position of Acts.

Prescripts, Conclusions, Superscriptions. Some manuscripts of Acts omit the words "he was taken up" in the prescript of Acts (1:2). As Acts was brought into a collection of sacred Scriptures that also included Luke, the apparent tension between the ascension accounts was resolved by omitting the reference to the Ascension either in Luke 24:51 or Acts 1:2. At any rate, we have here some evidence of the canonical shaping of Acts.

The title of the book most likely also is a canonical product.

The title "The Acts of the Apostles" has puzzled scholars for centuries. Gerhard Krodel's comments are typical: "The title itself is misleading, because it does not indicate that Acts is volume two of our author's literary work. Moreover, this book does not deal with the acts of the apostles, plural. Its two main figures are Peter and Paul, and the latter is not really an apostle according to Luke."[74]

Almost certainly the book did not carry the title from the time of its composition; in fact, it is unlikely the document was titled at all. More likely, however, is the view that the title probably corresponds to the acceptance of Acts in some communities as authoritative Scripture. Robert Wall has noted:

> . . .the effect of the title's "of the apostles" is to shift the attention away from the Spirit, as Luke would have it, toward the apostles, as the canonizing community would have it. Indeed, such a shift parallels the ecclesial movement during the first and second centuries away from charismatic authority to institutional authority, away from pneumatic claims (via revelation) to those rooted in the notion of apostolicity.[75]

Further, the title may reflect already the canonical function of Acts—it stands as a bridge between the Gospels, Paul's Epistles, and the writings of the other apostles. As F. F. Bruce has noted, "The title 'The Acts of the Apostles' may have been intended to point out that Paul was not the only faithful apostle of Christ (even if much more is said about him than about the others in Acts)."[76] This canonical function might explain then what some scholars, like Krodel, have emphasized about the inappropriateness of the title.

Though the ending of Acts does not reveal any text-critical problems that might be construed as evidence for canonical shaping, the ending does hint at the canonical function of Acts. The book ends enigmatically with the word "unhindered" (28:31) and emphasizes that the message of the Gospel marches forward unrestrained even when the messenger is under house arrest. Ending as it does with Paul preaching in Rome, Acts is also the logical introduction to Paul's letter to the Romans, which stands at the head of the Pauline corpus.

The Function of the Addressee. Whoever Theophilus may have been historically speaking—Luke's benefactor, a Roman dignitary, etc.—in the canonical context of Acts, Theophilus is the "lover of God" and functions to invite the reader to enter the story world of Acts. No longer just an historical figure, Theophilus functions as a hermeneutical bridge between the text and the reader. To read Acts in its canonical context, the reader must become a "lover of God," a theophilus.

The Canonical Position of Acts: Acts as "Canonical Bridge." Adolf Harnack observed long ago, "A canon which comprised only the four Gospels and the Pauline Epistles would have been at best an edifice of two wings without the central structure, and therefore incomplete and uninhabitable."[77] Interestingly, Brevard Childs has argued that "the canonical function of Acts was not determined by the order of its placement within the New Testament collection."[78] Robert Wall, on the other hand, observes, "The idea that Acts links the fourfold gospel on the one hand and the apostolic letters on the other is not new to canonical criticism; it is an old insight whose time has come."[79] In what follows, I attempt to uncover what insights are available from the assumption that the canonical position of Acts is indeed significant (*pace* Wall; *contra* Childs).

Acts as a Bridge to the Gospels. Despite the traditional use of Acts by the church to provide a geographic and chronological framework for reading Paul's letters, we should note that Acts is first found among New Testament manuscripts attached to the "fourfold Gospel." In fact, the oldest copy of the fourfold gospel, p^{72} (dated ca. A.D. 200), also contains Acts. Hence, historically speaking, Acts first found its place among authoritative Christian Scriptures in relationship to the Gospels, not Paul's letters. That the story of the founder of the Christian movement should be followed by the story of his successors is not unexpected. The commission of the resurrected Lord, found with variations in all four canonical Gospels (Mt 28:19–20; [Mk 16:15–18]; Lk 24:44–49; Jn 20:19–29), is found also in Acts (1:8). The rest of Acts then records the fulfillment of this commission by the apostles and Paul.

We might also consider the way in which the canonical portrait of Mary, the mother of Jesus, is completed by Acts. Though Luke's infancy account depicts Mary as a faithful and obedient servant of God, Mary is also part of Jesus' family who stand as outsiders to his ministry (see Mk 3:20–35; Mt 12:46–50; Lk 8:19–21). Jesus himself intensifies this struggle between his family of flesh and his family of faith when he responds to the report that his mother and brothers are outside asking for him

(Mk 3:32): " 'Who are my mother and brothers?' And looking around on those who sat about him, he said, 'Here are my mother and brothers! Whoever does the will of God is my brother, and sister, and mother' " (vv. 33–35 RSV).

In John's Gospel, Jesus resolves this canonical tension between his mother of flesh and his brother in faith. Among his last words in the Fourth Gospel are the poignant words he directs first to his mother and then to the "Beloved Disciple": "When Jesus saw his mother, and the disciple whom he loved standing near, he said to his mother, 'Woman, behold your son!' Then he said to the disciple, 'Behold, your mother!' (19:26–27 RSV). Fulton Sheen once referred to the first half of this saying, "Woman, behold your son," as the "second nativity," and he suggested that, in John's Gospel, Mary could not follow Jesus as Savior until she gave him up as Son.

Was Jesus' radical realignment of kinship successful? The Fourth Gospel gives only a cryptic summary: "From that hour the disciple took her to his own home" (19:27 RSV). But the canonical reader needs only to turn the page of the Bible to read that those who had returned to Jerusalem to pray after Jesus' ascension included not only the eleven apostles, but Jesus' mother and brothers (Ac 1:13–14). The limits of Jesus' family of faith, the church, had been extended to include also his family of flesh. What is promised in John, from a canonical perspective, is fulfilled in Acts.[80] The story of the transformation of Jesus' earthly family is canonically concluded by the presence of two epistles in the canon attributed to Mary's sons and Jesus' brothers, James and Jude.

Acts as a Bridge to the General Epistles. This last passing reference to the epistles of James and Jude brings us to consider the next group of writings for which Acts serves as a canonical coordinate, the General Epistles. Though p[72] groups Acts with the fourfold Gospel, most of the other earliest manuscripts place Acts before the so-called General Epistles. As Robert Wall has noted, "This canonical reality implies that Acts found its significance as the context for understanding the non-Pauline apostolic witness."[81] The canonical effect of Acts is that it "envisages a 'universalist' James, Cephas and John, thereby universalizing the non-Pauline collection. . . ."[82] The title found in some manuscripts, "The Acts of *All* the Apostles," supports this universalizing tendency.

By the time of the collection of the General Epistles, it was "the Jewish apostolate of James, Cephas, and John, which needed legitimating," not Paul.[83] Further, by including James and Jude in the collection, the apostolic writings were extended to include Jesus' family. Acts, with its favorable depictions of James, Peter, and John, served to provide the canonical legitimation of the Jewish mission against the onslaught of Marcion, Gnostics, and others in the second century who would have happily cut Christianity away from its Jewish roots. In a sense, then, the tensions between John and Peter (see Jn 21) and between James and Paul are resolved both by the narrative of Acts and by the presence of writings attributed to John, Peter, and James in the New Testament canon. And, of course, Acts serves to resolve the tension between the Jewish mission of the Jerusalem apostles and the gentile mission of Paul.

Acts as a Bridge to the Pauline Corpus. Acts is most typically seen to function as a bridge between the Gospel and the Apostle (as the four Gospels and Paul's letters were called in the early church). Traffic on the bridge, in this instance, travels in both direction. Acts serves as a canonical framework for the Pauline corpus, providing a narrative sequence into which these letters may be placed. On the other hand, Acts may be read in light of Paul's letters.

Acts also serves as the canonical coordinate between the Pauline collection and the General Epistles. Robert Wall noted that Acts functions "as the context within which the canonical conservation between the Pauline and the non-Pauline collection is understood."[84] He further says:

> Thus, sharply put, Acts interprets the two collections of letters in a more sectarian fashion: the Pauline corpus reflects the gospel of the gentile mission, while the non-Pauline collection reflects the gospel(s) of the Jewish mission. However, rather than causing division within the church, such a theological diversity is now perceived as normative and necessary for the work of a God who calls both Jews and gentiles to be the people of God.[85]

Acts, then, as a canonical bridge between the Pauline corpus and the General Epistles, provides a hermeneutical context for finding unity in the midst of theological diversity.

Acts As a Canonical Process:
The Historical Factors in the Canonization
of the Acts of the Apostles

What can be said about the historical process that led to the canonization of Acts? As in our discussion of Acts as a canonical product, my comments here should be taken as initial probings in this area, not as definitive conclusions. The point is to show how canonical criticism might address such questions.

Childs has commented on the canonical effect of Luke and Acts: "Luke became part of the fourfold Gospel collection and received its interpretation within the context of this corpus. Acts was assigned another position as bearer of the apostolic witness which was clearly distinguished from that of the evangelists."[86] Older scholars argued that the two works, Luke and Acts, were divided at the time of canonization, perhaps to employ Acts as canonical glue to hold together the "Gospel" and "Apostle," as early Christian writers called them. Earlier scholars argued that the conclusion of Luke and the beginning of Acts were later interpolations. Kirsopp Lake held that the ascension narrative in Luke 24 had been added later when the two works were divided. Amos Wilder and Hans Conzelmann supported this view, and Phillipe Menoud further suggested that both ascension accounts were interpolations added when the one-volume work of Luke-Acts was divided upon its acceptance into the canon.[87]

This hypothesis never gained a broad following. Ernst Haenchen has argued forcefully against the supposition that Luke's work was originally one volume and was divided upon canonization: ". . .the works were not taken into the canon by an ecclesiastical authority able to ensure the simultaneous alteration of all existing copies; their acceptance was, rather, a long drawn-out process. Nowhere have any traces come to light of the hypothetical older book."[88]

Haenchen's view is supported by the presence of the so-called Western Text of Acts. This text, of which Codex Cantabrigiensis (D) is the exemplar, is nearly ten percent longer than the Alexandrian version. Such unrestrained growth in the tradition may be taken as an indicator of a relatively late date for ecclesial acceptance of Acts as canonical Scripture—certainly much later than the Gospel of Luke. Childs is surely right in his observation: "It seems far more probable that Luke was first assigned a canonical sanctity and only subsequently did Acts acquire a similar status."[89]

Further support of the relatively late date for the church's acceptance of Acts as Scripture is found in the work of the church father Irenaeus (ca. A.D. 180). On the basis of the so-called "we" passages in Acts, Irenaeus clearly identifies Luke as a companion of Paul. After summarizing Paul's speech to the elders in Ephesus in Acts, Irenaeus writes, "But if any should reject Luke, on the ground that he did not know the truth, he plainly throws over the gospel of which he claims to be a disciple" (*Adv. Haer.* iii.14.3).

Irenaeus then describes some of the material in the Gospel that is distinctly Lukan and concludes:

> It is necessary, therefore, that they should accept also the other things that were said by Luke or that they should give up these as well. For it is not permitted to them by those who have sense, to accept as being true some of the things that were said by Luke [in his gospel], but to reject certain others [in Acts], as if he had not known the truth. . . . But if they are compelled also to accept the whole, paying heed to the entire gospel and to the teaching of the apostles, they must repent, in order to be saved from danger. (*Adv. Haer.*, iii.14.4).

Refuting especially the followers of Marcion and Valentinus, Irenaeus brilliantly argues on the basis of the common authorship of Luke and Acts that the veracity of the two works must stand or fall together. For Irenaeus, Acts is the bottleneck through which one must pass if the two major portions of the New Testament, the "Gospel" and the "Apostle," are to be held together—and for Irenaeus they must be held together. The comment by Cadbury about the place of Acts in the early church is especially true of the role it plays for Irenaeus: "The book of Acts is the only bridge we have across the seemingly impassable gulf that separates Jesus from Paul, Christ from Christianity, the gospel of Jesus from the gospel about Jesus."[90]

Though such historical testimony about Acts probably tells us little about the reasons for its composition,[91] it does inform us about the historical process that led to the canonical shape and function of Acts. Acts was an essential defense against Marcion, the Gnostics, and others who would have eliminated certain Christian writings as authoritative Scripture. Certainly much more work must be done on the historical factors that led to the formation and closure of the Christian canon. But this brief study does suggest that a theory of canon that accounts for both the theological and historical problems of the New Testament canon is in order and that Acts is a critical piece of that historical puzzle.

Summary

Frederick Danker once observed, "Who can assess the impediments to the understanding of Luke's thought that were erected through canonical interposition of John's gospel between the two sections of Luke's work? Centuries passed until Henry Cadbury finally cleared the way for perception of the distinctive literary features and their rationale in Luke-Acts."[92] If we are to take seriously the canonical shape of Luke and Acts as Childs insists we do, I would like to turn Danker's question back on the scholars who have followed Cadbury and ask, "Who can assess the impediments to understanding Luke's thought and the distinctive literary features of Luke and Acts that were erected when Henry Cadbury made 'Luke-Acts'?" Canonical criticism, as practiced here, at least *begins* to ameliorate the effect of seventy-five years of historical-critical study that has sought to override the canonical shape of Luke and Acts—the only shape of those writings the church has ever had.

CONCLUSION

In *The New Testament as Canon*, Brevard Childs concluded that his canonical approach is one that "seeks to sketch a different vision of the biblical text which profoundly affects one's concept of the enterprise, but which also makes room for the continuing activity of exegesis as a discipline of the church."[93] This vision begins to take shape as the theologians of the church wrestle with the Scriptures of the Christian canon. So much about this method of interpretation is new, and so much is still left to be worked out. That canonical criticism will not replace other interpretive tools in biblical study is clear to me.[94] But that canonical criticism will take its rightful place alongside other methods of interpretation, often as a corrective to the thoroughgoing historicism of traditional approaches, is equally clear.

The call to accept the canon as normative for theological exegesis is a healthful corrective to those approaches that have been either antipathetical or antithetical to interpretation within a confessional context. Canonical criticism, with all its flaws and potential weaknesses, does allow the exegete and his or her believing community to encounter more fully the living Lord to whom the Christian Scriptures bear witness, both individually and collectively as the canon.

BIBLIOGRAPHY

Barr, James. *Holy Scripture: Canon, Authority, Criticism*. Oxford: Clarendon, 1983.

Barton, John. *Reading the Old Testament: Method in Biblical Study*. Philadelphia: Westminster, 1984.

Childs, Brevard. *Introduction to the Old Testament as Scripture*. Philadelphia: Fortress, 1979.

_____. *The New Testament as Canon: An Introduction*. Philadelphia: Fortress, 1985

Horizons in Biblical Theology, 2 (1980): 113–211; 4 (1982): 13–60. (Articles by Bruce C. Birch, Brevard Childs, Douglas Knight, James Mays, David Polk, James Sanders, James Dunn.)

Journal for the Study of the Old Testament, 16 (1980): 2–60. (Articles by James Barr, J. Blenkinsopp, H. Cazelles, Brevard Childs, Bonnie Kittel, George M. Landes, R. E. Murphy, and Rudolf Smend.)

Morgan, Donn F. "Canon and Criticism: Method or Madness?" *Anglican Theological Review*, 68 (1986): 83–94.

Oss, Douglas A. "Canon as Context: The Function of Sensus Plenior in Evangelical Hermeneutics," *Grace Theological Journal*, 9 (1988): 105–27.

Sanders, James. *Torah and Canon*. Philadelphia: Fortress, 1972.

_____. *Canon and Community: A Guide to Canonical Criticism*. Philadelphia: Fortress, 1984.

_____. *From Sacred Story to Sacred Text*. Philadelphia: Fortress, 1987.

Spina, Frank. "Canonical Criticism: Childs Versus Sanders," in *Interpreting God's Word for Today: An Inquiry into Hermeneutics from a Biblical-Theological Perspective*. Eds. W. McCown and J. E. Massey. Anderson, Ind.: Warner, 1982, pp. 165–94.

NOTES

[1]This is especially true of Christopher Tuckett's otherwise fine introduction to New Testament study, *Reading the New Testament: Methods of Interpretation* (Philadelphia: Fortress, 1987). Tuckett treats canonical criticism, along with the more recent literary criticism, in the last chapter of the book under the title, "Other Approaches." He claims (p. 170), ". . . however much is claimed for the value of the new approach, the results are often rather meagre."

[2]See, for example, the following historical-critical works by Childs: *Myth and Reality in the Old Testament*, SBT, Vol. 27 (London: SCM, 1960); *Memory and Tradition in Israel*, SBT, Vol. 37 (London: SCM, 1962); *Isaiah and the Assyrian Crisis*, SBT, 2d series, Vol. 3 (London: SCM, 1967), and numerous articles. For a full bibliography and more detailed biographical statement, see Gene Tucker, David Petersen, and Robert Wilson, eds., *Canon, Theology, and Old Testament Interpretation: Essays in Honor of Brevard S. Childs* (Philadelphia: Fortress, 1988).

[3]See Brevard Childs, "Interpretation in Faith: The Theological Responsibility of an Old Testament Commentary," *Int* 18 (1964): 432–49.

[4]See Stendahl's article, "Biblical Theology," in *IDB*, George Buttrick, ed. (New York: Abingdon, 1962), Vol. I, 418ff.

[5]Childs, "Interpretation in Faith," 433.

[6]I have taken the first part of the following headings "A New Kind of. . ." from Frank Spina's article, "Canonical Criticism: Childs Versus Sanders," in *Interpreting God's Word for Today: An Inquiry into Hermeneutics from a Biblical-Theological Perspective*, eds. W. McCown and J. E. Massey (Anderson, Ind.: Warner, 1982), 165–94. The headings and subheadings, however, are not worked exactly the same as Spina's.

[7]Brevard Childs, *Biblical Theology in Crisis* (Philadelphia: Westminster, 1970). In the meantime, Childs continued to develop his new approach of theological exegesis. See, for example, his article, "Psalm 8 in the Context of the Christian Canon," *Int* 23 (1969): 20–31, which was reprinted in chapter nine of his *Biblical Theology in Crisis*.

[8]Typical of the concerns of the American Biblical Theology Movement was G. E. Wright, *God Who Acts: Biblical Theology as Recital* SBT, Vol. 18 (London: SCM, 1958). Some, like James Smart, however, seriously questioned whether such a movement ever existed. See *The Past, Present and Future of Biblical Theology* (Philadelphia: Fortress, 1979).

[9]Childs, *Biblical Theology*, 110.

[10]Ibid., 122. Childs pursues this interest in Old Testament theology in a more recent book, *Old Testament Theology in a Canonical Context* (Philadelphia: Fortress, 1986).

[11]Childs, *The Book of Exodus: A Critical, Theological Commentary*, OTL (Philadelphia: Westminster, 1974). A recent editorial review in *Expository Times* (98 [1988]: 359–63) of commentaries on Exodus said of Childs' commentary: "It is without doubt the best modern commentary at present."

[12]Childs, *Exodus*, ix.

[13]Brevard Childs, *Introduction to the Old Testament as Scripture* (Philadelphia: Fortress, 1979).

[14]John F. Priest, "Canon and Criticism: A Review Article," *JAAR*, 48 (1980): 265.

[15]R. N. Whybray, "Reflections on Canonical Criticism," *Theology*, 84 (1981): 29. For other reviews see the 1980 issue of *JSOT*, 16 (1980), which also contains a response by Childs.

[16]Childs, *Introduction*, 45.

[17]Ibid., 78.

[18]Ibid., 74.

[19]Barton, *Reading the Old Testament: Method in Biblical Study* (Philadelphia: Westminster, 1984), 154. Barton goes on in chapter eleven to argue that Childs' canonical approach is therefore open to the same criticisms as New Criticism. See my evaluation below.

[20]See the excursus, "The Canonical Approach and the 'New Yale Theology,'" in *The New Testament as Canon: An Introduction* (Philadelphia: Fortress, 1985), 541–46.

[21]Mark I. Wallace, "The New Yale Theology," *CSR*, 17 (1987): 154–70. For a list of writings by the Yale theologians, see Wallace, 155 n.1.

[22]Childs, *The New Testament as Canon*, 541.

[23]Wallace, "The New Yale Theology," 154. Wallace offers a critique of the New Yale Theology and poses "a major question regarding the Yale School" that remains unanswered: "Is the biblical world the sole theological determinant of what reality is, as the Yale theologians sometimes assert, or, as they also seem to indicate, is the biblical world simply one language-game (Lindbeck, Holmer) or literary picture (Frei) amidst other games and pictures, none of which has priority over any other?" (155).

[24]See Sanders, *From Sacred Story to Sacred Text* (Philadelphia: Fortress, 1987), 1–3, for a brief autobiographical statement by Sanders.

[25]Ibid., 3.

[26]James Sanders, *Torah and Canon* (Philadelphia: Fortress, 1972).

[27]See, e.g., "The Vitality of the Old Testament: Three Theses," *USQR*, 21 (1966): 161–84; *The Dead Sea Psalms Scroll* (Ithaca, N.Y.: Cornell University, 1967), 157–58; "Cave 11 Surprises and the Question of Canon," *McCQ*, 21 (1968): 284–98. For the most current listing

to date of Sanders' work on canonical criticism, see *From Sacred Story to Sacred Text*, 198–99.

[28]Brevard Childs, "A Call to Canonical Criticism," *Int* 27 (1973): 89.

[29]James Sanders, *Canon and Community: A Guide to Canonical Criticism* (Philadelphia: Fortress, 1984). See the review by Everett Kalin, "A Book Worth Discussing: *Canon and Community. A Guide to Canonical Criticism*," *CMT*, 12 (1985): 310–12.

[30]See "Hermeneutics in True and False Prophecy," in *Canon and Authority: Essays in Old Testament Religion and Authority*, eds. George W. Coats and Burke O. Long (Philadelphia: Fortress, 1977); reprinted as chapter five in *From Sacred Story to Sacred Text*.

[31]Sanders, *From Sacred Story to Sacred Test*, xii. See the reviews by Bernhard Anderson and Sibley Towner in *Religious Studies Review*, 15 (1989): 97–103.

[32]Ibid., 175.

[33]Ibid., 190.

[34]Ibid., 187.

[35]Ibid., 3.

[36]See the attempt by Garland Young to connect Sanders with Whiteheadian philosophy, "The Role of the Spirit in Texts: James Sanders, Paul Achtemeier, and Process Theology," *PerRelSt*, 13 (1986): 229–40.

[37]See Sanders' discussion of this issue in "Response to Lemcio," 123.

[38]Childs, *Introduction to the Old Testament*, 82. The editors' assignment of the title to my article, "Canonical Criticism," was felicitous.

[39]Sanders, *From Sacred Story*, 171; also Sanders, "Response to Lemcio," 123.

[40]See James Barr's scathing criticisms of Childs in *Holy Scripture: Canon, Authority, Criticism* (Oxford: Clarendon, 1983).

[41]Childs, "The Sensus Literalis of Scripture: An Ancient and Modern Problem," in Herbert Donner, et. al., eds. *Beiträge zur Alttestamentlichen Theologie* (Göttingen: Vandenhoeck & Ruprecht, 1977), 80–93.

[42]David Steinmetz, "The Superiority of Pre-critical Exegesis," in Donald K. McKim, ed., *A Guide to Contemporary Hermeneutics* (Grand Rapids: Eerdmans, 1986), 65–77.

[43]Ibid., 77.

[44]F. F. Bruce, *The Canon of Scripture* (Downers Grove, Ill.: InterVarsity, 1988), 322. This quotation is taken from Appendix II in this book, which is a reproduction of Bruce's 1976 Peake Memorial Lecture, "Primary Sense and Plenary Sense." See especially the section, "The Complexity of 'Primary Sense,'" 322–26.

[45]Steinmetz, "The Superiority of Pre-critical Exegesis," 77.

[46]See W. C. Kaiser, Jr., *Toward an Exegetical Theology* (Grand Rapids: Baker, 1981); *idem*, "Evangelical Hermeneutics: Restatement, Advance or Retreat from the Reformation?" *CTQ*, 46 (1982): 167–80; *idem*, "A Response to 'Author's Intention and Biblical Interpretation,'" *Hermeneutics, Inerrancy, and the Bible*, eds. E. D. Radmacher and R. D. Preus (Grand Rapids: Zondervan, 1984), 444–45.

[47]See Douglas A. Oss, "Canon as Context: The Function of *Sensus Plenior* in Evangelical Hermeneutics," *Grace Theological Journal*, 9 (1988): 105–27. See the footnotes of this article for bibliography on other discussions of the function of *sensus plenior* in biblical hermeneutics. On *sensus plenior*, see also R. E. Brown, "The History and Development of the Theory of a *Sensus Plenior*," *CBQ*, 15 (1953): 141–62; *idem*, "The *Sensus Plenior* in the Last Ten Years," *CBQ*, 25 (1963): 262–85.

[48]Ibid., 107.

[49]Ibid., 107–8.

[50]Ibid., 115.

[51]Bruce, *The Canon of Scripture*, 334 (my emphasis).

[52]Oss has offered a full articulation of this view of the *sensus plenior* in his article. He defends this canonical approach for evangelical hermeneutics against its critics. Though I am unable to explicate this issue fully in this essay on canonical criticism, I am in essential agreement with Oss's position, differing only on minor points. Oss claims to have offered this essay as the "basis for dialogue" (127), and I encourage the reader to weigh Oss's proposal against others who offer proposals for developing an "evangelical hermeneutic."

[53]Bruce, *The Canon of Scripture*, 331.

[54]I should note that Robert Wall has also used the two foci of process and product, though with different emphases, in "The Problem of the Multiple Letter Canon of the New Testament," *HBT*, 8 (1986): 1–31; so my approach is not entirely idiosyncratic.

[55]Donn F. Morgan, "Canon and Criticism: Method or Madness?" *ATR*, 68 (1986): 83–94. For an example in New Testament studies of a canonical exegesis of units smaller than a book, see Eugene Lemcio's treatment of the Beatitudes and the Great Commandment in "The Gospels and Canonical Criticism," *BTB*, 11 (1981): 114–22.

[56]Childs, *New Testament as Canon*, 49.

[57]Ibid.

[58]See Ralph Martin, *2 Corinthians*, Word Biblical Commentary, Vol. 40 (Waco: Word, 1986).

[59]See Childs' remarks, *The New Testament as Canon*, 291–95.

[60]Ibid., 49.

[61]Ibid.

[62]See Reginald Fuller, et. al., *Hebrews, James, 1 and 2 Peter, Jude, Revelation*, Proclamation Commentaries, ed. Gerhard Krodel (Philadelphia: Fortress, 1977), 1.

[63]Childs, *New Testament as Canon*, 52.

[64]Ibid., 52.

[65]Other issues raised by Childs include the problems of anonymity and pseudonymity from a canonical critical perspective. See the essay on pseudonymity by Thomas D. Lea in this volume.

[66]Morgan, "Canon and Criticism," 88.

[67]Ibid.

[68]E. J. Goodspeed, *The Formation of the New Testament* (Chicago, 1926).

[69]In the words of J. Weingreen, cited by John Sheehan in "Canonical Criticism: A Place on Which to Stand in Doing Theology," *Essays and Discovery: Essays in Honor of Karl Rahner, S.J.*, ed., William J. Kelley, S.J. (Milwaukee, Wisc.: Marquette University, 1980), 355.

[70]See, e.g., the essay by my colleague Robert Sloan elsewhere in this volume.

[71]W. Ward Gasque, *A History of the Criticism of the Acts of the Apostles* (Grand Rapids: Eerdmans, 1975), 309.

[72]Henry J. Cadbury, *The Making of Luke-Acts* (London: SPCK, 1958), x.

[73]See the monograph on this subject by Mikeal C. Parsons and Richard I. Pervo, *Rethinking the Unity of "Luke-Acts"* (Philadelphia: Fortress/Augsburg, forthcoming).

[74]G. Krodel, *Acts* (Philadelphia: Fortress, 1981), 1.

[75]Robert W. Wall, "The Acts of the Apostles in Canonical Context," *BTB* 18 (1988): 21–22.

[76]See F. F. Bruce, *The Acts of the Apostles* (Grand Rapids: Eerdmans, 1986), 17.

[77]A. Harnack, *History of Dogma*, Vol. II, ET (London, 1896), 48, n.2.

[78]Childs, *The New Testament as Canon*, 239.

[79]Wall, "Acts in Canonical Context," 17.

[80]This canonical portrait of Mary is not to suggest that Jesus' redefinition of kinship is unhistorical, but to make the point that the transformation of Jesus' earthly family is in fact a canonical one, i.e., known only through the canon taken as a whole.

[81]Wall, "Acts in Canonical Context," 20.

[82]Ibid.

[83]Ibid.

[84]Ibid.

[85]Ibid., 21.

[86]Childs, *The New Testament as Canon*, 239.

[87]Amos Wilder, "Variant Traditions of the Resurrection in Acts," *JBL* 62 (1943): 311; Hans Conzelmann, *The Theology of St. Luke* (Philadelphia: Fortress, 1961), 94; Phillipe Menoud, "Remarques sur les textes de l'ascension dans Luc-Actes," *Neutestamentliche Studien für Rudolf Bultmann* (BZNW 21; ed. W. Eltester; Berlin: Töpelmann, 1957), 148–56. Menoud, however, eventually changed his mind and accepted

the authenticity of the verses in question. See *idem*, "Pendant quarant jours (Actes i 3)," in *Neotestamentica et Patristica*, Cullmann Festschrift (Leiden: E. J. Brill, 1962): 148–56.

[88]Haenchen, *The Acts of the Apostles: A Commentary* (Philadelphia: Westminster, 1971), 99. He further argued (ibid.): "Second, it was daring enough to provide the gospel with a sequel in the shape of a book on the apostolic age, but is downright unthinkable that, instead of closing the gospel with the Resurrection and Ascension, Luke should prolong it until Paul's arrival in Rome; for him the life of Jesus was a self-contained epoch in the history of salvation, one distinct from the period which followed."

[89]Childs, *The New Testament as Canon*, 236.

[90]Cadbury, *Making of Luke-Acts*, 2.

[91]Contra John Knox, "Acts and the Pauline Letter Corpus," in *Studies in Luke-Acts*, eds. Leander E. Keck and J. Louis Martyn (Nashville: Abingdon, 1966), 279–87.

[92]Frederick W. Danker, *JBL*, 106 (1987): 143–44.

[93]Childs, *The New Testament as Canon*, 53.

[94]For a similar perspective, see James D. G. Dunn, "Levels of Canonical Authority," *HBT*, 4 (1982): 13–60.

Chapter Ten

Sociological Criticism

M. Robert Mulholland, Jr.

M. Robert Mulholland, Jr.

M. Robert Mulholland, Jr., is Vice President and Provost of Asbury Theological Seminary in Wilmore, Kentucky. He is a graduate of the United States Naval Academy (B.S.), Wesley Theological Seminary (M.Div.), and Harvard Divinity School (Th.D.). He has also pursued post-doctoral studies at Duke University. His articles have appeared in *Biblical Archaeology Review*, *The Asbury Herald*, *Beacon Dictionary of Theology*, and *Christian Home*. He is also the author of *Shaped by the Word: The Power of Scripture in Spiritual Formation* (The Upper Room) and *Revelation: Holy Living in an Unholy World* (Zondervan). He is also general editor of the Francis Asbury Press Commentary series (Zondervan).

Chapter Ten

Sociological Criticism

The reality of the growing importance of Sociological Criticism of the New Testament was impressively portrayed in a recent catalog of scholarly books. In the seven pages of New Testament works appeared nine works from a socio-critical approach, all published since 1978, six since 1985. It is almost impossible to open a catalog of works by New Testament scholars without finding books from a socio-historical, socio-political, socio-linguistic, sociological, or other social science frames of reference. Sociological Criticism is clearly a significant twentieth-century development in New Testament scholarship.

HISTORY AND DEVELOPMENT[1]

Most of twentieth-century New Testament scholarship has operated in the shadow and perspective of nineteenth-century "history of religions" approach to the New Testament. The main thrust of the history of religions approach has been to categorize the abundance of historical and literary religious phenomena of the New Testament period, to clarify the "universal" religious principles that were clothed by these categories, and then to understand the emergence of Christianity within the established paradigm of categories and principles. The clearest example of how this approach manifested itself in twentieth-century scholarship is the work of Rudolph Bultmann. Bultmann reduced Christian experience to the "universal principles" of Heideggerian existentialism that, in the New Testament, he found clothed in the mythological categories of a first-century worldview.

Under the broad umbrella of the history of religions

perspective, critical methodologies were generally developed within a larger humanistic/naturalistic worldview that tends to see all phenomena as objects to be grasped and utilized for the observer's agenda. Parker Palmer describes this condition well: "We are well-educated people who have been schooled in a way of knowing that treats the world as an object to be dissected and manipulated, a way of knowing that gives us power over the world. . . . In my own way I have used my knowledge to rearrange the world to satisfy my drive for power, distorting and deranging life rather than loving it for the gift it is."[2] In such a process, the prevailing perceptual framework of the scholarly guild shapes the individual scholar's approach to the data, and the perspective of the guild tends to emerge from the analysis of the data.

This ambience of scholarship follows Berger's sociological analysis of the world-building process that also related to how humans build their epistemological world.[3] According to Berger, *externalization* established a relationship with a world of data, experience, and ideas by structuring that world in a way that gives it an order and coherence that it does not appear to contain in and of itself. The categories of the history of religions perspective and the "universal principles" clothed in those categories are an example of such a structuring by which the history of religions school sought to bring order and coherence to the wealth of information about and discoveries of the New Testament period that mushroomed in the late eighteenth and throughout the nineteenth centuries.

Next, in Berger's analysis, "objectification" occurs when the structured world assumes the character of an object "out there" that is separate and distinct from the individual. Such statements as "scholarly consensus" or "the assured results of critical scholarship" reflect an objectification of a perceptual framework that, though it may have been critically developed, is uncritically assumed to be the only viable frame of reference for understanding a body of data.

Finally, *internalization* occurs when the now objectified structures that emerged from the process of externalization become the shaping dynamic of consciousness. When this process is complete, both the subjective and objective worlds are shaped by a unified epistemological paradigm that becomes normative for all those working within that field of study. Berger calls such a paradigm the "nomos" that is maintained and passed on by the authority figures in the field. While minor alterations of the nomos may take place over time, alternate perceptual frameworks are generally rejected and radical paradigm shifts are vigorously resisted.

In the latter half of the twentieth century, a growing number of New Testament scholars have chafed under what has been perceived to be the restrictive and inadequate paradigm of the historical-critical methodology, which represents the matured form of the history of religions perspective. Some have prematurely announced the demise of the historical-critical method.[4] One new methodology, structuralism, which is built upon the structuralist anthropology of Claude Levi Strauss, the linguistic studies of A. J. Greimas, and especially the structural linguistics of Ferdinand de Saussure, has largely chosen to ignore the sweep of historical-critical methodologies and to inaugurate a new paradigm that claims to disclose the deep meaning of texts.[5] Still others, however, have chosen to build upon the positive contribution of historical-critical methodologies but to move beyond the restrictions and inadequacies of the method by developing new dimensions of the paradigm. Sociological Criticism is one such effort.

Since the latter part of the last century, scholars have realized that understanding of the New Testament on theological grounds alone is woefully inadequate. The social setting of the New Testament and early Christianity has been seen as an indispensable ingredient in holistic interpretation. Even many of the most conservative scholars, who relied almost totally upon linguistic and grammatical methods of interpretation, have come to realize that language and grammar operated within a social matrix that shapes their function and meaning.

Realization of the significance of social setting for New Testament interpretation has led, in this century, to a wealth of resources that aim to put the flesh of social data upon the skeleton of New Testament history.[6] Much of this work is, however, descriptive rather than analytical. It tends to describe, often in the paradigmatic categories of the history of religions school, the characteristics of the New Testament world without utilizing social theory to analyze the dynamics of the Roman-Hellenistic world in general and its religious movements in particular. It is this weakness in historical-critical methodology that Sociological Criticism seeks to correct.

As early as 1960, but especially since 1970, we have seen a

virtual explosion of studies on the sociological dimensions of the New Testament. E. A. Judge's *The Social Pattern of Christian Groups in the First Century* was one of the earliest attempts to utilize social description to understand early Christianity. Judge sought to clarify the social situation of the original readers of the New Testament writings by an analysis of the different groups within which Christianity emerged, both in Palestine and in the larger Roman world, and the interaction of these groups within their larger culture. More recently Derek Tidball has provided a similar study[8] with an excellent synopsis and evaluation of the ways social theories have been used to study the New Testament together with his own study of the Christian community as a sect and its social status.

Judge and Tidball, along with numerous other scholars, have worked more along the lines of social description. In addition, a large number of scholars have begun to apply various sociological theories to the study of the New Testament and early Christianity. One of the pioneers in this endeavor is Gerd Theissen. His *Sociology of Early Palestinian Christianity*[9] studied the role of the charismatic leader in religious communities with a focus upon the role of Jesus in the early Christian community and the role Jesus assigned to the disciples. While this study did not move strongly into social theory, his work *The Social Setting of Pauline Christianity*[10] did, looking at the leadership dynamics and community organizational structures of the Pauline churches.

Anthony Saldarini has moved even more strongly into the use of sociological theory, building upon the work of Eisentadt, and Lenski on social stratification and differentiation[11] to analyze the roles of the Pharisees, scribes, and Sadducees in Palestinian Judaism of the New Testament period in order to illuminate the conflicts both Jesus and the early Christians encountered with these groups.[12] Along similar lines, Richard Horsley and John Hanson have built upon sociological studies of conflict within peasant societies to analyze those groups whom Josephus and the New Testament called "brigands," conflict that caused social and political instability in Palestine in the first century.

New Testament scholars such as Saldarini, Horsley, and Hanson build upon work in the field of social theory and utilize many of the hypothetical models that have been developed to assist in the analysis of the sociological dynamics of a culture.

The work of such social scientists as Max Weber,[13] Emile Durkheim,[14] Louis Kriesberg,[15] and Clifford Geertz[16] have provided the foundation of sociological theory upon which New Testament scholars have built. In addition to theories of social stratification and social conflict noted above, sociological theories of group development, group self-identity, religious dynamics, religious communities, and organizational structures have been used, along with a wide diversity of sociological hypotheses, to study the first-century Jewish and Roman-Hellenistic world and the Christian communities that emerged within that diverse sociological matrix.

Of particular interest from an anthropological frame of reference are the studies of the origins and growth of millenarian groups. These studies analyze marginalized groups formed by prophetic/charismatic leaders that expected a divine intervention that would vindicate the group's perspective and ethos and inaugurate a utopian era of divine rule in which the group would have a focal place. Early studies of these phenomena were conducted by Leon Festinger,[17] Norman Cohn,[18] and Peter Worsley.[19] Such studies have provided the inspiration for analyzing the early Christian movement as a millenarian movement. John Gager[20] and Howard Kee[21] are two New Testament scholars who have undertaken such study.

A somewhat faulty use of cultural anthropology for sociological analysis of the New Testament has been employed by Bruce Malina. In *The New Testament World: Insights from Cultural Anthropology*, [22] Malina uses helpful insights from cultural anthropology but fails to discern the tremendous diversity of social and cultural dynamics that constituted the Roman world in the first century. In a later work, *Christian Origins and Cultural Anthropology: Practical Models for Biblical Interpretation*, [23] he employs rather uncritically and inappropriately the group/grid scheme of Mary Douglas. Malina applies Douglas' scheme as a means of classification of data into sociological categories rather than utilizing the scheme as a means of sensitization to sociological dynamics as Douglas intended.[24]

Another area of Sociological Criticism that has gained significance in New Testament study is the field of sociolinguistics. Scholars have come to realize that language not only provides the linguistic symbol system of a culture, but is itself an integral part of the sociological matrix of the culture in which it is used. Language provides the symbolic world of a linguistic community by which that community orders and maintains its "world" as well as confirms and communicates it. As a simplistic example, consider the perceptual/experiential cultural matrix that operates when the word "gay" is used in the latter years of the twentieth century as opposed to the closing years of the nineteenth century.

The philosophical work of Gadamer[25] and Wittgenstein[26] has established the foundations for sociolinguistics. One of Gadamer's formative insights is that language operates within a particular sociological "horizon" that encompasses the worldview of the community and the symbol system employed by the community to describe and communicate its worldview. Linguistic communication across horizons becomes difficult because language does not function in the same way within every horizon. Wittgenstein developed the ideas of the "language game." By this he implied that in any given community and at any given point in time there is an agreed upon set of assumptions (the "rules" of the language game) within which communication (the "game") takes place.

One of the best applications of the work of Wittgenstein and Gadamer to the study of the New Testament is by Anthony Thiselton,[27] who utilizes Gadamer's two horizons to illustrate how the modern interpreter "hears" the language of the New Testament from within the culturally shaped horizon of her or his own sociological matrix and must learn to discern the sociological/cultural horizon of the original writers/readers if the hermeneutical fusion of horizons is to be accomplished, a fusion that is essential to any adequate understanding of the text. Thiselton also builds upon Wittgenstein's "language game" to emphasize the necessity of understanding the "language game" of the writer and original readers if accurate interpretation is to take place.

As a witness to the significance of socio-linguistics, Eugene Nida, one of the fathers of the field, has recently produced a new type of lexicon that will enable interpreters and exegetes to access the insights of socio-linguistics in their work with the New Testament.[28] This resource organizes the vocabulary of the New Testament in ninety-three semantic domains and provides the interpreter an entrée into the perceptual framework of the writer whose work is being studied.

PRINCIPLES OF SOCIOLOGICAL CRITICISM

Five general levels operate interactively in the utilization of Sociological Criticism in New Testament interpretation.

First, the preliminary level is the study of the social setting of the New Testament. This level is almost entirely descriptive, defining from textual, archaeological, and inscriptional evidence the political, economic, cultural, religious, social, educational, and communal structures of the New Testament period.

Second, and more analytical, is the description of the sociological dynamics of the New Testament world, understanding the interactions between the various social structures that either maintain the balance of the status quo or bring about disequilibrium and subsequent change (growth, decline, or the emergence of new social structures). Care must be taken to avoid neatly packaged descriptions that avoid the anomalous realities of any human social matrix. Balance and disequilibrium, growth and decline, old established structures and new emergent structures can and often do exist in the same sociological matrix.

Third, and both descriptive and analytical, is the use of sociological models to help define and analyze the ways in which groups and individuals exist and function within the multifaceted sociological matrix of their world. These models help to analyze such sociological characteristics as the relationships between individuals, the relationships between individuals and groups, the relationships between groups, the structures of groups (definition, formation, ethos and discipline, support structures, rituals, worldview and its symbol system, conflict and its resolution, differentiation and stratification, leadership and authority, mechanisms for change), and the social stratification of the culture.

Fourth, as part of the process of coming to some grasp of the sociological matrix of the New Testament world and the dynamics of the Christian movement within that matrix, the text of the New Testament is studied within the sociological context of the Christian communities in the Roman world of the first century. Meaning of the words and symbols of the text are sought within the sociological matrix of the New Testament world and not in a set of "external, unchanging meanings" inherent in the terms and symbols themselves. Especially, the meaning of the terms and symbols of the New Testament are not understood within the sociological matrix of the interpreter.

Fifth, throughout the process of Sociological Criticism a careful distinction must be maintained between the sociological horizon of the interpreter and that of the text. The interpreter, through Sociological Criticism, seeks to enter into the life-matrix of the text and its community of faith and to draw out the meaning of the text within that life-matrix. Once this has been accomplished, even during the process of its accomplishment, the analogues in the interpreter's own sociological matrix can begin to be perceived and the transfer of meaning from the sociological matrix of the text to that of the interpreter can begin.

As can be seen from this brief survey of the history and principles of Sociological Criticism, the field is teeming with life and vitality. The discipline has great potential for enhancing our ability to enter more fully into the matrix of life that shaped the life and perception of the early church, thus enriching our understanding of the New Testament and its significance for Christian discipleship in our own matrix of experience. As with any scholarly discipline, however, there are benefits to be gained and pitfalls to be avoided in the use of the methodology in the interpretation of the New Testament.

WEAKNESSES OF SOCIOLOGICAL CRITICISM

One of the primary weaknesses of any behavioral methodology applied to the Scriptures is the almost overpowering tendency to view the realities of spiritual experience from within a human-centered frame of reference. If, for instance, some aspect of the Christian community as portrayed in the New Testament has its parallels in the sociological dynamics of the Roman-Hellenistic world, it is a great temptation to presume that this feature is simply a common sociological phenomenon of the time and to explain away any claims of unique spiritual experience as simply the theologizing of the Christian community.

Take as an example Paul's use of terminology drawn from the mystery religions of the Roman world.[29] The mystery religions, with their dying and rising redeemer figures, with their promise of salvation in this world and the next, with their clearly defined rites of passage into the community of the redeemed that separated "insiders" from "outsiders," with their regular calendar of liturgy and even daily office constantly to reinforce the worldview and ethos of the mystery in the lives of the adherents provide a sociological phenomenon with strong parallels to the life of the Christian communities. From a sociological perspective, it would be easy to conclude that Christianity was simply another Hellenistic mystery religion with its roots in Jewish messianism rather than Greek mythology. But Paul signifies something more than this. His use of mystery terminology breaks the pattern of its use and meaning in the Roman world. Paul speaks of the mystery that has been revealed, and he proclaims the mystery to *all*, something that would have been anathema to the mystery religions. Further, the center of this mystery is not some ancient deity encrusted with ages of mythological clothing, but a historical figure of the time, a man who had lived in Palestine and whose life, death, and resurrection inaugurated a new community of people who have experienced the reality of God's transforming presence in their lives. To be sure, the incarnation of this experience in human community follows something of the sociological pattern of the mystery religions. But to understand the phenomenon only within the limits of the sociological pattern is to miss the radically different reality that is incarnate in the pattern.

Another potential weakness in Sociological Criticism is to apply to the world of the New Testament sociological paradigms developed in the present world whose social, political, economic, and cultural dynamics are radically if not totally alien to the Roman world of the first century. This practice can sometimes be found in the work of liberation theologians when they impose the sociological paradigms of their *Sitz im Leben* (life-setting) upon the text of the Bible in ways that overlook the sociological matrix of the text and violate the integrity of that matrix for interpretation of the text.

Another weakness, as noted above in reference to the work of Malina,[30] is to employ sociological models and/or methods in a Procrustian manner that trims the evidence to fit the parameters of the model/method, often casting aside evidence whose presence is crucial for an accurate understanding of the sociological dynamics so necessary for a full understanding of the text.

Perhaps the most subtle weakness in Sociological Criticism, implicit in all that has been said, is the tendency toward sociological reductionism. It is possible for the process of sociological criticism to be employed wisely, sensitively, accurately, and with care to avoid the weaknesses noted above, but to arrive at conclusions that leave the reality of God's presence, power, and purpose out of the interpretive equation. The witness of the text is understood as a sociological phenomenon only, and even if the reality of a supernatural element is acknowledged, it is subordinated to sociological phenomena. For example, in his excellent survey of sociological criticism, Kee applies Berger's analysis of the sociology of knowledge as a pattern of social appropriation relevant to the New Testament. After sketching Mark's portrayal of Jesus' understanding of his role, Kee states, "To the extent that his followers commit themselves to this understanding, it becomes the motivation for their lives. And as a group they have a new mode of social identity, which they pass on by preaching and teaching."[31] While such an understanding is sociologically sound, it omits the presence and work of God in the lives of the followers. They do not simply commit themselves to an understanding; they commit themselves to a transforming relationship with God. Understanding of the relationship is secondary to the relationship itself, and it is the reality of the relationship that becomes the motivation of their lives, not simply their understanding of it. They do indeed have a new mode of social identity, but one whose sociological dimensions are subordinate to the profound reality of their experience of God as the one who has bonded them together in this new community. Preaching and teaching are not merely sociological methods for promulgating an understanding, but vehicles for inviting others into the fellowship of this relationship with God.

STRENGTHS OF SOCIOLOGICAL CRITICISM

One strength of Sociological Criticism is its ability to help us distinguish between our own sociological matrix and that of the New Testament. Without this ability, we are very likely to succumb to the eisegesis of reading the New Testament through the eyes of our own life-matrix and interpreting it in the light of our own frame of reference. Another obvious strength is the ability to clarify the sociological matrix of the New Testament world and the life and activities of the Christian communities within that world. These strengths confront us, however, at one of the major areas of weakness in the study of the New Testament—the tendency to read the New Testament as a text from our own life-matrix. It is much easier simply to presume that the New Testament's frame of reference is the same as ours and to interpret it from within that matrix. Such interpretation results in the cultural captivity of the Scripture.

At this point someone is bound to ask, "But if we read the New Testament from within the sociological matrix of the first-century Roman world, are we not making it captive to that culture?" Not any more than God's incarnation in Jesus is captive to the sociological matrix of first-century Palestinian Judaism. "But," you will say, "Jesus brought something transformingly new to that cultural matrix. He transcended the cultural matrix, 'broke out' of the sociological 'box' of Palestinian Judaism." That may be true, but we can understand the true dimensions of these aspects of the Incarnation only if we first comprehend the sociological matrix from within which the Incarnation broke forth into the world.

The same is true of the New Testament's account of the primitive Christian movement. While God was definitely doing a "new thing" in the formation of the Christian movement, the movement was formed, developed, and grew within the sociological matrix of the first-century world. Its radical experience can best be understood only when the sociological matrix of its life and witness is understood.

Another important strength is Sociological Criticism's insights into the essentially sociological dimension of language. This was illustrated above by the term "gay" as used at the end of the nineteenth as opposed to its use at the end of the twentieth century. As a New Testament example, take the term "gospel."

The term "gospel" is one that gives us extreme difficulty from a sociological perspective. Our first problem is that we hear the term from within our own well-established sociological frame of reference. The term has a variety of particular religious denotations, each of which may carry an additional number of connotations within our own particular subculture. It can mean, variously, "Scripture," "preaching," a biblical book, something "true," a type of music, and so forth.[32] No matter what our individual frame of reference for understanding "gospel" may be, it bears little relationship to the frame of reference in which Paul used it.

"Gospel" was a term that carried significant sociological dynamics in the Roman world. These dynamics clustered around the emperor. The emperor's birthday was celebrated throughout the empire as a "gospel" (Greek *evangelion*, "good news"). The anniversary of his accession to the throne occasioned an empire-wide celebration of a "gospel." Thus "gospel" was intimately associated with the emperor as the one in whom the welfare, stability, and preservation of the status quo resided. The entire complex of sociological dynamics that shaped the Roman Empire were inseparably linked to the emperor in the worldview of the Roman world.

It becomes apparent that when Paul used "gospel" it carried far different dimensions for his first-century hearers than it does for us. We will look at some of those dimensions in the illustration of Sociological Criticism that closes this chapter.

Perhaps the greatest strength of Sociological Criticism is its focus upon the incarnational reality of human life. Sociological Criticism awakens us to the reality that all human existence is lived within specific, even if tremendously multifaceted and confusingly interactive, sociological matrices. This means that Christian life is not lived in some kind of spiritual cocoon but in the full-orbed sociological matrix of any given age with all the ebb and flow of its political, economic, social, religious, educational, institutional, and cultural dynamics. Human experiences with God take place within and are informed by the sociological matrices within which they occur.

Here again we see the mystery of incarnation. God chooses to indwell human communities of faith that are clothed in the sociological dynamics of their world. In a sense, God chooses to submit to the shaping of human sociological dynamics. While there is a body of divine reality beneath the sociological clothing of any human community of faith, we must be careful not to mistake the clothing for the body nor to isolate the body from the clothing as an abstraction that captures God within our own conceptualization.

Sociological Criticism can be an effective means of radical encounter with God by enabling us to enter into the life-matrix of the community of faith, understand the reality of God's incarnation in that particular sociological milieu, and open ourselves and our community of faith to the same kind of relationship with God in our own life-matrix. Ultimately, the meaning of a biblical text is not a "truth" to be learned but a reality of relationship with God to be incarnated again in the sociological matrix of a human community of faith. The purpose of the Scripture is not information but transformation, an encounter with God that is fully known only incarnationally within a specific sociological matrix.

ILLUSTRATION OF SOCIOLOGICAL CRITICISM

Philippians 1:27–28 provides an excellent insight into the need for and the contribution of Sociological Criticism. Translations vary somewhat, but none do justice to the sociological dimensions of this brief passage. A faithful rendering of the Greek text would be:

> Live as worthy citizens of the gospel of Christ so that whether I am present or absent I will hear things about you that indicate you are standing in one spirit, striving together with one soul for the faith of the gospel, and not frightened in anything by those who oppose you, which is proof to them of their destruction but your salvation, and this from God.

Even this translation, however, cannot begin to convey the tremendous significance of what Paul is saying to the Philippians in this brief passage. A number of meaningful sociological factors must be introduced to provide the full weight of Paul's exhortation.

First, the social setting of Philippi is crucial, as are the sociological dynamics of the setting that shaped the daily life of the Philippians. Philippi became a Roman colony in 42 B.C., established by Mark Antony after the victorious battle he and Octavian (who later became the Caesar Augustus of Lk 2:1) waged against Brutus and Cassius on the plains of Philippi following the assassination of Julius Caesar. As one of the first cities in the eastern Mediterranean to receive this prized status, Philippi would have been proud of this privileged bond with Rome and careful to protect this highly prized status that exempted it from taxes, tribute, and duties and allowed it to have the Roman polity. For the first eighty-eight years of its life as a colony, Philippi was the last military outpost between the Roman Empire and the incursions of the restless and warlike peoples of Thrace, who were not subdued and made a Roman province until 46 A.D. As such, Philippi had a long history of standing united against those who threatened the Roman way of life.

Those fortunate enough to be citizens of a colony, either by birth to parents who possessed citizenship or in recognition of meritorious service to the colony or empire, were also extended members of one of the tribes that constituted the citizenship of the city of Rome. As such, the welfare of Rome and the welfare of the colony were one and the same. Colonies were extremely careful to follow Rome's lead in all matters of life whether political, social, economic, religious, or cultural. Whatever Rome did, the colony followed suit lest it be seen as fractious if not seditious.

This probably accounts for the strange fact that Paul finds the Jewish community of Philippi worshiping "outside the gate at the riverside" (Ac 16:13). The only gate in Philippi near a river was the triumphal arch of Antony that marked the western boundary of the pomerium, the sacred precinct that constituted a Roman colony. Only licit religions were allowed to worship within the pomerium. What is puzzling in this case is that Judaism was a licit religion in the Roman Empire. Paul does not have to go outside the pomerium of the colonies of Pisidian Antioch or Corinth to find the synagogue. Why in Philippi? Chronologically, Paul appears to arrive in Philippi sometime in the latter part of 49 A.D., the year in which the emperor, Claudius, expelled the Jews from Rome.[33] Rome, historically, took such action against the Jews whenever there were disturbances of the social order usually caused by proselytizing.[34] It is significant that the charges against Paul and Silas in Philippi were: "These men are Jews, they are disturbing the city, they are advocating customs that are not lawful for us Romans to practice" (Ac 16:20–21). It would appear that Philippi had followed Rome's lead and expelled the Jewish community from the sacred precincts of the colony.

To be a colony was to be a microcosm of the sociological dynamics that shaped the life of the city of Rome. A number of those sociological dynamics inform Paul's exhortation to the Philippians.

The phrase "live as worthy citizens" translates a term that, for Paul, related to life lived as faithful members of God's covenant community,[35] and that for the Philippians who lived in a Roman colony would also have indicated a life conformed to the full range of sociological dynamics that shaped the

Roman worldview and lifestyle. It means to be thoroughly Roman in thought, word, and deed; to have every aspect of one's life shaped by the ethos of the Roman culture: political, economic, religious, educational, even linguistic (all the official inscriptions at Philippi are in Latin rather than Greek!). When Paul uses the term in addressing the Philippians, this is the larger sociological context within which they would hear it.

We have already seen that the word "gospel" operated in a totally different sociological milieu in Paul's world than in ours. Can you begin to understand the radical dimensions of Paul's exhortation to the Philippians to "live as worthy citizens of the gospel of Christ"? When informed by sociological analysis, Paul's call is radically and ultimately seditious in the setting of the Roman world. He is implying that Christ is the embodiment of a new order of being, a new context of life, a new matrix of existence, and that the Christians of Philippi should live out lives shaped by the ethos of this new realm. Paul's exhortation is profoundly countercultural when its sociological dimensions are clear.

Paul further highlights the countercultural nature of Christian existence in the world in Philippians 3:20, when he reminds the Philippians that their citizenship[36] is in heaven from where they await a Savior, the Lord Jesus Christ. Here the Christians' matrix of existence is clearly alternative to that of the Roman world whose savior and lord was the emperor.[37]

In the remainder of our passage (1:27–28), Paul indicates that the Philippians' posture toward the Roman world is not simply one of an alternative lifestyle. He again employs terminology that creates for his readers images that are rooted in the sociological dynamics of the Roman world. Paul's military images ("standing in one spirit," "striving together with one soul," "not frightened by those who oppose you") play upon the community spirit and solidarity that would have energized a Roman colony in the face of a threat to its way of life. The myth of Roman invincibility in the first century might well have alleviated fear in the face of opposition. For the Christians of Philippi, however, their reliance was to be upon the invincibility of a new order of being "gospel" in which the Spirit of God established a new matrix of existence for community solidarity.

Perhaps the most radical portion of Paul's exhortation is his affirmation of the "destruction" of the opponents. The word

Paul uses for "destruction" (*apōleias*) means, literally, to be un-citied, to experience the loss of that matrix of life that gives meaning, value, identity, and purpose to the community and the individual. Paul is implying that the entire sociological matrix of the Roman world is doomed to fail, but that the Christian matrix of existence will endure. What an impact this would have upon Christians living in a Roman colony in the golden age of Rome's glory!

Discerning the sociological dimensions within which Paul is working to convey meaning to his readers is only half of the role of Sociological Criticism. Another sociological aspect relates to the community to which Paul writes. How does that community identify itself within the larger community of Philippi? How does it understand its role in the midst of the Roman matrix? What is its worldview, its ethos?

We must remember that this community appears to have emerged out of ostracism and persecution. As Jews, they appear to have been expelled from the colony as far as their worship was concerned and, as Paul's trial in Philippi reveals, the political leadership of the colony couldn't distinguish between Jews and Christians. The fact that their "founder" had been beaten, imprisoned, and subsequently banished from the colony certainly would not enhance their status as a community within the colony. The fact they operated out of the house of a foreign woman would not serve to allay suspicions. It appears, then, that the Christian community in Philippi found itself at least marginalized within the sociological matrix of the colony if not alienated from that matrix. In such a situation it is easy for a group to feel isolated, alone, and powerless in the face of what appears to be the overwhelming superiority of the surrounding community.

It is no wonder that Paul describes his own imprisonment in more detail in Philippians than in any of the imprisonment epistles and calls the readers his partners in his imprisonment and the defense and confirmation of the gospel (1:7). Paul reminds them that they are engaged in the same conflict that they saw (Paul's imprisonment in Philippi) and now hear to be his (his present imprisonment in Rome). Paul is especially careful to note the Roman context of his imprisonment (the praetorian guard), and that it is a witness for Christ in the midst of Roman power (1:13). It is in this context that he calls them to be worthy citizens of the gospel of Christ.

Paul is reminding the Philippians of the new matrix of their existence in Christ that provides them with their identity as a community in the midst of a Roman colony. They are citizens of a new order of being whose reality will endure while Rome's will crumble. Their role in the midst of the Roman order is to live as worthy citizens of the new order, and the bulk of Paul's letter provides them the worldview and ethos of citizenship in this new order.

The space of this chapter prohibits a more in-depth analysis of this portion of Paul's letter to the Philippians, to say nothing of how it relates to other sociological dynamics that inform the rest of the letter. What we have looked at, however, should provide an introduction to the need for and the value of Sociological Criticism for the interpretation of the New Testament.

BIBLIOGRAPHY

Elliott, John H. *A Home for the Homeless: A Sociological Exegesis of 1 Peter*. Philadelphia: Fortress, 1981.

Gager, John G. *Kingdom and Community: The Social World of Early Christianity*. Englewood Cliffs, N.J.: Prentice-Hall, 1975.

Kee, Howard Clark. *Knowing the Truth: A Sociological Approach to New Testament Interpretation*. Philadelphia: Fortress, 1989.

Malherbe, Abraham J. *Social Aspects of Early Christianity*. Philadelphia: Fortress, 1983.

Malina, Bruce. *The New Testament World: Insights From Cultural Anthropology*. Atlanta: John Knox, 1981.

Meeks, Wayne A. *The First Urban Christians: The Social World of the Apostle Paul*. New Haven: Yale University Press, 1983.

_____. *The Moral World of the First Christians*. Philadelphia: Westminster, 1986.

Theissen, Gerd. *The Sociology of Early Palestinian Christianity*. Philadelphia: Fortress, 1978.

Tidball, Derek. *The Social Context of the New Testament*. Grand Rapids: Zondervan, 1984.

NOTES

[1]For a succinct yet comprehensive synopsis of the development of Sociological Criticism, see Howard Clark Kee, *Knowing the Truth: A Sociological Approach to New Testament Interpretation* (Minneapolis:

Augsburg Fortress, 1989). For an earlier survey, see Robin Scroggs, "The Sociological Interpretation of the New Testament: The Present State of Research," *New Testament Studies* 26, No.2 (1980): 164–79.

[2]Parker Palmer, *To Know as We Are Known* (San Francisco: Harper, 1983), 2.

[3]Peter Berger, *The Sacred Canopy: Elements of a Sociological Theory of Religion* (Garden City, N.Y.: Doubleday, 1969). Cf. 3–21 for what follows.

[4]Gerhard Meier, *The End of the Historical-Critical Method* (St. Louis: Concordia, 1977).

[5]Cf. Robert M. Polzin, *Biblical Structuralism: Method and Subjectivity in the Study of Ancient Texts* (Philadelphia: Fortress, 1977); Roland Barthes, et. al., *Structural Analysis and Biblical Exegesis*, (Pittsburgh Theological Monograph Series, 3 (Pittsburgh: Pickwick, 1974); Daniel Patte, *What is Structural Exegesis?* Guides to Biblical Scholarship (Philadelphia: Fortress, 1976); for a succinct overview of structuralism, see Raymond F. Collins, *Introduction to the New Testament* (Garden City, N.Y.: Doubleday, 1983), chapter seven.

[6]Cf. such works as Bo Reicke, *The New Testament Era* (Philadelphia: Fortress, 1968); F. F. Bruce, *New Testament History* (London: Nelson, 1969); Joachim Jeremias, *Jerusalem in the Time of Jesus* (Philadelphia: Fortress, 1975); Eduard Lohse, *The New Testament Environment* (Nashville: Abingdon, 1976); Helmut Koester, *Introduction to the New Testament*, Vol. 1, *History, Culture, and Religion of the Hellenistic Age* (Philadelphia: Fortress, 1982); Everett Ferguson, *Backgrounds of Early Christianity* (Grand Rapids: Eerdmans, 1987).

[7]London: Tyndale, 1960.

[8]Derek Tidball, *The Social Context of the New Testament* (Grand Rapids: Zondervan, 1984).

[9](Philadelphia: Fortress, 1978).

[10]Trans. John H. Schuetz (Philadelphia: Fortress, 1982).

[11]S. N. Eisenstadt, *Social Differentiation and Stratification* (Glenview, Ill.: 1971); Gerhard E. Lenski, *Power and Privilege: A Theory of Social Stratification* (New York: McGraw-Hill, 1966).

[12]Anthony Saldarini, *Pharisees, Scribes and Sadducees in Palestinian Society: A Sociological Approach* (Wilmington: Michael Glazier, 1988).

[13]*The Methodology of the Social Sciences*, trans. E. R. Shils and H. A. Finch (New York: Free Press of Glencoe, 1949).

[14]*The Elementary Forms of the Religious Life* (New York: Free Press of Glencoe, 1965).

[15]*The Sociology of Social Conflict* (Englewood Cliffs, N.J.: Prentice-Hall, 1973).

[16]*The Interpretation of Cultures* (New York: Basic Books, 1973).

[17]Leon Festinger, Henry W. Reicken, Stanley Schachter, *When Prophecy Fails: A Social and Psychological Study of a Modern Group that Predicted the Destruction of the World* (New York: Harper, 1956).

[18]*Pursuit of the Millennium: Revolutionary Millenarians and Mystical Anarchists of the Middle Ages* (New York: Oxford University Press, 1970).

[19]*The Trumpet Shall Sound* (New York: Schocken Books, 1968).

[20]John G. Gager, *Kingdom and Community: The Social World of Early Christianity* (Englewood Cliffs, N.J.: Prentice-Hall, 1975).

[21]Howard Clark Kee, *Community of the New Age: Studies in Mark's Gospel* (Philadelphia: Westminster, 1977).

[22](Atlanta: John Knox, 1981).

[23](Atlanta: John Knox, 1986).

[24]Douglas sees two dynamics of social structure: group and grid. Group relates to the level of individual commitment to the social matrix; grid relates to the level of control of the individual by the group. For example, a low group/low grid community would be characterized by a high level of individualism, whereas a high group/high grid community would be characterized by a strong hierarchical structure in which loyalty is paramount. Douglas sees this analytical method as a means for discerning the sociological matrix within which a group lives out its worldview, but not as a means for establishing categories by which phenomena are classified. Cf. Mary Tew Douglas, *Natural Symbols: Explorations in Cosmology* (London: Barrie and Jenkins, 1973); Mary Douglas, ed. *Essays in the Sociology of Perception* (London: Routledge and Kegan Paul, 1976).

[25]Hans Gadamer, *Truth and Method*, trans./ed. Garrett Barden and John Cumming (New York: Seabury, 1975); *Philosophical Hermeneutics*, trans. and ed. David E. Linge (Berkeley: University of California Press, 1976).

[26]Ludwig Wittgenstein, *On Certainty*, ed. Anscome and Wright, trans. Paul and Anscome (Oxford: Blackwell, 1969); *Philosophical Investigations*, trans. G. E. M. Anscome (New York: Macmillan, 1968).

[27]Anthony Thiselton, *The Two Horizons: New Testament Hermeneutics and Philosophical Description* (Grand Rapids: Eerdmans, 1980).

[28]Eugene A. Nida and Johannes P. Louw, eds., *Greek-English Lexicon of the New Testament Based on Semantic Domains*, 2 vols. (New York: United Bible Societies, 1988). See also J. P. Louw, ed., *Sociolinguistics and Communication* (UBS Monograph Series 1; New York: United Bible Societies, 1986).

[29]Paul repeatedly speaks of the "mystery" (Ro 16:25; 1Co 2:7, 4:1, 13:2(?); Eph 1:9, 3:3–4, 3:9, 6:19; Col 1:26–27, 2:2, 4:3; 1Ti 3:9, 3:16), especially the mystery revealed (Ro 16:25–26; 1Co 2:7–10; Eph 1:9, 3:3–4, 6:19; Col 1:26–27), which is now proclaimed to all (Ro 16:26; Eph 3:9, 6:19) and of which Paul is a "steward" (1Co 4:1)—a technical phrase used of the chief functionaries of the Hellenistic mystery religions.

[30]See notes 22 and 23.

316 | M. Robert Mulholland, Jr.

[31]Howard Clark Kee, *Knowing the Truth: A Sociological Approach to New Testament Interpretation* (Minneapolis: Augsburg Fortress, 1989), 52.

[32]"And so forth" is itself a phrase that indicates the speaker presumes the hearers share a common sociological frame of reference within which they can fill out what is implied.

[33]Suetonius, *Claudius* 24.5; cf. Acts 18:2.

[34]In about 139 B.C., there appears to have been an expulsion of Jews from Rome due to the spread of Judaism through proselytizing (The Epitome of Paris, *Valerius Maximus* i, 3.3). In 19 A.D., Jews were again expelled from Rome. Although the accounts of Tacitus (*Annals* ii, 85, 5), Suetonius (*Tiberius* 36.1), Dio (lvii, 18, 5a), and Josephus (*Antiquities* xviii, 65–84) vary, they all agree that proseltyizing lay at the heart of the problem. (For a full development of this Roman posture toward the Jews, see M. Robert Mulholland, Jr., *Revelation: Holy Living in an Unholy World* [Grand Rapids: Zondervan, 1990], Appendix.)

[35]Ernest C. Miller, Jr., *"politeuesthe* in Philippians 1:27: Some Philological and Thematic Observations," *Journal for the Study of the New Testament* 15 (1982): 86–96. Note also Paul's use of *politeuma* in 3:20. Only in Philippians does Paul use these two terms that would have carried added significance for people living in a Roman colony.

[36]*politeuma* = the full matrix of sociological factors that structured community life.

[37]In fact, the term "savior" represented one who either established, maintained and defended, or reestablished the sociological matrix within which the community and individuals found its meaning, value, purpose, identity, and welfare.

Chapter Eleven

Structuralism

Bill Stancil

Bill Stancil

Bill Stancil is Associate Professor of Christian Theology at Midwestern Baptist Theological Seminary in Kansas City, Missouri. He previously taught at the International Baptist Theological Seminary in Buenos Aires, Argentina, and at Beeson Divinity School in Birmingham, Alabama. He holds the B.A. from Memphis State University and the M.Div. and Ph.D. from Southwestern Baptist Theological Seminary. He has also studied at Texas Christian University. His articles have appeared in *The Quarterly Review, Southwestern Journal of Theology, The Baptist Standard*, and several other publications.

Chapter Eleven

Structuralism

Several new methods of biblical criticism have appeared in recent years, including sociological criticism, canonical criticism, and structuralism. Doubtless, structuralism is the most puzzling with its esoteric language, ubiquitous grids and charts, and frustrating forays into nonbiblical disciplines. One scholar decries its "penchant for neologisms and awkward expressions."[1] Another, most probably the victim of a request from an editor for an article, marvels that anyone would enter the "mine-field" of structuralism without some "professional constraint" or "inexplicable compulsion."[2] Whether by constraint or compulsion, the goal of this chapter is to lead readers safely through the minefield called structuralism with as few casualties as possible.

What makes structuralism so perplexing to the uninitiated is its radical departure from the presuppositions, terminology, and exegetical methods of more conventional types of biblical criticism. Traditionally, such methods as form, source, and redaction criticism have been utilized by scholars to uncover literary units that make up a text, to discover sources lying behind a text, and to disclose theological presuppositions that influenced the writer/redactor in giving shape to a text. These traditional critical methods give attention to such matters as the theology, motives, and historical circumstances of the writer. The text is not interpreted apart from a thorough consideration of those historical and theological factors that are, in a sense, extraneous to the text itself, but are nonetheless deemed essential for understanding the meaning of the text. In structuralism, however, the text itself takes center stage. Matters such as author, historical circumstances, and pre-literary traditions are at best of secondary importance.

DEFINITION AND DEVELOPMENT

Structuralism is both an ideology and a methodology. As an ideology, structuralism has been decried by some and embraced by others. It is interdisciplinary in application and has been used in such varied fields as linguistics, anthropology, psychology, literature, philosophy, and biblical studies. Its chief exponents reside in France, Germany, and the United States. Because of the eclectic nature of structuralism, stellar figures associated with the history of the movement are largely unknown to those who have worked in traditional biblical studies.

Structuralism had its beginnings with the Swiss linguist Ferdinand de Saussure (1857–1913), who taught at the University of Geneva from 1906–1911. In 1916 two of Saussure's students compiled his notes and published them posthumously as *Cours de linguistic générale*.[3] Another student of Saussure's carried back to his native Russia the linguistic theories learned at Geneva. The Russian Formalists, as they came to be called, applied these theories to literature and poetry. The most important advance to emerge from this school was the application of structuralism to folktales in a 1928 book by Valdimir Propp.[4] Another line of influence emanating from Saussure's work has been that of Russian Roman Jakobson and the so-called Prague Circle.[5]

Claude Lévi-Strauss pioneered the use of structuralism in the field of anthropology, especially in his work on myths from the cultures of the world.[6] A. J. Greimas has been at the forefront of the structural analysis of narratives.[7] The works of Tzvetan Todorov[8] and Roland Barthes[9] have also influenced American biblical scholars including Daniel Patte, Dan O. Via, Edgar McKnight, and others. Parables have especially been the focus of structural exegesis, and this work has been carried forward in the Scholars Press journal *Semeia: An Experimental Journal of Biblical Criticism*.

In its purest form structuralism seeks textual meaning independent of historical and cultural factors. As such, it is an "abandonment of history as a category of meaning."[10] Causal relationships and authorial intention are unimportant in structuralism. Meaning is contained in the deep structures of the text that reflect unconscious constraints that impinge on the writer. Most biblical scholars, however, view structuralism not as an ideology but as a method for analyzing texts. Those who use it generally do so alongside more traditional forms of biblical criticism. Thus, one need not be an enemy of history or reason to appreciate the contribution structuralism can make to biblical studies.

The goal of structural exegesis is to uncover the underlying structure that was responsible for producing the visible patterns of text. The word "structure," then, is not used in the traditional sense of the author's outline, pattern, or internal organization of the material. Rather, the structure to be uncovered is the deep, underlying configuration that exists below the surface of the text. This deep structure, unlike a surface outline or pattern, is not obvious to the casual reader. In fact, even the author himself was likely unaware of the many factors that presided over the creation of the text.

Anthropologist Edmund Leach, one of the earliest to use structuralism on biblical texts, points to the importance of this deeper structure when he argues that "sacred texts contain a religious message which is other than that which can be immediately inferred from the manifest sense of the narrative. Religious texts contain a mystery; the mystery is somehow encoded in the text; it is decodable."[11] Structuralism, then, proposes to uncover the "hidden or underlying configuration that can offer some explanation for the more or less visible or obvious pattern in the text."[12]

The purpose for uncovering these underlying structures is to awaken the imagination, evoke a vision of life, and release the power of the text to the reader today.[13] Meaning is not found as a result of a critical study of the text's historical background because meaning is not found "*behind* the text which creates distance" but rather "*in front of* the text which demands involvement."[14] Structuralism is "reader-oriented."[15] No original meaning for a text can be determined in isolation from the involvement of the reader.

In structuralism, deep structures are said to be self-sufficient and independent of outside forces such as social setting or the theological perspectives of the speaker/writer. These "structures of consciousness underlie and are mediated through language,"[16] implying an element of universality in deep structures that transcends the particularities of history. From where does this unconscious, universal meaning system originate? Are deep structures like Jungian archetypes that are universally a product of the collective human mind? Structuralists themselves disagree. Saussure locates the deep structures in the human brain, which he believes functions in certain universal patterns.[17] Jean Piaget and Claude Lévi-Strauss allow for a coalescence of both conscious behavior and unconscious infrastructures in the brain.[18] Regardless of how the presence of the deep structures is explained, if the universality of such structures holds true and can be demonstrated, then structuralism will have important implications for many different kinds of humanistic studies.

LANGUAGE AS CODE

Drawing on Saussure's terminology and theories, structuralists make an important distinction between language as code and language as speech. The word "langue" is used to refer to language as a system or a code, while the term "parole" refers to a specific speech-act. At the level of langue, speech is a closed system of codes that are governed by fixed rules. At the level of parole, these codes give rise to specific speech-acts. Speaking involves both aspects. When I say, "rain revives the parched earth," I am making actual (parole) a system that is theoretical (langue).

According to Saussure, language as system (langue) is no less concrete than language as message (parole).[19] Linguistic signs are contained in the brain and form part of the collective storehouse of those who speak the same language. Langue and parole are interrelated because "language is necessary if speaking is to be intelligible and produce all its effects; but speaking is necessary for the establishment of language, and historically its actuality always comes first."[20] An integral system of linguistics would require the interrelatedness of the two.

> . . . while language as a structure, as an ideal entity, is ontologically dependent on historical acts of usage, of speech-acts, which in each actual occurrence mean something new and different from anything which has ever previously been uttered, these same speech-acts logically presuppose the already ideally and objectively established

formal laws *according to* which acts of linguistic meaning can take place.[21]

Yet for all their interrelatedness, fundamental differences exist between language as code and language as message. Philosopher Paul Ricoeur, a critic of the linguistic/philosophical foundations of structuralism, notes that speech-acts are individual and intentional, unlike a code, which is anonymous and unintended. Further, speech-acts have a historical context unlike the ahistorical, virtual system of a code. Most important, a code lends itself to the kind of scientific analysis practiced by structuralism, whereas a specific speech-act or discourse must take into account other factors such as sociology and history.[22]

Language inscribed in a text (parole) is subject to the same analysis as speech. In its attempt to discover underlying structures, structuralism focuses on the linguistic code (langue) of a text in order to lay bare the arrangement or structure of the system of signs. The text is decomposed at the semiotic (sign) level in order to discover those elements that have impinged upon the creation of the particular text being studied. In fact for some structuralists, to explain the code of the text *is* to interpret the text. That is, meaning is not sought at the historical level of the author's message but at the ahistorical level of the linguistic code.

THE LINGUISTIC SIGN

In older hermeneutical systems the Cartesian subject/object dichotomy was held intact so that the goal of the exegete was to study the text objectively in order to learn what the author meant. Based on the objective meaning of the text, the exegete would then make application to contemporary life. Since the time of the pioneering hermeneutical work of Friedrich Schleiermacher and Wilhelm Dilthey,[23] interpreters have recognized that the meaning of a text cannot be objectively determined independent of the reader's experience of it. This is commonly stated in such ways as, "We do not stand in judgment of the text but rather the text stands in judgment of us," or "We do not seek to explain the text so much as we allow it to explain us."

The following three statements from James Smart, Rudolf Bultmann, and Amos Wilder, respectively, typify this breakdown of the subject/object division: One cannot really say what a text means without standing "in an immediate personal relation to what is proclaimed" in the text.[24] "The exegete is to 'interpret' Scripture after he has responsibly 'heard' what Scripture has to say."[25] The interpreter is not "on the balcony but the stage. If he looks at the world, the world looks at him. It is no longer a question of his apprehending only, but of his being apprehended."[26]

Structuralism goes beyond this generally accepted notion that the interpreter is actively involved in the meaning of the text. It suggests that texts are not only open to multiple understandings but that no one particular understanding takes precedence over another, not even the "intended" meaning of the author. This idea is again rooted in the theories of Saussure who taught that a linguistic sign is a "double entity" involving both signifier (*signifiant*) and signified (*signifié*).[27] The signifier might be a sound, gesture, or written pattern but is always considered to be arbitrary in the sense that it has "no natural connection with the signified."[28] The signified refers to the "psychological imprint of the sound, the impression that it makes on our senses."[29] That is, the signified is not so much the actual thing itself but a mental representation, including all it connotes or symbolizes. Together these two make up the sign.

In some forms of structuralism the signifier (text) is studied as a closed system of codes with no reference to the reader. Most biblical scholars who work with structuralism, however, believe the text is open to multiple signifieds (understandings). As noted, the author's intended meaning (signified) does not necessarily take precedence over other meanings. In fact, the author himself may not have known what he "intended" since the decoding of the text can reveal unconscious deep structure that may have guided the creation of the text. Meaning is multiple (polysemous or polyvalent) and includes not only the preunderstanding of the interpreter but any new understandings that are opened up as a result of a reader's encounter with the text. Since a sign is valid only when both signifier and signified are in operation, meaning is a product of both the structure of the text and the interpreter.

BINARY OPPOSITIONS

Phonemes are the smallest units of speech in any language and serve to distinguish one sound from another. There are no limits to the sounds that can be emitted within the framework of the "pitch, intensity, emphasis, and intonation which the human vocal apparatus is capable of producing."[30] Even the same individual never reproduces the exact sound twice because of the infinite number of variations. Since no single language ever uses the total range of possible speech sounds available to it, linguists try to identify the phonemes that are functional in a given language. Even the International Phonetic Alphabet, which serves as a standard for linguists, is not absolute but is only a tool for showing contrasts and relationships between languages.[31]

Phonemes exist as binary opposites because they are described in terms of contrasts (one sound higher or lower than another). The theory behind binary oppositions is that a phoneme is able to hold its position in the linguistic system by virtue of its opposition to another phoneme. A phoneme, then, is defined negatively on the basis of its relationship or opposition to other elements. Saussure compares this phenomenon to a chess game where the "respective value of the pieces depends on their position on the chessboard." In the same way, a "linguistic term derives its value from its opposition to all the other terms."[32]

After encountering these linguistic theories in 1941, anthropologist Claude Lévi-Strauss began to apply the concept of binary oppositions to the study of myths in South American cultures. Using this grammatical model, Lévi-Strauss taught that human behavior has its own grammar or set of rules and that it is impossible to speak of a myth's meaning without understanding the rules or grammar of behavior inherent in the human mind. He concluded that life's deepest concerns are structured around binary oppositions, and that societal myths function as a way to mediate these oppositions. Moreover, some oppositions are secondary in nature because they shield cultures from facing the more metaphysical and basic ones. For example, according to Lévi-Strauss such oppositions as life/death, heaven/earth, god/man are so threatening that they are deeply embedded in the myths of the cultures and the interpreter can do little more than uncover secondary expressions of these oppositions. In his groundbreaking studies on myth, Lévi-Strauss has documented the role of myth-making in mediating such oppositions as sacred/profane, male/female, raw/cooked, up/down, and others.[33]

Biblical structuralists have made extensive use of the concept of binary oppositions, especially in relation to the transformation and generating (production) of texts.[34] In his analysis of the women at the tomb, Louis Marin uncovers several sets of oppositions including light/darkness, sacred/profane, nocturnal/diurnal, presence/absence, and living body/dead body.[35] Dan O. Via finds four binary oppositions in his analysis of 1 Corinthians 1:18–2:5: foolishness/wisdom, weakness/power, death/life, and cross/boasting.[36] In his study of Genesis, Edmund Leach uncovers such oppositions as life/death, male/female, and human/divine.[37]

SYNCHRONIC RELATIONSHIPS

Critical methods that focus on changes occurring in a text as it develops through its various stages are said to be diachronic. Diachronic studies are evolutionary in nature, because the text is interpreted in light of developments and modifications that have occurred over the years. What comes before a text and what comes after is of paramount importance, since the meaning of the text is impacted by historical factors that are in flux. Most traditional methods of biblical criticism take a diachronic approach.

Synchronic relationships, on the other hand, refer to those that exist by virtue of elements belonging to the same system or structure, regardless of their chronological order or diachronic relationship. In synchrony, time is immobilized or frozen. Chronology is of little importance and often reflects no more than the natural sequence suggested by the genre of the literature. Edmund Leach speaks of the gospels in this way:

> From a structuralist point of view the gospel story does not have a beginning and a middle and an end; it all exists in synchrony as in a dream. The beginning refers to the end, the end refers to the beginning. The total structure is metaphoric. The sequences in the story are simply a by-product of the nature of narrative. The text can only say one thing at a time but what it says next is very likely just the same as what it has said before but with the imagery twisted around.[38]

The synchronic study of a biblical text is advantageous for at least two reasons. First, the chronological relationship between certain materials in the Bible is often tenuous. For example, the gospel writers, for reasons other than chronology, often locate material at different places in the text regardless of its diachronic relationship to other materials. John's recounting of the cleansing of the temple early in his gospel (2:13–22) has always presented a problem diachronically, in light of the fact that the synoptics position this incident during the final week of the life of Christ. If one looks at this pericope synchronically, however, it becomes merely another example of the opposition Jesus encountered with the Jewish religious leaders and can be interpreted independent of its chronological relationship to other pericopes in the text.

A second reason synchronic studies are important is because they give the interpreter a picture of the total system. In fact, it is only by seeing the total structure or system that one can understand the relationships of change in a system through the passing of time. Diachrony and synchrony "are interlinked and complement one another, with the structural vision actually forming the foundation for the best historical understanding."[39] Structuralist Robert Polzin uses the analogy of a house. If we really want to know about the house we will not only inquire how it was built (diachrony), but we will examine the house itself to learn what it is made of (synchrony). "Biblical criticism traditionally has confined itself to a search for internal signs of construction within the biblical house and has failed thereby to exploit many of the relationships that exist between the house's parts, as they now exist."[40]

VERTICAL AND HORIZONTAL AXES

Structural exegesis utilizes both horizontal and vertical axes to chart out the diachronic and synchronic relationships in a text.[41] Following the concepts of Saussure, a sentence is understood as a linear sequence of signs that includes the "signification" (the signifier and the signified) and its "value" or its relationship to other signs in the system.[42] The linear relationship between the various elements in a sentence can be placed on the horizontal axis of a grid. The elements that make up the linear sequence are said to be in a syntagmatic relationship.

Within any linear sequence of signs, however, other signifiers exist that are possible substitutes for the ones actually utilized. These signifiers are legitimate substitutes because they belong to the same system. Those elements that form a part of the system of signifiers that could serve as legitimate substitutes are said to exist in a paradigmatic relationship to one another and are placed on the vertical axis of a grid.

For example, the words in the sentence "war threatens life" form a linear sequence of signs (syntagm). Each word has value or holds its position in the sentence by virtue of its opposition to the others. On the level of syntagm, substitutions of words are possible but only according to the rules that make the sentence acceptable and intelligible.

Along with the linear sequence, however, other relationships are possible. For example, I might write "war endangers life" or "war jeopardizes life," and in each case the words "endangers" and "jeopardizes" are permissible substitutes without any loss of coherence because they form part of the same system of words and share a paradigmatic relationship. In fact, structuralism would emphasize that not only are these substitutes permissible, but they are necessary corollaries in understanding the full significance of the original word, since all of the words are associated in the memory.

Thus, the paradigmatic axis focuses not on the evolution of a word through its history nor on the linear relationship of one word to another. Rather, its emphasis is on all words that exist within a given system, without which the full identity and meaning of a specific word cannot be known. Again, this concept is indebted to Saussure's understanding of the sign as a double entity that includes not only the mental representation of the thing referred to but all that the representation connotes or symbolizes.[43] On a grid the above example would show syntagmatic and paradigmatic relationships in this way:

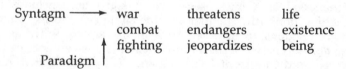

```
Syntagm ——→   war          threatens     life
              combat       endangers     existence
           ↑  fighting     jeopardizes   being
Paradigm  |
```

A non-linguistic example of these relationships might be that of a meal served in a restaurant that follows this order: appetizer, main course, desert, after-dinner drink. The elements belonging together on the paradigmatic axis are almost innumerable.

	Main		
Syntagm ⟶ *Appetizer*	*Course*	*Desert*	*Drink*
shrimp cocktail	steak	pie	coffee
cheese sticks	chicken	cake	brandy
salad	veal	ice cream	mocha

Paradigm ↑

Lévi-Strauss has extensively used this method for studying myths. He writes:

> . . .it is impossible to understand a myth as a continuous sequence. This is why we should be aware that if we try to read a myth as we read a novel or a newspaper article, that is line after line, reading from left to right, we don't understand the myth, because we have to apprehend it as a totality and discover that the basic meaning of the myth is not conveyed by the sequence of events but—if I may say so—by bundles of events even although these events appear at different moments in the story.[44]

Whether one is studying biblical narratives or cultural myths, in structuralism no one specific text (syntagm) has a privileged position. One text may be more complete than another but no version is superior. Each is unique in its structure and will contribute elements that belong together logically because of their paradigmatic relationships. In fact, syntagm and paradigm interact when dealing with multiple accounts of the same narrative or myth. "In a given version of a myth, if a sequence A is accompanied by a sequence B, and if this combination is found again in the form A′B′ in a second version, A″B″ in a third, etc., one can define A by the totality of its relations to B,B′,B″, and so on."[45] The same holds true for structuralist interpretations of biblical narratives. Such questions as the relationship of the synoptics and their sources are irrelevant for structuralism, since each gospel and each recension of the gospels is unique.

Using the actantial model of A. J. Greimas, Daniel Patte constructs a nondiachronic reading of the parable of the Good Samaritan composed of a series of six actants or spheres of action. The actants of the narrative are: "sender," "object," "receiver," "helper," "subject," and "opponent." In this particular parable the sender is not named but might be an abstract entity such as God, destiny, or conscience. The object is health for the receiver, who is the wounded man. The helper is represented by the know-how, oil, wine, donkey, money, and innkeeper. The subject is the Samaritan, and the opponent the robbers and effects of their action. Since the parable at its surface level reflects a diachronic order and not a structural one, it is divided into additional lexies or reading units in order to make clear the relationships between the various sequences. Subsequences within lexies further define the structure of the story.[46]

THE GENERATING OF TEXTS

In speaking or writing, why would one word be chosen over another or one myth used instead of another to express the deepest concerns of life? If historical factors are secondary to the unconscious deep structures that are at work in discourse and writing, how then are speech and texts generated (created)?

Noam Chomsky's theories of generative grammar and linguistic competence have added another ingredient to the stew that is structuralism.[47] Chomsky believes that form and meaning "are determined by the 'language faculty,' which is understood to be a particular component of the human mind."[48] Erhardt Güttgemanns and the "generative poetics" of Bonn, who have been at the forefront of the biblical study of the generating of texts, understand this "language faculty" as a structure in the human mind that allows a person to function linguistically without consciously being aware of the rules of the language.[49] Such "linguistic competence" makes certain that "the language structure used will conform to the given set of rules within the historical context of the writer."[50]

Chomsky has shown that complex sentences derive from the creative transformations of basic sentences. All languages have common deep structures that are governed by these transformational rules that "provide the organizing principles that make language learning possible."[51] These structures are made explicit in discourse or texts. Inherent, then, in structures is the element of change (transformation). In fact Jean Piaget, emphasizing the fact that elements of structures undergo change, defines a structure as a "system of transformations."[52] Lévi-Strauss, as noted above, has also discovered transformations operative at the level of myth when cultures transform basic metaphysical binary oppositions such as life/death to secondary oppositions such as agriculture/hunting.[53]

The linguistic competence of a speaker/writer in making transformations should not be confused with his "linguistic performance." The difference between the two somewhat parallels the difference between langue and parole. The speaker/writer is limited in the discourse or text he can produce (parole) since he can only generate discourse or texts within his linguistic competence (langue). The historical factors impinging upon a writer fade into the background and are not considered by structuralists to be the primary influences in the production of a text. Rather, the various transformations that occur at the linguistic level are the primary forces at work to produce the text.

For example, in form criticism the historical and sociological milieu of the early church is understood to be preeminently important for understanding the development of the gospels. In structuralism, however, emphasis would be placed on the creation of the gospels as a result of the linguistic competence of the particular speaker or writer at that time. One scholar points out that according to this theory of textual formation, pericopes of gospel tradition could not have been passed around by various writers because the material would have been useful only to those whose linguistic competence would have made them open to receiving such material.[54] As noted, this would imply that no text has priority over another since each is generated according to the linguistic competence of the writer. Some versions of a pericope may be more complete than others, but a specific performance text is nothing more than one actualization of the writer's linguistic competence within the rules of his specific historical context. The task of the interpreter is to discover those transformations that account for the generating of the text and those points of his own linguistic competence where legitimate transformations can occur.

AN EVALUATION OF STRUCTURALISM

The goal of biblical hermeneutics is to gain insight into the meaning of the Bible. What, however, does the word "meaning" mean?[55] Is meaning to be construed of as the original intention of the author, the world that is opened up to the reader who interacts with the text, or the structural arrangement of the linguistic signs of the text? Can any one of these alone exhaust the meaning of a text? The various answers to this question reflect the diversity found in hermeneutical theories today. In some way or another, the center of attention is either on the author, the reader, or the text, or a combination of these three.

Traditional exegetical methods have clearly centered on the referential and intentional meaning of Scripture, that is, the theological and historical entities and the personal circumstances, motives, and interests of the writers and readers themselves.[56] The focus of structuralism, however, is on the symbolic dimension of meaning as contained in the text itself.[57] This surely is one of structuralism's greatest strengths as a methodology. Because it is able to combine texts in ways that do not depend on relationships of sequence and history, the result is new insight into the meaning of the text. By arranging different texts, or elements within the same text, on the basis of a correlation of elements that belong to the same system (paradigm), new hermeneutical slants are gained that, when used with other forms of biblical criticism, can provide the reader with a new understanding about humankind, the world, and himself.

Some are skeptical about the value of structuralism in light of its meager output to this point. Is structuralism worth all the trouble? Thus far, in the opinion of James Barr, it has "produced no large body of profound and convincing results" and its results are "paltry, insubstantial." Structural exegesis, says Barr, often leaves us with a "sense of disappointment" because it is unclear what we have discovered that we might not have known before. "Is structuralism really a way that will lead to a new set of powerful insights and results in biblical study, or is it rather an expression of a new outlook of scholars, who are going to express themselves in a new way but will have essentially banal things to say?"[58] Barr thinks the source of this weakness lies in the fact that structuralism has a linguistic model as its basis.

Three comments are in order. First, it is probably unfair to judge structuralism on the basis of whether its body of results is large or small. The most obvious reasons for the paucity of results are the recent advent of the methodology and the small number of biblical scholars working in the field. Second, more and more scholars who work with structuralism are becoming eclectic in approach and moving away from a strictly linguistic model. Third, whether structuralism is worth the effort for the results produced can be answered only by each exegete. Each type of biblical methodology has something to offer in terms of hermeneutics. Some require more effort than others. Some are complex, involving detailed and expert knowledge in history, sociology, languages, and archaeology. Each has its own specialized vocabulary. Though structuralism differs greatly from traditional methods, its contributions can be valued and appreciated by diligent scholars.

An ongoing problem in biblical scholarship has been that of explaining in what way the various parts of the Bible form a whole. The early and medieval church fathers sought unity through allegory and typology. In the first half of this century scholars sought unity in such diverse concepts as covenant, salvation history, eschatology, and others. Much of modern scholarship has tended to despair of finding such unity, though the unity-in-diversity question has taken on a slightly different focus with the current emphasis on canonical criticism. This approach has called attention to the unity of the biblical texts as formed, shaped, and used by the communities of faith.[59] Structuralism might play an additional role in the unity-in-diversity question by its search for unity at a deeper level than the surface text. Since fundamentally structuralism *is* a quest for "invariant elements among superficial differences,"[60] such unity would not depend on the various layers that went into the final formation of the canon but on deep structures that reflect a unity of mind.

The search for universal invariants could also have important implications for the relationship between biblical and nonbiblical texts. Life is a "network of relations, where things have meaning not in themselves but as they stand within that network."[61] Since structuralism ranges across various disciplines and intellectual currents, it could become a powerful force in humanistic studies for bringing to light the condition of humankind. It might especially be helpful in disclosing deep structures shared by religions that differ greatly on the surface.[62]

Structuralism should be evaluated on the basis of its ability to give rise to and answer significant questions about the texts it analyzes. The questions that traditional methods of biblical criticism ask of the text include such things as who wrote it, to whom was it written, what were the sources used by the author, and what theological motives were at play in the mind of the writer. What one comes away with from the text is already limited by the kinds of questions asked and the way they are framed. Structuralism is valuable because it gives us "a new set of eyes."[63] It cannot be evaluated fairly if we try to make it answer the same questions raised by conventional methods. Unlike structuralism, traditional methods have not been principally concerned about such matters as deep structures, synchronic relationships, binary oppositions, and transformations.

For example, Edmund Leach points out that it can be misleading to fragment textual materials into different genres. When materials are studied only through the grid of the preconceived characteristics of a specific genre, the exegete fails to see that some sections are structural transformations of others and cut across the conventional genre distinctions.[64] This does not, as Leach himself points out, preclude using other critical methodologies in fruitful ways to discover other levels of meaning in the text. Texts are meaningful at a variety of levels. The point is, by asking new questions and arranging textual materials in novel ways, new levels of meaning are opened up.

The reintroduction of the text as the center of biblical studies must be viewed as a positive contribution of structuralism.[65] James Barr believes that a certain dissatisfaction has resulted from purely historical explanations of texts "even if all the critical analyses and divisions were correct." These explanations have failed to "furnish a proper account of the meaning of the texts" because they do not "speak of the meaning of texts *as they are*."[66] Structuralism affirms that meaning can be found in the text as it is, independent of historical matters extraneous to the text. As noted, it would be incorrect to say that all biblical scholars who use structuralism do so with no regard for author, reader, *Sitz im Leben*, and other concerns of traditional critical methods. Commitment to the principle of multiple meanings requires variety in critical methods, and for many a structuralist reading is only one among many necessary for understanding a text.

One of the chief criticisms leveled against structuralism is its emphasis on the "semantic autonomy" of the text. This phrase refers to the freedom of the text from either author (the subject who thinks and intends) or referent (the world about which the author writes).[67] To what extent must the interpreter be concerned about the original intention of the author? Can the text be truly autonomous, cut loose from its historical moorings?

Paul Ricoeur has shown that texts always exhibit characteristics of semantic autonomy because the author's intention, what he meant, is tied in with the finite horizon and psychology unique to him. Ricoeur warns, however, that the semantic autonomy of the text understood by itself is dangerous. He cautions against two fallacies: the "intentional fallacy" and the "absolute text fallacy." The former views the author's intention as the criterion for valid interpretation while the latter hypostasizes the text as an entity without an author. "If the intentional fallacy overlooks the semantic autonomy of the text, the opposite fallacy forgets that a text remains a discourse told by somebody, said by someone to someone else about something."[68] The relationship between the two is dialectical.

At the forefront lobbying for the rights of the original author has been E. D. Hirsch, Jr. In his influential 1967 book *Validity in Interpretation*, Hirsch argues that "the theory of authorial irrelevance"[69] has "encouraged willful arbitrariness and extravagance in academic criticism" and has called "into doubt the possibility of objectively valid interpretation."[70] In contrast to the structuralist view, Hirsch points out that almost any word sequence can "legitimately represent more than one complex meaning," but that "meaning is an affair of consciousness not of words. . . . A word sequence means nothing in particular until somebody either means something by it or understands something from it. There is no magic land of meanings outside human consciousness."[71] When a text is interpreted only as an immanent (closed) system of signs with author and referent banished, then all that remains is the "absolute givenness of the aesthetic work."[72] To lose the author, according to Hirsch, is to create confusion:

> Thus, when critics deliberately banished the original author, they themselves usurped his place, and this led unerringly to some of our present-day theoretical confusions. Where before there had been but one author, there now

arose a multiplicity of them, each carrying as much authority as the next. To banish the original author as the determiner of meaning was to reject the only compelling normative principle that could lend validity to an interpretation.[73]

Hirsch concedes that texts always contain implied meanings, unconscious meanings, and sometimes the author's response to what he originally wrote can change. Nor does Hirsch preclude the evaluation of a critic to determine whether or not the text produced actually accomplished what the author intended. But even the ability to judge whether a writer has succeeded or failed in his purpose is to imply some knowledge of the author's intention.[74] In a later work Hirsch, while not repudiating his previous position, acknowledges that there is nothing in the nature of the text itself that would require the interpreter to choose authorial intention as the norm.[75] However, since a choice of an interpretative norm is necessary, such choice belongs to the realm of ethics and the interpreter "falls under the basic moral imperative of speech, which is to respect an author's intention."[76]

Hirsch's clarifications in his later book would make clear the need for some sort of "reader-oriented criticism" that emphasizes not just movement from author to text but from text to reader. Once the text leaves the author it takes on a life unto itself, and the determiner of meaning can no longer be limited exclusively to the intention of the author. We see this in the Bible in cases where Paul's letters are addressed to a specific community of faith but are circulated to others (cf. Col 4:16). The meaning of the text could not be identical for different communities since the contexts are different. No pure subject/object dichotomy can exist in interpreting a text, since meaning is always related to the world or horizon created by the consciousness of the reader.

If we are to avoid the dangers of both the intentional fallacy and the absolute text fallacy (and certainly evangelicals have been more susceptible to the former), both structuralism and traditional critical methods are needed in order to provide valuable checks and balances. The danger inherent in structuralism is to lose sight of historical factors that provide legitimate parameters for interpretation. Structuralists argue that we "need not be afraid of being trapped into wild or fanatic illegitimate prophetic interpretations; the text rigorously delimits the field in which its various legitimate hermeneutics may unfold, and a structural exegesis of this text shows what this field is."[77] Though McKnight admits that "this vision of pluralism may be a nightmare,"[78] he also argues that the use of structuralism

> does not mean that "anything goes," for systems of interpretation involve components that must be correlated with each other and with the reader-components that are dynamic in themselves as well as parts of a dynamic system. These components include a world view that constrains the sort of meaning desirable and possible, methods that are capable of discerning those sorts of meaning, and meanings and interpretations that are consistent with the world view and the methods employed and which satisfy the reader.[79]

But not all structuralists take a moderating view as does McKnight. Edmund Leach writes, "Structuralists' analyses do not yield solutions which are 'right' or 'wrong'; they demonstrate the existence of partial patterns."[80] There is no "correct version"[81] according to Leach, nor is there a point at which the interpreter feels he understands it all. "At best he can simply feel that he understands rather more than when he started out. The whole process is dialectical; a provisional enquiry which then provokes further enquiry. What is revealed is not the truth but the basis for looking at familiar materials in a new way."[82] The prospect for abuse is obvious, not only in the direction of wild and fanatic interpretations but also "sane and interesting ones."[83]

In structuralism the question of multiple recensions takes on new meaning. The attempt of traditional biblical criticism to get back to the original (autograph) text insofar as possible is seen as unnecessary in structuralism. If no single text is in a privileged position, including those closer to the autographs, then structuralism must address these questions: to what extent are deep structures the product of the original text and the mind of the original writer(s)/redactor(s)? How were subsequent redactions guided by unconscious constraints? How does structuralism affect our understanding of inspiration? Will the idea of the inspiration of Scripture be "culturally and linguistically relativized" or should we posit God's involvement at the level of linguistic structures?[84]

In spite of the fact the Bible is a book that reflects the faith of its writers, the religious or dogmatic element is secondary in structuralism. Meaning is reduced to structure and is not a reflection of the faith of the writers. For example, when structuralism is used in the study of cultural myths, the actual symbols of the myth are less important than their structure or order. In biblical studies the same problem obtains. Structuralism fails to provide the kind of reading of the Bible that takes into account the theological factors dealt with in the text. Can structuralism "fit with the nature of the Christian faith as a religion?" asks James Barr. Christianity is not only a particular understanding of the Bible but involves actual persons and events, that is, a historical element. "Thus the structuralism that worked purely on the level of the Bible as a text would be ambiguous in its relation to theology and the codes that it uncovered might be the codes of biblical society rather than the lineaments of the affirmations of the faith."[85]

Structuralists have not been able to show to the satisfaction of most that signs governed by fixed rules on the semiotic level are applicable at a higher level. This is especially true in the use of binary oppositions. Doubtless, texts can be analyzed with reference to the closed system of signs where each element in the system stands in opposition to another. As phenomenologists have pointed out, however, this approach is limited when one moves beyond the basic levels of language to the higher level of sentences or a text. Ricoeur warns that to deal only at the level of the closed system of signs is to miss the fact that the ultimate purpose of language is to communicate or mediate "between minds and things."[86] Structuralism, he believes, excludes "the primary intention of language, which is to say something about something."[87]

Moreover, does literature really work this way, or is structuralism too neat and scientific for "so lively and unpredictable a creature as art?"[88] Barr suggests that relations are complicated, not simple, and involve a multitude of possibilities. For example, in the area of syntax one does not "find clear and simple oppositions but rather vague and fluid ones," and "in most cases we are dealing with a continuum of vaguely related, partly overlapping, terms, and with a greatly extensive series of possibilities rather than a closed matrix."[89] Even if the principle of binary oppositions were to hold true at higher linguistic levels, it would be far from certain that this is an appropriate model for describing the fundamental realities of life. Again, not all who use structuralism in biblical exegesis would reduce meaning to linguistic codes.[90] Yet binary oppositions commonly become the grid imposed on the text.

CONCLUSION

Structuralism is still "a house half built,"[91] and what position it might have in the panoply of critical methods in the future is yet uncertain. At first glance it might appear to be a safe haven to protect religiously conservative views from rigorous historical study. After all, conservative scholars have always been suspicious of attempts to explain the Bible in purely historical terms. Yet, if a structuralist reading of a text is really independent of history, then the text provides no reliable information historically,[92] and the value-judgments associated with a conscious decision to produce a text are swallowed up by a kind of preconsciousness that antecedes all knowledge.[93]

The price of such concessions is too high. A structuralist reading of the Bible, independent of any other kind of reading, can ultimately lead to ahistoricism and antirationalism. Ironically, evangelicals have often given up history and reason anyway by opting for subjective interpretations of the text.[94] The direction for the future seems to be one that includes structuralism as one viable method among others for understanding a text, but not as the exclusive determiner of meaning. Hermeneutics cannot afford to lose any element of the triad of author, reader, and text.[95]

BIBLIOGRAPHY

Barr, James. "Biblical Language and Exegesis—How Far Does Structuralism Help Us?" *King's Theological Review* 7 (1984): 48–52.

Cahill, Joseph. "A House Half Built." *Religious Studies Bulletin* (September 1982): 143–53.

Hirsch, E. D., Jr. *Validity in Interpretation*. New Haven: Yale University Press, 1967.

Leach, Edmund. *Genesis as Myth and Other Essays*. London: Jonathan Cape, 1969.

McKnight, Edgar V. *The Bible and the Reader*. Philadelphia: Fortress, 1985.

Patte, Daniel. *What Is Structural Exegesis?* Philadelphia: Fortress, 1976.

Polzin, Robert M. *Biblical Structuralism.* Missoula, Mont.: Scholars Press, 1977.

Ricoeur, Paul. *Interpretation Theory: Discourse and the Surplus of Meaning.* Fort Worth: The Texas Christian University Press, 1976.

Spivey, Robert A. "Structuralism and Biblical Studies: The Uninvited Guest." *Interpretation* 28 (April 1974): 133–45.

Stancil, Bill. "Structuralism and New Testament Studies." *Southwestern Journal of Theology* 22 (1980): 41–59.

NOTES

[1]Robert M. Polzin, *Biblical Structuralism* (Missoula Mont.: Scholars Press, 1977), 41.

[2]Joseph Cahill, "A House Half Built," *Religious Studies Bulletin* (September 1982): 143.

[3]Ferdinand de Saussure, *Course in General Linguistics*, trans. Wade Baskin, eds., Charles Bally and Albert Sechehaye (New York: Philosophical Library, 1959). Good surveys of the development of structuralism can be found in Edgar V. McKnight, *Meaning in Texts* (Philadelphia: Fortress, 1978), 95–143 and Susan Wittig, "The Historical Development of Structuralism" *Soundings* 58 (Summer 1975): 145–66.

[4]Vladimir Propp, *The Morphology of the Folktale* (Austin: University of Texas Press, 1970).

[5]Roman Jakobson, *Selected Writings* (The Hague: Mouton, 1966); and *Word and Language* (The Hague: Mouton, 1971).

[6]Claude Lévi-Strauss, *Structural Anthropology*, trans. Claire Jacobson and Brooke Grundfest Schoepf (New York: Basic Books, 1963).

[7]A. J. Greimas, *Sémantique structurale* (Paris: Larousse, 1966).

[8]Tzvetan Todorov, *Littérature et signification* (Paris: Larousse, 1967).

[9]Roland Barthes, *Elements of Semiology*, trans. Annette Lavers and Colin Smith (Boston: Beacon, 1964).

[10]*New Dictionary of Theology*, s.v. "Structuralism," by C. E. Armerding.

[11]Edmund Leach, "Introduction," in Edmund Leach and D. Alan Aycock, *Structuralist Interpretations of Biblical Myth* (Cambridge: Cambridge University Press, 1983), 2.

[12]Dan O. Via, Jr., *Kerygma and Comedy in the New Testament* (Philadelphia: Fortress, 1975), 7.

[13]Daniel Patte and Aline Patte, *Structural Exegesis: From Theory to Practice* (Philadelphia: Fortress, 1978), 4.

[14]Edgar V. McKnight, *The Bible and the Reader* (Philadelphia: Fortress, 1985), xviii.

[15]Edgar V. McKnight, *Post-Modern Use of the Bible: The Emergence of Reader-Oriented Criticism* (Nashville: Abingdon, 1988).

[16]Brian W. Kovacs, "Philosophical Foundations for Structuralism," *Semeia* 10 (1978): 88.

[17]See *The Westminster Dictionary of Christian Theology*, s.v. "Structuralism," by Raymond F. Collins.

[18]Jean Piaget, *Structuralism*, trans., ed., Chaninah Maschler (New York: Basic Books, 1970), 138.

[19]Saussure, *Course in General Linguistics*, 15.

[20]Saussure, cited by Wittig, "Historical Development of Structuralism," 149.

[21]James M. Edie, *Speaking and Meaning: The Phenomenology of Language* (Bloomington: Indiana University Press, 1976), x.

[22]Paul Ricoeur, *Interpretation Theory: Discourse and the Surplus of Meaning* (Fort Worth: The Texas Christian University Press, 1976), 3.

[23]On the contributions of Schleiermacher and Dilthey see Paul Ricoeur, "The Task of Hermeneutics," *Philosophy Today* 17 (1973): 112–20.

[24]James Smart, *The Interpretation of Scripture* (Philadelphia: Westminster, 1961), 41.

[25]Rudolf Bultmann, *Essays Philosophical and Theological* (London: SCM, 1955), 261.

[26]Amos N. Wilder, "New Testament Hermeneutics Today," in *Current Issues in New Testament Interpretation*, eds. William Klassen and Graydon F. Synder (New York: Harper, 1962), 45.

[27]Saussure, *Course in General Linguistics*, 65–78.

[28]Ibid., 69.

[29]Ibid., 66.

[30]Edie, *Speaking and Meaning*, 24.

[31]See Robert A. Hall, *Introductory Linguistics* (Philadelphia: Chilton Books, 1964), and John T. Waterman, *Perspectives in Linguistics* (Chicago: University of Chicago Press, 1963).

[32]Saussure, *Course in General Linguistics*, 88. See also the discussion in Jean Calloud, "A Few Comments on Structural Semiotics: A Brief Review of a Method and Some Explanation of Procedures," trans. John C. Kirby. *Semeia* 15 (1979): 55–56.

[33]See Claude Lévi-Strauss, *Structural Anthropology* (New York: Basic Books, 1963); *The Savage Mind* (Chicago: University of Chicago Press, 1966); *The Raw and the Cooked* (New York: Harper, 1969); *Myth and Meaning* (New York: Shocken Books, 1979); and *Anthropology and Myth* (Oxford: Basil Blackwell, 1987).

[34]See infra, 16–19 for a discussion of this.

[35]Louis Marin, "The Women at the Tomb: A Structural Analysis Essay of a Gospel Text," in *The New Testament and Structuralism*, trans. and ed. Alfred M. Johnson, Jr. (Pittsburgh: Pickwick, 1976), 73–96.

[36]Via, *Kerygma and Comedy*, 44.

[37]Edmund Leach, *Genesis as Myth and Other Essays* (London: Jonathan Cape, 1969).

[38]Edmund Leach, "Against Genres: Are Parables Lights Set in Candlesticks or Put Under a Bushel?" in Edmund Leach and D. Alan Aycock, *Structuralist Interpretations of Biblical Myth* (Cambridge: Cambridge University Press, 1983), 98.

[39]James Barr, "Biblical Language and Exegesis—How Far Does Structuralism Help Us?" *King's Theological Review* 7 (1984): 50.

[40]Polzin, *Biblical Structuralism*, 9.

[41]For brief discussions of this subject see McKnight, *The Bible and the Reader*, 6–7, and Bill Stancil, "Structuralism and New Testament Studies," *Southwestern Journal of Theology* 22 (Spring 1980): 49–50.

[42]Saussure, *Course in General Linguistics*, 111–22.

[43]Ibid., 66.

[44]Lévi-Strauss, *Myth and Meaning*, 44–45. See also Lévi-Strauss, *Anthropology and Myth*, 200–201.

[45]Lévi-Strauss, *Anthropology and Myth*, 201.

[46]Daniel Patte, *What Is Structural Exegesis?* (Philadelphia: Fortress, 1976), 41–50.

[47]See Noam Chomsky, *Syntactic Structures* (The Hague: Mouton & Co., 1957); *Aspects of the Theory of Syntax* (Cambridge, Mass.: MIT Press, 1965); *Knowledge of Language: Its Nature, Origin, and Use* (New York: Praeger, 1986). For a discussion of whether or not Chomsky has influenced structuralism in its development or merely in its terminology see Jonathan Culler, *Structuralist Poetics* (Ithaca: Cornell University Press, 1975), 7–8.

[48]Chomsky, *Knowledge of Language*, 3.

[49]Much of Güttgemanns' writing appears in the journal he edits entitled *Linguistica Biblica: Interdisziplinäre Zeitschrift für Theologie und Linguistik*. See also *Offene Fragen zur Formgeschichte des Evangeliums* (München: Christian Kaiser, 1970); *Studia Linguistica Neotestamentica* (München: Christian Kaiser, 1971). Some English translations of his ideas can be found in Vol. 6 of *Semeia*.

[50]Stancil, "Structuralism and New Testament Studies," 50.

[51]Cited by Edie, *Speaking and Meaning*, 63. For a fuller discussion see ibid., 57–69.

[52]Piaget, *Structuralism*, 5.

[53]See supra, 9–11.

[54]William Doty, "Linguistics and Biblical Criticism," *Journal of the American Academy of Religion* 41 (March 1973): 115.

[55]See Ricoeur's discussion in *Interpretation Theory*, 11–23.

[56]James Barr, *The Bible in the Modern World* (New York: Harper, 1973), 61–63.

[57]Patte and Patte, *Structural Exegesis*, 4.

[58]Barr, "Biblical Language and Exegesis," 50.

[59]See Brevard S. Childs, *The New Testament as Canon: An Introduction* (Philadelphia: Fortress, 1984); James A. Sanders, *Torah and Canon* (Philadelphia: Fortress, 1972); James A. Sanders, *Canon and Community* (Philadelphia: Fortress, 1984); and the essay by Mikeal C. Parsons in this volume (pp. 255–94).

[60]Lévi-Strauss, *Myth and Meaning*, 8.

[61]Barr, "Biblical Language and Exegesis," 52.

[62]Robert A. Spivey, "Structuralism and Biblical Studies: The Uninvited Guest," *Interpretation* 28 (April 1974): 143–44; David Jobling, "Structuralism, Hermeneutics, and Exegesis: Three Recent Contributions to the Debate," *Union Seminary Quarterly Review* 34 (Spring 1979): 143; and Cahill, "A House Half Built," 151.

[63]Jobling, "Structuralism, Hermeneutics, and Exegesis," 139.

[64]Leach, "Against Genres," 93.

[65]See Stancil, "Structuralism and New Testament Studies," 54, and *New Dictionary of Theology*, s.v. "Structuralism," by Armerding.

[66]Barr, "Biblical Language and Exegesis," 48.

[67]See Edie, *Speaking and Meaning*, 149.

[68]Ricoeur, *Interpretation Theory*, 30.

[69]E. D. Hirsch, Jr., *Validity in Interpretation* (New Haven: Yale University Press, 1967), 3.

[70]Ibid., 2.

[71]Ibid., 4.

[72]This phrase is used by Roman Jackobson, cited by Doty, "Linguistics and Biblical Criticism," 115.

[73]Hirsch, *Validity in Interpretation*, 5.

[74]Ibid., 10–14.

[75]E. D. Hirsch, Jr., *The Aims of Interpretation* (Chicago: University of Chicago Press, 1976), 7. For a discussion of this book see McKnight, *The Bible and the Reader*, 96–100.

[76]Hirsch, *The Aims of Interpretation*, 92.

[77]Patte and Patte, *Structural Exegesis*, 111.

[78]McKnight, *Post-Modern Use of the Bible*, 61.

[79]McKnight, *The Bible and the Reader*, 133.

[80]Leach, "Introduction," 4–5.

[81]Leach, "Against Genres," 92.

[82]Leach, "Introduction," 5.

[83]Elizabeth Struthers Malbon, "The Theory and Practice of Structural Exegesis: A Review Article" *Perspectives in Religious Studies* 11 (Fall 1984): 276.

[84]Vern S. Poythress, "Structuralism and Biblical Studies," *Journal of the Evangelical Theological Society* 21 (September 1978): 237.

[85]Barr, "Biblical Language and Exegesis," 52. Thiselton also argues that structuralism tends to reduce the particular events of God's saving activities in history to the level of "general truths about the nature of the human mind." See Anthony C. Thiselton, "Structuralism and Biblical Studies: Method or Ideology?" *Expository Times* 84 (August 1978): 334.

[86]Ricoeur, *Interpretation Theory*, 6.

[87]Paul Ricoeur, "Structure, Word, Event," in *The Conflict of Interpretations*, trans. Robert Sweeney, ed. Don Ihde (Evanston: Northwestern University Press, 1974), 84.

[88]John Gardner, *On Moral Fiction* (New York: Basic Books, 1978), 129.

[89]Barr, "Biblical Language and Exegesis," 51.

[90]McKnight, *The Bible and the Reader*, 13.

[91]Cahill, "A House Half Built," 153.

[92]Barr, "Biblical Language and Exegesis," 49.

[93]See Brian W. Kovacs, "Philosophical Foundations for Structuralism," *Semeia* 10 (1978): 93.

[94]Grant Osborne, "Interpreting the Bible: New Testament," in *The Proceedings of the Conference on Biblical Interpretation* (Nashville: Broadman, 1988), 143.

[95]McKnight, *The Bible and the Reader*, xviii. Cf. also McKnight's comment concerning the "impossibility of an approach in which neither historicity nor individual valuation plays a part." *Post-Modern Use of the Bible*, 144.

PART THREE

SPECIAL ISSUES IN NEW TESTAMENT INTERPRETATION

Chapter Twelve

Background Studies and New Testament Interpretation

David E. Garland

David E. Garland

David E. Garland is Professor of New Testament Interpretation at Southern Baptist Theological Seminary in Louisville, Kentucky. He is a graduate of Oklahoma Baptist University (B.A.) and Southern Baptist Theological Seminary (M.Div., Ph.D.). He has also done post-doctoral work at the University of Tübingen. He is the author of *The Intention of Matthew 23* (Brill) and *Galatians: A Bible Study for College Students* (Convention Press). He has also co-authored two books with Diana R. Garland: *Beyond Companionship: Christians in Marriage* (Westminster) and *Marriage: For Better or Worse* (Broadman). His numerous articles have been published in such journals as *Review and Expositor, Interpretation, Novum Testamentum,* and *Criswell Theological Review.* In addition to contributing to several dictionaries and symposiums, he is presently writing *The Sermon on the Mount* (Harold Shaw) and *Reading Matthew* (Crossroad).

Chapter Twelve

Background Studies and New Testament Interpretation

INTRODUCTION

Much of the basic story in the New Testament would be incomprehensible if the reader did not possess some knowledge about the ancient world, its beliefs, practices, and political history. When one reads, for example, the statement, "We have found the Messiah" (Jn 1:41), one needs to have some inkling about what "Messiah" means to understand the import of this discovery. The same is true of other titles that appear in the Gospels, such as Christ, Son of David, Son of Man, and Lord. Luke's mention of Pontius Pilate, a Roman, as the governor of Judea (3:1–2), immediately raises the question for the reader of the political situation of Palestine when John the Baptist and Jesus began their ministries. What brought about such a turn of events that Romans were governing Judea and that Jesus' opponents could attempt to ensnare him with a question about whether it was lawful to pay tribute to Caesar (Mt 22:15–22)? When Jesus announces in the Sermon on the Mount, "Unless your righteousness exceed that of the scribes and Pharisees you will in no way enter the kingdom of heaven" (Mt 5:20), the astute reader must ask who the scribes and Pharisees were and what their righteousness was that must be excelled?

The New Testament writers also record many details that might mystify a modern reader. The evangelist Matthew assumes that his readers will be familiar with what he is describing when he recounts that those who collected the temple tax (*didrachma*) asked Peter whether his teacher paid it (17:24), and when he relates Jesus' indictment that the scribes and Pharisees, who sit on the seat of Moses, make their phylacteries broad, their fringes long, and their proselytes double sons of Gehenna (23:2, 5, 15). Who today can understand these references without some acquaintance with Jewish religious habits in Jesus' time? Other questions also emerge as one reflects on the story. Why was eating with toll collectors and sinners such an issue for Jesus' opponents (Lk 5:30; 7:34; 15:1)? Why was eating with Gentiles such a volatile matter for Jewish Christians (Ac 11:3; Gal 2:11–14)? Why does the issue of eating meat sacrificed to idols so vex some at Corinth (1Co 8–10)? How was "Christ crucified" a stumbling block to the Jews and foolishness to the Greeks (1Co 1:23)? These are only a sampling of the myriad questions that may stump a modern reader of the New Testament or give pause for thought. They illustrate that when one studies the New Testament one needs also to be a student of early Judaism and of the Greco-Roman world.

The study of the world of Mediterranean antiquity today attracts many different interests. But as students of the New Testament we want to know how knowledge of that world can better inform our understanding of the biblical text. This last sentence assumes that what the New Testament describes did not take place in a vacuum. Language operates in a historical context. All of us are people of our own time and place. When we explore the social and cultural milieu in which the New Testament took shape, we are trying to get a sense of its time and place.[1]

To read the New Testament well we need to distinguish who the players are in the story. This pursuit calls for more than mastering facts such as names and dates; it requires attempting to understand the world of those names and dates. What were the historical, political, cultural, and socioeconomic factors that formed the stage setting?[2] What were the semantic codes employed by the writers and the hearers? What were the social roles that were taken for granted in their world that might be foreign to us? In probing for answers to these kinds of questions, one may discover not only what people thought in the time of Jesus or Paul, but how *they* thought as well—how they constructed their world and made sense of things, how they infused their world with meaning and emotion. The goal of discovering the so-called background of a text is to make as clear as possible what it says in its historical context.

Ascertaining the background ("foreground" might be a better term) of a text in the New Testament is not a simple task.[3] The sources we have are extensive and frequently arcane. One quickly realizes how vast the sources are by venturing to read through collections of inscriptional evidence, the Greek Old Testament (the Septuagint), the Pseudepigrapha, the Dead Sea Scrolls, the rabbinic corpus, the Nag Hammadi library, the Hermetica, the assortment of Greek and Latin authors conveniently published in the Loeb Classical Library, and the many writers not included in any of the above. It is difficult to become a master of any one body of this literature, let alone all. The investigation of the ancient world can also yield a multiplicity of options for understanding a New Testament passage. Often the best one can do is to rule out some alternatives and clarify the possibilities. The variety of alternatives challenges the interpreter to decide as carefully as possible which are legitimate and which are not. For example, what background best informs our understanding of the hymn in Philippians 2:6–11? Should it be read in light of the terminology found in classical Greek philosophers, the suffering servant hymns in Isaiah 40–55, the enthronement of the son of man in Daniel 7, Jewish speculation about the two Adams (see Ro 5:12–21; 1Co 15:45–49), a so-called Gnostic redeemer myth, or Wisdom motifs? All have been proposed; not all are likely. Possibly, none may be correct or even helpful for understanding the text. The range of options means that the student must frequently live by the educated guess and the power of imagination when assessing the backdrop of a passage in the New Testament. One's conclusion may be refuted by the next archaeological discovery or by a reevaluation of old data.

In what follows, I will briefly summarize some of the ancient sources available for studying the world of the New Testament and will provide an example of how these sources might shed light on our understanding of something in the New Testament. The examples given are not the last word on a passage but are intended only to be illustrative. The purpose is to show how attention to literature outside the New Testament opens up new angles of vision for examining what the text says.

EPIGRAPHY AND ARCHAEOLOGY

A wealth of inscriptions (written documents on stone, clay, or papyrus) has been recovered that casts light on the everyday world of the New Testament.[4] The mounds of papyri found in the sands of Egypt have helped to illumine the nature of the language of the New Testament.[5] Two separate inscriptions from the balustrade in the temple help to make sense of the rhubarb that erupted when the Jews from Asia accused Paul of taking a Gentile into the temple and defiling it (Ac 21:27–35). These inscriptions read:

> Let no foreigner enter within the screen and enclosure surrounding the sanctuary. Whosoever is taken will be the cause that death overtaketh him.[6]

Paul's description of his escape from Damascus in 2 Corinthians 11:30–33 may sound daring and dramatic. It takes on a different hue when read against the backdrop of one of the highest Roman military honors, the *corona muralis* (wall crown).[7] This distinction was awarded to the valorous commander who first ascended the wall of an enemy city. A head of the Roman goddess, Fortuna (fortune), adorned with the crown that resembles the turreted wall of a city and dating from the first or second century, has been discovered in Corinth. What Paul describes in his escape may be viewed as an ironic reversal of military bravery. He was not the first one up the wall but the first one down. The image in this context becomes another token of Paul's humiliation and weakness. But he declares that he will only boast about his weakness and how God is able to work through that weakness.

According to Matthew 27:51–54, Jesus' death is accompanied by earthquakes, the splitting of rocks, the opening of tombs, and the resurrection of holy ones. Earthquakes, splitting rocks, and resurrection were apocalyptic motifs associated with the great day of the Lord and can be documented from the Hebrew Scriptures and other ancient Jewish writings (e.g., Eze 37:1–14; 38:18–19; Isa 24:18–23; Da 12:1–2). That most Jews would have recognized the apocalyptic import of these events can be surmised from a wall mural from a third-century synagogue uncovered at Dura-Europos, a frontier town in Babylon. One panel related to prophecies from Ezekiel shows a split mountain with an olive tree, possibly representing the

Mount of Olives (see Zec 14:4), and ten men dressed in white rising from tombs that have been opened by the earthquake. The portentous events that Matthew reports, along with the splitting of the temple veil and the confession of the soldiers, would have underscored the apocalyptic import of Jesus' death for the Jewish reader. One might conclude that Matthew noted these events because he wished to convey that Jesus' death marked the long awaited turn of the ages.

THE DEAD SEA SCROLLS

Between 1947 and 1960, scrolls and crumbled fragments written in Hebrew and Aramaic and dating from 250 B.C.E. to the time of the first revolt against Rome were found at Khirbet Qumran and its vicinity beside the Dead Sea. Eventually over seven hundred texts, including ten complete scrolls, were recovered from eleven caves at Qumran where they had been stashed. The scrolls include every book in the Hebrew Scriptures except Esther, non-canonical books we classify as Apocrypha and Pseudepigrapha, Aramaic translations of the Hebrew Scriptures, and literature distinctive to the sect: collections of regulations, psalms, commentaries, and even a treasure map. Because of the vagaries of the way the publication of the literature was assigned to scholars, some four hundred other writings and fragments have yet to be published forty years after their discovery![8] But those that have been published provide us with an unprecedented first-hand glimpse into the diversity of Judaism in the time of Jesus that cannot be overestimated.[9]

It was probably to be expected that when the scrolls first came to light scholars would begin to see answers to every question in the New Testament in terms of something from Qumran. Real and imagined parallels between the Gospels and the scrolls led some to argue that Jesus had been directly influenced by the sect. A famous essay by Samuel Sandmel warns of the dangers in using parallels carelessly.[10] He challenges what he labels "parallelomania" and defines it as "that extravagance which first overdoes the supposed similarity in passages and then proceeds to describe source and derivation as if implying literary connection."[11] Sandmel makes the important point that ideas do not flow in pipelines. It is fallacious to argue from similarities to direct influence. The parallels one may see between two bodies of literature may simply be independent manifestations of a common heritage or shared atmosphere. Parallels should not be allowed to cloud one's vision to significant differences that might also exist.

For example, both John the Baptist and the Qumran community dwelt in the Judean wilderness.[12] Both were interested in water rites. Both were preoccupied with the imminence of divine judgment and lived ascetically. Before arguing for any direct connection between John and the sect at Qumran one should also note the considerable dissimilarities. John expressed no interest in creating an exclusive, priestly dominated sect that was fundamental to the covenanters at Qumran. The ritual baths at Qumran were limited to members of the sect and were repeated daily to achieve Levitical purity. John's baptism was open to everyone who repented. It had nothing to do with Levitical cleansing but was designed to prepare for the coming judgment of God and did not need to be repeated. The parallels do not necessarily indicate any direct association between John and Qumran, but may only reflect the fact that they shared similar expectations that were in the religious air at that time.

The literature found at Qumran also contains phrases that appear in the New Testament, such as "sons of light" and "sons of darkness," "the church of God" (1QM 4:9; see 1Th 2:14), "the righteousness of God " (1QS 11:12, in a context that speaks of justification by faith), "the mysteries of God" (1QpHab 7:8; see Eph 5:32), and meditations on Melchizedek (11AMelch 6–8; see Heb 7:1). But Sandmel also warns that one cannot rigidly assume that the New Testament can mean only what the parallel means.[13] One must be careful to understand what each term means in its own context. With these caveats in mind concerning parallels to the New Testament, the Dead Sea scrolls have shed enormous light on the diversity of Judaism in the time of Jesus and have contributed much to our understanding of the New Testament.

An important Christological issue pertains to the use of the title "son of God" in the scrolls. No Palestinian extra-biblical text before the New Testament had been uncovered where the title was used for the expected Messiah.[14] The title was not uncommon, however, in the Hellenistic world.[15] Consequently, many scholars claimed that the application of the title to Jesus originated when Christianity moved out into Hellenistic environment and was subjected to a supposed syncretistic paganization. Hans Conzelmann concludes, "All the passages with the title 'the Son' are thus demonstrably community christology."[16]

This assertion can no longer be held after the significant appearance of the title in the Qumran literature where it is directly connected to the Messiah. 4QFlorilegium 10–13 (a collection and commentary on selected biblical passages) contains a messianic interpretation of 2 Samuel 7:11–14. The author explicitly identifies "my son" as "the shoot of David" who will sit on David's throne and save Israel in the last days. In a fragment, 4QpsDan^a) (4Q 246), a human being (unidentified) is called son of God and son of the Most High, which directly parallels Luke 1:32–35.[17] James Charlesworth comments:

> We now have abundant and persuasive evidence that Jews roughly contemporaneous with Jesus did use the technical term "son" or "son of God." They attributed this title to paradigmatic holy individuals, including the long awaited Messiah, in God's drama of salvation. It simply will no longer suffice to attribute all references to "son" or "Son of God" to the needs and proclamations of the church."[18]

While this may be overstated, it can be affirmed "that the title 'son of God' was as much at home in Palestinian Judaism as in the contemporary Hellenistic world of the eastern Mediterranean."[19]

This affirmation is also true of the title "Lord." Rudolf Bultmann claimed that the absolute use of "the Lord" as a title for God could not originate in a Palestinian setting but was something borrowed from the Hellenistic world, where the title was commonly used to refer both to gods, particularly in mystery cults, and to human rulers (see 1Co 8:5; Ac 25:26). Bultmann wrote, "At the very outset the unmodified expression 'the Lord' used of God is always given some modifier; we read: 'the Lord of Heaven and earth,' 'our Lord,' and similar expressions."[20] An Aramaic translation of Job from Qumran belies this assertion. It refers to God absolutely as "the Lord" (11QtgJob 24:6–7; see also 11Qps 28:7; Josephus, *Ant.* 13.3.1 ¶68; 20.4.2 ¶90). This testimony means that the absolute use of "Lord" need not have been the creation of Hellenistic Christian missionaries but was at home in a Palestinian setting.[21]

JOSEPHUS AND PHILO

Josephus

Josephus was a Jew born into a priestly family (around 37–38 C.E.) and later led a contingent of troops in the revolt against Rome. He was captured early in the war by the Roman general Vespasian, and managed to ingratiate himself by correctly prophesying that the commander would become emperor. He later produced, under the ruling family's patronage, a seven-volume account of the war (*The Jewish War*) and a twenty-volume survey of Jewish history (*The Antiquities of the Jews*). He also wrote an autobiography and a work that attempts to refute slanders against the Jews (*Against Apion*). Josephus is obviously the primary source for Jewish history in this period.

In Josephus' account of Herod Antipas, he makes a passing reference to John the Baptist that forms an instructive parallel to the New Testament references to John:

> Herod had him put to death, though he was a good man and had exhorted the Jews to lead righteous lives, to practise justice towards their fellows and piety towards God, and so doing to join him in baptism. In this view this was a necessary preliminary to baptism if baptism was to be acceptable to God. They must not employ it to gain pardon for whatever sins they committed, but as a consecration of the body implying that the soul was already thoroughly cleansed by right behavior. When others too joined the crowds about him, because they were aroused to the highest degree by his sermons, Herod became alarmed. Eloquence that has so great an effect on mankind might lead to some form of sedition, for it looked as if they would be guided by John in everything that they did. Herod decided therefore that it would be much better to strike first and be rid of him before his work led to an uprising, than to wait for an upheaval, get involved in a difficult situation and see his mistake. Though John, because of Herod's suspicions, was brought in chains to Machaerus, . . . and there put to death, yet the verdict of the Jews was that the destruction visited upon Herod's army was a vindication of John, since God saw fit to inflict such a blow on Herod (*Antiquities*, 18.5.2 ¶117–119).[22]

Philo

Philo was a wealthy Jew who lived from 20 B.C.E. to 50 C.E. in Alexandria. He interpreted the law of Moses through the lens of Greek (Platonic) philosophy as he sought to bridge the gap between his biblical faith and his Hellenistic culture. His prolific writings were preserved by Christians, and his allegorical exegesis had an impact on later church Fathers such as Clement of Alexandria and Origen. Many links between Philo and John have been adduced (the use of the concept of the Logos, the imagery of God as Light, Shepherd, and fountain of living water). Philo's discussion of the Logos reflects the development of one strain of Jewish thinking about it in the New Testament era that forms a suggestive parallel to the Fourth Gospel:

> To His Word, His chief messenger, highest in age and honour, the Father of all has given the special prerogative, to stand on the border and separate the creature from the Creator. This same Word both pleads with the immortal as suppliant for afflicted mortality and acts as ambassador of the ruler to the subject. He glories in this prerogative and proudly describes it in these words 'and I stood between the Lord and you' (Dt 5:5), that is neither uncreated as God, not created as you, but midway between the two extremes, a surety to both sides; to the parent, pledging the creature that it should never altogether rebel against the rein and chooses disorder rather than order; to the child, warranting his hopes that the merciful God will never forget His own work. For I am the harbinger of peace to creation from that God whose will is to bring wars to an end, who is ever the guardian of peace (*Who is the Heir* 205–06).[23]

Striking parallels between Philo and Hebrews are also plentiful. The same words and the same ideas appear in both, but they are used in quite different ways. Philo is primarily important because he reflects a milieu that has been identified, for want of better terminology, as Hellenistic Judaism. This Greek-speaking and Greek-thinking Judaism influenced many strands of tradition since it comprised the audience for much of what was written in the New Testament.

THE APOCRYPHA AND PSEUDEPIGRAPHA

The Apocrypha

The Old Testament Apocrypha is a small part (the standard count is fifteen) of a vast number of books that were recognized as Scripture by Greek-speaking Jews but were not included in the Hebrew canon. They were preserved only by Christians. The term "Apocrypha" is misleading because it means "concealed" or "hidden," but some of the books are straightforward histories, like 1 Maccabees. For a time, the term had a pejorative connotation of "spurious" or "heretical." Since many modern translations of the Bible now include the Apocrypha, the term has become a neutral one that, for Protestants, means "non-canonical." Catholics refer to these writings as deuterocanonical because they were recognized as authoritative at a later date.

The books in the Apocrypha, with the exception of 2 Esdras, predate 70 C.E. and were interspersed throughout the Greek Old Testament, the Bible of the early Christians. As a bridge between the Hebrew Scriptures and the New Testament, they provide us with a glimpse of the development of postexilic Judaism, its religious practices, beliefs, and history amidst the invasion of Hellenistic culture.[24]

A passage from the Wisdom of Solomon concerning the righteous man forms an instructive backdrop for the taunting of Jesus on the cross:

> Let us see if his words are true, and let us test what will happen at the end of his life; for if the righteous man is God's son, he will help him, and will deliver him from the hand of his adversaries. Let us test him with insult and torture, that we may find out how gentle he is, and make trial of his forbearance. Let us condemn him to a shameful death, for, according to what he says, he will be protected (2:17–20, RSV).

The Pseudepigrapha

The popular piety of the first century was not represented by the legal debates found in the literature of the later rabbis. If anything might reflect that piety, it would be what is contained in the Pseudepigrapha. This term is applied broadly by some. James Charlesworth, who headed an international team of experts to produce an English translation of these ancient Jewish works,[25] includes sixty-five documents composed by Jews or Christians in Hebrew, Aramaic, and Greek between 200 B.C.E. and 200 C.E. Others would use the term more restrictively and exclude writings after 100 C.E. The name Pseudepigrapha means "with false superscription" and derives from the fact that most of the writings are attributed to some ideal hero in Israel's past. Some would reject the term Pseudepigrapha altogether and prefer to designate these writings simply as apocryphal Old Testament. Many of these religious writings were influential, but none was included in any official canon. They embody varying styles and genres that can be sorted into five broad literary categories: apocalyptic literature that purports to reveal what is occurring in the heavens and will occur on the earth in the near future; "Testaments," in which a patriarch delivers his last words from his death bed; legendary expansions of the Hebrew Scriptures;[26] wisdom and philosophical literature; and prayers, psalms, and odes. Again, these works were preserved, transmitted, and some possibly recast by early Christians.

The writings contained in the Pseudepigrapha reflect the wide spectrum of Jewish literary activity and the reservoir of inherited ideas, expressions, themes, and perceptions that would have been familiar to New Testament authors.[27] They can be particularly helpful in interpreting such difficult passages as 1 Peter 3:18–22. This passage poses several questions for the interpreter: Who are the spirits in prison? When did Christ preach to them? Where is the prison? What is the direction of Christ's journey? And what is the content of his preaching? The average person today would probably interpret this passage in terms of the Apostles' Creed and assume that it refers to Christ's descent into hell. But acquaintance with writings from the Pseudepigrapha lead most commentators to interpret this text differently.

Second Enoch 7 relates how Enoch is taken up into the second heaven where he sees dark looking angels in their prison. They are identified as the evil rebels who disobeyed God's commands by taking counsel with their own will and conspiring with their prince, who is fastened in the fifth heaven. In torment, they await the great and boundless judgment (see also *TLevi* 3:2; *1En* 10; 18:14; Jude 6; 2Pe 2:4). I would not suggest any dependence between 1 Peter and 2 *Enoch*, but I do propose that the writers shared inherited religious motifs. One might infer from the parallels between 2 *Enoch* and 1 Peter concerning the prisoners that 1 Peter does not have in view deceased human beings but some disobedient angelic or demonic beings. This would mean that the direction of Jesus' journey is up to the nether gloom of the heavens where these spirits await the final judgment.[28] 1 Peter could hardly have in view some great revival meeting in hell where Christ calls the dead to repentance; instead, the author depicts Christ announcing to the disobedient spirits his victory over the powers hostile to God.

RABBINIC LITERATURE

Rabbinic literature is the largest and probably the most difficult source to utilize for trying to understand the New Testament.[29] In the past, the rabbinic corpus has been employed largely for polemical motives. Excerpts were taken out of their original context and sometimes used as a foil to demonstrate the superiority of the teaching of Jesus.[30] Or an anthology of sayings was compiled to show that the teaching of Jesus was already contained in the Talmud.[31] Until recently, little attempt was made by Christian scholars to study rabbinic literature on its own terms, perhaps because it is such a daunting task.[32] The literature is difficult to understand and to interpret. One specialist compared the Talmud to a primeval, dense forest in which a person will lose his way without a skillful guide. Another averred, "Talmudic hermeneutics is about as simple as higher mathematics."[33]

The diversity of the corpus adds to the difficulty of using it. The writings range in time from 220–550 C.E. and even later. They consist of markedly different forms: Midrash, Targum, and Mishna and Gemara. The midrashic literature consists of verse-by-verse commentaries on the Hebrew Scripture. The targums are Aramaic translations of the Scriptures. The Mishna is a compendium of oral law that supplements scriptural law and was published around 200. The Babylonian Talmud (sixth century) is a commentary (gemara) on the Mishna that sought to make the Palestinian Mishna applicable to Babylonian Jewry. Both contain traditions from a variety of times and contexts without any regard for chronological order or historical context. Both derive from "an ongoing process of teaching, interpretation and application, of revision and expansion of earlier teachings" in light of later concerns.[34] The traditions contained in the Talmud will therefore not infrequently reflect a time later "than the period of which they claim to speak."[35] Consequently, the danger of anachronism always lurks in using these texts to understand or to illustrate something from the first century.

Scholars now recognize that one can no longer think of rabbinic Judaism as representing a so-called "normative" Judaism of the first century (or even of the second century). The society of scholars that produced the Mishna, for example, was in all probability a distinctive intellectual elite. Important breaks in the history of Judaism after the failed revolts in 70 and later in 135 (about which we know very little) created new sociological and political situations. One cannot assume that what the rabbis projected should be the case in Jewish social, economic, and religious life was in fact practiced in the time of Jesus. One can assume, however, that because the rabbis changed in their social position and gained more influence their religious preoccupations changed as well during the time that the traditions were developed. It is likely that they misremembered some traditions because of later changes in practice or that they deliberately misrepresented the tradition to aid changes in practice or that they simply idealized the past. Consequently, "Rabbinic texts cannot be taken . . . to represent the entirety, or even necessarily the mainstream, of pre-rabbinic Judaism."[36]

The recognition of this fact would help, for example, to avoid some invalid conclusions about the trial of Jesus as reported in the Gospels. Tractate *Sanhedrin* in the Mishna purports to contain procedures for the courts charged with the conduct of capital cases. According to *Sanhedrin* 4:1 capital cases are to be held in the daytime, and the verdict is to be reached in the daytime. A verdict for conviction cannot be reached on the same day of the trial. Therefore, a capital trial is not to be held on the eve of a Sabbath or feast day. According to *Sanhedrin* 5:2, when witnesses disagreed, their evidence was null and void; and, in 5:4, it is decreed that attempts be made to find witnesses on behalf of the accused. According to *Sanhedrin* 7:5, the blasphemer is not guilty unless he expressly pronounces the Name; and, in 11:2, it reports that the great court met in the Hall of Hewn Stone in the temple.

The trial of Jesus before the Sanhedrin in Mark comes off as both highly irregular and illegal when compared with this list of regulations in the Mishna. In Mark's account, the trial is conducted in the house of the high priest at night on the eve of Passover, and the guilty verdict is given on the same day as the trial. What Jesus says in response to the high priest could not technically be construed as blasphemy. The conflicting witnesses are not nullified, and no defense is presented on Jesus' behalf.[37]

Because of the discrepancies between what Mark records and what tractate *Sanhedrin* ordains, some scholars argue that the Jewish trial in Mark is a fiction invented by Christians who, for apologetic reasons, wanted to shift blame for Jesus' death from the Romans, who crucified Jesus, to the Jews, who were innocent of his death. None of the legal particulars derived from the Mishna, however, are pertinent for drawing such a conclusion. In this instance, the Mishna records prescription not description. Tractate *Sanhedrin* treats the council as if it were an all-powerful body not subject to any other external power. It is said to have the authority to judge the king and the high priest, to set boundary lines, and to declare war (*m.Sanh.*1:5). That is what the compilers of the tradition thought should be the case, but it certainly was not the way it was in the first century. In the time of Jesus, the high priest was a political appointee of the Romans; and, according to Josephus (*Ant.* 20.9.1 R 202), the Sanhedrin did not even have authority to assemble without the governor's permission. The high priest was left to run local administrative matters as he saw fit, and the evidence indicates that he was hardly under the thumb of the relatively uninfluential Pharisees and their legal judgments. The accuracy of the trial of Jesus in the gospel accounts cannot be discredited by appeal to regulations in the Mishna.

Can one appeal to rabbinic literature when interpreting the New Testament? Jacob Neusner has made a notable contribution as an interpreter and translator of these texts, making some of them available in English for the first time to the nonspecialist. He believes, however, that the New Testament and rabbinic literature differ so greatly in their overall perspective of their piety that they can hardly illuminate one another in their detail.[38] I would not be so pessimistic.[39] Details concerning Jewish practices and beliefs mentioned in the New Testament can be clarified by cautiously comparing it to information contained in the rabbinic literature.

For example, it is informative to relate Jesus' teaching in the Sermon on the Mount about being struck on the right cheek (Mt 5:39) with a Mishnaic discussion on indemnities for violence:

> If a man cuffed his fellow he must pay him a *sela* [four *zuz*].
> R. Judah says in the name of R. Jose the Galilean: One
> hundred *zuz*. If he slapped him he must pay 200 *zuz*. If [he
> struck him] with the back of his hand he must pay him 400
> *zuz* (m. B. Qam. 8:6).

Being struck on the *right* cheek envisions being slapped with
the back of the hand. Jesus is not simply urging that we turn
the other cheek when someone aims a blow at us but when
someone assaults us with insulting violence. Such a calculated
indignity is considered to be at least four times as injurious in
the Mishna, which reflects the outlook of a shame/honor
society.

The text may also be illuminated by comparing the two
pieces of literature. In *Mishna Berakot* 5:5 (a tractate dealing with
prayers), it is told of Hanina ben Dosa "that he used to pray
over the sick and say, 'This one will live,' or 'This one will die.'
They said to him, 'How knowest thou?' He replied, 'If my
prayer is fluent in my mouth I know that he is accepted and if it
is not I know that he is rejected.'"

This saying has a parallel in the Babylonian Talmud (*b. Ber.*
34b). When the two are compared, the later text, compiled
some three hundred years after the Mishna, seems to contain
the original context for the saying. In the Mishna, the context
has to do with the ramifications of making a mistake in reciting
a prescribed prayer. The tradition about the venerable Hanina
is given and interpreted as proof that even he made mistakes in
prayer and nothing evil befell him. The original setting for the
saying, however, probably had to do with the miraculous cure
of the son of R. Gamaliel, which the Babylonian Talmud
preserves:

> Our Rabbis taught: Once the son of R. Gamaliel fell ill. He
> sent two scholars to R. Hanina b. Dosa to ask him to pray for
> him. When he saw them he went up to an upper chamber
> and prayed for him. When he came down he said to them:
> Go, the fever has left him; They said to him: Are you a
> prophet? He replied: I am neither a prophet nor the son of a
> prophet, but I learnt this from experience. If my prayer is
> fluent in my mouth, I know that he is accepted: but if not, I
> know that he is rejected. They sat down and made a note of
> the exact moment. When they came to R. Gamaliel, he said
> to them: By the temple service! You have not been a moment

too soon or too late, but so it happened: at that very moment the fever left him and he asked for water to drink.

This story immediately brings to mind Jesus' healing of the official's son who was ill with a fever (Jn 4:46–54). For us today, fever is viewed as a symptom of an illness. In the time of Jesus, it was considered to be a separate affliction. Some deemed fever, in view of Deuteronomy 28:22, to be a divine chastisement that could be cured only by God. In the Babylonian Talmud we find a tradition from R. Alexandri who said in the name of R. Hiyya bar Abba:

> Greater is the miracle wrought for the sick than for Hananiah, Mishael and Azariah. [For] that of Hananiah, Mishael and Azariah [concerned] a fire kindled by man, which all can extinguish; whilst that of a sick person is [in connection with] a heavenly fire, and who can extinguish that? (b. Ned. 41a).

The implied answer to the question is that none can extinguish fever, a heavenly fire, except God.

In light of these passages, it is important to note that Hanina does not effect the cure himself. His statement about the fluency of his prayer meant that the words he uttered were not his own but were words placed in his mouth by God. When the words were placed in his mouth so that they flowed out, it was a sign to him that it was heaven's will for the sick person to recover. When that did not occur, it was a sign that heaven did not intend to provide the cure.[40] Whichever was the case, it is assumed that the cure was entirely dependent on heaven, not on Hanina's powers or even his prayers.

The differences with the parallel in John are significant. Jesus does not pray for healing but simply proclaims that the son will live. The emphasis is on the father's belief in Jesus' word and on the fact that Jesus' announcement marked the time when the fever left him (4:50, 52). Jesus is portrayed differently from Hanina as one who possesses divine power to effect the cure. Jesus' power is even more graphically displayed in the healing of the fever of Peter's mother-in-law (Mk 1:30–31). He raises her up by seizing her hand, and the fever forsook her. Again, Jesus does not pray for healing. By seizing her hand and raising her up, he is able *directly* to extinguish a heavenly fire. Those who are aware of Jewish presuppositions concerning fever are able to recognize that Jesus is shown doing something that only God or God's agent could do. The miracle makes a decided Christological statement.

THE TARGUMS

The targums are Aramaic translations of the Hebrew canon. They were developed on behalf of the Aramaic-speaking Jews to accompany the reading of the Hebrew text in the synagogue. The translations sometimes were paraphrases that included extensive interpretations.[41] The extant targums are rabbinic (except for those found at Qumran), but we have no reliable data about their authorship or the circumstances of their compilation. None probably predate 200 C.E. In spite of this fact, many scholars contend that they "preserve many exegetical traditions which would have circulated in the Jewish community of the first century."[42] and perhaps even earlier because they were subject to less thorough revision than other rabbinic texts such as the Mishna.[43]

The targums were designed for devotional use in the synagogue and not for professional study in the academy, and this purpose is what makes them valuable for the interpretation of the New Testament. They contain oral exegetical traditions that were more likely to have been familiar to the religious masses of the first century than the intricate academic debates of the sages. We therefore may learn from them what the average synagogue worshiper understood about the Scripture. The language is also more akin to the vernacular spoken by early Christians in Galilee.

Attention to a targum may offer an explanation for the difficult verses in Ephesians 4:8–10. Psalm 68:19 is quoted in 4:8: "When he ascended on high, he led a host of captives, and he gave gifts to men." It is then inferred from the ascent that a descent must have occurred to "the lower parts of the earth." Many have interpreted this as another reference to Christ's harrowing of hell. "He ascended on high" is taken to refer to his resurrection, and the "lower parts of the earth" is assumed to refer to the underworld, the antithesis of the supreme heights. This view comes to grief over three problems. First, the text clearly has ascension in view, not resurrection. Second, if the captives refer to the principalities and powers, they are located in "the heavenlies" in the cosmology of Ephesians (see 1:21; 2:2; 6:12) and not in the lower parts of the earth. Third, the immediate context has to do with Christ's gifts (4:7–8, 4:11–12), and a descent to Hades would have little relevance for the bestowal of gifts upon the community (4:7–8 and 4:11–12). The passage implies that a descent was necessary for these gifts to be given.

B. G. Caird examines how the use of Psalm 68 might help to clarify this passage and offers a suggestion that reveals how the use of the targums can elucidate the New Testament.[44] The quotation in Ephesians 4:8 significantly differs from the Greek and the Hebrew text of the Psalm. Instead of the second person, "you did ascend," referring to God, it has the third person, "he ascended." Instead of receiving gifts from the vanquished, it states that he "gave gifts." It therefore does not have in view God's ascent on Mt. Zion, but the wording has been altered so that it refers to Christ's ascent to the heavenlies. But why then use the Psalm at all?

According to a tradition from the Babylonian Talmud, Psalm 68 was used in the Jewish liturgy for the day of Pentecost and also was associated with the giving of the law to Moses on Mt. Sinai (b. Pesah. 68b). A targum interprets the Psalm specifically to refer to Moses:

> Thou hast ascended to heaven, that is Moses, the prophet; Thou hast taken captivity captive, thou hast learnt the words of the Torah; Thou hast given it as gifts to men, and also with the rebellious, if they turn in repentance, the Shekina of the glory of the Lord dwells.

This targum states that Moses ascended to heaven to receive the law, and one must infer that he descended later in order to give the law as gifts to men. According to Caird, the logic of the exegesis reflected in the targum of this Psalm is similar to that in Ephesians. But in Ephesians the Psalm has been "Christianized" to refer to Christ rather than to Moses. As Jews interpreted this Pentecostal Psalm to refer to Moses' giving of the law, Christians may have reread it as a celebration of the ascension of Christ on high (Lk 22:51; Ac 1:9) and his return at Pentecost to shower spiritual gifts on his church. This explains why a descent was inferred from an ascent and also why the writer insists on the fact that the identity of the one who ascended is the same as the one who descended. The Christ who ascended above the heavens did not abandon his people but returned to bestow spiritual gifts on them (see

Ac 2:33) to insure that God's purpose to unite all things in him might be achieved. While this interpretation may not be correct, it does show how attention to the way Jews interpreted the Scripture as it is preserved in the targums does open up new, if perhaps unfamiliar, ways of understanding difficult passages in the New Testament.

NAG HAMMADI

A collection of thirteen bound papyrus volumes written in Coptic, a late Egyptian language that uses Greek characters, was discovered in 1945 in northern Egypt. The collection contained forty-five works of varied genre that were translations of documents originally composed in Greek, some perhaps dating to the first century, but most from the second and third century.[45] The later discovery of the Dead Sea Scrolls overshadowed the significance of this library that provides primary evidence for current debates about the nature and dating of Gnosticism. The most famous of the works, The Gospel of Thomas, is a series of sayings of Jesus without a narrative context. It has been considered by some scholars to preserve early traditions of Jesus' teaching. It is my opinion, however, that the Nag Hammadi documents do not reflect pre-Synoptic traditions.[46] They do provide interesting comparison reading when studying the Gospels. For example, the parable of the lost sheep takes on a different emphasis in the Gospel of Thomas 107 from that in Luke's account:

> Jesus said: the kingdom is like a shepherd who had a hundred sheep. One of them went astray; it was the largest. He left the ninety-nine (and) sought for the one until he found it. After he had exerted himself, he said to the sheep, I love you more than the ninety-nine.

THE GRECO-ROMAN WORLD

Christianity emerged from Judaism, but it had great success as an urban movement in a world dominated by Hellenistic culture. Therefore, the student has much to learn from non-Jewish literature of the age.

Paul's second letter to the Corinthians offers good examples of how understanding the literary and cultural conventions of the time contributes to a better understanding of his letter. Paul gives the theme of his letter in 1:13–14. He hopes that they will come to understand fully that he is their boast in the day of the Lord Jesus (see 13:6). In 5:11–12, he says that he wants to give them a basis for being proud of him. This statement suggests that Paul is engaged in self-commendation, not because the congregation has failed to value Paul's gifts adequately, but because he wants to restore the broken relationship between them and instill their confidence in him again. He wants to give the church ammunition (the facts) that they can in turn use against those who boast "in the face and not in the heart" (2Co 5:12). If he fails, he may lose the congregation to interloping false apostles.

Obviously, self-commendation is a touchy subject. It borders on self-advertisement, which Paul roundly condemns (2Co 10:13–18). Plutarch (50?–120 C.E.) wrote an essay on the very subject, entitled *On Praising Oneself Inoffensively*. Paul's response to the Corinthians reveals some awareness of the conventions regarding self-commendation that Plutarch described. Charles Talbert offers a convenient listing of the guidelines regarding self-praise that are used by Paul. One should mix in one's faults or shortcomings (2Co 11:30–33, 12:8–9). One should express care or worry over others (2Co 11:1–4, 28–29; 12:19). One should include exhortation for the good of the hearer (2Co 13:5, 11). One may point out differences between oneself and others whose influence may be harmful (2Co 10:13–18; 11:12–15, 23–29).[47] In spite of the fact that Paul's self-commendation would have qualified as legitimate self-praise given the conventions of the day, Paul expresses his discomfort about what he is doing throughout the letter. He makes it clear that he is boasting only as a fool and has been forced to do so by the circumstances (2Co 11:23; 12:1; 11). Talbert and others point out that the use of the rhetorical device of self-praise illustrates the serious strain in Paul's friendship with the congregation.

An awareness of social conventions of the time also helps to clarify why one of the bones of contention between Paul and the church at Corinth arose out of his refusal to accept financial support from them. Paul worked to support himself but apparently did accept gifts from the Macedonian churches (2Co 11:9). Most churches today would be more than glad to accept free ministry; why would the Corinthians be so annoyed by

Paul's refusal to accept their offers of financial assistance (2Co 11:10; 1Co 9:15)?

The answer to this question is to be found in the Corinthians' cultural context. Most considered manual labor to be degrading and unseemly for a philosopher.[48] To make matters worse, Paul hints that his earnings hardly sufficed and that he was in need (2Co 11:9; see Php 4:12; 1Co 4:10–12). His poverty would hardly persuade others of the power of his gospel. A second irritant stems from Paul's acceptance of aid from the much poorer Macedonians (2Co 11:9; see 8:2). This must have struck the Corinthians as a sign of Paul's inconsistency and as demeaning to them (2Co 11:8–9a). The congregation's status was involved. Peter Marshall has shown how one's standing and influence in Roman societal structure was affected by the number of one's clients. His study also elucidates the protocol associated with the giving and receiving of benefactions. He established that spurning a benefaction was tantamount to a refusal of friendship and would have been construed as an act of social enmity.[49]

The reasons for Paul's intransigence on this issue can also be enlightened by reflecting on his environment. It is possible that he wanted to distinguish himself from the professional sophists, rhetoricians, and mystagogues who were well known for constantly having their hands out. He did not want to be known as a "peddler of the word of God" (2Co 2:17; 4:2). A satirical example of this religious greed is found in an incident from an ancient novel by Apuleius, *Metamorphosis* or *The Golden Ass*. After a troop of eunuch priests of "the Great Goddess of Syria" put on a public exhibition of religious ecstasy, the audience is said to vie "with one another in showering coins (not only copper but silver also) into the opened folds of the performers' gowns. . . . All these presents the priests greedily smuggled at once into bags kept ready for such alms."[50] Still another factor in Paul's refusal may have been his desire to remain independent of anyone's patronage—something that would have been particularly important in a congregation as divided as Corinth's. Accepting support might imply that Paul was in a client relationship to certain patrons in the church. If he wanted to remain the apostle of the entire congregation, he needed to avoid any appearance of being sponsored by one of the factions.

Another way that the Greco-Roman world can shed light

on the New Testament is in studying the usage of words or images in other texts. The use of the metaphor *paidagōgos* for the function of the law in Galatians 3:24–25, for example, has been subject to different interpretations. Some translations render it with an educative metaphor (KJV, "schoolmaster"; NEB and NASB, "tutor"; TEV, "instructor"). This interpretation assumes that the object of the law was to ready the child for maturity in Christ. Other versions opt for a custodial metaphor (RSV, "custodian"; JB, "guardian"; Goodspeed, "attendant"; see also Moffatt, "the law held us as wards in discipline," and Phillips, "the law was like a strict governess in charge of us"). This interpretation assumes that the law functioned in some way as a guardian. Which view is correct?

While it is always essential to try to understand the meaning of a term in the context of Paul's argument, it is also fruitful to investigate the semantic range of the expression in other writers.[51] The age of computers has opened up whole new opportunities for doing this. The *Thesaurus Linguae Graecae* project makes available some sixty-three million words of ancient Greek from some three thousand authors, ranging from Homer to beyond the Byzantine period. The addition of a database from nonliterary papyrus citations will add another five million words. This project adds a whole new dimension to the study of such words as *paidagōgos*. One can now review nearly every extant occurrence of a word.

Such a study of the word *paidagōgos* reveals the social background of the metaphor. The *paidagōgos* was normally a trustworthy, usually aged slave attendant, who was charged by upper-class families with the duty of supervising the life and morals of their young sons. Boys were not allowed to step out of the house without their *paidagōgos* tagging along to watch out for them and to keep them from mischief. Libanius (a fourth-century orator) wrote, "For pedagogues are guards of the blossoming youth, they are keepers, they are a fortified wall; they drive out undesirable lovers, thrusting them away and keeping them out, not allowing them to fraternize with the boys, they beat off the lovers' assaults, becoming like barking dogs to wolves."[52]

The evidence that can only be summarized here indicates that the *paidagōgos* is to be clearly distinguished from the teacher. He led the child to the teacher and, if he did teach, gave only informal instruction in basic etiquette. He was frequently caricatured for his severity as a stern taskmaster. In pictures on Greek vases he often has a stick in his hand, and in Greek plays he was stereotyped as harsh and stupid. Paul contrasts the harsh discipline of the *paidagōgos* with the milder discipline of the father, "You have 10,000 *paidagōgoi* in Christ, but not many fathers" (1Co 4:15). He continues the image in 4:21, "Am I to come to you with a rod in my hand [like a *paidagōgos*] or in love and a spirit of gentleness [like a father]?"

The context of Paul's other statements about the law in Galatians 3 requires that we understand the image of the *paidagōgos* as something that performs a temporary function and then is no longer needed. This is where the educative translation fails. One cannot say that the law "no longer" instructs us about Christ. The fact that Paul continues to cite from the law to make his case to the Galatians proves that the law does not cease to educate us in Christ. The common usage of the term *paidagōgos* in the ancient world, however, makes it clear that the image has to do with one who guards someone who is underage, a young child. When one comes of age, one no longer needs the protection of a *paidagōgos*. This fits the parallel argument in 4:1–8: when one reaches maturity, one no longer needs an overseer. From this background, Paul would be saying that the law served for a time as a guardian of the Jews (separating them from the Gentiles, protecting them from their idolatries). Now with the coming of Christ, they no longer need to be under the custody of the law but are free. They no longer need to be fenced off from Gentiles but have become co-heirs with them.

CONCLUSION

I have given brief descriptions and illustrations of how a variety of sources may be used in interpreting the New Testament. The task of understanding the New Testament in its world is challenging but incredibly exciting and rewarding. There is no substitute for first-hand acquaintance with the primary sources. It is best to read and study them as wholes in their own context and not as repositories of data waiting to illumine some individual New Testament phrase or concept. Stepping into their world is sure to help bring to life the world of the New Testament.

BIBLIOGRAPHY

Barrett, C. K. *The New Testament Background*. New York: Harper, 1957.

Bruce, F. F. *New Testament History*. Garden City: Doubleday, 1971.

Cohen, S. J. D. *From the Maccabees to the Mishnah*. Philadelphia: Westminster, 1987.

Ferguson, Everett. *Backgrounds of Early Christianity*. Grand Rapids: Eerdmans, 1987.

Hengel, Martin. *Judaism and Hellenism*. 2 vols. Trans. John Bowden. Philadelphia: Fortress, 1974.

Jeremias, Joachim. *Jerusalem in the Times of Jesus*. Trans. F. H. and C. H. Cave. Philadelphia: Fortress, 1969.

Kee, Howard Clark. *The New Testament in Context: Sources and Documents*. Englewood Cliffs, N.J.: Prentice-Hall, 1984.

Koester, Helmut. *Introduction to the New Testament*. Vol. I. *History, Culture, and Religion of the Hellenistic Age*. Philadelphia: Fortress, 1982.

Reicke, Bo. *The New Testament Era*. Trans. D. E. Green. Philadelphia: Fortress, 1974.

Safrai, S. and M. Stern, eds. *The Jewish People in the First Century*. 2 vols. Philadelphia: Fortress, 1974, 1976.

Schuerer, E. *The History of the Jewish People in the Age of Jesus Christ* (175 B.C.–135 A.D.). Rev. and ed. G. Vermes and F. Millar. 3 vols. Edinburgh: T. and T. Clark, 1973–1987.

Stephens, William H. *The New Testament World in Pictures*. Nashville: Broadman, 1987.

NOTES

[1]Some recent attempts to bring together a wide variety of sources are: C. K. Barrett, *The New Testament Background: Selected Documents* (rev. ed.; San Francisco: Harper, 1987); D. R. Cartlidge and D. L. Dungan, *Documents for the Study of the Gospels* (New York: Collins, 1980); and H. C. Kee, *The Origins of Christianity: Sources and Documents* (Englewood Cliffs, N.J.: Prentice-Hall, 1973).

[2]For excellent sources on Jewish history, see E. Schürer, *The History of the Jewish People in the Age of Jesus Christ*, rev. and ed. by G. Vermes, F. Millar, and M. Goodman, 3 vols. (Edinburgh: T. & T. Clark, 1973–1987); and multi-volume series such as the *Compendia Rerum Iudaicarum ad Novum Testamentum* (Fortress); the *Library of Early Christianity* (Westminster); and Cambridge *Commentaries on the Writings*

of the Jewish and Christian World (Cambridge University Press). Early Judaism and its Modern Interpreters, ed. R. A. Kraft and G. W. E. Nickelsburg (Philadelphia: Fortress, 1986) provides an excellent overview of developments in the study of Judaism and its literature.

[3]The best way to be able to reconstruct the world of the New Testament is to have as broad an orientation as possible. This necessitates familiarity with the primary sources. One cannot understand Judaism in the first century, for example, by reading an anthology of texts, even though that might be a good place to start.

[4]Examples may be found in W. Dittenberger, Sylloge Inscriptionum Graecarum 4 vols. (1915–1924); and G. H. R. Horsley, New Documents Illustrating Early Christianity (Sydney: The Ancient History Documentary Research Centre Macquarie University, 1981–87). See also H. Koester and H. L. Hendrix, Archaeological Resources for New Testament Studies (Philadelphia: Fortress).

[5]See A. Deissmann's classic work, Light from the Ancient East, 4th ed. (Grand Rapids: Baker, 1978, originally 1922).

[6]Ibid., 80.

[7]E. A. Judge, "The Conflict of Educational Aims in New Testament Thought," Journal of Christian Education 9 (1966): 44–45; see also V. P. Furnish, II Corinthians, AB 32a (New York: Doubleday: 1984), 542.

[8]For English translations of the Scrolls, see G. Vermes, The Dead Sea Scrolls in English, 2d ed. (New York: Penguin, 1975); and A. Dupont-Sommer, The Essene Writings from Qumran (London: Basil Blackwell, 1961). For research on the Scrolls, see J. A. Fitzmyer, The Dead Sea Scrolls: Major Publications and Tools for Study, SBS 8 (Missoula, Mont.: Scholars, 1977).

[9]The works are cited by cave number (1Q–11Q), the genre of the work when appropriate (p means pesher or commentary; t means targum, Aramaic translation), and the abbreviation of the Hebrew title of the work, or, if untitled, a number. The sigla a, b, c, d, are used to designate more than one copy of a text.

[10]S. Sandmel, "Parallelomania," JBL 81 (1962): 1–13.

[11]Sandmel, "Parallelomania," 1.

[12]Isaiah 40:3 is quoted in 1QS 8:13–14.

[13]Sandmel, "Parallelomania," 5.

[14]The title "son of God" can be found in literature prior to the gospels, Sirach 4:10, Wisdom of Solomon 2:18; 1 Enoch 105:2; Ezekiel the Tragedian; Testament of Levi 4:2; Joseph and Asenath 6:3, 5; 13:13; 18:11; 21:4; 23:10. See the discussion in M. Hengel, The Son of God (Philadelphia: Fortress, 1976).

[15]For a convenient summary, see J. A. Fitzmyer, The Gospel According to Luke I–IX, AB 28 (New York: Doubleday, 1981), 205–6.

[16]H. Conzelmann, An Outline of the New Testament Theology (New York: Harper, 1969), 127.

[17]See J. A. Fitzmyer, "The Contribution of Qumran Aramaic to the Study of the New Testament," NTS 20 (1974): 391–94.

[18]J. H. Charlesworth, Jesus Within Judaism: New Light from Exciting Archaeological Discoveries (New York: Doubleday, 1988), 152.

[19]Fitzmyer, Luke, 206–7.

[20]R. Bultmann, Theology of the New Testament (New York: Scribner's, 1951), 1:51. He overlooked Psalm 114:7.

[21]See Fitzmyer, Qumran Aramaic, 386–91.

[22]LCL IX:81–83. Trans. L. H. Feldman.

[23]LCL IV:385–86. Trans. F. H. Colson and G. H. Whitaker.

[24]For further reading, see B. M. Metzger, An Introduction to the Apocrypha (New York: Oxford University Press, 1957); and G. W. E. Nickelsburg, Jewish Literature Between the Bible and the Mishnah: A Historical and Literary Introduction (Philadelphia: Fortress, 1981).

[25]J. H. Charlesworth, ed., The Old Testament Pseudepigrapha, 2 vols. (New York: Doubleday, 1983, 1985). See also H. F. D. Sparks, ed., The Apocryphal Old Testament (Oxford: Clarendon, 1984).

[26]The Letter of Aristeas is an exception as an apologetic explanation of the creation of the Septuagint.

[27]J. H. Charlesworth, The Old Testament Pseudepigrapha and the New Testament, SNTSMS 54 (Cambridge: Cambridge University Press, 1985), 80.

[28]See W. Dalton, Christ's Proclamation to the Spirits: A Study of 1 Peter 3:18–4:6, AB 23 (Rome: Biblical Institute Press, 1965).

[29]For an introduction to the literature, see H. L. Strack and G. Stemberger, Einleitung in Talmud und Misdrasch, 7th ed. (Munich: C. H. Beck, 1982), a needed revision of the old edition of Strack's Introduction to the Talmud and Midrash translated into English in 1931. Jacob Neusner has written a number of useful introductory texts: Invitation to the Talmud, rev. ed. (San Francisco: Harper, 1984); The Oral Torah: The Sacred Books of Judaism (San Francisco: Harper, 1986); Invitation to Midrash (San Francisco: Harper, 1989).

[30]J. Lightfoot, A Commentary on the New Testament from the Talmud and Hebraica, 4 vols. (Grand Rapids: Baker, 1979, repr. from 1859 ed.). H. L. Strack and P. Billerbeck (Kommentar zum Neuen Testament aus Talmud und Midrasch, 5 vols. (Munich: C. H. Beck, 1926) published a collection of rabbinic texts that were grouped around New Testament texts they were regarded to elucidate. It remains an impressive compendium of material but needs to be used carefully.

[31]C. G. Montefiore and H. Loewe, A Rabbinic Anthology, repr. (New York: Schocken, 1974).

[32]The exception was G. F. Moore's masterful but now challenged Judaism in the First Centuries of the Christian Era, 2 vols. (Cambridge: Harvard University Press, 1927).

[33]P. S. Alexander, "Rabbinic Judaism and the New Testament," ZNW 74 (1983): 244, n. 8.

[34]B. M. Bokser, "Talmudic Form Criticism," *JJS* 31 (1980): 46.

[35]J. Neusner, *Rabbinic Traditions About the Pharisees Before 70* (Leiden: Brill, 1971), 1:6.

[36]W. Horbury, "Keeping Up With Recent Studies V. Rabbinic," *ExpT* 91 (1980): 238. This is not to say that old material is not preserved. S. Cohen ("Jacob Neusner, Mishnah, and Counter-Rabbinics: A Review Essay," *Conservative Judaism* 37 [1983]: 54) writes, ". . . the Mishnah contains ideas and traditions which were first formulated centuries before its redaction and which it could not neglect any more than it could neglect Scripture itself." It does mean, however, that "It is necessary to demonstrate rather than assume the antiquity of a given tradition. . . ." (Horbury, "Keeping Up," p. 238).

[37]The tradition recorded in *b. Sanh.* 43a may be an apologetic response to accusations of illegalities in the trial of Jesus:

> On the eve of the Passover Yeshu was hanged. For forty days before the execution took place, a herald went forth and cried, "He is going forth to be stoned because he has practised sorcery and enticed Israel to apostasy (sic). Any one who can say anything in his favour, let him come forward and plead on his behalf." But since nothing was brought forward in his favour he was hanged on the eve of Passover (cited from *Soncino* ed., p. 281.)

[38]J. Neusner, "The Use of the Later Rabbinic Evidence for the Study of First-Century Judaism," *Approaches to Ancient Judaism: Theory and Practice*, BJS 1 (Missoula, Mont.: Scholars, 1978), 223.

[39]See G. Vermes, "Jewish Literature and New Testament Exegesis: Reflections on Methodology," *Jesus and the World of Judaism* (Philadelphia: Fortress, 1983), 87.

[40]G. Vermes, *Post-biblical Jewish Studies* (Leiden: E. J. Brill, 1975), 179–81.

[41]Martin McNamara is directing a project, *The Aramaic Bible: The Targums*, published by Michael Glazier, to translate the targums into English.

[42]R. Le Dèaut, *The Message of the New Testament and the Aramaic Bible (Targum)*, SB 5 (Rome: Biblical Institute Press, 1982), 24.

[43]Vermes, "Jewish Literature," 76.

[44]G. B. Caird, "The Descent of Christ in Ephesians 4, 7-11," *SE II* (TU 87; 1964): 537–41.

[45]J. M. Robinson, ed., *The Nag Hammadi Library*, 3d ed. (San Francisco: Harper, 1988) provides an introduction and English translation.

[46]See C. Tuckett, *Nag Hammadi and the Gospel Tradition* (Edinburgh: T. & T. Clark, 1986).

[47]C. Talbert, *Reading Corinthians: A Literary and Theological Commentary on 1 and 2 Corinthians* (New York: Crossroad, 1987), 118–19.

⁴⁸See R. F. Hock, *The Social Context of Paul's Ministry: Tentmaking and Apostleship* (Philadelphia: Fortress, 1980).

⁴⁹P. Marshall, *Enmity at Corinth: Social Conventions in Paul's Relations with the Corinthians*, WUNT 2/23 (Tübingen: Mohr, 1987), 12–202; 242–47.

⁵⁰The translation is from Apuleius, *The Golden Ass*, trans. J. Lindsay (Bloomington, Ind.: Indiana University Press, 1960).

⁵¹See the investigations of R. N. Longenecker, "The Pedagogical Use of the Law in Galatians 3:19-4:7," *JETS* 25 (1982): 53–62; L. L. Belleville, " 'Under the Law': Structural Analysis and the Pauline Concept of Law in Galatians 3.2–4.11," *JSNT* 26 (1986): 53–78; D. J. Lull, " 'The Law Was Our Pedagogue': A Study in Galatians 3:19–25," *JBL* 105 (1986): 481–95; N. H. Young, "Paidagōgos: The Social Setting of a Pauline Metaphor," *NovT* 29 (1987): 150–76; T. D. Gordon, "A Note on *PAIDAGŌGOS* in Galatians 3.24–25," *NTS* 35 (1989): 150–54.

⁵²Qr. 58:7; cited by Young, *PAIDAGŌGOS*, 159.

Chapter Thirteen

The Study of
New Testament Greek
in the Light of Ancient
and Modern Linguistics

David Alan Black

David Alan Black

David Alan Black is Scholar in Residence at the Lockman Foundation and Adjunct Professor of New Testament at Talbot School of Theology in La Mirada, California. He formerly served as Professor of New Testament and Greek at Grace Theological Seminary's West Campus in Long Beach, California. He holds the B.A. from Biola University, the M.Div. from Talbot School of Theology, and the D.Theol. from the University of Basel. He also did post-doctoral studies at the Institute of Holy Land Studies in Jerusalem. A founding editor of *Filologia Neotestamentaria* (Journal of New Testament Philology), he has contributed articles to that journal as well as to several others, including *Novum Testamentum, New Testament Studies, Biblica, Westminster Theological Journal,* and *The Bible Translator.* His other publications include *Paul, Apostle of Weakness: Astheneia and Its Cognates in the Pauline Literature* (Lang), *Linguistics for Students of New Testament Greek* (Baker), and *Scribes and Scripture: New Testament Essays in Honor of J. Harold Greenlee* (editor; Eisenbrauns). He is currently completing *Using New Testament Greek in Ministry: A Practical Guide for Students and Pastors* for Baker Book House and *The Language of the New Testament: An Introductory Grammar* for Broadman Press.

Chapter Thirteen

The Study of
New Testament Greek
in the Light of Ancient
and Modern Linguistics

INTRODUCTION

Students of the New Testament are generally expected to have a knowledge of the language of the New Testament. Many of these students will find themselves exposed at the same time to the principles and methods of linguistics—the scientific study of language. While several textbooks deal with the application of modern linguistics to the study of New Testament Greek, there is little written on the history of language study and how that history influences the study of Greek today. The present essay is a brief synopsis of this subject, appraising the historical factors that have led to the present state of New Testament Greek studies and calling attention to issues that both scholars and students will face in the years ahead.[1]

WHERE IT ALL STARTED: THE ANCIENT GREEKS

Although there is evidence of language study from an earlier time—the oldest extant work of a linguistic nature is the admirable Sanskrit grammar of the Indian Panini (fifth century B.C.)—it was the ancient Greeks who initiated the formal study of language. That the history of grammar can be traced back to the writings of the early Greeks should come as no surprise, for it is a common pattern in the history of Western culture.

Somewhat less well known is the fact that the earliest works on grammar came not from grammarians but from philosophers who speculated upon a number of subjects, among them the nature of language. Living in an age in which problems were attacked by thinking them through instead of gathering data in a laboratory, the Greeks did not examine their language with the objectivity of a scientist. Instead, they thought about language, and in the course of philosophizing on the subject they made several important—if at times also inaccurate—observations.

Plato and the Physis-Nomos Controversy

One of the earliest philosophical questions about language is still with us today: how do words in particular, and language in general, acquire meaning? Plato (429–347 B.C.) devoted one of his dialogues, the *Cratylus*, to this question. This dialogue, sometimes called Plato's dullest, is actually fascinating because it contains several important insights about language. In *Cratylus* much of the dialogue is carried on by Socrates, who is asked to settle a dispute between Hermogenes and Cratylus. Cratylus believes that the name (*onoma*) of a thing is a consequence of the *nature* of the thing named, and thus that language has meaning "naturally" (*physei*, "by nature"), whereas Hermogenes denies this assumption and holds that names stand for things only through *agreement* among speakers, that is, through "convention" (*nomǭ*, "by law [of usage]"). In the view of Cratylus, the phonetic composition of a thing named should reflect the composition of the thing itself so that words can be examined as being true or false in themselves. In Hermogenes' view, any word is the correct word so long as there is general agreement among its users about its meaning.

Exactly how Plato himself felt about the controversy is not clear, although he has Socrates champion both sides of the argument with equal vigor. Socrates discusses two sorts of words in the dialogue, those that are compound, and those that are simple, noting that one must use a different method to analyze the two types. A compound word should be examined by first dividing it into its constituent parts. Taking the name of the Greek god Poseidon as an example, Socrates suggests that its constituents could be *posi* ("for the feet," dative plural of *pous*, "foot") and *desmos* ("chain"), since the one who first used the name might have contemplated that walking through the water would have been difficult for Poseidon. He notes further that the name is not simply a combination of these two parts, since some of the letters have been added or dropped for the sake of euphony (beauty of sound).

In the case of simple words Socrates says we must ask what the single letters imitate. One can classify letters into consonants, vowels, and semivowels (diphthongs) and then examine their qualities, much like an artist would examine the colors on a pallet. A letter like *r* seems apt to express motion, since the tongue moves rapidly when pronouncing it; it would therefore be an appropriate sound to use in a word like *rhoein* ("to flow"). On the other hand, *s*, *x*, and *ch* are pronounced with a great expenditure of breath, and so are well used in *seisthai* ("to shake"), *xeon* ("seething"), and *psychron* ("shivering"). The *l* sound, because of its gliding movements, is aptly used in *leios* ("slippery") and *olisthanei* ("he slips"). Then Socrates cites contrary examples, such as the oddity of finding a *l* in the word for "hardness" (*sklērotēs*), which is complicated when it is discovered that this word in the Eritrean dialect is *sklērotēr*, suggesting an inexplicable equivalence of *s* and *r*. Socrates concludes that since some names are more accurately descriptive than others, the one who depends on names to learn about the nature of their referents is risking receiving unreliable information. Thus Socrates is portrayed by Plato as taking a middle ground in this popular *nature versus convention* controversy.

Although the physis-nomos controversy seems pointless today, a remnant of the controversy can still be seen. Descendants of the "naturalist" school still argue for the dependence of grammatical distinctions on real distinctions in the human mind, while supporters of the "conventionalist" school deny a resemblance between symbol (word) and referent (object), except in scattered cases of onomatopoeia (words such as *buzz* or *crack*). We should emphasize that the Greeks studied only their own language. To them, all foreigners were *barbaroi*, people who did not talk but merely "babbled." Thus, not having evidence of words with the same meaning but completely different pronunciations in other languages, it was relatively easy for the naturalists to maintain their position. But today, with the linguistic descriptions of many languages available, the natural view is clearly untrue for the great majority of words found in all languages. In nearly every case, the conventional view that the relationship between sound and meaning is arbitrary provides the most valid and accurate position.

A number of other concepts of language that are important in modern grammatical study can also be found in Plato. As we have seen, his discussion of phonology included the breaking of sounds into consonants, vowels, and semivowels. He also distinguished different dialects of Greek, letters from their names, native Greek words from those borrowed from other languages, and a sound sequence as either a word or a combination of words, depending on the accent.

Plato also seems to have been the first person to distinguish between larger constituents that today are called *nouns* and *verbs*. In his *Theatetus*, Plato defines language as a combination of *onomata* and *rhēmata*. The expressions *onomata* (plural of *onoma*) and *rhēmata* (plural of *rhēma*) correspond to expressions used in both ordinary language and the vocabulary of grammar and logic. In ordinary language *onoma* can mean "name," but in the vocabulary of grammar it can mean "noun," "nominal," or "subject," and in logic it corresponds to "logical subject." In ordinary language *rhēma* can mean "phrase" or "saying"; in grammar it may mean "verb," "verbal," or "predicate," and in logic it corresponds to "logical predicate." These definitions come very close to our understanding of "subject" and "predicate" in traditional grammar. The *onoma* and *rhēma* were, in Plato's usage, the basic members of a *logos*, which can mean "nature," "plan," "argument," "clause," "sentence," and "proposition." But Plato did not distinguish the vocabulary of ordinary language, grammar, and logic, so that the translation of *logos* as "sentence" must be viewed with caution.

Plato would hardly have considered himself a linguist. Yet through his writings we catch a first glimpse of the foundations of linguistics and also the first formulations of problems that have been discussed by linguists ever since. Although his studies were destined to be modified and corrected, they remain a helpful revelation of some of the speculation out of which our thinking today on the question of grammar grew.

Aristotle

Aristotle (384–322 B.C.), like his predecessor Plato, was a grammarian only in the sense that philosophers of the time considered language to be a valid object of philosophical inquiry. He wrote no single essay on language, but referred to the structure of language in a number of works. In Aristotle's *Poetics, On Interpretation,* and *Rhetoric* we have the first grammatical sketch of the Greek language known to us. This sketch is mainly an attempt to systematize the observations made on language by Plato and other philosophers. But it had far-reaching consequences. In the centuries following, and especially during the Middle Ages preceding the Renaissance, the works of Aristotle came to be considered second only to the Bible as the final authority on all topics.

Aristotle's *Poetics*, although a treatise on dramatic criticism, includes an analysis of grammar blended with a description of the "virtues" and "barbarisms" of various literary works. Aristotle discussed types of letters, the division of sounds into consonants, vowels, and semivowels, and such categories as gender, number, case, and sentence. These categories represented a major step forward in the systematization of grammar, although it is questionable how much of it is due to Aristotle's original observations.

Another important work of Aristotle was *On Interpretation*, which he wrote as an introduction to and background for his system of logic. It is also the clearest formulation of his general theory of language. In it Aristotle defined noun and verb, and discussed noun cases and verb tenses as well as types of sentences. Aristotle defined the *word* as the minimal unit of language, incapable of being divided into smaller parts, a concept that modern morphologists have revealed to be inadequate. He also stated that words, in and of themselves, are not significant but must be used in combination with other words. Although this is related to the modern concept of structural meaning and the need for completeness, it ignores the fact that some utterances are composed of single words only: "Hi!"; "John" (in answer to "What's your name?").

The most interesting work of Aristotle for our purposes is the *Rhetoric*. In most other works Aristotle took a conventionalist view of language, emphasizing the role of custom and convention in language usage, but in the *Rhetoric* he tried to correct and improve usage. In describing correctness, Aristotle distinguished the same units as Plato did but added another word class that Plato had discussed (without naming) in *On Interpretation*: the *conjunction* (*ho syndesmos*). To Aristotle, conjunctions were all words that are not nouns or verbs. They differ from the latter in that they have no independent meaning but are simply used to tie sentences together. This division of words into those that do and those that do not have lexical (dictionary) meaning represents an early attempt to divide all words into two groups that are known today as *structure* and *content* classes.

The Stoics

After Plato and Aristotle, the first real advances in grammar were made by the Stoics, a group of philosophers and logicians who flourished from about the beginning of the fourth century B.C. until the rule of the Roman Emperor Marcus Aurelius (A.D. 161–180). Known today for their poker-faced attitude toward life, the Stoics were in fact the first real grammarians, producing the earliest purely linguistic monographs we know about in the Greek world. Unfortunately, not a single work of theirs is extant, and what we do have preserved are scattered quotations by other authors, mostly opponents of the Stoic school. But in spite of the scanty material and the problems connected with interpreting it, there is no doubt that the Stoic contribution to the development of linguistics was significant and in many areas of fundamental importance.

The Stoics sought to improve on Aristotle's definitions and to add still more to the general knowledge about Greek grammar. They expanded Aristotle's three classes to four (noun, verb, conjunction, article). Within the category of conjunction, the Stoics seem to have differentiated between prepositions and conjunctions, and in the article category between pronouns and articles. The Stoics were also the first to study number and agreement in nouns and verbs, to study the case in the noun, and to discuss voice, mood, and tense in the verb. They distinguished five cases: nominative, genitive, dative, accusative, and vocative. The Stoic theory of tenses was fairly elaborate, based for the most part on the principle of opposition. The present and imperfect were "opposed" to the perfect and pluperfect; these four tenses were opposed to the aorist and the future; and the aorist in particular was opposed to the perfect and pluperfect. The present and imperfect were called duratives, the perfect and pluperfect completives, and the aorist and future indeterminates.

We are not particularly concerned here with a complete list of Stoic contributions to Greek grammar. It is sufficient to call attention to the Stoic practice of dividing their data into as many distinguishable parts as they could and of assigning a technical term to each division. Much of their terminology has become a basic part of our linguistic heritage. For instance, Aristotle did not use (and probably did not know about) specific names for different cases. It was the Stoics who gave them the names they have kept to the present day. The Stoics seem further to have established the definite name for the neuter gender of nouns, namely *oudeteron*, "neither [masculine nor feminine]." Aristotle had simply called it *metaxu*, "in the middle."

But the Stoics are probably best known for their contribution in an entirely different area of grammar. Unlike Aristotle, the Stoics held that there was, in the remote history of the Greek language, a natural, necessary connection between the sounds of the language and the things for which the sounds stand, although they could see that the present forms of their language did not fully justify their claim. They therefore undertook to search for the original forms, the "roots" or *etyma* of current expressions, thus initiating the study called *etymology*.

The Alexandrians and the Analogy-Anomaly Controversy

After the Stoics, the center of grammatical thought in the West shifted to the Alexandrian school, founded by Alexander the Great at Alexandria, then the capital of Egypt. The famous library of this school started from the personal collection of Aristotle, teacher of Alexander. Many scholars settled in Alexandria and conducted research in varied fields, including mathematics (Euclid), physics (Archimedes), and astronomy (Ptolemy). From this school also came two of the most famous and influential books in the world: the *Elements* of Euclid and the *Grammar* of Dionysius Thrax. It was during the Alexandrian period that grammar finally gained status as an independent discipline.

An important debate among the Alexandrians concerned the problem of how language is related to logic—a question that had been discussed, in less sophisticated terms, in the older physis-nomos controversy. Some scholars held that language should be *analogous* to logic, and that it should be consistent in construction and free from illogical usages such as inconsistent verb endings or irregular noun forms. Examples of consistent patterns in English are the plural forms created by adding *s* to the singular form, as in *books, maps, characteristics,* and *effects*. Other Greek philosophers believed that language was full of *anomaly*, or irregularity in form. They were less concerned with consistency than with how language was actually spoken. In English, words that do not conform to the general pattern for plural formation include *men, sheep,* and *children*. Those who stressed the regularity of language were known as *analogists*, while those who emphasized the presence of irregularity were called *anomalists*. The analogists felt their duty was to "correct" inconsistencies in language and to make them conform to a logical pattern, whereas the anomalists saw their function as that of students and recorders of language.

In one respect, the Greek interest in regularity and irregularity was extremely fortunate for the study of Greek, since the analogists of Alexandria expended a great deal of effort to construct *kanones*, or lists of regularities in the forms of Greek, thereby establishing a form of grammatical description that survives today. However, because they concentrated on the final, single letter of forms, they were unable to show the complete regularities of noun declensions and verb conjugations, so that their lists were always subject to the attacks of the anomalists. As an example of what the analogists considered an exception, we can give the parallel declension of two Greek nouns—*aspis*, "shield," and *logos*, "word":

Nom.	aspis	logos
Gen.	aspidos	logou
Dat.	aspidi	logǭ
Acc.	aspida	logon

Since the nominative of these forms ends in the same letter, *s*, the analogists thought that they should be the "same" form and, therefore, be declined alike. Because of their misguided preference for the nominative case, they were unable to show the regularity of *aspis* (stem *aspid-*). Later on it became obvious that the best selection of the stem of *aspis* is one of its other cases, whereas it makes little difference for *logos*.

The analogist-anomalist controversy was never completely resolved in the ancient world. Today the debate can be seen in the differing approaches of those who would teach correct usage (prescriptive grammar) and those who feel that grammar is a matter of studying language analytically to see how it functions (descriptive grammar).

Dionysius Thrax

Alexandrian scholarship lasted for centuries in the grammatical field, beginning with the work of Xenodotus Philadelphus (284–257 B.C.) and culminating in the work of Apollonius Dyscolus (A.D. 180). The most influential and well-known Alexandrian grammarian was Dionysius Thrax, whose *Grammar* (100 B.C.) became the standard textbook on Greek grammar for the next 1800 years. Although it made no original contributions, it was the most comprehensive treatment of the Greek language to date, classifying and codifying the grammatical thinking of the time. It was largely through Dionysius that the Greek grammar of Plato and Aristotle was transmitted to later generations of students.

The entire text of Thrax's treatise consists of only twenty-five brief paragraphs dealing with what linguists today would call the phonology and morphology of the language. In the section of phonology Thrax discusses *grammata*, "letters," a terminological confusion that does not explicitly distinguish between the sounds and the symbols used to represent them. The textbook also discusses such topics as a definition of grammar, accenting, punctuation, syllables, parts of speech, and declension and conjugation. Thrax listed the article and the participle among the eight parts of speech, omitting the adjective and interjection. Otherwise, his classifications are similar to those used in modern grammar texts, except that many of his definitions have become revised.

Originally written in Greek, Thrax's volume was translated into Latin as the *Arts Grammatica* by Remmius Palaemon in the first century A.D. From this work came many of the technical terms currently employed in formal grammar. Thus the *Grammar* of Dionysius Thrax has had an influence in inverse proportion to its brevity and clarity. It became the subject of a great number of commentaries, known as scholia, which sometimes contain very valuable linguistic information. Its one great weakness, however, was a lack of information about syntactic constructions, a gap partially filled later by the work of Apollonius Dyscolus.

Summary of the Greek Contribution

Before we turn our attention to the Roman grammarians, we may briefly summarize the major characteristics associated with Greek grammatical thought. First, the story of Greek linguistics is identical with the study of the Greek language alone. Aristotle, for example, being at heart a philosopher, examined language to derive "universal" principles. Using the Athenian speech he knew so well, he could not have imagined how limited his sample was. Egyptian and Hebrew were nearby, as were the Greek dialects, but these were largely ignored. It was therefore inevitable that Greek language study became mainly a study of local Greek.

Second, being concerned with the effective use of language, the Greeks were interested in what language "should" be, not what language was. Following Aristotle's lead, the Alexandrian scholars fostered the idea that it is the duty of the grammarian to improve language, to formulate rules by which language usage will become more logical and persuasive. The informal use of language was of no interest to these rhetoricians; they were interested only in literature and oratory.

Finally, this admiration for literature led to the totally unwarranted assumption that the language of literature was somehow "better" or "more pure" than the everyday speech of men and women. Common speech was assumed to be a corrupt form of the language. This unfortunate side-effect of Alexandrian scholarship has continued down to our own times.

A TRADITION DEVELOPS: THE ROMAN GRAMMARIANS

The linguistic situation in Italy was in several respects different from that in Greece. Unlike the majority of Greek scholars, the Romans were not philosophers, and as Greek culture gave way to Roman it was the poets and politicians who were occupied with grammatical studies. Moreover, Italy was a multilingual country with several literary languages besides Latin, including Oscan, Umbrian, and Etruscan. Finally, the widespread knowledge of Greek among educated Romans gave Roman linguistics a comparative perspective unknown to the Greek grammarians.

Nevertheless, these differences had little effect on the Roman linguists, whose basic outlook was no broader than that of their Greek predecessors and contemporaries. The Romans observed what they could scarcely have failed to notice—that their native tongue, Latin, closely resembled Greek. Minor differences there were, but these did not require a complete overhaul of the grammatical system. As a result, the descriptive categories of the Alexandrian grammarians, based on Greek attitudes and Greek structures, were simply transferred from the Greek language to Latin.

The most influential and well-known Roman grammarians followed the Alexandrian tradition of concentrating on the language of literature instead of describing the Latin used by their contemporaries. They also shared the Greek attitude toward "barbarians"—excluding themselves, of course, from this undesirable category. Roman scholars also used the same terms and forms of description as the Greeks had several centuries before. On the whole, this superimposition of Greek grammar on the structure of Latin worked fairly well, for there are many similarities between the two languages. Perhaps if Latin and Greek had contained major structural differences, the Romans might have been forced to study Latin independently. But because of the affinities between the two languages, and because the Romans tended to view Greek culture as foundational, it seemed natural to assume that one system of grammar could serve both languages.

Varro

Probably the first Roman to study the Latin language as a specific object of inquiry was Marcus Terentius Varro (116–27 B.C.), whose *De Lingua Latina* was published near the middle of the first century B.C. It consisted of twenty-five books on Latin structure, of which only Books V to X have been preserved.

Varro dealt with etymology, inflection, the analogy-anomaly controversy, parts of speech, and syntax.

The evaluation of the extant books of *De Lingua Latina* reveals many interesting insights. In Book VIII, for example, Varro divided the words of the Latin language into four classes: those with case forms (nouns), those with tense (verbs), those with neither case nor tense (adverbs), and those with both case and tense (participles). This classification represents an advance over those who defined parts of speech according to meaning, for one can debate the meaning of the terms "noun" and "verb," but one cannot deny that Latin nouns have case and that verbs have tense.

On the subject of analogy-anomaly, Varro took a middle-of-the-road position. He assumed the presence of some patterns in language, but also recognized gaps or anomalies that could not be integrated into any linguistic pattern. He argued, for example, that while the words *nox* ("night") and *mox* ("soon") look alike, they are incompatible, since *nox* is a declinable form and *mox* is invariable. But he then went on to force other words into a regular pattern. An example of this is Varro's wholesale invention of the form *esum* ("I am") to make a regular pattern out of the present active indicative singular of the Latin verb *esse* ("to be"), which is *sum, es, est*.

Varro's grammatical system, if incomplete and inaccurate by today's standards, represented advanced thinking for his time. He attempted to use the *structure* of a word (inflection) to classify it as to type rather than basing his observations on function alone. He divided verbs into past, present, and future, and subdivided these into complete and incompleted action, as well as active and passive. But his discussion of Latin was not intended as a grammar in the same sense as Thrax's, and his work therefore remained outside of the Latin pedagogical tradition.

Quintilian

Marcus Fabius Quintilianus (A.D. 35–97), a famed educator and orator, wrote a treatise on rhetoric entitled *Institutio Oratoria*. Quintilian assumed that grammar, among other things, should be included as part of the orator's training, an assumption that remains unquestioned by many teachers to this day. He also stated that grammar should be based on reason, authority, and usage. Much of his text was therefore devoted to rooting out "barbarisms" (improper uses of a word) and "solecisms" (errors in syntax).

In addition to the elementary teaching of grammar, the *Institutio* included some etymological observations and a few more subtle points belonging to a more advanced analysis of language. For example, Quintilian recommended the admission of a seventh case in Latin and a sixth in Greek, since the Latin ablative and the Greek dative often have an "instrumental" meaning, different from the "usual" meaning of these cases. He also sought to improve the phonetic analysis of vowels and to introduce a classification of the Latin passive forms.

The basis of Quintilian's whole curriculum was an emphasis upon correctness and respect for authority, and his work gave great impetus to the analogist (prescriptive) approach to language. With Rome the center of the civilized world, it was natural that people throughout the Roman Empire would want to acquire a knowledge of educated Latin. The outline for the elementary teaching of grammar given by Quintilian would form the basis for the teaching of grammar up to the present century.

Donatus and Priscian

The Roman heritage of Varro and Quintilian was transmitted to us by those grammarians who succeeded them, the most famous of these being Donatus and Priscian. Aelius Donatus was a fourth-century grammarian whose short Latin grammar became a standard text throughout the Middle Ages. As evidence of its influence and popularity, it was the first book to be printed by means of wooden type.

But the most complete and authoritative description of the Latin language to emerge from this period is that of Priscian, a Latin who taught Greeks in Constantinople in the sixth century A.D. Priscian divided his *Institutiones Grammaticae* into eighteen books, of which the first sixteen deal with morphology and the last two with syntax. Along with the shorter grammar of Donatus, Priscian's work became the authority not only for Latin but for the discussion of language in general among scholars of the Middle Ages.

Priscian's work is important for two reasons. First, it is the most complete and accurate description of Latin by a native speaker of the language. Second, his grammatical theory is the foundation of the traditional way of describing language. An examination of Priscian's parts of speech reveals that much of our current grammatical theory was in fact formulated fifteen hundred years ago, and that only minor refinements have been added to this basic concept of the classification of words.

While Priscian's work is still a valuable and accurate source of information about Latin, it can be criticized from a linguistic point of view for several reasons. Chief among these is Priscian's use of both semantic and formal criteria in defining parts of speech, but never in any consistent way. For example, by denying that the form *vires* ("men") is analyzable into *vir-* and *-es*, Priscian was guilty of one of the grammarian's greatest mistakes, since *vir-* and *-es* are clearly distinguishable morphemes in Latin. The reason for Priscian's error was his insistence that "meaning" is the cardinal criterion of grammatical work. The result of this view is to make the study of language a study of vocabulary rather than the study of those individual units of meaning that make up words. Likewise, Priscian defined the verb as "a part of speech with tense and mood, but without case-inflection, signifying action of being acted upon." This definition begins by examining the *form* of the verb but concludes with its *meaning*. On the other hand, Priscian's sections on syntax, declension of nouns, and conjugations of verbs were highly satisfactory, even though he followed Thrax in defining the word as the minimal unit of utterance.

This survey of the Roman contribution to linguistics has dealt with only the most prominent Latin grammarians among the ancients—and certainly not even all of them, as a glance at one of the larger specialized handbooks will reveal. The Latins followed faithfully the method of analysis marked out by the Greeks. Although we must examine briefly the achievements of the Middle Ages, we shall find little actually new in the study of language until we reach the nineteenth century.

AFTER THE FALL:
MEDIEVAL AND RENAISSANCE LINGUISTICS

After the fall of Rome, grammar became firmly established as one of the major subjects of study during the Middle Ages, the leader of the *trivium* of grammar, rhetoric, and dialectic. The

Middle Ages were dominated by Christian theism, respect for authority and tradition, and theology. With Latin firmly established as the language of the church, with monasteries scattered throughout Europe, and with the Christianization of new nations, the teaching of Latin took on renewed importance.

Training of the clergy involved the grammars of Donatus and Priscian, although a textbook written in 1199 by Alexander de Villa Dei entitled *Doctrinale Puerorum* eventually became the standard school grammar of the Middle Ages. Around A.D. 1000 Aelfric, Abbot of Enysham, England, wrote a Latin grammar for English speakers. This text was presumed by the author to be applicable to Old English as well as Latin. Thus the tradition of imposing the grammar of one language on another was carried into English, and as this was one of the earliest grammars for English speakers, it established the basic curriculum for many years of scholarship.

The Modistae

Scholarship in medieval Europe was almost entirely confined to Latin. Greek had all but disappeared—which explains how *Graecum non est legitur*, the forerunner of "It's Greek to me," became a catch phrase among scholars.

About the middle of the twelfth century, however, Greek language and literature were rediscovered and translated. With the study of the classical authors, particularly Aristotle, grammatical thinking throughout Europe became more prescriptive, more logical, and more authoritative as grammarians renewed their search for a universal system. This attempt to formulate a unified theory of human language was part of the dominant thinking of the age, generally known as *scholasticism*. A number of writers of this time wrote commentaries entitled *De Modis Significandi*, from which these scholars became known as the *Modistae*. The Modistae believed that since language is governed by a system of rules, thought and therefore language are also rule-governed. Furthermore, the Modistae concluded that since the universe, including humankind, is everywhere the same, the ways in which humankind attains knowledge are everywhere the same, and language, as a means of expressing this knowledge, must also be universal. The Modistae's interest in a universal theory of language was continued by the rationalistic philosophers of the sixteenth, seventeenth, and eighteenth centuries, and the questions they asked about the nature of language are strikingly similar to those of modern scientific linguists.

The Renaissance

The Modistae's faith in a universal grammar typified the school of grammatical thought that dominated the late Middle Ages. The Renaissance, however, introduced an age of greater tolerance for divergent ideas as well as an emphasis on humanity rather than on the divine. Hitherto grammar had consisted of the study of Latin, with a system based on Greek, but now other languages were being scrutinized, including Hebrew and Arabic. This new interest in the Semitic tongues helped break the exclusive hold of Latin on the attention of European scholars, and by the sixteenth century studies of vernacular languages were beginning to appear. In 1606 the Frenchman Etienne Guichard compiled an etymological dictionary of Hebrew, Chaldean, Syriac, Greek, Latin, French, Italian, Spanish, German, Flemish, and English. Other scholars produced grammars of their own language. As expanding commerce created rivalries among nations, these grammars came to reflect pride in one's nation and the desire to promote a particular language. Probably the most celebrated linguistic chauvinist was the Swede Andreas Kemke, who maintained that in the Garden of Eden God spoke Swedish, Adam Dutch, and the serpent French.

The Medieval and Renaissance eras—that is, the period until about the end of the eighteenth century—witnessed a tremendous increase in the amount of information about language, even though the methods of analysis were still firmly rooted in the classical tradition. A new school of thought would be required to do what Newton did for physics or what Calvin did for theology; but this linguistic revolution had to wait until the nineteenth century. There were, however, important precursors, and one of these—Sir William Jones—calls for special attention.

Sir William Jones

Many people regard the year 1786 as the birth date of modern linguistics. On September 27, British judge Sir William Jones (1749–1794) read a paper to the Royal "Asiatick" Society in Calcutta pointing out that the resemblances of Sanskrit to Greek and Latin are too close to be coincidental and therefore show that all three "have sprung from some common source which, perhaps, no longer exists." This is the first recorded recognition of language kinship as recognized by modern linguistics, and it set off a veritable chain reaction of comparative studies extended throughout the nineteenth century.

Before this time, others had drawn attention to the importance of Sanskrit, but their observations had fallen on unfertile soil, like "discoveries" of America prior to Columbus. Attempts to derive one known language from another often produced ludicrous results. Thus, one might have tried to show how Latin was derived from Greek or Greek derived from Sanskrit in some kind of linear order:

Sanskrit ⟶ Greek ⟶ Latin

What Jones proposed is that all three languages evolved more or less independently from a common ancestor, in which case our diagram would look like:

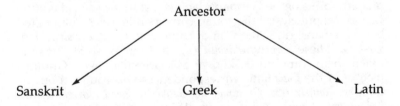

Moreover, Jones suggested that the ancestor "might no longer exist." What he meant was that the ancestor might not be attested or written down. The concept of an unrecorded common ancestor freed language students from having to explain everything in language history exclusively by what is found in written documents.

THE NINETEENTH CENTURY: HISTORICAL AND COMPARATIVE LINGUISTICS

With Sir William's discovery, the way was clear to approach the study of language from a new perspective. Scholars came to understand that language is in a constant state of flux, that it has history, and that its genesis and development can be studied from the historical point of view. For the next hundred years, linguistic thinking was centered largely around historical and comparative "philology" (as it was called), as linguists began to piece together a picture of the evolution of languages—tracing, comparing, and classifying them into families.

Indo-European Philology

For the Indo-European languages, the beginning of systematic comparison was Rasmus Rask's *Investigation of the Origin of Old Norse or Icelandic* (1814), which offered a complete classification of Indo-European languages and even a statement of the Germanic consonant shifts that was later more fully formulated by J. Grimm. Franz Bopp's *Ueber das Conjugationssystem der Sanskritsprache* (1816) did for comparative morphology what Rask had done for comparative phonology. Beginning with 1819 and ending with 1840, Jacob Grimm (of fairy tale fame) published a series of editions of his *Deutsche Grammatik*, where he sketched the grammatical structures of the older and modern forms of the Germanic languages. In the second edition Grimm set out clearly the sound correspondences he had noted between Sanskrit, Greek, and Latin and the Germanic languages. These *Lautverschiebungen*, or "sound shifts," as he called them, came to be known as "Grimm's Law." Grimm's picture of the Germanic correspondences was rounded out by Bopp's *Comparative Grammar of Sanskrit, Zend, Greek, Latin, Lithuanian, Gothic and German* (1833) and by Karl Verner's discovery of the role played by the position of the accent in consonantal development, first made public in an essay entitled, "An Exception to the First Consonant Shift" (1875).

Interest in comparative linguistics led to the investigation of other language families and also to the beginning of the linguistic treatment of contemporary languages without regard to history. In 1836 Friedrich Diez produced a comparative grammar of the Romance languages, in 1852 Franz von Miklosich wrote a grammar of the Slavic languages, and in 1853 Johann Kaspar Zeuss began the study of Celtic. But the most impressive achievement of comparative linguistic scholarship was the monumental *Outline of the Comparative Grammar of the Indo-European Languages* by Karl Brugmann and Berthold Delbrück, first published in 1886. Although later studies have disclosed errors in it, the second edition of this massive work is still quoted today.

The Neo-Grammarians

The emphasis on language change eventually led to a major theoretical advance. In the last quarter of the century, a group of linguists headed by Karl Brugmann formulated the theory that all sound change takes place in accordance with regular laws that have no exceptions. This so-called *Neo-Grammarian* group was attacked by various linguists who denied the functioning of these *Lautgesetze*, or "sound laws." The stand of the *Neo-Linguists*, as this group called itself, was that sound changes are sporadic and individualistic phenomena. The strength of the neo-grammarian approach was its insistence upon methodological rigor and its determination to deal only with the physical phenomena of language. This approach seemed to imply, however, that language had a sort of independent existence and that it was governed by forces beyond the power of human direction. Although the claims made by the Neo-Grammarians have been modified to some extent today, it was an important step forward for linguists to realize that language changes were not just optional tendencies, but definite and clearly stateable laws.

The Accomplishments of the Philologists

A detailed description of the work of the nineteenth-century philologists is beyond the scope of this essay. Let us, however, attempt to summarize here some of the most important results of this century of work.

The Discovery of Indo-European. By the beginning of the nineteenth century, theories propagating a Hebraic or Hellenic origin of all extant languages had been proven to be untenable. Instead, based upon correspondences too regular to be coincidental, the philologists saw that Sanskrit, Greek, Latin, the Germanic, Celtic, and Slavonic languages had developed from an *Ursprache*, a common ancestor, no longer extant. To this language they gave the name *Indo-European*, subdividing it into nine groups, including the Greek branch. Indo-European is only one of many language families studied from a historical perspective in the nineteenth century as well as more recently.

Comparative Studies. Working from a variety of recorded sources, comparative philologists began to build up details of regular sound changes, and, to a lesser extent, changes in grammatical forms. From the detailed evidence of certain sound shifts, the philologists formulated conclusions about the regularity of such shifts. The most famous of such formulations, "Grimm's Law," demonstrates how certain consonants of the original Indo-European underwent a change in the Germanic languages, and how another shift took place in the division of German into High German and Low German. It is the most spectacular (and for our understanding of the relation between English and Greek, the most important) of hundreds of similar shifts that occurred when languages gradually broke off from their parent language.

The Classification of Languages. As the work of the philologists spread into other language families, there developed an attempt to classify all languages according to their basic structural features. Probably the best-known effort in this direction is the classification of languages into the categories of isolative, agglutinative, and inflectional. Some philologists advanced the theory that languages passed from one stage to the next in the order given above, the inflectional languages (like Greek and Latin) being the "most highly advanced." However, this hypothesis represented an oversimplified view of language, and today most linguists reject the notion of the superiority of inflected languages. Yet the view that Greek or Latin is the "best" language still occasionally crops up in studies of historical linguistics.

Advance in New Testament Greek Grammar. When the light of historical-comparative philology was turned upon the language of the New Testament, it revealed that New Testament Greek is nothing other than a natural development in the long history of the Greek language. It also revealed that Greek is not an isolated language, but one that sustains vital relations with a great family of languages. These conclusions were first stated by the German philologist George Winer, who in 1822 inaugurated a new era in New Testament studies with the publication of his *Neutestamentliches Sprachidiom*. Winer's thesis that New Testament Greek was not a special "Holy Ghost" language but the ordinary tongue of the day was truly epoch-making. Further progress was made by Alexander Buttmann (1859) and Friedrich Blass (1890), whose grammars were based on Winer's fundamental premise. In 1895 Adolph Deissmann published his *Bibelstudien*, and his *Neue Bibelstudien* followed in 1897. These "Bible Studies" condemned the isolation of biblical Greek from the so-called "profane Greek." Deissmann based his conclusions on the witness of Greek inscriptions and papyri to the language of the New Testament. In 1896 J. H. Moulton began the formal application of the new light from the papyri to the Greek New Testament in his *Introduction to the Study of New Testament Greek*. Moulton's subsequent *Grammar* (1906), as well as the mammoth work by A. T. Robertson, *A Grammar of the Greek New Testament in the Light of Historical Research* (1914), are works of greatest linguistic interest. Even though some of the conclusions drawn by these scholars are open to doubt, their demonstration that "Bible Greek" is vernacular Koine remains of permanent value. Nigel Turner's recent attempt in *Christian Words* (1980) to return to the pre-Deissmann era in the study of New Testament vocabulary is a demonstrable cul-de-sac.

THE TWENTIETH CENTURY: DESCRIPTIVE AND GENERATIVE LINGUISTICS

While the nineteenth century was dominated by the historical-comparative and diachronic approach to linguistics, the twentieth century has been dominated by the descriptive and synchronic approach. Problems of language theory in general, as distinct from the study of individual languages, have also come to the fore, along with philosophical discussions on the nature of language very similar to those of the ancient Greeks. In America, linguistics began as an offshoot of anthropology, while in Europe structuralism was exerting a major influence in the field of linguistics.

American Descriptivism

While nineteenth century Europe was engrossed in the comparative method of language study and the interest was largely in historical matters, in America a tradition was developing of studying languages whose history and relationships were unknown. As early as the seventeenth century, Roger Williams in Rhode Island was describing an Algonkian language under the rubric "the language of America." When the American Philosophical Society was founded by Benjamin Franklin, a number of its members, including Thomas Jefferson, showed a genuine interest in American Indian languages and their description. Around the beginning of the twentieth century, anthropologists began to record the culture of the fast-dying Indian tribes, and the American Indian languages were an aspect of this research. The work of those early scholars was, for the most part, haphazard and lacking cohesion, primarily because there were no firm guidelines for linguists to follow when they attempted to describe exotic languages.

This state of affairs changed with the emergence of the Yale linguists Edward Sapir (1884–1939) and Leonard Bloomfield (1887–1949). Sapir became the leading theoretical linguist in the field of American Indian languages, producing many important studies. Bloomfield began his career as a comparative linguist, but soon began to take an interest in American Indian languages and in the whole American descriptivist approach. In 1914 he published a general work in linguistics which he later rewrote into a new work entitled simply *Language* (1933). Bloomfield's *Language* was quickly acknowledged as the best general introduction to linguistic science and the descriptive method. During the Bloomfieldian era large numbers of linguists, including many students of Sapir and Bloomfield, concentrated on writing descriptive grammars of both written and unwritten languages.

Saussure and Structuralism

As linguists in the United States became involved in the study of American Indian languages during the late nineteenth and early twentieth centuries, it became increasingly clear that the historical orientation of nineteenth-century European linguistics was no longer adequate. If any one person can be held responsible for this change in perception, it was the Swiss scholar Ferdinand de Saussure (1857–1913), whose *Cours de Linguistique Général* was published after his death from notes compiled from his students. Saussure's crucial contribution was his explicit statement that all language items are essentially interlinked—an aspect of language that had not been stressed before. This approach to language is today called *structural* or *descriptive linguistics*. All linguistics since Saussure has been structural, as "structural" in the broad sense merely means the recognition that language is a system of interdependent elements rather than a collection of unconnected individual items.

Structuralism and New Testament Greek

With the publication of A. T. Robertson's *Grammar*, the American application of historical-comparative philology to New Testament Greek had reached its apex. Once the analytical methods for a philological approach to the language had been derived, however, scholars began shifting their attention to the new revolution in structural and descriptive linguistics. Although the achievements here have not been as unambiguous as in the area of historical-comparative linguistics, no less effort has been expended.

Characteristic of this new direction in New Testament studies is the three-volume *A Beginning-Intermediate Grammar of Hellenistic Greek* (1973) by Robert Funk, who earlier gave New Testament scholars an English edition of Blass (Debrunner). Funk's *Grammar* is a rigorous and scholarly attempt to organize all of New Testament Greek linguistics into a single body of theory and practice. A similar emphasis upon descriptive linguistics can be found in Eugene Van Ness Goetchius's *The Language of the New Testament* (1965), William Sanford LaSor's *Handbook of New Testament Greek* (1973), and Ward Powers's *Learn to Read the Greek New Testament* (1979). The morphemic analysis of New Testament words receives special attention in Bruce Metzger's *Lexical Aids for Students of New Testament Greek* (1969) and more recently in J. Harold Greenlee's *A New Testament Greek Morpheme Lexicon* (1983). Each of these works is a serious attempt to update grammatical study, and LaSor's work in particular is an important advance over traditional grammars. Despite these promising beginnings, however, the descriptive approach to New Testament Greek grammar has not proved to be the dominant new tradition.

Chomsky and Generative Grammar

This history of the development of linguistics cannot be told without one more episode. In 1957 Noam Chomsky's *Syntactic Structures* presented a method of linguistic analysis that not only breaks sentences down into constituent morphemes but also reveals more of the inner structure of the language than any other method available at the time. It was Chomsky' theory that grammar should be more than a system for classifying the elements in sentences already produced, but a system of generating sentences in the first place. By what process, he asked, is a sentence changed from active to passive voice, from simple to compound, from singular to plural, from present to future? Chomsky theorized that a great variety of sentences can be generated by transforming certain elements of the sentence—by interchanging, adding, or deleting linguistic forms; by reversing word order; or by combining two or more structures into one. In his words, a grammar will be "a device which generates all the grammatical sentences of a language and none of the ungrammatical ones." This theory is known as transformational-generative grammar or, more simply, TG.

The Chomskian revolution has pervaded all areas of linguistics, with its greatest impact on the study of syntax. In the spirit of this new approach, several works have attempted to apply TG to New Testament Greek, including Theodore Mueller's *New Testament Greek: A Case Grammar Approach* (1978), Reinhard Wonneberger's *Syntax und Exegese* (1979), Daryl Dean Schmidt's *Hellenistic Greek Grammar and Noam Chomsky: Nominalizing Transformations* (1981), and J. P. Louw's *Semantics of New Testament Greek* (1982). TG grammar has also been an important element in the theory of translation developed by Eugene Nida in *Toward a Science of Translating* (1964), and has been used extensively in the seminars and institutes on translation conducted by the United Bible Societies. However, studies such as these have tended to be specific applications of earlier results achieved in linguistics, and as such have made a contribution to exegesis more than to the study of grammar.

CONCLUSION: WHERE DO WE GO FROM HERE?

Today the field of New Testament Greek philology has expanded beyond the wildest imaginings of previous generations. But this expansion of knowledge has ushered us into an age of new complexities, new patterns, and new challenges. In challenging the old assumptions, linguists have opened up a Pandora's box of fresh problems. After criticizing the traditional approach for being inconsistent, unscientific, and impractical, linguists have had difficulties standardizing their terminology, simplifying their discipline to a level realistic for classroom use, and demonstrating that the new grammar will aid exegesis and interpretation.

This last statement should be softened somewhat in that numerous linguists from the ranks of biblical scholarship have not been slack in bringing modern linguistics into the theological arena. Non-linguistic views of theology and biblical language were initially criticized by James Barr, whose *Semantics of Biblical Language* (1961) mercilessly revealed that not all was apple pie in Exegesisland. Barr's writings have done much to reorder certain methods of biblical research along the lines of contemporary linguistic theory. Since Barr we have seen many innovations in the grammars of the biblical languages. But they have been innovations, for the most part, within the framework laid down centuries ago by a naive and simplistic society. This framework has confined the pursuit of knowledge in the universities to certain traditional areas of learning, with innovation limited to changes in emphasis from one area to another, or a change in instructional methods or materials.

To the extent that both traditional and linguistic grammars are descriptive disciplines, there is no reason why each could not profit from the experience of the other. Adherence to the linguistic point of view entails a preference for a more revealing and exact description, and eventually explanation, of linguistic facts, but it need not entail a rejection of traditional values and emphases. Since it is a descriptive discipline, linguistics does not, because it cannot, prove or undermine any theological or philosophical position. But this rejection of "mentalism" in the study of language is the rejection of a grammatical method and not necessarily of a theological or philosophical commitment to the Bible as the Word of God. The most recent developments in biblical linguistics have, in fact, returned to the traditional goals of exegesis, but with the rigor of the scientific methods developed by linguists over a period of years. Periodicals such as *The Bible Translator* (United Bible Societies), *Notes on Translation* (Summer Institute of Linguistics), *Neotestamentica* (South African Bible Society), *Linguistica Biblica* (Bonn), and *Filologia Neotestamentaria* (Córdoba), along with textbooks such as Moisés Silva's *Biblical Words and Their Meaning* (1983), Peter Cotterell and Max Turner's *Linguistics and Biblical Interpretation* (1989), and the present writer's *Linguistics for Students of New Testament Greek* (1988) demonstrate that interest in this interdisciplinary territory is alive and growing.

Nevertheless, important challenges remain. Significant scholarly discussion continues unabated, and of the numerous issues currently under investigation the following seem to me to be among the most critical:

(1) The problem of the reticence to break the traditional mold and strike out for newer and more productive territory. No longer can students of Greek be considered knowledgeable if they still believe *the* grammar they were taught; it is now painfully obvious that there are *many* grammars—traditional, structural, transformational, etc.—and that each of these comes in a wide variety of sizes and shapes. And it seems a reasonable assumption that more will follow.

(2) The problem of the atomization of methods currently employed in New Testament philology. To take just one example, in the United States, Chomskian linguistics seems to hold the day, but there are several other methods being employed, such as Kenneth Pike's tagmemics, Charles Fillmore's case grammar, and Sydney Lamb's stratificational grammar. This diversity, including significant terminological confusion, remains a problem, and this situation is only exacerbated by the recent influx of methods currently in vogue in Europe.

(3) The present crisis over the nature of "New Testament Greek." What is to be done about the strongly Semitic character of New Testament Greek, and can one speak of New Testament Greek as a linguistic subsystem when a comprehensive grammar of Hellenistic Greek has yet to be written?

(4) The problem of defining the relationship between linguistics proper and New Testament "philology," which itself can refer both to *Literaturwissenschaft* (the study of the New Testament as a part of ancient Greek literature) and *Sprachwis-*

senschaft (the study of the Greek of the New Testament). This duel between diachronic and synchronic approaches must, it seems to me, be resolved if New Testament scholarship is to arrive at a synthesis capable of utilizing the best of both approaches to language.

(5) The riddle of the Greek verbal system: Can the tense structure of New Testament Greek continue to be described in terms of a rigid time structure when the latest research indicates that verbal *aspect* is the predominant category of tense (see especially the recent ground-breaking works by Buist Fanning and Stanley Porter)?

(6) The challenge posed by "rhetorical criticism" in taking us beyond hermeneutics and structuralism. The recent revival of interest in rhetoric in New Testament studies bodes well for the future of our discipline, but neither James Muilenburg nor his school has produced a workable model of rhetorical criticism (though F. Siegert's 1984 dissertation is a positive step in the right direction).

(7) Finally, the mention of structuralism raises the onerous hermeneutical question concerning surface and deeper linguistic meaning in the interpretation of New Testament texts, a question posed most radically by Erhardt Güttgemanns (1978) but certainly not by him alone.

These and other challenges will be around for some time to come, and will offer plenteous grist for the scholar's mill. It may be hoped that these and other questions regarding New Testament Greek studies will inspire a new generation of Greek students to meet its destiny—aware of its opportunities, mindful of its responsibilities, eager to make fresh contributions. More than ever before, it now appears to be more than wishful thinking that the best of both traditional and linguistic approaches can be combined for a more exact and productive understanding of the biblical languages.

BIBLIOGRAPHY

Arlotto, Anthony. *Introduction to Historical Linguistics*. Boston: Houghton & Mifflin, 1972.

Barr, James. *The Semantics of Biblical Language*. London: Oxford University Press, 1961.

Black, David Alan. *Linguistics for Students of New Testament Greek: A Survey of Basic Concepts and Applications.* Grand Rapids: Baker, 1988.

_____. *Using New Testament Greek in Ministry: A Practical Guide for Students and Pastors.* Grand Rapids: Baker, forthcoming.

Costas, Procope S. *An Outline of the History of the Greek Language.* Chicago: Ares, 1936.

Cotterell, Peter and Max Turner. *Linguistics and Biblical Interpretation.* Downers Grove, Ill.: InterVarsity, 1989.

Erickson, Richard J. "Linguistics and Biblical Language: A Wide-Open Field." *JETS* 26 (1983): 257–63.

Fanning, Buist M. *Verbal Aspect in New Testament Greek.* Oxford: University Press, 1990.

Funk, Robert W. *Language, Hermeneutic, and Word of God: The Problem of Language in the New Testament and Contemporary Theology.* New York: Harper, 1966.

Louw, J. P. *Semantics of New Testament Greek.* Philadelphia: Fortress, 1982.

Nida, Eugene A. "Implications of Contemporary Linguistics for Biblical Scholarship." *JBL* 91 (1972): 73–89.

Palmer, L. R. *The Greek Language.* Atlantic Highlands, N.J.: Humanities Press, 1980.

Porter, Stanley. *Verbal Aspect in the Greek of the New Testament, With Reference to Tense and Mood.* New York: Lang, 1989.

Schmidt, Daryl Dean. "The Study of Hellenistic Greek Grammar in the Light of Contemporary Linguistics." *PRS* 11 (1984): 27–38.

Siegert, F. *Argumentation bei Paulus gezeigt an Röm 9–11.* WUNT 34. Tübingen: Mohr [Siebeck], 1985.

Silva, M. *Biblical Words and Their Meaning: An Introduction to Lexical Semantics.* Grand Rapids: Zondervan, 1983.

Sweet, H. *History of Language.* New York: Macmillan, 1900.

NOTES

[1]For a bibliography of works consulted in the preparation of this essay, see the list at the end of this article and the writer's *Linguistics for Students of New Testament Greek* (Grand Rapids: Baker, 1988) 22, 141, 168–69. Chapter 6 of the latter work deals in greater detail with the subject of historical-comparative linguistics.

Chapter Fourteen

The Use of the Old Testament in the New

Klyne Snodgrass

Klyne Snodgrass

Klyne Snodgrass is Dean of the Faculty and Paul W. Brandel Professor of New Testament Studies at North Park Theological Seminary in Chicago, Illinois. He holds the B.A. from Columbia Bible College, the M.Div. from Trinity Evangelical Divinity School, and the Ph.D. from the University of St. Andrews. He also studied at Princeton and Tübingen universities. His articles have appeared in such journals as *New Testament Studies*, *Journal of Biblical Literature*, *Journal for the Study of the New Testament*, *Covenant Quarterly*, and *The Second Century*. He has also authored *The Parable of the Wicked Tenants* (Mohr [Siebeck]) and *Between Two Truths* (Zondervan).

Chapter Fourteen

The Use of the Old Testament in the New

No subject is perhaps more important for the understanding of the Christian faith than the use of the Old Testament in the New Testament. The Hebrew and Aramaic Scriptures were, of course, the only Bible the early Christian thinkers and writers had. Many of these Christians were transformed Jews and would have known Hebrew. Other early Christians would have known the Jewish Scriptures only in Greek translation. Regardless of their language, however, all Christians would have been engaged in relating the two most important realities of their lives—the Scriptures and Jesus Christ.

At every point early Christians attempted to understand their Scriptures in the new light of the ministry, death, and resurrection of Jesus Christ. They used the Old Testament to prove their Christian theology and to solve Christian problems. The Old Testament provided the substructure of New Testament theology.[1] The Old Testament also provided the language and imagery for much of New Testament thought, although this is not always obvious to a casual reader. Therefore, New Testament concepts must be understood from Old Testament passages. Virtually every New Testament subject must be approached through the contribution of the Old Testament. As Augustine observed, "The New Testament is in the Old concealed; the Old Testament is in the New revealed."[2]

However, not everything in the Old Testament is brought into the new faith. There is both continuity and discontinuity between the Old Testament and the New Testament. That is, while some parts of the New Testament are direct extensions of the Old Testament message, some parts of the Old Testament message have been superseded. Even so, none of the New Testament writers ever suggests that the Old Testament is less than fully the Word of God.

The analysis of this continuity and discontinuity is a much more fascinating and intriguing study than many people have realized. Too often Old Testament texts are considered as only so many prophecies to be calculated and at which to marvel. Any serious reading will show that the way the New Testament uses the Old Testament is far different from what we expected or have been led to believe. The New Testament writers have been disturbingly creative in their use of the Old Testament. Not only do New Testament quotations of the Old Testament sometimes differ from the Hebrew and Aramaic Scriptures on which our translations are based, the New Testament writers also have applied texts in surprising ways. For example, why does Matthew 2:18 view Jeremiah 31:15 as a prophecy of Herod's slaying of innocent babies, while Jeremiah's words obviously relate to the Babylonian invasion of Judea? Do the New Testament writers twist the Old Testament Scriptures, as some have charged?[3]

In addition to being fascinating, the study of the use of the Old Testament in the New Testament is comprehensive and demanding. To enter this arena is to be engaged in studies on the history of the text. Serious study requires the knowledge of Hebrew, Greek, and Aramaic because one has to compare the New Testament wording with the Masoretic Hebrew text, the Septuagint (the translation of the Old Testament into Greek), information from the Dead Sea Scrolls, the targums (Aramaic paraphrases of the Old Testament), and other Jewish or Christian uses of the Old Testament. Do not think that this is an exercise in tedium, however, for the use of the Old Testament in the New Testament also engages a person in hermeneutics, exegesis, and theology, study that in many cases will require adjustment of previous conclusions. How the Old Testament is viewed is *the* theological issue dividing many Christians. Dispensational theology, which views God as operating in different ways in different eras, and covenant theology, which emphasizes the unity of God's action throughout history, divide from each other and also from other approaches specifically over this issue.[4]

Our subject also has the potential of being a troublesome one. There are issues here that have not been treated adequately. We often proclaim our theories about Scripture in the abstract, but the use of the Old Testament by New Testament writers raises questions about our theories. Are all the discussions about inerrancy or other labels irrelevant in view of the selectivity by which the New Testament writers use the Old Testament? Obviously there are numerous Old Testament texts that were and are ignored by Christians, and we would argue that many are not to be implemented.[5] Why?

BRIEF HISTORICAL CONSIDERATIONS

The question of how the Old Testament should be appropriated exists already with the teaching of Jesus. His way of reading the Old Testament angered the religious authorities, for he did not focus on sabbath keeping and laws of purity as they did. In fact, according to the Gospels, Jesus appeared to flaunt violation of the purity code by touching lepers, a woman with an issue of blood, and corpses, and by eating with defiled people (note especially Mt 8–9 in contrast with Lev 13; 15:19f.; and Ezr 10:11). He argued that *sin* defiled a person, not eating with unclean hands (Mt 15:10–20). Mark 7:19 extends Jesus' teaching so that all foods are clean.[6] So much for dietary laws! Jesus focused on the intent of the law in the love commands and on the theme of mercy. Still, he claimed that none of the Scripture was set aside (Mt 5:17–20) and complained that the Jewish authorities substituted human traditions for the commands of God (Mt 15:3).[7] In Luke 24:44–45 the risen Christ claimed that all three sections of the Hebrew Scriptures (law, prophets, and writings) find their fulfillment in him. He then opened the mind of his disciples to understand the Scriptures. Clearly the issue both for the earthly and risen Christ is *how* the Hebrew Scriptures are to be interpreted correctly. The usual reading of the religious authorities was not sufficient.

The same question dominated the life of the early church. When asked whether he understood the text from Isaiah 53, the Ethiopian eunuch replied, "How am I able unless someone should guide me?" Beginning from that text Philip then proclaimed Christ to him (Ac 8:26–35). This account points both to the Christological way in which the early church interpreted the Old Testament and to the need of guidance in understanding.

One crucial issue for the early church was the question

how to treat the Old Testament commands on circumcision. At the "Jerusalem Council," surprisingly, explicit Old Testament commands on circumcision were set aside because of Christian experience *and other Old Testament texts* focusing on the inclusion of the Gentiles (Ac 15). One can well ask how Paul could say, "Circumcision is nothing and uncircumcision is nothing, but keeping the commands of God is what counts" (1Co 7:19), when circumcision was obviously an Old Testament command. Clearly it was no longer a relevant command for him. Still, the discussions of law in the epistles to the Galatians and to the Romans show how much the debate continued over the right use of the Old Testament. However, even when conclusions were drawn that a command was not binding, they were made from the Old Testament itself and with no thought of nullifying the Word of God.

In the second century a radical solution to the problem of the Old Testament emerged. Marcion of Sinope, influenced by Gnosticism, argued that the whole Old Testament should be rejected, even though he found value in some sections of the Old Testament. Marcion repudiated the God of the Old Testament as the creator of evil and sought to separate Christianity from anything Jewish. Consequently, he accepted as canonical only Paul's epistles (excluding the Pastorals) and the Gospel of Luke. In addition, he expurgated sections of these books that he felt were influenced too much by the Old Testament.[8] Unfortunately, there are still those around who are essentially Marcionite in their approach.

Most Christians, thankfully, did not follow Marcion. Instead, they sought to extend the interpretive practices of the New Testament writers and appropriate the Old Testament for Christian purposes in new ways. The Old Testament was combed for passages that could be understood of Christ and his church. Christians used the Old Testament to teach morality, to explain who Jesus was, and to provide illustrations of Christian thought. Unfortunately, however, usually there was little historical sensitivity or treatment of extended texts. Instead, the Old Testament was viewed as prophecy about Christ, as providing types of Christ, or as holding hidden ideas and symbols that may be spiritually understood through allegory.[9] Justin Martyr, for example, and numerous others found references to Christ in places most of us could hardly imagine. The stone cut out without hands in Daniel 2:45 was understood as a reference to the Virgin Birth. Nearly every stick, piece of wood, or tree was understood as pointing to the Crucifixion.[10]

In the centuries that followed, the Old Testament and New Testament were interpreted along two diverge New Testament paths. The Antiochean School, represented by John Chrysostom and Theodore of Mopsuestia, argued against allegorizing and engaged in fairly straightforward exegesis. Far more influential, but far more unacceptable from a modern viewpoint, was the Alexandrian School represented by Origen and Augustine. This school engaged in allegorical exegesis, by which a spiritual meaning could be assigned to a text, especially if that text were troublesome.[11] Allegorizing made it easy to read Christian theology into Old Testament texts. Allegorical exegesis was dominant until the Reformation and is still encountered today as pastors read into texts spiritual meanings that have nothing to do with the original purposes of the authors.

The Protestant reformers turned away from allegorical exegesis to focus on the plain meaning of the text, although Martin Luther on occasion still allegorized. Both Luther and John Calvin were aware of the unity and the differences between the Testaments. Luther stressed the discontinuity between the Testaments because of his distinction between law and gospel. Calvin, on the other hand, focused on continuity between the Testaments and argued for a "third use" of the law.[12] By this he argued what Luther was not ready to accept, that the law still has a role in guiding Christian morality. These differences in understanding the Old Testament have characterized the followers of Luther and Calvin to the present day.

How the Old Testament should be viewed in relation to the New Testament is still a matter of debate. In his *Two Testaments: One Bible*, D. L. Baker presented eight modern solutions to the problem of the relation of the Testaments.[13] Some of these solutions, such as that by A. A. Van Ruler, place priority on the Old Testament.[14] Some are much more negative in the assessment of the Old Testament, such as the view of Rudolf Bultmann, for whom the Old Testament is the necessary presupposition of the New Testament, but in actuality is only a history of Israel's *failure*.[15] The other solutions all view both Testaments positively, but vary in the degree to which they see the Old Testament as Christological, how they deal with Old

Testament history, and how they balance continuity and discontinuity.

The main problem for modern readers in the New Testament use of the Old Testament is the tendency of New Testament writers to use Old Testament texts in ways different from their original intention. A particular expression came into use to provide a solution. *Sensus plenior* is a Latin term popular among Roman Catholics and also among some evangelicals. It refers to the "fuller sense" God intended for a text beyond the human author's intention. The New Testament writers are viewed as inspired by the Spirit to understand and apply this fuller sense.[16] For some this is a solution; for others it is an obfuscation.

The questions that emerge from this historical overview cannot be neglected. Is the Old Testament really revelation for Christians? Can it be appropriated without being violated? To what degree does it tell of Jesus Christ? How do we deal with the discontinuity?

DISTRIBUTION AND FREQUENCY OF THE USE OF THE OLD TESTAMENT IN THE NEW TESTAMENT

Interesting results derive from an examination of Old Testament quotations and allusions printed in bold print in the United Bible Society's first edition of *The Greek New Testament*.[17] Three-fourths of the 401 quotations and allusions appear in the Gospels, Acts, Romans, and Hebrews. Of those 401 uses of the Old Testament, 195 have some type of accompanying formula such as "it is written" to inform the reader that a Scripture text is being cited.[18] In the remaining uses the only way the reader would know the Old Testament was being cited is by knowing the wording from the Old Testament text.

How and where the Old Testament is used depends on the author's purposes. Whereas Matthew focused on Jesus as the fulfillment of the Old Testament, Paul did not use this language, even though he believed it (Ro 1:2). Paul's use of the Old Testament is clearly circumstantial. When he discussed the relation of Jews to salvation in Christ in the epistle to the Romans, he quoted the Old Testament fifty-four times. But in several of his letters he makes little or no reference to the Old Testament. Colossians, for example, does not have any explicit reference to the Old Testament. The author of Revelation never quotes the Old Testament, but he uses wording of the Old Testament as much as any other writer. He merely reuses Old Testament language and images to make his point. The more an author attempts to explain the identity of Jesus or address Jews, the more likely the Old Testament will be used. To the degree that the identity of Jesus is assumed or that Gentiles are addressed, there is usually less use of the Old Testament.[19] The New Testament books with the most dependence on the Old Testament are Hebrews, Revelation, and 1 Peter.

METHODS AND HERMENEUTICAL ASSUMPTIONS

The fascinating aspect of this subject is the *way* in which Old Testament texts are used. As is clear already, not all New Testament writers use the Old Testament in what we would consider straightforward ways. Straightforward uses do occur, of course. Old Testament texts are used as direct prophecy (Mt 2:5–6) or as direct logical proof of an argument (Mt 4:4f.; Ro 4). New Testament writers adapt the words of the Old Testament for new purposes in easily understood ways. Analogies to the ministry of Jesus are found in Old Testament events (Jn 3:14). Words of judgment in Hosea 13:14 become words of victory in 1 Corinthians 15:54–55.[20] Such uses are easily justified as merely the rhetorical adaptation of familiar language. It is easy to understand the use of an Old Testament text as an illustration (1Co 10:7f.). It is not so easy to understand how a text that was not intended as messianic (Dt 18:15) becomes understood as messianic (Ac 3:22–23).[21] This is not a straightforward use. It is also not easy to see how Hosea 11:1, which refers to the exodus of Israel from Egypt, can be fulfilled by Joseph taking Jesus and Mary to Egypt (Mt 2:15). Nor is it easy to see how words clearly addressed to Isaiah (6:9–10) are seen as fulfilled in Jesus (Jn 12:39–41). Such examples of unexpected uses of the Old Testament could be multiplied easily.

The key to understanding the New Testament writers' use of the Old Testament is in understanding the presuppositions and exegetical methods by which they operated. Most of this necessary framework can be gleaned from the New Testament itself, but the discovery of the Qumran Scrolls has provided helpful insight and parallels to the practices of the New Testament writers.

The first presupposition about which we need to know is

corporate solidarity.[22] This expression refers to the oscillation or reciprocal relation between the individual and the community that existed in the Semitic mind. The act of the individual is not merely an individual act, for it affects the community and vice versa. The individual is often representative of the community and vice versa. Achan sinned and the nation suffered (Jos 7). An individual speaks in Psalm 118:10, but almost certainly he is representative of the nation. The "servant" is a collective term for the nation (Isa 44:1), but it also refers to the remnant (Isa 49:5) and probably also to an individual. Corporate solidarity should not be viewed as strange, for it is the basis for Paul's understanding of the atonement: "One died for all; therefore, all died" (2Co 5:14).

The representative character of Jesus' ministry, which is closely related to corporate solidarity, is one of the most important keys in understanding him and the way Old Testament texts are applied to him. The Christological titles "Servant," "Son of Man," and "Son of God" were all representative titles that were applied to Israel first. Jesus took on these titles because he had taken Israel's task.[23] He was representative of Israel and in solidarity with her. God's purposes for Israel were now taken up in his ministry. If this were true, what had been used to describe Israel could legitimately be used of him.

The second presupposition is *correspondence in history*, which is sometimes referred to as "typology."[24] Correspondence in history is actually a conviction about God and the way he works. The presupposition is that the way God worked in the past is mirrored in the way he works in the present and future. There is a correspondence between what happened to God's people in the past and what happens now or in the future. Climactic events in Israel's history become the paradigms by which new events are explained. For example, the Exodus was the climactic event by which God saved his people. Later writers use exodus terminology to describe God's saving his people from Assyria (Isa 11:6) or salvation generally. The suffering of a righteous person (Ps 22) finds correspondence in the crucifixion of Jesus (Mt 22:39–46).[25]

The important point about correspondence in history is that the text is not used *up* by a single event. Isaiah 40:3 was understood as a classic expression of God's salvation from Babylon. Malachi 3:1 reused the language to express the promise of future salvation. The New Testament writers saw

John the Baptist as the one in whom this verse finds its climax.[26] He was the voice crying in the wilderness to prepare the way before the Lord for ultimate salvation (Lk 3:4–6). Still, Luke 9:52 can adapt the words of Isaiah 40:3 to the disciples who prepare the way for Jesus as he goes to Jerusalem.[27] Those same words from Isaiah can even be applied to others who prepare the way.[28] Often words that find their climax in Jesus find further correspondence in his followers. If Jesus is the fulfillment of Isaiah 49:6 as the light to the Gentiles (Lk 2:32), the words can still be applied to Paul (Ac 13:47). If Jesus is a living stone, partly on the basis of Isaiah 28:16 and Psalm 118:22, his followers are living stones (1Pe 2:4–5). If he is the anointed One, they too are anointed (2Co 1:21). If 2 Samuel 7:14 can be interpreted of Jesus in Hebrews 1:5, it can also be applied to Christians in 2 Corinthians 6:18. We have not interpreted a text appropriately until we have determined how it corresponds or does not correspond with our present situation.

A third presupposition of the early church is that they lived in the days of *eschatological fulfillment*.[29] They believed that the end time had dawned upon them (1Co 10:11). This presupposition has a near parallel in the beliefs of the people of the Qumran community. They and many other Jews had an eschatological focus in their reading of the Hebrew Scriptures. Whereas for some Jews the end time belonged to an unknown future, the people at Qumran believed they were an end-time community from whose gates God would break out very soon in victorious conquest over his enemies. The early Christians viewed themselves as an end-time community as well, but there are major differences. For Christians, the end time was not just soon to appear. It had *already* appeared in the ministry of Jesus and especially in his resurrection and the pouring out of the Spirit. They could look at these events and know that God's kingdom had broken into their midst, even though its full realization was yet to come.

Old Testament texts that were viewed eschatologically were, therefore, texts that were descriptive of the reality they experienced. This presupposition can be seen clearly in a text like 1 Peter 1:12, where the author states that it was revealed to Old Testament prophets that, not to themselves but to his readers, they were ministering their prophecies. If the Scriptures find their *climax* in Christ, surely what is written there is especially for his followers. Similar expressions of this hermeneutical presupposition are seen in Romans 15:4; 1 Corinthians 9:10; and especially 10:11 ("These things happened to those people as an example, and they were written for our admonition upon whom the ends of the ages has come").[30]

The fourth presupposition is actually inherent in the third, but needs to be made explicit. The early church, like most of Judaism, assumed that the Scriptures were *Christological*. Texts that may have been general statements about the nation, prophets, priests, or kings were often *idealized* in anticipation of God's end-time deliverer who would fill the categories as no one else had. David had been the king *par excellence*, but one day there would be a king like him, only better.[31] The early church applied such texts to Jesus because of their conviction about his identity. The conviction about his identity did *not* derive from the Old Testament. They did not find texts and then find Jesus. They found Jesus and then saw how the Scriptures fit with him. They were not *proving* his identity in the technical sense so much as they were demonstrating how the Scriptures fit with him. Often they were merely following his lead in pointing to texts that summarized his ministry.[32]

Before examples of how these presuppositions are evidenced in specific New Testament quotations of Old Testament texts, another point needs to be made. Too often people look only at Old Testament texts and New Testament quotations without asking what those Old Testament texts had become in the history of Judaism. Specifically because of Christological or eschatological concerns, texts had a "life" in Judaism that led to their being understood in specific ways. These traditional interpretations have influenced the way Jesus and the early church adapted texts. Many times they are only picking up or adapting common understandings so as to make their point. They were only entering into the conversation of their hearers. The Dead Sea Scrolls have been particularly helpful in showing how texts were understood in the time of Jesus.

With these presuppositions, and with the awareness that there were traditional interpretations, we can understand why Old Testament texts were adapted the way they were. The presuppositions of corporate solidarity and correspondence in history are both at work in the application to Jesus of Hosea 11:1 ("Out of Egypt I called my son," Mt 2:15). Since Jesus, like Israel, is Son of God, there is parallelism between what happens to these two "sons." The application of Jeremiah 31:15

to the slaying of babies by Herod is also understandable. This is not merely correspondence between two sets of mothers who cry. Jeremiah 31 is an eschatological text, and the words immediately following 31:15 are words of comfort and hope for salvation that climax in 31:31–34 with the focus on the new covenant. Matthew and his readers know that Jesus has ushered in that eschatological time.[33] There is both correspondence and fulfillment.

The application of Isaiah 6:9–10 to the ministry of Jesus is another example of correspondence in history. This Old Testament text was spoken specifically to Isaiah about the hardness of heart of his hearers. Other Old Testament prophets picked up the language of Isaiah 6:9–10 so that these words became the classic expression of hardness of heart (cf. Jer 5:21; Eze 12:2). In the Synoptic Gospels the words are applied to Jesus' ministry as evidence of the hardness of heart of Jews in not responding to his teaching in parables (Mt 13:14–15//Mk 4:12//Lk 8:10). They are applied in a similar way in John 12:39–40 as a summary statement marking the rejection of Jesus by the Jews. Interestingly, these words are also addressed to the *disciples* in Mark 8:18 to ask whether they have hardened hearts. Isaiah 6:9–10 finds further correspondence as a description of the rejection of the Jews in Paul's ministry (Ac 28:26–27).[34]

Such examples suggest that the statement "Jesus is the fulfillment of the Scriptures" might be more adequately expressed as "Jesus is the *climax* of the Scriptures." His identity and ministry are mirrored there in unique ways, but "fulfillment" suggests a singularity and a focus on predictive prophecy that does justice only to some texts. Many Old Testament texts had other initial referents and also found later referents after Jesus. They find their coherence and true brilliance in him. This suggestion is not an effort to diminish the importance of predictive prophecy. It is merely a recognition that other uses of the Old Testament are common in the New Testament.

The use of Deuteronomy 18:15–19 is a good example of a text that had a life in Judaism. This text was not messianic originally, but the promise of a prophet like Moses became idealized (possibly because of Dt 34:10) so that hope emerged for an eschatological prophet. In both the Samaritan Pentateuch and in 4Q Testimonia of the Dead Sea Scrolls, Deuteronomy 18:18 is understood messianically. This expectation of an eschatological prophet is obvious in John 1:21, where John the Baptist is asked whether he is *the* prophet, and in 6:14, where people exclaim that Jesus is "truly *the* prophet, the one coming into the world." In Acts 3:22 Peter uses this expectation to define the identity of Jesus for his hearers.[35] Such usage arises from a context where certain assumptions were held about a text and where those assumptions become the tools to describe something else.

PESHER AND MIDRASH

In addition to the Jewish presuppositions we have mentioned, an interpreter of the New Testament's use of the Old Testament needs to be aware of other Jewish methods of treating the Scriptures. One method of appropriating Scripture for some Jews, particularly Jews from Qumran, was *pesher*. This practice does not seek to explain a text so much as it seeks to show where a text fits. The word *pesher* derives from an Aramaic root meaning "solution." The presupposition is that the text contains a mystery communicated by God that is not understood until the solution is made known by an inspired interpreter. With *pesher*, the starting point for understanding is not the Old Testament text, but a historical event or person. By viewing a text in the framework of an event, a *pesher* interpretation provides a solution to the mystery involved in understanding. In effect, *pesher* says "This [event or person] is that [of which the Scripture speaks]."[36] For example, the Qumran *Pesher* on Habakkuk understands the judgment spoken against Babylon (Hab 2:7–8) to refer to a wicked priest in Jerusalem who caused trouble for the Qumran community (1QpH 8.13f.).

Pesher also occurs in the New Testament. The most obvious example is Acts 2:17.[37] The event of the pouring out of the Spirit provided a framework for understanding Joel 2:28f. The event is seen as an actualization of the text.

The more common method of interpreting Scripture among Jews, however, was *midrash*. *Midrash* derives from a Hebrew word meaning "to seek" and refers to interpretive exposition. The starting point is the text itself, and the concern is to provide practical instruction so that people may understand God's Word and live accordingly. If *pesher* says "This is that," *midrash* says "That [Scripture] has relevance to this [aspect of life]." In the earlier rabbinic material, midrashic interpretation is fairly straightforward, but later rabbinic practices often focused more on individual words and even letters. The result is a "creative" exegesis in which the original concern of the text is often lost.[38] Even where the midrashic interpretation is fairly straightforward, the focus with *midrash* is on the application of the text rather than with understanding the text itself. *Midrash* is not usually a commentary on the text.

Still, *midrash* is not arbitrary application of the text. There are rules to guide an interpreter that legitimated an interpretation. The early rabbinic practices were guided by seven rules of exposition, which later were expanded until eventually there were thirty-two.[39] The seven rules are fairly logical and may have derived from Hellenistic rhetoric.[40] Such procedures have frequently been adopted by expositors of texts. These seven rules merit repetition and consideration, for at least some of them are observable in the New Testament.[41]

> *Qal wahomer*—"light and heavy," meaning what applies in a less important case applies also in a more important case and vice versa.
>
> *Gezerah shawa*—"an equivalent regulation," meaning where the same words are applied in two separate cases the same considerations apply.
>
> *Binyan ab mikathub 'ehad*—"constructing a family from one passage," meaning that where texts are similar a principle derived from one of them applies to the others.
>
> *Binyan ab mishene kethubim*—"constructing a family from two texts," meaning that where texts are similar a principle derived from two texts can be applied to the others.
>
> *Kelal uferat*—"general and particular," meaning that a general rule may be applied to a particular situation and vice versa.
>
> *Kayotse bo bemaqom 'aher*—"something similar in another passage," meaning that a text may be interpreted by comparison with a similar text.
>
> *Dabar halamed me'inyano*—"explanation from the context."

Such midrashic techniques are observable in the New Testament. When Jesus argued that if God cared for the birds, surely he cared much more for humans (Mt 6:26), he was arguing in good rabbinic fashion from the less important case to the more important. Similarly, when Jesus justified his disciples' eating grain on the Sabbath by pointing to the eating of the showbread by David and his men, he was arguing on the basis of an equivalent regulation (or possibly also from a less important case to a more important).[42] When Paul quoted several Old Testament texts with common key words, as he does in Galatians 3:8–14,[43] he was following the midrashic technique of bringing texts together to provide explanation. Such grouping of texts as a method of argumentation occurs often.[44]

TESTIMONIA

One further Jewish practice that must be noted is the use of *testimonia*. If one analyzes the use of Old Testament passages in the New Testament, very quickly one sees that certain Old Testament passages are quoted by several New Testament writers. In addition, sometimes the New Testament writers agree in using combinations of texts, and sometimes they even agree in wording that does not agree with the Septuagint or other known texts. The best example of these interesting phenomena is the agreement between 1 Peter 2 and Romans 9. First Peter 2:6–10 uses Isaiah 28:16; Psalm 118:22, Isaiah 8:14; parts of several other texts and Hosea 2:23. Romans 9:25–33 uses Hosea 2:23, other texts from Isaiah, and then a conflation of Isaiah 28:16 and 8:14 in the same non-Septuagintal form that 1 Peter has.[45] Should we account for such instances by arguing that one writer copied from the other?[46] Furthermore, there are a few places where Old Testament texts seem to have been joined in unexpected ways. For example, Mark 1:2–3 attributes to Isaiah words that appear to be a combination of Exodus 23:20; Malachi 3:1; and Isaiah 40:3.[47]

An attractive explanation of these phenomena is the argument that early Christians used *testimonia*. That is, they used collections of Old Testament texts that had been grouped thematically for apologetic, liturgical, and catechetical purposes. While it would be easy to overstate the case for *testimonia*,[48] their existence and use seem to be beyond doubt. Pre-Christian Jewish *testimonia* have been found at Qumran.[49] Evidence of the continued use and growth of *testimonia* in the patristic period also is without question.[50] For the New Testament itself, the argument that one author copied from the other is often far too simplistic to account for the data.[51] Rather, there were collections of Old Testament texts that were useful to the church in a variety of ways. Such collections would have circulated in *both* written and oral forms and would have offered practical resources for both itinerant preachers and gentile congregations.

The stone *testimonia*, then, would have been a pre-Christian Jewish collection that was adopted by Christians. The frequent use of Psalm 8 and Psalm 110 in combination reflects Christological *testimonia* brought together by the church.[52] The most common uses of *testimonia* were Christological and apologetic, but catechetical and liturgical uses are present as well. Romans 3:10–18 possibly is a grouping of *testimonia* on sin.[53] Romans 15:9–12 may reflect *testimonia* thematically arranged around the subject of the Gentiles.

Testimonia provide a window into the way the early church did its theology and ministry. They also provide insight into Old Testament quotations that are otherwise anomalies. Therefore, when an Old Testament quotation occurs, one must inquire about its use and textual form elsewhere in the New Testament and, if possible, in Judaism and the patristic period as well.

Example One—An Important Allusion
John 1:14–18

John 1:14–18 is a marvelously rich theological text on almost any reading, but a reading that does justice to the Old Testament background increases the significance of this text considerably. There is no Old Testament quotation in these verses, but there is an important allusion. Without an awareness of the Old Testament background on which the author frames his material, not only will much of the theological significance of this passage be lost, but one will not know why the author has chosen these words. There often is argument about whether a New Testament writer is alluding to an Old Testament text,[54] but there is such a constellation of words drawn from Exodus 33:17–34:6 that there can be no doubt that John 1:14–18 is based on this passage.[55]

Exodus 33:17f. is about Moses seeking a revelation of God's glory. Moses was told that neither he nor any other human could see God and live. He was allowed to see all God's goodness pass before him and, as it were, also to see the "back" of God. In this context Moses received the two tables of the law and was told that God is, among other things, full of lovingkindness and truth (*hesed veʾemet*). More than any text, this Old Testament passage defined who God was for Israel, and this event was viewed by Jews as the supreme revelation of God.

In John 1:14 the author claims to have seen the glory of the Word (*logos*), who was full of grace and truth. "Glory" is frequently to be understood as that which makes God visible.[56] Although "grace" (*charis*) is not often used to render the Hebrew word for lovingkindness (*hesed*), clearly the intention in John 1:14 is to say that in the *logos* made flesh, we encounter a revelation of God. He is the unique one from the Father in whom we encounter the very character of the Father, grace and truth.

Similarly in John 1:17, the intention of the author is clear with an awareness of the background in Exodus. The law, a valid revelation, was given through Moses. The true revelation of the Father, however, was given through Jesus Christ. There is a contrast with the revelation of Moses, but there is not a rejection of that revelation. In effect, this verse says, "Revelation did take place through Moses, but the supreme revelation of God is to be found in Jesus Christ."

John 1:18 expresses the whole of Johannine theology in a nutshell. The assertion that no human can see God and live is drawn from Exodus 33:20 and is an important theme throughout the gospel.[57] No one, not even Moses, has ever seen God, but the unique God,[58] the one in the bosom of the Father, has revealed him. To see him is to see the Father (Jn 14:9).

Example Two—An Important Quotation
Luke 4:18–19

Like John, the other Gospel writers use Old Testament quotations early in their writing to establish the identity of Jesus. The reader knows who Jesus is right from the start in every Gospel. In addition, Luke 4:18–19 established the character of Jesus' ministry through the quotation of Isaiah 61:1–2. This Old Testament text was the focus of Jesus' preaching in Nazareth.[59] Luke has placed this incident first in his account of Jesus' ministry to provide a programmatic description of Jesus' task. The importance of Isaiah 61:1–2 for Luke is obvious. He has moved this narrative to the beginning of his account of Jesus' ministry, whereas Matthew and Mark had it much later. Also, many of the main themes of Lukan theology are evidenced in this quotation (the Spirit, proclamation of the good news, the *aphesis*—which is both release and forgiveness, the poor and oppressed, and eschatology).

The words of Isaiah 61 are obviously important, but this text is another example of an Old Testament passage with a life in Judaism. The ideas associated with this text would have made it even more significant for Jesus and his hearers. Isaiah 61, with its focus on the "acceptable year of the Lord," would have alluded both to the "Year of Jubilee" described in Leviticus 25 and to God's end-time salvation.[60] The interpretation of Isaiah 61 in 11Q Melchizedek with reference to the "end of days" is clear proof of the eschatological association this text had. When people heard Isaiah 61, they understood it as a classic text describing end-time salvation. In effect, Jesus proclaimed to his hearers that God's end-time salvation had been fulfilled in their hearing. Their surprise is understandable.[61]

GUIDELINES

We have looked at a few examples of the significance of the Old Testament quotations in the New Testament. Other examples could be multiplied easily. Given that the use of the Old Testament in the New Testament is one of the most important issues in understanding the New Testament, certain guidelines will be helpful for studying those quotations.

1) Determine the original intention of the Old Testament passage. Close attention must be given to the context and to the theology at work in the Old Testament text.

2) Analyze the form of the text. To the degree that one is able, comparison should be made between the New Testament quotation and Old Testament text and various witnesses to it. Is the New Testament reference a precise quotation, a quotation from memory, a paraphrase, or an allusion? Does the New Testament agree with the Masoretic text or the Septuagint or some other witness such as a targum? Are any insights to be gained from the form of the

quotation? Even when one cannot make an independent comparison of other forms of the text, good commentaries will provide summaries of such comparisons.

3) Determine, if possible, how the Old Testament text was understood and used in Judaism. Again, where personal investigation is not practical, good commentaries will provide such information.

4) Determine the hermeneutical or exegetical assumptions that enabled the use of the Old Testament text. Is the use straightforward from our standpoint, or is there an assumption such as corporate solidarity or correspondence in history that makes the usage possible? Have any rabbinic techniques or wordplays made the Old Testament text attractive?

5) Analyze the *way* the New Testament writer uses the Old Testament text. Is the text being used as divine proof of the validity of his statement? Are words from the Old Testament used to enlighten, but with no thought of providing validation (as Jn 1:14–18)? Are the words adapted and used for rhetorical effect in the writer's own argument (as in 1Pe 1:3)? Is the New Testament writer only using an analogy based on an Old Testament text (Jn 3:14)?

6) Determine the theological significance and relevance of the use of the Old Testament text. For example, the Christological importance of the adaptation of Isaiah 8:12–13 to Christ in 1 Peter 3:14–15 is enormous. An Old Testament text that was explicitly about "*Yahweh* of hosts" has been applied to Christ without hesitation or any sense of need for explanation. That Paul could interpret Isaiah 49:8 eschatologically of his own ministry (2Co 6:2) is important in understanding both him and our own ministries.

7) Note which Old Testament texts are used in the New Testament and which are not.[62] Most of the New Testament references to the Old Testament come from parts of the Pentateuch, the Psalms, and a few of the prophets, especially Isaiah. Clearly all the Hebrew Scriptures were considered the Word of God, but what theological conclusions should be drawn with regard to texts that were set aside (as the food laws) or ignored? On what ground did Jesus and the New Testament writers find the essence of their gospel in certain texts, especially those that focused on God's promises, love, and mercy rather than those that focused on separation and the exclusiveness of Israel?

Beyond these guidelines, a further question must be mentioned. In view of the fact that the New Testament writers use Old Testament passages in ways that we find surprising, should we interpret the Old Testament the same way they did? In other words, can we use their technique to find Christian significance in Old Testament texts, or were they operating from a revelatory stance in ways that we cannot?[63] This question is crucial, for the abuse of the Old Testament message is all too common in Christian history. Clearly the proximity of the apostles to the ministry, death, and resurrection of Jesus places them in a unique category. Also, the eschatological significance of Jesus' ministry and his identity have been marked out in ways that, even though they may be enhanced, do not need improvement. We should not expect to see new instances of verses applied to Jesus on the basis of corporate solidarity or eschatological or messianic presuppositions.

With great fear of possible abuse, however, I would not want to argue that the apostles could be creative because of their context, but that we are confined to more mundane methods. In terms of approaching the text, whether Old Testament or New Testament, we must be guided by the author's intention. We do also, however, read the Scriptures in light of the person and work of Christ. We must resist superimposing Christian theology on Old Testament texts and should feel no compulsion to give every Old Testament text, or even most of them, a Christological conclusion. But we will have failed if we do not ask how Old Testament texts function in the whole context of Scripture. Without allegorizing the Old Testament, we must seek to understand God's overall purpose with his people. I am not impressed with the concept of *sensus plenior*, but neither am I willing to isolate texts from God's overall purpose.

Specifically, I have become convinced that the concept of correspondence in history is particularly valuable in interpretation. We have not completed the interpretive task until we have determined how a text does or does not correspond with Jesus' ministry or the ministry of the church.[64] The writers of the New Testament seem to have looked for patterns of God's working in the Hebrew Scriptures, in the life of Jesus, and in their own experience. Our reading of the Scriptures should do no less. Noting such patterns is a far cry from the abusive interpretation of allegorizing.

The New Testament writers were immersed in their Scriptures. The Scriptures were the frame of reference for their theology and provided many of the tools for their thinking. The same should be true of us.

BIBLIOGRAPHY

Anderson, Bernhard W., ed. *The Old Testament and Christian Faith*. New York: Herder and Herder, 1969.

Baker, D. L. *Two Testaments: One Bible*. Downers Grove, Ill.: InterVarsity, 1976.

Bock, Darrell L. *Proclamation From Prophecy and Pattern*. Sheffield: *JSOT*, 1987.

Bruce, F. F. *The New Testament Development of Old Testament Themes*. Grand Rapids: Eerdmans, 1968.

Carson, D. A. and H. G. M. Williamson. *It Is Written: Scripture Citing Scripture*. Cambridge: Cambridge University Press, 1988.

Dodd, C. H. *According to the Scriptures*. New York: Scribner's, 1952.

Efird, James M., ed. *The Use of the Old Testament in the New*. Durham, N.C.: Duke University Press, 1972.

Ellis, Earle E. *Paul's Use of the Old Testament*. Grand Rapids: Eerdmans, 1957.

————. *Prophecy and Hermeneutic in Earliest Christianity*. Grand Rapids: Eerdmans, 1978.

Feinberg, John S., ed. *Continuity and Discontinuity: Perspectives on the Relationship Between the Old and New Testaments*. Westchester, Ill.: Crossway, 1988.

France, R. T. *Jesus and the Old Testament*. London: Tyndale, 1971.

Goppelt, Leonhard. *Typos: The Typological Interpretation of the Old Testament in the New*. Trans. Donald H. Madvig. Grand Rapids: Eerdmans, 1982.

Juel, Donald. *Messianic Exegesis: Christological Interpretation of the Old Testament in Early Christianity*. Philadelphia: Fortress, 1988.

Lindars, B. *New Testament Apologetic*. Philadelphia: Westminster, 1961.

Longenecker, Richard N. *Biblical Exegesis in the Apostolic Period*. Grand Rapids: Eerdmans, 1975.

Westermann, Claus, ed. *Essays on Old Testament Hermeneutics*. English trans, ed. James Luther Mays. Richmond: John Knox, 1963.

NOTES

[1]C. H. Dodd, *According to the Scriptures: The Sub-structure of New Testament Theology* (London: Nisbet, 1952).

[2]Augustine, *Quaestionum in Heptateuchum libri Septem* 2.73.

[3]See S. Vernon McCasland, "Matthew Twists the Scriptures," *JBL*, 80 (1961): 143–48.

[4]See the collection of essays edited by John S. Feinberg, *Continuity and Discontinuity: Perspectives on the Relationship Between the Old and New Testaments* (Westchester, Ill.: Crossway, 1988). The main problem is how promises to the nation of Israel should be treated.

[5]No one would argue that we should test a suspected adulteress with "bitter waters" (Nu 5:11f.) or that we should execute heretics (Dt 13:6f.) or Sabbath breakers (Ex 31:15). The number of such texts is not small.

[6]See Robert Banks, *Jesus and the Law in the Synoptic Tradition* (Cambridge: Cambridge University Press, 1975), 132–46. Is Jesus' thought from Proverbs 4:23? See also Acts 10:9–16; Romans 14:14; 1 Corinthians 10:26f; and 1 Timothy 4:4, which place Christian conclusions in opposition with dietary restrictions in the Old Testament.

[7]On the question of Jesus and the law in Matthew, see my "Matthew and the Law," *Society of Biblical Literature 1988 Seminar Papers*, ed. David J. Lull (Atlanta: Scholars, 1988), 536–54.

[8]See Irenaeus, *Against Heresies* 1.27.2; Tertullian, *Against Marcion* 4.5–7 and 5.2–4; Richard N. Longenecker, "Three Ways of Understanding Relations Between the Testaments: Historically and Today," *Tradition and Interpretation in the New Testament*, ed. Gerald F. Hawthorne with Otto Betz (Grand Rapids: Eerdmans, 1987), 22–23; and E. C. Blackman, *Marcion and his Influence* (London: SPCK, 1948), 23f., 42f., and 113–24.

[9]For information on the early church's treatment of the Old Testament, see R. P. C. Hanson, "Biblical Exegesis in the Early Church," *The Cambridge History of the Bible*, ed. P. R. Ackroyd and C. F. Evans (Cambridge: Cambridge University Press, 1970), I, 412–53; Robert M. Grant with David Tracy, *A Short History of the Interpretation of the Bible* (Philadelphia: Fortress, 1984); Karlfried Froehlich, *Biblical Interpretation in the Early Church* (Philadelphia: Fortress, 1984); and James L. Kugel and Rowan A. Greer, *Early Biblical Interpretation* (Philadelphia: Westminster, 1986).

[10]See Justin, *Dialogue with Trypho* 70 and 76 (on the stone of Da 2) and 86 and 90–91 (on wood and trees and other symbols of the cross).

[11]On the Antiochean and Alexandrian schools of interpretation, see Richard N. Longenecker, "Three Ways of Understanding Relations between the Testaments: Historically and Today," 22–32; and Grant with Tracy, 52–72.

[12]For the approaches of Luther and Calvin, see Grant with Tracy, 92–99; Roland Bainton, "The Bible in the Reformation," *The Cambridge History of the Bible*, ed. S. L. Greenslade (Cambridge: Cambridge University Press, 1963), III, 1–37; Paul Althaus, *The Theology of Martin Luther*, trans. Robert C. Schultz (Philadelphia: Fortress, 1966), 86–102; Wilhelm Niesel, *The Theology of Calvin*, trans. Harold Knight (Philadelphia: Westminster, 1956), 104–9. On the third use of the law, see *Calvin: The Institutes of the Christian Religion*, ed. John T. McNeill; trans. Ford Lewis Battles (Philadelphia: Westminster), 2.7.12.

[13]D. L. Baker, *Two Testaments: One Bible* (Downers Grove, Ill.: InterVarsity, 1976).

[14]Arnold A. van Ruler, *The Christian Church and the Old Testament*, trans. Geoffrey W. Bromiley (Grand Rapids: Eerdmans, 1971).

[15]Rudolf Bultmann, "The Significance of the Old Testament for the Christian Faith," *The Old Testament and Christian Faith*, ed. Bernhard W. Anderson (New York: Herder and Herder, 1969), 8–35, especially 14–15; and "Prophecy and Fulfillment," *Essays on Old Testament Hermeneutics*, ed. Claus Westermann; English trans. ed. James Luther Mays (Richmond: John Knox, 1963), 50–75, especially 75.

[16]On *sensus plenior*, see Raymond Edward Brown, *The Sensus Plenior of Sacred Scripture* (Baltimore: St. Mary's University, 1955); "The History and Development of the Theory of a Sensus Plenior," *CBQ*, 15 (1953): 141–62; "The *Sensus Plenior* in the Last Ten Years," *CBQ*, 25 (1963): 262–85; William Sanford LaSor, "The *Sensus Plenior* and Biblical Interpretation," *Scripture, Tradition, and Interpretation*, ed. W. Ward Gasque and William Sanford LaSor (Grand Rapids: Eerdmans, 1978), 260–77; and Douglas Moo, "The Problem of *Sensus Plenior*," *Hermeneutics, Authority, and Canon*, ed. D. A. Carson and John D. Woodbridge (Grand Rapids: Zondervan, 1986), 179–211.

[17]The first edition UBS Greek New Testament has more passages in bold print and a much better index than later editions.

[18]The actual statistics of usage in the first edition UBS text are: Matthew, sixty-two quotations or allusions in bold print with thirty-two of them having an introductory formula; Mark, thirty with eleven having an introductory formula; Luke, thirty-nine with fifteen; John, eighteen with fourteen; Acts, thirty-seven with twenty-three; Romans, fifty-four with forty; 1 Corinthians, sixteen with ten; 2 Corinthians, twelve with five; Galatians, eleven with five; Ephesians, ten with one; Philippians, one with zero; Colossians, zero; 1 Thessalonians, one with zero; 2 Thessalonians, four with zero; 1 Timothy, two with one;

2 Timothy, one with zero; Titus, zero; Philemon, zero; Hebrews, fifty-nine with thirty; James, six with four; 1 Peter, fifteen with three; 2 Peter, two with zero; 1 John, zero; 2 John, zero; 3 John, zero; Jude, one with one; Revelation, twenty with zero. There are, of course, other allusions besides the ones in bold print in the UBS text, and other editions will assess quotations differently. There are a variety of introductory formulae. See Joseph A. Fitzmyer, "The Use of Explicit Old Testament Quotations in Qumran Literature and in the New Testament," NTS, 7 (1960–1961): 299–305.

On the extent of the canon in the first century, see Roger Beckwith, The Old Testament Canon of the New Testament Church (Grand Rapids: Eerdmans, 1985). It is significant that there are no quotations from the apocryphal and pseudepigraphal writings. There are, however, allusions to these writings.

Helpful treatments of the use of the Old Testament in the New Testament can be found in C. K. Barrett, "The Interpretation of the Old Testament in the New," The Cambridge History of the Bible, ed. P. R. Ackroyd and C. F. Evans (Cambridge: Cambridge University Press, 1970), I, 377–411; E. Earle Ellis, "How the New Testament Uses the Old," New Testament Interpretation (Grand Rapids: Eerdmans, 1978), 199–219; and D. Moody Smith, "The Use of the Old Testament in the New," The Use of the Old Testament in the New and Other Essays, ed. James M. Efird (Durham: Duke University Press, 1972), 3–65.

[19]First Corinthians is an exception.

[20]Hosea 13:14 should be translated, as in the New English Bible, with questions and a call for death to bring its plagues. The passage expects judgment.

[21]Deuteronomy 18:15f. refers to prophets in general who serve as spokespersons for God to the community. Note that 18:20f. refers to prophets who speak falsely.

[22]See Richard N. Longenecker, Biblical Exegesis in the Apostolic Period (Grand Rapids: Eerdmans, 1975), 93–94; E. Earle Ellis, "Biblical Interpretation in the New Testament Church," Mikra, ed. Martin Jan Mulder and Harry Sysling; Compendia Rerum Iudaicarum ad Novum Testamentum, sec. 2, pt 1 (Philadelphia: Fortress, 1988), 716–20; H. Wheeler Robinson, Corporate Personality in Ancient Israel (Philadelphia: Fortress, 1964); and Russell Philip Shedd, Man in Community (Grand Rapids: Eerdmans, 1964).

[23]N. T. Wright, "Jesus, Israel, and the Cross," Society of Biblical Literature 1985 Seminar Papers, ed. Kent Harold Richards (Atlanta: Scholars, 1985), 75–96, especially 83f.

[24]On correspondence in history, see Ellis, "Biblical Interpretation in the New Testament Church," 713–16; Baker, 239–70; Gerhard von Rad, "Typological Interpretation of the Old Testament," Essays on Old Testament Hermeneutics, ed. Claus Westermann; English trans. ed. James Luther Mays (Richmond: John Knox, 1963), 17–39; Leonhard

Goppelt, *Typos: The Typological Interpretation of the Old Testament in the New*, trans. Donald H. Madvig (Grand Rapids: Eerdmans, 1982). "Correspondence in history" is to be preferred to "typology"; the latter is too restricting and too associated with abuse.

[25]Jesus' cry of dereliction no doubt expressed the initial awareness of correspondence with Psalm 22. This psalm must be seen as the lament of a righteous sufferer and not as a prophecy of Jesus' death.

[26]In John 1:23 it is John the Baptist himself who uses Isaiah 40:3 as a description of his role.

[27]Isaiah 40:3 was also used at Qumran as a description of the role of the community. See my "Streams of Tradition Emerging from Isaiah 40:1–5 and Their Adaptation in the New Testament," *JSNT*, 8 (1980): 24–45, for a discussion of the use of Isaiah 40:3.

[28]Even if they are not applied in the same way.

[29]On eschatological fulfillment as a hermeneutical presupposition, see Ellis, "Biblical Interpretation in the New Testament Church," 710–13; Longenecker, *Biblical Exegesis in the Apostolic Period*, 95; Donald Juel, *Messianic Exegesis* (Philadelphia: Fortress, 1988), 49–56; F. F. Bruce, *Biblical Exegesis in the Qumran Texts* (London: Tyndale, 1960), especially 9–19.

[30]Romans 4:23–24 is slightly different, but also represents an eschatological presupposition.

[31]The Jews' expectation of an idealized Davidic king is well known. Note especially Jeremiah 23:5–8; 33:15–18; Psalm 89; and 4Q Florilegium. See Juel, 59–88.

[32]There are several Old Testament texts that seem to have provided the framework for Jesus' understanding of his ministry. Of primary significance are Psalm 118:22–26; Isaiah 61:1–3; Daniel 7:13–14. The impact of Isaiah 53 is debated but seems probable.

[33]On the infancy quotations in Matthew, see Longenecker, *Biblical Exegesis in the Apostolic Period*, 140–47; Raymond E. Brown, *The Birth of the Messiah* (Garden City: Doubleday, 1979), 96–116, 143–53, 184–88, and 219–25.

[34]See Craig A. Evans, *To See and not Perceive: Isaiah 6:9–10 in Early Jewish and Christian Interpretation* (Sheffield: JSOT, 1989).

[35]See Richard N. Longenecker, *The Christology of Early Jewish Christianity* (London: SCM, 1970), 32–38; and Howard M. Teeple, *The Mosaic Eschatological Prophet* (Philadelphia: Society of Biblical Literature, 1957). Note also John 7:40.

[36]See Bruce, 7–11; and Longenecker, *Biblical Exegesis in the Apostolic Period*, 39–45. On the interpretation of Scripture more generally at Qumran, see Daniel Patte, *Early Jewish Hermeneutic in Palestine* (Missoula, Mont.: Scholars, 1975), 211–314.

[37]Note also Acts 4:11 and Luke 4:18–21. Longenecker, *Biblical Exegesis in the Apostolic Period*, 70–75 and 100–101, lists several other

passages that he would categorize as New Testament *pesher* interpretations of Old Testament texts.

[38]On *midrash*, Rimon Kasher, "The Interpretation of Scripture in Rabbinic Literature," *Mikra* ed. Martin Jan Mulder and Harry Sysling; *Compendia Rerum Iudaicarum ad Novum Testamentum*, sec. 2, pt 1 (Philadelphia: Fortress, 1988), 560–77; Longenecker, *Biblical Exegesis in the Apostolic Period*, 32–38; Ellis, "Biblical Interpretation in the New Testament Church," 702–9.

[39]On hermeneutical rules for exposition, see Kasher, 584–94; Ellis, "Biblical Interpretation in the New Testament Church," 699–702; and Hermann L. Strack, *Introduction to the Talmud and Midrash* (Cleveland: World, 1963), 93–98.

[40]See David Daube, "Rabbinic Methods of Interpretation and Hellenistic Rhetoric," *HUCA*, 22 (1949): 239–64.

[41]Ellis, "Biblical Interpretation in the New Testament Church," 700–702, would argue that all seven are used in the New Testament.

[42]Matthew 12:1–8; see Ellis, "Biblical Interpretation in the New Testament Church," 700.

[43]Note the use of *epikataratos* in Galatians 3:10 (quoting Dt 27:26) and 3:13 (quoting Dt 21:23), *poiēsai auta* in 3:10 (from Dt 27:26) and *poiēsas auta* in 3:12 (from Lev 18:5), and *zēsetai* in 3:11 (quoting Hab 2:4) and 3:12 (quoting Lev 18:5).

[44]Note Acts 2:25, 30, and 34; 13:34–35; Romans 4:2 and 7; 9:33 and 11:9; 1 Corinthians 15:54–55; and Hebrews 1:5, 6–7.

[45]Psalm 118:22 also occurs in Matthew 21:42 and parallels and in Barnabas 6.4.

[46]See, for example, C. Leslie Mitton, *The Epistle to the Ephesians* (Oxford: Clarendon Press, 1951), 186–89.

[47]Note a similar example in Matthew 27:9–10, where a conflation of Zechariah 11:12–13 and Jeremiah 32:6–9 is attributed to Jeremiah. Such combinations of texts and their attributions to a specific author ought not be considered "errors."

[48]As Rendel Harris did with his "testimony book" hypothesis. See Rendel Harris, with the assistance of Vacher Burch, *Testimonies* (Cambridge: Cambridge University Press, 1916–1920), 2 vols.

[49]Note 4Q Testimonia and 4Q Florilegium. See Joseph A. Fitzmyer, "'4Q Testimonia' and the New Testament," *TS*, 18 (1957): 513–37.

[50]See Barnabas 6.2–4 for an example, and cf. Pierre Prigent, *Les Testimonia dans le christianisme primitif: L'Epître de Barnabé I–XVI et ses sources* (Paris: J. Gabalda et Cie, 1961), *passim*. Note also Cyprian, Treatise 12 ("Three Books of Testimonies Against the Jews").

[51]See my "I Peter II.1–10: Its Formation and Literary Affinities," *NTS*, 24 (1978), 97–106, especially 101–3.

[52]Note 1 Corinthians 15:25–27; Ephesians 1:20–22; and Hebrews 1:13 and 2:6–8. Psalm 110:1 is used in several other places, and is used

in the New Testament more than any other Old Testament text. On the use of Psalm 110, see David M. Hay, *Glory at the Right Hand* (Nashville: Abingdon, 1973).

[53]As several commentators have suggested. See, e.g., Ernst Käsemann, *Commentary on Romans*, trans. Geoffrey W. Bromiley (Grand Rapids: Eerdmans, 1980), 86. Note that this grouping of Old Testament texts on sin is present in the Septuagint version of Psalm 14:2–3. This could be due to Christian influence, but it seems more likely that these verses had earlier been collected in Judaism.

[54]What constitutes an allusion? Is one word in common between New Testament and Old Testament texts sufficient? Certainly not unless there is something in the New Testament context that suggests dependence on the Old Testament text. Does an allusion have to be a conscious allusion? Does it have to be an allusion that one could expect the readers to recognize? Frequently allusions are suggested that require a stretch of the imagination to accept.

[55]See Morna Hooker, "The Johannine Prologue and the Messianic Secret," *NTS*, 21 (1975): 52–56; and Anthony T. Hanson, "John i.14–18 and Exodus XXXIV," *NTS*, 23 (1977): 90–101.

[56]S. Aalen, "Glory, Honour," *The New International Dictionary of New Testament Theology*, ed. Colin Brown (Grand Rapids: Zondervan, 1976), II, 45.

[57]Cf. 5:37; 6:46; 12:41; and 14:8–9. Note also 1 John 4:12–20.

[58]*Theos*, not *huios*, is the correct reading.

[59]Note that while Luke's quotation is basically septuagintal, part of Isaiah 61:1 is omitted and part of Isaiah 58:6 is inserted.

[60]The Jubilee included four elements: 1) return of all property to the original owner; 2) release of all Jewish slaves; 3) cancellation of all debts; 4) allowing the land to lie fallow.

[61]See the discussion of this text in Robert B. Sloan, Jr., *The Favorable Year of the Lord* (Austin, Tex.: Schola Press, 1977); John Howard Yoder, *The Politics of Jesus* (Grand Rapids: Eerdmans, 1972), 34–40 and 64–77.

[62]Note Dodd's summary, *According to the Scriptures*, 107–8.

[63]Note the discussions in Longenecker, *Biblical Exegesis in the Apostolic Period*, 214–20; "Can We Reproduce the Exegesis of the Apostles," *Tyndale Bulletin*, 21 (1970): 3–38; and G. K. Beale, "Did Jesus and his Followers Preach the Right Doctrine from the Wrong Texts?" *Themelios*, 14 (1989): 89–96.

[64]See my "Streams of Tradition Emerging from Isaiah 40:1–5 and Their Adaptation in the New Testament," 39–40. For example, I would argue that the application of Lamentations 1:12 to the ministry of Jesus is legitimate on the basis of correspondence between the suffering of the nation and the suffering of Christ. This is not a text referring to Christ; it is a text applicable to Christ.

Chapter Fifteen

Unity in Diversity: A Clue to the Emergence of the New Testament as Sacred Literature

Robert B. Sloan

Robert B. Sloan

Robert B. Sloan is the George W. Truett Chair in Evangelism at Baylor University in Waco, Texas. He is a graduate of Baylor University (B.A.), Princeton Theological Seminary (M.Div.), and the University of Basel (D.Theol.). He also studied at the University of Bristol in England. Before going to Baylor, he taught at Southwestern Baptist Theological Seminary in Fort Worth, Texas. He has authored *The Favorable Year of the Lord* (Scholars Press), *Discovering I Corinthians* (Guideposts), and articles in such journals as *The Biblical Illustrator*, *Southwestern Journal of Theology*, *Novum Testamentum*, *Evangelical Quarterly*, and *Criswell Theological Review*. He currently serves as New Testament editor for *The New American Commentary* (Broadman), to which he is contributing the volume on Romans. He is also editing *Perspectives on John* for Mercer University Press.

Chapter Fifteen

Unity in Diversity: A Clue to the Emergence of the New Testament as Sacred Literature

The New Testament may be known and studied in terms of both its unity and its diversity. While professional New Testament scholarship typically busies itself with details of literary and theological diversity, the ordinary Christian worshiper more likely thinks of the New Testament in terms of its unitary status as a sacred book pertaining to religious faith and practice. But just as the unity of the New Testament should be neither ignored nor preemptively ruled out by New Testament scholarship, so ought not the rich diversity of the New Testament be overlooked by anyone. We have, for example, many different kinds of literature in the New Testament: Gospels, histories, hymns, prayers, confessions, letters, sermons, and of course a very stirring piece of apocalyptic at the end. Indeed, the diversity of the New Testament goes deeper than the types of literature. It is also reflected in the *messages* of those various books. In the Gospels we read of Jesus the great miracle worker, preacher, and teacher. In the Acts of the Apostles we hear of the work of the Spirit in the life of the early church. In the Epistles we find pastoral exhortations regarding both theological and behavioral problems in the early churches. And in the Revelation we read, in words of strange and wondrous imagery, of a rider on a white horse, a conquering Lord who will appear to rescue his beleaguered people. The more one pursues issues related to the variety of thought and expression in the New Testament, the more the question of coherence thrusts itself upon us. Therefore, without overlooking—indeed, rather presuming—the multiformity of the New Testament in terms of both style and content, the burden of this study relates more to the unity of the New Testament, and, more specifically, the role that the forces of coherence may have played in the emergence of the New Testament canon.

What, then, if it exists at all, is the unity of the New Testament? What is its "center"? What holds these books together? Or, to put it another way, why should we have bothered to bind these twenty-seven—in many ways very different—books with one cover? What, for example, do the rather Jewish-sounding epistle to the Hebrews—in which Jesus is a high priest after the order of Melchizedek—and the rather gentile-sounding Gospel of Mark—in which a Roman soldier declares, "Truly this was the Son of God"—have to do with each other?

In spite of the obvious literary and theological variety in the New Testament, I am convinced that the New Testament *is* dominated by a center: the message of the crucified and risen Lord Jesus. The first four books of the New Testament, for example, which could just as easily have been called biographies, were not called biographies; they were called Gospels.[1] And they were called Gospels precisely because they are devoted primarily to the gospel: the message of the crucified and risen Lord. It is the gospel, the story of that fateful week in Jerusalem, when Christ was crucified and raised, that dominates each Gospel. Turning from the Gospels to Acts, we may similarly note a kind of gospel centrality, for Acts is more than the history of the early church: it is a theological history of the progress of the gospel to the uttermost parts of the earth. In the same vein, the Epistles, which represent pastoral exhortations regarding doctrine and behavior in the early church, have as their fundamental pattern and basis for exhortation the fact of Christ's death and resurrection for us. Since, for example, Christ has conquered sin and death, we must lay aside our evil practices (e.g., 1Co 5:7–8; 15:20–58; Col 2:8–3:17; Heb 12:1–13:17; 1Pe 4:1–6). Since Christ has been raised from the dead, we too must walk in newness of life (Ro 6:4; cf. 1Pe 3:13–22). Since Christ in his death and resurrection has fulfilled the ancient scriptural promises of salvation for Israel and the nations, thereby ushering in a new aeon of life and peace, Jew and Gentile may now live together in a *koinōnia* of God's Spirit (Ro 14:1–15:13, Eph 2:11-3:15). Similarly, in the Revelation, we soon discover that it is no strange and unknown figure who appears to John on the Isle of Patmos and later rides forth to rescue a suffering people. No, indeed, both the mysterious Son of Man (1:13) and the rider on the white horse (19:11–16) are none other than the risen Lord himself, who, because he was slain, is worthy to receive all glory, dominion, power, and majesty (5:9–14).

Thus, with all the rich variety of expression in the New Testament, the gospel—the message of the crucified and risen Lord—stands as a kind of coherent center, a theological core, of early Christian literature. The books of the New Testament, as diverse literary expressions, were each intended to meet the specific needs of specific people in light of the grand and glorious center, the news that God had acted decisively to save his people through the crucified and resurrected Jesus. If this is so, however, this gospel unity is more than an interesting historical fact about the New Testament, and it is certainly not an artificially deduced synthesis of a collection of ancient, diverse books. Rather, it reflects what may have been the heart and *theological criterion* of a (perhaps unconscious) way of living and thinking in normative, early Christian experience.

Seen in this way, I am convinced that the problem of unity and diversity offers a significant clue to the reconstruction of at least some of the historical processes that led to the emergence of the New Testament as sacred literature. Indeed, I will argue that the theological core of the New Testament constituted a *theological* canon—a kind of conceptual organizing principle— that explains the development of the *literary* canon, i.e., the placement of the individual books of the New Testament into a single collection of sacred literature. Or, to put it the other way around, the proper starting point for any discussion of the theological and literary diversity of the New Testament is the historical fact of its unity in the form of a canon: i.e., as an established list of authoritative books suitable for use by the churches. What, however, were the forces that produced this collection and thus, in some sense, presupposed and/or drew upon some level of coherence among the individual books?

HISTORICAL PARAMETERS

I will start with two relatively fixed points. The first is the beginning of the Christian movement, or the church, sometime around the advent of the fourth decade of the first century A.D. The other is the Easter Letter of Athanasius, bishop of Alexandria, written in A.D. 367. The rise of the church may no doubt be attributed to the stupendous events that occurred in connection with the life of Jesus of Nazareth. A charismatic preacher, miracle worker, friend of sinners, and innovative interpreter of Jewish law, this Jesus was put to death at the instigation of the Jewish authorities during the procuratorship of Pontius Pilate. A series of dramatic resurrection appearances that began three days later, coupled with the fact of the empty tomb, convinced his disillusioned followers that he had been raised by God to absolute life. This fact, coupled with the profound religious experiences of the following Pentecost, propelled the new movement into the Roman world. Using what Christians now call the Old Testament as their Scriptures, these followers of the risen Lord formed churches, engaged in worship and benevolence, and especially through the impetus of persecution and their own sense of divinely ordained mission began to spread the message of the crucified and risen Lord throughout the Mediterranean world.

Some three centuries later, by the time of Athanasius, it could be written down—and was in fact (rather casually) in his Easter Letter of A.D. 367—that there were certain books (the twenty-seven that we now call the New Testament) acceptable for reading in worship. How we got from a movement that had only the Old Testament as its Scriptures to one that widely accepted a second collection of twenty-seven books as an addition to its Scriptures is another way of approaching the central question of this paper. That is, what were the forces, however diverse, that led toward and made possible the unified collection of sacred books we call the New Testament canon?

THE RISE OF INDIVIDUAL BOOKS
FROM APOSTOLIC TRADITION

In tracing the processes that led to the rise of given books of the New Testament, it is essential to understand that the early church had a theology before it had a New Testament. This point is rather obvious to those of us who spend our lives studying the origins of Christianity, but it is a point worth considering. Confessionally and doctrinally, of course, it is the other way around. We are accustomed to speaking of theology as a derivative of the New Testament. But, we must remember, it was not always the case that Christians had a New Testament. Assuming for the sake of argument that 1 Thessalonians, written about A.D. 50 or 51, represents the earliest of our twenty-seven New Testament documents, and assuming that Jesus died no later than the year A.D. 33, we are confronted with a period of nearly two decades in which early Christians prayed, preached, sang, worshiped, evangelized, and generally experienced the presence of the risen Lord in their midst without having at their disposal even one document of what we call the New Testament. Of course, even by the year A.D. 50, we are still decades away from a situation in which the books of the New Testament have in any significant way been copied, exchanged, circulated, and thus generally used in the major Christian congregations. Nonetheless, from the very beginning, the earliest Christians had a theology. The book of Acts, it may be recalled, specifically suggests that from Pentecost on there were certain things preached and believed by the leaders of early Christianity, convictions that set the Christian movement apart theologically from its Jewish and/or Hellenistic culture. Indeed, there is a substantial enough pattern (see below) in the entire collection of sermons in Acts to suggest to us that the early preachers shared a fairly consistent core of proclamation and belief.[2]

Not only do the early sermons attest to a common core—designated here as "apostolic theology"—of early Christian belief, but literary analysis of other portions of the New Testament has revealed that embedded within the documents are portions of early Christian hymns, confessions, and other tradition material that reflect the theology and beliefs of the very earliest generation of Christian teachers. For example, most New Testament scholars assume, based upon literary analysis of the passage, that Philippians 2:6–11 represents a hymn commonly sung by early Christians.[3] The same conclusion can be drawn concerning 1 Timothy 3:16 and 2 Timothy 2:11–13, where we find, in rhythmic Greek, passages that are specifically introduced as common confessional material. Apart from the interesting fact that these statements suggest that the highest Christology in the New Testament is in fact the earliest, and thus give the lie to evolutionary models of Christological development,[4] for current purposes I refer to these examples to confirm my earlier point: A consistent pattern of theology and belief that dates from the earliest period of Christian experience is reflected in the New Testament. That is, the pattern was established many decades prior to the New Testament documents themselves.[5]

Thus, though one finds variations of detail, analysis of the sermons in Acts as well as the confessional material throughout the New Testament suggests that early Christian teachers were convinced of several things,[6] particularly (1) that in connection with the events surrounding the person of Jesus, God had been acting in fulfillment of the ancient Jewish Scriptures; (2) that the crucifixion of Jesus had been ordained by God and was moreover a mighty act of conquest and deliverance for his people, as confirmed by God's vindication of Jesus in the Resurrection; (3) that this same crucified and risen Jesus had been exalted to a heavenly throne at the right hand of God and was thus installed as both Messiah and Lord, the supreme agent and executor of the kingdom of God; (4) that Jesus had poured out the Spirit of God upon his people and was thus himself present in their midst as the living Lord; (5) that this same Jesus would again be manifested to the world to vindicate his people and judge all the earth; and (6) that to participate in the saving work of God through Christ and thus to be included among the people of God, one must turn from sin and believe on the risen Christ as Messiah and Lord, confessing him through baptism in his name.

If it is asked where these early Christian leaders got their theology, the simple answer is that their theology reflects their own Jewish heritage on the one hand and their encounter with the life, teachings, and exaltation of Christ on the other. Wherever they obtained it, however much it continued to develop, as certainly it did with the passage of time, and however diverse it was in nuance and detail from one teacher/preacher to the next, a core of apostolic theology was nonetheless there from the beginning of the church. This core served as both historical predecessor of and intellectual substructure for the New Testament books, whose emergence in the context of varied historical situations we will now consider.

The Correspondence Literature

Let me begin by suggesting that we divide the New Testament into two parts: the narrative/historical material, and the correspondence material.[7] The narrative/historical material covers the four Gospels and Acts, the correspondence literature the rest of the New Testament. As to why the correspondence literature is written, the simple answer is that the given author could not be present to deliver his remarks in person.[8] The geographical expansion of Christianity had made the use of writing materials inevitable. The "epistle" was—most scholars agree—essentially a substitute for the apostolic presence.[9]

But that doesn't answer the question entirely. There were also circumstances in the life settings of both the recipients and the authors of the correspondence literature that called forth a given document. At Corinth, for example, we see that problems and questions related to division within the community, church discipline, lawsuits, sexual immorality, meat offered to idols, women praying and prophesying without their heads covered, drunkenness and quarreling at the Lord's table, the resurrection of the dead, and a proposed offering for Christians in Jerusalem, all contributed to the writing of what we now call 1 Corinthians. So it was for most of the correspondence literature. Questions and problems of a theological nature, sometimes of a very practical nature, concerns related to worship, heresy, church leadership, persecution, and the return of the Lord—all were factors contributing to the historical causes for given pieces of literature. Everything from a thank-you note for a gift of money (Philippians) to a highly symbolic answer to the question, "How long, O Lord, must we wait?" (Revelation), could be cited as reasons for writing.

The point being developed here, however, is really twofold. On the one hand, it is true to say that the New Testament literature is not a "systematic theology." That is, it does not represent a meticulous, systematic laying out of early Christian doctrine by topical arrangement. The literature was called forth by specific needs in either the life of the writer or the lives of the recipients, or in both. It is what we call "occasional literature," written to meet specific needs, for specific people, at a specific time in history. On the other hand, however, when we say that the New Testament writers did not write a systematic theology, we do not mean that they are not systematic *thinkers*. As I have already argued, from the very earliest days of the church, there was something I prefer to call "apostolic theology." There was a core of theological belief that when confronted with specific problems and needs, was able to adapt itself in response. At least one of the literary fruits of that theological, pastoral adaptation of the early theology to specific needs is the correspondence literature of the New Testament.

The Narrative/Historical Literature

The situation with regard to the narrative/historical material is somewhat different, though not completely unrelated. The Gospels and Acts are not so obviously pastoral or hortatory as the Epistles, but the teachings of Jesus and the apostles, as well as the example of their lives, certainly served a teaching function for early Christians, a fact that no doubt contributed to both the emergence and shape of the Gospels. The story of Jesus had an inherent value for those who confessed him as Lord. Accounts of his life, words, death, and resurrection were no doubt repeated to eager audiences countless times by those who had either seen and heard the Lord, or else knew those who had.[10] Eventually, various and concurrent factors such as the geographical spread of the gospel, the desire to preserve as accurately as possible the testimony of the apostles, the need to instruct new converts even in the absence of eyewitnesses, and conflict with alien religious forces both from within and without churches led to the production of what we now call Gospels.

The Gospels were something of a theological narrative of the essential (especially gospel) elements of the history of Jesus. That is, the story of Jesus was important as the background and basis of the apostolic preaching.[11] Indeed, the opening line of the Gospel of Mark describes the forthcoming literary production as "the beginning of the gospel of Jesus Christ." Thus, according to its expressed intention, what follows in Mark is *the historical genesis (the beginning) of the apostolic message about Jesus Christ*.[12] The Gospel of Luke likewise has its roots in the apostolic preaching, as seen from Luke's reference to the sources of his literary product as being those who were "eyewitnesses and ministers of the word" (1:2), where "word" is a common Lukan expression for the preached gospel (Ac 8:4; 14:25; 16:6; 17:11). Though probably not originally conceived as correspondence, that is, to be sent from one place to another,[13] the Gospels reflect the felt need in at least some early Christian communities to have an account of the words and deeds of Jesus. Believers desired particularly an account of the events of the last days leading up to and including his death and resurrection, events that constituted the historical basis of early Christian preaching and catechesis.

Thus, Gospel accounts of the teachings of Jesus, coupled with the events of his ministry, suffering, and resurrection, likewise reflect the "apostolic theology" of early Christianity, especially *vis-à-vis* its historical roots in the person and history of Jesus. Therefore, though the Gospels were no doubt written a number of decades after the lifetime of Jesus, it was the continued apostolic *preaching* of the death and resurrection of Jesus that gave decisive shape to the Gospels as we now have them, a reality attested by the fact that the central themes of early Christian preaching and teaching were also emphasized in the Gospels. It is no secret to anyone who has looked at the Gospels that the focus is upon the last eight days of Jesus' life, the period from Palm Sunday to Easter Sunday. His life and teachings prior to that were, of course, important for early Christians and certainly received significant, though differing, amounts of emphasis in our four Gospels. But it is no accident that the Gospels were given titles very early in Christian history (the Gospel According to Matthew, the Gospel According to Mark, etc.) that reflect the then still current assumption of a singular Christian message (the gospel[14]) with its focus upon certain central events, namely, the death and resurrection of Jesus for our salvation.[15]

As for Acts, its reason for being was also related to the gospel as the oral message of early apostolic preaching. If the "former treatise" (1:1) related, as "handed down" from those "who were eyewitnesses and ministers of the word" (Lk 1:2), the *historical basis* of the gospel—Luke's version "from the beginning" (Lk 1:3) of "the things accomplished among us" (Lk 1:1), especially with respect to what Jesus "did and taught" (1:1)—Acts, as its sequel,[16] is the subsequent history of the *progress* of the apostolic preaching. That is, Acts is an account of the spread of the gospel from its Jewish beginnings in Jerusalem to its acceptance by Gentiles in "the uttermost parts of the earth" (1:8). Luke's Gospel represents the historical basis of the "word"; Acts, its historical progress.[17] But for both works, the "word," the preached gospel, is the confessional behind each literary historical product. In both works, the "word" is operative as a shaping force in the author's present experience.

Summary and Conclusion

The great diversity of historical settings and circumstances standing behind the books of the New Testament accounts for its obvious theological variety. But underlying the evident theological and historical variety reflected in the New Testament is also a profound unity. The unity lies not in our ability to derive a classical, systematic theology from the New Testament. Rather, the unity of the New Testament is seen in the proclaimed theology—recovered by various historical, exegetical, and other critical means—that lies behind the New Testament. Thus, it could be argued that the New Testament as *literature* is the *product* of New Testament theology, where the latter expression suggests the earliest, theological sense of the phrase "New Testament." We, of course, from our later vantage point, must use the New Testament, as a literary collection, as the basis of New Testament theology. But we must always remember that behind these documents were Christian preachers and thinkers who had a consistent core of faith and belief. It is these central convictions that a proper New Testament theology seeks.

THE COEXISTENCE OF NEW TESTAMENT LITERATURE AND APOSTOLIC TRADITION

The Primacy of Christian Oral Tradition

What I have called "apostolic theology" is also called the "tradition of Christ" (cf. Col 2:6, 8) or simply "tradition" (1Co 11:2; 2Th 2:15; 3:6; cf. Ro 6:17; 1Co 11:23; 15:1, 3; Gal 1:9, 12; Php 4:9; 1Ti 1:18; 2Ti 2:2; Jude 3) in the New Testament period. The word "tradition" usually has negative connotations for us, but in the New Testament literature "tradition" may be either positive or negative. Certainly Jesus loudly criticized the tradition of the Pharisees because he believed that they had thereby subverted the clear intent of the Scriptures (Mt 15:1–8). Paul, too, for example, warned the Colossians against the "traditions of men" (2:8). On the other hand, the gospel is also referred to as tradition (1Co 15:1, 3; Gal 1:9, 12), and it is this word that in fact still captures for us the character of much that happened in the earliest decades of the first century A.D.

The man Jesus appeared on the Jewish scene as a miracle

worker and teacher of dramatic, if not provocative, presence. Though the reasons for his break with the religio-political leaders of Judaism were no doubt many, in tracing the cause of his eventual death at their hands one must surely begin with an account of his *halakah*, that is, his interpretations of Jewish Scripture, law, and tradition, which to them were utterly unacceptable. His teaching tradition, moreover, was dramatically reinforced by his lifestyle. His outspoken criticism of the rabbinic traditions of scriptural exegesis (Mt 5:17–48; Mk 7:1–13), his mockery of the Pharisees for their ritual observances done in the absence of "the weightier matters of the law" (Mt 23:23), his numerous run-ins with religious authorities regarding Sabbath-keeping—including his willingness not only to heal on the Sabbath (Lk 6:6ff.; 13:10–17; 14:1–6) but to permit his disciples to gather grain on the Sabbath and then justify their actions by calling himself "Lord of the Sabbath" (Mk 2:23–28)—and his disconcerting words about the status and future of the temple in Judaism (Mt 2:16; Jn 2:19; cf. Mt 26:61) put him on a certain collision course with the religious authorities. To be sure, his willingness to accept the ritually impure into the kingdom of God, his belittling of pharisaical fastidiousness, his nonascetical view of life, and his willingness to eat and drink with sinners made him popular with the crowds. But the same actions served only to deepen the religious establishment's resentment and fear of him. The Galilean rabbi had to be suppressed.

It must be noticed that Jesus nowhere seems to have disagreed with the religious authorities on questions of inspiration, text, or canon. No doubt he was accused of rejecting Moses and the Scriptures, but such accusations are commonly made of those whose interpretations of Scripture are being rejected. Besides, Jesus seems to have countered such accusations with his own declarations of faithfulness to the Law and the Prophets (Mt 5:17–20). Of course, he criticized the religious establishment for *their* traditions that, he argued, functionally supplanted the Scriptures (Mt 15:1–12). But the arguments of each were nonetheless essentially arguments regarding matters of interpretation: the authority, tradition, and/or law of Jesus on the one hand[18] versus the authority and traditions of the elders (Mt 15:2; Mk 7:3) on the other. Jesus himself could often be heard asking the teachers of the Law, no doubt with irony, if not sarcasm, "Have you not read. . . ?" (Mt 12:3; 21:42; 22:31;

Mk 2:25). Ultimately, his tradition, his teaching, his *torah*, were too radical, too different, and too threatening to their perceptions of Jewish identity to go unchallenged. And that is to say nothing of the political threat that it posed for them *vis-à-vis*, their status in Jewish/Roman society.

With regard to a distinctive tradition, the same was true of the followers of Jesus. The "tradition of Jesus" (meaning *both* the interpretive tradition handed down by him and the apostolic interpretation of him[19]), which received its decisive illumination in his death and resurrection, stands as the point of division between primitive Christianity and Judaism. Of course, Christianity was first regarded as a sectarian movement *within* Judaism, but its theological claims soon tested the limits of official Judaism's patience. Christian views became but marginally tolerable, if at all. But even Jewish sanctions against Christianity reflect the latter's identity as an *internal* threat to the traditional faith of Judaism and force us to ask historically for the causes of the burgeoning split, at least some of which must have been the too radical, apparently anti-torah nature of the new "teaching" (Ac 4:18; 5:28, 40; cf. 6:13–14). The new sectarian movement experienced the arrest and flogging of some of its teachers (Ac 4, 5) and, rather early, even the death of one of its most dynamic—indeed, incitive—preachers (Ac 6–8). Among other things, i.e., various political developments that converged around the year A.D. 37,[20] the death of Stephen was certainly brought on as well by his theological challenge to the traditional role and ongoing authority of the law and the temple cultus in Jewish life (Ac 6:10–14; 7:46–50), a challenge that Stephen, according to Luke, provocatively and theologically tied to the betrayal and death of Jesus at the hands of the Jewish leaders (Ac 7:51–53).

The story of Philip's encounter with the Ethiopian eunuch (Ac 8:26–39) likewise illustrates this conflict of traditions between established first-century Judaism on the one hand and emergent (though still within Judaism) Christianity on the other.[21] The Ethiopian court official had been to Jerusalem to worship. He had surely heard the conflicting assertions of the historically brash and exegetically novel traditions of the followers of the crucified Nazarene over against the established orthodoxies of the more traditional scribes and Pharisees. When Philip first met the Ethiopian, the latter was already reading what was no doubt, by that time, a much-disputed text in

Jerusalem, i.e., the text of Isaiah 53 regarding the humble servant of Yahweh whose life "is removed from the earth" (v. 8). In Jerusalem the argument must have raged between Christians and Jews regarding the identity of the speaker. Did the prophet speak of himself (as no doubt many Jews had begun to argue), or did his enigmatic words refer to someone else (as no doubt the Christians had insisted)? There was no question as to which side of the debate Philip would take. Invited to join the Ethiopian in his chariot, Philip gave the text a decidedly Christocentric interpretation. Luke tells us that "beginning from this Scripture, he preached Jesus to him" (Ac 8:35).

Thus, in the earliest years, the conflict between church and synagogue did not *center upon* the authority, text, or canon of Scripture. Of course, the widespread Christian use of the Septuagint, the Greek Old Testament, led to Jewish reticence about the LXX in later years and eventually brought about its displacement for Jews by the Greek version of Aquila. Indeed, Jewish efforts at fixing the Hebrew Scriptures and canon toward the end of the first century A.D. may likewise be attributed in part to the emergence of Christianity and co-opting by Christians of the LXX, which had previously enjoyed significant popularity among most Jews.[22] But that debate over the authentic text and/or translation of the (Old Testament) Scriptures was for later generations. In the earliest days, Christians and Jews did not argue over the authority, text, or canon of Scripture. It was the *interpretation* of Scripture that divided them. Early Christians, believing that the resurrection of Jesus had vindicated him before his detractors (he is Lord of all), as a matter of course accepted as authoritative the tradition of Jesus—that is, *his* understanding of the mysteries, ways, and laws of God as revealed in Holy Scripture. The word of Jesus was authoritative. It was a law/Torah/tradition that included his teachings, the events of his life, and the culminating expression/vindication of his interpretation(s) of Scripture and his messianic mission in his death and resurrection.[23] Early Christian tradition, therefore, had the gospel events at its heart, which of necessity also involved the Christian understanding of the ancient Scriptures—an interpretive perspective that in its central features was no doubt learned from Jesus.[24]

Therefore, with regard to religious authority, it seems that the earliest formative/normative center of the Christian movement lay in the apostolic *theology*, a largely oral tradition of preaching and teaching. But the apostolic message did not stand alone as a merely conceptual/doctrinal authority unto itself. Rather, it was the early consensus interpretation—seen against the backdrop of the Jewish Scriptures[25]—of *certain historical events* that were believed to be divine acts of salvation. That is, the apostolic tradition had its historical roots in the life, i.e., teachings, death, and resurrection, of Jesus of Nazareth. The tradition was proclaimed and preserved by a body of eyewitnesses and/or bearers of the authentic tradition, and was both interpretively shaped by early Christian teachers in the spiritual experience of the church (cf. Eph 2:19–3:11) and continually reapplied, either in person or in writing, to new situations of life encountered by the earliest groups of believers.

While we may assume, therefore, that the letters, for example, of the New Testament were not thought of as Scripture by the original authors or readers of those documents, they were nonetheless literary applications of apostolic tradition and thus were both certainly perceived and intended from the beginning as *authoritative* pieces of communication. In this regard, it may be noted that apostolicity was nearly always a significant feature of the correspondence literature. The letters, then, are a kind of literary crystallization of the apostolic tradition at a given point in time, in response to a given situation. The correspondence literature is, therefore, in occasional form, a specialized case, or subset, if you will, of the primitive tradition. Again, though the letters were certainly not thought of as Scripture either by the original authors or recipients, they were certainly intended—and no doubt regarded—as possessing religious authority. With the exception of Hebrews, all the correspondence literature of the New Testament had the name of a noteworthy apostle attached to it. In fact, even Hebrews, with its somewhat checkered canonical career, may in part owe its inclusion in the canon to its presumed Pauline authorship; that would be so in some early circles at any rate. To be sure, the book does show some connection with the Pauline circle of theology.

Much the same can be said for the narrative literature. However different the situations may have been that called forth the narrative literature, especially the Gospels, they represent in narrative form the historical basis of early Christian tradition and thus surely reproduce much of the early Christian teaching and/or catechesis. As such, the Gospels, like the Epistles, were an "occasional" literary subset of the broader, authoritative, and oral, apostolic tradition.

The Decline of the Oral Tradition

The next stage in the transition from tradition to Scripture may be seen in the passing of time and the natural consequences thereof. The spread of the gospel into areas that were geographically remote from its origins, the loss of first-generation apostolic presence and apostolic memory as well as the fact that *writing*, in the very nature of the case, *tends to displace memory*[26] are all factors that led to the eventual decline of the authoritative oral traditions. They were superseded by the written apostolic tradition, which was rapidly becoming indispensable. A brief look at Ignatius of Antioch and Papias of Hierapolis will serve to illustrate and somewhat demonstrate the transition from oral to written tradition with respect to the increased investment in the latter of religious (theological and historical) authority.[27]

Ignatius, the bishop of Antioch, whose death may be dated in either A.D. 108 or 116,[28] seems clearly on the one hand to have known much of the New Testament literature (especially Matthew, Johannine traditions, and the letters of Paul). But on the other hand he seems to have *preferred* the living prophetic voice (*Phld.* 6.1; 8.2; 9.2; *Smyrn.* 5.1; 7.2). Certainly Ignatius never referred to any of the New Testament materials as Scripture nor did he associate what appear to us to be New Testament literary traditions[29] with the traditional categories and/or formulas suggestive of the use of Scripture. Papias, fragments of whose work are preserved for us only by Eusebius, was bishop of Hierapolis and a contemporary of Ignatius, though Papias outlived him some fifteen to twenty years. Papias clearly stated his preference for the "living voice" of tradition (EH 3.39.4), but it is not clear that such a preference had to do with oral sayings of Jesus over against their written form, as some have interpreted the purpose of his no longer extant five-volume work on the *Explanation of the Sayings of the Lord* (*logiōn kuriakōn exēgēsis*). Papias's preference may have been more a general statement about historical method with respect to his examination of the origins and meaning of certain already existent *written* "reports" (*logia*), i.e., our Gospels. That is, Papias, in his investigation of the historical background of the Gospels, preferred, as a matter of historical caution, the voice of those elders who were in a historical line with the Lord and/or the disciples of the Lord as opposed to either wordy or secondary written sources. However, whatever view one takes of the purpose of Papias' work, whether it was to recover unrecorded sayings of Jesus or to comment upon the meaning and origin of certain already existent texts (our Gospels), we may conclude that by about A.D. 120 not much oral material was left to be found that was not already included in the Gospels. This view assumes that Eusebius or others who had access to Papias' work would have preserved for us other sayings of Jesus that are not in the Gospels, as was apparently the case with the fertility logion.[30] A.D. 120 is a convenient and reliable approximation of the final decline of the oral tradition and the emerging dominance of the written traditions for other reasons as well. In this connection, the use of the word "gospel" also provides an illuminating window into that historical transition.

The evidence is strong that generally in second-century papyri the four canonical Gospels were called, "The Gospel According to Matthew," "The Gospel According to Mark," and so on. It is evident that the use of the word gospel had a kind of collective, or unitary, function in these titles. That is, "gospel" was a reference to the basic Christian message. Its use in the second-century titles of our Gospels implies the individual quality of each book as a version of that preached message otherwise known as the "gospel." In other words, we have "Matthew's Version of the Gospel," or "Mark's Version of the Gospel." Or we could speak of "The Message that We Preach According to the Testimony of Luke" or ". . . John." Similar conclusions may be drawn for the word gospel as employed in the New Testament itself, where the noun is found seventy-seven times and is *always* used in a collective/unitary sense to refer to a preached, oral message. Thus, the collective notion of "gospel," as reflected in the New Testament documents, is still in use at the time of the application of the titles in the second century.[31]

The Apostolic Fathers, a general designation for referring to the earliest post-biblical literature up to about the year A.D. 120, likewise continued this unitary, or collective, sense of the word "gospel." In the *Didache*, the *Epistle of Barnabas*, and Ignatius, where the noun "gospel" is used, it is found *only in the collective sense* of the good news preached by Jesus and the early church. In fact, it is this pattern in the Apostolic Fathers that convinces many scholars (including me) that the traditional titles of our four Gospels must have been given sometime not much later than the beginning of the second century, i.e., around A.D. 100. By the middle of the second century, however, the situation had changed. Justin Martyr, who died around A.D. 165, clearly uses "gospel" to refer to a book (see *Apology* 1.66.3 and *Dialogue* 100.1). Similarly, Irenaeus, about A.D. 180, referred to the "four Gospels" (*Against Heresies* 3.1.1). Therefore, in the first part of the second century (up to about A.D. 120), "gospel" still seems exclusively to have referred to a message. As such it would seem to bear witness to the continued existence, as late as the first or second decade of the second century, of a living Christian tradition that *was not yet completely displaced* by those literary products, *though it coexisted* with some important and no doubt influential written expressions of that tradition (various New Testament documents).

But the memory of the apostolic voice was soon to fade. Indeed, as stated earlier, the mere fact that apostolic tradition had been written down—i.e., had taken on varied literary embodiments depending upon the occasions that called it forth—likely contributed early on to the beginning of the process of the decline of the oral tradition. By A.D. 150, the authoritative apostolic writings had become indispensable. The Gospels, at least, were being read in worship alongside the writings of the prophets (Justin, *Apology,* 1.67) and could be appealed to with the religiously pregnant phrase, "it is written" (Justin, *Dialogue,* 100.1), a traditional introductory formula for Scripture. Eventually, the apostolic literature (various New Testament documents) became, among other things, the final link to the older, eyewitness generation. With such indispensability also undoubtedly came increased religious stature.

By the time of Irenaeus (ca. A.D. 180), the Gospels are sacred books and may be referred to as "Scripture" (*Against Heresies,* 1.1.3; 3.1.1). The same may be said of the letters of Paul (*Against Heresies,* 1.3.4). Indeed, if anything, for Irenaeus, the "living voice" is secondary, if not suspect, having been claimed by Gnostics as their authoritative key (*Against Heresies,* 3.2.1).

The Literary Traditions as Scripture

The transition from written, authoritative apostolic tradition to Scripture is the final stage in a process that extended from A.D. 33 until the middle of the second century A.D. Though the description of the apostolic writings as "Scripture" was not inevitable, it was not unnatural once the writings themselves, grouped in various collected bodies[32], in the absence of apostolic memory and with the continued loss of connection between church and synagogue, not only continued to be read alongside Old Testament Scripture in the churches but also finally became indispensable as the last link to the apostolic generation.

Some movement in that last step toward the label "Scripture" may also have come with the increased threat of the various gnostic movements in the second century. It is interesting to note in this connection that, as far as we know, the first commentary on a portion of the New Testament can be dated to the middle of the second century. Though his work is known to us only in fragmentary fashion through the work of Origen, the gnostic teacher Heracleon, who flourished from A.D. 145 to 180, is known to have written a commentary on the Gospel of John. Whether it was the emergence of actual written commentaries on New Testament books that encouraged the final shift in nomenclature (i.e., the use of the term "Scripture" with reference to various New Testament books) cannot be decided with certainty. Perhaps it was due to the kind of disputed interpretation and analysis of the apostolic literature that was already going on orally before the production of actual written commentaries and is only reflected in the written commentaries. It seems, however, that the rise of groups such as the various gnostic communities, which incorporated Christian language and confession into their alien metaphysical and mythological structures, must certainly have contributed to the emergent status of the various New Testament writings as Scripture.[33]

Of course, the gnostic connection and its mutual interpenetration with Judaism preceded the Christian era. Indeed, gnostic authors no doubt commented upon Old Testament Scripture before they did upon the authoritative apostolic literature. But a gnostic commentary on an apostolic document may well have created a new religious (ecclesiastical and theological) crisis. For when Ignatius, for example, was confronted by docetic teachers who appealed to written records, presumably Old Testament Scripture, he could appeal to the authoritative apostolic tradition, i.e., the traditional core of belief that included the birth of Jesus and his true suffering and resurrection. What, however, was to be done when it was no longer the Old Testament Scriptures that were misinterpreted, but *the apostolic traditions themselves*—that is, the very materials that had originally served as the hermeneutical/interpretive guidelines for understanding Old Testament Scripture?[34] One solution was to develop and/or employ theological summaries—themselves apparently comprised of traditional confessional material—*as the hermeneutical keys to the apostolic literature.*

We would suggest that the dying out of apostolic memory and oral tradition, and the thereby emergent status of the *written* (and collected) apostolic traditions as indispensable—as the only vital link to the early eyewitness generation—made inevitable the onset of debate over what we now call the New Testament materials, i.e., the written apostolic traditions themselves. As long as the apostolic traditions were oral, they were certainly authoritative, but were themselves not so much the object of scrutiny as they were the authoritative witness to other highly scrutinized matters: either the interpretation of Old Testament Scripture or historical events and words pertaining to Jesus and/or the apostles. But it is almost in the nature of the case that written materials themselves not only soon displace oral material, but themselves become the object of interpretive analysis.

In this same period of time, about the middle of the second century, a series of labels and/or categories *emerged to refer to the correct interpretation of the apostolic tradition itself.* Iranaeus and Tertullian refer to such things variously as "the rule of faith" (*regula fidei*),[35] "the truth" (*alētheias/veritatis*),[36] or "the canon/rule of truth" (*kanon tēs alētheias/regula veritatis*).[37] These labels do not refer so much to any given confession per se but to interpretive material that, while sounding like creedal material, had not yet been formalized as a creed. However, the "rule of faith" seems on a historical trajectory that began with what I have called the apostolic theology, was itself expressed early on in various confessional forms, and ended in some of the more classical creeds, for example, the Apostles' Creed. To be sure, the sociological function of the rule of faith was not unlike that of later, more formalized creeds, i.e., it served as an interpretive guideline to distinguish acceptable from unacceptable theology and thus to reveal those who are truly within the church and those who are heretics. But, more specifically, for Irenaeus the rule of faith served, among other things, as the standard for judging whether or not one had correctly interpreted *Scripture*, especially the apostolic Scriptures that, as both written and indispensable, were themselves now the object of both focus and abuse (*Against Heresies*, 1.8.1, 9.1, 9.4). Indeed, it may well be that the rise of a more formalized language and/or theological vocabulary of "inspiration" as applied to the apostolic (New Testament) documents was itself not only a natural outgrowth of the long-existent function of those texts, but also a response to the interpretive abuse of them by those outside the theological parameters of the *regula fidei*. The connection between the rule of faith and the interpretation of Scripture was still being evidenced by the beginning of the third century when Origen declared himself at liberty to interpret the Scriptures in his own "higher," "spiritual" senses, so long as he did not deny the ground floor of belief, that is, the rule of faith.[38]

In summary, I would suggest that the transition in religious status for the various New Testament writings—from authoritative literary tradition to Scripture—took place for several reasons. First, it *could* happen because the once oral, but always authoritative, apostolic tradition became reflected in written (albeit "occasional") form. Second, a complex of factors relating to the geographical expansion of Christianity, the collection/grouping of the materials, a growing distance between church and synagogue, and the loss of apostolic presence and memory led to the increased functional status of the written materials over the oral traditions inasmuch as the written materials became an indispensable link to the authoritative apostolic tradition. Third, as the collected materials themselves became indispensable, indeed, once they began to function as such (i.e., as an indispensable collection) within the life and especially the worship of the church, they began de facto to function on a par with Old Testament Scripture and may well in that setting have first received the appellation of "Scripture." Finally, once the written materials themselves became no longer the interpretive key to the Old Testament Scriptures, but became also themselves the object of reflection and analysis, it was not unnatural to see the written traditions given the authoritative title "Scripture." This phenomenon was made necessary first of all by the ever-increasing distance between the original authors/settings and those who used the materials, and, second, by sectarian debate. What had already begun to function as Scripture had to be defended as Scripture.[39]

FROM SCRIPTURE TO CANON

The path toward Athanasius and his Easter Letter of A.D. 367 was thus set by virtually the middle and/or end of the second century A.D. Of course, a great deal of sorting and sifting out was still to be done. The arduous task of preserving, copying, collecting, excluding, and sharing the apostolic materials was still in its infancy, but the use of the label "Scripture" to refer to portions of what we now call the New Testament came into practice. Issues related to the number, order, and textual shape of the New Testament materials were still in various stages of transition. The core, however, was already established. Athanasius no more created the canon than modern day politicians create opinion; rather, he reflected the emerging consensus. His letter was only one result of a long process that had gone on at much lower levels in the life and related experiences not of "the" church, but of hundreds of communities of faith scattered about the Mediterranean world.

The core of what eventually came to be the list of authoritative books was functionally set probably no later than the earliest decades of the second century. Many scholars have argued that Marcion was the driving force behind the creation of an orthodox canon of Scripture, but Marcion probably played no more a part, and possibly less, than the gnostic and other heretical movements of the second century in forcing the more traditional churches to establish as clearly as possible their historical links with Jesus and the apostles.[40] The four Gospels and the traditional Pauline corpus were already being collected by the beginning of the second century, a phenomenon that itself certainly facilitated their eventual perception as Scripture.[41] The very fact that the Gospels were given titles suggests that they were being used and/or bound together. There are signs in the New Testament itself that some at least of the Pauline letters were being collected, perhaps even within his lifetime, and circulated among various churches (Gal 1:1; Eph 1:1; Col 4:16; cf. 2Ti 4:13 and 2Pe 3:15, 16[42]). Certainly the beginning of the second century is not too early to assume some sort of collection of most of what we call the traditional Pauline letters. The rest of the New Testament books had greater or lesser degrees of success in finding acceptance, with 2 Peter, Hebrews, and James having perhaps the greatest difficulties.[43] But even these books were ultimately, if not originally, associated with the names of leading apostles and therefore were being widely used in the second century.

To be sure, materials that are not a part of our New Testament were also used in the churches. The *Shepherd of Hermas*, *First Clement*, and the *Didache*, for example, were widely read and appreciated in the second century.[44] Ultimately, however, a number of criteria coalesced to leave us with the twenty-seven documents that comprise our current list. I would highlight the three factors of apostolic theology, apostolic connection (which was the guarantee of apostolic tradition and thus its handmaiden), and use in the churches as being the three major, mutually interrelated criteria that finally led to the various lists of authoritative books that began to circulate from the middle to late second century[45] and ultimately to the list referred to by Athanasius in A.D. 367.

The canonical process was precisely that—a process. The books of the New Testament did not become authoritative because they were canonical. Rather, they became canonical because they were already authoritative. That is, they were regarded first as authoritative, then as Scripture, and finally as canonical (exclusively acceptable for use in worship as Scripture). This was so because they contain the apostolic theology,[46] and they represented in the face of heretical challenges a link to the generation of Jesus and the apostles (the link itself being the guarantee of the authoritative traditions), and because the sheer experience of repeated use in the churches caused people to affirm the religious value of these books as media for the voice of God.

CONCLUSIONS

This study began by alluding to the importance of this topic for Christian thinking and confession today. I propose to conclude my remarks by returning to that arena and therefore offer the following three observations.

First, I'm convinced that the discussion in some circles over the authority of the original manuscripts, though well-intended, is theologically shortsighted. Certainly, there is a meaningful sense in which one can speak of original manuscripts and their inspiration. That is, if we have a document now, then sometime, at some place, someone must have put pen to paper and, with the use of some combination of sources and literary creativity, produced something that we could legitimately call an "original"—i.e., an ultimate textual forefather—in relationship to the given document in our possession. But it seems to me that such statements often imply too severe a stricture upon the fuller process that Christians have traditionally regarded as the work of God. To speak of the authority of the New Testament is to refer not only to the nature of the given texts, but to say something about a *collection* of texts, and thus to imply something about the limits of that collection. But as we have seen in this study, the acknowledged authority of the individual documents (an authority both perceived and intended even from their inception, as I would argue) and/or various subcollections of those documents was a phenomenon that historically *preceded* the final shaking out of the limits of that collection, i.e., the historical emergence of consensus regarding the canon. This means that in probably every case it was not an original manuscript that was first called "Scripture" and/or later deemed canonical by Christians of the second, third, and fourth centuries A.D.; rather, it was no doubt copies of the originals, handed down for decades, if not in some cases a couple of centuries, that were first regarded as Scripture. We must not preemptively cut God out of the longer historical process of canonization, which, ironically, is precisely what they do who limit theological authority to the original manuscripts.

The *limits* of the canon are just as important religiously and theologically as the inspiration and authority of the individual literary parts. Put another way, in the case of Scripture, divine authority is not only tied to inspiration (*if* that term may be limited to activities related to the *production* of "original" texts) but also to canonicity. This is so where canonicity relates to the historically worked out delimitation—with the use all through the earliest decades of what were no doubt *not* original manuscripts—of what in fact could and could not be regarded as Scripture and thus as authoritative. Though the authority of the individual books preceded their canonicity, it was ultimately the latter that, at least in the implicit if not explicit act of excluding certain documents, pronounced limits upon the extent and nature of their *collective* authority. Thus, we may and should confess the authority of the *canonical* Scriptures.[47] Such a confession of course does not obviate the text-critical task; indeed, it makes it all the more significant, for such a confession places us squarely within the tradition of our earliest Christian forebears who confessed the inspiration and authority of their non-original but historically received texts. However we deal (as they at some level must have done as well) with and critically analyze our received texts,[48] it is still the "received as canonical" text—and not by a now hopelessly irretrievable original text—that we confess to be true and faithful. It is the Scripture we read in church which, when rightly interpreted, tell us the truth about God, ourselves, the world, and salvation.

Second, speaking of interpretation, if anything is to be learned from the study of canon it is the importance of interpretation. Early Christians did not regard themselves as Christian simply because they possessed an authoritative text. No doubt they were glad to have their sacred collection of books (initially only what we now call the Old Testament), as indeed we should be to have ours. Most Christians are unashamed to confess their commitment to the authority of the Bible. But we must not assume that, having declared our commitment to the authority of Scripture, we have now made ourselves fully, or even adequately, Christian. In the history of Christendom, virtually every branch, limb, and twig of the visible church has pronounced upon its commitment to the authority of the Scriptures. Such commitments are commonly attested among the ranks of Baptists, Lutherans, Roman Catholics, Methodists, and Jehovah's Witnesses. But surely none would disagree to the proposition that there are significant theological differences among, say, Baptists, Jehovah's Witnesses, and Roman Catholics. One sometimes hears a kind of ecumenically pious maxim that suggests that as long as you believe in the authority of the Bible, it does not matter how you interpret it. I disagree. It seems to me possible to make the parameters of faith and fellowship either too broad or too narrow, but in either case there are interpretive parameters being employed, however much we continue to work, as we must, toward the enunciation and clarification of those parameters. What is at stake in such matters is the appropriation of historically and theologically *legitimate* parameters. If the Scriptures themselves are to provide any relevant clues in these matters, it would seem that what has herein been called the "apostolic theology" is historically and theologically the proper place to start. Put another way, good theology must not only confess biblical authority, but it must have a biblical "shape." This writer believes in the authority of the Bible, *as correctly interpreted*, and thus not necessarily in every interpretation of those who loudly proclaim its authority. We must do our best to seek the center of the New Testament, to research its own internal parameters of interpretation, and, under the guidance of God's Spirit, to live our lives together as faithful witnesses to its truths.

Third, I think the canon still has a valuable role to play in both Christian confession and scholarly research. Its value for Christian confession will certainly continue, if for no other reason but by the sheer dint of tradition. But more than that, a list of authoritative books has value not only for confession but also for historical research by virtue of the fact that the canon stands as a literary witness to a theological unity. Put another way, the fact is that we have a canon. For some set of reasons, at least one of which must be theological, these books have been bound together. It is just as important for the historian/theologian as it is for the believer to understand the conceptual unity that underlies this collection of diverse literature. There is a unity underlying this diversity. I hasten to add, however, that the unity lies not so much on the literary level as it does on a historical/theological level. That is, when we focus our attention both as worshipers and as scholars upon this particular collection of literature, we must remember that we are not purely literary critics. There are people, situations, and living ideas that lie behind and underneath these texts. Indeed, I've discovered that the problem of the canon for both theology and confession is that the distinctives of the various books tend to be flattened out when what was originally an isolated literary piece is transplanted to a new setting, i.e., a literary *collection*. The various problems and specific historical needs that brought each individual piece into being can easily be obscured when individual books are studied only in the light of one another. When either academic research or ecclesiastical confession becomes focused upon these documents only as collected documents, and ignores the history, the people, and the particularities, i.e., the social and political environments in which the documents emerged, it becomes stultified. For confession, the preempted result can be interpretive schemas that may have a certain inner-canonical coherence but are in fact misrepresentations of the texts due to anachronisms and/or other failures at the point of historically responsible reading. For research, a kind of scholasticism can emerge that never truly discovers new models of understanding even though it may develop new labels for old methods. Ultimately this must fail because, often under the guise of "literary" analysis, it ignores the complexities of life behind the texts, as mandated to research by, for example, the historic function of the texts themselves within the lives of people and communities of faith.

On the other hand, while the tendency of literary collections to overwhelm the historical distinctives of the individual pieces must be respected, it ought to be neither exaggerated nor feared. The academic tendency to eliminate the canon for the sake of recovering the historical particularity of each individual piece also brings an immeasurable loss, one that is both confessional and historical in significance. The fact that individual works could be put into a unified collection tells us not only something about the historical forces that drove toward coherency, but also something about the individual pieces themselves and the way in which they were historically understood. Moreover, the unified religious, historical, and theological experiences and convictions that gave rise to the individual literary pieces themselves were probably not completely unlike those that also preserved and collected the individual works. History, theology, and canon are inextricably linked. The existence of this literature in a collection is a historical fact, and we are obligated to understand why such diverse texts should have been bound together. Certainly, one of those reasons is the core of apostolic theology and tradition that existed from the earliest days of Christianity, a core that had its own historical beginnings—the history, teachings, suffering, and resurrection of Jesus. The study of the New Testament canon as a canon of sacred Scripture brings us back precisely to the very beginnings, not only of Christian history, but also of Christian confession. We are brought back to the historical person of Jesus Christ. As a devoted student of (Old Testament) Scripture himself, he is the adhesive binding of this new collection of sacred books. The crucified, risen, and exalted Lord is both the originating influence and the reflective object of the theology that eventually gave rise to the New Testament literature itself. In this as in other matters, he must forever stand at the center.

BIBLIOGRAPHY

Bruce, F. F. *The Canon of Scripture.* (Downers Grove, Ill.: InterVarsity, 1988).

_____ *Tradition Old and New.* (Grand Rapids: Zondervan, 1970).

Dunn, James D. G. *Unity and Diversity in the New Testament.* (Philadelphia: Westminster, 1977).

Goppelt, Leonhard. *Theology of the New Testament.* 2 vols., trans. John Alsup (Grand Rapids: Eerdmans, 1981, 1982).

Meade, David G. *Pseudonymity and Canon.* (Grand Rapids: Eerdmans, 1987).

Morris, Leon. *New Testament Theology.* (Grand Rapids: Zondervan, 1986).

Moule, C. F. D. *The Birth of the New Testament.* 3d rev. ed. (San Francisco: Harper, 1982).

Stendahl, Krister. "Biblical Theology," in *Interpreter's Dictionary of the Bible.* A–D (1962), 432–37.

NOTES

[1]Though this is not to deny that Greek *bios* literature may well provide the closest literary analogy for purposes of genre comparison, and for reading and understanding our Gospels. See Charles Talbert, *What is a Gospel?* (Philadelphia: Fortress, 1977). For a more nuanced view, see David E. Aune, *The New Testament in Its Literary Environment* (Philadelphia: Westminster, 1987), especially 17–76.

[2]See Bo Reicke, *Glaube und Leben der Urgemeinde* (Zürich: Zwingli, 1957), 39, where he refers to the speeches in Acts as representing that which is theologically "characteristic" of the early church. See also F. F. Bruce, *The Acts of the Apostles* (Grand Rapids: Eerdmans, 1951; repr., 1986), 18–21.

[3]See Ralph Martin, *Carmen Christi: Philippians ii:5–11 in Recent Interpretation and in the Setting of Early Christian Worship* (Cambridge: Cambridge University Press, 1967).

[4]Cf. C. F. D. Moule, *The Origin of Christology* (New York: Cambridge University Press, 1977), 1–10.

[5]This is not to deny the diversity, both literary and theological, alluded to earlier.

[6]Similar to C. H. Dodd, *The Apostolic Preaching and Its Developments* (London: Hodder and Stoughton, 1944), 17.

[7]Cf. W. G. Kümmel, *Introduction to the New Testament*, trans. A. J. Mattill, Jr. (Nashville: Abingdon, 1966), 9–11. Kümmel does not include the Apocalypse with the correspondence literature, though it clearly has certain epistolary features.

[8]Romans, which is best understood as a kind of advance letter (cf. also 2Co 10–13), is thus not strictly a substitute for the apostolic presence—i.e., it is its designed forerunner. My colleague Mikeal Parsons also suggests to me that Philemon likewise accomplishes things in apostolic absence that could not be so well done with apostolic presence. With these qualifiers, however, I think the general point about the apostolic letters serving as a substitute for the apostolic presence still stands.

[9]See Robert W. Funk, "The Apostolic *Parousia*: Form and Significance," in *Christian History and Interpretation: Studies Presented to John Knox*, ed. W. R. Farmer, C. F. D. Moule, and R. R. Niebuhr (Cambridge: Cambridge University Press, 1967), 249–68. See also Nils A. Dahl, "Letter," *Interpreter's Dictionary of the Bible*, suppl. vol. (Nashville: Abingdon, 1976), 538–41.

[10]A "problems"-oriented way of discussing the occasionality of a given piece should not be allowed to overwhelm the significance of other historical factors, e.g., sheer curiosity, devotion, etc. See T. W. Manson, *Studies in the Gospels and Epistles*, ed. Matthew Black (Philadelphia: Westminster, 1962), 3–12.

[11]Dodd, *Apostolic Preaching*, 30–31, 36–56.

[12]Bo Reicke, *The Roots of the Synoptic Gospels* (Philadelphia: Fortress, 1986), 152.

[13]This fact is perhaps, at least initially, the best suggestion as to why the Gospel authors do not state their names, in addition to the fact that they probably do not think of themselves as authors. See the discussion of these and related issues in Martin Hengel, *Studies in the Gospel of Mark* (Philadelphia: Fortress, 1985), 64–84.

[14]Again, note well that the word "gospel" in each title functions as a reference to the gospel as *message*, not a literary genre.

[15]See below for further discussion regarding the titles to the Gospels.

[16]Mikeal C. Parsons, "The Unity of the Lukan Writings: Rethinking the Opinio Communis," in *The Acts of the Apostles*, ed. Naymond H. Keathley (Waco, Tex.: Baylor University Press, forthcoming).

[17]Cf. W. C. van Unnik, "The 'Book of Acts' the Confirmation of the Gospel," *Novum Testamentum* 4 (1960): 26–59.

[18]It does not seem historically inappropriate to refer to Jesus' teachings with the word "law" given (a) the nature and contextual

force of his teachings as reported in the Matthean Sermon on the Mount, where not only do the introductory warnings (5:17–20) propose the words of Jesus as the fulfillment of the Law and the Prophets and as constituting a righteousness that is "greater" than that of the scribes and Pharisees but, more specifically, the "but I say to you" references are rhetorically juxtaposed to the commonly received interpretations of the Mosaic Law (5:21, 27, 33, 43); and (b) the repeated use of the term "law" in James (1:25; 2:8–12; 4:11, 12; 5:7–9) with at least some connection to the teachings of Jesus (cf. Mt 7:1–2). See Robert B. Sloan, "The Christology of James," *Criswell Theological Review* 1:1 (1986): 22–29.

[19]The apostolically interpreted gospel events (*about* Jesus) of the cross and Resurrection cannot finally be separated from the Jesus traditions initiated by him, e.g., Jas 1:18, 25; 2:8–12; 4:11, 12; 5:7–9, where gospel as "the word of truth" is called, or at least related to, the "law," the "law of liberty," the "royal law," etc., which are in turn related to some extent related to the teachings of Jesus. Sloan, ibid.; cf. Brevard S. Childs, *The New Testament as Canon: An Introduction* (Philadelphia: Fortress, 1984), 67–69, where Childs argues that (there is canonical significance in the fact that) in Matthew "the time of Jesus and the time of the church have been fused."

[20]Bo Reicke, *The New Testament Era*, trans. David E. Green (Philadelphia: Fortress, 1968), 190–91.

[21]See F. F. Bruce, *Tradition Old and New* (Grand Rapids: Zondervan, 1970), 74–86, for a helpful elaboration of this issue, especially the relationship between competing interpretive traditions that claim a common body of sacred text.

[22]See S. Jellicoe, *The Septuagint and Modern Study* (Ann Arbor: Eisenbrauns, 1978), 74–77.

[23]See note 19.

[24]"It is individual minds that originate. Whose was the originating mind here? . . .[T]he New Testament itself avers that it was Jesus Christ himself who first directed the minds of His followers to certain parts of the scriptures as those in which they might find illumination upon the meaning of His mission and destiny. . . . To account for the beginning of this most original and fruitful process of rethinking the Old Testament we found need to postulate a creative mind. The Gospels offer us one. Are we compelled to reject the offer?" C. H. Dodd, *According to the Scriptures* (New York: Scribner's, 1953), 110.

[25]The significance of the Scriptures for understanding the theology of Jesus and/or early Christianity would be difficult to overestimate. For an impressive illustration of this fact as well as an excellent treatment of intertextuality in Paul, see Richard B. Hays, *Echoes of Scripture in the Letters of Paul* (New Haven: Yale University Press, 1989).

[26]Regarding the relationship between orality and written materials, see Walter J. Ong, *Orality and Literacy* (London: Methuen, 1982).

[27]Dependence on the magisterial work of Reicke will be evident to those familiar with it; see Reicke, *The Roots of the Synoptic Gospels*, 45–47, 155–74.

[28]The A.D. 116 date is to be preferred. See Glanville Downey, *A History of Antioch in Syria* (Princeton: Princeton University Press, 1961), 292ff.

[29]This cautious way of referring to Ignatius' *apparent* use of New Testament materials is necessary because we may not often be certain that what looks to us in Ignatius to be a New Testament *literary* citation, allusion, or echo may not in fact have come to Ignatius in the form of an *oral* tradition. See Christian Maurer, *Ignatius von Antiochien und das Johannesevangelium* (Zürich: Zwingli, 1949).

[30]Irenaeus, *Adversus Haereses* 5.33.3, 4.

[31]Regarding these issues, see Hengel, *Studies in the Gospel of Mark*, 64–84; Reicke, *The Roots of the Synoptic Gospels*, 150–54; and the more recent work by Helmut Koester, "From the Kerygma-Gospel to Written Gospels," *New Testament Studies* 35 (1989): 361–81.

[32]Though not sufficient to explain the use of the term "Scripture" with regard to various New Testament documents, the fact of their collection seems to have been historically integral to the emergent process of their being so described. The religious value of the apostolic witness in terms of both personal authority and theological normativity—both a function of historical connection to Jesus—had been immediately accorded various individual documents and led no doubt to their repeated use and preservation. But the label "Scripture" seems historically to have been connected to *bodies* of sacred literature. The evidence seems to suggest that one document, unless it were presumed to be part of and/or inextricably linked to a larger collection of literature, would not be called "Scripture." Religious authority and value seem historically to have preceded canonicity, but the label "Scripture" seems to have required the process of collecting (which itself required the "collectibility" of the individual documents) as a necessary antecedent to its use. As suggested earlier, the preservation and ongoing use of individual documents may be explained in terms of their intrinsic historical and theological worth. Their *collection* (i.e., being grouped together in bodies or anthologies—great or small—of literature) seems to imply historical and theological commonalities among the documents. Once collected, however, fresh possibilities emerged, not the least of which was the functional (and increasingly favorable) comparison of the new apostolic literature with the ancient (Jewish) Scriptures.

[33]The role of Marcion has been reevaluated by several scholars in *The Second Century: A Journal of Early Christian Studies* 6 (Fall 1987–1988): Gerhard May, "Marcion in Contemporary Views: Results and Open Questions," 129–51; Han J. W. Drijvers, "Marcionism in Syria: Principles, Problems, Polemics," 153–72; R. Joseph Hoffmann, "How

Then Know This Troublous Teacher? Further Reflections on Marcion and his Church," 173–91. See also David Salter Williams, "Reconsidering Marcion's Gospel," *Journal of Biblical Literature* 108 (1989): 477–96.

[34]If the Gospel of John, as was certainly the case by the mid-second century, was part of a collected body of literature, the threat to one document may well have been felt as a threat to all and thus to the larger historical and theological traditions standing behind them.

[35]Tertullian, *De Praescriptione Haereticorum* 13; *De Virginibus Velandis* 1.3; *Adversus Praxean* 2:1–2.

[36]Irenaeus, *Adversus Haereses* 1.10.1; 3.2.1; 3.24.2; 4.26.2.

[37]Irenaeus, *Adversus Haereses* 1.9.4; 3.2.1.

[38]*De Principiis*, 1.Praef.2.

[39]The author is aware of the many attempts to use 2 Timothy 5:18 and 2 Peter 3:15, 16 as evidence that within the New Testament some portions refer to other portions as Scripture; see, e.g., Wayne Grudem, "Scripture's Self-Attestation and the Problem of Formulating a Doctrine of Scripture," in *Scripture and Truth*, ed. D. A. Carson and John D. Woodbridge (Grand Rapids: Zondervan, 1983), 46, 48; but the issues involved in each case are manifold and not easily resolved. In the case of 1 Timothy 5:18, the allusion to the saying contained in Luke 10:7 (assuming Luke's Gospel as the literary source for the saying) could well represent, taking the *kai* as epexegetic, the standard Christian interpretation (learned from Jesus) of Deuteronomy 25:4, so that the reference to "Scripture" in 1 Timothy 5:18 is a reference to Deuteronomy 25:4 and not Luke 10:7. In the case of 2 Peter 3:15, 16, the reference to "the rest of the Scriptures," an expression that seemingly includes the letters of Paul, may, but need not, be so understood. See Charles Bigg, *Epistles of St. Jude and St. Peter* (Edinburgh: T. & T. Clark, 1902), 301f.; see also Robert Sloan, "Response to David F. Wells," in *Evangelical Affirmations*, ed. Kenneth S. Kantzer and Carl F. H. Henry (Grand Rapids: Zondervan, 1990), 177–90.

[40]See note 33.

[41]See note 32.

[42]Of course, with 2 Peter, a lot depends on the date of the document. While I do not think Paul's letters are referred to in 3:15, 16 as "Scripture" (see note 39 above), it is nonetheless evident that at least some of Paul's letters were being collected, and presumably thereby accorded some kind of authoritative status by the time of 2 Peter's composition.

[43]See Theodor Zahn, *Grundriss der Geschichte des Neutestamentlichen Kanons*, 2d corr. ed. (Leipzig: A. Deichert, 1904), 14–35. See also Kurt Aland, *The Problem of the New Testament Canon* (Oxford: A. R. Mowbray, 1962), 8–13.

[44]Zahn, *Grundriss*, 22–27.

[45]F. W. Grosheide, ed., *Some Early Lists of the Books of the New Testament* (Leiden: Brill, 1948).

[46]To summarize: I am suggesting that the apostolic theology not only gave the individual books an intrinsic confessional and theological value but also served as a cohesive force that tended to draw the books together into intellectually and historically associated collections.

[47]See the essay by Mikael Parsons elsewhere in this volume.

[48]The task of analysis/interpretation is never done, beginning with the texts we receive and extending through all the processes of reading, exegesis, and synthesis which culminate in the proclamation of the Word.

Chapter Sixteen

The Development of Doctrine in the New Testament

Jerry W. McCant

Jerry W. McCant

Jerry W. McCant is Professor of Religion and Christian Education at Point Loma Nazarene College in San Diego, California. He holds the B.A. from Trevecca Nazarene College, the M.Div. from Nazarene Theological Seminary, and the Ph.D. from Emory University. Prior to his present position he held pastorates in North Carolina, Kentucky, and Georgia. His articles have appeared in *New Testament Studies*, *Wesleyan Theological Journal*, *Journal of Christian Education*, and numerous other journals. He has also authored *The Meaning of Church Membership* and *Teens and Self-Esteem*, both published by Nazarene Publishing House.

Chapter Sixteen

The Development of Doctrine in the New Testament

Doctrine is at the same time the most pervasive and the most elusive feature of New Testament interpretation.[1] If "theology" is the fundamental reason for most New Testament research,[2] one would expect doctrine to be both obvious and well-defined. However, even a cursory review of the New Testament reveals this to be a false assumption. Until the early 1800s, the church gave no attention to New Testament theology as a separate and distinct discipline.

What does one find in the New Testament? Three Synoptic Gospels have similar "Jesus stories" in narrative form. John contains discourses, signs, and revelation speeches of Jesus. Acts offers a "history" of the early church in Jerusalem and Paul's missionary journeys. Fourteen letters are attributed to Paul; seven general or catholic letters are attributed to other apostles. The last document in the canon[3] is an apocalypse.

Scholars have concluded that the New Testament "arose in response to quite particular needs or ambitions."[4] Everywhere in the New Testament we meet "theological conflicts and fierce quarrels between opponents."[5] Doctrine is certainly presupposed in the New Testament, but none of the documents provide abstract, systematic, or fully developed doctrines. Historical changes forced Christians to formulate doctrines that in the New Testament had been barely glimpsed. Doctrine is often implied but it is always "task theology," that is, "theology being written for or brought to bear on the task at hand."[6]

"Development of doctrine" is a phrase requiring elucidation. I do not claim that one can place New Testament doctrines on a linear scale extending from the simple teachings of Jesus to "higher" forms of the doctrine.[7] Nor am I interested in development that will ascertain what was "placed on the lips of Jesus" by the church.[8] At the same time, history is important, and we cannot explain all historical development by taking refuge in a doctrine of "progressive revelation."[9]

What is later is not necessarily better than nor superior to what is early in the New Testament. Among New Testament critics, there is a consensus that Philippians 2:5–11 is a pre-Pauline Christ hymn.[10] Christ hymns in Colossians 1:15–20 and John 1:1–18 are supposedly later, but they do not, in fact, represent "higher" Christologies. In this essay, "development" is meant to be a neutral and relatively value-free term.

Many books bear such titles as *A Theology of the New Testament*. However, New Testament theologians take freedom in discarding large sections of the canon. In Rudolf Bultmann's two-volume *Theology of the New Testament*, the word "theology" applies only to Pauline and Johannine literature.[11] W. G. Kümmel seeks theology in the major New Testament witnesses: Jesus, Paul, and John. But except for the section on Paul, "theology" is missing in all his chapter headings.[12]

Similarly, Hans Conzelmann seems to think Paul is the only theologian among New Testament writers.[13] Alan Richardson's work is based on a purely thematic approach.[14] With a thematic outline, Donald Guthrie goes to the authors who speak to the various themes.[15] Leon Morris treats all sections of the New Testament in a roughly chronological order, but within each section he reverts to a thematic approach.[16]

At the end of the last century, William Wrede argued that "the name New Testament theology is wrong in both its terms."[17] First, Christian literature is not restricted to the New Testament. Second, he argued that the New Testament is concerned with religion, not theology. A better subject, he said, would be "early Christian history of religion" or "the history of early Christian religion and theology."[18] J. Weiss[19] and W. Bousset[20] attempted approaches similar to Wrede's proposal. Wrede's goal was in the end unattainable, but some New Testament scholars still share his skepticism about the possibility of a theology of the New Testament.[21]

Whitehead defined speculative philosophy as "the endeavor to frame a coherent, logical, necessary system of general ideas in terms of which every element of our experience can be interpreted."[22] If theology assumes a coherent, logical, and necessary system, one can hardly speak of a New Testament theology. Boers has correctly observed that "Bultmann's theology of Paul may more appropriately be called a theology, not of Paul, but based on Paul, that is, a theology developed theoretically by Bultmann on the basis of hints provided by Paul."[23] Doctrinal elements abound in the New Testament, but there is no fully developed doctrine by a single New Testament author. Christian doctrine has been developed from the theological raw material of the New Testament.

DIVERSITY IN THE NEW TESTAMENT

That there is diversity in the New Testament is axiomatic among biblical scholars. Hardly anyone familiar with New Testament literature would challenge this claim. The most obvious form of diversity is literary: Gospels, Acts, Letters, and Apocalypse. Within each of these genres, other literary forms can be identified. In the Gospels one discovers sayings, parables, pronouncement stories, aphorisms, and passion-resurrection narratives. The letters employ exhortations, prayers, benedictions, apologies, healing stories, aretalogies, fools' speeches, diatribes, household codes, allegories, hymns, and other forms.

Prior to this century, the generally accepted view of orthodoxy was that in the earliest stages there was a single, clearly defined faith that separated Christians from heretics. Walter Bauer shattered that view and demonstrated that no "pure" form of Christianity existed in the second century.[24] Diverse forms of the Christian faith sometimes competed for the loyalties of believers. James D. G. Dunn[25] has pushed diversified Christian options all the way back to the New Testament itself.

Dunn finds four major streams in earliest Christianity.[26] In earliest Christianity, belief in Jesus marked a Jew as peculiar, but otherwise both they and their opponents considered them fully Jewish. By the end of the second century, however, Jewish Christians (i.e., Ebionites and Nazareans[27]) were heretics. Still, Christians canonized the Hebrew Bible and Jewish documents like Matthew and James. Hellenistic Christianity had its place, but its influence became intolerable in the form of gnosticism.[28] John's Gospel, the Corinthian correspondence, Colossians, the

Pastorals, and even Jude provide evidence of the influence of the Hellenistic stream.

Apocalyptic Christianity was canonized by the inclusion of 1 and 2 Thessalonians and Revelation. Some scholars argue that apocalyptic had a pervasive influence on the New Testament and that it is "the mother of Christian theology.[29] Early Catholicism is most evident in the Pastoral letters.[30] Convinced that we owe a great debt to early Catholicism, Elaine Pagels is of the opinion that

> had Christianity remained multiform, it might well have disappeared from history, along with dozens of rival religious cults of antiquity. I believe we owe the survival of Christian tradition to the organizational and theological structure that the emerging church developed. Anyone as powerfully attracted to Christianity as I am will regard that as a major achievement.[31]

Bultmann drew attention to this diversity of doctrinal interests in the New Testament era and observed that "a norm or an authoritative court of appeals for doctrine" is lacking throughout this period.[32] He quoted Käsemann with approval: "The New Testament canon . . . is the foundation of the multiplicity of confession."[33] Käsemann thinks John represents a "naive doceticism,"[34] and that Diotrophes in 3 John is orthodox while the elder is a "Christian gnostic."[35] Charlot goes so far as to say that "no theological position . . . is common to all writers and levels of tradition in the New Testament."[36] Is theological pluralism, then, the norm in the New Testament?

Only if one buries one's head in the sand is it possible any longer to deny the presence of doctrinal diversity in the New Testament. Mark's Jesus appears first as an adult, while Matthew and Luke have virgin birth stories; in Matthew, the Virgin Birth fulfills Isaiah 7:14, but not in Luke. John's Jesus was a preexistent Logos (i.e., "Word")[37] who appears first on the earthly scene as an adult, not as the Christ Child. The evangelists are interested in the historical Jesus,[38] but Paul is more concerned with the Christ of faith. James barely mentions Jesus (1:1, 2:1), and 3 John never even mentions Jesus.

Hebrews has a unique high priesthood Christology and discusses Jesus' heavenly ministry of intercession after the exaltation. In 1 Corinthians Paul mentions the practice of praying for the dead, and 1 Peter tells of Jesus' descent to

Hades between the time of the Crucifixion and the Resurrection.[39] Only in 2 Peter does the New Testament teach that heaven and earth will melt with fervent heat. John's Gospel has been described as "naive docetism," but 1 John is clearly and fiercely opposed to docetic Christology.

John urges the born-again experience but says almost nothing about sin, while Paul says much about sin but does not mention being born again. Synoptic evangelists stress the kingdom of God; John emphasizes eternal life; and Paul writes about being "in Christ."[40] Jesus is "Son of Man" in the Synoptics, "the Servant of God" in Acts; Paul called him "the second Adam" and Hebrews "the eternal high priest" like Melchizedek.

Diversity in the New Testament is important, and serious students of the New Testament should not minimize its importance. We cannot force every New Testament author to speak to every doctrinal issue, and we need not force authors to agree on every subject. However, we do need to consider seriously the possibility of unity in diversity in the New Testament. Students of the New Testament must not become so enchanted with analytical study that diversity is overemphasized. Stressing diversity for its own sake may become a form of pseudosophistication and pseudocritical scholarship.

UNITY IN THE NEW TESTAMENT

As early as 1931 E. H. Hoskyns and Noel Davey were saying that all the evidence converges on a single point: that in Jesus God was revealed for the salvation of humankind.[41] In his inaugural lecture at Cambridge, C. H. Dodd called for a new emphasis on the unity of the New Testament to replace the severely analytical approach of the preceding century. Dodd found the unity of the New Testament in the kerygma: the proclamation that the New Age has come in the person and mission of Jesus.[42] In later works, Dodd further developed his thesis.[43]

Floyd Filson contends that the New Testament's unity is found in Jesus' resurrection.[44] He thinks New Testament theology should understand New Testament history theologically, i.e., from the resurrection of Christ. A. M. Hunter argues for *Heilsgeschichte* (Ger., "story of salvation") as the basis for New Testament unity. *Heilsgeschichte* includes Christology, soteriology, and ecclesiology, "and these three are at bottom one—three strands in a single unity."[45]

Hunter is convinced of the New Testament's unity and that "NT study is making it ever plainer."[46] He concludes that "Of the analytic textbooks with their 'separate-compartment' chapters, each bearing its label—Synoptic, Pauline, Johannine, etc.—we have already more than enough."[47] Interestingly, when asked to write an introduction to New Testament theology, Hunter's structure served to highlight the diversity of the New Testament within its basic unity.[48]

Heilsgeschichte is for Cullmann a common conception of time and history and places Christ at the center of time.[49] "This age" has passed away, and in Christ "the age to come" is already present. Cullmann thinks there can be no *Heilsgeschichte* without Christology and no Christology without *Heilsgeschichte*.[50] This concept is the unifying force of the New Testament. "It is not as if the New Testament were a series of monographs like Kittel's theological wordbook."[51]

A few years ago G. E. Ladd confidently announced: "The analytic fashion of an earlier generation is now passé."[52] A quick review of scholarly New Testament literature since 1964 does not confirm Ladd's opinion.[53] He said, "The modern biblical theologian can no longer be satisfied to conclude his work with the reconstruction of a number of separate, independent theologies of *Lehrbegriffe*."[54] Unity in the New Testament is seen as "the visitation of men in the person and mission of Jesus Christ; diversity exists in the progressive unfolding of the divine visitation and in the various ways the one revelatory, redeeming event is capable of being interpreted."[55] For Ladd this means "the kingdom of God" = "Eternal Life" = "in Christ." In *A Theology of the New Testament* Ladd's consistent point of reference for unity is the kingdom of God.[56]

Donald Guthrie staunchly defends the unity of the New Testament.[57] He thinks the central figure of New Testament theology (i.e., Jesus) is the clue to unity. However, this is not enough because some scholars point to plural Christologies in the New Testament. Guthrie contends that Christological pluralism is "a misleading understanding of the evidence."[58] Christology unifies the New Testament, and Guthrie argues for only one Christology in the New Testament. So-called divergent Christologies only point to various aspects of Christology.

In his recent *New Testament Theology*, Leon Morris pleads

for unity. Using the words of A. M. Hunter, he argues that New Testament authors used "different idioms and different categories of thought." All diversities will "resolve themselves into a satisfying unity."[59] For him the canon itself argues for unity because "exactly the same twenty-seven books were practically universally accepted."[60] Indeed, "if there had not been some kind of unity, the various books would not have been accepted into the canon."[61] Thus, that which unites the canon is the conviction "that God had acted in Jesus of Nazareth, especially in his death and resurrection."[62]

Although he sees great doctrinal diversity in the New Testament, Bultmann has observed that "unity of doctrine was assured by the canon and not by some normative system of dogmatics."[63] Kümmel, who seeks for the "heart of the NT" from the "central" witnesses of the New Testament, comes to this conclusion:

> The question, to be posed in conclusion, of the common message of the major New Testament witnesses thus does not thrust itself upon us from the involvement with the proclamation of these witnesses themselves, who stand in no direct connection with one another, but from the awareness of their common membership in the canon of the New Testament.[64]

By canonizing diversities, the church assumed a kind of unreflected unity in the New Testament.

For centuries Christians assumed the unity of the New Testament. First, with Luther and since the middle of the eighteenth century, biblical studies have been done with historical-critical methodologies. Such study revealed that New Testament authors do not always say the same thing.[65] Boers reminds us that through the Middle Ages Christian theology did not try to think the thoughts of the biblical writers as distinct from their own. "They thought their own thoughts, which they took for granted as being in continuity with those of the biblical writers."[66] Apparently no one challenged the unity of the New Testament before the Reformation.

The Reformers insisted on Scripture alone as the basis and norm for all Christian life and thought. They wanted to establish the Bible's authority more firmly as the norm over against the church and its traditions. With the loss of tradition, however, the Bible was no longer an integral, contemporary part of the living tradition but was separated from it by an intervening history. Historical consciousness and the use of critical tools forced a confrontation with the question of unity.

Is there, then, any unity beyond that of the relative canonical unity conceded by Bultmann? In spite of the development of thought, Kümmel finds a certain unity in Jesus. The major witnesses, he says, agree on a twofold message:

> That God has caused his salvation promised for the end of the world to begin in Jesus Christ, and that in this Christ God has encountered us and intends to encounter us as the Father who seeks to rescue us from imprisonment in the world and to make us free for active love.[67]

All major witnesses in the New Testament proclaim a common message that in Jesus God has come to us in our world. Indeed, "Jesus is the central reference of all the books"[68] in the New Testament. Even Käsemann, who speaks of outright contradictions in the New Testament, believes that the revelation of Christ is the real clue to the New Testament. He has concluded that "all the documents, with varying degrees of explicitness and clarity of outline, are designed to witness to the lordship of Jesus."[69]

After a lengthy discussion of diversity in the New Testament and even of contradictions, Dunn offers a strong defense for "unity in diversity." He finds unity in nine areas: kerygma, primitive confession, tradition, use of the Old Testament, ministry, worship, sacraments, Spirit, and Christology.[70] Dunn admits many differences in the documents under these categories, but he consistently finds something commonly agreed upon, and held by all—a unified voice. Christology emerges as the most decisive feature from the previous eight considerations. Reference to Jesus unifies the New Testament documents. He concludes that "the argument of the different kerygmata in affirming that Jesus of Nazareth and the exalted Christ are one and the same, is the unifying core round which the diversity of New Testament Christianity coheres."[71]

AN APPROACH TO DEVELOPMENT

Since there is both unity and diversity in the New Testament, how may one demonstrate doctrinal development? Several approaches to the subject are available.[72] First, one may discuss the documents in their canonical order. Second, one may look at the various contexts of the church. Third, one may trace doctrinal developments in the New Testament's major witnesses. Fourth, it is possible to take several major doctrinal themes and survey what New Testament authors have to say.[73] Fifth, approaching the subject chronologically, one may trace doctrinal developments as the New Testament was written. Any of these approaches could yield helpful results.

My own approach will be slightly different from any of the aforementioned. There is a discernible unity in the New Testament, but within that unity one finds much diversity. Also, as Leon Morris has observed, "We cannot write a theology of Peter or James or even Paul, for in no case do we have sufficient material, or even an indication that the writer is giving us what he sees as most important for Christian theology."[74] No New Testament writer is a systematic theologian; no Christian doctrine is fully developed by a single author. Reference to and concern for Jesus binds the New Testament in canonical unity. Within that unity, there is diversity and development. I propose to trace that development of doctrinal concern for Jesus in roughly chronological order as the documents themselves developed, beginning with the Pauline corpus and concluding with the General Letters.[75]

DOCTRINAL DEVELOPMENT IN THE NEW TESTAMENT

Scholars, both liberal and conservative, generally agree that the Pauline letters are the earliest writings in the New Testament.[76] It is generally agreed that 1 Thessalonians was the first of these documents, but after that opinion varies as to the order of the letters. This problem is not serious since all of Paul's letters were written within about one decade, thus allowing little time for any substantial development in his doctrinal positions.[77] If one accepts only seven Pauline letters as authentic, it is possible for 1 Thessalonians to be first and Romans last. However, I accept all of the prison letters[78] as authentic and thus the last of Paul's letters.

The Pauline Letters

1. 1 Thessalonians. This letter is addressed to "the church of the Thessalonians in God the Father and the Lord Jesus

Christ" (1:1).[79] The combination "Lord Jesus Christ" occurs fifty-four times in Paul's letters. Both "Lord" and "Christ" are titles, but Paul nominalized them and they became names for Jesus. The Thessalonians were focusing on the death, resurrection, and return of Jesus. Paul had preached to them "the gospel of Christ" (3:2). Jesus traditions are everywhere presupposed in this letter (cf. 2:13).[80]

The "Lord Jesus" was killed by Jews (2:15), but "the Lord Jesus Christ" died for us (5:10).[81] Only in 4:14 does Paul ever say that "Jesus died and rose again" (as if by Jesus' own power); the efficiency of the Resurrection is elsewhere attributed to God (cf. 1Th 1:10; Gal 1:1; 1Co 6:14; 2Co 4:14; Ro 4:24; 8:11; 10:9). This same Jesus is expected to return (4:13–5:10; 5:23) at which time "the dead in Christ shall rise first" (4:16) and with the living they will be raptured away (4:17).[82] In 1 Thessalonians Christology is basically eschatological. The Christian life is primarily concerned with the expectation of the Parousia.[83]

2. 2 Thessalonians.[84] Pauline theology is predominantly Christology.[85] There are some definite shifts in emphasis from 1 Thessalonians. Readers still hear "our gospel" (2:14) and are exhorted "to hold to the [Pauline?] traditions" (2:15), but the death and resurrection of Jesus are not emphasized. Jesus is primarily "Lord" in 2 Thessalonians (1:1, 2, 7, 8, 9, 12; 2:1, 8, 13–14, 16; 3:1, 3, 4, 5, 6, 12, 16, 18). The great use of "Lord" may suggest an early date and Pauline authorship for 2 Thessalonians.[86] Paul implies the equality of Jesus with God (1:1; 2:16; 3:6).

False teachers had forged Paul's name on a letter and taught a kind of overrealized eschatology (2:2) that led to a libertarian ethic (3:6–15). In 1 Thessalonians Paul appears to believe the Parousia is imminent, even in his lifetime (4:15). But 2 Thessalonians (2:1–12) declares a delay in the Parousia; the "man of lawlessness" and apostasy must first come.[87] A restraining force was preventing the "man of lawlessness" from coming. When the restraint is removed, he will come and Jesus will slay him "with the breath of his mouth" (2:8). Jesus will punish persons who are afflicting Christians (1:5–10; cf. Rev 16:5–7); he will be accompanied by "his mighty angels with flaming fire" (1:7), "dealing out retribution" (1:8), but he will be "glorified in his saints" (1:10).

3. *Galatians.* An apologetic letter,[88] Galatians is a defense of "the gospel of Christ" (1:7) and of Paul's apostleship. The "apostle . . . of Jesus Christ" (1:1)[89] is so impassioned that the thanksgiving appearing in all of his other letters is missing. Jesus "gave himself for our sins" (1:4), and God "raised him from the dead" (1:1). The Galatians had deserted "the grace of Christ" for a "different gospel" (1:8), which is a distortion of "the gospel of Christ" (1:8). Anyone preaching a "different gospel" is twice cursed by Paul (1:8–9). Paul says that God revealed "his son in me that I might preach him among the Gentiles" (1:16).[90]

Here we first meet the Pauline phrase "justified by faith" (2:16).[91] Christ brought an end to the law, and if one is justified by the law, "Christ died needlessly" (2:21). Justification comes by "faith in Jesus Christ" (3:22); even Abraham and Hebrew Scripture with the Sarah-Hagar allegory "proves" his point (3:8; 3:11; cf. Hab. 2:4). Law served as a *paidagōgos* to "lead us to Christ" (3:24). In Christ there is complete equality (3:27–28) as Abraham's offspring (3:29). Circumcision is "the stumbling-block of the cross" (5:11) for persons wishing to avoid being "persecuted for the cross of Christ" (6:12), but Paul's only boast is "in the cross of our Lord Jesus Christ" (6:14). Paul's doctrine of Christ in Galatians is soteriological—the death of Christ and justification by faith.

4. *1 Corinthians.*[92] "Task theology" in 1 Corinthians is Christocentric. An allusion to Jesus' teaching is the basis for forbidding divorce (7:10–11; Mk 10:2–12). The apostle carefully distinguishes his opinions from the Lord's commands (7:6, 10, 12, 25, 40b). Here we have the earliest known record of the Lord's Supper (11:23–24). Paul preaches "the cross of Christ" (1:17–18) and "Christ and him crucified" (1:23; 2:2). Christ's death was salvific—he "died for our sins" (15:3)[93] and "you were justified in the name of our Lord Jesus Christ" (6:11). Tied to Paul's Jewish understanding, Christ is "our Passover" (5:7) and "the spiritual rock" (10:4) in the wilderness.

Jesus Christ is the foundation of the Corinthian church (3:11), and the church is "Christ's body" (12:27). Christians "belong to Christ" (3:23) because they "have been bought with a price" (6:20). Since Christ is not divided (1:13), the Corinthians are called to unity "by the name of Jesus Christ our Lord" (1:10), and the exhortation continues in chapters 12–14. Christians assemble for worship "in the name of our Lord Jesus

Christ" (5:4). Already Paul knows Christian traditions (11:2), and the most extensive New Testament treatment of the Resurrection is based on a traditional creedal statement (15:3–5; cf. 6:14).[94] Christ is "the last Adam" who is a "life-giving spirit" (15:45). Paul knows the early Christian confession "Jesus is Lord" (12:3). Believing Jesus will soon return (7:29), Paul recommended maintaining the status quo (7:17–24, 26), which is Paul's rule "in all the churches" (7:17). In his closing remarks Paul utters an Aramaic prayer: *Maranatha*—"Our Lord, come!" (16:22). Paul's doctrine of Christ in 1 Corinthians becomes the "solution" for dealing with local church problems.

5. *2 Corinthians.*[95] An "apostle of Jesus Christ" (1:1) and "ambassador of Christ" (5:20) defends his apostleship.[96] We now hear of "Christ's suffering" (1:5) and being crucified "because of weakness" (13:4). God's Son is God's "yes" (1:19) to the people of a new covenant, unlike that of Moses (3:7–15) because in Christ the veil has been removed. Christ is "the image of God" (4:4) and we have seen "the radiancy of the knowledge of the glory of Christ" (4:6). God raised "the Lord Jesus" and will also raise us (4:14).

Christ died and was raised "on their behalf" (5:15), and everyone "in Christ" is a "new creature" (5:17). But Christ also has a "judgment seat" (5:10). "God was in Christ reconciling the world to himself" (5:19) and became poor [preexistence?] so we could become rich (8:9). Christ's death and resurrection are the basis for Paul's apostolic defense (12:9–10; 13:4).

6. *Romans.*[97] A descendant of David, Jesus "was declared the Son of God with power by the resurrection from the dead" (1:3–4). Sin (chaps. 1–3) is met with redemption, "a propitiation" in the blood of Christ (3:25). Justification (3:25–30; chaps. 4–5) receives its fullest expression in Romans. Abraham and David were justified by faith, and promises made to Abraham were fulfilled in Jesus (4:24–25). Love caused Jesus to die for sinners (5:8) so that one might be "justified by his blood" (5:9).[98] Through Adam, sin entered the world (5:12), but Christ, the second Adam, countered sin with grace (5:19). Baptized persons, crucified and buried with Christ, are dead to sin (6:11). Justification results in eternal life (6:23).

Through Jesus Christ, who is "the end of the law" (10:4), believers have died to the law (7:6) and are free from any condemnation (8:1; cf. 5:18). Jesus died, was raised, and "is at the right hand of God, who also intercedes for us" (8:34).[99]

Paul's fellow-Jews have largely rejected Christ (chap. 9), but *anyone* who confesses "Jesus is Lord" will be saved (10:9), and finally "all Israel will be saved" (11:26). The church is "one body in Christ" (12:5) and fulfills the law with love (13:8). To be justified means to be "in Christ" (16:3; 7–13).

7. *Ephesians.*[100] God is "the Father of our Lord Jesus Christ" (1:3; cf. 1:17). Through Christ, there is adoption as the children of God (1:5) as well as "redemption through his blood, the forgiveness of our trespasses" (1:7). God raised Jesus from the dead and "seated him at his right hand in the heavenly places" (1:20). Christ is both the church's head (1:22–23; 4:15) and its cornerstone (2:20). Justification is by faith in Jesus Christ (2:5–10), by "the blood of Christ" (2:13).

Jesus has abolished the "dividing wall" (2:14) between Jews and Gentiles, reconciling them "through the cross" (2:15–16). The "mystery of Christ" is that Gentiles may also claim the covenant promise (3:3–6). The Jesus of Ephesians descended "into the lower parts of the earth" but then ascended "far above all the heavens" (4:9–10). Christ dwells in the hearts of believers (3:17), who are sealed in Christ by the Spirit (1:13) "for the day of redemption" (4:30). Christ loved the church and "gave himself up for us, an offering and sacrifice" (5:2), and the church is the bride of Christ (5:22–23). In Ephesians, Christology serves Paul's ecclesiology.[101]

8. *Philippians.*[102] Paul is still expecting the Parousia—"the day of Christ" (1:6, 10; 2:16), and apocalyptic hope is still present (3:20–21). A reference to "the Spirit of Jesus Christ" (1:19) raises the question of the relationship of the exalted Christ to the Spirit. The suffering, death, and resurrection of Jesus are important to the apostle (3:10), and he acknowledges that his righteousness is "through faith in Christ" (3:9). Atypical for Paul, the Lord Jesus Christ is also called "Savior" (3:20). It is Paul's testimony that Christ strengthens him to "do all things" (4:13).

The Christ hymn (2:5–11) is the richest source of the doctrine of Christ in this letter. From the hymn we learn that Jesus was preexistent, divine, and equal to God (2:6). Jesus emptied himself (i.e., kenotic Christology) and became human (2:7; i.e., Incarnation). Humility brought obedience, which Christ "learned" to the point of death on a cross (2:8). God has exalted Jesus and given him the name "Lord" (2:9–11)—every knee *should* bow and every tongue *should* confess that "Jesus Christ is Lord."

9. Colossians. As in Ephesians, God is "the Father of our Lord Jesus Christ" (1:3). Jesus is God's "beloved Son, in whom we have redemption, the forgiveness of sins" (1:13–14). Reconciliation has come through the Incarnation—"in his fleshly body through death" (1:22). Baptism (i.e., being buried with Christ in Romans) is the true circumcision in Colossians. Jesus took our "certificate of debt" and "nailed it to the cross" (2:14). The "revealing of Christ" (3:4) points again to the parousia. For "Christ is all and in all" (3:11).

As in Philippians, a Christ hymn (1:15–20) is a rich source for the doctrine of Christ. Jesus is divine because he is "the image of the invisible God" (1:15a) and the "firstborn of all creation" (1:15b). As the preexistent Creator, "all things have been created by him and for him" (1:16). It is he who holds the universe together (1:17). The "head of the church," Jesus is also "the firstborn from the dead" (1:18). Both human and divine, "all the fulness" is in him (1:19), that is, "in him, all the fulness of Deity dwells in bodily form" (2:9). A cosmic Christ, he has reconciled all things to himself "through the blood of the cross" (1:20).

10. Philemon. Any doctrine of Christ in Philemon is implicit,[103] but the whole letter presupposes Christ. Paul, "a prisoner of Christ Jesus," (1:1) was responsible for the conversion of both Onesimus (v. 10) and Philemon (v. 19). Conversion to Christ, according to Paul, has made one who was "useless" before "useful both to you and me" (v. 11).[104] The apostle forfeits his right to apostolic authority and "requests" that Philemon receive Onesimus back, not as a slave, but as "a beloved brother" (v. 16). Paul perceived that faith in Jesus Christ would reset all social relationships. That Philemon was included in the canon may suggest that Paul was right. In his letter to Ephesus (1:3; 2:1; 6:2), Ignatius mentions a Bishop Onesimus of Ephesus.

The Synoptic Gospels.[105]

Because the first three Gospels are so similar they are called *synoptic*. The "synoptic problem" is the literary problem of accounting for the similarities and dissimilarities of these Gospels. All of the synoptic accounts are "Jesus stories" but not biographies. Except for infancy narratives in Matthew and Luke, the Synoptic Gospels are accounts of the ministry, suffering, death, and resurrection of Jesus. The question that motivated the evangelists to write was "Who was Jesus?" The Synoptic Gospels emphasize Jesus' parables, his self-designation as "Son of Man," and his proclamation of the kingdom of God. Marcan priority is generally assumed because together Matthew and Luke repeated ninety-three percent of Mark's gospel.

1. Mark. Only Mark designated his document as a "gospel." Mark's Jesus is both human (6:3) and divine. At the beginning (1:1) and the end of his gospel (15:39), Jesus is designated as "Son of God." Only twice does Mark record a divine voice (1:11; 9:7), and both times God calls Jesus "beloved Son."[106] Jesus' self-designation, "Son of Man," occurs fourteen times.[107] Jesus is called "the Christ" seven times, perhaps the most significant being Peter's confession (8:29). Jesus is said to have taught "as one having authority" (1:22). He had authority over demons (1:27, 39), disease (2:1–3:6), sin (2:5–10) and nature (6:30–42, 45–52; 8:1–10). Mark's interpretation depicts Jesus as a divine and powerful Savior.

Mark is interested in Jesus' passion; the Cross is central to his understanding of Jesus.[108] Every major section of the Gospel (3:6; 6:6; 8:21; 10:45; 12:44) ends on a note pointing to the Passion, and the central section of Mark (8:27–10:45) interprets the passion of Jesus. Judas betrayed him; Peter denied him and the others fled in Jesus' hour of death. Women who become surrogate disciples fail him in the end (16:8). The Marcan Jesus is a suffering Son of Man Messiah. In this first Gospel, the Parousia is imminent.[109]

2. Matthew.[110] While Matthew is interested in the church (16:16–19; 18:15–18), "The gospel must be explained primarily in terms of Christology, not in terms of ecclesiology."[111] To Mark's account infancy stories are added (chaps. 1–2), but from infancy till Jesus' entry into the ministry we hear nothing. When Mark's description of Jesus appears to be negative Matthew corrects him, and even the disciples fare better at the hands of Matthew than of Mark. The Matthean Jesus is called "Son of God," "Son of David," "Christ," "Wisdom," and "Son of Man." Matthew has "Jesus" 150 times and "Christ" only seventeen times; the human name used so many times suggests the full humanity of Jesus.

Matthew summarized Jesus' ministry as teaching, preaching, and healing (4:23). Jesus is a descendant of Abraham and David; Hebrew Scripture demonstrates that Jesus is the promised Messiah.[112] The Matthean Jesus performed about twenty miracles, and his miracles are seen as fulfillment of Scripture (8:17; 12:15–21). But miracles do not compel commitment. Matthew depicts Jesus primarily as a teacher; the disciples are not allowed to teach until Jesus is gone. Five major discourses underscore Jesus' teaching ministry. Like a new Moses, Jesus gives the Sermon on the Mount; his revelation surpasses that of Sinai. He came to "fulfill the law" (5:17). The ever-present Jesus is "Emmanuel" (God is with us, 1:22–23) who promises to be present when the church assembles (18:20) and to be with the disciples always (28:20). A program of evangelizing the world (28:19–20) indicates the Parousia has already been delayed.

3. Luke.[113] Like Matthew, Luke adds extensive birth narratives to Mark's account (chaps. 1–2) and a quick glimpse of Jesus at the temple when he was twelve. The Lukan Jesus was a warm, winsome personality who was thoroughly human. He developed normally (2:52), became hungry (4:2), was sometimes astonished (7:9), and wept over Jerusalem (19:41). Jesus is "Son of God," "Son of Man," "Son of David," "the Christ," and most often (103 times) "Lord." Other titles given to him include "Teacher," "Master," "Rabbi," "Savior," "King," and "Prophet."

That Jesus is the universal Savior is indicated when his genealogy is traced back to Adam. A human Jesus, he favors the outcasts, i.e., women, children, lepers, tax collectors, and sinners. He was called "a friend of sinners" (7:34), and his mission was "to seek and to save that which was lost" (19:10). The parables of Jesus reveal a gentle and sensitive man. In the parables (cf. chap. 15), Jesus speaks as one sent from God with authority to speak for God. He clearly understands himself as a messianic fulfillment of Isaiah 61:1–2 (cf. Lk 4:21). On the cross Jesus promises paradise to a dying thief and prays for his executioners' forgiveness. Luke understands the Cross in terms of salvation. The ascension of Jesus occurs on Easter Sunday (24:51). The Parousia has been delayed indefinitely—after all, Luke wrote Acts!

4. Acts.[114] Moving from Luke to Acts, "The proclaimer has become the proclaimed."[115] Jesus proclaimed the kingdom of God, but the church proclaimed Jesus. Unlike the Synoptics,

Acts displays little interest in the historical Jesus, but there are Jesus traditions in Acts (cf. 1:21–22, 2:22, 36; 3:14; 6:14; 7:59–60; 10:36–39; 13:24–25; 13:28; 19:3–4, 20).[116] Sometimes Jesus is even quoted (11:16; 20:35). The Resurrection is more important in Acts than the death of Jesus (2:24, 31, 36; 13:13–14; 17:3, 18, etc.). The resurrected Jesus appeared only to believers (10:41; 13:31). There is hardly a theology of Jesus' death in Acts; with the exception of 10:28 we hear nothing of salvation through his death. Jesus' death is not interpreted soteriologically, but no opportunity is missed to blame the Jews for his death (2:23, 36; 3:1–15; 4:10; 5:30; 7:52; 10:39; 13:27ff.).

Practically everything relating to Jesus (i.e., his ministry, death, resurrection, exaltation) is attributed to God (e.g., 2:22, 32; 3:26; 5:30ff.; 10:38, 40). Aside from 1:10–11 and 3:20, there is no reference to the Parousia; the imminent Parousia is missing.[117] The tension between fulfillment and the imminent consummation, so important in Jesus' message and Paul's proclamation, is completely lacking in Acts. In Acts Jesus is called "the Christ," "Jesus," "Jesus, the Nazarene," "Jesus Christ, the Nazarene," "the Holy and Righteous One," "Lord," "a prince and a Savior," "Son of Man," "the Lord Jesus," "Jesus of Nazareth," "a Savior, Jesus," "King, Jesus," and "servant."

God has made the exalted Jesus "both Lord and Christ" (2:36) and elevated him to "the right hand of God " (5:31; 7:55) to "grant repentance to Israel, and forgiveness of sins" (5:31). Everything is done "in the name of Jesus": baptism (2:38; 8:16; 19:5), healing (3:16), being saved (4:12), teaching (5:40), preaching (8:12), and even dying (21:13). Almost exclusively, Jesus is interpreted through the lens of the Hebrew Bible. Unquestionably, in Acts there is continuity between the historical Jesus and the Christ of faith (cf. 9:5, 22; 17:3). Jesus' resurrection is proclaimed, repentance is urged, and forgiveness is promised in Acts.

5. Hebrews.[118] No document in the New Testament is more thoroughly Christological than Hebrews. A sonship Christology is developed in 1:1–4:13, and 4:14–13:2 contains a high priest Christology. Christ is a fulfillment of prophecy (1:1) and is God's final revelation (1:2a). Hebrews 1:2–4 is reminiscent of the Colossian Christ hymn. Christ was preexistent; he was creator and now reflects God's glory. He is the exact image of God, and it is he who upholds the universe. Hebrews refers to

Jesus as "Son," "Apostle," "Pioneer," "Christ" and "Son of God."

A key word in Hebrews is "better"; as a son, Jesus is better than angels (1:4), Moses (3:3, 6), and Joshua (4:8ff.). The Incarnation and full humanity of Jesus are affirmed (2:14–18; 4:15); humanity, not divinity, qualifies Jesus to be an effective heavenly high priest. The human Jesus remains sinless (4:15; 5:9; 7:26–27). The Cross and redemption through the blood of Christ are central to Hebrews' understanding (9:14, 22; 10:19, 29). By his death, Jesus "tasted death for everyone" (2:9), rendered Satan powerless (2:14), and effected a "once-for-all" sacrifice for sin (7:27; 9:28; 10:10, 14, 18).

Having made a once-for-all sacrifice for sin, Jesus was exalted to the right hand of God (1:3; 8:1; 10:12). Through the human experience Jesus *became* a high priest who is merciful and faithful (2:17–18) as well as compassionate (4:15). Chapters 5–6 advance the argument from a sonship Christology to a high priesthood Christology and enunciate the author's thesis: Jesus is a high priest forever after the order of Melchizedek. Chapters 7:1–10:18 elaborate the thesis with a series of comparisons and contrasts. Priesthood Christology is unique to Hebrews, and only here in the New Testament do we find a Christology concerned with the heavenly ministry of the exalted Christ. The once-for-all sacrifice is the ground of his continued ministry of intercession (7:25) and permanent priesthood (7:24). Interestingly, Hebrews refers to the Parousia only once (9:28); and almost as an afterthought it once refers to the Resurrection (13:20).

The Johannine Writings

1. The Johannine Gospel.[119] Immediately Jesus is revealed as Christ, the Son of God[120] who is superior to John the Baptist (1:19–51). The man from heaven, Jesus is preexistent but appears on the human scene as an adult. Unlike the Marcan Jesus, he declares himself to be Messiah (4:26) and is the Son of Man who descended from above (8:23). After a brief earthly sojourn (7:33), he returned to his Father (3:13–15; 6:62; 8:14; 16:28). He declared himself one with God (10:30; 13:32; 16:7, 14, 20, 28; 17:1, 3; 18:36–38) but was subordinate to the Father (14:28) and dispenses judgment (5:22, 27) and eternal life (3:13–56; 6:27, 54). The revelation of God (13:31), Jesus will be "lifted up" (3:13–15; 8:28; 13:34–36) on the cross and in the Ascension. God's only Son (3:16) is from another world (8:23), and seven "I am" sayings reveal that the Johannine Jesus is God.

In the "Gospel of Signs" (chaps. 1–12) seven of Jesus' miracles are reported, but there were others (2:23; 20:30). Until 12:37 and again in 20:30–31, miracles are intended to evoke faith (2:11; 4:53; 6:14; 7:31; 11:45, 47b–48; 12:37–38; 20:31). Faith is a prerequisite for synoptic miracles (e.g., Mk 6:5–6); miracles produce faith in John, but not everyone believes (12:37). A human Jesus (1:14), he is a "man" (e.g., 4:29; 5:12; 7:46; 9:16; 11:47). He became weary (4:6) and thirsty (4:6–7), and was troubled by impending death (12:27). He knew "his hour had come to depart this world to the Father" (13:3).

Jesus could say, "I lay down my life. . . . No one has taken it from me" (10:17–18). Like a servant, he washed his disciples' feet, tells them he is going away, and promises to send the Holy Spirit. On Easter Sunday Jesus ascended to the Father (20:7) but appeared to his disciples a few days later for the "Johannine Pentecost" (20:22). In a sense, John practically dispensed with the Parousia. The realities of eschatology were already present in Christ. To be sure, there is a futurist element in Johannine eschatology (cf. 5:28–29; 6:39–40, 44, 54; 12:48), but eternal life is present eschatology and that is dominant in John's account of Jesus.

2. The Johannine Letters. From the first word the author of 1 John affirms an incarnational Christology (1:1–3). He is reacting against docetics in the church (2:19) who deny that Jesus is the Christ, the Son of God (2:22–23), specifically that he came in the flesh (4:2–3). The heretics are called antichrists and liars (2:18, 22; 4:3); "antichrist" in the New Testament appears only in 1 and 2 John. Denial of the Son alienates one from the Father (2:23) and forfeits eternal life (5:11–12). Jesus is the Son of God (4:15, 5:5) and the Christ (5:2); a Christian believes "in his name" (3:23; 5:13).

"The blood of Jesus" cleanses every sin (1:7), and Jesus is an Advocate (*Paraklētos*) with the Father for one who sins (2:1–2). Jesus came to "take away sins" (3:5), to be an "expiation" for the sins of the whole world (2:2), and to "destroy the works of the devil" (3:8). He is "the Savior of the world" (4:14; cf. Jn 4:42). Through Jesus believers have eternal life (5:11) and forgiveness of sins (1:9; 2:12). John knows it is "the last hour" (2:18), but only in 3:2 does he explicitly refer to the Parousia.

2 John presupposes the same doctrinal issue as 1 John but while the docetics of 1 John are still in the church, they are outside the church in 2 John. They deny that Jesus came in the flesh (v. 7). The church is again warned against the docetics (i.e., antichrists, vv. 7–11). Thus, the Incarnation is implicit in the theology of 2 John. The author, who identifies himself only as "the Elder," assumes the equality of Jesus and the Father.

3 John reflects schismatic difficulties in the Johannine community (v. 9), but the problems apparently are not related to Christology. In fact, Jesus (by any name!) is not even mentioned in 3 John unless one takes the reference to "the Name" (v. 7) to mean "Jesus." Because this Christian "note" was canonized, it is probably safe to assume the presupposition of a Johannine Christology in 3 John.

3. The Johannine Apocalypse.[121] Things "which must shortly take place" are promised in "a revelation of Jesus Christ" (1:1), and there is a greeting from Jesus Christ for the readers. Jesus is eternal (1:4), firstborn from the dead, ruler of kings, and he redeems by blood (1:5). Jesus is the Alpha and Omega (1:8; 21:6) and is coming again (1:7). The only fact about the historical Jesus mentioned in Revelation is his death, which is interpreted redemptively and not as victimization.

John's first vision is one of the Lord in all his glory (1:12–20). Jesus is supreme Lord, "the first and the last and the living one" (1:17–18), and he holds the keys of death and hades (1:18). The Son of God (2:18), he has "the key of David" (3:7) and is "the ruler of God's creation" (3:14). He is called "the lion of the tribe of Judah, the root of David," (5:5) and "a lamb standing as though slain" (5:6, 9, 12).[122] There always seems to be a chorus of praise for the Lamb who is worthy (6:1, 3). As the overcoming Lamb, he promises rewards to overcomers in the seven churches (chaps. 2–3).

The "one who sits on the throne" (5:1) is the Lamb (5:5) who is judged to be worthy to open the seven seals. His death is no last-ditch effort, because he was "slain from the foundation of the world" (13:8). Throughout Revelation, Jesus is treated as the functional equivalent of God (1:1–2, 13–16; 4:1–5:6, etc.). He sits on God's throne (3:21; 7:9–10, 17; 12:5; 22:1, 3; 22:3). God rules but he manifests his rule in Jesus (11:15). Chapter 19 lets us hear the "Hallelujah Chorus" in praise of Jesus; he is King of kings and Lord of lords (19:16). Satan will be bound and Christ will reign with his saints for one glad millennium (20:4, 6). There will be a marriage supper for the Lamb and his bride, the church (19:7–10). Christ will return "with a robe dipped in blood" (19:13; cf. 19:11–20). Jesus promises to come "quickly" (22:12, 20). "Come, Lord Jesus!" (22:20).

The Pastoral Letters[123]

Jesus was confessed to be the living Lord (1Ti 6:13–16) who came to redeem sinners (1Ti 1:15) and abolish death (2Ti 1:10) by giving himself "as a ransom" (1Ti 2:6). He is still living (2Ti 2:8), desires that "all come to the knowledge of truth" (1Ti 2:4), and is a mediator "between God and men" (1Ti 2:5). There is a sense of Jesus' presence with Christians even as they look for his return (1Ti 5:21; 6:13), which is "the blessed hope" (Tit 2:13). God is "our Savior" (1Ti 1:1; 2:3; 4:10; Tit 1:3; 2:10; 3:4) and so is Christ (Tit 2:13); "God the Savior" is "Christ the Savior" (Tit 2:13). Christ as Savior shares equality with God, exercises lordship, and is divine.[124]

Concern for orthodoxy becomes Christological with the claim that "sound words" are from Christ (1Ti 6:3, 13–14; Tit 2:10). Right doctrines have been given by the Holy Spirit and lead to salvation through Jesus Christ (2Ti 3:14–15). False doctrine confronted in the Pastorals seems to be gnosticism, both libertinist (Tit 1:10–12) and ascetic (2Ti 2:8); it might even be docetic (1Ti 3:16). The Christ hymn (1Ti 3:16) is clearly incarnational; 1Ti 2:5 refers to "the man, Christ Jesus" who testified before Pontius Pilate (1Ti 6:13).

The urgency of an imminent Parousia is gone, but the church knows about "the day of the Lord" (2Ti 1:12, 18; 4:8) and "the appearing of our Lord Jesus Christ" (1Ti 6:14; 2Ti 4:1, 8; Tit 2:13). Perhaps some even believe they are living in the last days (1Ti 4:1; 2Ti 3:1), but 2 Timothy 4:3 suggests the last days have not yet begun. At any rate the apocalyptic fervency is gone (2Ti 2:2); Christ will come, but only "at the proper time" (1Ti 6:15).

The General Letters

1. *James.* Neither a letter nor a sermon, James is parenesis (i.e., exhortation). In its 108 verses, there are fifty-four imperatives.[126] This document betrays little, if any, interest in doc-

trine,[127] including Christology. There is almost nothing distinctively Christian in James. Jesus is mentioned only twice (1:1; 2:1), and some scholars say these are Christian interpolations in an otherwise Jewish document.[128] There is, however, no textual evidence of interpolations, and the church did canonize James as a Christian document. Some scholars find allusions in James to Jesus' teaching, especially the Sermon on the Mount (e.g., compare Jas 5:12 with Mt 5:36–37; Jas 1:5, 17 with Mt 7:7–12, etc.).[129] If it is a Christian document, 5:7 may refer to the Parousia. Even so, a doctrine of Christ does not exist in this document.

2. 1 Peter. Doctrine and parenesis are so interwoven that it is difficult to extricate the one from the other. At 1:2 is a remarkable combination of trinitarianism, predestination, and the blood of Jesus. Christians have been "born again" through the resurrection of Jesus (1:3) and the Word of God (1:23).[130] Prophets predicted Christ's suffering and glory (1:11). Redemption is effected by Jesus' "precious blood" (1:2, 19). Preexistence is claimed for Jesus who "has appeared in the last times" (1:20). God raised Jesus from the dead and glorified him (1:21). Jesus is the "cornerstone" (2:6) of the church but is also the "rejected stone" (2:7).

Jesus' suffering is interpreted as a paradigm for Christians who should "follow in his steps" (2:21). Christians should expect to "share Christ's sufferings" (4:13). Jesus, the sinless one, never sought revenge on his tormentors (2:22–23). The theology of the Cross incorporates the Incarnation: Jesus bore our sins in his body on the cross and was wounded for our healing (2:24). He was "put to death in the flesh" (3:18) and then went and preached to the "prisoners" in hades (3:19). Although the urgency of the imminent Parousia is gone, Peter believes that "the end of all things is at hand" (4:7). Jesus, "the Chief Shepherd," is coming again (5:4).

3. Jude.[131] A vitriolic, polemical Christian tract, Jude "does not contain any message of Christ at all."[132] However, its several references to Christ assure the reader it is a document written for Jesus people. A "bondservant of Jesus Christ" wrote to persons who were "kept for Jesus Christ" (1:1). Jude's opponents "deny [the humanity of?] our only Master and Lord, Jesus Christ" (v. 4). The orthodox faith (v. 3) is what was spoken "by the apostles of our Lord Jesus Christ" (v. 17). Jude assumed that he was living in "the last times" (v. 18) and anxiously awaited "the mercy [Parousia? cf. Tit 2:13] of our Lord Jesus Christ to eternal life" (v. 21). Readers are commended "to the only God our Savior, through Jesus Christ our Lord" (v. 25). Despite his lack of doctrinal interest, it is certain that Jude was interested in Jesus.

\ **4. 2 Peter.**[133] "An apostle of Jesus Christ" (1:1) can write about "our God and Savior Jesus Christ" (1:1) or "our Lord and Savior Jesus Christ" (1:11; 2:20; 3:18). Christ possesses "divine power" (1:3), and "those who have received faith" (1:1) have been made "partakers of the divine nature" (1:4). Peter affirms the "coming of our Lord Jesus Christ" (1:16) and claims to have been an eyewitness of the transfiguration of Jesus (1:16–18).

Peter wants to stir up his readers' memories (1:13) because Christ has revealed to him that his death is imminent (1:14). He charges his readers to remember "the commandment of the Lord and Savior spoken by your apostles" (3:2). They are living in "the last days" because the mockers of the Parousia have arrived (3:3). In defense of the delayed Parousia, Peter argues on the basis of Psalm 90:4 that God's concept of time is different: one day is as a thousand years. God's apparent "slowness" in sending Jesus is an act of mercy for sinners (3:9). It is certain that "the day of the Lord will come" (3:10) and Peter's readers should "look for" it and "hasten the day of God" (3:12). While they wait they should "grow in the grace and knowledge of our Lord Jesus Christ." (3:18).

CONCLUSION

Interest in and concern for Jesus is the basis for laying claim to unity in the New Testament. Every document in the New Testament except for James, Jude, and 3 John, has considerable interest in Jesus. On the other hand, no single document in the New Testament will provide us with a fully developed doctrine of Christ. Despite the distaste some scholars have for harmonization, it is necessary to harmonize the various aspects of the doctrine of Christ in the New Testament if we wish to have a developed New Testament Christology.

Only the dullest, most unreflective student of the New Testament would deny its doctrinal diversity. However, our awareness of diversity is no cause for crying, "Foul!" or, "Contradictions!" Certain tensions do exist, but the diverse views enrich rather than diminish our understanding of Christ. John and Paul give us preexistence, but without Matthew and Luke we would not have the birth narratives of Jesus. Paul emphasizes the Resurrection, but only Hebrews tells us about the heavenly, high priestly ministry of the exalted Christ. Based on their writings available to us, no author of the New Testament could have written the Nicene Creed! To understand the various aspects of the doctrine of Christ, we need all of our New Testament documents.

Doctrine in the New Testament did not develop in a linear, progressive pattern. Paul, our first New Testament author, had little interest in the historical Jesus; the evangelists, writing some twenty to twenty-five years later, were vitally interested in the ministry and teachings of Jesus. But Hebrews, appearing about the same time as the Synoptic Gospels, was interested neither in biographical details of Jesus nor in his resurrection. Starting with Paul, here is a declining intensity with regard to Parousia expectations, but 2 Peter, perhaps the last New Testament document to be written, has considerable interest in the Parousia even if the "delayed Parousia" has been accepted. The Pastoral letters are "late," but the Christology is not advanced; ecclesiology is much more important in these letters.

Personally, I am grateful for the rich diversity within the unity of the New Testament's understanding of Jesus. Such diversity allows me to tap into the resources of the New Testament according to my own particular needs at any given time. The unity of the New Testament that focuses on Jesus reminds me that Jesus is the essence of both Christianity and its canon. The diversity of the New Testament reminds me to be charitable with fellow pilgrims who defend their "biblical position" on doctrines in tension with my own theology. Indeed, the New Testament canon, which is a strong basis for unity, at the same time is an excellent paradigm of the diversity that has always existed in the Christian community.

BIBLIOGRAPHY

Walter, Bauer. *Orthodoxy and Heresy in the New Testament.* Philadelphia: Fortress, 1979 (German original, 1934).
Hendrikus Boers. *What Is New Testament Theology?* Philadelphia: Fortress, 1979.

John Carmody, Denise Lardner Carmody, Gregory A. Robbins. *Exploring the New Testament*. Englewood Cliffs, N.J.: Prentice-Hall, 1986, pp. 374–423 especially.

James D. G. Dunn. *Unity and Diversity in the New Testament*. Philadelphia: Westminster, 1977.

Archibald M. Hunter. *The Message of the New Testament*. Philadelphia: Westminster, 1944. (Published in 1943 in London under the title, *The Unity of the New Testament*.)

Ernst Käsemann. "The Problem of a New Testament Theology." *New Testament Studies* 19(3), April, 1973, pp. 238ff.

G. E. Ladd. *The Pattern of New Testament Truth*. Grand Rapids: Eerdmans, 1964.

Walter A. Liefeld. "The Development of Doctrine in the New Testament." *The International Bible Commentary*. Ed. F. F. Bruce. Grand Rapids: Marshall Pickering/Zondervan, rev. ed. 1986, pp. 1091ff.

Leon Morris. *New Testament Theology*. Grand Rapids: Zondervan, 1986.

James M. Robinson and Helmut Koester. *Trajectories Through Earliest Christianity*. Philadelphia: Fortress, 1971.

NOTES

[1]Substituting "doctrine" for "theology," I am quoting Hendrikus Boers, *What is New Testament Theology?* (Philadelphia: Fortress, 1979), 7.

[2]Hendrikus Boers, *What is New Testament Theology?*, 7. In this essay the terms "doctrine" and "theology" are used interchangeably.

[3]Canon (*kanōn*, literally "a measuring rod") refers to a list of books authoritatively accepted as comprising the New Testament. See Norman Perrin, *The New Testament: An Introduction*. Rev. by Dennis C. Dulling (San Diego: Harcourt, Brace, Javonavich, 1982), 435.

[4]John Carmody, Denise Lardner Carmody, Gregory A. Robins, *Exploring the New Testament* (Englewood Cliffs, N.J.: Prentice-Hall, 1986), 10.

[5]Ernst Käsemann, "The Problem of a New Testament Theology," *New Testament Studies*, 19 no. 3 (April 1973): 238. If there had been no conflicts to settle, would New Testament authors have written anything, or if they had written abstract theology, what might have been important enough to write?

[6]Gordon D. Fee and Douglas Stuart, *How to Read the Bible for all Its Worth* (Grand Rapids: Zondervan, 1982), 46.

[7]Most critical scholars seem to presuppose a linear, progressive development. Cf. Norman Perrin, *The New Testament: An Introduction*,

400ff. and Willi Marxsen, *Introduction to the New Testament*, Trans. G. Buswell (Philadelphia: Fortress, 1968).

[8]Rudolf Bultmann, *Theology of the New Testament*. vol. 1. (New York: Scribner's, 1951 and 1955), 29. Also see his *The History of the Synoptic Tradition* (New York: Harper, 1968).

[9]Walter A. Liefeld, "The Development of Doctrine in the New Testament." *The International Bible Commentary*, ed. F. F. Bruce (Grand Rapids: Marshall Pickering/Zondervan, rev. ed., 1986), 1059. Cf. Harvie M. Conn, ed. *Inerrancy and Hermeneutic* (Grand Rapids: Baker, 1988), 57, 88–90, 93, 98, 182, 201, 223.

[10]However, see David Alan Black, "The Authorship of Philippians 2:6–11: Some Literary-Critical Observations," *Criswell Theological Review*, 22 (1966): 269–89 for a defense of the Pauline authorship of Philippians 2:6–11.

[11]Rudolf Bultmann, *Theology of the New Testament*.

[12]W. G. Kümmel, *The Theology of the New Testament According to Its Major Witnesses: Jesus—Paul—John* (Nashville: Abingdon, 1973). Kümmel believes these witnesses give us "the central proclamation of the New Testament" (p. 322).

[13]Hans Conzelmann, *Outline of the Theology of the New Testament* (London: SCM, 1969).

[14]Alan Richardson, *An Introduction to the Theology of the New Testament* (New York: Harper, 1958). This book is based on dogmatic propositions, not on a critical investigation of the New Testament.

[15]Donald Guthrie, *New Testament Theology* (Leicester, England: InterVarsity, 1981).

[16]Leon Morris, *New Testament Theology* (Grand Rapids: Zondervan 1986).

[17]William Wrede, "The Task and Methods of New Testament Theology," reprinted in Robert Morgan, *The Nature of New Testament Theology* (London, 1973), 116.

[18]Ibid.

[19]Johannes Weiss, *Earliest Christianity*, ed. Frederick C. Grant (New York: Harper Torchbooks, reprinted 1959; original 1917).

[20]Wilhelm Bousset, *Kyrios Christos* (Nashville: Abingdon, 1970; original 1913).

[21]See Herbert Braun, "The Problem of a Theology of the New Testament," *Journal for Theology and the Church*, 1 (1965): 169–83; Ernst Käsemann, "The Problem of a New Testament Theology"; Hendrikus Boers, *What Is New Testament Theology?*

[22]Alfred North Whitehead, *Process and Reality* (New York: Macmillan, 1929), now a Harper Torchbook, The Academy Library TB 1033Q (New York: Harper, 1960), 4.

[23]Hendrikus Boers, *What is New Testament Theology?*, 82.

[24]Walter Bauer, *Orthodoxy and Heresy in Earliest Christianity* (Philadelphia: Fortress, 1971; German original, 1934).

[25]James D. G. Dunn, *Unity and Diversity in the New Testament* (Philadelphia: Westminster, 1977).

[26]Ibid., 235–366.

[27]See Hans von Campenhausen, *The Foundation of the Christian Bible* (Philadelphia: Fortress, 1972), 62–102.

[28]See Pheme Perkins, *The Gnostic Dialogue* (Ramsey, N.J.: Paulist, 1980).

[29]Ernst Käsemann, "Primitive Christian Apocalyptic," *New Testament Questions of Today* (Philadelphia: Fortress, 1969; original, 1964), 137.

[30]See Hans von Campenhausen, *Ecclesiastical Authority and Spiritual Power in the Church of the First Three Centuries* (Stanford: Stanford University Press, 1979).

[31]Elaine Pagels, *The Gnostic Gospels* (New York: Random House, 1979), 142.

[32]Rudolf Bultmann, *Theology*, II, 135.

[33]Ibid., 142.

[34]Ernst Käsemann, *The Testament of Jesus* (SCM Press, 1968; original, 1966).

[35]Ernst Käsemann, "Ketzer und Zeuge: zum johanneischen Verfasserproblem," (1951), *Exegetische Versuche und Besinnungen* (Göttingen: Vandenhoeck und Ruprecht I (1960): 168–87.

[36]J. Charlot, *New Testament Disunity: Its Significance for Christianity Today* (New York: Dutton, 1970), 111. H. E. W. Turner, *The Pattern of Christian Truth* (London: Mowbray, 1904), 9.

[37]Besides doctrinal differences, the Synoptics have Jesus' ministry in Galilee for about one year while John places it mostly in Jerusalem for a period of three years.

[38]Despite the valuable work of Charles Talbert, *What is a Gospel?* (Philadelphia: Fortress, 1977), the New Testament gospel accounts are not biographies in any modern sense of the word.

[39]Paul's statement about praying for the dead (1Co 15:29) is strangely reminiscent of 2Mc 12:45, the Roman Catholic prooftext for purgatory.

[40]In *The Unity of the New Testament* (London, 1943), 14–15, A. M. Hunter suggests that terms like "kingdom of God" (Synoptics), "eternal life" (John), and "in Christ" (Paul) represent only "different idioms, different categories of thought" to express the same idea. Leon Morris, *New Testament Theology*, 16, still defends the same position. While there is a basis for "unity in diversity," their position may be indefensible on exegetical grounds.

[41]E. H. Hoskyns and Noel Davey, *The Riddle of the New Testament* (London: Faber and Faber, 1931).

[42]C. H. Dodd, *The Present Task of New Testament Studies* (1936). *The Apostolic Preaching and Its Developments* (New York: Harper, 1964) is a

pioneering study of speeches in Acts as examples of the early Christian kerygma.

[43]See C. H. Dodd, *The Interpretation of the Fourth Gospel* (Cambridge: Cambridge University Press, 1953) and *The Parables of the Kingdom* (Cambridge: Cambridge University Press, 1935).

[44]See F. V. Filson, *One Lord, One Faith* (London: Black, 1943) and his *Jesus Christ the Risen Lord* (New York: Abingdon, 1956).

[45]A. M. Hunter, *The Message of the New Testament*, 11.

[46]Ibid., 9.

[47]Ibid., 121.

[48]A. M. Hunter, *Introducing New Testament Theology* (London: SCM, 1954).

[49]Oscar Cullmann, *Christ and Time* (London: SCM, 1951; original, 1949).

[50]Oscar Cullmann, *The Christology of the New Testament*, rev. ed. Trans. Shirley C. Guthrie and Charles A. M. Hall. (Philadelphia: Westminster, 1963; original 1956), 9.

[51]Ibid.

[52]G. E. Ladd, *The Pattern of New Testament Truth* (Grand Rapids: Eerdmans, 1964), 9.

[53]See, for instance, Ernst Käsemann, "The Problem of a New Testament Theology," 1973; Herbert Braun, "The Problem of a Theology of the New Testament"; Hendrikus Boers, *What is New Testament Theology?*; Hendrikus Boers, "Where Christology is Real," *Interpretation*, 26 (July 1972): 300–327; J. Charlot, *New Testament Disunity: Its Significance*; James M. Robinson and Helmut Koester, *Trajectories Through Earliest Christianity*; James D. G. Dunn, *Unity and Diversity in the New Testament*. Many other articles and books could be cited; critical scholarship is still very much concerned with diversity in the New Testament.

[54]G. E. Ladd, *The Pattern of New Testament Truth*, 9. He considers only the Synoptics, John, and Paul.

[55]Ibid., 14.

[56]G. E. Ladd, *A Theology of the New Testament* (Grand Rapids: Eerdmans, 1974).

[57]Donald Guthrie, *New Testament Theology*.

[58]Ibid., 54.

[59]Leon Morris, *New Testament Theology*, 16.

[60]Ibid., 12.

[61]Ibid., 16.

[62]Ibid.

[63]Rudolf Bultmann, *Theology*, II, 141. Alfred Wikenhauser, *New Testament Introduction* (New York: 1958), 57, reminds us that the Peshitta, a Syrian version of the New Testament dating from the fifth century, omits 2 Peter, 2 and 3 John, Jude, and Revelation. The Eastern half of the Syrian church still holds to this canon.

[64]W. G. Kümmel, *Theology*, 322–23.

[65]Ibid., 323.

[66]Hendrikus Boers, *What is New Testament Theology?*, 16.

[67]W.G. Kümmel, *Theology*, 332.

[68]Carmody, Carmody, Robbins, *Exploring the New Testament*, 417.

[69]Ernst Käsemann, "The Problem of a New Testament Theology," 244.

[70]James D. G. Dunn, *Unity and Diversity*, 11–231.

[71]Ibid., 229. For further considerations of unity, see Carmody, Carmody, Robbins, *Exploring the New Testament*, 409–11.

[72]See Walter L. Liefeld, "The Development of Doctrine in the New Testament," 1060–62.

[73]This approach is used by Walter Liefeld, "The Development of Doctrine in the New Testament," 1062–71.

[74]Leon Morris, *New Testament Theology*, 11. Of course, Morris knows that scholars have written "theologies" of the various authors. There is no end of books proposing to give theologies of Paul.

[75]I say "roughly chronological" because our dates are at best educated guesses and one should not be dogmatic about such matters. The "Pauline Corpus" refers to the collection of Paul's letters.

[76]For examples, see Willi Marxsen, *Introduction to the New Testament* and Leon Morris, *New Testament Theology*.

[77]Leander E. Keck, *Paul and His Letters*. Proclamation Series (Philadelphia: Fortress, 4th printing, 1979), 4. For a different view of development in Paul, see Charles Buck and Greer Taylor, *Saint Paul: A Study of the Development of His Thought* (New York: Scribner's, 1969). But see the criticisms of Buck and Taylor in Victor Paul Furnish, "Development in Paul's Thought," *Journal of American Academy of Religion*, 30 (1970): 289–303.

[78]Philippians, Philemon, Ephesians, and Colossians are the Prison (sometimes called Christological) letters. Many scholars reject Ephesians and Colossians as well as 2 Thessalonians as authentic Pauline letters.

[79]Paul uses the term "Christ" 379 times (72% of the 529 uses in the New Testament). The name "Jesus" appears 214 times and "Lord" 270 times in Paul's writings.

[80]Joseph A. Fitzmeyer, *Paul and His Theology* (Englewood Cliffs, N.J.: Prentice-Hall, 1987), 34.

[81]Paul always seems to assume continuity between the Jesus of history and the Christ of faith.

[82]1 Thessalonians 4:17 with its language of "being caught up . . . in the air" is the basis for the doctrine of the rapture in the New Testament.

[83]*Parousia* is a Greek term meaning "presence" or "coming." It is considerably later before Christians use the expression "second coming" (*deuteros parousia*).

[84]Second Thessalonians is rejected as authentically Pauline by many scholars; rejection is based primarily on theological and stylistic considerations. If Pauline, it was written about A.D. 50, but Marxsen, *Introduction to the New Testament*, p. 44, places it soon after 70; Perrin, *The New Testament: An Introduction*, pp. 208–9, places it a generation after Paul, about the same time as Revelation.

[85]Joseph A. Fitzmeyer, *Paul and His Theology*, 38.

[86]Ibid., 51ff. According to Bultmann, it is "unthinkable" that Jews would have called God "Lord," so he thinks this designation for Jesus is Hellenistic.

[87]There is no exegetical basis for identifying the "lawless one" with the antichrist, as R. H. Fuller, *A Critical Introduction to the New Testament* (London: Duckworth), 57, does. The term "antichrist" appears in the New Testament only in 1 and 2 John.

[88]H. D. Betz, *Galatians*, Hermeneia Series (Philadelphia: Fortress, 1979), 14–25, analyzes this genre in great detail.

[89]With the exception of Philippians, 1 & 2 Thessalonians, and Philemon, the superscription of all his letters reveals that Paul wrote in the official capacity of *apostolos*.

[90]Martin Hengel, *Between Paul and Jesus* (Philadelphia: Fortress, 1983), 31, 39–40, suggests that Paul's essential Christology was formed on the Damascus Road.

[91]Paul never said "by faith alone." Joachim Jeremias, *The Central Message of the New Testament* (New York: Scribner's, 1983), 58, observes that surprisingly the full formula "justification by faith" or "to be justified by faith" is limited to three letters: Galatians, Romans, and Philippians.

[92]For a good commentary, see Hans Conzelmann, *1 Corinthians*, Hermeneia Series (Philadelphia: Fortress, 1975).

[93]The first instance we have of this statement.

[94]Donald J. Selby, *Introduction to the New Testament* (New York: Macmillan, 1971), 368, says 1 Corinthians 15 is "One of the half-dozen most important chapters in the New Testament."

[95]Ralph P. Martin, *2 Corinthians*, Word Biblical Commentary (Waco, Tex.: Word, 1986) is an excellent commentary on 2 Corinthians.

[96]Stanley K. Stowers, *Letter Writing in Greco-Roman Antiquity*, Library of Early Christianity, ed. Wayne A. Meeks (Philadelphia: Westminster, 1986), 173, correctly calls 2 Corinthians as "ironic apology."

[97]See Ernst Käsemann, *Commentary on Romans* (Grand Rapids: Eerdmans, 1980).

[98]The blood of Jesus (Ro 3:25; 5:9) is not often mentioned in Paul's letters.

[99]Ernst Käsemann, *Romans*, p. 213, says Paul is the first to relate the doctrine of the Spirit to the doctrine of Christ. Cf. Hebrews 7:25 on the intercession of Jesus.

[100]Some scholars reject the Pauline authorship of Ephesians and date it toward the end of the first century. I accept it as Pauline, written from prison in Rome about A.D. 60–62 (the same for Philippians, Colossians, and Philemon).

[101]Norman Perrin, *Introduction*, p. 220, notes that in Ephesians "ecclesiology swallows the christology."

[102]Most scholars accept Philippians as Pauline, but some see it as composite of three letter fragments: 1:1–31; 3:2–4:9; 4:10–20.

[103]J. B. Lightfoot, *St. Paul's Epistles to the Colossians and to Philemon*, rev. 9th ed. (New York: Macmillan, 1890), 314, mentions a strong bias against the letter in the fourth century because it was thought to be concerned with personal trivia without theological substance. We can be happy it was finally canonized.

[104]With the words "useful" and "useless," Paul employs a pun to make his point.

[105]The first three New Testament gospels were designated "synoptic gospels" by J. J. Griesbach in 1778.

[106]Martin Kähler's definition of gospel is well-known: "A Passion-resurrection narrative with an extended introduction."

[107]D. E. Nineham observes that "it is as Son of God rather than as teacher or prophet that St. Mark presents our Lord." *The Gospel of St. Mark*, Pelican Gospel Commentaries (Harmondsworth: Penguin, 1963), 48. See J. D. Kingsbury, *The Christology of Mark's Gospel* (Philadelphia: Fortress, 1983).

[108]See Morna D. Hooker, *The Son of Man in Mark* (Toronto: Toronto University Press, 1967).

[109]Ralph P. Martin, *Mark: Evangelist and Theologian* (Grand Rapids: Zondervan, 1972), 117.

[110]J. D. Kingsbury, *Matthew: Structure, Christology, Kingdom* (Philadelphia: Fortress, 1975).

[111]Georg Strecker, *The Interpretation of Matthew*, ed. Graham Stanton (Philadelphia: 1983), 77.

[112]"Formula quotations" are used to show how Jesus is a fulfillment of messianic promises in the Hebrew Bible.

[113]See Hans Conzelmann, *The Theology of St. Luke*, trans. Geoffrey Buswell (New York: Harper, 1961; original, 1953) and Jerome Kodell, *The Gospel According to Luke* (Collegeville, Minn.: Liturgical Press, 1983).

[114]See Ernst Haenchen, *Acts of the Apostles* (Philadelphia: Westminster, 1971) for an excellent commentary.

[115]Bultmann, *New Testament Theology* I, 33.

[116]The historical Jesus is not Luke's consuming passion but Dunn (*Unity and Diversity in the New Testament*), p. 17, overstates the lack of interest in Acts.

[117]It can be argued, however, that community sharing programs in Acts 2 and 4 reflect belief in an imminent Parousia.

[118]For a good commentary see Ernst Käsemann, *The Wandering People of God* (Minneapolis: Augsburg; Reginald H. Fuller, "The Letter to the Hebrews," *Hebrews, James, 1 and 2 Peter, Jude, Revelation,* ed. Gerhard Krodel (Philadelphia: Fortress, 1977).

[119]See Raymond E. Brown, *The Gospel According to John,* 2 vols. (Garden City, N.Y.: Doubleday Anchor, 1966).

[120]In the same chapter, one also meets "the Word," "Lamb of God," "Rabbi," "Messiah," "Jesus," and "King of Israel."

[121]See Elizabeth Schüssler-Fiorenza, *Invitation to the Book of Revelation* (Garden City, N.Y.: Doubleday-Anchor, 1981). Norman Perrin, *Introduction,* p. 112, calls Revelation "A prophetic-apocalyptic letter."

[122]The Greek term *arnion* (lamb) is used by John twenty-nine of the thirty times it occurs in the New Testament.

[123]An overwhelming majority of critical scholars regard the Pastorals as deutero-Pauline. See R. H. Fuller, *Critical Introduction,* p. 133. But some reputable scholars (e.g., Joachim Jeremias, *Die Briefe an Timotheus und Titus,* NTD [Göttingen: Vandnhoeck und Ruprecht, 1954] and J. N. D. Kelley, *The Pastoral Epistles,* BC, [London: Black, 1963]) still defend Pauline authorship. My own reluctance to grant authenticity to the Pastorals is an historical judgment that does not call biblical inspiration into question.

[124]See Oscar Cullmann, *The Christology of the New Testament,* trans. Shirley C. Guthrie and Charles A. M. Hall (Philadelphia: Westminster, 1963), 241–45, and Richard N. Longenecker, *The Christology of Early Jewish Christianity,* Studies in Biblical Theology, Second Series, 17 (Naperville, Ill.: Allenson), 141–44.

[125]The General or Catholic Letters are letters that were supposedly not written for a specific church or concrete situation. That characterization has been called into question, but the category has remained a helpful way of distinguishing the Pauline letters from the non-Pauline. There are seven general letters: James; 1 and 2 Peter; 1, 2, 3 John and Jude. The Johannine epistles, however, were treated under the Johannine literature.

[126]Willi Marxsen, *Introduction,* 226.

[127]Donald Guthrie, *New Testament Theology,* p. 54, admits that James is short on theology.

[128]This hypothesis goes back to F. Spitta, "Der Brief des Jacobus," in *Zur Geschichte und Literatur des Urchristentums,* II (1896): 1ff.

[129]See Norman Perrin, *Introduction,* 373.

[130]The concept of being born again occurs in the New Testament only here and John 3, but Peter and John do not use the same Greek word.

[131]Since Jude 4–16 is repeated in 2 Peter 2, the majority of scholars believe Jude was written first and is thus treated here before 2 Peter.

[132]Werner Georg Kümmel, *Introduction*, 426.

[133]Some Bible students still argue for Petrine authorship and a date in the early 60s. However, there is a consensus among critical scholars that 2 Peter is the latest writing in the New Testament (Kümmel, *Introduction*, 434), and some (e.g., Norman Perrin, *Introduction*, p. 381) argue for a date as late as A.D. 140.

Chapter Seventeen

The Diversity of Literary Genres in the New Testament

Craig L. Blomberg

Craig L. Blomberg

Craig L. Blomberg is Assistant Professor of New Testament at Denver Seminary in Denver, Colorado. He holds the B.A. from Augustana College, the M.A. from Trinity Evangelical Divinity School, and the Ph.D. from the University of Aberdeen. He previously taught at Palm Beach Atlantic College in Florida. From 1985-1986 he was Senior Research Fellow at Tyndale House in Cambridge, England. He has authored *The Historical Reliability of the Gospels* (IVP), *Interpreting the Parables* (IVP), and articles in such journals as *Westminster Theological Journal*, *Themelios*, *Journal of the Evangelical Theological Society*, *Journal for the Study of the New Testament*, and *Trinity Journal*. He is currently writing the volume on Matthew for *The New American Commentary* (Broadman).

Chapter Seventeen

The Diversity of Literary Genres in the New Testament

Casual readers of Scripture often treat the Bible itself as if it were all a book of Proverbs. They quote, interpret, and apply their favorite verses with little awareness of the contexts in which those texts appear. More serious readers often know enough to interpret a verse in light of the paragraph in which it appears and in view of the overall structure and themes of the particular book in which it is found. But even people who have been studying the Bible for years often do not realize that one cannot treat a passage in Joshua the same way one deals with a Psalm, a portion of Romans, or a section of the book of Revelation. Each of these four biblical books represents a different literary "genre" and each has distinctive principles that must guide legitimate interpretation. A genre may be defined as "a group of texts that exhibit a coherent and recurring configuration of literary features involving form (including structure and style), content, and function."[1]

In the New Testament four primary genres appear: gospels, a book of "acts," epistles, and an apocalypse. As obvious an observation as this is, it is remarkable that the vast majority of New Testament surveys and introductions, commentaries, and guides to hermeneutics say next to nothing about the distinctives of these four genres. But times are changing. In the last decade, a spate of specialized studies has appeared, spawning a new discipline in biblical study often known as "genre criticism." This article can only survey some of the high points of recent research, but its goal is to demonstrate how crucial it is for correct interpretation and application to be able to answer the questions: What is a gospel? What is an "acts"?

What is an epistle? What is an apocalypse? The reader who desires more detail at a foundational level should consult the introductory handbooks by Gordon D. Fee and Douglas Stuart (*How to Read the Bible for All Its Worth*)[2] and by Leland Ryken (*How to Read the Bible as Literature*[3] and *Words of Life: A Literary Introduction to the New Testament*[4]), works designed especially with the layperson in mind. The most thorough survey of technical research, but still readable for the average theological student, is David Aune's *The New Testament in Its Literary Environment*.[5]

WHAT IS A GOSPEL?

At first glance, most readers would probably call the gospels biographies of Jesus. On closer inspection, they would discover that none of the four gospels looks like the modern biographies with which they are familiar. For example, Mark and John say nothing about Jesus' birth, childhood, or young adult years. Luke 1–2 and Matthew 1–2 include selected incidents related to his birth and one episode about his teaching in the temple at age twelve, but otherwise they too are silent. On the other hand, all four gospels devote a disproportionately large amount of their space to the last few weeks and days of Christ's life. Almost half of John's gospel (chaps. 12–21) deals with the period of time beginning from "Palm Sunday" (five days before his crucifixion). The main events of Jesus' life that are recorded appear in different orders in the different gospels. Many of the details vary too. Only John reveals that Jesus' ministry occupied a three-year period or longer, and all four gospel writers are only rarely concerned to tell us how much time elapsed between any two events.

As a result, most modern scholars have abandoned the identification of the gospels with the genre "biography." Most also have given up believing that the gospels may be viewed as historically reliable, except in certain places. Instead, they conclude that Matthew, Mark, Luke, and John wrote to express their theological understandings of the person and work of Christ, and to record instructions relevant for the Christian communities to whom they wrote. The four evangelists had scarcely any historical or biographical intentions in mind. Contradictions of many kinds, scholars would allege, appear on virtually every page of a gospel synopsis. But one may look beyond the disagreement and discover key themes on which all the writers agree and which reflect the heart of early Christian faith.

If the gospels are for the most part neither historical nor biographical, what then do contemporary critics believe them to be? Several proposals have competed with one another. A few have identified the gospels with well-known genres of Greco-Roman fiction. Some have called the gospels "aretalogies"— accounts of episodes from the life of a "divine man," usually embellishing and exaggerating the feats of some famous hero or warrior of the past.[6] Some have applied to them language of the playwrights, associating the gospels with "comedies" (stories with a triumphant ending) or "tragedies" (stories in which the protagonist is defeated, despite having shown signs of ability and knowledge to do better).[7] But more differences than similarities appear between the gospels and these various genres so that none of these identifications is widely held today. Most would probably term them unique literary creations that defy classification. W. G. Kümmel's summary represents the views that a majority would endorse:

> Viewed as a literary form the Gospels are a new creation. They are in no way lives after the manner of Hellenistic biographies, since they lack the sense of internal and external history (as in lives of heroes), of character formation, of temporal sequence, and of the contemporary setting. Neither do the Gospels belong to the genre, memoirs, in which the collected stories and sayings from the lives of great men are simply strung together. Nor do they belong to the genus, miracle stories, in which the great deeds of ancient wonder-workers are glorified in a more or less stylized manner.[8]

Nevertheless, several other possibilities merit consideration, as there is a growing minority of scholars who believe that the gospels should be equated with a known genre from the Hellenistic world of the first century.

One of these proposals is that the gospels are a kind of Jewish "midrash." Midrash is a Hebrew word for "commentary" and referred especially to a type of Jewish writing in which sacred traditions were retold, elaborated, and embellished in a mixture of history and fiction, designed to communicate important theological beliefs. Robert Gundry took the evangelical world by storm in the early 1980s when he advocated viewing Matthew as just such a midrash, which combined the historical information of Mark and Q (material common to Matthew and Luke not found in Mark) with various kinds of legendary additions of Matthew's own creation. For example, Matthew has turned Luke's shepherds (Lk 2:6) into "magi" or wise men (Mt 2:1). Because Gundry believed this was a recognized and accepted genre of writing, he believed that Matthew could still be said to be inerrant, that is, truthful in all he intended to affirm, since his audiences would have recognized that where he deviated from his sources, he was not intending to communicate historical information.[9] Most evangelicals reacted by denying that Matthew fit the Jewish genre of midrash; many insisted that it was impossible to believe what Gundry did and consistently affirm inerrancy at the same time. The latter charge seems unfounded, but the first response is well taken. There is not sufficient evidence to demonstrate that Matthew's community would have known Mark and Q well enough to distinguish fact from fiction. Nor is evidence available that these two sources would have developed the same authoritative status for as long a period as Old Testament Scripture had by the time Matthew wrote. Thus he could not feel free to treat them in the same way Jews sometimes treated well-established canonical texts.[10]

A second, even more influential proposal has grown up in more liberal theological circles. Werner Kelber has proposed that the gospels, especially Mark, be seen as a type of parable. Mark 4:11–13 does not just refer to Jesus' teaching but to Mark's understanding of the entire gospel—both concealing and revealing. Those who first wrote down the gospels, Kelber believes, were rebelling against the apostolic authority that had been preserving the tradition orally. And "for a language that asserts itself by distanciation from the received mode of communication, parable is the ultimate metaphor."[11] Now to be sure, Kelber has demonstrated that metaphor and mysteriousness are more pervasive in the gospels than many have recognized, but it is doubtful if any entire gospel deserves the label "parable." Most of Kelber's argument depends on a false dichotomy between oral and written traditions that recent research into the acquisition of literacy by preliterate societies has been exposing. Mark looks more like a nonparabolic narrative that has had parabolic elements woven into it.[12]

Are other options left? Luke 1:1–4 provides the most

important clues to the gospel genre. In these verses, Luke describes his work in language closely paralleled in other Greco-Roman historical and biographical texts. What led modern interpreters away from a historical or biographical genre was that the gospels did not seem to match up to *modern* conventions for these types of works. But when they are compared with various ancient sources, the gospels compare quite favorably. Ancient historical standards of precision in narration and in selection and arrangement of material were much less rigid than modern ones. Few if any ancient works were written merely for the sake of preserving the facts; almost all were trying to put forward and defend certain ideologies for morals. But propaganda need not distort the facts, though it sometimes does. As a result, several recent studies have begun to swing the pendulum back in the direction of viewing the gospels as a kind of history or biography. Not all of these are equally confident of how much of that history may be viewed as trustworthy. C. H. Talbert, for example, is still fairly skeptical of the level of historical reliability; for him, calling the gospels biographies means that they have a mythical structure, an origin in the legends of the "cult" or ritual of a religious community devoted to the traditions of its founder, and an optimistic, "world-affirming" perspective reacting against the many pessimistic philosophies of the day.[13] On the other hand, Martin Hengel associates the gospels with those kinds of biographies that supplied a "relatively trustworthy historical report,"[14] while Terrence Callan finds the closest parallels to Luke's preface in the histories of Herodotus, Tacitus, Arrian, Dio Cassius, Sallust, and Josephus, all of whom are generally viewed by modern historians as more reliable than not in what they record.[15]

Perhaps the best term to use to describe what a gospel is, then, is "theological biography." One may not excuse the apparent contradictions among the gospels by denying a historical intention on the part of the four evangelists. Apparent contradictions must be evaluated. In fact, when this is done, plausible resolutions of all of them may be discerned. One cannot always prove what the best solution is in any given case, but there are no "contradictions" or "errors" that necessarily impugn the integrity of any of the gospel writers or that threaten the trustworthiness of what they have written.[16] At the same time, none of the evangelists was a mere chronicler of information. Virtually every teaching and episode from Jesus' life that they have included was included for a theological reason—to teach us something about who Jesus was and how people should live.

Implications for interpreters are numerous. As one is studying any individual passage in the gospels, one must try to understand it in light of that author's overarching purposes and not immediately obscure those purposes by comparing it with parallel information in other accounts. The reason the gospels differ as they do is because the four evangelists were each trying to emphasize different aspects of the gospel. Reading Matthew's account of the Resurrection should make one aware of his concern to answer Jewish charges that the disciples had stolen Christ's body (27:62–66; 28:11–15). Reading Mark's account should highlight the initial fear and silence of the women who came to Jesus' tomb (16:8). Luke stresses that the Resurrection was a fulfillment of all of the Jewish Scriptures (24:25, 44, 46–47). John emphasizes Jesus' encounter with Thomas to prove that Jesus was God himself (20:24–28). Each of these four emphases fits in closely with a dominant emphasis of the gospel in which it appears. Each emphasis is also fairly distinctive to the gospel in which it appears. All four themes are usually missed when one deals with a composite "harmony" of the various Resurrection accounts. Yet such a harmony is also valuable in demonstrating that none of the four accounts contradicts another.

Recognizing the gospels as theological biographies also affects the way one relates a particular passage to its larger context. The individual events in the gospels do not always appear in chronological order. Many times, the four evangelists write topically. Much of Mark 1–8 falls into just such an outline. Mark 1:21–45 presents a series of Jesus' healings. Mark 2:1–3:6 gives a series of controversies with the Jewish leaders. Mark 4:1–34 links together several of Jesus' parables. Mark 4:35–6:6 tells of several of Jesus' more dramatic miracles over the forces of nature (and concludes by contrast with his inability to work them in Nazareth because of widespread disbelief there). When one sees where several of these passages appears in the other gospels, it is clear that all of them cannot be in chronological order. So it is safe to assume that no chronology is implied unless it is explicitly present in the text (and unfortunately English translations often use the word "then" when the Greek need only be translated as "and"). For example, one dare not assume that Luke 9:51–18:14 represents one consecutive series of Jesus' teachings as he traveled from Galilee to Jerusalem (even though it is often called the Perean ministry as if this were the case). For one thing, that would mean that he had already arrived at Jerusalem's outskirts (Bethany) in 10:38–42 (cf. John 11:1, which tells where Mary and Martha lived) but was somehow back north again on the border between Samaria and Galilee in 17:11. Rather, this nine-chapter section of Luke's gospel, almost exclusively devoted to Jesus' sayings, is a topically arranged collection of Jesus' teaching "under the shadow of the cross" (9:51). The significance of the order of Luke 11:1–14, 5–8 and 9–13 is therefore that they are all teachings about prayer, not necessarily that they were all spoken in the same place, or that order, or one right after the other.[17]

It is amazing how often students of Scripture miss either the historical or theological element in the gospels, or, worse still, pit one against the other. Both are present and they do not conflict. In fact, it is often precisely when one understands an evangelist's theological rationale for a given version of an episode from Christ's life that apparent contradictions with parallel accounts evaporate.[18] For example, Luke's account reverses the order of the second and third of Christ's temptations by Satan. Matthew ends with Jesus seeing all the kingdoms of the world (4:8–10); Luke, with Jesus being tempted to throw himself off the temple (4:9–12). But Luke never says the "third" temptation happened after the "second." Most likely, he has arranged the temptations in the order he has to end with a climax of Jesus at the temple in Jerusalem, since Luke is the gospel writer most interested in Jesus' relationship with the temple and with Jerusalem. There is no contradiction, but the change in sequence is not arbitrary. Luke wants to highlight Jesus as the one whose ministry zeroed in increasingly more narrowly on the Jewish people and finally in on Jerusalem, as well as to underscore Jerusalem as the center from which the gospel subsequently went out to all the world (Ac 1:8).[19]

WHAT IS THE ACTS OF THE APOSTLES?

As the second volume in Luke's two-part work, one should expect Acts closely to resemble the gospels in genre. If the gospels are best described as theological biographies, then Acts is best described as a theological history.[20] Instead of focusing on one main character, Jesus, as in a biography, Acts broadens its scope to present key episodes in the lives of several early church leaders. Still, the title Acts of the Apostles is misleading, since most of the apostles disappear very quickly from view after the opening chapters. Most of Luke's narrative is focused on Peter and Paul, with subordinate characters such as the deacons, Stephen, and Philip, garnering the next greatest amount of attention. The "Acts of the Holy Spirit" might be a more descriptive title, since Luke sees the coming of the Spirit at Pentecost and his subsequent filling of believers as constitutive of the expansion and growth of the fledgling Christian community.

As with the Gospels, most interpreters have tended to create false dichotomies between theology and history. Throughout the past century, two clearly discernible "camps" have competed with one another in interpreting Acts. One group of commentators, primarily British, compared Acts favorably with the more reliable ancient Greek historians as Herodotus and Thucydides, and argued for a substantial measure of historicity. The trailblazer for this group was the British archaeologist, Sir William Ramsey, whose turn-of-the-century excavations in Asia Minor converted him from a skeptic to one who was extremely confident of Luke's historical intentions and success in carrying them out.[21] But these commentators, followed by many North American evangelicals, often missed the key theological emphases of the Acts.

A second group of scholars, primarily German, has given Luke very poor marks as a historian but has concentrated instead on his theological concerns, though even they are finding him largely inferior to the epistles of Paul both in his presentation of Christianity in general and in the credibility of his portrayal of Paul in particular. Ernst Haenchen's massive commentary on Acts has been foundational for this group,[22] and most North American liberal scholarship has followed in his footsteps.

In the past decade, a third, primarily American group, has emerged. Elaborated at greatest length by Richard Pervo, this approach classifies Acts as a historical novel.[23] In other words, Luke had more in common with other Greco-Roman writers of fiction than he did with authors of history or biography. Pervo believes his approach is a helpful advance on the stalemate of the history vs. theology debate. He underlines the elements of adventure and excitement in Luke's narrative style and points out numerous features that Acts shares with other ancient novels. But all of these features appear in genuine histories as well. When one reads Pervo's work closely, it becomes apparent that, despite his disclaimers to the contrary, his case ultimately depends on a series of implausibilities that he identifies in the narratives of Acts. As with the so-called contradictions in the gospels, all of these "implausibilities" have been plausibly explained by more conservative commentators, though Pervo ignores most of these explanations. A better solution to the theology/history debate is to affirm an element of both at the same time rather than to look for a third alternative.

When one turns to implications for interpretation, one discovers that Acts is much more concerned to narrate events in chronological order than is any of the gospels. Still there are occasions when Luke reverts to a topical sequence. Josephus (*Ant.* xx,ii.5; xix, viii.2), for example, makes it plain that the famine that Luke records in Acts 11:27–30 occurred about two to three years after the death of Herod Agrippa (Ac 12:1–24). Luke has told the story of the famine earlier probably because Agabus predicted it in Antioch, and in Acts 11:19–26 Luke has just been relating information about the development of Christianity in Antioch. So readers dare not assume that the events at the beginning of Acts 12 somehow depend on those at the end of chapter 11, since in fact they occurred at a later date.

Sensitivity to Luke's theological concerns, without denying his trustworthiness as a historian, also helps contemporary readers to recognize Luke's main emphases within any given passage. In light of modern debates about water baptism, baptism in the Spirit, and eternal security, readers of Acts 8 usually raise such questions as: Why didn't the Spirit come immediately when the Samaritans believed Philip's preaching? Was Simon Magus ever really saved, and if so did he lose his salvation? Is it significant that Philip baptizes the Ethiopian eunuch as soon as the chariot in which they are riding passes a sufficiently large body of water? Although all of these are legitimate questions, probably none was in Luke's mind as he penned this chapter of Acts. Once one realizes that the outline for his book (Ac 1:8) is concerned with the expansion of

Christianity into successively less and less Jewish circles, the two most striking features of Acts 8 become the reception of the gospel by Samaritans and by a eunuch, both considered highly unclean by orthodox Jews. The main applications of Acts 8 for Christian living today should therefore not center around the pros and cons of the charismatic movement nor debate the issue of believers' vs. infant baptism. Rather they should call all Christians today to determine who are the Samaritans and eunuchs in modern society. Whoever today's "untouchables" or outcasts are, these are the ones on whom significant Christian ministry should center.

WHAT IS AN EPISTLE?

An epistle is obviously a letter. So what else needs to be said? For a long time, New Testament scholars said very little else, except to note that most of the New Testament epistles followed typical Hellenistic convention by beginning with a greeting and statement of the author and persons being addressed, by continuing with an appropriate prayer or thanksgiving, by often containing a section of instruction or exhortation toward the end, and by concluding with further greetings and a farewell formula. In just the last decade or so, however, interest in analyzing the body of a given New Testament letter has increased dramatically. Today, several good introductions to a whole host of subgenres of Hellenistic letters are available,[24] while a significant number of helpful classifications of specific New Testament epistles enhance the interpreter's ability to understand the biblical writers' original intentions.

For most of this century the work of Adolf Deissmann has dominated scholarship on the epistles. Based on his study of Egyptian papyri, Deissmann subdivided the letter genre into "real" and "non-real" letters. Real letters, like the papyri, were private, non-literary, informal, and artless, addressing specific circumstances. Non-real letters, like more classical Greek treatises, were public, deliberately literary, and designed to address a general audience without regard to occasion. For Deissmann, Paul's letters were real, private, nonliterary, and artless.[25] But these distinctions proved to be too cut and dried. Deissmann's dichotomy was based exclusively on materials from one Egyptian province and did not take into account the literary nature either of other papyri or of Paul's letters. At the same time, general letters often tended "to avoid or even suppress typically epistolary forms and styles for other types of discourse."[26]

Although Deissmann's categories remain widely influential, recent genre criticism of the epistles has tended to head in two somewhat different directions. Some scholars have tried to classify the epistles functionally according to specific subgenres of letter writing. Others have analyzed the rhetoric of the epistles, associating various New Testament letters with one or more of the major forms of Greco-Roman rhetoric used in a variety of different kinds of speaking and writing, including letter writing.

Two functional categories of epistle that are represented in the New Testament are the parenetic letter and the letter of recommendation. First Thessalonians is a good example of a parenetic or exhortational letter.[27] This kind of epistle is designed primarily to persuade or dissuade an audience concerning a specific action or attitude. Many readers of 1 Thessalonians have been surprised at how much praise Paul lavishes on this particular church throughout chapters 1–3, even though he has some very pointed moral instruction to give them in 4:1–12 and crucial theology to correct in 4:13–5:11. When 1 Thessalonians is seen as a parenetic letter, Paul's strategy makes excellent sense. One of the key features of this kind of letter is that the author establishes his friendship with his audience and emphasizes how well they are doing and how little they really need any further instruction. But, in fact, they do need additional encouragement to correct beliefs and lifestyle. So the author has tactfully prepared his readers for the exhortation with which the letter concludes.

The Pastoral Epistles, especially 1 and 2 Timothy, are additional examples of parenetic letters.[28] Here Paul relies heavily on personal reminders of his past behavior to encourage Timothy to imitate his example. Inasmuch as the church at Ephesus, where Timothy is ministering, is troubled by false teachers, this exhortation becomes all the more crucial. Other New Testament letters do not correspond so closely to the formal style of a parenetic letter but do contain substantial portions of exhortation. First Peter is perhaps the best example of this kind of writing.[29]

Philemon provides an excellent illustration of a letter of recommendation (also called a letter of introduction or intercessory letter). This kind of letter was common among the papyri, designed to introduce the bearer of the letter to its recipient and then to request a favor. Often the writer of the letter was a close friend or relative of the recipient and was promising to return the favor in some way.[30] Thus, Paul is asking Philemon to welcome his runaway slave, Onesimus, back home without punishing him. Paul promises to pay any damages Philemon has incurred and reminds him of the debts he owes Paul. The entire epistle is a masterpiece of tact and persuasion as Paul steers a delicate course between pleading and demanding. Since it was a well-established genre of writing, Philemon could have been expected to recognize the kind of letter Paul sent and to comply with his requests. Third John appears to be a second canonical letter of recommendation—on behalf of the traveling Christian missionaries whom John encourages Gaius to welcome.[31]

More common among genre criticism of the epistles has been rhetorical analysis. The three major kinds of rhetoric that Greco-Roman writers identified were judicial (forensic, apologetic), deliberative (symbouleutic, hortatory), and epideictic (demonstrative, laudatory). Judicial rhetoric sought to convince an audience of the rightness or wrongness of a past action. Deliberative rhetoric tried to persuade or dissuade an assembly concerning the expediency of a future action. Epideictic rhetoric used praise and blame in order to urge a group of people to affirm a point of view or set of values in the present. A full-blown rhetorical speech would contain all of the following features, though often one or more sections might be missing.

exordium (proemium)—stated the cause and gained the hearer's attention and sympathy

narratio—related the background and facts of the case

propositio (divisio, partitio)—stated what was agreed upon and what was contested

probatio (confirmatio)—contained the proofs, based on the credibility of the speaker, appeals to the hearer's feelings, and/or logical argument

refutatio (confutatio)—refuted opponents' arguments

peroratio (conclusio)—summarized argument and sought to arouse hearers' emotions[32]

The most well-known example of an application of rhetorical genre to the New Testament epistles appears in Hans-Dieter Betz's major commentary on Galatians.[33] Betz believes that Galatians is an apologetic letter, using judicial rhetoric to defend Paul's past actions in preaching independently of the Jerusalem apostles, and to summon his audience to side with him and against the Judaizers who are currently infiltrating Galatia. This analysis implies that Paul's primary thrust is not so much an exposition of the doctrine of justification by faith as a polemic against legalism in which he attempts to justify himself. Several studies, reacting to Betz, have agreed that rhetorical analysis greatly helps one's understanding of Galatians, but prefer to analyze it in terms of deliberative rhetoric.[34] The exhortational material in 5:1–6:10 fits in more with the purpose of a speaker who is trying to convince his audience to act a certain way in the future than with one who is simply defending himself. And even 1:12–2:14, the most autobiographical section of Galatians, is more a defense of the divine origin of Paul's gospel than of Paul's personal behavior or motives.

Second Thessalonians affords a second probable example of deliberative rhetoric.[35] Here Paul wishes to dissuade his readers from believing that the day of the Lord had already come (2:2) or was so imminent that they could stop working (3:6–15). In fact, many of the New Testament letters have elements of deliberative rhetoric in them because one of the primary purposes of the epistle writers was to tell people how to act or how not to act in the Christian life.

Epideictic rhetoric has proved helpful in an analysis of Romans. Commentators have long recognized various points of uniqueness in this epistle—it reads more like a theological treatise than a personal letter, yet chapters one and sixteen frame the epistle with numerous personal and informal remarks. Romans also divides abruptly into theological (1:16–11:36) and ethical material (12:1–15:13). Epideictic rhetoric provides a structure that incorporates all of these disparate sections into a coherent whole. The features of a personal letter at beginning and end established Paul's credibility and a relationship with the Romans. In between appear the *propositio* (1:16–17) and *confirmatio* (1:18–15:13).[36]

Robert Jewett has narrowed down the genre of Romans even more specifically—it is an ambassadorial letter. Paul is paving the way for a hoped-for visit to Rome by commending his understanding of the gospel to the church there and by explaining the purposes of his travels. One application of this genre identification is that it makes the long list of greetings in chapter 16 an integral part of the letter rather than a hypothetical fragment of some other letter (such as Ephesians) as has often been proposed.[37] Stanley Stowers has also identified the rhetoric of Romans more specifically, pointing out that most of chapters 1–11 form a diatribe. A diatribe was a conversational method of instruction among ancient philosophers and religious teachers in which hypothetical objections from opponents were regularly considered and answered. So when Paul frequently discusses how someone might reply to his presentation of the gospel (e.g., 2:1, 9; 4:1; 6:1, 15; 7:7), one must not assume that such objectors were actually present in the Roman church. Rather, Paul is anticipating the type of response he could imagine his letter eliciting and answering those charges before they ever arise.[38]

Functional and rhetorical genre criticism also support the case for the unity of several epistles that have often been viewed as a collection of independent fragments of letters. Duane Watson, for example, has shown that the outline of Philippians closely corresponds to that of a deliberative letter, although he has to bracket 2:19–30 as an epideictic digression.[39] Linda Belleville has suggested that 2 Corinthians 1–7 follows the paradigm for an apologetic, self-commendatory letter, with the body opening in 1:8 and the transition to the request section in 6:1.[40] I have elsewhere proposed that these same seven chapters may also be seen as a chiasmus (inverted parallelism): 1:12–22 and 7:13b–16 both deal with proper boasting; 1:23–2:11 and 7:8–13a, grief and comfort regarding an offender whom the Corinthians have punished; 2:12–13 and 7:5–7, Paul's looking for Titus in Macedonia; 2:14–4:6 and 6:11–7:4, a series of contrasts between belief and unbelief; and 4:7–5:10 and 6:1–10, surviving and triumphing despite every hardship. The center, which is the climax of a chiasmus, is Paul's discussion of his ministry of reconciliation in 5:1–11.[41] Of course, it is always possible that a later editor has imposed one of these structures on the various fragments of letters that he inherited. But the main reason Philippians and 2 Corinthians are usually seen as composite letters is because there seems to be no overarching outline to unite the different sections of the epistles as they currently stand. Once this objection is removed, there is really no good reason to continue to see them as composite collections of fragments.

Genre criticism of Hebrews, James, Jude, and the epistles of Peter and John proves somewhat more daunting. Several of these letters lack the conventional openings or closings and may not be ordinary epistles at all. Hebrews, for example, refers to itself as "a word of encouragement" or exhortation (13:22). The only other place this phrase occurs in the New Testament is in Acts 13:15, where it refers to a sermon. Hebrews is therefore best understood as a sermon or homily. It may well have been written to be preached before it was given an epistolary closing and used as a letter.[42] If this is the case, then it goes without saying that Hebrews should be taken seriously as a text to be preached today. Among other things, this means that it is unlikely that the numerous warnings against apostasy throughout the letter (esp. 2:1–4; 3:7–4:11; 6:4–12; 10:19–39; 12:14–29) are merely hypothetical. The writer of Hebrews seriously believed that at least some in his congregation were in danger of abandoning their profession of Christian faith. Whether or not such people were ever truly believers is not an issue that genre criticism can solve, but it at least suggests that the debate is not academic!

Perhaps the most significant recent study of the genre of James is Peter Davids' analysis of the letter as a complex chiasmus. Three themes dominate the epistle: trials and temptations, wisdom and speech, and wealth and poverty. James 1 introduces each of these themes twice, while chapters 2–5 unpack them in greater detail in inverse order.[43] Even if Davids' outline requires modification at a few points, it refutes two widely held notions about the letter. First, James is not simply a collection of teachings loosely strung together, like the book of Proverbs. Second, James's main concern is not faith vs. works, though that has been the primary preoccupation of commentators ever since Martin Luther. Important as it is, James's discussion of a faith that produces no works as being dead (2:18–26) is actually a subordinate point under the larger and more crucial topic of the right use of one's material resources (see 2:14–17 and 1–13).

First John neither begins nor ends like a letter. Of several proposals that have been made, perhaps David Aune's is the best: it is a "deliberative homily."[44] Like Hebrews, it resembles a sermon more than a letter. Like other forms of deliberative rhetoric, it is designed to persuade the Ephesian church, to which it was probably addressed, to side with John and embrace true Christian doctrine and practice over against the false teachers who have promoted heresy and ungodliness and begun to split the church (2:19).

Richard Bauckham has broken fresh ground with his detailed analysis of 2 Peter. Taking his cue from 1:14–15, Bauckham identifies 2 Peter as a testament.[45] This was a well-known Jewish and Greco-Roman form of address depicting the final instructions of an aged leader or teacher to his sons or followers shortly before his death. Numerous other details of 2 Peter match features prominent in such books as the Testaments of the Twelve Patriarchs (an important collection of intertestamental Jewish writings). Now most ancient testaments were pseudonymous. That is to say, they were not actually written by the revered individuals to whom they were ascribed. But no deceit was intended in this attribution of authorship and no one was misled by the literary convention, any more than modern audiences object to or are misled by ghostwriters. In fact, in many instances such pseudonymity was an ascription of honor to a teacher to whom one owed credit for his ideas. Bauckham thus believes that the early church would have recognized and accepted 2 Peter as a testament written by one of Peter's disciples in the generation following his death (usually assumed to be in the late 60s) to contemporize Peter's message for the church of a later date (probably near the end of the first century).[46]

Pseudonymity has traditionally been a difficult concept for evangelicals to accept. This is largely because arguments for pseudonymity have usually depended on interpretations of certain passages in a given biblical book that place them in opposition to portions of other biblical writings believed to be authentic.[47] Sometimes scholars have flatly declared that certain portions of Scriptures were forgeries.[48] But these approaches to pseudonymity, though still widespread, are increasingly giving way to hypotheses like those of Bauckham, in which the integrity of the unknown writers is in no way impugned, and in which the unity and consistency of Scripture may still be maintained. It is doubtful if Bauckham's hypothesis may be considered to be proved, but it is at least an option that evangelicals should seriously consider and not dismiss out of hand as by definition incompatible with a high view of Scripture. If an ancient writer could have written "Peter" and expected his readers to realize that it was not Peter writing (as for example if he were already dead) but that the thoughts of the letter were those the writer could have imagined Peter speaking if he were alive, then such a practice is morally no more objectionable than when a modern author uses a pen name or when a public figure writes an "autobiography" that was really composed by a professional assistant to whom he told his life story. But the jury is still out on whether or not such practice was deemed acceptable in the earliest years of Christianity. From the mid-second century on, it often was not, because of the proliferation of heretical literature under the guise of apostolic authorship.[49]

WHAT IS THE BOOK OF REVELATION?

The great reformer John Calvin admitted that he wasn't sure what to do with the book of Revelation and therefore did not write a commentary on it, even though he had completed volumes on the rest of the New Testament. Readers throughout the ages have shared Calvin's perplexity, and not a few commentators on the book might have done better to follow in his footsteps. Still, genre criticism can help the careful student sift the more likely from the less likely interpretations in a maze of opinions that compete for attention.

Formally, Revelation shares features with three distinct genres—prophecy, apocalyptic, and epistle. As a letter, to be circulated among seven churches in Asia Minor, John addressed contemporary circumstances that his audience was undergoing. Chapters 2–3, which most specifically address these seven congregations, contain various enigmas that are deciphered when one studies the historical background of each individual city.[50] When, for example, John calls the Laodicean church to be either hot or cold and not lukewarm (3:15–16), he is not encouraging them to take a clear stand either for or against Christ. Both hot and cold water are positive metaphors. Laodicea did not have its own water supply and so depended on water piped in either from the cold mountain streams near Colossae or from the natural hot springs at Hierapolis. Unfortunately, by the time it arrived at Laodicea, the water was often lukewarm and insipid. The church was resembling its water supply, and John was commanding them to become either therapeutically warm or refreshingly cool.

As prophecy, one can also expect Revelation to refer to actual events that will occur at some time in the future. Old Testament prophecies that were fulfilled in New Testament times sometimes unfolded as the literal occurrence of events previously predicted (e.g., Mic 5:2; cf. Mt 2:6). Frequently, however, the New Testament writers found merely a typological correspondence between ancient prophecy and contemporary events (e.g., Hos 11:1; cf. Mt 2:15)—that is to say, patterns of history were repeating themselves in ways too "coincidental" not to be attributed to the hand of God.[51] So to say that Revelation depicts certain events that had not yet happened at the time of its writing does not enable one to determine how literally they were being described. There is an approach to interpreting Scripture that requires that all texts be taken literally unless there is clear evidence of the use of figures of speech, but however helpful this approach may be for other literary genres, it is almost certainly more misleading than helpful when one approaches prophecy. What John records represents what he actually saw in his visions, but to what extent those visions can be compared to photographs of what will happen in the end times or to what extent God used well-known imagery and symbolism that John and his readers would have understood (much like the political cartoons of today that picture the United States as an eagle and the Soviet Union as a bear) cannot be determined apart from meticulous study and research.

The most significant genre for interpreting Revelation is apocalyptic. Apocalyptic works were common in both Jewish and Greco-Roman circles in antiquity. A somewhat technical but nicely comprehensive definition of an apocalypse is that of John J. Collins:

> "Apocalypse" is a genre of revelatory literature with a narrative framework, in which a revelation is mediated by an otherworldly being to a human recipient, disclosing a transcendent reality which is both temporal, insofar as it envisages eschatological salvation, and spatial insofar as it involves another, supernatural world.[52]

Other good examples of apocalypses from ancient Jewish and Christian writers include 4 Ezra, 2 Baruch, the Apocalypse of

John the Theologian, and the Apocalypse of Peter. Apocalypses regularly used highly unusual, even bizarre or grotesque imagery to communicate truths about the last days. They tended to believe that the world would end with a cataclysmic intervention by God, who would bring justice and create a perfect society. They often encouraged a beleaguered religious community to persevere during times of persecution. All of these features recur in the book of Revelation.

On the other hand, Leon Morris nicely summarizes seven key differences between Revelation and typical apocalypses: (a) regular references to the book as prophecy; (b) typically prophetic warnings and calls for repentance; (c) lack of pseudonymity; (d) an optimistic worldview; (e) no retracing of history in the guise of prophecy; (f) realized eschatology (the end times have begun with the first coming of Christ); (g) little interpretation by angels; and (h) belief that the Messiah has already come and made atonement.[53]

When people misinterpret Revelation, therefore, it is usually because they focus too exclusively on either the prophetic or the apocalyptic element. Many liberal commentators do not adequately take into account the prophetic element. Thus Adela Collins, for example, writes that "a hermeneutic which takes historical criticism seriously [by which she means understanding Revelation as apocalyptic] can no longer work with an interventionist notion of God."[54] In other words, modern readers cannot seriously expect the world to end with God's supernatural intervention by means of the various plagues and tribulation that Revelation describes and certainly not by the universally visible and bodily return of Jesus Christ from heaven. Yet it is precisely this that an understanding of Revelation as prophecy must affirm, however much different schools of interpretation disagree concerning other details. It is an antisupernatural bias, not a correct use of historical (or genre) criticism, that leads Collins to her conclusions. On the other hand, many conservative commentators, especially popular writers like Hal Lindsey, do not adequately take into account the apocalyptic element when they try to find detailed counterparts in current events to each of the different images in Revelation. Ironically, such interpretation often eliminates the supernatural element just as much as more liberal views do. For example, Lindsey's famous interpretation of the locusts in Revelation 9 as armed helicopters[55] misses the point that these are not human creations, but demonic, otherworldly creatures coming up from the Abyss (9:1–3, 11), described in terms designed to horrify ancient readers accustomed to the ravages of locust plagues but wholly ignorant of the methods of twentieth-century warfare.

Fortunately, more and more scholars of both conservative and liberal persuasions are coming to recognize Revelation as a mixture of prophecy and apocalyptic.[56] Several recent international colloquia on apocalyptic writings have begun to rectify the previous, widespread lack of interest in Revelation on the part of most scholars.[57] Works like those of Robert Mounce, George Ladd, and G.-R. Beasley-Murray offer students a good spectrum of plausible evangelical commentary.[58] Numerous details still remain puzzling, and there is room for tolerating a fair amount of disagreement. But for an interpretation of a given passage in Revelation to be relatively convincing, several criteria must be satisfied.[59]

(1) When John interprets a particular symbol, that interpretation must be preferred to any other speculations (e.g., the lampstands of 1:12 are the seven churches to whom John writes [v. 20]). (2) When key Old Testament texts, or for that matter other Jewish texts well known in the first century, use imagery in a consistent way that John seems to echo, those meanings should be carried over into Revelation (e.g., the "son of man" in 1:13 almost certainly hearkens back to Daniel 7:13). (3) When other historical information accessible to first-century Asian readers sheds light on particular details, it should be utilized (e.g., the five months of 9:5 was the average life cycle for a locust, and therefore not necessarily a literal reference to the length of demonic persecution during the tribulation, but merely a length appropriate for symbolism involving locusts). (4) When imagery seems merely to support the central truth of a passage, no specific, allegorical interpretation should be given to it (e.g., all the jewels adorning the walls of the new Jerusalem simply reinforce the picture of its magnificence and do not each stand for some particular attribute [21:19–21]).

Above all, any interpretation that could not have been deduced by John's original readers must be rejected out of hand.[60] When details seem cryptic, it is more likely the modern reader who is missing something that would have been more clear to Revelation's original recipients. To be sure, when the prophet-apocalpyticist Daniel described his visions, there were elements even he did not understand. And the angel told him to seal up the words of his scroll until the end, when all would become clear (12:4, 8–10). But Revelation deliberately reverses this strategy, with the angel's caution to John "not to seal up the words of the prophecy of this book, because the time is near" (22:10). John wrote to encourage persecuted Christians to persevere because God would soon avenge their ill treatment, and he used a combination of well-established genres (however strange they may seem to people today) to inform them in language they were meant to understand about what would happen at the end of history.[61]

CONCLUSION

Understanding the genre of a particular New Testament book scarcely solves all the interpretive issues arising from it. But it does help readers avoid some basic errors that come from a lack of appreciation of literary form. At the level of individual portions of a book, it is widely realized that one cannot interpret a parable the same way as a miracle story or prose in the same fashion as poetry. At last, more and more students of Scripture are recognizing that the same is true when comparing a gospel with an epistle or the book of Acts with the book of Revelation. Genre criticism is still in its infancy as a discipline, and further refinements are surely to be expected. It also runs the risk of overemphasizing the similarities between Scripture and noncanonical writings, just as traditional Christianity has often overemphasized the differences. But the study of genre is here to stay, and it should be welcomed by all serious Bible readers even as they examine each individual hypothesis with a healthy measure of skepticism.

BIBLIOGRAPHY

Aune, David E. *The New Testament in Its Literary Environment*. Philadelphia: Westminster, 1987.

Fee, Gordon D. and Douglas Stuart. *How to Read the Bible for All Its Worth*. Grand Rapids: Zondervan, 1982.

France, R. T. and David Wenham. *Gospel Perspectives III: Studies in Midrash and Historiography*. Sheffield: JSOT, 1983.

Guelich, Robert. "The Gospel Genre." In *Das Evangelium und die Evangelien*. Ed. Peter Stuhlmacher. Tübingen: Mohr, 1983. Pp. 183–219.

Hellholm, David, ed. *Apocalypticism in the Mediterranean World and the Near East*. Tübingen: Mohr, 1983.

Kennedy, George A. *New Testament Interpretation Through Rhetorical Criticism*. Chapel Hill, N.C.: University of North Carolina Press, 1984.

Pervo, Richard I. *Profit with Delight: The Literary Genre of the Acts of the Apostles*. Philadelphia: Fortress, 1987.

Ryken, Leland. *Words of Life: A Literary Introduction to the New Testament*. Grand Rapids: Baker, 1987.

Stowers, Stanley K. *Letter Writing in Greco-Roman Antiquity*. Philadelphia: Westminster, 1986.

Unnik, W. C., van. "Luke's Second Book and the Rules of Hellenistic Historiography." In *Les Actes des Apôtres: Traditions, réaction, théologie*. Ed. Jacob Kremer. Gembloux: Duculot, 1979. Pp. 37–60.

NOTES

[1]David E. Aune, *The New Testament in Its Literary Environment* (Philadelphia: Westminster, 1987), 13. The term "genre" is used in a variety of ways in biblical and literary criticism. A balanced review and assessment of its various uses appears in Grant R. Osborne, "Genre Criticism—Sensus Literalis," *Trin J* n.s. 4 (1983): 1–27.

[2](Grand Rapids: Zondervan, 1982).

[3](Grand Rapids: Zondervan, 1984).

[4](Grand Rapids: Zondervan, 1987).

[5]See note 1. An important collection of samples of Greco-Roman literary genres most relevant for interpreting the New Testament appears in David E. Aune, ed., *Greco-Roman Literature and the New Testament* (Atlanta: Scholars, 1988).

[6]E.g., Morton Smith, "Prolegomena to a Discussion of Aretalogies, Divine Men, the Gospels and Jesus," *JBL* (1971): 174–99.

[7]E.g., respectively, Dan O. Via, Jr., *Kerygma and Comedy in the New Testament* (Philadelphia: Fortress, 1975); Gilbert Bilezikian, *The Liberated Gospel: A Comparison of the Gospel of Mark and Greek Tragedy* (Grand Rapids: Baker, 1977).

[8]Werner G. Kümmel, *Introduction to the New Testament* (Nashville: Abingdon, 1975), 37. The most recent detailed survey of proposals for the genre of the gospels comes to a similar conclusion. See Robert A. Guelich, "The Gospel Genre," in *Das Evangelium und die Evangelien*, ed. Peter Stuhlmacher (Tübingen: Mohr, 1983), 217.

[9]Robert H. Gundry, *Matthew: A Commentary on His Literary and Theological Art* (Grand Rapids: Eerdmans, 1982).

[10]For a more detailed and incisive critique of Gundry, see esp. Philip B. Payne, "Midrash and History in the Gospels with Special Reference to R. H. Gundry's "Matthew," in *Gospel Perspectives*, vol. 3, ed. R. T. France and David Wenham (Sheffield: JSOT, 1983), 177–215.

[11]Werner Kelber, *The Oral and the Written Gospel* (Philadelphia: Fortress, 1983), 131.

[12]See esp. James G. Williams, *Gospel Against Parable* (Sheffield: Almond, 1985).

[13]C. H. Talbert, *What is a Gospel?* (Philadelphia: Fortress, 1977). Philip L. Shuler, *A Genre for the Gospels: The Biographical Character of Matthew* (Philadelphia: Fortress, 1982) classifies Matthew as encomium or laudatory biography but is not overly optimistic about the amount of accurate history it contains.

[14]Martin Hengel, *Acts and the History of Earliest Christianity* (London: SCM, 1979), 16. Cf. Aune, *New Testament*, 64–65.

[15]Terrence Callan, "The Preface of Luke-Acts and Historiography," *NTS* 31 (1985): 576–81.

[16]I have defended this claim at length in my book, *The Historical Reliability of the Gospels* (Leicester: IVP, 1987), which is heavily indebted to the six-volume series, *Gospel Perspectives*, ed. R. T. France, David Wenham, and Craig Blomberg (Sheffield: JSOT, 1980-86).

[17]Cf. esp. my "Midrash, Chiasmus, and the Outline of Luke's Central Section," in *Gospel Perspectives*, vol. 3, 217–61.

[18]Cf. esp. my article, "The Legitimacy and Limits of Harmonization," in *Hermeneutics, Authority, and Canon*, ed. D. A. Carson and John D. Woodbridge (Grand Rapids: Zondervan, 1986), 139–74.

[19]Cf. esp. K. R. Wolfe, "The Chiastic Structure of Luke-Acts and Some Implications for Worship," *SWJT* 22 (1980): 60–71.

[20]Cf. I. H. Marshall, "Luke and His Gospel," in *Das Evangelium und die Evangelien*, 289–308; W. C. van Unnik, "Luke's Second Book and the Rules of Hellenistic Historiography," in *Les Actes des Apôtres: traditions, rédaction, théologie*, ed. Jacob Kremer (Gembloux: Duculot, 1979), 37–60.

[21]William Ramsay, *St. Paul the Traveller and Roman Citizen* (London: Hodder & Stoughton, 1895).

[22]Ernst Haenchen, *The Acts of the Apostles* (Oxford: Blackwell, 1971).

[23]Richard I. Pervo, *Profit with Delight: The Literary Genre of the Acts of the Apostles* (Philadelphia: Fortress, 1987).

[24]John L. White, *Light from Ancient Letters* (Philadelphia: Fortress, 1986); Stanley K. Stowers, *Letter Writing in Greco-Roman Antiquity* (Philadelphia: Westminster, 1986); and Abraham J. Malherbe, *Ancient Epistolary Theorists* (Atlanta: Scholars, 1988).

[25]Adolf Deissmann, *Light from the Ancient East* (London: Harper, 1922⁴), 146–251.

[26]Aune, *New Testament*, 218. Cf. Stowers, *Letter Writing*, 18–19.

[27]See esp. Abraham J. Malherbe, *Paul and the Thessalonians: The Philosophic Tradition of Pastoral Care* (Philadelphia: Fortress, 1987), 68–78. Cf. B. C. Johanson, *To All the Brethren: A Text-Linguistic and Rhetorical Approach to 1 Thessalonians* (Stockholm: Almqvist & Wiksell, 1987), who sees the letter as a combination of parenetic and deliberative forms.

[28]See esp. Benjamin Fiore, *Personal Example in the Socratic and Pastoral Epistles* (Rome: BIP, 1986). Cf. Stowers, *Letter Writing*, 97.

[29]Aune, *New Testament*, 121–22.

[30]Ibid., 211–12; Stowers, *Letter Writing*, 155.

[31]Ibid., 156.

[32]George A. Kennedy, *New Testament Interpretation Through Rhetorical Criticism* (Chapel Hill, N.C.: University of North Carolina Press, 1984), 24.

[33]Hans-Dieter Betz, *Galatians* (Philadelphia: Fortress, 1979). See also Bernard H. Brinsmead, *Galatians—Dialogical Response to Opponents* (Chicago: Scholars, 1982).

[34]Robert G. Hall, "The Rhetorical Outline for Galatians: A Reconsideration," *JBL* 106 (1987): 277–87; Francois Vouga, "Zur rhetorischen Gattung des Galaterbriefes," *ZNW* 79 (1988): 291–92; Joop Smit, "The Letter of Paul to the Galatians: A Deliberative Speech," *NTS* 35 (1989): 1–26.

[35]Robert Jewett, *The Thessalonian Correspondence: Pauline Rhetoric and Millenarian Piety* (Philadelphia: Fortress, 1986), 63–87; G. S. Holland, *The Tradition That You Received From Us: 2 Thessalonians in the Pauline Tradition* (Tübingen: Mohr, 1988), 6.

[36]Wilhelm Wuellner, "Paul's Rhetoric of Argumentation in Romans: An Alternative to the Donfried-Karris Debate over Romans," in *The Romans Debate*, ed. Karl P. Donfried (Minneapolis: Augsburg, 1977), 168. Cf. Kennedy, *Rhetorical Criticism*, 152–56.

[37]Robert Jewett, "Romans as an Ambassadorial Letter," *Int* 36 (1982): 5–20.

[38]Stanley K. Stowers, *The Diatribe and Paul's Letter to the Romans* (Chicago: Scholars, 1981).

[39]Duane F. Watson, "A Rhetorical Analysis of Philippians and Its Implications for the Unity Question," *NovT* 30 (1988): 57–88.

[40]Linda L. Belleville, "A Letter of Apologetic Self-Commendation: 2 Cor. 1:8–7:16," forthcoming in *NovT*.

[41]Craig L. Blomberg, "The Structure of 2 Corinthians 1–7," *Criswell Theological Review* 4.1 (1989): 3–20.

[42]William L. Lane, "Hebrews: A Sermon in Search of a Setting," *SWJT* 28 (1985): 13–18.

[43]Peter H. Davids, *The Epistle of James* (Grand Rapids: Eerdmans, 1982). Cf. J. M. Reese, "The Exegete as Sage: Hearing the Message of James," *BTB* 12 (1982): 82–85.

[44]Aune, *New Testament*, 218. An attractive but perhaps slightly anachronistic alternative is Stephen S. Smalley's label "paper"—i.e., "a consideration, for purposes of teaching and further discussion, of the christological and ethical issues which were causing debate and even division within the Johannine church" (*1, 2, 3 John* [Waco: Word, 1984], xxxiii).

[45]Richard J. Bauckham, *Jude, 2 Peter* (Waco: Word, 1983), 131–63. Duane F. Watson, *Invention, Arrangement and Style: Rhetorical Criticism of Jude and 2 Peter* (Atlanta: Scholars, 1988) finds 2 Peter a combination of testamentary genre and deliberative rhetoric.

[46]Cf. esp. Richard J. Bauckham, "Pseudo-Apostolic Letters," *JBL* 107 (1988): 469-94.

[47]The best recent example is Mark Kiley, *Colossians as Pseudepigraphy* (Sheffield: JSOT, 1986). But see George E. Cannon, *The Use of Traditional Materials in Colossians* (Macon: Mercer, 1983), 136–66, who uses genre criticism to compare the rhetorical structure of Colossians with the undisputed Pauline letters, discovering parallels that would not easily be imitated by a different writer.

[48]The best recent example is Lewis R. Donelson, *Pseudepigraphy and Ethical Argument in the Pastoral Epistles* (Tübingen: Mohr, 1986), who even argues that this trait characterized an entire pseudepigraphic genre.

[49]The most important recent evangelical treatment of pseudepigraphy is David G. Meade, *Pseudonymity and Canon* (Grand Rapids: Eerdmans, 1987), who argues that before the mid-second century it was generally acceptable. For further discussion, see Thomas D. Lea's essay on pseudonymity in this volume.

[50]See esp. Colin J. Hemer, *The Letters to the Seven Churches of Asia in Their Local Setting* (Sheffield: JSOT, 1986).

[51]See esp. R. T. France, *The Gospel According to Matthew* (Grand Rapids: Eerdmans, 1985), 40.

[52]John J. Collins, "Introduction: Morphology of a Genre," *Semeia* 14 (1979), 9. Cf. Jean Carmignac, "Qu'est-ce que l'Apocalyptique? Son emploi à Qumran," *RQ* 10 (1979): 3–33.

[53]Leon Morris, *The Book of Revelation* (Grand Rapids: Eerdmans, 1987²), 25–27.

[54]Adela Y. Collins, "Reading the Book of Revelation in the Twentieth Century," *Int* 40 (1986): 242.

[55]Hal Lindsey, *There's A New World Coming* (Santa Ana, Calif.: Vision House, 1973), 124.

[56]The pioneering study was George E. Ladd, "Why Not Prophetic-Apocalyptic?", *JBL* 76 (1957): 192–200. Cf. David Hill, *New Testament Prophecy* (London: Marshall, Morgan & Scott, 1979), 70–93; Elisabeth S.

Fiorenza, *The Book of Revelation: Justice and Judgment* (Philadelphia: Fortress, 1985), 133–56.

[57]Results are published in *Semeia* 14 (1979); 36 (1986); and David Hellholm, ed. *Apocalypticism in the Mediterranean World and the Near East* (Tübingen: Mohr, 1983).

[58]Robert H. Mounce, *The Book of Revelation* (Grand Rapids: Eerdmans, 1977); George E. Ladd, *The Revelation of John* (Grand Rapids: Eerdmans 1972); G.-R. Beasley-Murray, *The Book of Revelation* (London: Oliphants, 1974).

[59]One of the best and most readable guides to principles for interpreting Revelation is A. B. Mickelsen, *Daniel and Revelation* (Nashville: Nelson, 1984).

[60]Fee and Stuart, *How to Read the Bible*, 209–10.

[61]For excellent and recent evangelical summaries of the message and application of Revelation, see Donald Guthrie, *The Relevance of John's Apocalypse* (Grand Rapids: Eerdmans, 1987); and Graeme Goldsworthy, *The Gospel in Revelation* (Exeter: Paternoster, 1984).

Chapter Eighteen

Pseudonymity and the New Testament

Thomas D. Lea

Thomas D. Lea

Thomas D. Lea is Associate Professor of New Testament at Southwestern Baptist Theological Seminary in Fort Worth, Texas. He holds degrees from Mississippi State University (B.S.) and Southwestern Baptist Theological Seminary (M.Div., Th.D.). He has also studied at Regent College in Vancouver, British Columbia. His articles have appeared in such journals as *Criswell Theological Review*, *Journal of the Evangelical Theological Society*, *Southwestern Journal of Theology*, and *Theological Educator*. He has also authored (with Curtis Vaughan) *1 Corinthians* and *1 Peter, 2 Peter, and Jude* in the *Bible Study Commentary* (Zondervan). He has just completed the volume on 1 and 2 Timothy for *The New American Commentary* (Broadman).

Chapter Eighteen

Pseudonymity and the New Testament

Many contemporary New Testament scholars accept the pseudonymous authorship of such New Testament writings as Colossians, Ephesians, the Pastoral Epistles, James, and 1 and 2 Peter. Pseudonymous authorship of a New Testament writing would occur if a writer deliberately used a name other than his own in producing a book of the New Testament. Supporters of this view feel that the writer used pseudonymity for a variety of purposes. Some scholars feel that writers gained acceptance for their opinions by attributing them to venerated authors of antiquity. Others feel that writers used pseudonymity to conceal the source of unpopular opinions that might endanger their author.

In discussing pseudonymity we must begin by admitting anonymity. All of the Gospels, Acts, and Hebrews are anonymous. None of these writings claims an author within the book. The question of pseudonymous authorship arises only when an author willfully uses the name of someone other than himself as the author of a work.

Many justify the presence of pseudonymous writings in the New Testament by pointing to the widespread acceptance of the practice in extrabiblical writings. Many others, including this writer, find ethical, psychological, historical, and theological objections to the acceptance of the practice in the New Testament.

To understand the problem, we will first investigate historically the development of the issue and then study contemporary opinions about pseudonymity in the New Testament. Finally we will suggest various approaches to understanding the issue. We will also investigate the authorship of the Pastoral Epistles in order to relate the application of the concept of pseudonymous authorship to New Testament study.

HISTORICAL DEVELOPMENTS
IN THE STUDY OF PSEUDONYMITY

A study of the practice of pseudonymity in literary history can provide perspective for understanding the subject. We will investigate the practice of pseudonymity among the Jews and references to the practice in the New Testament itself. It will be important to observe the discussion about the practice among the Ante-Nicene Fathers and in the writings of that largely pseudonymous literature known as the New Testament Apocrypha. We will also study the opinions of biblical scholars on this subject up through the year 1950.

Pseudonymity in Jewish Writings

Pseudonymity among the Jews appeared more frequently in apocalypses than in epistles. Names such as Enoch, Baruch, and Ezra were attached to apocalyptic productions, presumably to gain acceptance for the writing. Two letters prior to the Christian era also employed pseudonymity, a rare practice among the Jews. The *Epistle of Jeremy* uses the name of the prophet Jeremiah to supplement the canonical book and provides a penetrating denunciation of idolatry. Guthrie feels that the epistle "was issued under Jeremiah's name because it was intended to supply a supposed deficiency in the canonical treatment of Babylonian idolatry."[1] The *Letter of Aristeas* represents a defense of the Jews for a gentile environment. The author is difficult to identify precisely, but he writes to his brother Philocrates about the Jewish effort to translate the Hebrew Old Testament into Greek. Readers of the letter would link the writer with the production of the LXX in the time of Ptolemy II Philadelphus of Egypt (285–247 B.C.). The writer of the letter presents himself as involved in the mission of Scripture translation, but Charlesworth dates the writing between 250 B.C. and A.D. 100.[2]

The presence of these examples of epistolary pseudepigraphy among the Jews should not lead us to assume that Christian writers adopted this literary genre. Christians placed a high value on the practice of truthfulness and honesty. This emphasis makes it questionable that Christians would uncritically adopt a practice of debatable virtue. Also, we must inquire whether the church historically accepted the practice of pseudonymity.

Internal New Testament Evidence Concerning Pseudonymity

The New Testament contains little evidence concerning the views of early Christians on the subject of pseudonymity. However, the existing evidence does not support the idea that New Testament writers accepted the practice.

In 2 Thessalonians 2:2 Paul warned against the acceptance of the teaching of a letter "supposed to have come from us." In 3:17 he states that the greeting in his own handwriting provided a sign of the authenticity of the letter. Paul's chief reasons for proscribing acceptance of the pseudonymous writing was the doctrinal heresy of the letter. However, it seems unlikely that Paul would sanction the use of pseudonymity in the service of orthodoxy when he had attacked its usage in the spread of heresy.

Paul warned in 1 Timothy 4:1–2 against accepting the teaching of "hypocritical liars" and "deceiving spirits." These pungent words would seem to apply in prohibiting the acceptance of literary forgeries that intended to spread false teaching. As Candlish says, "A false report of his word might proceed from a mere mistake; but a letter wrongly ascribed to him could only be a fiction designed to deceive."[3]

Many New Testament writings contain an appeal for truth that could not harmonize with the mental approach of a willful pseudonymous writer. In Ephesians 4:15 Paul directs his readers to "speak the truth," and in Colossians 3:9 he says, "Do not lie to each other." In Ephesians 4:25 Paul directs his readers to "put off falsehood and speak truthfully." Guthrie has warned that "pseudepigraphic hypotheses must assume that the author's notion of the truth contained nothing inconsistent with a literary method which he must have known would deceive many if not all his readers."[4]

The Ante-Nicene Writers and Pseudonymity

What criteria did writers after the New Testament era use to determine which books were genuine and which were false? Both "genuine" and "false" relate to the identity of the stated author rather than to the content of the book. Did it matter to post-apostolic Christians whether their writings carried the name of the correct author?

Serious discussion of the apostolic authorship of Christian writings would normally take place only for those writings produced in the period before Nicea. After this period writings would be so far distant from the apostolic period that an audience would normally see that a document that claimed apostolic authorship was spurious.

Christians evidently took seriously the claim for authorship in a book and applied several tests to writings to determine their acceptability. Although Eusebius is not classed among the Ante-Nicene Fathers, he does relate incidents that come from that period. He discusses the authenticity of the *Shepherd of Hermas* and indicated that the acceptability of the book hinged on the certainty of authorship. Some identified Hermas with the disciple by the same name in Romans 16:14. Others disputed the identification. Eusebius said that because of the uncertainty on this issue the book was not "placed among those of acknowledged authority" by those who rejected the identity of the two men.[5] Known pseudonymous authorship of this book would have led to its rejection from the list of accepted books.

Eusebius also related the story of Serapion and the Gospel of Peter. In the late second century Serapion, bishop of Antioch, wrote a letter to the church at Rhosse in Cilicia concerning their use of the apocryphal Gospel of Peter. Serapion had initially allowed the church to use the book, but that was before he had read it himself. When he realized that this writing also contained heresy, he banned its usage. He explained, "We, brethren, receive Peter and the other apostles as Christ himself. But those writings which falsely go under their name, as we are well acquainted with them, we reject, and know also, that we have not received such handed down to us."[6] Both doctrinal deviation and the pseudonymous authorship of the book were factors in Serapion's rejection of the Gospel of Peter.

Tertullian insisted that orthodox teaching of Christianity should come only from the apostles. He says, "It remains, then, that we demonstrate whether this doctrine of ours, of which we have now given the rule, has its origin in the tradition of the apostles, and whether all other *doctrines* do not ipso facto proceed from falsehood."[7] Tertullian insisted that both the authorship and the content of the writings demanded scrutiny before acceptance.

Tertullian also referred to the writing of the apocryphal *Acts of Paul* by an elder of Asia. He noted that the elder had written the fictional material from a love for Paul to increase Paul's fame. Despite his good intentions, the church removed the elder from office.[8] It is true that Tertullian questioned the acceptance of the book because it provided an example of women's teaching and baptizing. It is hard to feel that he was indifferent to the pseudonymous authorship of the book. However, Tertullian's discussion does suggest that the church was greatly concerned about the fictional nature of the book. The author of the book did not claim to be Paul, but he presented himself as a friend of Paul and elaborated some of the accounts about Paul that he had received. The church greeted the fictional writing, even for the positive purpose of honoring Paul, as an offense deserving of removal from office.

Supporters of the practice of pseudonymity in Scripture have sometimes seized a statement of Tertullian to support their views. Tertullian suggested that "it may well seem that the works which disciples publish belong to their masters."[9] Some supporters of the practice of pseudonymity have taken this statement to support their view that a disciple of Paul penned Ephesians pseudonymously in Paul's name. They understand Tertullian to teach that the public would attribute the work of disciples to their masters without seeing any moral inconsistency.

Tertullian used the statement to prove the canonicity of the Gospels of Mark and Luke. Since neither writer was an apostle, Tertullian established their dependency on Peter and Paul respectively. This dependence by Mark and Luke on the apostles confirmed the authority and canonicity of their writings. This statement of Tertullian must not be used as a broad, sweeping defense of the practice of pseudonymity. We should limit its usage to a confirmation of the authority of Mark and Luke.[10]

In his discussion of the corporeality of God, Origen referred to the *Doctrine of Peter*. He rejected the use of the writing because he indicated that the book "was not composed either by Peter or by any person inspired by the Spirit of God."[11] Presumed pseudonymity of the writing was a factor in Origen's rejection of it.

Some students of the New Testament suggest that early Christian writers may have been indifferent to the practice of pseudonymity due to their precritical mindset. Dionysius' intelligent discussion of the authorship of Revelation dispels this idea. Dionysius admitted that the author of Revelation was a holy, inspired man named John. He questioned apostolic authorship with the words:

> . . . I could not so easily admit that this was the apostle, the son of Zebedee, the brother of James, and the same person with him who wrote the Gospel which bears the title *according to John*, and the catholic epistle. But from the character of both, and the forms of expression, and the whole disposition and execution of the book, I draw the conclusion that the authorship is not his.[12]

Dionysius examined the book with techniques that resembled those of modern criticism. He reflected no gullibility or a precritical mindset. He rejected apostolic authorship of the Revelation, but he did not embrace pseudonymous authorship of the book. He was not sure of the identity of the author, but he was certain that a follower of Jesus named John was the author.

The *Constitutions of the Holy Apostles* was sometimes seen as the work of Clement, bishop of Rome. Students of the book have found it to be a document of the third century with additions that could be dated later.[13] The document contained laws or instructions on various moral issues and directives for bishops, presbyters, and deacons. Some sections provided encouragement to those who faced martyrdom. One section warned against pseudonymous writings with the words:

> . . . you are not to attend to the names of the apostles, but to the nature of the things, and their settled opinions. For we know that Simon and Cleobius, and their followers, have compiled poisonous books under the name of Christ and of His disciples, and do carry them about in order to deceive you who love Christ, and us His servants.[14]

These words indicate the attitude of an unknown early Christian writer on the subject of pseudonymity. It is unlikely that this writer would have accepted as genuine a writing known to come from a pseudonymous author. This view would seem to represent the view of Christian orthodoxy on the practice of pseudonymous writings.

Evidence from the early Fathers suggests that two factors were important in judging the authenticity of a writing. A book espousing heresy faced rejection. A writing known to be pseudonymous also faced rejection. These twin criteria seemed to fit together just as the obverse and converse sides of coins. Evidence indicates that the church would reject the writings of apostles if they contained error. The church would also reject known pseudonymity even if it taught orthodoxy. F. F. Bruce surveys the criteria of canonicity and suggests that "it is doubtful if any book would have found a place in the canon if it had been *known* to be pseudonymous. . . . Anyone who was known to have composed a work explicitly in the name of an apostle would have met with . . . disapproval."[15]

Pseudonymity in the New Testament Apocrypha

Schneemelcher defines the New Testament Apocrypha as:

> Writings which have not been received into the canon, but which by title and other statements lay claim to be in the same class with the writings of the canon, and which from the point of view of Form Criticism further develop and mould the kinds of style created and received in the NT. . . .[16]

Much of this literature is pseudonymous in its claims to authorship. Several motives led authors to employ pseudonymity. Some of the literature intended to supplement material in the canonical writings. The *Infancy Gospels* use meager hints from the canonical Gospels in order to provide expanded fictional information about the life of Christ. Some of the apocryphal writings contain variant teachings and traditions that appeared in early Christianity. The *Gospel of Thomas*, an acknowledged product of Gnostic circles, demonstrates this feature. Other writings, such as the *Acts of Paul*, glorified the figures of the apostles for various reasons. Hennecke's two-volume work presents over seventy-five examples of apocryphal fragments and documents that present some information relating to the history of the New Testament or its doctrines.

The church exercised discernment in rejecting these writings as spurious. There is some uncertainty concerning the precise principles used by the church to determine genuineness, but Schneemelcher says, "What was fundamental and apostolic was given precedence, but what was apostolic was determined by what was fundamental, i.e., by the confession and faith of the Church."[17] The twin criteria of orthodoxy and apostolicity were used in testing these writings for genuineness.

Two lists of the canonical writings of the New Testament also provide help in assessing the criteria used by the church in determining the genuineness of writings. The Muratorian Canon bears the name of its discoverer L. Antonio Muratori, who published it in 1740. Metzger feels that the document is the product of someone living in or near Rome near the close of the second century.[18] The author lists those writings believed by his part of the church to belong to the New Testament.

The author of the list mentions an epistle to the Laodiceans and also to the Alexandrians. He describes them both as "forged in Paul's name."[19] He is unwilling to receive them into the canon accepted by the church. Strangely the writer accepts the intertestamental *Wisdom of Solomon* but expresses reluctance about the use of the *Apocalypse of Peter*. The only clear criterion advanced by the writer seems to be a demand that no forgeries be admitted into the canon. He would clearly oppose pseudonymous authorship.

Eusebius provides a list of canonical writings in his *Ecclesiastical History*. He divided the books into the categories of "recognized," "disputed," and "spurious."[20] The recognized books included the four Gospels, Acts, thirteen Epistles of Paul (without an individual listing), 1 John, and 1 Peter. The disputed books included James, Jude, 2 Peter, and 2 and 3 John. He mentioned that some leaders accepted Revelation as a recognized writing, but he also indicated that some listed it as spurious. He omitted mention of the Epistle to the Hebrews, but he may have viewed it as authored by Paul and included among these writings.

Eusebius described the spurious books as those in which "the character of the style also is far removed from apostolic usage, and the thought and purport of their contents are completely out of harmony with true orthodoxy and clearly show themselves that they are the forgeries of heretics."[21] The term "forgery" described that which was fictional or fabricated. Eusebius rejected those writings whose contents were heretical and whose authorship was known to be pseudonymous.

We may view Eusebius's statements as indicative of the techniques used by other Christian leaders in distinguishing the true writings from the false. The dual themes of orthodoxy and apostolic authorship appear as the criteria by which canonical writings are distinguished from the false.

Views About the Practice of Pseudonymity (up to 1950)

The Reformation produced a resurgence of interest in Bible study, and with this renewed interest it was inevitable that questions about pseudonymity would arise. Luther, for example, excluded James from his canon, but not because of pseudonymous authorship. He felt that James failed to present a clear affirmation of Christ. He commented, "That which does not teach Christ is still not Apostolic, even if it were the teaching of St. Peter or St. Paul. Again that which preaches Christ, that were Apostolic, even if Judas, Annas, Pilate, and Herod 'preached it.' "[22] Presumably a pseudonymous writing that preached Christ would be acceptable to Luther regardless of its authorship.

Calvin's approach to 2 Peter suggests his acceptance of a secretary as the author of the writing. He says:

> If it is received as canonical, we must admit that Peter is the author, not only because it bears his name, but also because he testifies that he lived with Christ. . . . Therefore I conclude that if the epistle is trustworthy it has come from Peter; not that he wrote it himself, but that one of his disciples composed by his command what the necessity of the times demanded.[23]

The questions raised by Luther and Calvin regarding authorship were words from questioners who were confident of the high authority of Scripture. Many German critics of the nineteenth century were more suspicious of the historical trustworthiness of Scripture.

F. C. Baur attacked the authenticity of the Pastorals with

the words, "What gives these Epistles their claim to the name of the apostle is simply the circumstances that they profess to be Pauline, and make the apostle speak as their author."[24] Baur felt that the presence of pseudonymity in the Pastorals should prepare students of the New Testament to expect it in other places. He refused to call the practice willful forgery or deception, but he betrayed a pejorative attitude toward the writings by referring to the "forging of such Epistles."[25] So extravagant did Baur become in his rejection of the apostolic origin of most of Paul's writings that he viewed even Philemon as a work of "Christian fiction." Instead he regarded it "as a Christian romance serving to convey a genuine Christian idea."[26]

Adolph Jülicher followed the suggestions of Baur in looking for examples of pseudonymity in the New Testament, but he attempted to justify the presence of the genre with more detailed descriptions. He rejected the term "forgery" as the proper term to use in describing pseudonymous writings. He attributed the presence of pseudonymous writings to the "boundless credulity" of Christians and to the fact that believers frequently borrowed from books without considering the practice dishonest. He indicated that writers put whatever words they desired into the mouth of a respected apostle without regarding themselves as deceivers. He believed that early Christians "were quite indifferent as to the form in which it was clothed."[27] He cites the presence of pseudepigraphical literature in both Greek and Jewish civilization. It was not so much that these examples spurred early Christians to produce pseudonymous writings, but the widespread presence of the practice shows the naivete and lack of literary concern in these civilizations. Jülicher did not follow the almost total skepticism of some German scholars in rejecting all of the Pauline Epistles except Romans, the Corinthian Epistles, and Galatians. He felt that "Paul must first have written his Epistles and these Epistles have won repute and influence, before those who had not the courage to appear openly under their own names could attempt to influence Christendom in the customary form of the didactic letter."[28] Jülicher's ideas are important because they represent an approach to the practice of pseudonymity that is still used in defending the practice today.

Martin Dibelius was another influential German writer in the early twentieth century. He was instrumental in popularizing a form critical approach to the Gospels. His views concerning the practice of pseudonymity in the New Testament were not so comprehensive as those of Jülicher, but he felt that the practice was indisputably present in the New Testament. In discussing the authorship of 2 Peter he said, "Obviously in this case we have the beginning of pseudonymity in the literary sense."[29] After investigating the content of the Pastorals, he decided that the character of the language demonstrated that they were not authentic. He believes that a "Paulinist makes use here of conceptions which are foreign to the Pauline letters which have come down to us."[30]

Questions concerning the apostolic authorship of New Testament books were not limited to European scholars. The influential New Testament scholar James Moffatt, born in Great Britain but long a teacher in America, advocated the presence of pseudonymity in the New Testament. He explained the presence of pseudonymous writings by referring to Jewish and Greek literary antecedents. He felt that Christian writers innocently adopted a practice that was widespread in the ancient world. The type of pseudonymity in the New Testament, according to Moffatt, varied in the following instances:

> While 2 Peter represents in the NT Canon a pseudonymous epistle, pure and simple, the pastoral epistles, on the other hand, were composed by a Paulinist who must have had access to certain notes or papers of the great apostle, which he incorporated in his own writings.[31]

Moffatt felt that a chief motive for the appearance of pseudonymity was a modesty that prevented a follower of a noted master from presenting his own ideas about the master's teaching under his own name.[32] He explained the method of pseudonymity by appealing to examples in the practice of ancient Greek and Roman authors. He noted that classical historians felt no guilt over composing writings that were true to "the general spirit of the situation"[33] but that reflected the creative imagination of the author in its details. This practice in the world of ancient literature led to the composition of speeches in the New Testament that "consist of (a) compositions made up from previous materials, usually genuine in the main; and (b) more or less free compositions, which . . . represent what the writer's historical sense judged appropriate to the situation."[34] Moffatt assumed that Christian writers adopted a literary outlook that was similar to that of non-Christian writers. Evidence from both the New Testament and the practice of the early church renders this assumption questionable.

Another American, E. J. Goodspeed, made two observations about pseudonymity in his book *New Chapters in New Testament Study*.[35] First, he warned against studying each piece of literature in isolation and instead urged that they all "must be studied together from the point of view of its pseudonymous character."[36] The idea seems to be that an increase in the number of potentially pseudonymous writings makes the presence of additional pseudonymous writings more likely. Goodspeed begins with an assumption that Jude and 2 Peter are pseudonymous, and he progressively extends the designation to include Ephesians, 1 Peter, James, and the Pastorals. Second, he assumed along with Moffatt that it was normal "for a disciple to put forth his interpretation or restatement of his master's teaching under that master's name."[37]

The foregoing discussion has dealt largely with those who accepted and defended the practice of pseudonymity. Not all scholars readily recognized the presence of this literary convention in the New Testament. Two British scholars of the late nineteenth and the early twentieth centuries expressed their reservations about the practice.

J. S. Candlish carefully examined the historical response in the early church to pseudonymity and rejected the concept on an ethical basis.[38] He suggests that inspired writings could use whatever literary genre would be acceptable in secular writings of the day.[39] However, he excludes from the sweep of his statement those writings that use deliberate falsehood or deceit, for "the detection of these in any composition, designed to promote selfish or sectarian ends, is inconsistent with its being divinely inspired."[40]

R. D. Shaw included a section, "Pseudonymity and Interpolation," in a discussion of the Pastorals.[41] He followed Candlish in rejecting the concept of pseudonymous writings based on the ethical inconsistency of the act. He also found it incomprehensible that the New Testament era could produce a writer so skilled that he could pseudonymously produce a Pauline epistle that was universally received as authentic.[42] He strongly asserted that a writer who made a determined attempt to deceive his readers would violate a basic moral principle and that "the claim to a place in the canon must go with it."[43]

A survey of two German supporters of pseudonymity in the twentieth century will conclude this historical survey. Arnold Meyer wrote a brief but comprehensive study of pseudonymity and concluded that the ethical argument against pseudonymity was not convincing.[44] He viewed pseudonymity as an obvious literary device, harmless and not intended as deceitful.

F. Torm raised questions about the psychological problems underlying the practice of pseudepigraphy.[45] Torm studied the problem of authorship of the Pastorals. He concluded that it was easier to accept Pauline authorship than to accept a pseudonymous writer who became a shrewd, calculating trickster who attempted also to appear as a warm, deeply ethical believer. From a literary standpoint he felt that it was better to allow the author of a book to use nuances in his expressions than to create a pseudonymous personality who more resembled a phantom than a living human being.

Our survey has taken us from the Reformation to the mid-twentieth century. The supporters of pseudonymity varied in their intensity of support from a cautious acceptance of an amanuensis in writing 2 Peter to the rejection of all the Pauline epistles except Romans, 1 and 2 Corinthians, and Galatians. Supporters of the practice explained the practice as due to the credulity of the early church and to the influence of numerous examples from Greek and Jewish writings. Many supporters of pseudonymity refused to see the productions as forgeries and suggested that the use of the genre was not dishonest in any way.

Opponents of the practice viewed it as ethically incongruous with the profession by Christian writers of a deep moral concern. They also pointed out the psychological difficulties inherent in combining a practice of deceit with a profession of morality. They asked, "How could the craftsman of a pseudonymous writing be a warm, obedient believer?" These issues still constitute much of the focus in contemporary discussions of pseudonymity.

CONTEMPORARY DISCUSSIONS OF PSEUDONYMITY

In this section we will survey insights concerning pseudonymous authorship of New Testament writings contributed by scholars since the 1950s.

J. C. Fenton surveyed factors leading to the practice of pseudonymity in an article entitled "Pseudonymity in the New Testament."[46] The prevalence of numerous examples of pseudonymous writings in the ancient world made him assert that the practice was an accepted literary genre used by both the heretical and the orthodox. He felt that some writers published pseudonymously because they had encountered heresy and wanted to call their readers back to the trustworthy teaching of an apostle. Another motive inspiring pseudonymous writing came from a student who wished to attribute his work to his teacher.

Kurt Aland presented a discussion of the problem of pseudonymity that rejected ethical and psychological considerations and attempted to break new ground.[47] He considered the literature of the first two centuries in making his new proposal. In examining this literature he suggested that the Gospels and many other New Testament books first appeared anonymously. He included in his discussion of anonymity many examples from noncanonical writings. For example, he suggested that the author of the Epistle of Barnabas viewed himself as a channel for Spirit-inspired knowledge to flow to the readers.[48] Aland feels that the *Didache* helps to make a transition from anonymous writings to pseudonymous writings. He views the writer of the document as a charismatic who first proclaimed his message to a local congregation. The content of his message confirmed the claim, the church acknowledged the claim, and the *Didache* achieved widespread recognition in the church.[49] The author remained anonymous because the church felt that the true author of the material was the Holy Spirit. Aland's conclusion was that the use of pseudonymity was the logical conclusion from the presupposition of the Spirit's authorship. Since the Spirit and the apostles agree, Aland sees nothing wrong with the writer's attributing authorship to them. The result is that Aland accepts pseudonymity as normal, and the presence of the name of a true author as abnormal.[50]

Aland assumes that there is no difference in the sense of inspiration for writers of canonical and noncanonical literature. Also, as others have pointed out,[51] the logical result of Aland's idea is that the genuine Paul was less Spirit-filled than some nameless imitator who practices Spirit-filled pseudonymity. Further, Aland neglects not only the ethical and psychological dilemma of pseudonymity, but he also ignores the historical practices of the early church. He does not discuss evidence of the rejection of the practice of pseudonymity by the early church.

Norbert Brox is a contemporary German writer who uses a variety of principles to explain his acceptance of pseudonymity in the New Testament.[52] Brox's contribution does not represent a completely new approach but is a combination of several existing principles. He feels that the early Fathers were more concerned about the nature of the teaching than the identity of the author. He also emphasized that some writers sought to guarantee the authority of their statements by attributing them to an earlier age. Brox feels that they saw nothing wrong in using falsehood in the support of their religion.

David Meade has made the most complete recent attempt in English to explain the practice of pseudonymity in the New Testament. He has suggested that a Jewish background lies behind the practice of pseudonymity. He feels that the literary attribution to an author "must be regarded more as a claim to authoritative tradition . . . and less a claim to actual authorship."[53] He finds no moral culpability in the practice, for he feels that the actual author believed that his beliefs were faithful to and continuous with the teachings of the suggested author. Meade refuses to locate canonical authority in literary authorship or personal inspiration. He locates it in a religious community that interprets tradition and receives nurture from it.[54]

Meade's analysis does not profess to "prove or disprove pseudonymity . . . but to understand it."[55] Despite this claim, however, Meade writes with the assumption that pseudonymity is a fact and attempts to give a rationale for it. One reviewer has expressed this caution about Meade's analysis:

> [Meade's] confidence is a bit surprising since he engages in no literary analysis of the biblical texts, shows little apprehension of the complexity of the historical data and compositional techniques in the New Testament writings, and is occupied primarily in refereeing with remarkable speed various modern theories and interpretations as they bear upon his thesis.[56]

In a pertinent article Bruce Metzger has provided much helpful material for understanding the practice of pseudepigraphical writing.[57] He admits the circulation in antiquity of

many pseudonymous writings and presents motives for understanding their production. He concludes that patristic writers
condemned pseudonymous writings on both literary and
doctrinal grounds.[58] He surveys differing opinions about various pseudepigraphical literature and concludes that "the
prevalence of differing degrees of sensitivity to the morality of
such productions, should warn us against attempting to find a
single formula that will solve all questions."[59] Without providing a detailed discussion for accepting pseudonymity, he
nevertheless accepts that "it cannot be argued that the character
of inspiration excludes the possibility of pseudepigraphy
among the canonical writings."[60]

Those who reject the concept of pseudonymity in the New
Testament vary in their approach. J. I. Packer approaches the
issue theologically with the statement that "pseudonymity and
canonicity are mutually exclusive."[61] Michael Green has ethical
and historical objections to admitting the presence of pseudonymity in the New Testament. However, he speaks in a
conciliatory manner to those who might disagree with him:

> If . . . it could be conclusively proved that 2 Peter is that
> otherwise unexampled thing, a perfectly orthodox epistolary
> pseudepigraph, I, for one, believe that we should have to
> accept the fact that God did employ the literary genre of
> pseudepigraphy for the communicating of His revelation.[62]

Bruce rejects the concept of pseudonymity in the New
Testament and suggests that the criterion of apostolicity is still
relevant in determining the authorship of New Testament
books. He applies it in a different way. He does not seek to
ground the acceptance of such a Gospel as Luke on direct
apostolic influence, but he feels that Luke has based his record
on "authentic apostolic preaching" that he received from
eyewitnesses and others.[63]

Donald Guthrie is the most prolific contemporary writer
who opposes accepting the presence of pseudonymous material
in the New Testament.[64] Guthrie refrains from making a
theological affirmation that would exclude pseudonymous
material from the New Testament. He investigates the attitude
of the early church concerning the acceptance of pseudonymous writings and concludes that "where the pseudonymous
device was recognized it was not merely not tolerated but
emphatically condemned."[65] He also objects to the practice of

pseudonymity on ethical grounds. He finds that the "deception" involved in writing pseudonymous literature "is difficult to reconcile with the high spiritual quality of the New Testament writings concerned."[66] He also studies the psychological problem present when a man of profound religious convictions uses a literary style that would be dishonest at worst and questionable at best. He concludes that "psychological difficulties lie in the path of theories of pseudonymous authorship and advocates of them must come to grips with these problems in presenting their case."[67]

Those who find and accept pseudonymous writings in the New Testament show little concern over the ethical problem that this would create. They contend that the early church saw nothing dishonest in a writer's attributing his words to another author. They do not value psychological objections to pseudonymous authorship. They do not find the practice of the early church in questioning pseudonymous authorship a compelling feature to prevent the consideration of the concept. They generally feel that the early church was more concerned about correct doctrine than about literary origins. David Meade, the most important recent advocate in English of the idea of pseudonymity in the New Testament canon, suggests that the practice indicates only authoritative tradition, not literary authorship.

Opponents of the idea of pseudonymous authorship take the opposite position on most of these issues. Some rule out the possibility of pseudonymous writings with theological objections. Most opponents of the practice find the ethical objections to its existence insurmountable. Also, they feel that the practice of the early church would not have knowingly permitted the acceptance of a pseudonymous writing into the canon. Finally, they find psychological difficulties in picturing a writer who could actually turn out a writing under a false name.

CONCLUSION

Students of the subject of pseudonymous literature in the New Testament must consider several factors in arriving at a solution. First, they must consider both the internal evidence of a New Testament writing and the external evidence of the church's reception of that writing. Such eminent New Testament scholars as H. Conzelmann, M. Dibelius, and A. T.

Hanson have examined evidence for the Pauline authorship of the Pastorals and have concluded against apostolic authorship. However, scholars such as Gordon Fee, J. N. D. Kelly, and Donald Guthrie examine the same evidence and conclude for apostolic authorship. An observer can easily charge that both sides make subjective evaluations. It is important to ask how the church dealt with pseudonymous writings. Scholars must consider both internal and external evidence in assessing the practice of pseudonymity. Available evidence for the study of the church's attitude toward pseudonymous writings suggests that the church did not accept it.

Second, students of the practice of pseudonymity must not ignore the ethical dilemma that the acceptance of pseudepigraphy involves. It is difficult to accept the existence of a church that could urge its members to practice truth and at the same time condone the obvious deceit of pseudonymous writings. It appears inconsistent for the writer of Ephesians to urge his readers to "put off falsehood" (Eph 4:25) if he were not Paul.

Third, R. D. Shaw has written compellingly of the psychological difficulties in picturing a pseudonymous author when he said:

> This enthusiastic disciple, who considered himself a "genuine Paulinist," at once so skillful and so obtuse, following so closely yet differing so daringly, inventing impossible personal situations . . . while he yet breathes an air of the profoundest reverence for truth, conspicuously able and fruitful in an age of conspicuous feebleness and barrenness, pretending to honour his master, conjuring with his name, in the very act of flying in the face of his most solemn warnings and attenuating his most cherished doctrines—is an absolute chimaera.[68]

Fourth, many students of the development of the New Testament canon agree that apostolic authorship was important. R. Laird Harris has written that "the canonicity of a book of the Bible depends upon its authorship. . . . If it was a part of the New Testament, it was recognized as inspired if it had been written by an apostle—either by himself or with the help of an understudy or amanuensis."[69] Understanding how to apply the concept of apostolic authorship for a Gospel such as Luke or an anonymous writing such as Hebrews becomes difficult. The acceptance of the concept of a pseudonymous author for a canonical writing becomes an even more difficult exercise.

Finally, it is important to recognize that some New Testament writings are anonymous and not pseudonymous. The absence of the name of an author in the four Gospels and Hebrews indicates that these are anonymous writings. Pseudonymity occurs when we encounter the willful use of a name other than the genuine author. The attribution of Hebrews to Pauline authorship by the Eastern church was not an example of the acceptance of pseudonymous authorship. It was a case of mistaken identity. The church may have originally admitted Hebrews into the New Testament canon under the presumption of Pauline authorship. The acceptance of Hebrews as an authoritative document was a correct decision. The mistaken belief that Paul authored it was unfortunate. The writing is an example of anonymous literature.

PSEUDONYMOUS AUTHORSHIP AND THE PASTORAL EPISTLES

Many contemporary New Testament scholars are convinced that the name "Paul" in the Pastoral Epistles is a pseudonym. Advocates of pseudonymity suggest that an admirer of Paul penned the letters after Paul's death. His use of the name was either an effort to gain acceptance for his ideas or a tribute to Paul as the instructor of the writer. Proponents of the idea of pseudonymous authorship for the Pastorals base their case on five features.[70]

First, they find the vocabulary and style of the Pastorals different from other Pauline writings. Such words as "slave traders" (*andrapodistēs*, 1Ti 1:10); and "integrity" (*aphthoria*, Tit 2:7); are *hapax legomena*. Such a term as "godliness" (*eusebeia*, 1Ti 6:11) is a key term in the Pastorals but is unknown in the other ten Pauline writings. Such an important Pauline concept as the Cross is not discussed in the Pastorals. Supporters of pseudonymous authorship for the Pastorals feel that these facts indicate that the Apostle Paul did not write the Pastorals. Supporters of the authenticity of the Pastorals suggest that the length of the Pastorals is too brief to serve as a source of trustworthy information about the writing habits of the author.[71] Also, it is possible to explain the change in style as due to different subject matter, different needs among the readers, or the use of an amanuensis.

Second, defenders of the pseudonymity of the Pastorals date the heresy that the author opposed as later than the lifetime of Paul. Gnostic heretics arose in the second century to question Christ's resurrection and to practice a morality that alternated between moral license and asceticism. Supporters of pseudonymity feel that the terms "myths" and "genealogies" in 1 Timothy 1:4 refer to a developed Gnosticism. They also note that the Greek term for "opposing ideas" in 1 Timothy 6:20 (*antithesis*) is the title of a work in the second century by the heretic Marcion. This prompts some to date the Pastorals after Paul's lifetime. Opponents of the use of pseudonymity in the Pastorals observe that the heresy contains Jewish as well as Gnostic elements (1Ti 1:7; Tit 1:10). Also, many of them feel that the vague hints in the Pastorals about the identity of the heretics are not sufficient to link the system securely with Gnosticism.[72]

A third argument put forth in support of pseudonymous authorship in the Pastorals is the alleged late development of the ecclesiastical structure of the Pastorals. Some indicate that the authority given to elders in the Pastorals (1Ti 5:17) resembles that of second-century bishops in the time of Ignatius. If the insight were correct, it would make it likely that the Pastorals were a second-century production. Supporters of the apostolic authorship of the Pastorals feel that the broad authority given to the elders in the Pastorals was an effort to equip them to deal with the Ephesian heresy. They also deny that the interest in church organization in the Pastorals represents a Pauline obsession. They indicate that Paul had always shown an interest in and an awareness of church structure (Ac 14:23; Php 1:1).

A fourth objection raised against Pauline authorship of the Pastorals is the presence of historical circumstances that conflict with Acts. In 1 Timothy 1:3 Paul had left Timothy in Ephesus to deal with false teachers. In Titus 1:5 Paul had left Titus in Crete and traveled to Nicopolis (Tit 3:12), where he intended to spend the winter. By way of contrast, in Acts 20:4–38 Timothy had accompanied Paul during his journey to Ephesus and was not in Ephesus to receive a letter from him. In Acts, Paul visited neither Crete nor Nicopolis. These facts lead some to suggest that a pseudonymous author has added the above incidents to

Paul's life. The traditional answer to these observations is that Paul obtained release from the imprisonment of Acts 28, returned to the East, and later suffered arrest and imprisonment in Rome again. Under this view the Pastoral incidents do not harmonize with Acts because they occurred at a later time.

A final objection to Pauline authorship of the Pastorals concerns the theology of the Pastorals. Common Pauline doctrines such as the fatherhood of God, the believer's union with Christ, and the work of the Holy Spirit do not appear in the Pastorals. Some scholars assume that Paul could not have written letters that omitted these emphases. Further, they find a lack of discussion of the significance of Christ's death and the use of the term "faith" in reference to personal belief rather than to existential commitment to Christ (1Ti 3:9). Supporters of Pauline authorship find reference to God's fatherly goodness in 1 Timothy 6:17 and Titus 3:4. Paul could also speak of the "life that is in Christ Jesus" (2Ti 1:1) and made some references to the work of the Holy Spirit (1Ti 4:1; 2Ti 1:14). Discussion of Christ's death appears in 1 Timothy 2:6 and Titus 2:14. Paul also used the term "faith" in reference to Christian belief in Philippians 1:27 and Colossians 2:7.

The foregoing information comes from the internal content of the letters. In addition to this internal information is a long history of external attestation to the Pauline authorship of the Pastorals. The church historian Eusebius supported Pauline authorship of the Pastorals with the words, "The epistles of Paul are fourteen, all well known and beyond doubt. It should not, however, be concealed, that some have set aside the Epistle to the Hebrews."[73] Widespread uncertainty about Pauline authorship of the Pastorals did not appear until the nineteenth century.

In addition to these internal and external facts a study of the attitude of the early church toward pseudonymous authorship provides additional help in deciding about the authorship of the Pastorals. A knowledge of the ethical, historical, and psychological issues concerning pseudonymous authorship raises significant doubt in this writer's mind of its acceptability with the Pastorals.

The acceptance of apostolic authorship of the Pastorals is no guarantee that interpreters will avoid mistakes in their understanding and application of the writings. It can, however, allow students to approach the text with a decision already made in favor of its authenticity and trustworthiness. This is a minimum requirement for anyone seeking to understand and apply wisely the text of Scripture.

BIBLIOGRAPHY

Aland, Kurt. "The Problem of Anonymity and Pseudonymity in Christian Literature of the First Two Centuries." In *The Authority and Integrity of the New Testament*, 1–13. London: SPCK, 1965.

Bauckham, Richard. "Pseudo-Apostolic Letters." *JBL* 107 (September 1988): 469–94.

Bruce, F. F. *The Canon of Scripture*. Downers Grove, Ill.: InterVarsity, 1988.

Green, Michael. *The Second Epistle of Peter and the Epistle of Jude*. Tyndale New Testament Commentaries. Edited by R. V. G. Tasker. Grand Rapids: Eerdmans, 1968.

Guthrie, Donald. "Acts and Epistles in Apocryphal Writings." In *Apostolic History and the Gospel*, ed. W. Ward Gasque and Ralph P. Martin, 328–45. Grand Rapids: Eerdmans, 1970.

————. "The Development of the Idea of Canonical Pseudepigrapha in New Testament Criticism." In *The Authority and Integrity of the New Testament*, 14–39. London: SPCK, 1965.

————. "Epistolary Pseudepigraphy." Chap. in *New Testament Introduction*, 2d ed., 2:282–94. London: Tyndale, 1963.

Lea, Thomas D. "The Early Christian View of Pseudepigraphic Writings." *JETS* 27 (March 1984): 65–75.

Meade, David. *Pseudonymity and Canon*. Grand Rapids: Eerdmans, 1986.

Metzger, Bruce. "Literary Forgeries and Canonical Pseudepigrapha." *JBL* 91 (March 1972): 3–24.

NOTES

[1]Donald Guthrie, *New Testament Introduction*, 2d ed. (London: Tyndale, 1963), 2:184.

[2]James H. Charlesworth, ed., *The Old Testament Pseudepigrapha* (Garden City, N.Y.: Doubleday, 1985), 2:8.

[3]J. S. Candlish, "On the Moral Character of Pseudonymous Books," *The Expositor* 4, series 4 (1891): 105.

[4]Guthrie, *New Testament Introduction*, 292.

[5]Eusebius, *Ecclesiastical History* 3.3. References to Eusebius are taken from the translation by Christian Frederick Cruse, *The Ecclesiastical History of Eusebius Pamphilus* (Grand Rapids: Baker, 1955).

[6]Ibid., 6.12.

[7]Tertullian, *On Prescription Against Heretics* 21. All references to the writings of the Ante-Nicene Fathers are taken from Alexander Roberts and James Donaldson, eds., *The Ante-Nicene Fathers*, 10 vols. (New York: The Christian Literature Company, 1890; repr. Grand Rapids: Eerdmans, 1980).

[8]Tertullian, *On Baptism* 17.

[9]Tertullian, *Against Marcion* 4.5.

[10]For additional discussion see Donald Guthrie, "Tertullian and Pseudonymity," *Expository Times* 67 (August 1956): 341, 42.

[11]Origen, *De Principiis* Preface 8.

[12]Dionysius, *Extant Fragments* 1.4.

[13]Roberts and Donaldson, *The Ante-Nicene Fathers*, 7:387–90

[14]*Constitutions of the Holy Apostles*, 6.16.

[15]F. F. Bruce, *The Canon of Scripture* (Downers Grove, Ill.: InterVarsity, 1988), 261.

[16]Edgar Hennecke, *New Testament Apocrypha*, ed. Wilhelm Schneemelcher, trans. R. McL. Wilson (Philadelphia: Westminster, 1963), 1:27.

[17]Ibid., 36.

[18]Bruce Metzger, *The Canon of the New Testament* (London: Oxford, 1987), 194.

[19]Metzger provides a translation of the Muratorian Canon on pp. 305–7.

[20]These are the terms used in Metzger's Translation of Eusebius' list, pp. 309, 310. See also the listing in *Ecclesiastical History* 3.25.

[21]Metzger, 310.

[22]Quoted in B. F. Westcott, *The Canon of the New Testament* (London: Macmillan, 1889; Joplin, Mo.: College Press, Evangelical Reprint Library, 1972), 482.

[23]John Calvin, *The Epistle of Paul the Apostle to the Hebrews and the First and Second Epistles of St. Peter*, ed. David W. Torrance and Thomas F. Torrance, trans. William B. Johnston; *Calvin's Commentaries*, Vol. 12 (Grand Rapids: Eerdmans, 1963), 325.

[24]F. C. Baur, *Paul: The Apostle of Jesus Christ*, trans. by A. Menzies (London: Williams and Norgate, 1875), 2:109.

[25]Ibid., 110.

[26]Ibid., 84.

[27]Adolph Jülicher, *An Introduction to the New Testament*, trans. by Janet Penrose Ward (London: Smith, Elder & co., 1904), 53.

[28]Ibid., 54.

[29]Martin Dibelius, *A Fresh Approach to the New Testament and Early Christian Literature* (New York: Scribner's, 1936), 207.

[30]Ibid., 232.

[31]James Moffatt, Introduction to the Literature of the New Testament (New York: Scribner's, 1911), 41.

[32]Ibid.

[33]Ibid., 42.

[34]Ibid., 43

[35]Edgar J. Goodspeed, New Chapters in New Testament Study (New York: Macmillan, 1937).

[36]Ibid., 172.

[37]Ibid., 173.

[38]Candlish, 278.

[39]Ibid., 273, 274.

[40]Ibid., 276.

[41]R. D. Shaw, The Pauline Epistles: Introductory and Expository Outlines (Edinburgh: T & T Clark, 1903), 477–86.

[42]Ibid., 481.

[43]Ibid., 482.

[44]Arnold Meyer, "Die Pseudepigraphie als ethisch-psychologisches Problem," ZNW 35 (1936): 262–79.

[45]F. Torm, Die Psychologie der Pseudonymität im Hinblick auf die Literatur des Urchristentums (Gütersloh: C. Bertelsmann, 1932).

[46]J. C. Fenton, "Pseudonymity in the New Testament," Theology 58 (February 1955): 51–56.

[47]Kurt Aland, "The Problem of Anonymity and Pseudonymity in Christian Literature of the First Two Centuries," The Authority and Integrity of the New Testament (London: SPCK, 1965), 1–13.

[48]Ibid., 6.

[49]Ibid., 7.

[50]Ibid., 8.

[51]David G. Meade, Pseudonymity and Canon (Grand Rapids: Eerdmans, 1986), 13–14.

[52]Norbert Brox, Falsche Verfasserangaben zur Erklärung der frühchristlichen Pseudepigraphie (Stuttgart: KBW, 1975).

[53]Meade, 43.

[54]Ibid., 209.

[55]Ibid., 16.

[56]E. Earle Ellis, review of Pseudonymity and Canon, by David Meade, in Southwestern Journal of Theology 30 (Fall 1987): 57.

[57]Bruce Metzger, "Literary Forgeries and Canonical Pseudepigrapha," JBL 91 (March 1972): 3–24.

[58]Ibid., 15.

[59]Ibid., 19.

[60]Ibid., 22.

[61]J. I. Packer, 'Fundamentalism' and the Word of God (Grand Rapids: Eerdmans, 1958), 184.

[62]Michael Green, *The Second Epistle of Peter and the Epistle of Jude,* Tyndale New Testament Commentaries, ed. R. V. G. Tasker (Grand Rapids: Eerdmans, 1968), 33.

[63]Bruce, 276, 77.

[64]In addition to two previously cited articles he has written "The Development of the Idea of Canonical Pseudepigrapha in New Testament Criticism," *The Authority and Integrity of the New Testament* (London: SPCK, 1965),14–39, and "Acts and Epistles in Apocryphal Writings," *Apostolic History and the Gospel,* ed. W. Ward Gasque and Ralph P. Martin (Grand Rapids: Eerdmans, 1970), 328–45.

[65]Guthrie, *New Testament Introduction,* 290.

[66]Ibid., 291.

[67]Ibid., 294.

[68]Shaw, 477.

[69]R. Laird Harris, *Inspiration and Canonicity of the Bible* (Grand Rapids: Zondervan, 1957), 272.

[70]E. E. Ellis, *Paul and his Recent Interpreters* (Grand Rapids: Eerdmans, 1961), 49–57; *idem,* "Traditions in the Pastoral Epistles," *Early Jewish and Christian Exegesis,* ed. C. A. Evans and W. F. Stinespring (Atlanta: Scholars, 1987), 237–53. Also, John A. T. Robinson, who cannot be accused of being a traditionalist, has shown the uncertainty and historical difficulties of the ascriptions of pseudepigrapha to the documents of the New Testament. See *Redating the New Testament* (Philadelphia: Westminster, 1976), 63, 156, 169–99.

[71]Bruce M. Metzger, "A Reconsideration of Certain Arguments Against the Pauline Authorship of the Pastoral Epistles," *Exp Tim* 70 (December 1958): 94.

[72]J. N. D. Kelly, *A Commentary on the Pastoral Epistles* (London: A & C Black, 1963; Grand Rapids: Baker, 1981; Thornapple Commentaries), 11–12.

[73]Eusebius, *Ecclesiastical History* 3.3.

Chapter Nineteen

New Testament Interpretation and Preaching

C. Richard Wells

C. Richard Wells

C. Richard Wells is Associate Professor of Divinity at Beeson Divinity School in Birmingham, Alabama. He holds the B.A. from Florida Southern College, the M.A. from Stetson University, the M.Min. from Criswell College, and the Ph.D. from Baylor University. He is currently completing a second Ph.D. at the University of North Texas. He previously taught at Criswell College in Dallas, Texas, and has also held several pastorates. His essays have appeared in *The Indiana Baptist, Criswell Theological Review, Criswell Study Bible,* and *Reclaiming the Prophetic Mantle* (Broadman). He is currently writing *Understanding the Times: Ministry Megatrends at the End of the Twentieth Century* for Broadman Press.

Chapter Nineteen

New Testament Interpretation and Preaching

An old story tells about an uncut young seminary student who could not understand why he needed to study exegesis: "All I want to do," he protested, "is preach *Jesus!*" In truth, our mythical theologue may be saying what a great many evangelical preachers are thinking. For many, authoritative and persuasive preaching needs only the straightforward explication of the Bible. Scholars with nothing better to do may occupy themselves with hermeneutics, exegesis, and the complex of related disciplines called "criticism." But preachers live in the real world. They must preach sermons to people in the throes of life and death, not generate lively discussion on an esoteric topic. The wide gulf that has often separated the professional biblical scholar from the preacher[1] grows wider.

Something is sadly odd about this state of affairs. This generation of preachers has access to a range and depth of biblical scholarship unparalleled in the history of Christendom. The sciences of hermeneutics, exegesis, and textual and other critical studies are finely developed. Yet preaching is in crisis. We do well to recall, of course, that every age, even the nineteenth-century "golden age of preaching," has had its crisis.[2] But the contemporary crisis is, to put it bluntly, different: It is the seeming inability to preach biblically despite (or *because of* [?]) a full century of the most intense biblical scholarship ever known. In the words of David Buttrick: "Preachers drift out of seminaries trained in historical-critical method, practiced in homiletical techniques, yet at a loss to preach 'biblically.' "[3]

Depending on one's point of view, the current crisis

amounts either to a failure to make use of what is now available, a failure to be honest about known critical problems, or the demoralizing effect of critical approaches to Scripture. In any event, preaching is increasingly cut off from biblical scholarship in general and biblical criticism in particular.[4] Even when preachers accept certain critical findings, they seldom embrace critical methods and still less utilize them in any significant way.

THE BREACH BETWEEN PREACHING AND CRITICISM

Most evangelical seminaries as well as many undergraduate religion programs introduce critical scholarship to their students. It is a worthwhile question to ask, then, why so few graduates find any place for criticism in their preaching.

For some, the answer is time. In the article cited above, David Buttrick invites us to survey the study of a typical pastor. On the desk we will find "a stack of books—counseling, management, perhaps biblical theology. But on the same desk there are apt to be back issues of a 'homily service,' and on the shelves there may be commentaries gathering dust."[5] Time pressure ensures that most preachers consider themselves fortunate to show up on Sunday with anything at all to say. A few may stir up their exegetical skills with an occasional word study. But few indeed will venture far into the kingdom of the critics.

For others, the problem is expertise. A seminary-kind of acquaintance with critical approaches such as textual criticism, redaction criticism, source or form criticism does not guarantee the ability to interact with them discerningly, much less actually to utilize them in homiletical analysis.

Third, for many preachers critical study as a whole clouds the meaning and significance of Scripture rather than giving clarity. Writes Arthur Wainwright: "As ingenious theories pile on top of each other, the inventiveness of experts can make the Bible more difficult to understand than it was before."[6] Uncertainty is always unsettling. Small wonder many preachers shrink from modern critical scholarship that appears not only to create uncertainty but to revel in it.

Fourth, some preachers and congregations alike associate scholarship per se with poor preaching. Many a vibrant young preacher has been warned that "seminary will just ruin you!"

And many an anecdote highlights the perception of a scholar in the pulpit as hopelessly technical, largely irrelevant, and outrageously boring. Yet even more thoughtful people, including seminary-trained preachers, express the fear that critical study leads to detachment from the text of Scripture and from the living Word proclaimed therein.[7]

Others have yet more serious reservations about criticism. Those who have some awareness of the field often wonder about the legitimacy of historical-critical methodology per se for preaching. Harold Lindsell's remark is trenchant: "The historical-critical method is the Bible's greatest enemy."[8] And Lindsell, while outspoken, is not alone. An irenic scholar like Donald Guthrie can say, on the one hand, that it is "not impossible to sustain full biblical authority at the same time as using critical faculties to determine the historical background of the biblical texts."[9] Yet, on the other hand, he finds source, form, and redaction criticism so fraught with questionable assumptions that the evangelical must remain extremely cautious about the "dubious results of human propositions."[10]

Even more serious, however, is what O. C. Edwards has called the "failure of nerve" within historical-criticism itself. Increasingly, according to Edwards, critical scholars are raising questions about the capacity of the method to elucidate the text of Scripture or, for that matter, to salvage anything meaningful from it at all.[11]

Writing earlier than Edwards, Hendrikus Boers suggested that historical-critical scholarship could no longer evade the question "whether it still contributes fundamentally to the strengthening of the faith, or whether it is effecting its dissolution."[12] Indeed, Boers argued that historical-critical research and revelation are antithetical concepts. Despite the implications for faith, however, Boers was unwilling to abandon research. Ultimately the "New Testament scholar is compelled," he said, "to abandon also to the 'flames of critical scrutiny' the New Testament understanding that faith is grounded in the history of Jesus as the event of salvation."[13]

The lamentations of these scholars, and others like them,[14] bodes ill for preaching. For it is beyond question that preaching is "to deliver the message of God, a message from God to . . . people."[15] At best, critical scholars have not shown as clearly as they might just how contemporary scholarship enhances the church's life through the Bible. More ominously, preachers may be rejecting out-of-hand an approach they perceive to have profoundly negative consequences for the authority of the pulpit. And worse, they may sense that the critics themselves have lost the ability to say it is not so.

HOMILECTICS AND NEW TESTAMENT CRITICISM

Problems such as these prompt us to ask whether New Testament criticism has any value for preaching at all. In one sense, of course, the question is entirely moot. Any preacher who studies the text of Scripture is a critic of sorts. And any preacher who analyzes the text of Scripture in light of a wider study of its historical setting is engaged in historical-criticism. George Eldon Ladd meant precisely this when he observed that "The Word of God has been given to men through historical events and historical personages; and *this very fact demands historical-criticism*, unless the true nature of the Bible is to be ignored."[16] For Ladd, the negative presuppositions associated with historical-criticism (denial of the supernatural, for example) are not essential to the methods themselves:

> Criticism means making intelligent judgments about historical, literary, textual, and philological questions which one must face in dealing with the Bible, in the light of all available evidence, when one recognizes that the Word of God has come to men through the words of men in historical situations.[17]

Two Distinctions

We may assume that no one will quibble with Professor Ladd over this point. We may even assume general agreement with Edgar Krenz, writing from outside the evangelical fold, that "we cannot escape historical-critical study of the Bible."[18] But this agreement should not blind us to the real differences between a Ladd and a Krenz. We must begin, therefore, with some careful distinctions.

(1) The first is between homiletics (the science of preaching) and criticism. Clearly these two disciplines differ, but how exactly do they? One approach to this question is to regard them as aspects of exegesis. Exegesis, of course, is simply the work of biblical interpretation. It is closely related to hermeneutics, which, in fact, is the set of rules for exegesis. To borrow

Bernard Ramm's happy metaphor, hermeneutics is the rule-book, exegesis is the game.[19] In more scientific terms, hermeneutics is the "theory that guides exegesis," while exegesis is "the *practice* of and the set of *procedures* for discovering the author's intended meaning."[20]

By definition, however, interpretation means interpreting *something* (a document from the past) for *someone* (an audience in the present). Exegesis thus moves in two directions, toward the past (biblical history, Scripture) and toward the present (applicable truth, the contemporary audience in its culture). The clearest distinction between criticism and preaching is here. New Testament criticism is that side of exegesis that focuses on the original significance of the New Testament. Homilectics is that side of exegesis that focuses on the meaning of the New Testament for contemporary hearers in their culture.

In actuality, we should say that hermeneutics is a rule-book that governs the critical side of exegesis. On the homiletical side, theology (especially systematic theology) provides the framework. For preaching is nothing more than proclaiming the theological message of a text "*in the light of* the whole system of revealed truth [that is, systematic theology]."[21]

In short, criticism is merely a device for gathering the facts of a text in its setting. Hermeneutics gives the framework for interpreting those facts. Exegesis proper *is* the interpretation of them. Theology gives the framework for communicating the message to a contemporary audience in its culture. Homiletics brings that message to bear upon the facts of the present listener.

This way of understanding homiletics and criticism may help us formulate some guidelines for a profitable interface. Ernest Best wisely observes that "exegesis has a real but negative function. It cannot tell us how to move from a text to a new crystallization."[22] (The reader should note that "crystallization" comes close to what traditional homiletics calls "contemporary application.") Best means of course that the critical study of a text forces the preacher away from the audience. Yet this is crucial.

(2) Another clarification is between critical methods and methodology. Although it is not usually done this way, we should properly call the historical-critical approach to New Testament study "methodology." Accordingly, we should call the various critical tools such as form, source, redaction, or

rhetorical criticism "methods." The difference is exactly the same as the difference between hermeneutics and exegesis. A methodology is a philosophy, or theory, of methods. While methods are thus derived from methodology, they are not the same.

When evangelicals and non-evangelicals talk about historical criticism, they are talking about methodology—and they are frequently talking about different methodologies. True, their methodologies share common interests in historical background, textual variations (variants), dates, authorship, sources, literary types, and the like. But they diverge over the rules and assumptions that govern their investigations. In short, there are distinct historical-critical methodologies.

Two Implications

The value of criticism for preaching depends on our ability to distinguish methods and methodology. This becomes clear if we consider two major implications.

(1) Since methods and methodologies differ, we must judge the usefulness of methods in more than one way. Certainly, a given critic will utilize a chosen method in a way that meshes with an over-arching methodology. But the method itself is a technique for assessing the original significance of a New Testament text. The methods do not deal with the text at the same level, however. Some methods take the text in its present form (redaction and textual criticism are examples). Other methods deal with the precanonical form of the text. Source criticism is an example. Form criticism proceeds even farther back to a pre-text (oral) stage of a biblical tradition. More radical recent methods such as structuralism and literary criticism (New Criticism or narrative criticism) proceed further still, to the origins of a tradition in the dynamics of human consciousness.[23]

For evangelical preachers, the methods of criticism that deal with the text as it is have the greatest potential usefulness. Methods that attempt to go beyond or get behind the text are necessarily more speculative, and thus their results are more tenuous.[24] The levels at which critical methods function may serve, therefore, as a guide for the preacher in preparation.[25]

(2) Apart from the value of any specific method, evangelical preachers can utilize, indeed must utilize, historical-critical

methodology. Sidney Greidanus helps us think through what this means in his significant recent work, *The Modern Preacher and the Ancient Text*. Greidanus first carefully explains the threefold assumption of traditional historical-criticism, derived from Ernst Troeltsch, viz., that: (1) The historicity of events can be established only in terms of probabilities (Principle of Criticism); (2) The key to criticism is the analogy of present events with past events (Principle of Analogy); and (3) Any event must be understood in terms of cause/effect (Principle of Correlation). After his critique,[26] he proposes an alternative "Holistic Historical-Critical Method."[27]

The Holistic Method (methodology) embraces each of Troeltsch's assumptions but with crucial adaptations. Greidanus begins with the Principle of Correlation, affirming that it is a "valid principle only as long as it is open to all possible causes in history."[28] That is, the preacher may interpret historically and critically—looking for cause and effect relationships—as long as God is allowed among the causes. This proviso in turn recasts the Principles of Analogy and Criticism. The work of God means that all events in history are not similar to others and thus predictable. So the Principle of Analogy must account for events at two levels, the ordinary mediate level (where God works "unobtrusively through 'natural' causation"), and the immediate level (where God acts uniquely).[29] Further, because the work of God is presupposed, the preacher approaches the documents of Scripture from the perspective of trust, rather than of doubt, so that the historicity of the text becomes a matter to *understand* rather than to *determine*. Thus the Principle of Criticism is also reformulated.

The Informing Value of Critical Methodology

The distinctions drawn earlier, together with Greidanus's critique, suggest two informing values of historical-critical methodology for contemporary evangelical preachers. First, they highlight the urgency of an acquaintance with the methodology so as to make use of the literature in the field of New Testament studies. Not long ago, R. B. Crotty referred to training in historical-critical methods as a kind of initiation without which a good deal of significant material would be "quite inaccessible."[30] He was right, even if his list of potentially obscure material was too short. The truth is that a preacher will find much of almost any recent commentary, study aid, or background work "quite inaccessible" without some grasp of the historical-critical foundations upon which it rests.

The danger is twofold. On one hand, like a miner without a lamp, the preacher may pass over jewels there for the taking. On the other, the preacher may mistake a worthless stone for a gem. Worse still, he may grasp a scorpion. In short, some awareness of critical methodology opens a new world of study possibilities to the preacher. At the same time, it affords protection against latent distortion.

Second, they suggest a responsible use of criticism in homiletics. As a *methodology*, New Testament criticism is a way of studying the text. Certainly, it should be holistic, as Greidanus says. But it should also be seen for what it is—a medium for clarifying meaning, with the ultimate purpose of deriving significance.[31] In other words, the preacher will always begin and end with the significance of biblical revelation. Used holistically, criticism is useful but intermediary. By the way of criticism, the preacher will seek the *meaning* of the text in the most comprehensive way—grammatically, syntactically, contextually, verbally, historically, and theologically.[32]

Theoretically, then, almost any of the critical methods might help the preacher. For example, despite his radical demythologizing, Bultmann's form-critical approach could orient the preacher to some characteristic forms of Synoptic[33] literary units (pericopes). Similarly, a preacher might benefit from knowing that material common only to Matthew and Luke (the hypothetical Q source) tends to be more autobiographical and poetical, refers frequently to nature and common life, and consists mainly of the Lord's teaching.[34] The preacher might conceivably utilize even the methods of structuralism to clarify the peculiar structural unity of a text in its book context.[35]

A preacher is never free, however, to foreclose on the quest for significance. Criticism must remain the servant of homiletics, not its master, otherwise preaching degenerates into a kind of travelogue back into history. To borrow Paul Ricoeur's well-known steps in the critical use of Scripture, the preacher moves from an original naivete, to critical scrutiny, and back to a fresh and compelling second naivete.[36] An evangelical preacher ought to outstrip Ricoeur himself,[37] insofar as critical scrutiny does not dispel a "myth." It rather clarifies, deepens, and develops a matter of utmost, and authentic, historical importance. It enables the preacher to proclaim with the flush of sincerity a truth that, because it is understood thoroughly, has come to be appreciated profoundly.

We conclude, then, that New Testament criticism *informs* preaching. It enables the preacher to read the literature with discernment and profit. It gives some perspective to the homiletical process. It helps the preacher appreciate, indeed to enter, the historical context of the Bible. In short, it creates a mindset that (potentially at least) compels the preacher to seek the truth-intention of the biblical writer in order to speak the truth with power in a new age.

THE WORK OF THE PREACHER AND CRITICAL STUDY

Beyond this generalized, informing value, does New Testament criticism contribute specifically to the homiletical task? It is certainly true that the disciplines of critical study are, by and large, "too technical and too tedious for the parish preacher to practice on a regular basis."[38] But that does not mean the preacher ought to ignore critical study or that such study has not legitimate contributions to make.

Criticism Challenges a Preacher to Preach with Integrity

Some years ago A. J. M. Wedderburn of St. Andrews complained that the Bible (especially the Gospel portion) was being used dishonestly in evangelistic preaching. He objected to the practice, as he saw it, of invoking the face-value authority of the Bible, thus failing to appreciate (or perhaps just ignoring) real difficulties in the text.[39] What is particularly interesting about Wedderburn's critique is that, for him, it meant changing the way evangelistic preaching should be done (that is, as a witness, rather than as a barrister). It meant that instead of stringing texts together to present an irrefutable proof that then must be accepted, the evangelist must reckon with objections and difficulties. This might require that evangelism and preaching "should take place within the context of a whole educational programme."[40]

T. E. Brinnington rejoined that evangelism is no context for dealing with critical questions.[41] But Wedderburn's point is well taken, and in fact Brinnington affirmed it himself. He argued that Wedderburn's criticism of John Stott and Canon Michael Green was unwarranted: ". . . presumably when their evangelism presupposes certain conservative positions in gospel study, they have reached those positions *in light of all the evidence.*"[42]

At bottom, the issue dividing Brinnington and Wedderburn has more to do with how, not whether, critical problems must be taken into account. And that is our point here. To whatever degree it may be true that the sermon does not lend itself to the discussion of critical problems (we will take up this question later), these problems do need to be *considered*. Familiarity with critical methodology and methods challenges the preacher to deal forthrightly and honestly with the text. Sometimes critical study highlights issues and problems explicitly. Always, it encourages caution and humility.

Critical Study Develops the Scholarship of the Preacher

We have already drawn attention to the competing interests that vie for the precious time of every preacher. Indeed, time pressure is a major factor in the failure of preachers to benefit from contemporary critical scholarship. Quite simply, the preacher cannot resolve that dilemma without the sternest possible discipline—setting priorities, setting inviolable times and places for study, and so on. But given that, some attention to critical study will develop the preacher as a scholar.

This commitment to critical study is crucial, and not just in terms of thinking logically or of reasoning through an argument of Scripture.[43] For the preacher must first be a scholar of the Bible. A consistent, holistic critical approach develops that scholarship. Superficiality is the bane of preaching. Exploring the New Testament in light of critical studies will make it hard to stay on the surface. Such studies not only give the preacher a deep sense of the historical context of the text, but also an appreciation for its character as Scripture[44] and as literature.[45]

Critical Study Can Help the Preacher Develop a Preaching Strategy

When all is said and done, it may well be that critical study of the New Testament has accomplished only two things. It has enabled us (1) to recover some sense of its historical rootage and (2) to grasp the significance of its literary units. The preaching value of such insights is incalculable and nowhere more so than in the development of preaching strategy.

Every preacher has experienced the agony of searching for a preaching text (at least a sermon; the text may be optional!). Critical study will not relieve the agony. But once some basic choices are made, criticism can help flesh out a preaching program and refine a preaching text.

The basic choices to which we refer are those related to the direction a preacher will take over a course of time. Series preaching is the greatest ally here.[46] Whether based on whole books, character studies, thematic sections from books, lectionary texts, or otherwise (the possibilities are endless), a series identifies a text or texts for preaching and thus effectively eliminates the agony of constant choosing.

Criticism and Preaching Direction. Once the preacher establishes a basic preaching direction, critical study can begin to differentiate and integrate the sermonic material. Historical analysis will be the first step, as a way of giving the textual segment its proper context. In this process, the preacher should begin to formulate something of the theme, purpose, and theological message of the segment. In turn, a preaching strategy for the segment should begin to emerge.

In Philippians, for example, a cursory reading might suggest a series on joy, since the word appears in various forms some sixteen times.[47] The *Sitz im Leben* (historical setting) might suggest a more refined theme, however. Paul's imprisonment is a case in point. In 1:12 he says it "has really served the advance of the gospel."[48] But this advance has come in two different ways, viz., through the apostle's personal ministry to those around him (1:13) and, indirectly, through the preaching of others aroused by Paul's experience (1:14–15). Unfortunately, some of these are preaching "out of selfish ambition, not sincerely, supposing that they can stir up trouble for me while I am in chains" (1:17).

Following directly on this revelation is a reference to Paul's joy. It would be tempting, then, to short-circuit the interpretive process by developing a sermon around some such notion as "Paul was able to rejoice in difficult circumstances and so should we." In truth, Paul's rejoicing had specific content: "The important thing is that in every way, whether from false motives or true, Christ is preached. And *because of this* I rejoice" (1:18). The apostle's joy has nothing to do with "coping," "handling stress," or "positive mental attitude." His joy is that Christ is being preached, even at some considerable cost to himself. In point of fact, all the references to joy in Philippians draw their character from serving or ministry. Thus a preaching theme for the letter might take a form like this: "Joy is the by-product of ministering in Christ."[49]

Our point here is that the more deeply we probe the historical setting of the message, the more finely we can develop a preaching theme for a series (and thus for a sermon therein). Moreover, the historical setting gives preaching a sense of living reality. Exploring it, then reimaging it, enables the preacher to communicate something of the human pathos with which the theological truth of the text is bound together.

Critical Methods and the Preaching Program. In the case of the epistles generally, the task is a matter of fairly straightforward historical interpretation. But the other forms of New Testament literature, notably the Gospels, are not so easily mastered. Can critical study come to the aid of homiletics in these cases?

Our earlier discussion of the levels at which different critical methods function may help us think through this question. We assume that the preacher will read introductory material that can account for historical setting, background, audience, critical problems, and the like. Beyond this basic preparation, however, the serious preacher must engage the text itself. Are critical methods useful for this task? We maintain that they can be. Redaction criticism is one such possibility, and one which preachers at different levels of competence can take at their own pace.

Redaction criticism (see the chapter by Grant Osborne in this volume) begins with the text that we have. It assumes that the author was also an editor (redactor), working with some materials others had written and composing some himself.[50] The most significant pragmatic implication of redaction criticism is that the Gospel is thus a "theology."[51] If we are correct in saying that preaching is the proclamation of biblical theology, then redaction criticism would seem to give an ideal preaching focus to a book.

Of course, like all the historical-critical methods, redaction criticism is not without serious limitations.[52] And preachers will be hesitant to adopt the method wholesale with all its assumptive baggage. But it does give the preacher a way of looking at a Gospel in order to draw out its theme. In the words of Osborne, "a delineation of redactional emphases will aid the scholar in determining the special emphases of the evangelists."[53]

Given the profound reservations evangelicals must have, the homiletical value of the approach should not be overlooked. For a more skilled preacher, Osborne's two sets of criteria for using redaction criticism might be the place to start. Osborne speaks of external and internal criteria. The former asks, "How does the evangelist use his sources?" The latter asks, "What themes does the writer develop throughout his book?"[54] Osborne develops each of these criteria into interpretive steps.

For the majority of preachers for whom such detailed analysis is simply out of the question, we offer two alternative practical uses of the redactional approach in homiletics. First, carefully compare and contrast parallel gospel accounts.[55] Note the contexts in which they appear, the ways they are introduced and concluded, and any additions or omissions.

Consider, for example, the notoriously difficult passage concerning the Syro-Phoenician woman (Mt 15:21–28/Mk 7:24–30). Despite obvious similarities, the accounts differ in several ways. Matthew adds Jesus' saying that he is sent "only to the lost sheep of Israel." He also adds that the woman "came and knelt before him" and that the disciples urged Jesus to "send her away." Matthew has "Canaanite" in place of Mark's "Greek, born in Syrian Phoenicia." In Matthew the woman calls Jesus "Lord, Son of David," in Mark just "Lord."

Whatever else may be said, it is clear that Matthew emphasizes the contrast between Jewish unbelief and the gentile woman's faith. Mark, on the other hand, emphasizes her faith, not in contrast to Jewish unbelief, but in relation to her ethnic origin and status. Mark writes to Gentiles (note his explanations of Jewish peculiarities in 7:3, 11, for example). His emphasis falls on the universality of the gospel—"she believed, so can you." Matthew's falls on the culpability of Jews, who should have known better—"*she* believed, how can *you* of all people, fail to believe?" For the contemporary preacher, these differences have real value. A sermon from Mark's pericope might stress the *universality* of the gospel message of Christ. From Matthew, one might stress the *responsibility* of those who have the advantages of exposure to the gospel.

Second, construct a detailed (to paragraph level) outline of the entire gospel (or book).[56] This kind of theological outline will differ from a grammatical outline or a syntactical display[57] of a text in that it will highlight the flow of a whole book, rather than the syntax, grammar and vocabulary of a unit. The former is *macro*-preparation—telescopic and comprehensive. The latter is *micro*-preparation—microscopic and particular.

The homiletical value of this practice is fourfold. First, it will help the preacher clarify the theme of a book. Second, it will expose preaching units, that is, blocks of material that hang together and contribute to the development of the overall theme. Third, it emancipates the preacher from slavish dependence on secondary sources in sermon preparation. The text is engaged firsthand and with scrutiny. Fourth, the observant preacher will be able to identify the literary forms (genres) and devices used in developing the book's theological theme. This will give direction to the study of the individual units.[58]

Historical criticism generally, and form criticism in particular, have called attention to literary units in the New Testament, especially the Gospels. The preacher who can plan a preaching program around such units will not only mitigate the agony of text selection but will also naturally encourage *coherence*, not only within an individual sermon but over an extended period of preaching. And unity, as Broadus said long ago, "is indispensable to the best efforts of discourse."[59]

PREACHING AND NEW TESTAMENT CRITICAL PROBLEMS

To this point, we have dealt almost exclusively with the use of New Testament criticism in the *preparation* of sermons. Suppose we turn our attention for a moment to sermon *delivery*.

Virtually all contemporary preachers are at least conscious of some problems created by critical study for sermon delivery. Even with no knowledge whatsoever of formal critical methods, a preacher nowadays is likely to know, for example, that a modern translation differs at several points with the King James Version as well as with other modern translations. Any preacher who undertakes serious exposition, moreover, must come to grips with the problem of problems, handling critical questions in the pulpit. In this last section, I will suggest a couple of guidelines. I begin with guidelines for the various kinds of problems a preacher is likely to encounter. Then I will suggest some general procedural guidelines that are applicable to all or most of the problems.

Kinds of Critical Problems

Textual (Lower-Critical) Problems. Those exposed to the study of textual criticism in seminary are well aware that the Greek text, or better, the Greek texts, contain hundreds of variants (see the chapter in this volume by Michael Holmes). Most of these readings are insignificant, either because they clearly lack much substance or because they differ only slightly from one another. And none have any bearing on fundamental doctrines. But, as noted above, translations differ because of these variants. Since preachers and congregations may use several different translations among them, the homiletic problem is real.

A striking case is 1 John 5:7–8. Verse 7 of the KJV is eliminated in most modern translations, as are the words "in earth" in verse 8.[60] There are less dramatic cases, of course, that might still have fairly weighty implications. For example, Colossians 1:14 in KJV reads "redemption through [Christ's] blood," while most modern translations delete "in his blood" since these words do not appear in many of the oldest Greek manuscripts. Likewise, in Matthew 5:22 the KJV has "angry with his brother without a cause." Most modern translations delete the words "without a cause."

We could multiply examples. The point is that text-critical questions exist. And the contemporary proliferation of translations ensures that the preacher and the congregation will have occasion to notice differences that are sometimes fairly significant. Given the hundreds of variants and the insignificance of most, how do preachers decide when to handle one in a sermon?

The best guide is the translations themselves. Harold Scanlin reminds us that translation is a means of communicating New Testament textual criticism to the public.[61] Nowadays, a congregation will ordinarily be divided between users of the KJV and users of various modern versions. Obviously, the preacher will focus attention only on significant differences between the KJV and the modern translations. Most of these differences are reflected in footnotes in the contemporary versions. The NIV contains the fewest number of these (129), the NASB has 209, others have more.[62] Paying attention to the important translation differences has the double benefit of limiting the field and of providing a reference (either a footnote or study Bible note) for the congregation. Even in those (increasingly rare) churches where pastor and people use the KJV exclusively or (perhaps less likely) use the same modern translation, the preacher should be alert to the major text-critical questions identified by translation.

Higher-Critical Problems. We may lump together other historical-critical questions under this heading since they are commonly distinguished from lower-critical (textual) questions. To what extent should questions of authorship, date, the use of sources, occasion, and the like be raised in preaching? We are not yet ready to discuss the dynamics of raising them, only with *what* to raise, if we raise any. We risk two opposite errors. One is to introduce into our preaching scholarly discussions in which the average listener can find no value and has no conceivable interest. The other is to add nothing to the texts we preach so that they are devoid of a historical framework.

We offer three criteria for determining the kinds of critical questions to raise in preaching. First, we should raise those that contribute meaningfully to the interpretation of the text before us. Take as an example the oft-quoted intention of Luke "to write an orderly account" (1:3) of Christ's life and ministry. The fact that Luke knew of other accounts (1:1–2) proves the existence of sources. Since the use of sources contributes meaningfully to our understanding of Luke's Gospel, it seems appropriate to raise the source-critical issue. A sermon along these lines might stress Luke's concern for factuality, the human instrumentality (sources) in revelation, and/or the zeal of the early church to preserve and to communicate the glorious events that had taken place before their eyes (1:4).

Second, we should raise only those questions that we can resolve beneficially. Notice this does not mean solve completely or prove. It does mean that theological imperatives should not rest on disputed questions. It also means that uncertainties should not be preached as assured results (1Ti 3:8). It further means that the introduction of questions should serve some purpose other than curiosity. But most important, it means that the preacher should be able to give reasons for resolving a problem in a certain way and to tell *the difference it makes.*

The identity of Paul's opponents in Corinth is a case in point. A long debate continues over whether they were Jewish, Jewish Christian, Jewish Gnostic, Judaizing, or something else again. The problem likely cannot ever be solved, but it can be resolved beneficially. No matter who they were, they had "tendencies which were leading to an inadequate view of Christianity."[63] By dealing with the likely groups in light of the message of the letters, the preacher opens up vast possibilities for exploring *contemporary* alterations of the gospel. The homiletical value is immense.

Third, we should raise only the kinds of questions that lend themselves to sufficient explanation within the constraints of the sermon. If the problem requires tedious background and argumentation, most listeners simply will not (or cannot) hear it. A critical problem must never displace the Gospel in any sermon.

Some Procedural Guidelines

The preacher who takes the task of interpretation seriously wants also to preach authoritatively and honestly. We conclude our study of New Testament criticism and preaching, therefore, with considerations for handling the critical questions that necessarily emerge.

The Congregation. The first criterion is the ability and/or desire of the congregation to handle critical questions. An urbane, thoughtful congregation might soak up what others find bewildering, irrelevant, or boring. Of course, even the most sophisticated group may not be biblically literate or may not take much interest in the issues. And almost no one wants a steady diet of them. Above all, the preacher must never confuse personal critical interests with those of the congregation. The only point to preaching is to *communicate* the gospel. Everything must serve that end.

The Preacher. The preacher must question his or her motivation for raising issues. Is it to impress, to arouse curiosity, or to talk about a pet topic? Relatedly, does the preacher have the knowledge and skill to handle the issue honestly, accurately, and meaningfully?

The Context. Another consideration is what we might call the need to know. We noted this briefly in the discussion of textual problems. At issue here is whether raising the question intersects a congregational, denominational, or theological point of significance. Pauline authorship of the Pastorals, for example, bears on the nature and authority of Scripture, and thus deserves some investigation.

The Format. Generally speaking, a single sermon from an isolated text is a format unsuitable for the introduction of critical problems. Most such problems rise in connection with our understanding of a whole book. It seems best, therefore, to restrict them to series preaching. Sermons that introduce series are exceptionally well suited to handling these questions.

These criteria restrict our use of a good many tempting questions: Who wrote Hebrews? Where was Paul imprisoned when he wrote Ephesians? Which of the Synoptics came first? And many others. Within the guidelines we have considered any of these might arise. But we must confine ourselves by asking whether they help us preach the gospel deeply but clearly.

Over thirty years ago, Theodore Wedel reasoned that since Bultmann's demythologizing made the presuppositional pathway from the past to the present difficult, modern preachers must take a different route. We must, he declared, engage in "proclamation of kerygma as a present power to salvation and *then* win our hearers to an acceptance of its historical foundations."[64] Unfortunately, Wedel's affirmation seems to imply that we might confidently preach a gospel message and only later make those who have heard and believed aware that it has no roots in the soil of historical factuality. To an evangelical, this is duplicity, pure and simple. Yet it contains a germ of truth. For the sermon, first of all, is the word of God (1Th 2:13). And while every preacher should be and must be a critic, no preacher should ever forget that critical study serves homiletics. The test for any method, approach, or issue is whether it helps us "preach . . . the unsearchable riches of Christ" (Eph 3:8).

BIBLIOGRAPHY

Baker, D. L. *Two Testaments, One Bible.* Downers Grove, Ill.: InterVarsity, 1976.

Barr, James. *The Bible in the Modern World.* London: SCM, 1973.

Buttrick, David. *Homiletic.* Philadelphia: Fortress, 1987.

Fee, Gordon D. *New Testament Exegesis.* Philadelphia: Westminster, 1983.

Greidanus, Sidney. *The Modern Preacher and the Ancient Text.* Grand Rapids: Eerdmans, 1988.

Kaiser, Walter C., Jr. *Toward an Exegetical Theology.* Grand Rapids: Baker, 1981.

Packer, J. I. "Preaching as Biblical Interpretation." *Inerrancy and Common Sense.* Ed. Roger Nicole and J. Ramsay Michaels. Grand Rapids: Baker, 1980.

Stott, John R. W. *Between Two Worlds.* Grand Rapids: Eerdmans, 1978.

Thiselton, Anthony. *Two Horizons.* Grand Rapids: Eerdmans, 1980.

NOTES

[1] Robert E. Van Voorst, "The Dynamic Word: A Survey and Critique of Recent Literature in Preaching and the Bible" *Reformed Review* 37 no. 1 (Autumn 1983): 1.

[2] Clyde Fant, *Preaching for Today,* New Expanded Rev. Ed. (New York: Harper, 1975, 1987), 23–27.

[3] David Buttrick, "Interpretation and Preaching," *Interpretation* 35 (January 1981): 46.

[4] In his significant book *The Bible in the Pulpit: The Renewal of Biblical Preaching* (Nashville: Abingdon, 1978), Leander Keck makes this point explicitly: ". . . the most important factor in the present malaise of preaching is *the preacher's own ambivalence toward the Bible and toward biblical criticism*" (p. 22).

[5] Buttrick, 46.

[6] Arthur Wainwright, *Beyond Biblical Criticism: Encountering Jesus in Scripture* (Atlanta: John Knox, 1982), 9.

[7] D. A. Carson speaks of the inevitable "dislocation and disturbing distanciation" required by critical study. It is "difficult," he says, and "can be costly," but it can lead ultimately to a more robust Christian life and faith. Cf. *Exegetical Fallacies* (Grand Rapids: Baker, 1984), 22.

[8] Harold Lindsell, *The Bible in the Balance* (Grand Rapids: Zondervan, 1979), 275.

[9] Donald Guthrie, "Biblical Authority and New Testament Scholarship," *Vox Evangelica* 16 (1986): 10.

[10] Ibid., 20. Guthrie finds source and form criticism most tentative, while allowing for "some moderate use of redaction criticism"(p. 19).

[11] O. C. Edwards, Jr., "Historical-Critical Method's Failure of Nerve and a Prescription for a Tonic: A Review of Some Recent Literature," *Anglican Theological Review* 59 (April 1977): 115–16.

[12] Hendrikus Boers, "Historical-Criticism Versus Prophetic Proclamation," *Harvard Theological Review* 65 (1972): 393.

[13]Ibid., 414.

[14]Notably Peter Stuhlmacher, *Historical-Criticism and Theological Interpretation of Scripture: Towards a Hermeneutics of Consent*, trans. Roy A. Harrisville (Philadelphia: Fortress, 1977). Even earlier John Knox argued that many preachers "who have accepted the historical method in principle do not fully believe in it . . . we have accepted the method, not because we have gladly seen in it great creative possibilities, but because we have been forced. . . ." Cf. *Criticism and Faith* (New York/Nashville: Abingdon, 1952), 17–18.

[15]D. Martyn Lloyd-Jones, *Preaching and Preachers* (Grand Rapids: Zondervan, 1972), 53.

[16]George Eldon Ladd, *The New Testament and Criticism* (Grand Rapids: Eerdmans, 1967), 72.

[17]Ibid.

[18]Edgar Krenz, *The Historical-Critical Method*. Guides to Biblical Scholarship (Philadelphia: Fortress, 1975), 3.

[19]Bernard Ramm, *Protestant Biblical Interpretation* 3d ed. (Grand Rapids: Baker, 1970), 11.

[20]Walter Kaiser, *Toward an Exegetical Theology: Biblical Exegesis for Preaching and Teaching* (Grand Rapids: Baker, 1981), 47.

[21]Donald Macleod, "Preaching and Systematic Theology," in Samuel T. Logan, Jr., ed., *The Preacher and Preaching: Reviving the Art in the Twentieth Century* (Phillipsburg, N.J.: Presbyterian and Reformed, 1986), 248 [emphasis mine].

[22]Ernest Best, *From Text to Sermon: Responsible Use of the New Testament in Preaching* (Atlanta: John Knox, 1978), 109.

[23]I am indebted to John Reumann's analysis of criticism and text transmission, which suggested this kind of conceptualization to me. See his "Exegetes, Honesty and the Faith: Biblical Scholarship in Church School Theology," *Currents in Theology and Mission* 5 (February 1978): 16–32. Reumann sketched out nine stages in text-tradition development subsequent to the event that gave rise to it. He then correlated form, source, and redaction criticism with the first three stages. We have enlarged the scheme to include other methods of criticism.

[24]A good example, though drawn from the Old Testament, is the historical-critical analysis of 1 Samuel 13 *for preaching* by Thomas Smothers ("Historical Criticism as a Tool for Proclamation: 1 Samuel 13," *Review and Expositor* 84 [Winter 1987]: 23–32). After textual, source, tradition-history, and form critical studies, Smothers concludes that "the methods have not provided firm answers to the questions which matter most for interpretation" (p. 29). But at the outset Smothers had indicated that the discussions of these questions "*raise others*" (p. 24, emphasis mine) such as later additions. Alas, such questions *cannot* be answered!

[25]Not surprisingly, evangelical New Testament scholars have focused a good deal of attention on redaction criticism. Cf. Grant Osborne, "The Evangelical and Redaction Criticism: Critique and Methodology," *Journal of the Evangelical Theological Society* 22 no. 4 (December 1979): 305–22. They have given much less attention to other methods, except in textbook introductory fashion.

[26]Sidney Greidanus, *The Modern Preacher and the Ancient Text: Interpreting and Preaching Biblical Literature* (Grand Rapids: Eerdmans, 1988), 24–36; also Krenz, 55–57.

[27]Ibid., 37–47.

[28]Ibid., 37.

[29]Ibid., 42.

[30]R. B. Crotty, "Changing Fashions in Biblical Interpretation," *Australian Biblical Review* 33 (October 1985): 15.

[31]See on the difference Grant R. Osborne, "Preaching the Gospels: Methodology and Contextualization" *Journal of the Evangelical Society* 27 no. 1 (March 1984): 34–35; also E. D. Hirsch, *The Aims of Interpretation* (Chicago: University of Chicago, 1976).

[32]The work by Walter Kaiser, *Toward an Exegetical Theology* (Grand Rapids: Baker, 1981), 69–147, is an excellent guide to these different types of analysis. Cf. also Greidanus, 48–121, who discusses literary, historical, and theological interpretation.

[33]Rudolf Bultmann, *History of Synoptic Tradition* trans. John Marsh (New York: Harper, 1963).

[34]Cf. Donald Guthrie, *New Testament Introduction* 3d ed. (Downers Grove, Ill.: InterVarsity, 1970), 154–55.

[35]See Bill Stancil's chapter in this volume; also his "Structuralism and New Testament Studies," *Southwestern Journal of Theology* 22 no. 2 (Spring 1989): 53–54.

[36]Paul Ricouer, "Biblical Hermeneutics," *Semeia* 4 (1975): 85.

[37]For Ricouer the "first naivete" cannot stand by itself in a critical age. The "myth" to which it belongs, however, embodies meaning in its form irrespective of its actual connection with historical event. Cf. *The Symbolism of Evil* trans. E. Buchanan (Boston: Beacon, 1967), 18.

[38]William E. Hull, "The Synoptic Gospels," in James W. Cox, ed., *Biblical Preaching* (Philadelphia: Westminster, 1983), 176. Hull was referring to Synoptic studies. Doubtless it is equally appropriate for New Testament criticism generally.

[39]A. J. M. Wedderburn, "The Use of the Gospels in Evangelism—I," *The Evangelical Quarterly* (April–June 1977): 75.

[40]Ibid., 86–87.

[41]T. E. Brinnington, "The Use of the Gospels in Evangelism—II," *The Evangelical Quarterly* (April–June 1977): 93–94.

[42]Ibid., 94 (emphasis added).

[43]Broadus advocated a method of sermon preparation that developed this capacity for "logical analysis" since "few kinds of power are

so valuable to [the preacher]." Cf. *On the Preparation and Delivery of Sermons* New and Rev. Ed. Jesse B. Weatherspoon (New York: Harper, 1870, 1898, 1926, 1944), 134.

[44]See on this point Elizabeth Achtemeier, "The Artful Dialogue: Some Thoughts on the Relations of Biblical Studies and Homiletics," *Interpretation* 41 (January 1987): 21–22.

[45]See especially the readable volume from Thomas G. Long, *Preaching and the Literary Forms of the Bible* (Philadelphia: Fortress, 1989).

[46]Ian Pitt-Watson (*A Primer for Preachers* [Grand Rapids: Baker, 1986], 70) calls series "a blessed lifeline to sanity."

[47]Thus Jac J. Muller, *The Epistles of Paul to the Philippians and to Philemon* NICNT (Grand Rapids: Eerdmans, 1955), 20–21, citing Bengel's oft-quoted summary: "*Summa epistolae: guadeo, gaudete*" ("The whole of the epistle: I rejoice, you rejoice").

[48]All Scripture quotes of NIV unless otherwise indicated.

[49]In an actual sermonic use of this theme, we would recast the "ministering in Christ" into something like "life-giving living," using the sermon itself to explain what it means to "minister in Christ." We use "theme" as Greidanus (p. 131) does: "a summary statement of the unifying thought of the text." We agree further that it should be stated from the author's viewpoint and as a sentence (p. 135). Cf. also Haddon Robinson's "homiletical idea," in *Biblical Preaching* (Grand Rapids: Baker, 1980), 37–41; also Donald Miller, *The Way to Biblical Preaching* (Nashville: Abingdon, 1957), 53–55.

[50]The relative proportion of original authorship versus redaction is debated by redaction critics. All agree, however, that the Evangelist (in the case of the Gospels) has woven materials together.

[51]Cf. Werner H. Kelber, "Redaction Criticism: On the Nature and Exposition of the Gospels," *Perspectives in Religious Studies* 6 (Spring 1979): 11. Kelber goes on to argue that contrary to popular belief redaction criticism is not a mere extension of form criticism, for the very reason that it presupposes a theological design that form criticism specifically denies (pp. 12–13).

[52]For a helpful exposé, see D. A. Carson, "On the Legitimacy and Illegitimacy of a Literary Tool," in D. A. Carson and John D. Woodbridge, eds., *Scripture and Truth* (Grand Rapids: Zondervan, 1983), 123–37.

[53]Grant R. Osborne, "The Evangelical and Redaction Criticism: Critique and Methodology," *Journal of the Evangelical Theological Society* 22, no. 4 (December 1979): 313.

[54]Ibid., 316ff.

[55]See Carson, "Legitimacy," 140.

[56]Cf. Hull, 176.

[57]Kaiser, 99–104.

[58]For help here, a good introduction is Leland Ryken, *Words of Delight: A Literary Introduction to the Bible* (Grand Rapids: Baker, 1987).

[59]Broadus, 134.

[60]Other major changes include Acts 8:37, Mark 16:9–20, John 7:53–8:11, and Matthew 6:13. Most other changes involve words or phrases.

[61]Harold P. Scanlin, "Bible Translation as a Means of Communicating New Testament Textual-Criticism to the Public," *Bible Translator* 39, no.1 (January 1988): 101–13.

[62]Ibid., 113.

[63]Guthrie, *Introduction*, 424.

[64]Theodore D. Wedel, "Bultmann and Next Sunday's Sermon," *Anglican Theological Review* 39 (January 1957): 7.

Name Index

Subject Index

Scripture Index